W9-ATH-552

INTERNATIONAL ISSUES IN SOCIAL WORK AND SOCIAL WELFARE

SELECTIONS FROM CQ RESEARCHER

Los Angeles | London | New Delhi
Singapore | Washington DC

For information:

SAGE Publications, Inc.
2455 Teller Road
Thousand Oaks, California 91320
E-mail: order@sagepub.com

SAGE Publications Ltd.
1 Oliver's Yard
55 City Road
London EC1Y 1SP
United Kingdom

SAGE Publications India Pvt. Ltd.
B 1/I 1 Mohan Cooperative Industrial Area
Mathura Road, New Delhi 110 044
India

SAGE Publications Asia-Pacific Pte. Ltd.
33 Pekin Street #02-01
Far East Square
Singapore 048763

Printed in the United States of America

Library of Congress Cataloging-in-Publication Data

International issues in social work and social welfare: selections from CQ researcher.
    p. cm.
ISBN 978-1-4129-7940-5 (pbk.)
  1. Social service. 2. Social problems. I. CQ researcher.
HV40.I554 2010
361—dc22   2009024145

This book is printed on acid-free paper.

09   10   11   12   13   10   9   8   7   6   5   4   3   2   1

Acquisitions Editor:	Kassie Graves
Editorial Assistant:	Veronica Novak
Production Editor:	Laureen Gleason
Typesetter:	C&M Digitals (P) Ltd.
Cover Designer:	Candice Harman
Marketing Manager:	Stephanie Adams

Contents

Annotated Contents

Human Trafficking and Slavery: Are the World's Nations Doing Enough to Stamp It Out?

From the villages of Sudan to the factories, sweatshops and brothels of India and South Asia, slavery and human trafficking still flourish. Some 27 million people worldwide are held in some form of slavery, forced prostitution or bonded labor. Some humanitarian groups buy captives' freedom, but critics say that only encourages slave traders to seize more victims. Meanwhile, nearly a million people are forcibly trafficked across international borders annually and held in captivity. Even in the United States, thousands of women and children from overseas are forced to become sex workers. Congress recently strengthened the Trafficking Victims Protection Act, but critics say it is still not tough enough, and that certain U.S. allies that harbor traffickers are treated with "kid gloves" for political reasons.

Child Soldiers: Are More Aggressive Efforts Needed to Protect Children?

Since the mid-1990s, the world has watched in horror as hundreds of thousands of children and young teenagers have participated in nearly 50 wars, mostly in Africa and Asia. Children as young as 5 or 6 have served in combat, and thousands of abducted young girls were forced into sexual slavery. Some terrorist groups even strap explosive-rigged vests onto children and send them off as suicide bombers. Others have been recruited, sometimes forcibly, into the official armed forces or paramilitary units of several dozen countries. U.N. treaties prohibit the use of child soldiers, and the Security Council "names and shames" persistent violators. But only four former guerrilla commanders have been convicted by international tribunals, and some human-rights advocates urge more aggressive prosecution of perpetrators. However, some peace negotiators say threats of prosecution can obstruct cease-fire negotiations and prolong the fighting. In the U.S., where children under 18 serve in the military in non-combat roles, Congress is considering laws to combat the use of child soldiers overseas.

Women's Rights: Are Violence and Discrimination Against Women Declining?

Women around the world have made significant gains in the past decade, but tens of millions still face significant and often appalling hardship. Most governments now have gender-equality commissions, electoral gender quotas and laws to protect women against violence. But progress has been mixed. A record number of women now serve in parliaments, but only 14 of the world's 193 countries currently have elected female leaders. Globalization has produced more jobs for women, but they still constitute 70 percent of the world's poorest inhabitants and 64 percent of the illiterate. Spousal abuse, female infanticide, genital mutilation, forced abortions, bride-burnings, acid attacks and sexual slavery remain pervasive in some countries, and rape and sexual mutilation have reached epic proportions in the war-torn Democratic Republic of the Congo. Experts say without greater economic, political and educational equality, the plight of women will not improve, and society will continue suffering the consequences.

Rapid Urbanization: Can Cities Cope With Rampant Growth?

About 3.3 billion people — half of Earth's inhabitants — live in cities, and the number is expected to hit 5 billion within 20 years. Most urban growth today is occurring in developing countries, where about a billion people live in city slums. Delivering services to crowded cities has become increasingly difficult, especially in the world's 19 "megacities" — those with more than 10 million residents. Moreover, most of the largest cities are in coastal areas, where they are vulnerable to flooding caused by climate change. Many governments are striving to improve city life by expanding services, reducing environmental damage and providing more jobs for the poor, but some still use heavy-handed clean-up policies like slum clearance. Researchers say urbanization helps reduce global poverty because new urbanites earn more than they could in their villages. The global recession could reverse that trend, however, as many unemployed city dwellers return to rural areas. But most experts expect rapid urbanization to resume once the economic storm has passed.

Aiding Refugees: Should the U.N. Help More Displaced People?

Some 42 million people worldwide have been uprooted by warfare or other violence, including 16 million refugees who are legally protected because they left their home countries. Most live in refugee camps and receive aid from the United Nations or other agencies but cannot work or leave the camps without special permission. Another 26 million people who fled violence are not protected by international treaties because they remained in their home countries. The number of such "internally displaced persons" (IDPs) has risen in the last decade, largely due to wars in Africa, Iraq, Afghanistan and Colombia. Millions of IDPs live in harsh conditions, and many receive no aid. Some critics say the U.N. High Commissioner for Refugees should do much more for IDPs, but the agency already faces severe budget shortfalls and bleak prospects for more donations from wealthy nations. Meanwhile, scientists warn that the number of people displaced by natural disasters — now about 50 million a year —could rise dramatically in coming years due to climate change.

Disaster Preparedness: Is the U.S. Ready for Another Major Disaster?

The flawed response to Hurricane Katrina by local, state and federal officials has experts worried that the nation is unprepared for another major disaster. Nearly every emergency-response system broke down in the days immediately following the monster storm — the costliest disaster in American history. Some disaster experts say the government's preoccupation with terrorism — including the deployment of thousands of National Guard and Reserve troops in Iraq — has jeopardized domestic emergency-response capabilities. President Bush proposes putting active-duty troops in charge when states and local communities are overwhelmed by a disaster —whether manmade or natural — but many state officials don't want to give up control. Both Congress and the White House are investigating post-Katrina emergency operations to avoid similar mistakes next time. Meanwhile, disaster officials say Katrina showed the need for individual citizens to be prepared to serve as first-responders for their own families.

Wounded Veterans: Is America Shortchanging Vets on Health Care?

Early this year, *The Washington Post* exposed shockingly substandard treatment for wounded veterans at Walter Reed Army Medical Center's outpatient facilities. Follow-up investigations soon turned up evidence that problems extended beyond shabby conditions at the military's top-drawer hospital. On the battlefield, military surgeons are saving many more lives than ever before. But once they return home, men and women recovering from sometimes devastating war injuries confront a red-tape jungle of laws and regulations. Moreover, many wait months for treatment or benefits, and some even have had reenlistment bonuses withheld after wounds forced them out of active service. A history of disgraceful treatment of veterans of past wars, including the Vietnam conflict, looms over the issue. Amid the present uproar, a presidential panel on military and veterans' health care has called for far-reaching changes, but some critics say changes need to go deeper if the country is to live up to its promises to its troops.

Religious Fundamentalism: Does It Lead to Intolerance and Violence?

People around the world are embracing fundamentalism, a belief in the literal interpretation of holy texts and, among the more hard-line groups, the desire to replace secular law with religious law. At the same time, deadly attacks by religious extremists in India, Uganda, Somalia and Nigeria are on the rise — and not just among Muslims. Meanwhile, political Islamism — which seeks to install Islamic law via the ballot box — is increasing in places like Morocco and in Muslim communities in Europe. Christian evangelicalism and Pentacostalism — the denominations from which fundamentalism derives — also are flourishing in Latin America, Africa, Central Asia and the United States. Ultra-Orthodox Jewish fundamentalists are blamed for exacerbating instability in the Middle East and beyond by establishing and expanding settlements on Palestinian

lands. And intolerance is growing among Hindus in India, leading to deadly attacks against Christians and others. As experts debate what is causing the spread of fundamentalism, others question whether fundamentalists should have a greater voice in government.

Energy Nationalism: Do Petrostates Threaten Global Energy Security?

A world thirsting for imported oil and gas is seeking new supplies in Central Asia and Africa, where many nations have nationalized their energy resources. In a dramatic reversal from 30 years ago, government-owned or controlled petroleum companies today control 77 percent of the world's 1.1 trillion barrels of oil reserves. While the emergence of these rising petrostates has helped diversify the world's energy sources, many are considered oil "hot spots" — vulnerable to disruption from international terrorists or domestic dissidents. In addition, many of the petrostates are blending politics and energy into a new energy nationalism, rewriting the rules of the world's energy markets and restricting international oil corporations' operations. Russia's confrontational energy policies alarm its neighbors, and critics say a booming China is combing the world for access to oil and gas resources without concern for suppliers' corruption or human rights violations. Many also worry that growing competition for dwindling oil supplies will lead to greater risks of international conflict.

Oceans in Crisis: Can the Loss of Ocean Biodiversity Be Halted?

The world's oceans are in a dire state. Large predatory species are being decimated — including sharks, whales, tuna, grouper, cod, halibut, swordfish and marlin — and replaced by species with less commercial and nutritive value. In fact, a growing body of evidence suggests that the world's marine ecosystems have been altered so dramatically they are undergoing evolution in reverse, returning to a time when algae and jellyfish dominated the seas. The crisis is having an increasingly profound effect on humans. Fishing cultures from Newfoundland to West Africa are vanishing, and toxic algal blooms have closed beaches and recreational areas from Florida to the Black Sea. The damage is being caused by overfishing, climate change and destruction of habitat due to coastal development and pollution. Scientists and policy makers widely agree that a broad-based approach known as ecosystem-based management would help restore the oceans' productivity, but significant research and strong international cooperation are needed to bring about such a shift.

Avian Flu Threat: Are We Prepared for the Next Pandemic?

As deaths from bird flu continue to mount in Asia — and now threaten Europe — concern about a worldwide epidemic has prompted calls to action at the highest levels of government. Last month, in response to President Bush's emergency request, Congress approved $3.8 billion to develop new vaccines and stockpile anti-flu medications. Some critics say it's too little too late. If a pandemic hit tomorrow, the nation would have drugs to treat only very few people, no approved vaccine and a public health system that is woefully unprepared for a pandemic. With each new case of human infection, the danger increases that bird flu could easily pass among humans, health authorities warn. But some scientists doubt the virus will mutate into one that is easily transmitted from human to human. So far, most victims had close contact with poultry. But even skeptics agree a flu pandemic is inevitable at some point, and that the nation needs to shore up its response.

Anti Americanism: Is Anger at the U.S. Growing?

"We are all Americans," a banner headline in *Le Monde* declared after the terrorist attacks on Sept. 11, 2001. But the warm embrace from France and the rest of the global community was short-lived. The U.S. invasion of Iraq has unleashed a torrent of anger at the United States. Often directed at President George W. Bush and his policies, it takes aim at everything from the abuses at Abu Ghraib prison to the mounting death toll in Iraq to U.S. policies on climate change. Before the war, anti-Americanism had seemed the province of leftists who demonized capitalism, or those who resented America's unrelenting cultural influence — what some call the McGlobalization of the world. Now, anti-Americanism seems epidemic, especially in the Muslim world but also in Europe, Asia and Latin America. In European intellectual circles it has even become a badge of honor. Ironically, while resentment of the U.S. simmers, people seeking economic opportunity continue to emigrate to the U.S.

Preface

What is human trafficking and where does it occur? Is anti-Americanism and anger at the United States growing? How have other nations exploited children as child soldiers and what can be done about it? Has violence and discrimination against women increased or decreased globally over the past decade? Is religious fundamentalism on the rise? These questions and many more are addressed in a collection of articles for debate offered exclusively through *CQ Researcher,* CQ Press and SAGE. With a focus on articles that bring students up to date on timely global issues, this reader promotes in-depth discussion and helps students formulate their own positions on critical issues. Furthermore, it helps bring pressing international issues into the classroom for almost any course across the social work curriculum, as required by the new guidelines set forth by the Council on Social Work Education.

This first edition includes twelve up-to-date reports by *CQ Researcher*, an award-winning weekly policy brief that brings complicated issues down to earth. This collection was carefully crafted to cover a range of issues relevant to social workers and will help your students gain a deeper, more critical perspective of international issues and debates in social work.

CQ RESEARCHER

CQ Researcher was founded in 1923 as *Editorial Research Reports* and was sold primarily to newspapers as a research tool. The magazine was renamed and redesigned in 1991 as *CQ Researcher.* Today, students are its primary audience. While still used by hundreds of journalists and newspapers, many of which reprint portions of the reports, the *Researcher's* main subscribers are now high school, college and public libraries. In 2002, *Researcher* won the American Bar Association's coveted Silver Gavel award for magazine excellence for a series of nine reports on civil liberties and other legal issues.

Researcher staff writers—all highly experienced journalists—sometimes compare the experience of writing a *Researcher* report to drafting a college term paper. Indeed, there are many similarities. Each report is as long as many term papers—about 11,000 words—and is written by one person without any significant outside help. One of the key differences is that writers interview leading experts, scholars and government officials for each issue.

Like students, staff writers begin the creative process by choosing a topic. Working with the *Researcher's* editors, the writer identifies a controversial subject that has important public policy implications. After a topic is selected, the writer embarks on one to two weeks of intense research. Newspaper and magazine articles are clipped or downloaded, books are ordered and information is gathered from a wide variety of sources, including interest groups, universities and the government. Once the writers are well informed, they develop a detailed outline, and begin the interview process. Each report requires a minimum of ten to fifteen interviews with academics, officials, lobbyists and people working in the field. Only after all interviews are completed does the writing begin.

CHAPTER FORMAT

Each issue of *CQ Researcher*, and therefore each selection in this book, is structured in the same way. Each begins with an overview, which briefly summarizes the areas that will be explored in greater detail in the rest of the chapter. The next section chronicles important and current debates on the topic under discussion and is structured around a number of key questions, such as "Does corporate social responsibility really improve society?" or "Does corporate social responsibility restrain U.S. productivity?" These questions are usually the subject of much debate among practitioners and scholars in the field. Hence, the answers presented are never conclusive but detail the range of opinion on the topic.

Next, the "Background" section provides a history of the issue being examined. This retrospective covers important legislative measures, executive actions and court decisions that illustrate how current policy has evolved. Then the "Current Situation" section examines contemporary policy issues, legislation under consideration and legal action being taken. Each selection concludes with an "Outlook" section, which addresses possible regulation, court rulings and initiatives from Capitol Hill and the White House over the next five to ten years.

Each report contains features that augment the main text: two to three sidebars that examine issues related to the topic at hand, a pro versus con debate between two experts, a chronology of key dates and events and an annotated bibliography detailing major sources used by the writer.

ACKNOWLEDGMENTS

We wish to thank many people for helping to make this collection a reality. Tom Colin, managing editor of *CQ Researcher*, gave us his enthusiastic support and cooperation as we developed this edition. He and his talented staff of editors and writers have amassed a first-class library of *Researcher* reports, and we are fortunate to have access to that rich cache. We also wish to thank our colleagues at CQ Press, a division of SAGE and a leading publisher of books, directories, research publications and Web products on U.S. government, world affairs and communications. They have forged the way in making these readers a useful resource for instruction across a range of undergraduate and graduate courses.

Some readers may be learning about *CQ Researcher* for the first time. We expect that many readers will want regular access to this excellent weekly research tool. For subscription information or a no-obligation free trial of *CQ Researcher*, please contact CQ Press at www.cqpress.com or toll-free at 1-866-4CQ-PRESS (1-866-427-7737).

We hope that you will be pleased by this edition of *International Issues in Social Work and Social Welfare*. We welcome your feedback and suggestions for future editions. Please direct comments to Kassie Graves, Acquisitions Editor, SAGE Publications, 2455 Teller Road, Thousand Oaks, CA 91320, or kassie.graves@sagepub.com.

—The Editors of SAGE

Contributors

Brian Beary, a freelance journalist based in Washington, D.C., specializes in European Union (EU) affairs and is the U.S. correspondent for *Europolitics*, the EU-affairs daily newspaper. Originally from Dublin, Ireland, he worked in the European Parliament for Irish MEP Pat "The Cope" Gallagher in 2000 and at the EU Commission's Eurobarometer unit on public opinion analysis. A fluent French speaker, he appears regularly as a guest international-relations expert on television and radio programs. Beary also writes for the *European Parliament Magazine* and the *Irish Examiner* daily newspaper. His last report for *CQ Global Researcher* was "Race for the Arctic."

Peter Behr recently retired from *The Washington Post*, where he was the principal reporter on energy issues and served as business editor from 1987-1992. A former Nieman Fellow at Harvard University, Behr worked at the Woodrow Wilson Center for Scholars and is working on a book about the history of the U.S. electric power grid.

John Felton is a freelance journalist who has written about international affairs and U.S. foreign policy for nearly 30 years. He covered foreign affairs for the *Congressional Quarterly Weekly Report* during the 1980s, was deputy foreign editor for National Public Radio in the early 1990s and has been a freelance writer specializing in international topics for the past 15 years. His most recent book, published by CQ Press, is *The Contemporary Middle East: A Documentary History*. He lives in Stockbridge, Massachusetts.

Karen Foerstel is a freelance writer who has worked for the Congressional Quarterly *Weekly Report* and *Daily Monitor, The New*

York Post and *Roll Call*, a Capitol Hill newspaper. She has published two books on women in Congress, *Climbing the Hill: Gender Conflict in Congress* and *The Biographical Dictionary of Women in Congress*. Her most recent *CQ Global Researcher* report was "China in Africa." She has worked in Africa with ChildsLife International, a non-profit that helps needy children around the world, and with Blue Ventures, a marine conservation organization that protects coral reefs in Madagascar.

Sarah Glazer, a New York freelancer, is a regular contributor to *CQ Researcher*. Her articles on health, education and social-policy issues have appeared in *The New York Times*, *The Washington Post*, *The Public Interest* and *Gender and Work*, a book of essays. Her recent *CQ Researcher* reports include "Increase in Autism" and "Gender and Learning." She graduated from the University of Chicago with a BA in American history.

Peter Katel is a *CQ Researcher* staff writer who previously reported on Haiti and Latin America for *Time* and *Newsweek* and covered the Southwest for newspapers in New Mexico. He has received several journalism awards, including the Bartolomé Mitre Award for coverage of drug trafficking from the Inter-American Press Association. He holds an AB in university studies from the University of New Mexico. His recent reports include "New Strategy in Iraq," "Prison Reform" and "Real ID."

Samuel Loewenberg, now based in Berlin, is an award-winning freelance writer who has reported on global issues for *The New York Times*, *The Economist*, *The Washington Post* and *Newsweek*, among others. He covered the terrorist bombings in both Madrid and London as well as the anti-globalization movement in Brazil. He is a former Columbia University Knight-Bagehot Journalism Fellow.

David Masci specializes in science, religion and foreign policy issues. Before joining *CQ Researcher* in 1996, he was a reporter at Congressional Quarterly's *Daily Monitor* and *CQ Weekly*. He holds a law degree from The George Washington University and a BA in medieval history from Syracuse University. His recent reports include "Rebuilding Iraq" and "Torture."

Pamela M. Prah is a *CQ Researcher* staff writer with several years previous experience at Stateline.org, *Kiplinger's Washington Letter* and the Bureau of National Affairs. She holds a master's degree in government from Johns Hopkins University and a journalism degree from Ohio University. Her recent reports include "War in Iraq," "Methamphetamines" and "Labor Unions' Future."

Jennifer Weeks is a *CQ Researcher* contributing writer in Watertown, Massachusetts, who specializes in energy and environmental issues. She has written for *The Washington Post*, *The Boston Globe Magazine* and other publications, and has 15 years' experience as a public-policy analyst, lobbyist and congressional staffer. She has an AB degree from Williams College and master's degrees from the University of North Carolina and Harvard. Her previous *CQ Global Researcher* examined "Carbon Trading."

Colin Woodard has reported from more than 40 foreign countries on six continents and lived in Eastern Europe for more than four years. He is the author of *Ocean's End: Travels Through Endangered Seas*, a narrative, nonfiction account of the deterioration of the world's oceans. He also writes for *The Christian Science Monitor* and *The Chronicle of Higher Education*. His previous *CQ Global Researcher* report was on climate change.

Human Trafficking and Slavery

Are the World's Nations
Doing Enough to Stamp It Out?

David Masci

Tearful Eastern European women comfort each other after being freed in 2000 from an American-owned hotel in Phnom Penh, Cambodia, where they were forced to have sex with businessmen and government officials. Traffickers in Eastern Europe often lure young women into bondage by advertising phony jobs abroad for nannies, models or actresses.

AFP Photo/Philippe Lopez

From *CQ Researcher,*
March 26, 2004.

O ne morning in May, 7-year-old Francis Bok walked to the market in Nymlal, Sudan, to sell some eggs and peanuts. The farmer's son had made the same trip many times before.

"I was living a very good life with my family," he recalls today. "I was a happy child."

But his happy life ended that day in 1986. Arab raiders from northern Sudan swept into the village, sowing death and destruction. "They came on horses and camels and running on foot, firing machine guns and killing people everywhere," he says. His entire family — mother, father and two sisters — died in the attack.

The raiders grabbed Francis and several other children, lashed them to donkeys and carried them north for two days. Then the children were parceled out to their captors. Francis went to a man named Giema Abdullah.

For the next 10 years, the boy tended his "owner's" goats and cattle. He slept with the animals, never had a day off and was rarely fed properly.

"He treated me like an animal, he even called me an animal, and he beat me," Francis says. "There was no joy. Even when I remembered my happy life before, it only made me sad."

In 1996, Francis escaped to Sudan's capital, Khartoum; then he made his way to Cairo, Egypt, and eventually in 2000 to the United States, which admitted him as a refugee.

As all American students learn, the Civil War ended slavery in the United States in 1865. Internationally, the practice was banned by several agreements and treaties, beginning in

Where Human Trafficking Occurs

Human trafficking and slavery take place in virtually every country in the world, but the U.N. and other reliable sources say the most extensive trafficking occurs in the countries below (listed at right).

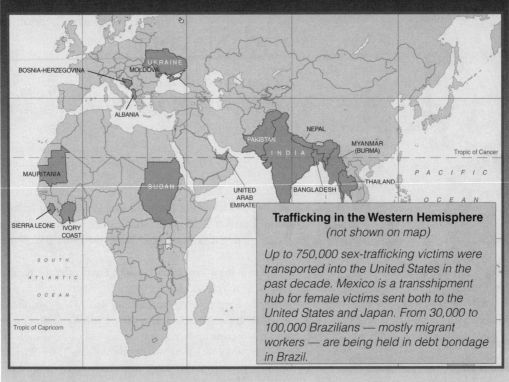

Trafficking in the Western Hemisphere
(not shown on map)

Up to 750,000 sex-trafficking victims were transported into the United States in the past decade. Mexico is a transshipment hub for female victims sent both to the United States and Japan. From 30,000 to 100,000 Brazilians — mostly migrant workers — are being held in debt bondage in Brazil.

Sources: Protection Project at Johns Hopkins University, U.S. State Department, Human Rights Watch, International Labour Organization, American Anti-Slavery Group

1926 with the Slavery Convention of the League of Nations. But for tens of millions of people around the world, including millions of children like Francis, slavery never ended. An estimated 27 million people currently are held in some form of bondage, according to anti-slavery groups like Free the Slaves.[1] From the villages of Sudan and Mauritania in Africa to the factories, sweatshops and brothels of South Asia, slavery in its rawest, cruelest form is very much alive in the 21st century.

Many of those in bondage were kidnapped, like Francis. Others go voluntarily to different countries, thinking they are heading for a better life, only to be forced into a nightmare of prostitution or hard labor. Many more work as bonded laborers, tied to lifetime servitude because their father or grandfather borrowed money they couldn't repay.

Trafficking people across international borders has become a $12-billion-a-year global industry that touches virtually every country. The U.S. government estimates that between 800,000 and 900,000 people are trafficked internationally every year, many of them women and children, transported as sex workers.[2] The total includes up to 20,000 people forcibly trafficked into the United

Europe	
Albania	Up to 90 percent of the girls in rural areas don't go to school for fear of being abducted and sold into sexual servitude.
Bosnia and Herzegovina	A quarter of the women working in nightclubs claim they were forced into prostitution. The U.N. police task force is suspected of covering up its involvement in the sex trade.
Moldova	Up to 80 percent of the women trafficked as prostitutes in Western Europe may be Moldovans.
Ukraine	Up to 400,000 Ukrainian women have been trafficked for sexual exploitation in the past decade, Ukraine says. Ukrainian sex slaves can fetch up to $25,000 in Israel.
Africa	
Ivory Coast	A girl can allegedly be bought as a slave in Abidjan for about $7; a shipment of 10 children from Mali for work on the cocoa plantations costs about $420.
Mauritania	Light-skinned Arab Berbers today are thought to exploit hundreds of thousands of black African slaves. Slave raids in the 13th century began systemic slavery in Mauritania.
Sudan	Muslim tribesmen from northern Sudan still stage slave raids on non-Muslim Dinka peoples in the south, taking thousands of women and children.
Asia	
Bangladesh	An estimated 25,000 women and children are trafficked annually from Bangladesh.
India	Parents have sold an estimated 15 million children into bonded labor in return for meager loans from moneylenders.
Myanmar	The ruling military junta coerces minorities into forced labor in factories that benefit the regime and foreign corporations.
Nepal	A major source of women trafficked into Indian brothels; in addition, an estimated 75,000 people are trapped as bonded laborers in Nepal.
Pakistan	Millions of Pakistanis, often members of religious minorities, are forced to work as brick makers or in the fields of feudal landowners.
Thailand	Children sold by their parents make up a significant percentage of prostitutes in Thailand, which is a prime destination for pedophile sex tourists.
United Arab Emirates	Many women trafficked from the former Soviet Union end up in the UAE.

States annually, according to the Central Intelligence Agency.[3] (*See sidebar, p. 12.*)

Lyudmilla's story is typical. Like many desperately poor young women, the single mother of three from the former Soviet republic of Moldova responded to an advertisement promising work in Italy. Instead she was taken to a brothel in Macedonia, where she spent two horrific years in sexual slavery before escaping in 2002.[4]

Venecija, a Bulgarian, also ended up in a Macedonian brothel. "We were so tired we couldn't get out of bed," she recalled. "But [we had to] put on makeup and meet customers," she said after escaping. Those who refused were beaten until they "changed their minds."[5]

John Eibner of Christian Solidarity International pays an Arab trader to free 132 slaves in Madhol, northern Sudan, in 1997. Critics of slave-redemption say it only encourages more slave-taking, but supporters say that not trying to free slaves would be unconscionable.

Traffickers control their victims through a variety of coercive means. In addition to rape and beatings, they keep their passports, leaving them with few options if they do manage to escape.

And the violence can follow those who do get away. Mercy, a young West African woman trafficked to Italy, escaped her tormentors only to see her sister killed in retribution after Mercy told human rights groups about her experience.[6]

The vast majority of slaves and victims of human trafficking come from the poorest parts of Africa, Asia, Latin America and Eastern Europe, where smooth-talking traffickers often easily deceive desperate victims or their parents into believing that they are being offered a "better life."

"Being poor doesn't make you a slave, but it does make you vulnerable to being a slave," says Peggy Callahan, a spokeswoman for Free the Slaves, based in Washington, D.C.

Some Christian groups and non-governmental organizations (NGOs) have tried to buy slaves out of bondage, particularly in Sudan, where two decades of civil war have stoked the slave trade. But many humanitarian groups argue that so-called slave redemption merely increases the demand for slaves.

International efforts to fight slavery and trafficking have increased dramatically over the last 10 years, with the United States playing a leading role. President Bush dramatized America's commitment in an address to the U.N. General Assembly on Sept. 23, 2003. The president had been expected to focus on security issues in the Middle East, but he devoted a substantial portion of his remarks to urging the international community to do more to fight trafficking.

"There is a special evil in the abuse and exploitation of the most innocent and vulnerable," Bush said. "Nearly two centuries after the abolition of the transatlantic slave trade, and more than a century after slavery was officially ended in its last strongholds, the trade in human beings for any purpose must not be allowed to thrive."[7]

The cornerstone of recent American anti-trafficking efforts is the 2000 Trafficking Victims Protection Act, which mandates the cutoff of most non-humanitarian U.S. aid for any nation deemed not trying hard enough to address the problem.

"The act breaks new ground because it actually tries to bring about changes in other countries," says Wendy Young, director of external relations for the Women's Commission for Refugee Women and Children in New York City.

"It's making a difference in countries all over the world," agrees Rep. Christopher H. Smith, R-N.J., one of the law's authors.

But critics contend the act is too weak to force real behavior changes. "It's very easy for countries to avoid sanctions just by taking a few largely meaningless actions," says Katherine Chon, co-director of the Polaris Project, an anti-trafficking advocacy group in Washington. She also accuses the administration of giving a pass to important allies, like Saudi Arabia, regardless of what they do to ameliorate their forced-labor practices.

All sides agree that many countries where trafficking occurs have a long way to go before they attain the level of economic, legal and political maturity needed to entirely eliminate the practice. "I don't think people realize just how desperately poor and chaotic many countries are today," says Linda Beher, a spokeswoman for the New York City-based United Methodist Committee On Relief, which assists trafficking victims.

A tragic consequence of this poverty is child labor, which many experts see as a cousin to slavery. In the developing world today, nearly 200 million children ages 5-14 are put to work to help support their families, according to the International Labour Organization

(ILO). Almost half are under age 12, and more than 20 million are engaged in highly hazardous work, such as tanning leather or weaving rugs, exposing them to unhealthy chemicals or airborne pollutants.[8]

Some humanitarian aid workers describe much child labor as inherently coercive, because young children often have no choice.

The ILO argues that eliminating child labor and sending children to school would ultimately benefit nations with child laborers by raising income levels. (*See graph, p. 6.*) But some economists counter that putting even a fraction of the working children in school would be prohibitively expensive.

As experts debate resolving what has been called one of the greatest humanitarian problems of the 21st century, here are some of the questions they are asking:

Does buying slaves in order to free them solve the problem?

In recent years, would-be Samaritans — from Christian missionaries to famous rock musicians — have worked to free slaves in Africa. Although slave trading occurs in many countries, the rescue efforts largely have focused on war-torn Sudan, where Muslim raiders from the north have enslaved hundreds of thousands of Christian and animist tribesmen in the south.

The Sudanese government has done virtually nothing to stop the practice and has even encouraged it as a means of prosecuting the war against the rebellious south, according to the U.S. State Department's 2003 "Trafficking in Persons Report."

Since 1995, Christian Solidarity International (CSI) and other slave-redemption groups operating in Sudan say they have purchased the freedom of more than 60,000 people by providing money for local Sudanese to buy slaves and then free them.[9]

Fighting the Traffickers

The 2000 Trafficking Victims Protection Act requires the State Department to report each year on global efforts to end human trafficking. Last year, 15 countries were placed in Tier 3, for those deemed to be doing little or nothing against trafficking. Countries in Tier 3 for three years in a row can lose all U.S. non-humanitarian aid. Tier 1 countries are considered to be actively fighting trafficking. Seventy-five countries are in Tier 2, indicating they are making some efforts against trafficking.

State Department Anti-Trafficking Ratings

Tier 1 — Actively Fighting Trafficking		
Austria	Hong Kong	Poland
Belgium	Italy	Portugal
Benin	South Korea	Spain
Colombia	Lithuania	Sweden
Czech Republic	Macedonia	Switzerland
Denmark	Mauritius	Taiwan
France	Morocco	United Arab Emirates
Germany	The Netherlands	United Kingdom
Ghana		

Tier 3 — Doing Little or Nothing		
Belize	Georgia	North Korea
Bosnia and Herzegovina	Greece	Sudan
Myanmar	Haiti	Suriname
Cuba	Kazakhstan	Turkey
Dominican Republic	Liberia	Uzbekistan

Source: "2003 Trafficking in Persons Report," Office to Monitor and Combat Trafficking in Persons, Department of State, June 2003

"Women and children are freed from the terrible abuse, the rape, the beatings, the forcible conversions [to Islam] — all of the horrors that are an inherent part of slavery in Sudan," said John Eibner, director of CSI's redemption program.[10]

Halfway around the world, *New York Times* columnist Nicholas D. Kristof had his own brush with slave redemption when he traveled to Cambodia and freed two female sex slaves. "I woke up her brothel's owner at dawn," he wrote of his efforts to purchase one of the prostitutes, "handed over $150, brushed off demands for interest on the debt and got a receipt for $150 for buying

Economic Benefits Cited for Ending Child Labor

Banning child labor and educating all children would raise the world's total income by 22 percent, or $4.3 trillion, over 20 years, according to the International Labour Organization (ILO). The principal benefit would be the economic boost that most countries would experience if all children were educated through lower secondary school, plus substantial but less dramatic health benefits. The ILO analysis assumes countries that banned child labor would pay poor parents for their children's lost wages, something critics say is unrealistically expensive.

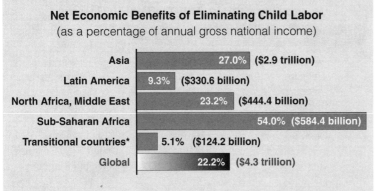

Net Economic Benefits of Eliminating Child Labor
(as a percentage of annual gross national income)

Asia	27.0%	($2.9 trillion)
Latin America	9.3%	($330.6 billion)
North Africa, Middle East	23.2%	($444.4 billion)
Sub-Saharan Africa	54.0%	($584.4 billion)
Transitional countries*	5.1%	($124.2 billion)
Global	22.2%	($4.3 trillion)

* Transitional countries — such as Taiwan, Singapore and Malaysia — are no longer considered "developing" but not yet classified as fully industrialized.

Source: "Investing in Every Child," International Programme on the Elimination of Child Labour, International Labour Office, December 2003

a girl's freedom. Then Srey Neth and I fled before the brothel's owner was even out of bed."[11]

While experts concede that slave redeemers are well-intentioned, many contend the practice actually does more harm than good. "When you have people running around buying up slaves, you help create market demand for more slaves," says Jim Jacobson, president of Christian Freedom International, a relief group in Front Royal, Va., that stopped its slave-repatriation efforts five years ago. "It's really just simple economics."

Kevin Bales, author of *Disposable People: New Slavery in the Global Economy* and president of Free the Slaves, agrees. "This is like paying a burglar to redeem the television set he just stole," says Bales, a noted expert on contemporary slavery. "It's better to find other ways to free people, like going to the police or taking them out of bondage by force."

Indeed, Jacobson says, redemption only puts more money in the pockets of unscrupulous and often violent slave traders. "These people end up taking the money and buying more guns and hiring more thugs to go out and take more slaves," he says.

In addition, the critics say, many "slaves" pretend to be in bondage to defraud Westerners. "If you talk to aid workers in these places, you'll find that [bogus slave traders] are literally picking up [already free] people from across town and 'selling' them an hour later," Free the Slaves' Callahan says.

"So much of it is a huge scam operation," agrees Jacobson. "A lot of these people aren't really slaves."

But supporters of redemption say it would be unconscionable not to attempt to free slaves, even if slavers will go out searching for new victims. "Slaves are treated so badly, especially the women and children, who have been beaten and raped," says William Saunders, human rights counsel for the Family Research Council, a conservative social-policy group, and co-founder of the Bishop Gassis Sudan Relief Fund, both in Washington. "How can you not try to free these people?"

Saunders and others also contend that slave buyers take steps to avoid creating a bigger market for slaves. "In the Sudan, they use the local currency, because a dollar or a [British] pound is the sort of powerful magnet that might give people incentives to take more slaves or present non-slaves," he says.

In addition, redemption supporters say, they usually cap what they will pay per person — typically $50. "There's a real effort to ensure that we don't inflate the value of slaves," says Tommy Ray Calvert, chief of external operations for the Boston-based American Anti-Slavery Group (AASG).

Calvert contends that the redemptions have helped decrease slave raids in Sudan. The redemptions "brought world attention to the issue and forced our government and others to start pressuring the Sudanese to stop this evil practice," he says.

Moreover, Saunders refutes the charge that redeemers simply set people free without trying to ensure that they are true slaves. "They try to repatriate these people directly to their villages," Saunders says. "They don't just buy their freedom and let them go."

But the critics remain dubious. "It's so hard to get anywhere in Sudan that there is no way that they could actually follow all of these people back to their home villages," Jacobson says. "It would take weeks or months."

Moreover, he says, "they don't have any idea whether the people they've freed have been coached or whether the village they're going to is really their village. It's simply impossible to know."

Is the Trafficking Victims Protection Act tough enough?

The $12 billion human-trafficking industry is now the world's third-largest illegal business, surpassing every other criminal enterprise except the drug and arms trades, according to the United Nations.[12]

In October 2000, the U.S. government zeroed in on the problem, enacting the Trafficking Victims Protection Act (TVPA), which targets the illegal trade both at home and abroad.[13] The law established the State Department's Office to Monitor and Combat Trafficking in Persons, which issues an annual report on what countries are doing to end trafficking.

The report uses a three-tiered system to rank countries — from states that actively fight trafficking (Tier 1) to those doing little (Tier 3). Countries classified as Tier 3 for three years in a row are subject to a cut-off of non-humanitarian U.S. aid. (*See sidebar, p. 12.*)

On the domestic side, the law allows U.S. authorities to charge alleged traffickers in the United States under the tough federal anti-racketeering law (RICO). According to the State Department, 111 persons have been charged with trafficking in the first three years since the law was enacted, a threefold increase over the three-year period before the TVPA went into effect.[14]

The law also makes it easier for trafficked victims to acquire refugee status in the United States and allows them to sue their victimizers for damages in civil court.

Rescuers return 14 children to their native Bangladesh after they were abducted to India. Children in poor countries sometimes are sold by their parents or kidnapped by traffickers and forced to work without pay, frequently in hazardous conditions.

AFP Photo

President Bill Clinton signed the bill into law on Oct. 28, 2000, saying it would provide "important new tools and resources to combat the worldwide scourge of trafficking."

Today, however, critics argue that while the act is "a step in the right direction," it is ultimately not tough enough to shake up the industry, especially internationally. "Of course, it's good that we have it, but frankly we have an awfully long way to go," says the Polaris Project's Chon.

She especially criticizes provisions requiring countries to fight trafficking or face American penalties. "It's just not strong enough because it allows countries to avoid sanctions with just superficial acts," she says.

For example, she says, Japan responded to U.S. pressure to curtail sex trafficking by "giving Cambodia a few million dollars in anti-trafficking aid and holding a symposium on trafficking." But the Japanese did "not really do anything to substantially crack down on their own widespread problem."

Yet, she adds, the United States has said Japan has been tackling trafficking enough to avoid a Tier 3 classification and the prospect of sanctions. "Japan is an important ally," she says. "Need I say more?"

Other critics allege that certain countries are treated with "kid gloves" for political reasons. "States like Saudi

Arabia and countries from the former Soviet Union, which are important American allies, have been pushed up to Tier 2 because stopping slavery isn't the priority [in U.S. foreign relations] it should be," says Calvert of the AASG.

Calvert is especially incensed that the government failed to classify Mauritania, on Africa's northwestern coast, in Tier 3, calling it instead a "special case" because of insufficient information to make an accurate determination. "This is a country with literally hundreds of thousands of people in chattel slavery and everyone knows it, and yet it gets a pass," he says. "That is just unbelievable to me."

But supporters contend that the TVPA, while not perfect, helps move problem countries in the right direction. "It's important to have a tool we can use to push foreign governments to act against this terrible abuse of human dignity, and this law does that," says Beher, of the United Methodist Committee On Relief.

In Japan, for instance, the law has helped make the fight against trafficking more effective, raising public awareness of the problem dramatically as a result of the debate over its ranking in the TVPA, supporters add.

"When Japan was dropped from Tier 1 to Tier 2, it was very embarrassing for them, and all of a sudden you saw this real public debate about the trafficking issue — which is a huge problem there," says Diana Pinata, a spokeswoman for Vital Voices, a global woman's advocacy group in Washington. "If nothing else, the [annual State Department trafficking] report and the threat of sanctions keeps the issue in the spotlight in these countries, and that's very positive."

Besides Japan, several other countries, including Russia, Saudi Arabia and Indonesia, have dramatically improved their anti-trafficking efforts as a result of pressure brought to bear by the TVPA, says John Miller, director of the Office to Combat Trafficking. "We've seen real efforts all over the world," he says. "Some have been more substantial than others, but there already has been a lot of progress."

Moreover, Miller rejects the charge of political favoritism. "Look at the Tier 3 list, and you'll see that there are U.S. allies like Greece and Turkey there," he says. "These decisions aren't being made on the basis of politics."

Pinata agrees. "When we speak to NGO workers and others in the field working on this issue, we get the sense

that the trafficking report's assessment of these countries is essentially correct," she says.

Should most forms of child labor be eliminated?

Zara Cigay, 12, and her two younger brothers don't go to school. Instead, they help their parents and extended family, migrant farm workers who pick cotton and other crops in southern Turkey.

"Wherever there is a job, we do it," said Huseyin Cigay, Zara's great-uncle. "The children work with us everywhere."[15]

More than 250 million children around the world between the ages of 5 and 17 are working, according to the ILO. Most are in developing countries in Africa and Asia, and nearly half work full time like Zara and her brothers.[16]

Many do strenuous farm labor. In cities, they do everything from retailing and domestic service to manufacturing and construction. In nations beset by civil wars, thousands of children have been forced to fight in rebel armies.[17]

A large portion of child labor is coerced, according to child-welfare experts. Children are often sold by their parents or kidnapped and forced to work virtually as slaves for no pay. In India, children are literally tied to weaving looms so that they cannot run away.

Labor experts uniformly condemn forced and bonded labor. But on the question of child labor in general, the experts are split over whether the practice should be condoned under certain circumstances.

Human rights advocates and others point to the ILO's 1999 Worst Forms of Child Labor Convention, which prohibits all full-time work and any work by children under 12 but sanctions part-time, non-hazardous labor for teenagers that does not interfere with their social development.[18]

"Under international law, children have a right to a basic education," says Karin Landgren, chief of child protection at the United Nations Children's Fund (UNICEF). "Work should never interfere with this."

In addition, Landgren says, "They need to have time to play and participate freely in their country's cultural and social life. This is vitally important if they are to develop into healthy adults."

A recent ILO report says that child labor negatively impacts all levels of society. "Child labor perpetuates poverty, because when children don't have an education and a real chance to develop to their fullest potential, they are mortgaging their future," says Frans Roselaers, director of the organization's international program on the elimination of child labor and author of the report.

Child labor also costs societies economically by producing uneducated adult workers, Roselaers says. "Countries with a lot of child workers are stunting their economic growth," he says, "because they will only end up producing an army of weak and tired workers with no skills."

But some economists counter that child labor, even full-time work, is often a necessity in developing countries. "In an ideal world, children would spend all of their time at school and at play, but poor people in poor countries don't have the kind of options that we in rich countries do," says Ian Vasquez, director of the Project on Global Economic Liberty at the Cato Institute, a libertarian think tank. "When you begin to restrict children's options for work, you can end up hurting children and their families."

Indeed, child labor often is the only thing that stands between survival and starvation, some experts say. "No parents want their child to work, but child labor helps families get by," says Deepak Lal, a professor of international-development studies at the University of California, Los Angeles. "When a country's per capita income rises to about $3,000 or $4,000, child labor usually fades away."

In addition, Lal says, working children often end up with a better education than those who don't work. "The public education system is a failure in many parts of the developing world and really doesn't offer much to the children who attend school," he says. "But if a child works and his family earns enough to send him or his siblings to private school, that can really pay off."

Finally, Vasquez argues that outlawing child labor would only drive the problem underground, where there is no government oversight, and abuses would increase. "In Bangladesh, girls were prevented from continuing to work in textile plants, so many ended up as prostitutes," he says. "People need to make money, and if you deny them one route, they'll take another."

But Roselaers counters that child workers would not be driven to more dangerous and demeaning jobs if the international community eased the transition from work to school. In the case of Bangladesh, he says, the threat of a consumer boycott by Western countries prompted textile factory owners to fire their child employees.

"The factory owners panicked and fired the kids, and so, yes, there were problems," he says. "But when groups like the ILO and UNICEF came in, we started offering the parents stipends to make up for the lost income and easing the children's transition from work to school."

Some 1 million children are now being helped to make the transition from work to school, according to a recent ILO report.[19] In India, for instance, the ILO and the U.S. Department of Labor are spending $40 million this year to target 80,000 children working in hazardous jobs.[20]

Nonetheless, Lal says, such a program could only make a small dent in the problem. "You can't give a stipend to each of the many millions of families that send their children to work," he says. "There isn't enough money to do this, so it's not a realistic solution, just a palliative that make Westerners feel good about themselves."

BACKGROUND

Ancient Practice

Slavery is as old as human civilization. All of the world's great founding cultures, including those in Mesopotamia, China, Egypt and India, accepted slavery as a fact of life.[21] The practice also was common in sub-Saharan Africa and the Americas.

Neither the Bible nor the great thinkers of Greece and Rome took firm positions against slavery. Some, like the Greek philosopher Aristotle, vigorously defended it.

It was not until Enlightenment philosophers like John Locke and Voltaire established new definitions of human freedom and dignity in the 17th and 18th centuries, that large numbers of people started questioning the morality of keeping another person in bondage.

Ancient societies typically acquired slaves from outside their borders, usually through war or territorial conquest. Captives and conquered people often served as agricultural workers or domestic servants.

Slavery probably reached its zenith in ancient Greece and then Rome, where human trafficking became a huge and profitable industry. In many Greek cities, including powerful Athens and Sparta, as many as half the residents

CHRONOLOGY

19th Century *After thousands of years, slavery is abolished in much of the world.*

1821 Congress enacts the Missouri Compromise, specifying which new U.S. states will allow slavery.

1833 England outlaws slavery throughout its empire.

1839 The world's first international abolitionist group, Anti-slavery International, is founded in England.

1848 Slavery abolished in French colonies.

1863 President Abraham Lincoln issues Emancipation Proclamation.

December 1865 The 13th Amendment abolishes slavery.

1873 Spain ends slavery in Puerto Rico.

1888 Brazil outlaws slavery.

1900-1990 *International treaties to halt slavery are adopted.*

1919 International Labour Organization (ILO) is founded.

1926 League of Nations outlaws slavery.

1945 United Nations is founded.

1946 U.N. Children's Fund is established.

1948 U.N.'s Universal Declaration of Human Rights prohibits slavery.

1951 International Organization for Migration is founded to help migrants.

1956 Supplementary Convention on the Abolition of Slavery, the Slave Trade, and Institutions and Practices Similar to Slavery outlaws debt bondage, serfdom and other forced-labor practices.

1978 Human Rights Watch is founded.

1983 Sudan's civil war begins, pitting the Muslim north against the Christian and animist south, leading to slave raids in the south.

1990s *The end of the Cold War and other geopolitical changes allow trafficking and slavery to expand.*

1991 Collapse of the Soviet Union leads to a dramatic rise in trafficking in Eastern Europe.

1994 American Anti-Slavery Group is founded.

1995 Christian and non-governmental organizations begin redeeming slaves in Sudan.

June 1, 1999 ILO adopts the Worst Forms of Child Labor Convention.

2000-Present *United States and other countries renew efforts to fight slavery and trafficking.*

March 2000 Free the Slaves is founded.

Oct. 28, 2000 President Bill Clinton signs the Trafficking Victims Protection Act.

Nov. 15, 2000 United Nations approves the Protocol to Prevent, Suppress and Punish the Trafficking in Persons.

Feb. 14, 2002 Polaris Project is founded to fight trafficking.

June 10, 2002 State Department's Office to Monitor and Combat Trafficking releases its first "Trafficking in Persons Report."

March 11, 2003 Brazilian President Luiz Inacio Lula da Silva unveils anti-slavery initiative.

Sept. 19, 2003 President Bush signs Trafficking Victims Protection Act Reauthorization.

Sept. 23, 2003 President Bush delivers a major anti-trafficking address at the U.N. General Assembly.

January 2004 U.N. launches year-long commemoration of anti-slavery movement.

Summer 2004 State Department's Fourth Annual "Trafficking in Persons Report" to be released.

were slaves. In Rome, slavery was so widespread that even common people could afford to have one or two.[22]

Slaves in the ancient world often did more than just menial tasks. Some, especially in the Roman Empire, became physicians and poets. Others achieved great influence, managing estates or assisting powerful generals or politicians.

Great Roman thinkers like Pliny the Younger and Cicero urged masters to treat their slaves with kindness and even to let them "share your conversations, your deliberations and your company," Cicero wrote.[23] Perhaps as a result, manumission, or the freeing of slaves by their masters, was commonplace, usually after many years of service.

Ultimately, however, Roman slavery was maintained by cruelty and violence, including the use of severe flogging and even crucifixion. Slave revolts, common in the first and second centuries B.C., were brutally suppressed.

The collapse of the western half of the Roman Empire in the 5th-century A.D. led to a new, more fragmented, power structure in Western Europe often centered around local warlords (knights) and the Catholic Church. The new order did not eliminate slavery, but in many areas slaves became serfs, or peasants tied to the local lord's land and could not leave without his permission.[24]

In the East, meanwhile, a new force — Islam — was on the rise. For the Arabs who swept into the Mediterranean basin and the Near East beginning in the 7th century, traditional slavery was a way of life, just as it had been for the Romans. In the ensuing centuries, the Arabs brought millions of sub-Saharan Africans, Asians and Europeans to the slave markets for sale throughout the Middle East.

Meanwhile, slavery remained commonplace elsewhere. In North America, Indians along the Eastern seaboard and in the Pacific Northwest often enslaved members of other tribes taken in war. The more advanced indigenous civilizations to the south, like the Aztec and Mayans in what is now Mexico, and the Inca of Peru, also relied upon slaves. And on the Indian subcontinent, the strict Hindu caste system held tens of millions in virtual bondage.

Slavery Goes Global

In the 15th century, European explorers and adventurers sailing to new territories in Asia, Africa and the Americas began a new chapter in the history of slavery.

By 1650, the Dutch, Spanish, Portuguese, French and English had established colonies throughout the world. The new territories, especially in the Americas, produced new crops such as sugar and tobacco, as well as gold and other minerals. Initially, enslaved indigenous peoples did the harvesting and mining in South America. But ill treatment and disease quickly decimated native populations, prompting the importation of slaves from Africa.

From the mid-1500s to the mid-1800s, almost 9 million Africans were shipped mostly to Latin America — particularly to today's Brazil, Haiti and Cuba — under the most inhumane conditions. About 5 percent — about 400,000 — of all the African slaves ended up in the United States.[25]

On the sugar plantations of the West Indies and South America, crushing work and brutal punishment were the norm. Although Spain and Portugal had relatively liberal laws concerning the treatment of slaves — they could marry, sue a cruel owner and even buy their freedom — they were rarely enforced.

In the British colonies and later in the United States, slaves enjoyed somewhat better working conditions and medical care. Nonetheless, life was harsh and in some ways more difficult. Since slaves in Latin America and the Caribbean usually outnumbered Europeans, they were able to retain more of their African customs. In British America, where by 1750 whites outnumbered slaves by more than four to one, Africans quickly lost many of their cultural underpinnings.

Most American slavery was tied to the great Southern plantations that grew tobacco, rice and other cash crops. Although slavery also was practiced in Northern states, it was never as widespread and had been largely abolished by 1800.

By the late 18th century, Southern slavery also appeared headed for extinction, as industrialization and other trends took hold, rendering the plantation system increasingly economically unfeasible. But Eli Whitney's invention of the cotton gin in 1793 gave American slavery a new lease on life. The gin made the labor-intensive process of separating the seeds from the cotton easy, enabling slaves to dramatically increase their output.[26]

Meanwhile, the rise of textile mills in England and elsewhere was creating a new demand for the fluffy, white fiber. By the early 19th century, many Southern plantations that had been unprofitably growing other crops

Fighting Trafficking in the United States

Seven men were sent to prison on Jan. 29, 2004, for holding several Latin American women against their will in South Texas, forcing them to work without pay and raping them repeatedly.

The case was the latest in a series of sex-trafficking cases prosecuted under the Trafficking Victims Protection Act (TVPA) of 2000, which established stiff penalties for human trafficking and provided mandatory restitution to victims.[1] In the last three years, the Justice Department has prosecuted 132 traffickers — three times the number charged in the three years before the law was enacted.[2]

Last year, Congress updated the law to make trafficking a racketeering offense and allow victims to sue their captors in U.S. courts.

"While we have made much progress in combating human trafficking . . . we have not yet eradicated modern-day slavery," reauthorization sponsor Rep. Christopher H. Smith, R-N.J., said during consideration of the bill by the House International Relations Committee on July 23, 2003.

The Central Intelligence Agency estimates that between 18,000 and 20,000 people are trafficked into the United States each year.[3] Many are women — kidnapped or lured here with promises of marriage or work as nannies, models, waitresses, factory workers and exotic dancers. Once they arrive, they are stripped of their passports and forced to work as sex slaves, laborers or domestic servants until their smuggling or travel "debts" are repaid. The average victim is 20 years old.[4]

"They tell them they'll make a lot of money, they'll be free, they'll have a beautiful life," says Marisa B. Ugarte, executive director of the Bilateral Safety Corridor Coalition, a San Diego organization that assists trafficking victims in Mexico and the United States. "But once they are here, everything changes."

Prior to passage of the TVPA, many of the victims were treated as criminals and subject to deportation. Today, they can apply to the Bureau of Citizen and Immigration Services for one of 5,000 "T" nonimmigrant visas available each year. The visas allow them to remain in the United States if they are assisting in the investigation or prosecution of traffickers. They may then apply for permanent residency if their removal would cause severe hardship.[5]

The Department of Homeland Security had received 721 T-status applications as of June 30, 2003: 301 were granted, 30 were denied and 390 are pending.[6]

Mohamed Mattar, co-director of the Protection Project, a human-rights research institute at Johns Hopkins University, said the visa program has been stymied by victims' reluctance to go to law enforcement authorities for help.

This fear is fed by the fact that many police officers remain unaware of the TVPA and are more likely to arrest the victims than the perpetrators, says Donna M. Hughes, an authority on sex trafficking at the University of Rhode Island.

"We need to start treating [Johns] like the perpetrators they are, and not like lonely guys," Hughes adds. "We need a renewal of ideas at the state and local level."

Under the TVPA, alien trafficking victims who do come forward can receive federal benefits normally available to refugees.

Historically, most trafficked victims have come from Latin America and Southeast Asia, smuggled across the porous Mexican border by "coyotes" or escorted by "jockeys" pretending to be a boyfriend or cousin.[7] Since the early 1990s, however, there has been an influx of women from the former Soviet Union and Central and Eastern Europe,

were now making plenty of money using slaves to pick and process cotton.

Around the same time, however, a movement to abolish slavery began to gather steam in the Northern states. For decades, Americans had debated the morality of slavery. During deliberations over independence in 1776, many delegates to the Second Continental Congress — including John Adams, Benjamin Franklin and Virginia slaveholder Thomas Jefferson — had pushed to make the elimination of slavery part of the movement for America's independence. But resistance from the South and the need for colonial unity against the British doomed the proposal.

The debate over slavery, however, did not go away. The issue complicated the new country's efforts to form

where trafficking rings recruit women with newspaper ads and billboards beckoning them to prosperous futures in the United States.

Undocumented migrant workers are also vulnerable to traffickers. On March 2, 2004, a federal district judge sentenced Florida labor contractor Ramiro Ramos to 15 years in prison for holding migrant workers in servitude and forcing them to work in citrus groves until they had paid off their transportation debts.[8]

In some instances, diplomats and international civil servants bring domestic workers — often illiterate women from Africa, Asia and Latin America — into the United States legally, but then force them to work long hours for almost no pay. In one case, an Ethiopian maid for an International Monetary Fund staffer says she worked eight years for seven days a week, 15 hours a day for less than 3 cents an hour.[9]

Although the employer claimed the maid was his guest, he disappeared before a lawsuit filed by the maid, Yeshehareg Teferra, could be prosecuted. "I was not their guest," Teferra told a reporter. "I was their slave "[10]

Foreign diplomats bring 3,800 domestic servants into the United States each year under special temporary work visas, which allow them only to work for the employer who sponsored them. The employer promises to abide by U.S. labor laws, but there is almost no oversight of the program, so the abuse of servants remains under law enforcement's radar screen, human rights advocates say.[11]

But foreign nationals are not the only victims of domestic trafficking. Homeless and runaway American children also are preyed upon by pimps, who troll malls and clubs in search of teenagers they can "turn." Typically, the pimps befriend the girls, ply them with drugs and then use their addiction to turn them into prostitutes.[12]

There are between 100,000 and 300,000 such citizen victims in the United States, though they're more often overlooked by police, says Derek Ellerman, co-founder of the Polaris Project, a grass-roots anti-trafficking organization. "There is a glaring bias in enforcement" of the Mann Act, which bans the transport of children and adults across state lines for prostitution, Ellerman says. "U.S. kids who are being targeted [by traffickers] just are not being protected."

For the traffickers — many of them members of gangs or loosely linked criminal networks — trafficking is much more lucrative than smuggling contraband items, because human slaves can provide a source of long-term income through prostitution and forced labor. "There's a market for cheap labor, and there's a market for cheap sex, and traffickers know they can make money in it," Michele Clark, co-director of the Protection Project, says.

— Kelly Field

---

[1] Department of Justice press release, Jan. 29, 2004.

[2] Department of Justice press release, March 2, 2004.

[3] Department of Justice, "Assessment of U.S. Activities to Combat Trafficking in Persons," August 2003, p. 3.

[4] Amy O'Neill Richard, "International Trafficking in Women to the United States: A Contemporary Manifestation of Slavery and Organized Crime," DCI Exceptional Intelligence Analyst Program, pp. 3-5.

[5] John R. Miller, "The United States' Effort to Combat Trafficking in Persons," *International Information Program Electronic Journal*, U.S. State Department, June 2003.

[6] Department of Justice, *op. cit.*, August 2003, p. 9.

[7] Peter Landesman, "The Girls Next Door," *The New York Times Magazine*, Jan. 25, 2004.

[8] Justice Department, *op. cit.*, March 2, 2004.

[9] William Branigin, "A Life of Exhaustion, Beatings, and Isolation," *The Washington Post*, Jan. 5, 1999, p. A6.

[10] Quoted in *ibid*.

11 Richard, *op. cit.*, p. 28,

[12] Janice G. Raymond and Donna M. Hughes, "Sex Trafficking of Women in the United States, International and Domestic Trends," Coalition Against Trafficking in Women, March 2001, p. 52.

---

its governing institutions and to expand westward, forcing increasingly abolitionist Northerners and slaveholding Southerners to craft tortured compromises to keep the nation together.

In 1789, delegates to the Constitutional Convention hammered out the infamous Three-fifths Compromise, permitting each slave to be counted as three-fifths of a person for purposes of apportioning the number of representatives each state had in the new Congress.[27] And in 1821, Congress passed the Missouri Compromise, drawing a line westward along the 36.30 parallel. The new Western states above the line would be admitted to the Union as "free" states, while those below the boundary would be so-called slave states.

Nearly 200 Million Young Kids Must Work

Nearly a fifth of the world's young children have to work, including 110 million in Asia and fully a quarter of all the children in sub-Saharan Africa.

Working Children, Ages 5 to 14, By Region
(in millions)

Region	Total Working	Percentage of children in region
Asia	110.4	18.7%
Latin America	16.5	17.0
North Africa, Middle East	9.0	10.2
Sub-Saharan Africa	37.9	25.3
Transitional countries*	8.3	14.6
Total	**182.1**	**18.5%**

* Transitional countries — such as Taiwan, Singapore and Malaysia — are no longer considered "developing" but not yet classified as fully industrialized.

Source: "Investing in Every Child," International Programme on the Elimination of Child Labour, International Labour Office, December 2003

Outlawing Slavery

Much of the rest of the world, however, was abolishing slavery. In the early 1800s, many of the newly independent nations of Spanish America won their independence and immediately outlawed human bondage. Simón Bolívar, who liberated much of Latin America, was a staunch abolitionist, calling slavery "the daughter of darkness."[28]

In Europe, the tide also was turning. Largely due to the efforts of abolitionist William Wilberforce, the British Empire outlawed the practice in 1833, although de facto slavery continued in India and some other colonies. In 1848, France also freed the slaves in its colonies.

However, in the United States, peaceful efforts at compromise over slavery failed, and the issue finally helped trigger the Civil War in 1861. In 1863, during the height of the conflict, President Abraham Lincoln issued the "Emancipation Proclamation," freeing all slaves in the Southern, or Confederate, states. Soon after the war ended with Union victory in 1865, the 13th Amendment to the Constitution abolished slavery altogether.[29]

After the Civil War, the worldwide abolition of slavery continued. Spain outlawed the practice in Puerto Rico in 1873 and in Cuba in 1886. More important, Brazil began dismantling its huge slave infrastructure in 1888.

Today, slavery is illegal in every country in the world and is outlawed by several treaties. "In international law, the outlawing of slavery has become what is called *jus cogens*, which means that it's completely accepted and doesn't need to be written into new treaties and conventions," says Bales of Free the Slaves.

The foundation of this complete acceptance rests on several groundbreaking international agreements, beginning with the 1926 Slavery Convention of the League of Nations, which required signatory countries to work to abolish every aspect of the practice.[30]

Slavery also is banned by the 1948 Universal Declaration of Human Rights, which holds that "no one shall be held in slavery or servitude; slavery and the slave trade shall be prohibited in all their forms."[31]

Other conventions prohibiting the practice include the 1930 ILO Convention on Forced Labor and a 1956 Supplementary Convention on the Abolition of Slavery, the Slave Trade, and Institutions and Practices Similar to Slavery.

More recently, the United Nations in 2001 approved a Protocol to Prevent, Suppress and Punish the Trafficking in Persons as part of a major convention on fighting organized crime. The protocol requires signatories to take action to fight trafficking and protect its victims. It has been signed by 117 countries and ratified by 45.[32] While the United States has not yet ratified the document, it has the support of the White House and is expected to win Senate approval in the near future.

CURRENT SITUATION

Human Trafficking

The poorest and most chaotic parts of the developing world supply most trafficking victims — often women and children destined for the sex trade.

In South Asia, young women and children routinely are abducted or lured from Nepal, Pakistan, India, Bangladesh, Cambodia and Myanmar (Burma) to work in brothels in India's large cities, notably Bombay, and the Persian Gulf states. Thousands also end up in Bangkok, Thailand's capital and an infamous sex-tourism mecca.

In Asia, the victims' own families often sell them to traffickers. "In Nepal, entire villages have been emptied of girls," says Pinata of Vital Voices. "Obviously, this could not have happened without the complicity between traffickers and the victims' families."

Parents sell their children for a variety of reasons — virtually all linked to poverty, Pinata says. "Some think the child will have a better life or that their daughter will be able to send money home," she says. "For some, it's just one less mouth to feed."

"Even when they have a sense of what their children will be doing, many parents feel they don't have a choice," adds UNICEF's Landgren. "They feel that literally anything is better than what they have now."

In Eastern Europe, traffickers often lure women into bondage by advertising in local newspapers for nanny positions in the United States or Western Europe. For instance, Tetiana, a Ukrainian woman, was offered 10 times her salary to be an au pair in Italy. Instead she was forced into prostitution in Istanbul, Turkey.[33]

Others are promised work as models or actresses. In some cases, the victims even put up their own money for their travel expenses, only to find themselves prisoners in a European brothel or in Mexico, awaiting transport across the border to the United States.[34]

Even those who understand at the outset that they are going to be prostitutes are not prepared for the brutality they face. "They're unaware of how much abuse, rape, psychological manipulation and coercion is involved," says the Polaris Project's Chon.

Eastern Europe is particularly fertile ground for sex traffickers, she says. The collapse of communism more than a decade ago has left many parts of the region, especially Ukraine, Moldova and Belarus, economically and politically stunted. "These countries are just full of desperate people who will do anything for a chance at a better life," she says.

To make matters worse, brothel owners prize the region's many light-skinned, blonde women. "Lighter women are very popular in places like the United States,

AFP Photo

Six-year-old Ratan Das breaks rocks at a construction site in Agartala, India, where he earns about 40 cents a day to supplement his widowed mother's 60-cents-per-day income. India has more child laborers than any other country — about 120 million — followed by Pakistan, Bangladesh, Indonesia and Brazil.

Europe and Asia," Chon says. "So these women are in demand."

In Africa, more people are trafficked for forced labor than as sex slaves. "In Africa, you have a lot of people being taken and sent to pick cotton and cocoa and other forms of agricultural labor," says Vital Voices' Pinata.

Regardless of their origin, once victims are lured into a trafficking ring, they quickly lose control over their destiny. "If they have a passport, it's usually taken from them and they're abused, physically and psychologically, in order to make them easier to control," says the United Methodist Committee On Relief's Beher.

When victims of trafficking reach their final destination, they rarely have freedom of any kind. "A 16-year-old girl who had been trafficked into Kosovo to be a prostitute told me that when she wasn't working in the bar, she was literally locked into her room and not allowed out," Beher says. "That's the sort of thing we see all the time."

Organized crime plays a key role in most human trafficking. "Most of what you are dealing with here is criminal networks," says Miller of the Office to Combat Trafficking. "You can't take someone out of the Czech Republic and drive her to the Netherlands and hand her over to another trafficker and then to a brothel without real cooperation."

A 16-year-old Cambodian girl rescued from a brothel peers from her hiding place in Phnom Penh. An estimated 300,000 women are trapped in slave-like conditions in the Southeast Asian sex trade. Cambodia recently agreed to join the first U.N. program aimed at halting the trafficking of women in the region.

AFP Photo/Rob Elliott

Indeed, smuggling rings often team up with criminal groups in other countries or maintain "branch offices" there. And most traffickers are involved in other criminal activities, such as drugs and weapons smuggling. "Many drug gangs in Southeast Asia are spinning off into trafficking because it's very low risk and very lucrative," says the Women's Commission's Young, who adds that unlike a shipment of drugs, human cargo can earn traffickers money for years.

These crime networks, especially in Eastern Europe and Asia, operate freely, in large part because they have corrupted many local officials. "So many people are being moved across borders that it's impossible to believe that government officials aren't cooperating," Young says. "Like drugs and other illegal activities, this is very corrupting, especially in poor countries where the police are poorly paid."

In addition to stepping up law enforcement, countries can do many things to fight trafficking, UNICEF's Landgren says. "For example, the United Kingdom has a new system that keeps tabs on children entering the country," she says. "By keeping track of children that come in from abroad, we can better protect them."

And in Brazil, where landowners often lure peasants to their farms with promises of work only to put them in debt bondage, President Luiz Ignacio Lula da Silva has stepped up efforts to free forced laborers. Lula, as the president is called, also has called for a change in the constitution to allow the confiscation of land for those convicted of enslaving workers.

Even countries that have long allowed trafficking are beginning to address the issue. Moldova, for instance, has begun prosecuting traffickers and has created a database of employment agencies that help people find legitimate work abroad.[35]

NGOs have also taken steps to help. For instance, some groups run safe houses where trafficking victims who escape can find shelter and security. "We provide them with medical and psychological care," says Beher, whose group operates a house in Kosovo's capital, Pristina. "We allow them to stay until they recover and then help them to get home, which is usually somewhere else in Eastern Europe, like Romania or Moldova."

The Polaris Project maintains three 24-hour hotlines (in English, Thai and Korean) in the United States to allow both victims and third parties to report trafficking activity. Polaris also has a trafficking database to help law enforcement and other officials gather information about potential cases.

But international organizations and NGOs can only do so much, says Beher, because impoverished, poorly governed countries will always be breeding grounds for trafficking. "Until the causes disappear, all we in the international aid community can do is fight the symptoms," she says.

"In order to really get rid of this problem," Beher continues, "you need political stability and a strong civil society, which in turn leads to the rule of law and stronger law enforcement. You know, there's a reason why there aren't a lot of Finnish people being trafficked."

But Calvert of the American Anti-Slavery Group says governments and international organizations could virtually shut down the trade in human beings if they wanted to. "The international community is in a state of denial and lacks the commitment to fight this," he says. "Look at Britain: They had whole fleets of ships devoted to stopping the slave trade on the high seas, and it worked."

Calvert says the United Nations and other international groups should be more aggressive and

AT ISSUE

Is the Trafficking Victims Protection Act tough enough?

YES
Rep. Christopher H. Smith, R-N.J.
Chairman, U.S. Helsinki Commission

Written for *The CQ Researcher,* March 15, 2004

Each year, nearly a million people worldwide are bought and sold into the commercial sex industry, sweatshops, domestic servitude and other dehumanizing situations.

In October 2000, President Clinton signed into law the Trafficking Victims Protection Act (TVPA), which I authored. It provided a multifaceted approach to halting human trafficking through law enforcement, prevention and aid to victims. It also represented two major policy changes: up to life in prison for those who traffic in humans and treatment of the people trafficked — largely women, children, and teenagers — as victims rather than as criminals. In 2003, the law was expanded and strengthened.

As President Bush noted in his historic speech at the United Nations in September 2003, the global community must do more to eradicate human slavery. But significant progress has been made in just a few years, thanks largely to the law's three-tier system and annual "Trafficking in Persons Report" mandated by the law.

When the first report came out, the State Department listed 23 nations in Tier 3 as the worst offenders. It pulled no punches and did not hesitate to name offending nations, including our allies, if they were not making "serious and sustained" efforts to fight trafficking. Naming names was a measure I fought hard to include in the law, even though it was initially opposed by the previous administration.

Thanks to the report and the threat of sanctions, most nations have improved their record on trafficking. Only 15 countries were in Tier 3 during the most recent 2003 report, and most of them made enough progress in the ensuing months to avoid economic sanctions. The State Department is continually improving the scope of the report so it will present the most accurate and thorough picture of the worldwide trafficking problem.

The message from the United States is loud and clear: If you are committed to the fight against human slavery, we welcome you as an ally. But if you continue to look askance when it comes to this horrible crime and pretend you don't have a trafficking problem, we're going to aggressively push you to make reforms, and we'll use economic sanctions as a means to that end.

NO
Tommy Calvert, Jr.
Chief of External Operations,
American Anti-Slavery Group

Written for *The CQ Researcher,* March 15, 2004

Most anti-slavery experts would agree the TVPA is a good law, but that slavery can be defeated in our lifetime only if we give the law priority in attention and funding — and apply it equally to friends and foes alike.

The "Trafficking in Person's Report" (TIPS) required by the law does not reveal the full story on global slavery, but only a snapshot. The criteria used to determine progress in the fight against slavery — by focusing on government action rather than on total slavery within a nation's borders — skew our view of realities on the ground.

South Korea, for example, has a serious problem with trafficking — an estimated 15,000 people trafficked per year — but it is ranked in Tier 1, the best ranking a government can receive. Nations can create many seemingly tough laws and programs to fight slavery. However, organized crime may still run thriving trafficking operations in the face of such policies, which may in reality be weak or ineffectual.

Last year marked the first time that countries designated by the "Trafficking In Persons Report" as the worst offenders — Tier 3 — would automatically be subject to U.S. sanctions, which can only be waived by the president.

The State Department gave wide latitude to the standards for Tier 2, perhaps to keep strategic allies from being hit with sanctions. Both Brazil and Saudi Arabia, for instance, received Tier 2 designations. But Brazil's president has launched one of the world's most ambitious plans to end slavery, while Saudi Arabia has no laws outlawing human trafficking and has prosecuted no offenders. Thus, the report's rankings equate a major national initiative to end slavery with royal lip service.

Some Middle Eastern and North African countries may have advanced in the rankings because they are being courted by the administration to support the war on terror and our plans for change in the region. But there is evidence these countries have not really progressed in the fight against human bondage.

The long-term effect of such discrepancies is to reduce the credibility of the report and lengthen the time it takes to eradicate slavery.

AFP Photo/Saeed Khan

Pakistani Minister for Education Zobaida Jalal and Deputy Labor Under Secretary for International Labor Affairs Thomas Moorhead sign an agreement in Islamabad on Jan. 23, 2002, calling for the U.S. to provide $5 million to help educate working children in Pakistan.

uncompromising in combating slavery. "They had weapons inspectors didn't they?" he asks. "Well that's what we need to fight this. We need that kind of action."

Slavery and Forced Labor

Slavery today bears little resemblance to earlier forms of bondage. For instance, 150 years ago in the American South, a healthy slave was a valuable piece of property, worth up to $40,000 in today's dollars, according to Free the Slaves.[36] By contrast, slaves today are often worth less than $100, giving slaveholders little incentive to care for them.

Although slavery exists nearly everywhere, it is most prevalent in the poorer parts of South Asia, where an estimated 15 million to 20 million people are in bonded labor in India, Pakistan, Bangladesh and Nepal.

Bonded labor usually begins when someone borrows money from someone else and agrees to work for that person until the debt is paid. In most cases, the debt is never paid and the borrower and his immediate family become virtual slaves, working in exchange for basic amenities like food and shelter.

"Often you see a whole family in bondage for three or four generations because once someone borrows a small amount of money you're trapped," says Callahan of Free the Slaves. "You don't pay off the principal of the loan, you just keep paying off the interest."

Bonded laborers work at jobs ranging from making bricks in Pakistan to farming, cigarette rolling and carpet making in India. In the western Indian state of Gujarat, some 30,000 bonded families harvest salt in the marshes. The glare from the salt makes them color-blind. When they die, the laborers cannot even be cremated, according to Hindu custom, because their bodies have absorbed too much salt to burn properly.[37]

Slavery is also widespread in sub-Saharan Africa, where the Anti-Slavery Group estimates that at least 200,000 people are in bondage. Besides Sudan, the largest concentration of African slaves is in Mauritania. For hundreds of years, Mauritania's lighter-skinned ruling elite kept their darker compatriots in a system of chattel slavery, with generations being born into servitude. Although the country formally outlawed slavery in 1980, the practice is thought to still be widespread.

"For the thousands of slaves who were legally freed in 1980, life did not change at all," Bales writes. "No one bothered to tell the slaves about it. Some have never learned of their legal freedom, some did so years later, and for most legal freedom was never translated into actual freedom." Today, slaves are still "everywhere" in Mauritania "doing every job that is hard, onerous and dirty."[38]

Slaves also pick cotton in Egypt and Benin, harvest cocoa and other crops in Ivory Coast and mine diamonds in Sierra Leone.

In addition, hundreds of youngsters are abducted each year and forced to become soldiers for rebel fighters in war zones like Uganda and Congo.

Child soldiers often are made to do horrible things. A girl in Uganda who was kidnapped at 13 was forced to kill and abduct other children during her five years in captivity.[39]

But slavery also flourishes beyond the developing world. Although the problem is not as widespread, forced labor and servitude also occur in Europe and the United States — in brothels, farms and sweatshops. "It's amazing, but there are slaves in the United States doing all kinds of things," says Miller of the Office to Combat Trafficking. "Recently authorities found a group of Mexican [agricultural workers] who had been trafficked to work for no pay in Florida. It's unbelievable."

Moreover, slavery is not confined to just seedy brothels or plantations. In upscale American neighborhoods too, people, usually from other countries, have been enslaved, often as domestics. Last year, for instance, a suburban Maryland couple was convicted of forced labor for coercing an illegal alien from Ghana to work seven days a week as a domestic servant without pay. And from time to time, foreign diplomats are found to be harboring unpaid domestic workers from their home countries who cannot leave to work for someone else because the diplomats hold their visas.[40]

OUTLOOK

Impact of Globalization

The increasing ease of travel and communication brought about by globalization has helped many industries, including illegal ones like trafficking and slavery.

"Globalization has certainly made trafficking and slavery easier, but it is a double-edged sword," says Jacobson of Christian Freedom International. "It has also helped us to more quickly and effectively shine a spotlight on the evil thugs who are doing these bad things."

Moreover, Jacobson says, as globalization improves the general standard of living in the developing world, it becomes harder for traffickers to prey on innocents. "When the boats are rising for everyone, poverty and despair are alleviated," he says. "When someone gets a job and education and health care, they are much less susceptible to being abused."

The Polaris Project's Chon is also optimistic, although for different reasons. "I'm very upbeat about all of this, because tackling these problems is a matter of political will, and I think the world is slowly beginning to pay more attention to these issues," she says. "I feel as though we're at the same point as the [American] abolitionist movement at the beginning of the 19th century, in that things are slowly beginning to move in the right direction."

Rep. Smith agrees. "There's a fever all over the world to enact new, tough policies to deal with this," he says. "Because the U.S. is out front on this, a lot of countries are beginning to follow suit."

Moreover, the optimists note, victims themselves are increasingly fighting for their rights. "There is a silent revolution going on right now, in places like India, where people are literally freeing themselves from slavery," says Callahan of Free the Slaves, referring to thousands of quarry slaves in northern India who recently have left their bondage and begun new lives. "If this kind of thing keeps up, in a few decades these problems will be blips on the radar screen compared to what they are today."

But Beher of the United Methodist Committee on Relief sees little change ahead because of continuing poverty and societal dysfunction. "The problems that lead to trafficking and slavery are very complicated, and there are no easy fixes," she says. "We need to build up the economies and the civil society of the places where these things happen in order to get rid of this once and for all. And I'm afraid that that is going to take many decades."

Indeed, "Things could get a lot worse before they get better," warns Young of the Women's Commission for Refugee Women and Children, comparing trafficking to the drug trade.

"It's so profitable, and there is so little risk in getting caught that it seems like there will be plenty of this kind of thing going on for the foreseeable future."

NOTES

1. See www.freetheslaves.net/slavery_today/index.html.

2. Figure cited in "2003 Trafficking in Persons Report," U.S. Department of State, p. 7.

3. Frank Trejo, "Event Underscores Scope, Toll of Human Trafficking," *Dallas Morning News*, March 4, 2003, p. 3B.

4. Richard Mertens, "Smuggler's Prey: Poor Women of Eastern Europe," *The Christian Science Monitor*, Sept. 22, 2002, p. A7.

5. Quoted in *ibid.*

6. "Trafficking in Persons Report," *op. cit.*, p. 6.

7. The entire text of President Bush's speech can be found at www.whitehouse.gov/news/releases/2003/09/20030923-4.html.

8. "IPEC Action Against Child Labour: 2002-2003," International Labour Organization, January 2004, p. 15; see also ILO, "Investing in Every Child," December 2003, p. 32.

9. Figure cited in Davan Maharaj, "Panel Frowns on Efforts to Buy Sudan Slaves' Freedom," *Los Angeles Times*, May 28, 2002, p. A3.

10. Quoted from "60 Minutes II," May 15, 2002.

11. Nicholas D. Kristof, "Bargaining For Freedom," *The New York Times*, Jan 21, 2004, p. A27.

12. Figure cited at "UNICEF Oral Report on the Global Challenge of Child Trafficking," January 2004, at: www.unicef.org/about/TraffickingOralreport.pdf.

13. Full text of the law is at: www.state.gov/documents/organization/10492.pdf. The law was reauthorized in December 2003.

14. Figures cited at www.state.gov/g/tip/rls/fs/28548.htm.

15. Richard Mertens, "In Turkey, Childhoods Vanish in Weary Harvests," *The Christian Science Monitor*, May 8, 2003, p. 7.

16. ILO, *op. cit.*

17. See Brian Hansen, "Children in Crisis," *The CQ Researcher*, Aug. 31, 2001, p. 657.

18. See: www.ilo.org/public/english/standards/ipec/ratify_govern.pdf.

19. ILO, *op. cit.*, January 2004, p. 37.

20. "With a Little U.S. Help, ILO Targets Child Labour," *Indian Express*, March 3, 2004.

21. Hugh Thomas, *World History: The Story of Mankind from Prehistory to the Present* (1996), pp. 54-55.

22. *Ibid.*, pp. 105-107.

23. Quoted in Michael Grant, *The World of Rome* (1960), p. 116.

24. Thomas, *op. cit.*, pp. 107-110.

25. Figures cited in *ibid.*, p. 279.

26. John Hope Franklin and Alfred A Moss, Jr., *From Slavery to Freedom: A History of African-Americans* (2000), p. 100.

27. *Ibid.*, p. 94.

28. From a speech before the Congress of Angostura in 1819. See http://www.fordham.edu/halsall/mod/1819bolivar.html.

29. Franklin and Moss, *op. cit.*, p. 244.

30. The full text of the convention can be found at www.unicri.it/1926%20slavery%20convention.pdf.

31. Quoted at www.un.org/Overview/rights.html.

32. A complete list of those countries that have signed and ratified the protocol are at www.unodc.org/unodc/en/crime_cicp_signatures_trafficking.html.

33. Sylvie Briand, "Sold into Slavery: Ukrainian Girls Tricked into Sex Trade," Agence France Presse, Jan. 28, 2004.

34. Peter Landesman, "The Girls Next Door, *The New York Times Magazine*, Jan. 25, 2004, p. 30.

35. "Trafficking in Person's Report," *op. cit.*, p. 107.

36. See www.freetheslaves.net/slavery_today/index.html.

37. Christopher Kremmer, "With a Handful of Salt," *The Boston Globe*, Nov. 28, 1999.

38. Kevin Bales, *Disposable People: The New Slavery in the Global Economy* (1999), p. 81.

39. Thomas Wagner, "Study Documents Trauma of Child Soldiers," Associated Press Online, March 11, 2004.

40. Ruben Castaneda, "Couple Enslaved Woman," *The Washington Post*, June 10, 2003, p. B1.

BIBLIOGRAPHY

Books

Bales, Kevin, *Disposable People: New Slavery in the Global Economy, University of California Press,* 1999.
The president of Free the Slaves and a leading expert on slavery offers strategies to end the practice.

Bok, Francis, *Escape From Slavery: The True Story of My Ten Years In Captivity and My Journey to Freedom in America, St. Martin's Press,* 2003.
A former slave in Sudan tells the gripping story of his ordeal and eventual journey to the United States.

Franklin, John Hope, and, Alfred Moss Jr., *From Slavery to Freedom: A History of African Americans, McGraw-Hill,* 2000.
Franklin, a renowned professor emeritus of history at Duke University and Moss, an associate professor at the University of Maryland, discuss the slave trade and slavery in the United States up to the Civil War.

Articles

"A Cargo of Exploitable Souls," *The Economist,* June 1, 2002.
The article examines human trafficking of prostitutes and forced laborers into the United States.

Bales, Kevin, "The Social Psychology of Modern Slavery," *Scientific American*, **April 2002, p. 68.**
A leading expert on slavery examines the psychological underpinnings that may drive both traffickers and slaveholders as well as their victims.

Cockburn, Andrew, "Hidden in Plain Sight: The World's 27 Million Slaves," *National Geographic*, **Sept. 2003, p. 2.**
A correspondent for London's *Independent* takes a hard look at slavery; includes chilling photographs of victims.

Hansen, Brian, "Children in Crisis," *The CQ Researcher*, **Aug. 31, 2001, pp. 657-688.**
Hansen examines the exploitation of children around the world, including sexual slaves and forced laborers.

Kristof, Nicolas D., "Bargaining For Freedom," *The New York Times*, **Jan. 21, 2004, p. A27.**
The veteran columnist describes how he "bought" and freed two sex slaves in Cambodia. The article is part of Kristof's series on his experiences in Southeast Asia.

Landesman, Peter, "The Girls Next Door," *The New York Times Magazine*, **Jan. 25, 2004, p. 30.**
Landesman's detailed exposé of trafficking focuses on the importation of young girls into the U.S. for prostitution.

Maharaj, Davan, "Panel Frowns on Efforts to Buy Sudan Slaves Freedom," *Los Angeles Times*, **May 28, 2002, p. 3.**
The article details the controversy surrounding the practice of slave redemption in Sudan.

Mertens, Richard, "Smugglers' Prey: Poor Women of Eastern Europe," *The Christian Science Monitor*, **Sept. 25, 2002, p. 7.**
The article examines the plight of Eastern European women trafficked into sexual slavery who manage to escape.

Miller, John, R., "Slavery in 2004," *The Washington Post*, **Jan. 1, 2004, p. A25.**
The director of the State Department's Office to Monitor and Combat Trafficking in Persons argues that the Trafficking Victims Protection Act has prodded other countries to act.

Power, Carla, *et al.*, **"Preying on Children,"** *Newsweek*, **Nov. 17, 2003, p. 34.**
The number of children being trafficked into Western Europe is rising, helped by more porous borders and the demand for young prostitutes.

Vaknin, Sam, "The Morality of Child Labor," *United Press International*, **Oct. 4, 2002.**
UPI's senior business correspondent argues that organizations opposed to most forms of child labor impose unrealistic, rich-world standards on the poorest countries.

Reports

"Investing in Every Child: An Economic Study of the Costs and Benefits of Eliminating Child Labor," *International Labour Organization*, **December 2003.**
The ILO contends that ending child labor would improve economic growth in the developing world.

"IPEC Action Against Child Labor: 2002-2003," *International Labour Organization*, **January 2004.**
The report charts the progress made by the ILO's International Program on the Elimination of Child Labor (IPEC), which funds anti-child labor initiatives around the world.

"Trafficking in Persons Report," *U.S. Department of State*, **June 2003.**
The annual report required by the Trafficking Victims Protection Act assesses global anti-trafficking efforts.

For More Information

American Anti-Slavery Group, 198 Tremont St., Suite 421, Boston, MA 02116; (800) 884-0719; www.iabolish.org.

Casa Alianza, 346 West 17th St., New York, N.Y. 10011; (212) 727-4000; www.casa-alianza.org. A San Jose, Costa Rica, group that aids street children in Latin America.

Christian Children's Fund, 2821 Emerywood Parkway, Richmond, VA 23294; (800) 776-6767; www.christian childrensfund.org. CCF works in 28 countries on critical children's issues.

Christian Freedom International, P.O. Box 535, Front Royal, VA 22630; (800) 323-CARE (2273); (540) 636-8907; www.christianfreedom.org. An interdenominational human rights organization that combines advocacy with human itarian assistance for persecuted Christians.

Christian Solidarity International, Zelglistrasse 64, CH-8122 Binz, Zurich, Switzerland; www.csi-int.ch/index .html. Works to redeem slaves in Sudan.

Defence for Children International, P.O. Box 88, CH 1211, Geneva 20, Switzerland; (+41 22) 734-0558; www .defence-for-children.org. Investigates sexual exploitation of children and other abuses.

Free the Children, 1750 Steeles Ave. West, Suite 218, Concord, Ontario, Canada L4K 2L7; (905) 760-9382; www .freethechildren.org. This group encourages youth to help exploited children.

Free the Slaves, 1326 14th St., N.W., Washington, DC 20005; (202) 588-1865; www.freetheslaves.net.

Human Rights Watch, 350 Fifth Ave., New York, NY 10118; (212) 290-4700; www.hrw.org. Investigates abuses worldwide.

International Labour Organization, 4, route des Morillons, CH-1211, Geneva 22, Switzerland; www.ilo.org. Sets and enforces worldwide labor standards.

Polaris Project, P.O. Box 77892, Washington, DC 20013; (202) 547-7990; www.polarisproject.org. Grass-roots organization fighting trafficking.

United Methodist Committee On Relief, 475 Riverside Dr., New York, NY 10115; (800) 554-8583; gbgm-umc .org. Worldwide humanitarian group.

United Nations Children's Fund (UNICEF), 3 United Nations Plaza, New York, NY 10017; (212) 326-7000; www .unicef.org. Helps poor children in 160 countries.

Women's Commission on Refugee Women and Children, 122 East 42nd St., 12th Floor, New York, NY 10168-1289; (212) 551-3088; www.womenscommission.org. Aids trafficking victims in the developing world.

World Vision International, 800 West Chestnut Ave., Monrovia, Calif. 91016; (626) 303-8811; www.wvi.org. A Christian relief and development organization established in 1950.

Child Soldiers

2

Are More Aggressive Efforts Needed to Protect Children?

John Felton

Former child soldier Ishmael Beah addresses a 2007 international conference on child soldiers. His best-selling autobiography about his horrific experiences in Sierra Leone has raised public awareness of the use of children in armed conflicts.

From *CQ Researcher*, July 2008.

I shmael Beah kept on the move in the bush for months with some of his friends to escape the chaos of war-torn Sierra Leone in the early 1990s. Their greatest fear was ending up in the clutches of rebel groups who abducted young boys to join them in fighting against the government and raping, murdering and mutilating civilians. Instead, they wound up in the hands of government soldiers, which wasn't much better.

"We were told that our responsibilities as boys were to fight in this war or we would be killed," he told a U.S. Senate committee last year. "I was 13 years old."[1]

Then, recalling his first day in battle, Beah told the panel that after less than a week of training in how to use AK 47s, M16s, machine guns and rocket-propelled grenades, the adult soldiers led him and his friends into the forest to ambush rebels. "My squad had boys who were as young as 7 . . . dragging guns that were taller than them as we walked to the frontlines."

At first, "I couldn't shoot my gun," he remembered. "But as I lay there watching my friends getting killed . . . I began shooting. Something inside me shifted and I lost compassion for anyone. After that day, killing became as easy as drinking water." For the next two years, Beah said, "all I did was take drugs, fight and kill or be killed."

Children always have been among the first victims of warfare, usually as innocent bystanders. Indeed, in most conflicts, more women and children die — from a combination of disease, starvation or violence — than soldiers. Children also have been pressed into service occasionally as fighters, often as the last, desperate resort of losing armies.[2]

Dozens of Countries Use Child Soldiers

Tens of thousands of children under age 18 — some as young as 5 — serve as soldiers or spies for rebel groups, government-linked paramilitary militias or government armed forces. Most are recruited or conscripted in Africa and Asia. Government armed forces in several industrialized countries induct under-18-year-olds but don't use them in combat.

Countries That Use Child Soldiers
(Between April 2004-October 2007)

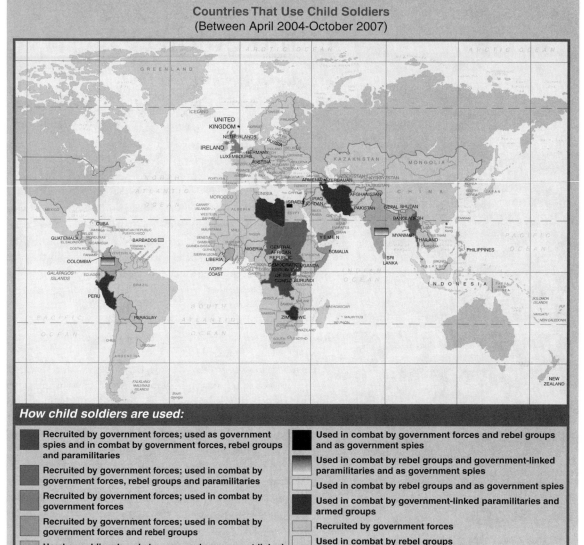

How child soldiers are used:

- Recruited by government forces; used as government spies and in combat by government forces, rebel groups and paramilitaries
- Recruited by government forces; used in combat by government forces, rebel groups and paramilitaries
- Recruited by government forces; used in combat by government forces
- Recruited by government forces; used in combat by government forces and rebel groups
- Used as soldiers by rebel groups and government-linked paramilitaries
- Used in combat by government forces and rebel groups and as government spies
- Used in combat by rebel groups and government-linked paramilitaries and as government spies
- Used in combat by rebel groups and as government spies
- Used in combat by government-linked paramilitaries and armed groups
- Recruited by government forces
- Used in combat by rebel groups

* Deployed children under 18 to Iraq, where they were exposed to risk of hostilities.

Source: "Child Soldiers: Global Report 2008," Coalition to Stop the Use of Child Soldiers

Laws and Resolutions Dealing with Child Soldiers

Several United Nations treaties make it illegal under international law for governments or rebel groups to recruit and use children in warfare, including:

- **Additional Protocols to the Geneva Conventions (1977)** — Establishes age 15 as the minimum for participation in armed combat by government forces or nongovernmental groups; applies both to international and domestic conflicts.
- **Convention on the Rights of the Child (1989)** — Prohibits the recruitment and use of children under 15 by armed groups; a compromise is reached after objection by the United States, Britain and the Netherlands to an 18-year-old standard. The United States and Somalia are the only countries that have not ratified it.[1]
- **Rome Statute (1998)** — Creates the International Criminal Court and defines as a war crime the recruitment or use in combat of children under 15.
- **Worst Forms of Child Labour Convention (1999)** — Adopted by member states of the International Labor Organization; defines a child as anyone under 18 and says child labor includes "forced or compulsory recruitment of children for use in armed conflict."
- **Optional Protocol to the Convention on the Rights of the Child (2000)** — Raises to 18 the minimum age for using children in conflicts, prohibits compulsory recruitment by governments or non-state groups of anyone under 18; allows governments to recruit 16- and 17-year-olds for military service if the recruitment is voluntary and approved by the parents or legal guardians. The United States ratified it in 2002.[2]

Since 1999, the U.N. Security Council has adopted six resolutions pertaining to children in armed conflict:

- **Resolutions 1261 (1999) and 1314 (2000)** — Calls on all parties to respect international law concerning the protection of children, including girls, in armed conflict.
- **Resolution 1379 (2001)** — Asks the U.N. secretary-general to create a blacklist of those who recruit child soldiers.
- **Resolutions 1460 (2003) and 1539 (2004)** — Calls for children to be included in programs designed to help former soldiers disarm, demobilize and reintegrate into society; suggests implementation of country-specific, targeted measures.
- **Resolution 1612 (2005)** — Creates a mechanism for monitoring and disseminating information on six types of child-rights violations; creates a Security Council Working Group to recommend measures on a per-situation basis; urges those using children in conflict to establish action plans for their release and reintegration.

---

[1] Available at www.unhchr.ch/html/menu2/6/crc/treaties/crc.htm.

[2] Available at www.unhchr.ch/html/menu2/6/crc/treaties/opac.htm.

But in recent times tens of thousands of children like Beah have been actively and regularly used in warfare. Since the closing decades of the 20th century, rebel groups and even government armies routinely have used children in combat or supporting roles throughout Africa, Asia, Europe and Latin America.

Many of these children were forced to participate in or witness acts almost beyond comprehension, including:

- The 1994 genocide in Rwanda during which at least 800,000 people were slaughtered within a few weeks, many hacked to death with machetes;

- Sierra Leone's civil war in which children were forced to kill their parents and cut off the hands and feet of civilians;

- Indiscriminate guerrilla attacks on noncombatants in Colombia and Sri Lanka;

- The forced murders of their own family members and neighbors, perpetrated at the direction of the Lord's Resistance Army (LRA), a rebel group led by fanatical recluse Joseph Kony in northern Uganda and neighboring countries.

- The use of children, in some cases preteens, as suicide bombers by several groups, including the Tamil

19 African Commanders Charged with Using Child Soldiers

A total of 19 former and current commanders — all from Africa — have been charged with enlisting children under age 15 as soldiers. Four are serving time in prison after being convicted. Six are on trial, while six have been charged but never captured. Most were accused of other war crimes as well, including murder, rape, abductions, forced labor and looting. No commanders from other countries have been charged for using child soldiers.

Country	Commander	Military Group*	Status
Democratic Republic of the Congo			
	Thomas Lubanga Dyilo	Union of Congolese Patriots	International Criminal Court trial indefinitely suspended 6/2008; his release is pending appeal
	Germain Katanga	Patriotic Forces of Resistance	ICC pre-trial hearings began 5/27/2008
	Mathieu Ngudjolo Chui	Front for National Integration	ICC pre-trial hearings began 5/27/2008
	Kyungu Mutanga	Mai-Mai	In Congolese custody
	Jean-Pierre Biyoyo	Mudundu 40	Sentenced to 5 years by Congolese military tribunal 3/2006; escaped
	Bosco Ntaganda	Union of Congolese Patriots	ICC warrants issued 8/22/2006
Liberia			
	Charles Taylor	Former president, Liberia	Trial continues at Special Court of Sierra Leone
Sierra Leone			
	Alex Tamba Brima	Armed Forces Revolutionary Council	Convicted, serving 50 years
	Brima Bazzy Kamara	Armed Forces Revolutionary Council	Convicted, serving 45 years
	Santigie Borbor Kanu	Armed Forces Revolutionary Council	Convicted, serving 50 years
	Allieu Kondewa	Civil Defense Forces	Convicted, 8-year sentence increased to 20 years, 5/2008
	Issa Hassan Sesay	Revolutionary United Front	Joint trial in Special Court of Sierra Leone expected to conclude in August
	Morris Kallon	Revolutionary United Front	
	Augustine Gbao	Revolutionary United Front	
Uganda			
	Joseph Kony	Lord's Resistance Army	ICC warrant issued 7/8/2005
	Vincent Otti	Lord's Resistance Army	Reportedly killed in 2007
	Raska Lukwiya	Lord's Resistance Army	Killed, 2006
	Okot Odiambo	Lord's Resistance Army	ICC warrant issued 7/8/2005
	Dominic Ongwen	Lord's Resistance Army	ICC warrant issued 7/8/2005

Lubanga
Katanga
Taylor
Kony
Otti

* The accused were serving with these groups at the time of their alleged crimes. Some are in other groups now.

Sources: United Nations; Human Rights Watch; Special Court of Sierra Leone, www.sc-sl.org/RUF-Casesummary.html

Tigers in Sri Lanka, the Taliban in Afghanistan and the Palestinian groups Hamas and Islamic Jihad.

Thousands of other children raided and burned villages, shouldered automatic weapons in combat or served as porters, spies or decoys. The girls were often forced to satisfy the sexual appetites of the guerrillas.

The U.N.'s Special Representative for Children and Armed Conflict, Radhika Coomaraswamy, says there are at least 250,000 child soldiers worldwide.[3] But other experts say the nature of civil conflicts makes it difficult to compile accurate records.

"It's absolutely impossible to determine the number of child soldiers with any accuracy," says Victoria Forbes Adam, executive director of the London-based Coalition to Stop the Use of Child Soldiers. "We think it is in the many tens of thousands, but that is a complete guesstimate." Leaders of armed groups, particularly rebels fighting in the bush, generally refuse to open their rosters to international inspection, she explains, and "children come in and out of conflicts, they die of illness, they die of injuries, or they may simply be missing from their communities."

However, many more children are recruited by official national armies than by rebel groups, according to some studies. About 500,000 under-18-year-olds serve at any given time in government armies and paramilitary groups in about 50 countries, according to P.W. Singer, a senior fellow at the Brookings Institution think tank in Washington, D.C., who has written widely on the problem. (*See map, p. 24.*) Most serve in reserve units until they are called into combat, Singer writes.[4]

The United Nations and human rights groups have accused some countries of forcibly recruiting children for their armies. The military government of Myanmar, for example, allegedly rewards recruiters with money and bags of rice for luring children into the army, according to Human Rights Watch (HRW).[5]

The presence of children in combat can make conflicts more persistent because conflicts involving children "are easier to start, more difficult to end, and more likely to resume," says Singer. Children are so readily available, cheap and expendable — from the viewpoint of leaders of armed groups — that using them can be an incentive to start conflicts and keep fighting even if success seems futile, he says.

Former Liberian President Charles Taylor, in handcuffs, arrives in the Netherlands in 2006 for his war crimes trial before the Special Court of Sierra Leone in The Hague. Taylor is accused of sponsoring and aiding rebels who carried out murders, sexual slavery, mutilations and the conscription of child soldiers during the civil war in Sierra Leone. The trial continues.

Defining a "child soldier" is a complex issue. Who is a child? And who is a soldier? As set out in several U.N. treaties since World War II, a child is anyone under 18. The most recent legal definition is contained in the 2000 Optional Protocol to the Convention on the Rights of the Child on the Involvement of Children in Armed Conflict — known as the "Optional Protocol." It allows governments to recruit 16- and 17-year-olds but prohibits them from serving in combat. The United States and 25 other countries recruit under-18-year-olds into their armed services, according to the Coalition to Stop the Use of Child Soldiers.[6] Under the Optional Protocol, "non-state actors" such as rebel groups, may not recruit anyone under 18.

But many rebel leaders around the world either ignore the prohibition or claim not to know the ages of their recruits. "They say, 'The children come to us without any birth certificates, so how are we to know how old they are?'" says U.N. Special Representative Coomaraswamy,

Former Girl Soldiers Get Little Aid

Many programs often ignore their needs

When she was 12 years old, Lucy Aol was abducted by the Lord's Resistance Army (LRA), a rebel group in northern Uganda. They made her walk several hundred miles to a hideout in southern Sudan.

"We were used like slaves," she recently recalled. "We used to work in the fields or collect firewood from 7 in the morning until 5 in the evening, and we were given no food. If you made a mistake or refused, they would beat us," she said. "The three girls who were taken from my village with me were beaten to death."

A year after she was abducted, Aol was forced to become the "wife" of a rebel commander. She and her "husband" later fled the rebel group together, but he was killed, and she discovered she was pregnant, and at age 16 she gave birth to a daughter. Now 21, Aol is studying environmental health at a college in Uganda.[1]

Similar stories could be told by thousands of girls in recent decades. Up to 40 percent of the children serving in some armed groups are girls.[2] A 2004 study found that girls served in 38 regional conflicts between 1990 and 2003 and were fighters in all but four.[3] Yet, the plight of young girls forced to join armed groups still isn't on the radar screens of many governments and world leaders — or even those working to reintegrate former male child soldiers into society.

Only in the last few years have aid programs taken girls' needs into consideration, and they still are not being given as much attention or help as the boys. Many girls also avoid official postwar reintegration programs for fear of being stigmatized.

"Boys might be called rebels, but girls are not just rebels. They may have been raped, they may feel spiritually polluted or unclean, and if they are mothers they may be called the mothers of rebel children, and so they are isolated," says Michael Wessells, a professor of psychology at Randolph-Macon College in Virginia who has aided former child soldiers in Africa and Asia for three decades. "But all they want is to be like other children."

"In many parts of the world, if you are female and you're not a virgin, you are not marriageable," says Neil Boothy, a professor at Columbia University who has developed and studied aid programs for former child soldiers for two decades. "And marriage remains the economic pathway for most women in most societies."

Only a few postwar integration programs, however, provide vocational training for both girls and boys. One exception is a program in northern Uganda run by local organizations supported by the Anglican Church. It allows both girls and boys who had been in armed groups to attend a technical school where they learn basic business skills and agricultural trades, such as beekeeping.

who has negotiated with many rebel leaders in Africa and Asia.

Perhaps the most precise definition of a child soldier was produced at a conference of scholars and representatives of various child-protection agencies, organized in 1997 by the United Nations Children's Fund (UNICEF). Convening in Cape Town, South Africa, the group developed the so-called Cape Town Principles, which define a child soldier as anyone under 18 "who is part of any kind of regular or irregular armed force" in any capacity, including cooks, porters, messengers and non-family members accompanying such groups. Also included were girls recruited for sexual purposes and those forced into marriage.[7]

However, David M. Rosen, a professor of anthropology and law at Fairleigh Dickinson University in Madison, New Jersey, argues that the age "when the young are fit to be warriors" varies from culture to culture.[8] In some societies, he wrote in a provocative 2005 book, "young people are deliberately socialized into highly aggressive behavior, and both individual and collective violence are highly esteemed." Other societies, he added, put more emphasis "on peaceful resolution of disputes." Rosen contends the United Nations and international humanitarian organizations have used the subject of child soldiers to advance their own agendas, including, in his view, protecting post-colonial governments in Africa and Asia against internal rebellion and denouncing Israel for its attacks on

A recent study of former LRA girl soldiers focused on several thousand girls and young women who had been forced to "marry" rebel commanders.[4] The study said the presence of forced wives in rebel units "served to bolster fighter morale and support the systems which perpetuate cycles of raiding, looting, killing, and abduction." Thus, says study co-author Dyan Mazurana, forcing girls to become commanders' wives is an integral part of how many armed groups conduct their business — not an incidental factor that can be ignored by governments and aid groups in their postwar negotiations with rebels.

The leaders of local communities often argue that the best way to deal with the forced wives of rebels after a war "is for them to stay with their captors," she continues. But the young women overwhelmingly reject that idea.

Grace Akallo — abducted by the LRA in 1996 but who escaped after seven months — says she "can't imagine" any girl wanting to stay with her captors. "We were all so anxious to get away from them, we would do anything to get

A Palestinian policeman teaches a girl how to use an AK-47 assault rifle in a Gaza refugee camp in southern Gaza Strip. Palestinian extremist groups reportedly have used children as suicide bombers.

away from them," says Akallo, now a college student in the United States.

Complicating the situation, says Wessells, are girls who joined armed groups voluntarily to avoid abusive parents, to escape arranged marriages or in hopes of finding a better life. These girls are often more reluctant than abducted girls to return to their communities after the war, so they are unlikely to seek help from official aid programs, Wessells says.

[1] "In the Tragedy of Child-soldiering in Africa, a Girl's Story Finds a Happy Ending," The Associated Press, Aug. 25, 2007.

[2] Hilde F. Johnson, deputy executive director, UNICEF, address to the Ministerial Meeting on Children and Armed Conflict, Oct. 1, 2007, a follow-up to the Paris Principles and Paris Commitments, formulated in February 2007, www.unicef.org/protection/files/Final-Paris-Principles-1Oct07-HFJ-speech.pdf.

[3] Susan McKay and Dyan Mazurana, "Where are the Girls? Girls in Fighting Forces in Northern Uganda, Sierra Leone, and Mozambique. Their Lives During and After War," International Centre for Human Rights and Democracy, Montreal, 2004, pp. 22, 25.

[4] Kristopher Carlson and Dyan Mazurana, "Forced Marriage within the Lord's Resistance Army, Uganda," Feinstein International Center, Tufts University, May 2008.

Palestinians while ignoring terrorist attacks perpetrated by Palestinian child soldiers.

Children end up in armies and rebel groups for a variety of reasons, depending on the circumstances. All too often, children are abducted from their villages or displaced-person camps or — like Beah — are swept up by government armies. Leaders of armed groups often use narcotics to dull the fears of their child soldiers or to stimulate them for combat. Beah's experiences were similar to those of Albert, a former child soldier who told Amnesty International he was forced to join a rebel group in the Democratic Republic of the Congo when he was 15.

"[T]hey would give us 'chanvre' [cannabis] and force us to kill people to toughen us up," he recalled. "Sometimes they brought us women and girls to rape. . . . They would beat us if we refused."[9]

Many young children join armed groups voluntarily because their families can't support them, or they're lured by the prospect of carrying a gun and wearing a snazzy uniform. Others are enticed by recruiters who make extravagant promises to the children and their families that they have no intention of keeping.

The child soldier problem has captured the world's attention intermittently over the past two decades — most often when children are found to engage in atrocities. Conflicts in the West African nations of Liberia and Sierra Leone during the 1990s seemed to represent the quintessential use of child soldiers in brutal circumstances.

Abducting Girls Is Most Widespread in Africa

Girls were abducted into either official armed forces or non-state armed groups in 28 countries between 1990 and 2003 — 11 of them in Africa.

Countries Where Girls Were Abducted into Armed Groups (1990-2003)

Africa	Americas	Sri Lanka
Angola	Colombia	Timor-Leste
Burundi	El Salvador	
Democratic	Guatemala	**Europe**
Republic of the	Peru	Federal Republic of
Congo		Yugoslavia
Ethiopia	**Asia**	Germany
Liberia	Myanmar	Northern Ireland
Mozambique	Cambodia	
Rwanda	India	**Middle East**
Sierra Leone	Indonesia	Iraq
Somalia	Nepal	Turkey
Sudan	Philippines	
Uganda		

Source: Susan McKay and Dyan Mazurana, "Where are the girls?" Rights & Democracy, March 2004

In Liberia, Charles Taylor rose to power at the head of a rebel army composed substantially of young fighters whom he sent out to rape, pillage and murder. In neighboring Sierra Leone, the Revolutionary United Front (RUF) — a rebel group armed and supported by Taylor — forced its child soldiers to mutilate victims in one of the most depraved civil conflicts in modern times. These wars spawned other conflicts in the region, notably in Guinea and the Côte d'Ivoire, sometimes involving child soldiers who crossed borders to keep fighting because it was the only life they knew.

Beah, who was fortunate enough to be removed from the Sierra Leone conflict by UNICEF, recounted his story in the gripping 2007 bestseller, *A Long Way Gone: Memoirs of a Boy Soldier.*[10] The book, and Beah's engaging media appearances, quickly drew more public attention to the child soldier issue than stacks of U.N. reports and resolutions had done.

Besides being an appealing advocate for child soldiers, Beah, now in his late-20s, shows that child soldiers can return to a normal life once they're removed from conflict and receive appropriate assistance from groups specializing in protecting children. Admittedly, as a ward of the U.N. system for several years, Beah had opportunities few other former soldiers enjoy. Even so, child-protection experts emphasize that even after committing heinous acts or suffering deep psychological or physical injuries, former child soldiers can be rehabilitated.

As governments and international organizations around the globe wrestle with the problem of child soldiers, here are some of the questions being addressed:

Does "naming and shaming" help prevent the use of child soldiers?

In his most recent report on children and armed conflict, released in January, United Nations Secretary-General Ban Ki-moon identified 40 governments or rebel groups, in 13 conflicts, that recruited and used child soldiers.[11] This report was a key component of the U.N.'s policy of publicly identifying those who recruit and use child soldiers — and condemning them for it. The U.N. has been in the "naming and shaming" business since November 2001, when the Security Council adopted Resolution 1379, asking the secretary-general to identify governments and groups that engaged in the practice.[12]

Secretary-General Kofi Annan submitted his first such report in 2002, and subsequent reports have been filed each year.

Human-rights advocacy groups, such as Amnesty International and HRW, also have made naming and shaming an important part of their campaigns to draw attention to the use and abuse of child soldiers. These groups issue their own reports on specific conflicts, and a collaboration of such groups, the Coalition to Stop the Use of Child soldiers, periodically publishes a comprehensive assessment of the use of child soldiers worldwide. The coalition's most recent report, "Child Soldiers Global Report 2008," was published in May.[13]

In his 2007 report, Secretary-General Ban said naming offending parties "has proven to have a deterrent effect" and has allowed the U.N. and other agencies to maintain political pressure and take action against those who are "persistent violators of child rights."[14]

U.N. Special Representative Coomaraswamy says it's also significant that the child soldier problem is the only "thematic issue" regularly addressed by the Security Council — as opposed to specific crises in individual countries. The council has established a "working group" that meets every two months to discuss the secretary-general's reports. On behalf of the Security Council, the working group condemns those who continue using child soldiers and praises those who agree to stop the practice.

"People do listen to the Security Council," Coomaraswamy says. "They may not always act in ways we wish they would, but they do listen, and this should not be dismissed."

Jo Becker, child rights advocacy director of HRW, agrees naming and shaming has had some impact, but mostly on governments. For example, she notes, governments in Chad, the Democratic Republic of the Congo and Myanmar have pledged to stop using child soldiers due to international pressure. And while these and other governments haven't always kept their promises, at least they have taken the first step of forswearing their use, she says.

Some rebels have responded to international pressure, such as the Tamil Tigers of Sri Lanka, who "promote themselves as a reputable group and rely very heavily on contributions from the international diaspora of Tamils," Becker points out. According to the U.N., the group has released some child soldiers — but certainly not all of them — and continued recruiting children well into 2007, although in lower numbers than in previous years.[15]

However, leaders of many other groups — such as Kony, of the Lord's Resistance Army — appear to have little or no regard for how they are seen internationally and are not swayed by having their names published in U.N. reports. "Kony's name was already mud and could hardly get any worse," says Christopher Blattman, an assistant professor of political science and economics at Yale University who has done extensive research on Kony.

An even more skeptical view comes from Singer at Brookings, who says most of those who use child soldiers see it as a purely pragmatic rather than a moral issue. "You can't shame the shameless," Singer says, "but you can create some sense of accountability by figuring out what their interests are, what drives their calculations and how you can alter their calculations." Prosecuting and imposing sanctions are more effective parts of a "cost structure" that can be imposed on those who use child soldiers, Singer says.

Some experts argue that naming and shaming can be useful in some cases but counterproductive in others. "If you are . . . trying to use communication and negotiations channels [with rebels] to get the release of child soldiers, it can be undermined by strident or hostile criticism of the group," says Michael Wessells, a professor of psychology at Randolph-Macon College in Virginia, who has worked with programs to aid child soldiers for nearly three decades. "The door closes, and the lives of children are damaged even further."

For instance, Blattman says pending International Criminal Court (ICC) indictments of Kony and four of his commanders may have helped persuade Kony to authorize aides to enter into peace negotiations with the Ugandan government in hopes the indictments would be lifted. But the court's insistence on maintaining the indictments "could now be an impediment to peace because it doesn't offer them [Kony and his commanders] much of an option," Blattman says. If Kony faces a choice of prison or lifetime exile, he probably will choose exile and continued conflict, Blattman adds, prolonging his two-decade-long war well into the future.

Nevertheless, Wessells says, it is "profoundly important to make clear that it is not OK for leaders of armed groups to say they can do whatever they want." Reflecting concerns about the potential negative consequences of naming and shaming, an international forum of experts on child soldiers, meeting in Switzerland in 2006, called for more research on the effectiveness of naming and shaming.[16]

Should the United States prosecute alleged child soldiers detained at Guantánamo Bay?

An alleged terrorist captured in Afghanistan when he was 15 could be the first person tried for war crimes

Girl soldiers serve with Maoist rebels near Kathmandu. According to a recent U.N. report, the group refuses to release its child soldiers on a regular basis despite signing an historic peace pact with the Nepalese government.

committed as a child. Omar Ahmed Khadr, now 21, is facing trial by a military commission after spending nearly six years in prison at the U.S. military base at Guantánamo Bay, Cuba.

The son of a financier for the al Qaeda Islamic terrorist group, Khadr is charged with murder, spying against the United States and other crimes. He allegedly threw a grenade that killed a U.S. soldier and injured others in Afghanistan on July 27, 2002.[17] Khadr was seriously wounded during the fighting and was transferred to Guantánamo in November 2002, where he was placed under the jurisdiction of the U.S. military commission created after the Sept. 11, 2001, terrorist attacks.

The commission in late 2007 and early 2008 rejected several motions filed by Khadr's attorneys challenging the proceedings, including one contending Khadr had been illegally recruited by his father into working as a translator at al Qaeda training camps in Afghanistan. Col. Peter Brownback, the commission's judge, dismissed that motion on April 30 on the grounds that Congress did not set a minimum age for defendants when it authorized the military commissions in 2006.[18] Khadr's trial is scheduled to begin in October.

HRW and other groups have denounced the government's handling of Khadr, noting that he was treated as an adult despite his age when he allegedly committed the crimes and has been held in "prolonged" periods of solitary confinement for more than

five years.[19] In an *amicus curiae* brief submitted to the commission on Jan. 18 on behalf of 23 members of Canada's parliament and 55 legal scholars from Canada, Sarah H. Paoletti, clinical supervisor and lecturer at the Transnational Legal Clinic at the University of Pennsylvania School of Law, argued that Khadr's prosecution "is in stark opposition to longstanding and well-established precedent under international law protecting the rights of children unlawfully recruited into armed conflict."[20]

Paoletti's brief said recent treaties and agreements suggest that former child soldiers should be offered rehabilitation and reintegration back into their communities rather than prosecution. For instance, the 1998 Rome Statute, which created the ICC, denied the court jurisdiction over anyone younger than 18 at the time of the alleged crime. This ban does not apply to courts or tribunals established by national governments.[21]

Similarly, a set of "principles" negotiated by representatives of countries and nongovernmental organizations in Paris last year suggested that former child soldiers should not be prosecuted but rather treated as "victims of offences against international law, not only as perpetrators. They must be treated in accordance with international law in a framework of restorative justice and social rehabilitation, consistent with international law, which offers children special protection through numerous agreements and principles."[22]

David M. Crane, former chief prosecutor at the U.N.-backed Special Tribunal for Sierra Leone, is one of the most prominent opponents of Khadr's prosecution. He says he decided not to prosecute child soldiers — even those who had committed "horrendous crimes" — because adults were the responsible parties. "Even if a child willingly goes along, he really has no choice in the matter, and this certainly appears to be true in the case of Khadr," who was under the influence of his father, Crane says.

The U.N.'s Coomaraswamy has appealed to the United States to halt the prosecution, saying "children should not be prosecuted for war crimes." She is pleased that Khadr's military lawyers are fighting the prosecution "tooth and nail."

The Pentagon has defended its prosecution on the grounds that none of the international treaties dealing with children and armed conflict expressly forbid a national government from prosecuting alleged child soldiers. In fact, a prosecution motion in the case argued that the Optional Protocol obligated the government to take legal action against Khadr. Al Qaeda itself violated that treaty by recruiting Khadr, the prosecution said, so dismissing the charges against him — as his defense lawyers argued — "would effectively condone that alleged violation by allowing Khadr to escape all liability for his actions and would further incentivize such actions."[23]

In another government defense of the Khadr case, the Pentagon official in charge of detention policy, Sandra L. Hodgkinson, told a U.N. committee on May 22 that the U.S. detention of Khadr and other juveniles in Afghanistan and Iraq reduces the threat that they will be used to carry out suicide bombings and other attacks. "If there is a sense that juveniles cannot be removed from the battlefield, there is a valid concern that the tactic of recruiting children will be further utilized against coalition forces and innocent civilians in Iraq and Afghanistan," she said.[24]

Although Khadr is a Canadian citizen by birth, Canada has refused to intervene on the grounds that he has been charged with a serious crime. Even so, the Canadian Supreme Court on May 23 denounced the early stages of the U.S. handling of his case. In a unanimous opinion, the court said U.S. legal processes at Guantánamo in 2002-03 "constituted a clear violation of fundamental human rights protected by international law." Moreover, the court said the Canadian government erred in turning over to U.S. authorities information about interviews with Khadr conducted by the Canadian intelligence service in 2003; Khadr's defense lawyers were entitled to see some of these documents, the court said.[25]

In a follow-up to that decision, a lower-court judge in Canada ruled on June 25 that Khadr's lawyers could be given a document and recordings describing alleged mistreatment of him by U.S. officials at the Guantánamo prison in 2004.

Another alleged child soldier held at Guantánamo, Mohammed Jawad, was captured in Afghanistan in December 2002 when he was either 16 or 17 and charged last January with attempted murder and intentionally causing bodily harm. The military alleges he threw a hand grenade into a vehicle carrying two U.S. soldiers and their Afghan interpreter.[26] Jawad's case is still in the early stages of consideration by a military commission at Guantánamo.

Hearings on both the Khadr and Jawad cases continued in mid-June despite a major Supreme Court ruling on June 12 that Guantánamo prisoners could challenge their detentions in U.S. federal court. The decision didn't directly go to the actions of the military commissions, but defense lawyers already have said they will use it to challenge a broad range of government actions concerning the detainees.

Should Congress pass legislation to combat the use of child soldiers overseas?

The child soldier issue has reached the U.S. Congress, which is considering two bills intended to put some force behind American criticisms of the use of child soldiers. The House-passed Child Soldier Prevention Act would bar U.S. military aid or arms sales to governments that recruit or use child soldiers (defined as children under 16 voluntarily recruited into an official army or under 18 forced to join an army). The U.S. president could waive the ban by declaring that it is in America's national interest to provide aid or sell weapons to governments that use child soldiers.

The Senate, meanwhile, passed the Child Soldiers Accountability Act, which would make it a crime under U.S. law for anyone, anywhere, to recruit a child under 15 into an armed group or use a child in combat. The measure also prohibits entry into the United States of anyone who recruits or uses child soldiers under 15.

Sen. Richard L. Durbin, D-Ill., one of the bill's sponsors, said it would help "ensure that the war criminals who recruit or use children as soldiers will not find safe haven in our country and will allow the U.S. government to hold these individuals accountable for their actions."[27] Senate aides say there has been no active opposition so far to either measure.

The House-passed measure potentially could prove controversial, however, because the national police force in Afghanistan — a key U.S. ally — has been accused of forcibly recruiting children under 18. The State Department cited the allegations in its 2007 human rights report on the country.[28]

Afghanistan was scheduled to receive about $8 million in military aid in fiscal 2008, according to the Center for Defense Information, a liberal think tank in Washington.

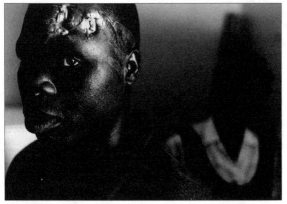

Simon, now 19, spent eight years as a child soldier with the Lord's Resistance Army (LRA) after being abducted from his home in northern Uganda. During that time he saw hundreds of people killed, including some who were hacked to death in front of him, and he was forced to kill other child abductees who tried to escape. Besides his psychological wounds, he is struggling to recover form a head wound received during combat. The LRA is led by Joseph Kony, a notorious, self-styled prophet who was indicted by the International Criminal Court in 2005 but remains at large.

The center said the bill could affect military aid to six other countries unless the president waived the provisions. The center compared the State Department's 2007 human rights reports — which dealt with child soldiers for the first time — and the administration's allocations of military aid as well as its arms sales to foreign countries. The six other countries that used child soldiers in some official capacity while receiving U.S. military aid were Chad, the Democratic Republic of the Congo, Somalia, Sri Lanka, Sudan and Uganda. Most of the aid programs were small and included only military training — generally considered the stepping stone to a broader relationship between the U.S. and foreign militaries.[29]

Sen. Durbin said the bill "would ensure that U.S. taxpayer dollars are not used to support this abhorrent practice by government or government-sanctioned military and paramilitary organizations." The United States could continue military aid if the president chose to do so, Durbin added, "but it would be used only to remedy the problem by helping countries successfully demobilize their child soldiers and professionalize their forces."[30]

Neither of the two measures has encountered any formal opposition in either chamber of Congress. Although the Bush administration has taken no formal position on either bill, congressional aides and lobbyists favoring the proposals say they expect the White House to oppose them as a matter of course because legislation limiting a president's flexibility in foreign policy is generally resisted.

BACKGROUND

Child Armies Proliferate

An explosion of civil conflicts around the globe during the last half of the 20th century was accompanied by several developments that ensured children would bear much of the burden of war. Chief among them was the invention of simple-to-use, lightweight weapons — especially automatic rifles and rocket launchers. Even a 10-year-old can carry and use the world's most ubiquitous weapon: the Kalashnikov assault rifle, or AK-47.

After the collapse of communism in Eastern Europe and the Soviet Union between 1989-91, millions of Kalashnikovs and other Soviet weapons fell into the hands of unscrupulous arms dealers, who sold them to rebel leaders and warlords around the world. They often paid with narcotics, diamonds or other resources plundered from their own countries.

Rebels claiming to be fighting for social justice or a host of other causes found they could easily fill their ranks with children. An official of the Chadian military explained their advantages: "Child soldiers are ideal because they don't complain, they don't expect to be paid and if you tell them to kill, they kill."[31]

Children also are easy to abduct or force into military service, especially if they live in unprotected villages or communal facilities, such as refugee camps, where they are often protected only by mothers and unarmed humanitarian workers. "All the boys in the village were asked to join the army," a former child soldier told author Singer. "There was no way out. If I left the village I would get killed by the rebels who would think that I was a spy. On the other hand, if I stayed in the village and refused to join the army, I wouldn't be given any food and would eventually be thrown out, which was as good as being dead."[32]

Social and economic conditions in many poor countries, such as poverty and lack of educational and job opportunities, make children susceptible to the call of combat. "Demagogues, warlords, criminals and others

C H R O N O L O G Y

1980s *Civil conflicts in Africa and Asia begin to use children in combat.*

1983 Tamil Tiger insurgency erupts in Sri Lanka. The group later gains notoriety for its use of suicide bombers and thousands of child soldiers.

1987 Joseph Kony's Lord's Resistance Army in Uganda begins abducting children for use as soldiers.

1989 U.N. General Assembly adopts Convention on the Rights of the Child, which establishes 15 as the minimum age for recruiting children into armed forces. Eventually, 190 countries ratify the treaty; the United States refuses to ratify it.

1990s *Genocide in Rwanda focuses global attention on child soldiers.*

1994 Thousands of children take part in Rwandan genocide.

1996 UNICEF's Landmark "Impact of Armed Conflict on Children" report focuses international attention on child soldiers.

1997 Zaire's dictator Mobutu Sese Seko is ousted by Laurent Kabila's rebel group, which uses several thousand child soldiers. Kabila's backers in Rwanda and Uganda later turn against him, setting off a war using tens of thousands of child soldiers. . . . Ugandan diplomat Olara Otunu becomes the U.N.'s first Special Representative for Children and Armed Conflict.

1998 Human-rights organizations form Coalition to Stop the Use of Child Soldiers.

1999 First U.N. resolution on child soldiers, Resolution 1261, condemns abduction and recruitment of children for combat.

2000s *U.N. steps up efforts to combat use of child soldiers.*

2000 U.N. "Optional Protocol" sets 18 as the minimum age for children in combat and bars non-state armed groups from recruiting or using children under 18.

2001 U.N. Security Council asks secretary-general to identify parties recruiting or using children in armed conflicts.

2002 U.S. Senate ratifies Optional Protocol.

2003 U.N. Secretary-General Kofi Annan submits first report listing groups recruiting and using children in armed conflicts. Security Council asks secretary-general to report on actions being taken by armed groups cited in his report to stop the use of children.

2004 Security Council calls for "action plans" to stop use of child soldiers.

2005 Security Council establishes monitoring and reporting mechanism on children and armed conflict. . . . International Criminal Court (ICC) issues war crimes arrest warrants for Lord's Resistance Army leader Kony and four commanders for forced recruitment and use of child soldiers in Uganda.

2006 ICC charges Thomas Lubanga Dyilo, leader of the rebel Union of Congolese Patriots, with using child soldiers.

2007 UNICEF and the French government sponsor a conference in Paris on preventing the use of child soldiers and aiding children in post-conflict situations. . . . *A Long Way Gone: Memoirs of a Boy Soldier*, by Ishmael Beah, becomes worldwide bestseller and focuses new attention on child soldiers. . . . Four former militia leaders are convicted by a U.N.-backed special tribunal on charges that they recruited and used child soldiers during the war in Sierra Leone — the first time an international court has addressed the use of child soldiers. . . . Former Liberian President Charles Taylor goes on trial at the Special Court of Sierra Leone (at The Hague) on 11 charges of war crimes and crimes against humanity, including conscripting children into the armed forces and using them in combat.

2008 Cease-fire agreement signed in January offers a potential end to fighting in eastern Congo, where the use of child soldiers is common. . . . ICC temporarily halts its first-ever case, against Congolese rebel leader Lubanga because of a dispute over the handling of confidential evidence.

Former Child Soldiers Can Become Good Citizens

But reintegration must be handled carefully by aid agencies

"**M**y parents ran away when they saw me. I had to follow them; they thought I would abduct them."

— Former girl child soldier, 15[1]

"We feel different because of the way other children look at us; it seems as if we are not children born from this land. They view us as though we come from a different place."

— Former boy child soldier, 17[2]

For many child soldiers, the end of a war can be nearly as traumatic as the conflict itself. Some cannot remember anything but warfare and have little concept of what normal civilian life is like. Others suffered serious physical wounds, and most endure at least short-term psychological problems, and sometimes drug addiction.

Returning child soldiers often find that one or both parents have been killed or may have moved elsewhere. Parents also are sometimes reluctant to accept a returning child whom they no longer know or understand, especially if the child was forced to commit atrocities — sometimes even against his own family.

Because their schooling has been interrupted, most former child soldiers have few job skills appropriate to civilian society. Governments and international aid agencies often include provisions for child soldiers in official programs to disarm, demobilize and reintegrate rebel fighters. But several experts in the field say many of these so-called DDR programs are underfunded, badly managed or lack appropriate resources to meet the special needs of children.

Many researchers consider economic opportunity as the greatest need faced by former child soldiers. "When they go home, their struggles are going to be largely economic — as much, if not more so, than mental health or some other concerns," says Neil Boothby, director of the Program on Forced Migration and Health at Columbia University. "They need to learn how to make a living in a peaceful and useful way. Their fights will be against poverty as much as to maintain mental health."

Boothby and other experts say research also refutes public perceptions — fostered by some news accounts — that former child soldiers are so deranged they cannot adapt to civilian life. At least two studies have found that former child soldiers tend to be good citizens once they are integrated back into their home communities. A long-term study of nearly 40 former child soldiers in Mozambique — all of them demobilized in 1988 — showed they have "turned out quite well," co-author Boothby says.[3] "They are perceived by their communities to be good neighbors, a high percentage are active in the equivalent of the PTA and many are leaders in their communities. It dispels the notion that there are lost generations" of former child soldiers. "The only time you lose generations is when you don't help them after a crisis."

Another study — of young Ugandans abducted by the notorious Lord's Resistance Army (LRA) — also found "a greater propensity toward engaged citizenry, including voting at higher rates and being more involved with community leadership" than their counterparts.[4] Christopher Blattman, a co-author of that study and an assistant professor from Yale University, says only a small minority of youth abducted by the LRA were so traumatized they could no longer function in society.

Grace Akallo, who was abducted at 15, says her personal experience demonstrates that children can overcome their past so long as they get help. "I suffered a lot in the LRA, but I went back to school and my family, and I am fine now. So long as a child gets an opportunity for a future, that child can be OK."

Experts who have assisted or studied former child soldiers say several important lessons have been learned during recent post-conflict experiences, including:

- Governments and aid agencies administering post-war reintegration programs should be cautious about making cash payments to former child soldiers. Giving returnees clothing, food, job training, medical aid and psychological counseling is appropriate, experts say, but in many circumstances giving them cash is not. "We know from many different contexts that when young people in these situations are given cash, bad things happen," says Michael Wessells, a psychology professor from Randolph-Macon College in Virginia, who has helped and studied child soldiers in Africa and Asia. "Commanders sometimes grab the cash and use it to recruit other children, so it runs counter to the intended purpose." A cash payment also can be seen as a reward for serving in an armed group, which is counterproductive, he says. On the other hand, Boothby says cash payments can help in some circumstances if they are carefully monitored to ensure the money benefits the children.

- Girls who have served with armed groups have different needs from boys, particularly if they return from the bush with children. Child soldier aid programs recently have begun to consider girls' special needs, such as child care, assistance with reproductive health matters and psychological aid to deal with the potential stigmatization in their home communities, where the girls are considered "unclean" because of their forced sexual relationships with rebel commanders.

- Reintegration programs should consider the needs of local communities, and community members should be involved in the process. Programs designed by officials in aid agencies or even by government officials in the conflict country often fail because they ignore local situations.

- Donor countries and aid agencies that fund reintegration programs should commit for the long haul. In several recent cases, money ran out before the bulk of former fighters returned from the bush, leaving thousands of youths feeling angry and betrayed. U.N. officials say that after the long war in the Democratic Republic of the Congo, for example, only about half of former child and adult fighters received assistance.[5]

- Targeting aid exclusively or primarily to former members of armed groups risks stigmatizing them and fostering jealousy among their neighbors. Thus, aid programs should be directed at entire communities, not just individuals, Wessells says. Moreover, all children who have

AFP/Getty Images/Sena Vidanagama

Former Sri Lankan Tamil Tiger fighters Velayutham Chuti, 18, (left) and 14-year-old Pulidha Logini (right) celebrate with their families after being released by a rival rebel group. The Hindu Tamil Tigers reportedly have used thousands of children in their long battle against the predominantly Buddhist government, making the Tigers one of the world's most persistent users of child soldiers.

served with armed groups — whether as porters, spies or as "wives" of commanders — should be eligible for reintegration aid, not just the fighters, experts say.

[1] "Returning Home: Children's Perspectives on Reintegration: A Case Study of Children Abducted by the Lord's Resistance Army in Teso, Eastern Uganda," Coalition to Stop the Use of Child Soldiers, February 2008, p. 14.

[2] *Ibid.*, p. 16.

[3] N. Boothby, J. Crawford and J. Halperin, "Mozambique Child Soldier Life Outcome Study: Lessons Learned in Rehabilitation and Reintegration," *Global Public Health*, February 2006.

[4] "Making Reintegration Work for Youth in Northern Uganda," The Survey of War Affected Youth, www.sway-uganda.org.

[5] "Report of the Secretary General on Children and Armed Conflict in the Democratic Republic of the Congo," June 28, 2007, pp. 14-15.

Congo Reintegrates the Most Child Soldiers

More than 104,000 child soldiers have been demobilized and reintegrated into society worldwide, including 27,000 in the Democratic Republic of the Congo — more than any other country. UNICEF estimates up to 33,000 children were involved in the long-running Congolese war — the biggest and deadliest since World War II. Uganda, where the Lord's Resistance Army notoriously relied on abducting children, has reintegrated 20,000 former child soldiers into their communities. Outside Africa, Sri Lanka has reintegrated more child soldiers than any other country.

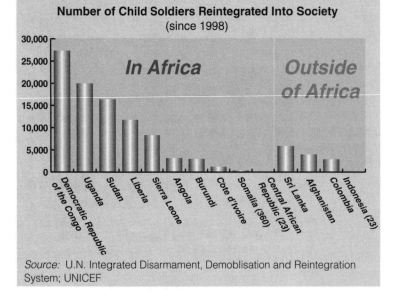

Number of Child Soldiers Reintegrated Into Society
(since 1998)

Source: U.N. Integrated Disarmament, Demoblisation and Reintegration System; UNICEF

find it easier to recruit when a large population of angry, listless young men fill the street," Singer said.[33]

Impressionable children also can find military life alluring. When a recruiter from the army or a rebel group shows up and offers an impoverished child the opportunity to wear a uniform and make himself feel powerful by carrying a gun, the sales pitch is often difficult to resist.

U.N. Roles

The task of curtailing the use of under-age fighters has fallen largely to the United Nations, which has had only limited success. The U.N. has taken a two-pronged approach: getting a treaty enacted making it illegal for governments and armed groups to use children under 18

in combat and establishing a system for identifying armed groups that recruit and use child soldiers. The Security Council has threatened to sanction more than a dozen persistent violators of the law but has taken that step only once, in Côte d'Ivoire in West Africa.

Several treaties and regulations adopted by the U.N. after World War II created a legal structure offering theoretical protection to children and discouraging their use in warfare, including the 1948 Universal Declaration of Human Rights, the Geneva Conventions of 1949 and Additional Protocols to those conventions adopted in 1977 and the 1989 Convention on the Rights of the Child. These treaties were strengthened substantially in 2000 with adoption of the Optional Protocol, which specifically barred non-state armed groups from recruiting or using any children under 18 but allowed governments to recruit children 16 or 17 as long as they weren't used in combat until they turned 18. In essence, the treaty made it illegal under international law for anyone to use a child under 18 in combat. In addition, the 1998 Rome Statute — which went into effect in 2002 and created the International Criminal Court — defined as a "war crime" the conscription or use in war of any child under 15.

Since 1996 the Security Council also has adopted six resolutions dealing specifically with children and armed conflict. The last four of these (Resolution 1379 adopted in 2001, Resolution 1460 adopted in 2003, Resolution 1539 adopted in 2004, and Resolution 1612 adopted in 2005) created a system under which U.N. officials monitor the impact of armed conflicts on children and publicly identify countries and groups that illegally recruit and use children in combat.

In some cases, when confronted by the U.N. with solid evidence about their use of child soldiers, warlords have promised to release them. Some have kept their promises, notably the leaders of three groups in Côte d'Ivoire who were subjected to Security Council sanctions in 2006.[34] Most others broke their promises. In Somalia, for example, the Union of Islamic Courts, which briefly held power in 2006, told U.N. officials they would stop using child soldiers, but didn't.[35]

Children at War

The United Nations, nongovernmental groups and academic experts have identified nearly 50 civil conflicts since World War II that have involved children, mostly in sub-Saharan Africa. The following examples are representative of recent or ongoing conflicts involving heavy use of child soldiers:

Colombia — The long-running, multifaceted civil conflict in Colombia has featured the most extensive use of child soldiers in the Americas. According to various estimates, 11,000 to 14,000 Colombians under 18 have been recruited into the country's armed groups.[36] Most are members of the two leftist guerrilla factions, the Revolutionary Armed Forces of Colombia (FARC) and the National Liberation Army (ELN). Several thousand underage fighters also have been associated with right-wing paramilitary groups aligned with the government, the military and major landowners; the largest paramilitary force is the United Self-Defense Forces of Colombia (AUC).[37]

The Colombian army also used under-18-year-olds as fighters until 2000, when it reportedly halted the practice after domestic and international protests. But there have been reports about the army's continued use of children. American journalist Jimmie Briggs said the army still recruits soldiers under 18 but assigns them to non-combat duty until they turn 18.[38] In its "2008 Global Report," the Coalition to Stop the Use of Child Soldiers cited the army for using captured children for intelligence-gathering.[39]

Significantly, since 1999 more than 3,300 former child soldiers (mostly from the FARC) have gone through the government-sponsored demobilization, disarmament and reintegration process — one of the few major demobilization efforts ever conducted during an ongoing conflict.[40]

Democratic Republic of the Congo — The Congolese war — the biggest and deadliest since World War II — took place in the former Zaire from about 1998 until 2003. It involved more than a dozen guerrilla groups and, at various points, the armies or paramilitary groups from Angola, Burundi, Rwanda, Uganda and Zimbabwe. The International Rescue Committee has estimated that up to 5.5 million people — about one-tenth of the Congo's population — may have died as a result of the conflict.[41]

Many of the armed groups used children as fighters or in support roles. In 2002, as part of the war was ending, UNICEF estimated that about 33,000 children were involved in the fighting — or 20 percent of active combatants.[42] In June 2007, U.N. Secretary-General Ban told the U.N. Security Council that 29,291 children had been released by armed groups during the previous three years under a U.N.-sponsored demobilization program. However, due to alleged mismanagement of the program and a failure by donor nations to fulfill their funding pledges, only about half of the former child soldiers had received aid to reintegrate into their communities, the report found.[43]

Although peace agreements were signed in 2002 and 2003, fighting has continued in parts of eastern Congo, where renegade Tutsi commander Laurent Nkunda leads a militia in fighting the Congolese army. Nkunda claims his group is protecting Congo's minority Tutsi population — an ethnic group that was slaughtered by the hundreds of thousands during the 1994 genocide in Rwanda.

The U.N. has accused Nkunda of forcibly recruiting hundreds, and possibly several thousand, children.[44] Nkunda, along with other rebels, signed a cease-fire agreement on Jan. 23, 2008, pledging to end the fighting.[45] Reports since then have suggested the cease-fire merely reduced the level of fighting rather than stopping it.[46] Government security forces also used child soldiers, at least through 2007, according to the U.S. State Department.[47]

Liberia — From the early 1990s until President Charles Taylor was ousted from power in 2003, Liberia was a focal point for several civil conflicts in West Africa, all involving child soldiers. During the early 1990s, Taylor led a rebel army, composed in large part of children, which controlled much of Liberia. After he became president in 1997, he also backed rebel groups in neighboring Côte d'Ivoire, Guinea and Sierra Leone.

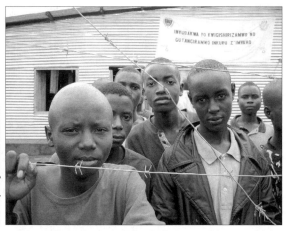

AFP/Getty Images/Esdras Ndikumana

Former child soldiers at a demobilization camp in Burundi wait to be reintegrated back into society. About 104,000 children worldwide have been reintegrated into their communities after serving in various rebel or government armed forces.

Taylor's support for the notorious Revolutionary United Front in Sierra Leone — in exchange for access to diamonds and other natural resources in rebel-controlled areas — was the basis for his indictment on 11 war-crimes charges by a U.N.-sponsored tribunal. His trial, which began in July 2007, is still under way. The regional impact of the war in Liberia and Taylor's sponsorship of neighboring rebel armies continued at least until 2005. According to the Coalition to Stop the Use of Child Soldiers, rebel groups in Guinea and Côte d'Ivoire were still recruiting child soldiers (and former child soldiers who had reached age 18) from Liberia.[48]

Myanmar — The U.N., HRW and other organizations say the secretive military government of Myanmar (formerly Burma) makes widespread use of children in its army even though the minimum recruitment age is 18.[49] According to HRW, government recruiters force boys under 18 to lie about their ages or falsify induction forms to meet quotas.[50] The government began recruiting children extensively in the 1990s, when it more than doubled the size of the army — from 200,000 to 500,000 — to combat an upsurge in a decades-old separatist insurgency in Karen state in southeastern Myanmar, the group said.[51]

Responding partly to pressure from the U.N., the government in 2004 created a committee to prevent the military recruitment of under-18-year-olds. Since then, government representatives have insisted the

army has no under-age soldiers. However, Secretary-General Ban wrote in a November 2007 report that recruitment continued unabated, with recruiters still rewarded with cash and a bag of rice for each new solider they produced, regardless of his age.[52]

U.N. and HRW officials do not know how many children now serve in the Myanmar military because the government severely restricts international access to the country. However, the HRW report quoted several former soldiers as estimating that 20 to 50 percent of the soldiers in their units had been underage.[53]

Many of the country's non-state military groups also use underage soldiers, but the extent is unknown, according to both the U.N. and HRW.[54]

Sri Lanka — The Liberation Tigers of Tamil Eelam (LTTE), better known as the Tamil Tigers, reportedly has used thousands of children in the Hindu group's long battle against the majority Sinhalese (mostly Buddhist) government, making it one of the world's most persistent users of child soldiers. A breakaway rebel faction, known as the Karuna group, which in recent years has been aligned with the government, also reportedly has used child soldiers.[55] A cease-fire negotiated by Norwegian diplomats in February 2002 helped reduce violence for more than three years, but several incidents in 2005 and 2006 led to an escalation of fighting, particularly in the north, which continues today. The cease-fire essentially collapsed in 2006, and the government formally withdrew from it in mid-January 2008. The U.N. had estimated a year earlier that at least 67,000 people had died in the quarter-century of conflict.[56]

The total number of children caught up in the conflict is unknown. However, a UNICEF database showed that between 2002 and 2007 the Tigers recruited 6,248 children, and up to 453 children were recruited by the Karuna group during the last three years of that period. UNICEF said these figures most likely understate the actual use of child soldiers, because the agency relies on voluntary reporting by parents and community leaders, who often withhold information because they fear retaliation.[57] Whatever the actual total, the Tamil Tigers have used children actively in fighting, including as suicide bombers — a technique the group introduced to the world in the 1980s.

U.N. officials and human rights groups have accused the government of complicity in the Karuna group's use of child soldiers and even allowing the group to recruit or abduct children in government-controlled areas. In some cases army units allegedly have participated actively in forcibly recruiting children.[58] The government has denied these accusations.

The Tamil Tigers pledged in 2007 to stop recruiting child soldiers and release all of those in its custody by the end of that year. As of January 2008, however, UNICEF listed 1,429 cases in which a recruited child soldier had not been released, including at least 168 children who were still under 18.[59]

Sudan — Africa's largest country has experienced two major conflicts and several smaller ones in recent years — all involving child soldiers. Secretary-General Ban reported in 2007 that more than 30 armed groups operated in Sudan.[60]

Ban's report and independent human rights groups have found that children have been recruited and used as soldiers by the government's Sudan Armed Forces, by the pro-government militias known as the Janjaweed (which operate in the western region of Darfur), by the main Darfur rebel groups — the Justice and Equality Movement (JEM) and the Sudan Liberation Army (SLA), which have both splintered into factions — and by armed groups in southern Sudan, including the region's main rebel group, the Sudan People's Liberation Army (SPLA).[61]

The Security Council's Working Group on Children and Armed Conflict has repeatedly — most recently in February 2008 — condemned the "continuous recruitment and use of children" by the government and armed groups in Sudan and demanded that the children be released so they could be reintegrated into their families and communities.[62]

In southern Sudan, the government and the SPLA signed a peace agreement in January 2005 ending a 20-year conflict. The agreement called for creation of a "government of national unity," but real unity has been elusive, as the Khartoum government and the former rebels continue to bicker about many of the same issues that fueled the war, including control over oil production in the region.[63]

Between 2001 and early 2006 the SPLA demobilized about 20,000 former child soldiers, but the Coalition to Stop the Use of Child Soldiers reported that as of late 2007 about 2,000 children remained under the militia's control.[64] Secretary-General Ban

The use of child soldiers, like these, by the Chadian military was officially prohibited in May 2007, but as a government official explained, using children is "ideal" because "they don't complain, they don't expect to be paid and if you tell them to kill, they kill."

reported in August 2007 that the SPLA had made "significant progress" by releasing at least 47 children in one of its units, but two armed groups associated with the government's army had not fulfilled their promises to release children.[65]

In Darfur, the fighting remains well below the peak of the conflict in 2002-03, but serious violence continues despite the presence of a U.N. peacekeeping mission. Ban's report found that nearly all armed groups in Darfur, including the Sudanese army and its related militias, continued to recruit and use children as fighters.[66]

The conflict in Darfur also has spilled into neighboring conflicts in Chad and the Central African Republic, where government armies and rebel groups (some supported by the Sudanese government) have recruited and used child soldiers. The Chadian government, in turn, reportedly participated in the forced recruitment in 2006 of nearly 5,000 Sudanese refugees, including several hundred children, by one of the Darfur rebel groups.[67]

Uganda — As in Sierra Leone, the use and abuse of child soldiers has reached a depraved level in Uganda, largely due to the fanatical Kony's Lord's Resistance Army. The United Nations has estimated that Kony, a violent, self-styled prophet, abducted or forced nearly 25,000 children into his army between 1986 and 2005.[68] However, independent experts have said the U.N. estimate counts only former LRA members who later turned themselves into Ugandan government reception centers. Researchers at Tufts University in Boston estimate that the LRA abducted at least 60,000 boys and girls, and that 15-20 percent of the boys and 5 percent of the girls died during the war, said Yale's Blattman, one of the researchers.

Human rights groups say the LRA continues to abduct children, although in lower numbers than earlier.[69] Blattman says his team believes the LRA now has fewer than 1,000 people—adults or children—in its ranks. The International Criminal Court in July 2005 issued arrest warrants for Kony and four of his aides, charging them with war crimes, including the use of child soldiers; at least one of the aides reportedly has since died.[70]

The LRA was one of several Ugandan groups that took up arms in 1986 against the new government of Yoweri Museveni, himself a former rebel leader who had used large numbers of child soldiers during a five-year war against President Milton Obote. Kony claimed to be fighting on behalf of his own ethnic group in northern Uganda, the Acholi people, but ultimately the Acholi became the principal victims in the two-decade-long war between the LRA and the government.[71] Kony reportedly claims his fight is ordained by God. At a 2006 meeting with Ugandan officials, Kony denied that his forces had committed atrocities and insisted "the tragedy that was taking place in Uganda was done by the Uganda government."[72]

The war developed a critical international dimension in the mid-1990s, when Sudan armed Kony's forces to help in its own war against the SPLA in southern Sudan. Kony used southern Sudan as a base from which to launch attacks against both the SPLA and the Ugandan army. He later established bases in the Democratic Republic of the Congo and the Central African Republic.[73]

The conflict in northern Uganda peaked after March 2002, when the Ugandan government launched an offensive against the LRA, which responded by targeting civilians as well as government forces. Over the next two years Kony increased the pace of abductions of children, forcing many of them to endure beatings and to carry out atrocities against each other and against civilians, sometimes even members of their own families. Girls were forced into virtual slavery, the youngest ones as servants and the older ones as "wives" of LRA commanders, says Grace Akallo, who was abducted at 15 and held for seven months until she escaped. Fearing such abductions,

thousands of children living in rural villages trudged long distances every evening to sleep in larger towns considered safe. Known as "night commuters," the children became the most visible symbols to the outside world of the horrors in northern Uganda.[74] Despite denials, the Ugandan government also recruited children into its army and local pro-government militias called the UPDF, according to U.N. officials and human rights groups.[75]

The fighting slowed significantly in 2005, when Sudan signed a peace accord with the rebels in southern Sudan and, reportedly, ended much of its support for Kony — a development that led to efforts to end the war in northern Uganda. Peace talks between Uganda and LRA representatives began in Juba, southern Sudan, in 2006. A cease-fire signed in August that year generally has held, resulting in the longest sustained period of peace in northern Uganda in more than two decades.[76] Although the LRA is no longer operating in northern Uganda, it is still present in the Central African Republic, Congo and Sudan and reportedly has continued abducting children well into 2008, according to a June 23 report by Secretary-General Ban.[77]

A diplomat negotiating on Kony's behalf initialed a peace agreement in February 2008, but Kony himself failed to show up for much-publicized signing ceremonies in April and May, reportedly fearing he might be arrested to face war crimes charges.[78] Uganda has offered to request that the charges against Kony be dropped so he could be tried in a local tribunal, but so far this has not been enough incentive for him to turn himself in.

CURRENT SITUATION

"Empty Threats"

United Nations officials and independent human rights groups say the U.N. Security Council risks losing credibility because of its failure to follow through on repeated threats to impose sanctions against governments and armed groups that persist in recruiting and using child soldiers.

In its last two resolutions on child soldiers — Resolution 1539 in 2004 and Resolution 1612 in 2005 — the Security Council threatened to impose "targeted measures" (primarily sanctions) against armed groups that defy international demands to stop using children in combat, but so far it has not taken any action. The council "needs to show that the threats they make are not empty threats," says Becker, of Human Rights Watch.

Top U.N. officials in recent months also have called on the council to follow through on its threats to punish those who use child soldiers. In his annual report on children and armed conflict, published in January, Secretary-General Ban suggested the council impose various measures, including banning the export or supplying of weapons, banning military assistance, imposing travel restrictions on government officials or leaders of armed groups, preventing armed groups and their leaders from accessing the international financial system and referring violators to the ICC for possible war-crimes punishment.[79]

And on Feb. 12, Special Representative Coomaraswamy confronted the council directly on the issue, pointing out that U.N. reports over the past five years had identified 16 "persistent violators" of international law, some of whom were "making efforts" to comply with the law, while others "remain in contempt of the council and its resolutions."[80]

She doubts the council will impose sanctions anytime soon, however, which she finds frustrating. "You have to realize that [imposing sanctions] is the most extreme action the Security Council can take in any context," she says. "And this is the Security Council, where there are always strong political considerations, and they are very cautious, so I think it will be some time down the road before they agree on sanctions."

Her comments reflect the fact that all actions by the Security Council require extensive compromise among countries with often-conflicting viewpoints, and the council cannot act unless there is unanimous agreement among all five of its permanent, veto-wielding members (Britain, China, France, Russia and the United States). In recent years China and Russia have been the most reluctant of the so-called "permanent five" to intervene in what they consider the domestic affairs of member states.

On the same day Coomaraswamy called for Security Council action, the council said it was "gravely concerned by the persistent disregard of its resolutions on children and armed conflict by parties to armed conflict." The council also said it "reaffirms its intention to make use of all the tools" provided in its previous resolutions. However, it did not mention sanctions nor did it

A young Congolese Patriotic Union soldier totes his rifle in the Democratic Republic of the Congo. In addition to rebel groups, Congo's government also uses child soldiers. Congo is one of seven countries — including Afghanistan, Chad, Somalia, Sri Lanka, Sudan and Uganda — that have used child soldiers while receiving U.S. military aid. Legislation pending before Congress would bar military aid to any country that uses child soldiers.

take any specific action — either then or in subsequent months.[81]

As Becker's comments suggest, independent human-rights groups are equally frustrated with the Security Council's lack of action. In two reports last January, the Watchlist on Children and Armed Conflict (a coalition of human rights groups) detailed several cases in which the council suggested it would act against violators but did not.[82] Becker says the council's reluctance to act

AT ISSUE

Should the U.S. prosecute alleged child soldiers at Guantánamo?

YES

David B. Rivkin, Jr.
Partner, Baker Hostetler LLP,
Washington, D.C.
Former Justice Department official and
Associate White House counsel during the
Reagan and George H.W. Bush administrations

Written for *CQ Global Researcher*, June 2008

In a challenge to the laws of war employed by the United States since 9/11, critics claim the military commission prosecution of Omar Ahmed Khadr is illegitimate. A Canadian national, Khadr is accused of committing war crimes while fighting with al Qaeda in Afghanistan when he was 15. His lawyers argue he is a "child soldier" and thus immune from liability. These claims have no legal or policy merit.

Although the Optional Protocol to the Convention on the Rights of the Child bars recruitment and use of juveniles for combat, terrorist groups are not likely to comply with the protocol or worry about potential liability for their non-compliance. But this is irrelevant to Khadr's liability.

As presiding Judge Peter Brownback has properly ruled, the Military Commissions Act of 2006 gave the commission jurisdiction to try war-related offenses committed by juveniles, and nothing in U.S. law or the Constitution contradicts that. He also has properly concluded that no international treaty, convention or customary law norm establishes age as a bar to war-crimes prosecutions. Indeed, Khadr's lawyers have not cited any international law supporting their extraordinary claim of legal immunity.

This leaves the United States with a choice of whether to continue with Khadr's prosecution or exercise prosecutorial discretion and dismiss all charges against him — even if his prosecution is legally permissible. But first one must ask whether prosecuting him makes policy sense or is fair and just. Would we not be better served by sending Khadr home to be reunited with his family?

The answer is no. The gravity of the alleged offenses and the fact that he chose to join al Qaeda, an unlawful enemy entity, strongly mitigate against granting him immunity. Plus, he performed these actions at 15 — an age old enough to assess the moral and legal implications of his behavior.

Moreover, proponents of immunity fail to see that it would only further incentivize the continued recruitment of child soldiers and the use of children in the commission of war crimes. This result would neither benefit juveniles involved nor help their victims, who usually are civilians.

More broadly, granting him immunity would further debase international laws against war crimes — laws that have taken centuries to develop and are absolutely necessary if 21st-century warfare is not to descend into unbridled barbarism and carnage, to the detriment of the civilized world.

NO

Jo Becker
Advocacy director, Children's Rights
Division, Human Rights Watch;
Founding chairman, Coalition to
Stop the Use of Child Soldiers

Written for *CQ Global Researcher*, June 2008

Since 2002 the United States has held at least 23 detainees who were under 18 at the U.S. military base at Guantánamo Bay, Cuba. Two of them, Omar Khadr and Mohammad Jawad, are being prosecuted before U.S. military commissions for allegedly throwing grenades at American soldiers in Afghanistan. Khadr was 15 when he reportedly killed U.S. Army Sgt. First Class Christopher Speer and injured other soldiers in a July 2002 firefight. Jawad was 16 or 17 in December 2002 when he allegedly tossed a grenade into a military vehicle and injured two U.S. soldiers and an Afghan translator.

During the more than five years that Khadr and Jawad have been detained at Guantánamo, the United States has ignored their juvenile status. In violation of international juvenile-justice standards, the two have been incarcerated with adult detainees, subjected to prolonged solitary confinement, denied direct contact with their families and refused educational opportunities or rehabilitation.

Under juvenile-justice standards and international guidelines for the treatment of former child soldiers, children should be treated according to their unique vulnerability, lower degree of culpability and capacity for rehabilitation. Although international law does not preclude prosecution of child soldiers for serious crimes, their rehabilitation and reintegration into society must be paramount.

America's treatment of Jawad and Khadr cannot be construed as rehabilitative. They are confined in small cells for 22 hours a day, with little more than a mattress, the Koran and toilet paper. Their attorneys say Jawad and Khadr have been tortured. Khadr says his interrogators shackled him in painful positions, threatened him with rape and used him as a "human mop" after he urinated on the floor during one interrogation session. Jawad was moved from cell to cell and deprived of sleep. Eleven months after arriving at Guantánamo, Jawad tried to hang himself with his shirt collar. His lawyer says he suffers from severe depression and appears to have lost touch with reality.

Under juvenile-justice principles, cases involving children must be resolved quickly and their detention be as short as possible. But Khadr and Jawad were held for more than three years before even being charged. Now, five years after their apprehension, there is no foreseeable end to their ordeal.

Guantánamo, with its flawed military commissions, is no place for children. The United States should either transfer their cases to U.S. federal court and apply fundamental standards of juvenile justice, or release them for rehabilitation.

means that "as long as governments and commanders of these groups know they can recruit and use child soldiers without serious consequences, in particular to them personally, they will do it. But if their visas are denied or their assets are frozen or they suffer some real penalties, they will at least think twice about it."

U.N. officials say they repeatedly have confronted government officials and leaders of armed groups with evidence of their use of child soldiers, often to be greeted with outright denials or with vague pledges to stop the practice. "Their justification is, 'We don't go out and recruit,' which of course is not true," says Coomaraswamy, who often meets with leaders of armed groups using child soldiers. "They say, 'The children are hanging out at the gates, they want to join, many of them are orphans, how can I send them away?' This is usually the line, along with, 'We give them food, they are so happy,' that kind of thing."

Prosecuting Violators

The international community has another, stronger weapon against government leaders and military commanders who use child soldiers: Prosecution for war crimes. So far 19 commanders — all from Africa — have faced charges or prosecution either at the International Criminal Court or in special war crimes tribunals. Five have been convicted; the others are either on trial, awaiting trial, still at large or have reportedly died.

Four of the five convictions were handed down by the U.N.-supported special tribunal on war crimes committed during the brutal civil war in Sierra Leone, which raged from 1991 to 2002. The Hague-based Special Court for Sierra Leone in June 2007 convicted and sentenced three members of the Armed Forces Revolutionary Council — Alex Tamba Brima, Brima Bazzy Kamara and Santigie Borbor Kanu — on charges the rebel group committed war crimes and recruited and used child soldiers. It was the first time an international tribunal had ruled on the recruitment of child soldiers. "These convictions are a ground-breaking step toward ending impunity for commanders who exploit hundreds of thousands of children as soldiers in conflicts worldwide," Human Rights Watch said at the time.[83] The three men were sentenced to prison terms ranging from 45 to 50 years, and those sentences were affirmed in February by the court's appellate division.

A fourth man, Allieu Kondewa, a member of the Civil Defense Forces militia, was convicted in August 2007 on several charges, including recruitment of child soldiers.[84] He was sentenced to eight years in prison, which has since been increased to 20 years.[85]

Crane, the Syracuse University law professor who was the first prosecutor at the Sierra Leone court, says those convictions established important precedents. "This tells the leaders of these kinds of groups all over the world, 'If you are committing international crimes like abducting children and making them kill people, you can be convicted and sent to prison for the rest of your life.' "

A tribunal in the Democratic Republic of the Congo in March 2006 convicted Jean-Pierre Biyoyo, former commander of the Mudundu 40 armed group, on charges of recruiting and using child soldiers. Although he was sentenced to death, the sentence was reduced to five years' imprisonment.[86] Three months later he escaped from prison and eventually joined rebel leader Nkunda in North Kivu province, according to the U.S. State Department.[87]

Among the dozen other officials and warlords charged with war crimes for using child soldiers, the most prominent defendant is Taylor of Liberia, who currently is on trial before the Special Court for Sierra Leone on 11 charges of war crimes and crimes against humanity, including the use child soldiers.[88]

The International Criminal Court has charged three former Congolese guerrilla leaders with various war crimes, including the use of child soldiers. Thomas Lubanga Dyilo, leader of the Union of Congolese Patriots, had been scheduled to be the first person ever tried by the court. He was charged in 2006 with enlisting, recruiting and using child soldiers during the long and bloody fighting in Ituri region in eastern Democratic Republic of the Congo.[89]

However, the case appeared on the verge of collapse in early July as the result of a dispute between the U.N. and the ICC judges over U.N. documents that the prosecution had used to develop its charges. The U.N. had given the documents to the prosecution on a confidential basis. The court's judges indefinitely halted the Lubanga case on June 13 because the documents contain "exculpatory material" that should have been made available to the defense. An initial attempt to work out a compromise failed, and the trial judges on July 2 ordered Lubanga's eventual release as the "logical consequence" of the earlier decision. The prosecution appealed the decision to halt the case, and the ICC's appellate chamber said on July 7 that Lubanga should remain in prison until it had ruled on that appeal. News reports said ICC officials were still hoping for a compromise on the documents issue.

Human Rights Watch expressed disappointment over the legal wrangling, saying the failure of the case would deny justice to the alleged victims of Lubanga's actions. "The victims are the ones who suffer as a result of these embarrassing legal difficulties at the ICC," HRW counsel Param-Preet Singh says. Even so, she adds, denying Lubanga a fair trial "would also be an injustice, and the ICC cannot afford that, either."[90]

The possible collapse of the Lubanga case also came as a disappointment to the U.N., which had expected the case to establish legal doctrines on punishing those who recruit and use child soldiers. In a statement after the June 13 decision to halt the trial, U.N. Special Representative Coomaraswamy urged that the trial "not be compromised for technical reasons" and noted that the case "is considered a major milestone in international attempts" to eradicate the practice of using child soldiers.

U.S. Legislation

Both of the U.S. bills concerning child soldiers have made some progress but are still pending, with time running out for action during an election year. The House approved the Child Soldier Prevention Act — which would bar military aid and arms sales to countries using child soldiers — on Dec. 4, 2007. It was included in a measure to reauthorize a 2000 anti-human-trafficking law.[91] The vote on the underlying bill was 405-2, with no opposition to the child soldier provisions. The Senate, by contrast, has passed the Child Soldiers Accountability Act, which criminalizes the use of child soldiers and bars entry into the United States by anyone using child soldiers. The measure was approved by unanimous consent on Dec. 18, 2007.

Senate sponsors combined both bills into one measure, the Child Soldier Accountability and Prevention Act of 2008 (S 3061), introduced on May 22 by Joseph R. Biden, D-Del., and Sam Brownback, R-Kan. The measure is pending before the Senate Judiciary Committee, after markup was delayed on June 26 by an unnamed Republican senator who put a hold on the bill.

OUTLOOK

Child Terrorists?

Some of the recent conflicts that have involved the most widespread and notorious use of child soldiers have ended with formal peace agreements or dwindled into low-level, sporadic fighting. Among them were the inter-related conflicts in West Africa; the huge, pan-African war in the Democratic Republic of the Congo; and civil wars in the Balkans, El Salvador and Indonesia. The latest global survey by the Coalition to Stop the Use of Child Soldiers said the number of countries where children were directly involved in conflicts declined from 27 in 2004 (when the group issued its previous report) to 17 by the end of 2007.[92]

Becker, of Human Rights Watch, says the decline is good news but does not mean the child-soldier problem has disappeared. "Some conflicts are ending, but that does not mean that children are no longer being used in war," she says. "When armed conflicts occur, children are almost inevitably involved." As examples, Becker cites new, or newly revived conflicts in the past two years in the Central African Republic, Chad and Somalia — all involving extensive use of children.

Moreover, new conflicts can be expected because the underlying conditions that led to most of the world's civil conflicts remain unresolved. "It's not like we have fewer poor kids today, fewer orphans who can be recruited by warlords," says Singer of the Brookings Institution. "You still have these problems on a global scale."

Specialists in the field, as well as government officials worldwide are particularly concerned about what appears to be the increasing use of children as terrorists, including as suicide bombers. The Tamil Tigers developed the tactic two decades ago, even fashioning suicide bomb vests in small sizes for children, according to some sources.[93]

Suicide bombing as a terrorist tactic has spread in recent years to other parts of South and Central Asia — including Afghanistan, India and Pakistan — to Colombia and to the Middle East, including extremist Palestinian factions, and Iraq.[94] Children in their early- and mid-teens have carried out, or attempted, suicide attacks in nearly all these places, sometimes causing large-scale fatalities. In Iraq, U.S military officials have said insurgents often use children to place the roadside bombs, known as "improvised explosive devices," that typically kill American troops.

Singer does not expect terrorism and the use of children by terrorists to diminish anytime soon, despite the efforts of the U.S. "war" against terrorism. In fact, he says, "we could see the use of children as terrorists globally, if you put yourself in the position of the planners of these attacks and how they might be looking to expand their operations."

As for combating the more conventional use of children in civil conflicts, the U.N.'s Coomaraswamy is optimistic the world is ready to act more decisively. "This is an issue on which you have a near-global consensus on the need for action, not just rhetoric," she says. "Not that we will be able to stop all recruitment and use of child soldiers, but I think we can lessen it quite a bit in the next decade."

She and other experts had hoped that the two most prominent cases involving use of child soldiers — the ongoing Taylor tribunal and the ICC case against Lubanga — would produce ground-breaking convictions demonstrating that the use of children in war will be punished.

The dismissal of the Lubanga case could give added importance to the Taylor trial, where Crane, the former special prosecutor in Sierra Leone, expects a guilty verdict. "That will have an incredible ripple effect, particularly on the dictators and warlords of the world," he says. "It says that the lives of their citizens matter. In particular, it shows Africans themselves that their lives matter."

NOTES

1. Testimony of Ishmael Beah, Senate Judiciary Subcommittee on Human Rights and the Law, hearing on "Casualties of War: Child Soldiers and the Law," April 24, 2007, http://judiciary.senate.gov/testimony.cfm?id=2712&wit_id=6387.

2. P. W. Singer, *Children at War* (2006), p. 23.

3. "Some 250,000 children worldwide recruited to fight in wars — UN official," United Nations Department of Public Information, Jan. 30, 2008, www.un.org/apps/news/story.asp?NewsID=25450&Cr=children&Cr1=conflict#.

4. Singer, *op. cit.*, p. 30.

5. "Sold to be Soldiers: The Recruitment and Use of Child Soldiers in Burma," Human Rights Watch, October 2007, www.hrw.org/reports/2007/burma1007/burma1007web.pdf.

6. "Child Soldiers Global Report 2008," Coalition to Stop the Use of Child Solders, p. 29, www.childsoldiersglobalreport.org/files/country_pdfs/FINAL_2008_Global_Report.pdf.

7. "Cape Town Principles and Best Practices," April 1997, UNICEF, p. 8, www.unicef.org/emerg/files/Cape_Town_Principles(1).

8. David M. Rosen, *Armies of the Young: Child Soldiers in War and Terrorism* (2005), p. 4.

9. "Childhood Denied: Child Soldiers in Africa," Amnesty International, available online under the title "Democratic Republic of Congo: Children at War," on p. 7, at www.amnesty.org/en/library/asset/AFR62/034/2003/en/dom-AFR620342003en.pdf.

10. Ishmael Beah, *A Long Way Gone: Memoirs of a Boy Soldier* (2007).

11. "Children and Armed Conflict, Report of the Secretary General," Dec. 21, 2007, pp. 40-45.

12. U.N. Security Council Resolution 1379, www.securitycouncilreport.org/atf/cf/{65BFCF9B-6D27-4E9C-8CD3-CF6E4FF96FF9}/CAC%20SRES%201379.pdf.

13. "Child Soldiers Global Report 2008," *op. cit.*

14. "Children and Armed Conflict," *op. cit.*, p. 33.

15. "Report of the Secretary General on Children and Armed Conflict in Sri Lanka," Dec. 21, 2007, pp. 3-7.

16. "International Forum on Armed Groups and the Involvement of Children in Armed Conflict: Summary of Themes and Discussion," Coalition to Stop the Use of Child Soldiers, August 2007, p. 16, www.child-soldiers.org/childsoldiers/Armed_groups_forum_report_August_2007_revision_0ct07.pdf.

17. "Military Commission Charges Referred," U.S. Department of Defense news release, April 24 2007, www.defenselink.mil/releases/release.aspx?releaseid=10779. For background, see David Masci and Kenneth Jost, "War on Terrorism," *CQ Researcher*, Oct. 12, 2001, pp. 817-848; also see Peter Katel and

Kenneth Jost, "Treatment of Detainees," *CQ Researcher*, Aug. 25, 2006, pp. 673-696.

18. "Ruling on Defense Motion for Dismissal Due to Lack of Jurisdiction Under the MCA in Regard to Juvenile Crimes of a Child Soldier," *United States of America v. Omar Ahmed Khadr*, April 30, 2008, www.defenselink.mil/news/d20080430Motion.pdf.

19. "Letter to U.S. Secretary of Defense Robert Gates on Omar Khadr," Human Rights Watch, April 2, 2008, www.hrw.org/english/docs/2008/02/01/usint17956.htm.

20. *Amicus curiae* brief contained in the April 30 ruling, note 19 above, pp. 108-146.

21. Rome Statute of the International Criminal Court, United Nations Doc. A/CONF.183/9, July 17, 1998.

22. "The Paris Principles: Principles and Guidelines on Children Associated with Armed Forces or Armed Groups," February 2007, section 3.6, www.diplomatie.gouv.fr/en/IMG/pdf/Paris_Conference_Principles_English _31_January.pdf.

23. "Government's Response to the Defense's Motion for Dismissal Due to Lack of Jurisdiction under the MCA in Regard to Juvenile Crimes of a Child Soldier," Jan. 25, 2008. p. 9, footnote 3.

24. Deputy Assistant Secretary of Defense Sandra L. Hodgkinson, testimony to the U.N. Committee on the Rights of the Child Concerning U.S. Implementation of the Optional Protocol on Children in Armed Conflict, May 22, 2008, p. 26, www2.ohchr.org/english/bodies/crc/docs/statements/48USA Opening_Statements.pdf.

25. Randall Palmer, "Top Court Says Canada Complicit in Guantánamo Base," Reuters, May 23, 2008.

26. "Military Commission Charges Referred," U.S. Department of Defense, Jan. 31, 2008, www.defenselink.mil/releases/release.aspx?releaseid=11655.

27. *Congressional Record*, Dec. 18, 2007, p. S15941.

28. "Country Reports on Human Rights Practices: Afghanistan," U.S. State Department, March 11, 2008. www.state.gov/g/drl/rls/hrrpt/2007/100611.htm.

29. "U.S. Military Assistance to Governments and Government-Supported Armed Groups Using Child Soldiers, 2002-2008," Center for Defense Information, April 2, 2008, p. 1, www.cdi.org/PDFs/CS_MilAssist08.pdf.

30. "Casualties Of War: Child Soldiers and The Law," Sen. Dick Durbin, April 24, 2007, http://durbin.senate.gov/showRelease.cfm?releaseId=280883.

31. "Report of the Secretary General on Children and Armed Conflict in Chad," United Nations, July 3, 2007, p. 7; also see "Early to War: Child Soldiers in the Chad Conflict," Human Rights Watch, July 2007, www.hrw.org/reports/2007/chad0707/.

32. Singer, *op. cit.*, p. 63.

33. *Ibid.*, p. 41.

34. "Security Council committee concerning Côte d'Ivoire issues list of individuals subject to measures imposed by Resolution 1572 (2004)," SC/8631, U.N. Department of Public Information, Feb. 7, 2006.

35. "Report of the Secretary General on Children and Armed Conflict in Somalia," May 7, 2007, p. 13, www.unhcr.org/cgi-bin/texis/vtx/refworld/rwmain?docid=4850fe4e2.

36. Jimmie Briggs, *Innocents Lost: When Child Soldiers Go to War* (2005), p. 41.

37. "Child Soldiers Global Report 2008," *op. cit.*, pp. 101-103; "Overcoming Lost Childhoods: Lessons Learned from the Rehabilitation and Reintegration of Former Child Soldiers in Colombia," YCare International, 2007, p. 4; "You'll Learn Not to Cry: Child Combatants in Colombia," Human Rights Watch, September 2003, www.hrw.org/reports/2003/colombia0903/.

38. Briggs, *op. cit.*, p. 56.

39. "Child Soldiers Global Report 2008," *op. cit.*, p. 101.

40. *Ibid.*, p. 102.

41. "Mortality in the DRC: An Ongoing Crisis," International Rescue Committee, January 2008, www.theirc.org/media/www/congo-crisis-fast-facts.html.

42. "Child soldier recruitment continues," United Nations Integrated Regional Information Network, Feb. 19, 2007.

43. "Report of the Secretary General on Children and Armed Conflict in the Democratic Republic of the Congo," June 28, 2007, pp. 14-15, http://daccessdds.un.org/doc/UNDOC/GEN/N07/390/16/PDF/N0739016.pdf?OpenElement.

44. *Ibid.*, pp. 3-6.

45. "MONUC welcomes the success of the Goma conference and the signing of its acts of engagement," United Nations Mission in the Democratic Republic of the Congo, Jan. 23, 2008, www.monuc.org/News .aspx?newsId=16531.

46. "After two key deals, what progress towards peace in North Kivu?" United Nations Integrated Regional Information Network, May 14, 2008, www.reliefweb .int/rw/rwb.nsf/db900sid/KKAA-7EN5EQ?Open Document&rc=1&cc =cod.

47. "Report on Human Rights, Democratic Republic of the Congo, 2007," U.S. Department of State, www .state.gov/g/drl/rls/hrrpt/2007/100475.htm.

48. "Child Soldiers Global Report," *op. cit.*, p. 212.

49. "Report of the Secretary General on Children and Armed Conflict in Myanmar," Nov. 16, 2007, pp. 4-5.

50. "Sold to be Soldiers," *op. cit.*

51. *Ibid.*, pp. 25-26.

52. "Report of the Secretary General on Children and Armed Conflict in Myanmar," *op. cit.*, pp. 5-6.

53. "Sold to be Soldiers," *op. cit.*, p. 60.

54. *Ibid.*, p. 94.

55. "Report of the Secretary General on Children and Armed Conflict in Sri Lanka," Dec. 21, 2007.

56. "United Nations Concerned by Civilian Deaths in Sri Lanka," U.N. Department of Public Information, Jan. 2, 2007, www.un.org/News/Press/docs/2007/ iha1248.doc.htm.

57. "No Safety, No Escape: Children and the Escalating Armed Conflict in Sri Lanka," Watchlist on Children and Armed Conflict, April 2008, p. 5.

58. "Complicit in Crime: State Collusion in Abductions and Child Recruitment by the Karuna Group," Human Rights Watch, January 2007, www.hrw.org/ reports/2007/srilanka0107/.

59. "Press Conference on Children and Armed Conflict in Sri Lanka," U.N. Department of Public Information, April 14, 2008, www.un.org/News/ briefings/docs/2008/080414_Children.doc.htm.

60. "Report of the Secretary General on Children and Armed Conflict in the Sudan," Aug. 29, 2007, p. 4, www.cfr.org/publication/11358/report_of_the_secretary

general_on_children_and_armed_conflict_in_the_ sudan.html.

61. *Ibid.*, pp. 5-6.

62. "Conclusions on Parties in the Armed Conflict in the Sudan," Working Group on Children and Armed Conflict, U.N. Security Council, Feb. 5, 2008, p. 1.

63. "Report of the Secretary General on the Sudan," Jan. 31, 2008, p. 2.

64. "Child Soldiers Global Report 2008," *op. cit.*, p. 319.

65. "Report of the Secretary General on Children and Armed Conflict in the Sudan," *op. cit.*, pp. 2, 5.

66. *Ibid.*, p. 6.

67. "Child Soldiers Global Report 2008", *op. cit.*, pp. 89, 93.

68. "Report of the Secretary-General on Children and Armed Conflict in Uganda," May 7, 2007, p. 3.

69. "Child Soldiers Global Report 2008," *op. cit.*, p. 347; "Uganda: LRA Regional Atrocities Demand Action," Human Rights Watch, May 19, 2008, www.hrw.org/ english/docs/2008/05/19/uganda18863.htm.

70. "Report of the Secretary-General on Children and Armed Conflict in Uganda," *op. cit.*, p. 4.

71. "Child Soldiers Global Report 2008," *op. cit.*, p. 347.

72. "The Shadows of Peace: Life after the LRA," IRIN news service, Sept. 18, 2006.

73. "Optimism prevails despite setback in peace talks," IRIN news service, April 18, 2008.

74. "Stolen Children: Abduction and Recruitment in Northern Uganda," Human Rights Watch, March 2003, www.hrw.org/reports/2003/uganda0303/.

75. "Report of the Secretary-General on Children and Armed Conflict in Uganda," *op. cit.*, pp. 2, 5.

76. "Living with the LRA: The Juba Initiative," IRIN news service, May 1, 2008.

77. "Additional report of the Secretary-General on children and armed conflict in Uganda," United Nations, p. 3, June 23, 2008, http://daccess-ods .un.org/access.nsf/Get?OpenAgent&DS=s/2008/ 409&Lang=E.

78. Charles Mpagi Mwanguhya, "Peace Deal Dissolves," Institute for War and Peace Reporting, May 19, 2008, www.iwpr.net/?p=acr&s=f&o=344708&apc_ state=henh.

79. "Report of the Secretary-General on Children and Armed Conflict," Dec. 21, 2007, p. 37.

80. "Statement in the Security Council by Special Representative of the Secretary General for Children and Armed Conflict Radhika Coomaraswamy," Feb. 12, 2008.

81. "Statement by the President of the Security Council," Feb. 12, 2008, http://daccess-ods.un.org/access .nsf/Get?Open&DS=S/PRST/2008/6&Lang= E&Area=UNDOC.

82. "Getting it Done and Doing It Right: A Global Study on the United Nations-led Monitoring and Reporting Mechanism on Children and Armed Conflict," Watchlist on Children and Armed Conflict, January 2008, www.watchlist.org/reports/pdf/global-v8-web .pdf; and "The Security Council and Children and Armed Conflicts: Next Steps towards Ending Violations Against Children," Watchlist on Children and Armed Conflict, January 2008.

83. Christo Johnson, "Sierra Leone tribunal issues historic verdicts," *The Independent* (London), June 21, 2007.

84. "Report of the Special Representative of the Secretary General for Children and Armed Conflict," Aug. 13, 2007, p. 5; Coalition to Stop the Use of Child Soldiers, www.child-soldiers.org/childsoldiers/ legal-framework.

85. See www.sc-sl.org/CDF-Timeline.html.

86. "Report of the Secretary General on Children and Armed Conflict in the Democratic Republic of the Congo," *op. cit.*, p. 27.

87. "Report on Human Rights, Democratic Republic of the Congo, 2007," U.S. State Department, www .state.gov/g/drl/rls/hrrpt/2007/100475.htm.

88. "Report of the Special Representative of the Secretary General for Children and Armed Conflict," *op. cit.*

89. "The Prosecutor v. Thomas Lubanga Dyilo," International Criminal Court, www.icc-cpi.int/cases/ RDC/c0106/c0106_doc.html.

90. "International Criminal Court's Trial of Thomas Lubanga 'Stayed,' " Human Rights Watch, http:// hrw.org/english/docs/2008/06/19/congo19163 .htm.

91. For background, see David Masci, "Human Trafficking and Slavery," *CQ Researcher*, March 26, 2004, pp. 273-296.

92. "Child Soldiers Global Report 2008," *op. cit.*, p. 12.

93. Singer, *op. cit.*, p. 118.

94. *Ibid.*, pp. 117-119.

BIBLIOGRAPHY

Books

Beah, Ishmael, *A Long Way Gone: Memoirs of a Boy Soldier, Sarah Chrichton Books*, 2007.
A former child soldier tells his compelling story of being recruited into one of Sierra Leone's rebel groups at age 13.

Briggs, Jimmie, *Innocents Lost: When Child Soldiers Go to War, Basic Books*, 2005.
A New York journalist provides first-hand reports about child soldiers in Afghanistan, Colombia, Sri Lanka and Uganda.

Rosen, David M., *Armies of the Young: Child Soldiers in War and Terrorism, Rutgers University Press*, 2006.
An American anthropologist examines legal and political issues surrounding the use of child soldiers.

Singer, P. W., *Children at War, University of California Press*, 2006.
A senior fellow at the Brookings Institution provides a comprehensive overview of the use of child soldiers.

Wessells, Michael, *Child Soldiers: From Violence to Protection, Harvard University Press*, 2006.
A professor of psychology at Randolph-Macon College examines issues involving child soldiers, drawing on his own three decades of experiences reintegrating former child soldiers into their former communities.

Articles

Boustany, Nora, "Report: Brokers Supply Child Soldiers to Burma," *The Washington Post*, Oct. 31, 2007, p. A16.
Burma's military government has been forcibly recruiting child soldiers through brokers who buy and sell boys to help the army deal with personnel shortages, according to a detailed report by Human Rights Watch.

Pownall, Katy, "In the Tragedy of Child-Soldiering in Africa, a Girl's Story Finds a Happy Ending," *The Associated Press*, Aug. 25, 2007.
A former female child soldier in Uganda is now studying environmental health at a university.

Reports and Studies

"Child Soldiers: Global Report 2008," *Coalition to Stop the Use of Child Soldiers*, May 2008, www .childsoldiersglobalreport.org/.
A nongovernmental organization offers its latest report on the use of child soldiers, including assessments of how well the United Nations and others are combating the problem.

"Children in Conflict: Eradicating the Child Soldier Doctrine," *The Carr Center for Human Rights Policy, Kennedy School of Government, Harvard University*, www.hks.harvard.edu/cchrp/pdf/ChildSoldierReport .pdf.
The center recommends international action to combat the use of child soldiers.

"Getting it Done and Doing It Right: A Global Study on the United Nations-led Monitoring and Reporting Mechanism on Children and Armed Conflict," *Watchlist on Children and Armed Conflict*, January 2008, www.watchlist.org/news/reports/pdf/global-v8-web.pdf.
A watchdog group critiques the U.N. Security Council's system of monitoring the impact of armed conflict on children, including child soldiers.

"Making Reintegration Work for Youth in Northern Uganda," *The Survey of War Affected Youth*, November 2007, www.sway-uganda.org/SWAY.ResearchBrief .Reintegration.pdf.

This report summarizes two phases of a long-term study of the economic, educational, social and other needs of former child soldiers in the Lord's Resistance Army in northern Uganda.

"The Security Council and Children and Armed Conflicts: Next Steps towards Ending Violations Against Children," *Watchlist on Children and Armed Conflict*, January 2008, http://watchlist.org/docs/Next_Steps_ for_Security_Council_-_Child_Soldiers_Coalition_ and_Watchlist_-_January_2008.pdf.
The watchdog group recommends that the U.N. Security Council take tougher measures against those who continue to use child soldiers.

"Soldiers of Misfortune: Abusive U.S. Military Recruitment and Failure to Protect Child Soldiers," American Civil Liberties Union, May 2008, www.aclu .org/intlhumanrights/gen/35245pub20080513.html.
A civil rights organization critiques U.S. policies toward the use of child soldiers, including voluntary recruitment of teenagers under 18 and detention of under-18-year-old alleged terrorists by the military.

U.N. Reports

"Children and armed conflict: Report of the Secretary-General," *U.N. Security Council*, Dec. 21, 2007, http://daccessdds.un.org/doc/UNDOC/ GEN/N07/656/04/PDF/N0765604.pdf?Open Element.
In his latest annual report to the U.N. Security Council, Secretary-General Ban Ki-moon listed 40 groups in 13 countries around the world that continue to use child soldiers. A complete list of other U.N. reports on conflicts affecting children is at www.un.org/children/conflict/ english/reports.html.

For More Information

Amnesty International, 1 Easton St., London WC1X 0DW, United Kingdom; 44-20-7413-5500; http://web.amnesty.org. Actively advocates on a wide range of human rights issues, including child soldiers.

Child Rights Information Network, c/o Save the Children, 1 St. John's Lane, London EC1M 4AR, United Kingdom; 44-20-7012-6866; www.crin.org. Advocates for enforcement of international legal standards protecting children; associated with Save the Children-UK.

Coalition to Stop the Use of Child Soldiers, 4th Floor, 9 Marshalsea Road, London SE1 1EP, United Kingdom; 44-20-7367-4110/4129; www.child-soldiers.org. A coalition of international human rights groups that sponsors conferences and issues regular reports on child soldiers in armed conflicts.

Human Rights Watch, 350 Fifth Ave., 34th Floor, New York, NY 10118-3299; (212) 290-4700; http://hrw.org/campaigns/crp/index.htm. One of the most active international groups pushing governments, the United Nations and other agencies to stop using child soldiers.

International Committee of the Red Cross, 19 avenue de la Paix, CH 1202 Geneva, Switzerland; 41-22-734-6001; www.icrc.org/web/eng/siteeng0.nsf/html/children!Open. Advocates on behalf of all victims of war, including child soldiers.

United Nations Children's Fund (UNICEF), UNICEF House, 3 United Nations Plaza, New York, NY 10017; (212) 325-7000; www.unicef.org. Monitors the impact of war on children, including the recruitment and use of child soldiers.

United Nations Special Representative of the Secretary-General for Children and Armed Conflict, United Nations S-3161, New York, NY 10017; (212) 963-3178; www.un.org/children/conflict/english/home6.html. The primary U.N. official dealing with children and armed conflict; works with governments and armed groups to develop action plans for releasing child soldiers and easing the burden of children in conflict; issues regular reports on the world's most serious conflicts.

Watchlist on Children and Armed Conflict, c/o Women's Commission for Refugee Women and Children, 122 East 42nd St., 12th Floor, New York, NY 10168-1289; (212) 551-3111; www.watchlist.org. Publishes studies and advocates strong international action to aid children caught up in armed conflict.

War Child International, 401 Richmond St. West, Suite 204, Toronto, Ontario, Canada M5V3A8; (416) 971-7474; www.warchild.org/index.html. A coalition of groups advocating on behalf of children caught in armed conflicts.

Women's Rights

Are Violence and Discrimination Against Women Declining?

Karen Foerstel

Iraqi teenager Du'a Khalil Aswad lies mortally wounded after her "honor killing" by a mob in the Kurdish region of Iraq. No one has been prosecuted for the April 2007 murder, even though a cell-phone video of the incident was posted on the Internet. Aswad's male relatives are believed to have arranged her ritualistic execution because she had dated a boy from outside her religious sect. The United Nations estimates that 5,000 women and girls are murdered in honor killings around the globe each year.

AFP/Getty Images

S he was 17 years old. The blurry video shows her lying in a dusty road, blood streaming down her face, as several men kick and throw rocks at her. At one point she struggles to sit up, but a man kicks her in the face forcing her back to the ground. Another slams a large, concrete block down onto her head. Scores of onlookers cheer as the blood streams from her battered head.[1]

The April 7, 2007, video was taken in the Kurdish area of northern Iraq on a mobile phone. It shows what appear to be several uniformed police officers standing on the edge of the crowd, watching while others film the violent assault on their phones.

The brutal, public murder of Du'a Khalil Aswad reportedly was organized as an "honor killing" by members of her family — and her uncles and a brother allegedly were among those in the mob who beat her to death. Her crime? She offended her community by falling in love with a man outside her religious sect.[2]

According to the United Nations, an estimated 5,000 women and girls are murdered in honor killings each year, but it was only when the video of Aswad's murder was posted on the Internet that the global media took notice.[3]

Such killings don't only happen in remote villages in developing countries. Police in the United Kingdom estimate that up to 17,000 women are subjected to some kind of "honor"-related violence each year, ranging from forced marriages and physical attacks to murder.[4]

But honor killings are only one type of what the international community calls "gender based violence" (GBV). "It is universal," says Taina Bien-Aimé, executive director of the New York-based

From *CQ Researcher*,
May 2008.

Only Four Countries Offer Total Equality for Women

Costa Rica, Cuba, Sweden and Norway receive the highest score (9 points) in an annual survey of women's economic, political and social rights. Out of the world's 193 countries, only 26 score 7 points or better, while 28 — predominantly Islamic or Pacific Island countries — score 3 or less. The United States rates 7 points: a perfect 3 on economic rights but only 2 each for political and social rights. To receive 3 points for political rights, women must hold at least 30 percent of the seats in the national legislature. Women hold only 16.6 percent of the seats in the U.S. Congress. The U.S. score of 2 on social rights reflects what the report's authors call "high societal discrimination against women's reproductive rights."

Status of Women's Rights Around the Globe

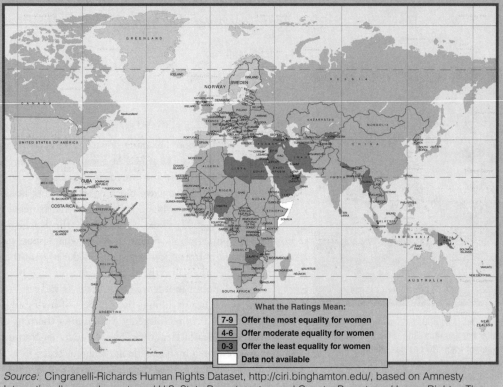

What the Ratings Mean:

7-9	Offer the most equality for women
4-6	Offer moderate equality for women
0-3	Offer the least equality for women
	Data not available

Source: Cingranelli-Richards Human Rights Dataset, http://ciri.binghamton.edu/, based on Amnesty International's annual reports and U.S. State Department annual Country Reports on Human Rights. The database is co-directed by David Louis Cingranelli, a political science professor at Binghamton University, SUNY, and David L. Richards, an assistant political science professor at the University of Memphis.

women's-rights group Equality Now. "There is not one country in the world where violence against women doesn't exist."

Thousands of women are murdered or attacked around the world each day, frequently with impunity. In Guatemala, where an estimated 3,000 women have been killed over the past seven years, most involving some kind of misogynistic violence, only 1 percent of the perpetrators were convicted.[5] In India, the United Nations estimates that five women are burned to death each day by husbands upset that they did not receive sufficient dowries from their brides.[6] In Asia, nearly 163 million females are "missing" from the population — the result of sex-selective abortions, infanticide or neglect.

And since the 1990s some African countries have seen dramatic upsurges in rapes of very young girls by men who believe having sex with a virgin will protect or cure them from HIV-AIDS. After a 70-year-old man allegedly raped a 3-year-old girl in northern Nigeria's commercial hub city of Kano, Deputy Police Chief Suleiman Abba told reporters in January, "Child rape is becoming rampant in Kano." In the last six months of 2007, he said, 54 cases of child rape had been reported. "In some cases the victims are gang-raped."[7]

Epidemics of sexual violence commonly break out in countries torn apart by war, when perpetrators appear to have no fear of prosecution. Today, in Africa, for instance, UNICEF says there is now a "license to rape" in eastern regions of the Democratic Republic of the Congo, where some human-rights experts estimate that up to a quarter of a million women have been raped and often sexually mutilated with knives, branches or machetes.[8] Several of the Congolese rapists remorselessly bragged to an American filmmaker recently about how many women they had gang-raped.[9]

"The sexual violence in Congo is the worst in the world," said John Holmes, the United Nations under secretary general for humanitarian affairs. "The sheer numbers, the wholesale brutality, the culture of impunity — it's appalling."[10]

In some cultures, the female victims themselves are punished. A report by the Human Rights Commission of Pakistan found that a woman is gang-raped every eight hours in that country. Yet, until recently, rape cases could not be prosecuted in Pakistan unless four Muslim men "all of a pious and trustworthy nature" were willing to testify that they witnessed the attack. Without their testimony the victim could be prosecuted for fornication and alleging a false crime, punishable by stoning, lashings or prison.[11] When the law was softened in 2006 to allow judges to decide whether to try rape cases in Islamic courts or criminal courts, where such witnesses are not required, thousands took to the streets to protest the change.[12]

Honor killings are up 400 percent in Pakistan over the last two years, and Pakistani women also live in fear of being blinded or disfigured by "acid attacks" — a common practice in Pakistan and a handful of other countries — in which attackers, usually spurned suitors, throw acid on a woman's face and body.

Women's Suffering Is Widespread

More than two decades after the U.N. Decade for Women and 29 years after the U.N. adopted the Convention on the Elimination of All Forms of Discrimination against Women (CEDAW), gender discrimination remains pervasive throughout the world, with widespread negative consequences for society.

According to recent studies on the status of women today:

- Violence against women is pervasive. It impoverishes women, their families, communities and nations by lowering economic productivity and draining resources. It also harms families across generations and reinforces other violence in societies.
- Domestic violence is the most common form of violence against women, with rates ranging from 8 percent in Albania to 49 percent in Ethiopia and Zambia. Domestic violence and rape account for 5 percent of the disease burden for women ages 15 to 44 in developing countries and 19 percent in developed countries.
- Femicide — the murder of women — often involves sexual violence. From 40 to 70 percent of women murdered in Australia, Canada, Israel, South Africa and the United States are killed by husbands or boyfriends. Hundreds of women were abducted, raped and murdered in and around Juárez, Mexico, over the past 15 years, but the crimes have never been solved.
- At least 160 million females, mostly in India and China, are "missing" from the population — the result of sex-selective abortions.
- Rape is being used as a genocidal tool. Hundreds of thousands of women have been raped and sexually mutilated in the ongoing conflict in Eastern Congo. An estimated 250,000 to 500,000 women were raped during the 1994 genocide in Rwanda; up to 50,000 women were raped during the Bosnian conflict in the 1990s. Victims are often left unable to have children and are deserted by their husbands and shunned by their families, plunging the women and their children into poverty.
- Some 130 million girls have been genitally mutilated, mostly in Africa and Yemen, but also in immigrant communities in the West.
- Child rape has been on the increase in the past decade in some African countries, where some men believe having sex with a virgin will protect or cure them from HIV-AIDS. A study at the Red Cross children's hospital in Cape Town, South Africa, found that 3-year-old girls were more likely to be raped than any other age group.
- Two million girls between the ages of 5 and 15 are forced into the commercial sex market each year, many of them trafficked across international borders.
- Sexual harassment is pervasive. From 40 to 50 percent of women in the European Union reported some form of sexual harassment at work; 50 percent of schoolgirls surveyed in Malawi reported sexual harassment at school.
- Women and girls constitute 70 percent of those living on less than a dollar a day and 64 percent of the world's illiterate.
- Women work two-thirds of the total hours worked by men and women but earn only 10 percent of the income.
- Half of the world's food is produced by women, but women own only 1 percent of the world's land.
- More than 1,300 women die each day during pregnancy and childbirth — 99 percent of them in developing countries.

Sources: "Ending violence against women: From words to action," United Nations, October, 2006, www.un.org/womenwatch/daw/public/VAW_Study/VAW studyE.pdf; www.womankind.org.uk; www.unfp.org; www.oxfam.org; www.ipu.org; www.unicef.org; www.infant-trust.org.uk; "State of the World Population 2000;" http://npr.org; http://asiapacific.amnesty.org; http://news.bbc.co.uk

Negative Attitudes Toward Women Are Pervasive

Negative attitudes about women are widespread around the globe, among women as well as men. Rural women are more likely than city women to condone domestic abuse if they think it was provoked by a wife's behavior.

| Location | Percentage of women in selected countries who agree that a man has good reason to beat his wife if: | | | | | | Women who agree with: | |
	Wife does not complete housework	Wife disobeys her husband	Wife refuses sex	Wife asks about other women	Husband suspects infidelity	Wife is unfaithful	One or more of the reasons mentioned	None of the reasons mentioned
Bangladesh city	13.8	23.3	9.0	6.6	10.6	51.5	53.3	46.7
Bangladesh province	25.1	38.7	23.3	14.9	24.6	77.6	79.3	20.7
Brazil city	0.8	1.4	0.3	0.3	2.0	8.8	9.4	90.6
Brazil province	4.5	10.9	4.7	2.9	14.1	29.1	33.7	66.3
Ethiopia province	65.8	77.7	45.6	32.2	43.8	79.5	91.1	8.9
Japan city	1.3	1.5	0.4	0.9	2.8	18.5	19.0	81.0
Namibia city	9.7	12.5	3.5	4.3	6.1	9.2	20.5	79.5
Peru city	4.9	7.5	1.7	2.3	13.5	29.7	33.7	66.3
Peru province	43.6	46.2	25.8	26.7	37.9	71.3	78.4	21.6
Samoa	12.1	19.6	7.4	10.1	26.0	69.8	73.3	26.7
Serbia and Montenegro city	0.6	0.97	0.6	0.3	0.9	5.7	6.2	93.8
Thailand city	2.0	0.8	2.8	1.8	5.6	42.9	44.7	55.3
Thailand province	11.9	25.3	7.3	4.4	12.5	64.5	69.5	30.5
Tanzania city	24.1	45.6	31.1	13.8	22.9	51.5	62.5	37.5
Tanzania province	29.1	49.7	41.7	19.8	27.2	55.5	68.2	31.8

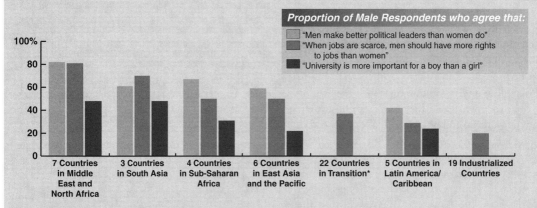

Proportion of Male Respondents who agree that:
- "Men make better political leaders than women do"
- "When jobs are scarce, men should have more rights to jobs than women"
- "University is more important for a boy than a girl"

7 Countries in Middle East and North Africa / *3 Countries in South Asia* / *4 Countries in Sub-Saharan Africa* / *6 Countries in East Asia and the Pacific* / *22 Countries in Transition** / *5 Countries in Latin America/Caribbean* / *19 Industrialized Countries*

* Countries in transition are generally those that were once part of the Soviet Union.

Sources: World Health Organization, www.who.int/gender/violence/who_multicountry_study/Chapter3-Chapter4.pdf; "World Values Survey," www.worldvaluessruvey.org

But statistics on murder and violence are only a part of the disturbing figures on the status of women around the globe. Others include:

- Some 130 million women have undergone female genital mutilation, and another 2 million are at risk every year, primarily in Africa and Yemen.
- Women and girls make up 70 percent of the world's poor and two-thirds of its illiterate.
- Women work two-thirds of the total hours worked by men but earn only 10 percent of the income.
- Women produce more than half of the world's food but own less than 1 percent of the world's property.
- More than 500,000 women die during pregnancy and childbirth every year — 99 percent of them in developing countries.
- Two million girls between the ages of 5 and 15 are forced into the commercial sex market each year.[13]
- Globally, 10 million more girls than boys do not attend school.[14]

Despite these alarming numbers, women have made historic progress in some areas. The number of girls receiving an education has increased in the past decade. Today 57 percent of children not attending school are girls, compared to two-thirds in the 1990s.[15]

And women have made significant gains in the political arena. As of March, 2008, 14 women are serving as elected heads of state or government, and women now hold 17.8 percent of the world's parliamentary seats — more than ever before.[16] And just three months after the brutal killing of Aswad in Iraq, India swore in its first female president, Pratibha Patil, who vows to eliminate that country's practice of aborting female fetuses because girls are not as valued as boys in India. (*See "At Issue," p. 75.*)[17]

Last October, Argentina elected its first female president, Cristina Fernández de Kirchner,* the second woman in two years to be elected president in South America. Michelle Bachelet, a single mother, won the presidency in Chile in 2006.[18] During her inaugural speech Kirchner

---

* Isabel Martínez Perón assumed the presidency of Argentina on the death of her husband, Juan Perón, in 1974 and served until she was deposed in a coup d'etat in 1976; but she was never elected.

admitted, "Perhaps it'll be harder for me, because I'm a woman. It will always be harder for us."[19]

Indeed, while more women than ever now lead national governments, they hold only 4.4 percent of the world's 342 presidential and prime ministerial positions. And in no country do they hold 50 percent or more of the national legislative seats.[20]

"Women make up half the world's population, but they are not represented" at that level, says Swanee Hunt, former U.S. ambassador to Austria and founding director of the Women and Public Policy Program at Harvard's Kennedy School of Government.

While this is "obviously a fairness issue," she says it also affects the kinds of public policies governments pursue. When women comprise higher percentages of office-holders, studies show "distinct differences in legislative outputs," Hunt explains. "There's less funding of bombs and bullets and more on human security — not just how to defend territory but also on hospitals and general well-being."

Today's historic numbers of women parliamentarians have resulted partly from gender quotas imposed in nearly 100 countries, which require a certain percentage of women candidates or officeholders.[21]

During the U.N.'s historic Fourth World Conference on Women — held in Beijing in 1995 — 189 governments adopted, among other things, a goal of 30 percent female representation in national legislatures around the world.[22] But today, only 20 countries have reached that goal, and quotas are often attacked as limiting voters' choices and giving women unfair advantages.[23]

Along with increasing female political participation, the 5,000 government representatives at the Beijing conference — one of the largest gatherings in U.N. history — called for improved health care for women, an end to violence against women, equal access to education for girls, promotion of economic independence and other steps to improve the condition of women around the world.[24]

"Let Beijing be the platform from which our global crusade will be carried forward," Gertrude Mongella, U.N. secretary general for the conference, said during closing ceremonies. "The world will hold us accountable for the implementation of the good intentions and decisions arrived at in Beijing."[25]

Spain's visibly pregnant new Defense minister, Carme Chacón, reviews troops in Madrid on April 14, 2008. She is the first woman ever to head Spain's armed forces. Women hold nine out of 17 cabinet posts in Spain's socialist government, a reflection of women's entrance into the halls of power around the world.

But more than 10 years later, much of the Beijing Platform still has not been achieved. And many question whether women are any better off today than they were in 1995.

"The picture's mixed," says June Zeitlin, executive director of the Women's Environment & Development Organization (WEDO). "In terms of violence against women, there is far more recognition of what is going on today. There has been some progress with education and girls. But the impact of globalization has exacerbated differences between men and women. The poor have gotten poorer — and they are mostly women."

Liberalized international trade has been a two-edged sword in other ways as well. Corporations have been able to expand their global reach, opening new businesses and factories in developing countries and offering women unprecedented employment and economic opportunities. But the jobs often pay low wages and involve work in dangerous conditions because poor countries anxious to attract foreign investors often are willing to ignore safety and labor protections.[26] And increasingly porous international borders have led to growing numbers of women and girls being forced or sold into prostitution or sexual slavery abroad, often under the pretense that they will be given legitimate jobs overseas.[27]

Numerous international agreements in recent years have pledged to provide women with the same opportunities and protections as men, including the U.N.'s Millennium Development Goals (MDGs) and the Convention on the Elimination of All Forms of Discrimination Against Women (CEDAW). But the MDGs' deadlines for improving the conditions for women have either been missed already or are on track to fail in the coming years.[28] And more than 70 of the 185 countries that ratified CEDAW have filed "reservations," meaning they exempt themselves from certain parts.[29] In fact, there are more reservations against CEDAW than against any other international human-rights treaty in history.[30] The United States remains the only developed country in the world not to have ratified it.[31]

"There has certainly been progress in terms of the rhetoric. But there are still challenges in the disparities in education, disparities in income, disparities in health," says Carla Koppell, director of the Cambridge, Mass.-based Initiative for Inclusive Security, which advocates for greater numbers of women in peace negotiations.

"But women are not just victims," she continues. "They have a very unique and important role to play in solving the problems of the developing world. We need to charge policy makers to match the rhetoric and make it a reality. There is a really wonderful opportunity to use the momentum that does exist. I really think we can."

Amidst the successes and failures surrounding women's issues, here are some of the questions analysts are beginning to ask:

Has globalization been good for women?

Over the last 20 years, trade liberalization has led to a massive increase of goods being produced and exported from developing countries, creating millions of manufacturing jobs and bringing many women into the paid workforce for the first time.

"Women employed in export-oriented manufacturing typically earn more than they would have in traditional sectors," according to a World Bank report. "Further, cash income earned by women may improve their status and bargaining power in the family."[32] The report cited a study of 50 families in Mexico that found "a significant proportion of the women reported an improvement in their 'quality of life,' due mainly to their income from working outside their homes, including in (export-oriented) factory jobs."

But because women in developing nations are generally less educated than men and have little bargaining power, most of these jobs are temporary or part-time, offering no health-care benefits, overtime or sick leave.

Women comprise 85 percent of the factory jobs in the garment industry in Bangladesh and 90 percent in Cambodia. In the cut flower industry, women hold 65 percent of the jobs in Colombia and 87 percent in Zimbabwe. In the fruit industry, women constitute 69 percent of temporary and seasonal workers in South Africa and 52 percent in Chile.[33]

Frequently, women in these jobs have no formal contract with their employers, making them even more vulnerable to poor safety conditions and abuse. One study found that only 46 percent of women garment workers in Bangladesh had an official letter of employment.[34]

"Women are a workforce vital to the global economy, but the jobs women are in often aren't covered by labor protections," says Thalia Kidder, a policy adviser on gender and sustainable livelihoods with U.K.-based Oxfam, a confederation of 12 international aid organizations. Women lack protection because they mostly work as domestics, in home-based businesses and as part-time workers. "In the global economy, many companies look to hire the most powerless people because they cannot demand high wages. There are not a lot of trade treaties that address labor rights."

In addition to recommending that countries embrace free trade, Western institutions like the International Monetary Fund and the World Bank during the 1990s recommended that developing countries adopt so-called structural adjustment economic reforms in order to qualify for certain loans and financial support. Besides opening borders to free trade, the neo-liberal economic regime known as the Washington Consensus advocated privatizing state-owned businesses, balancing budgets and attracting foreign investment.

But according to some studies, those reforms ended up adversely affecting women. For instance, companies in Ecuador were encouraged to make jobs more "flexible" by replacing long-term contracts with temporary, seasonal and hourly positions — while restricting collective bargaining rights.[35] And countries streamlined and privatized government programs such as health care and education, services women depend on most.

Globalization also has led to a shift toward cash crops grown for export, which hurts women farmers, who produce 60 to 80 percent of the food for household consumption in developing countries.[36] Small women farmers are being pushed off their land so crops for exports can be grown, limiting their abilities to produce food for themselves and their families.

While economic globalization has yet to create the economic support needed to help women out of poverty, women's advocates say females have benefited from the broadening of communications between countries prompted by globalization. "It has certainly improved access to communications and helped human-rights campaigns," says Zeitlin of WEDO. "Less can be done in secret. If there is a woman who is condemned to be stoned to death somewhere, you can almost immediately mobilize a global campaign against it."

Homa Hoodfar, a professor of social anthropology at Concordia University in Montreal, Canada, and a founder of the group Women Living Under Muslim Laws, says women in some of the world's most remote towns and villages regularly e-mail her organization. "Globalization has made the world much smaller," she says. "Women are getting information on TV and the Internet. The fact that domestic violence has become a global issue [shows globalization] provides resources for those objecting locally."

But open borders also have enabled the trafficking of millions of women around the world. An estimated 800,000 people are trafficked across international borders each year — 80 percent of them women and girls — and most are forced into the commercial sex trade. Millions more are trafficked within their own countries.[37] Globalization has sparked a massive migration of women in search of better jobs and lives. About 90 million women — half of the world's migrants and more than ever in history — reside outside their home countries. These migrant women — often unable to speak the local language and without any family connections — are especially susceptible to traffickers who lure them with promises of jobs abroad.[38]

And those who do not get trapped in the sex trade often end up in low-paying or abusive jobs in foreign factories or as domestic maids working under slave-like conditions.

Female Peacekeepers Fill Vital Roles

Women bring a different approach to conflict resolution.

The first all-female United Nations peacekeeping force left Liberia in January after a year's mission in the West African country, which is rebuilding itself after 14 years of civil war. Comprised of more than 100 women from India, the force was immediately replaced by a second female team.

"If anyone questioned the ability of women to do tough jobs, then those doubters have been [proven] wrong," said U.N. Special Representative for Liberia Ellen Margrethe Løj, adding that the female peacekeepers inspired many Liberian women to join the national police force.[1]

Women make up half of the world's refugees and have systematically been targeted for rape and sexual abuse during times of war, from the 200,000 "comfort women" who were kept as sex slaves for Japanese soldiers during World War II[2] to the estimated quarter-million women reportedly raped and sexually assaulted during the current conflict in the Democratic Republic of the Congo.[3] But women account for only 5 percent of the world's security-sector jobs, and in many countries they are excluded altogether.[4]

In 2000, the U.N. Security Council unanimously adopted Resolution 1325 calling on governments — and the U.N. itself — to include women in peace building by adopting a variety of measures, including appointing more women as special envoys, involving women in peace negotiations, integrating gender-based policies in peacekeeping missions and increasing the number of women at all decision-making levels.[5]

But while Resolution 1325 was a critical step in bringing women into the peace process, women's groups say more women should be sent on field missions and more data collected on how conflict affects women around the world.[6]

"Women are often viewed as victims, but another way to view them is as the maintainers of society," says Carla Koppell, director of the Cambridge, Mass.-based Initiative for Inclusive Security, which promotes greater numbers of women in peacekeeping and conflict resolution. "There must be a conscious decision to include women. It's a detriment to promote peace without including women."

Women often comprise the majority of post-conflict survivor populations, especially when large numbers of men have either fled or been killed. In the wake of the 1994 Rwandan genocide, for example, women made up 70 percent of the remaining population.

And female peacekeepers and security forces can fill vital roles men often cannot, such as searching Islamic women wearing burkas or working with rape victims who may be reluctant to report the crimes to male soldiers.

But some experts say the real problem is not migration and globalization but the lack of labor protection. "Nothing is black and white," says Marianne Mollmann, advocacy director for the Women's Rights Division of Human Rights Watch. "Globalization has created different employment opportunities for women. Migration flows have made women vulnerable. But it's a knee-jerk reaction to say that women shouldn't migrate. You can't prevent migration. So where do we need to go?" She suggests including these workers in general labor-law protections that cover all workers.

Mollmann said countries can and should hammer out agreements providing labor and wage protections for domestic workers migrating across borders. With such protections, she said, women could benefit from the jobs and incomes promised by increased migration and globalization.

Should governments impose electoral quotas for women?

In 2003, as Rwanda struggled to rebuild itself after the genocide that killed at least 800,000 Hutus and Tutsis, the country adopted an historic new constitution that, among other things, required that women hold at least 30 percent of posts "in all decision-making organs."[39]

Today — ironically, just across Lake Kivu from the horrors occurring in Eastern Congo — Rwanda's lower house of parliament now leads the world in female representation, with 48.8 percent of the seats held by women.[40]

"Women bring different experiences and issues to the table," says Koppell. "I've seen it personally in the Darfur and Uganda peace negotiations. Their priorities were quite different. Men were concerned about power- and wealth-sharing. Those are valid, but you get an entirely different dimension from women. Women talked about security on the ground, security of families, security of communities."

In war-torn countries, women have been found to draw on their experiences as mothers to find nonviolent and flexible ways to solve conflict. [7] During peace negotiations in Northern Ireland, for example, male negotiators repeatedly walked out of sessions, leaving a small number of women at the table. The women, left to their own, found areas of common ground and were able to keep discussions moving forward. [8]

"The most important thing is introducing the definition of security from a woman's perspective," said Orzala Ashraf, founder of Kabul-based Humanitarian Assistance for the Women and Children of Afghanistan. "It is not a man in a uniform standing next to a tank armed with a gun. Women have a broader term — human security — the ability to go to school, receive health care, work and have access to

The first all-female United Nations peacekeeping force practices martial arts in New Delhi as it prepares to be deployed to Liberia in 2006.

AP Photo/Mustafa Quraishi

justice. Only by improving these areas can threats from insurgents, Taliban, drug lords and warlords be countered."[9]

[1] "Liberia: UN envoy welcomes new batch of female Indian police officers," U.N. News Centre, Feb. 8, 2008, www.un.org/apps/news/story.asp?NewsID=25557&Cr=liberia&Cr1=.

[2] "Japan: Comfort Women," European Speaking Tour press release, Amnesty International, Oct. 31, 2007.

[3] "Film Documents Rape of Women in Congo," "All Things Considered," National Public Radio, April 8, 2008, www.npr.org/templates/story/story.php?story Id=89476111.

[4] "Ninth Annual Colloquium and Policy Forum," Hunt Alternatives Fund, Jan. 22, 2008, www.huntalternatives.org/pages/7650_ninth_annual_colloquium_and_policy_forum.cfm. Also see Elizabeth Eldridge, "Women cite utility in peace efforts," *The Washington Times*, Jan. 25, 2008, p. A1.

[5] "Inclusive Security, Sustainable Peace: A Toolkit for Advocacy and Action," International Alert and Women Waging Peace, 2004, p. 15, www.huntalternatives.org/download/35_introduction.pdf.

[6] *Ibid.*, p. 17.

[7] Jolynn Shoemaker and Camille Pampell Conaway, "Conflict Prevention and Transformation: Women's Vital Contributions," Inclusive Security: Women Waging Peace and the United Nations Foundation, Feb. 23, 2005, p. 7.

[8] The Initiative for Inclusive Security, www.huntalternatives.org/pages/460_the_vital_role_of_women_in_peace_building.cfm.

[9] Eldridge, *op. cit.*

Before the civil war, Rwandan women never held more than 18 percent of parliament. But after the genocide, the country's population was 70 percent female. Women immediately stepped in to fill the vacuum, becoming the heads of households, community leaders and business owners. Their increased presence in leadership positions eventually led to the new constitutional quotas. [41]

"We see so many post-conflict countries going from military regimes to democracy that are starting from scratch with new constitutions," says Drude Dahlerup, a professor of political science at Sweden's Stockholm University who studies the use of gender quotas. "Today, starting from scratch means including women. It's seen as a sign of modernization and democratization."

Both Iraq and Afghanistan included electoral quotas for women in their new constitutions, and the number of women in political office in sub-Saharan Africa has increased faster than in any other region of the world, primarily through the use of quotas. [42]

But many point out that simply increasing the numbers of women in elected office will not necessarily expand women's rights. "It depends on which women and which positions they represent," says Wendy Harcourt, chair of Women in Development Europe (WIDE), a feminist network in Europe, and editor of *Development*, the journal of the Society for International Development, a global network of individuals and institutions working on development issues. "It's positive, but I don't see yet what it means [in terms of addressing] broader gender issues."

Few Women Head World Governments

Fourteen women currently serve as elected heads of state or government including five who serve as both. Mary McAleese, elected president of Ireland in 1997, is the world's longest-serving head of state. Helen Clark of New Zealand has served as prime minister since 1999, making her the longest-serving female head of government. The world's first elected female head of state was Sirimavo Bandaranaike of Sri Lanka, in 1960.

Current Female Elected Heads of State and Government

Heads of both state and government:

 Gloria Macapagal-Arroyo — President, the Philippines, since 2001; former secretary of Defense (2002) and secretary of Foreign Affairs (2003 and 2006-2007).

Ellen Johnson-Sirleaf — President, Liberia, since 2006; held finance positions with the government and World Bank.

Michelle Bachelet Jeria — President, Chile, since 2006; former minister of Health (2000-2002) and minister of Defense (2002-2004).

Cristina E. Fernández — President, Argentina, since 2007; succeeded her husband, Nestor de Kirchner, as president; former president, Senate Committee on Constitutional Affairs.

Rosa Zafferani — Captain Regent, San Marino, since April 2008; secretary of State of Public Education, University and Cultural Institutions (2004 to 2008); served as captain regent in 1999; San Marino elects two captains regent every six months, who serve as co-heads of both state and government.

Heads of Government:

Helen Clark — Prime Minister, New Zealand, since 1999; held government posts in foreign affairs, defense, housing and labor.

Luísa Días Diogo — Prime Minister, Mozambique, since 2004; held several finance posts in Mozambique and the World Bank.

Angela Merkel — Chancellor, Germany, since 2005; parliamentary leader of Christian Democratic Union Party (2002-2005).

Yuliya Tymoshenko — Prime Minister, Ukraine, since 2007; chief of government (2005) and designate prime minister (2006).

Zinaida Grecianîi — Prime Minister, Moldova, since March 2008; vice prime minister (2005-2008).

Heads of State:

Mary McAleese — President, Ireland, since 1997; former director of a television station and Northern Ireland Electricity.

Tarja Halonen — President, Finland, since 2000; former minister of foreign affairs (1995-2000).

Pratibha Patil — President, India, since 2007; former governor of Rajasthan state (2004-2007).

Borjana Kristo — President, Bosnia and Herzegovina, since 2007; minister of Justice of Bosniak-Croat Federation, an entity in Bosnia and Herzegovina (2003-2007).

Source: www.guide2womenleaders.com

While Afghanistan has mandated that women hold at least 27 percent of the government's lower house seats and at least 17 percent of the upper house, their increased representation appears to have done little to improve women's rights.[43] Earlier this year, a student journalist was condemned to die under Afghanistan's strict Islamic sharia law after he distributed articles from the Internet on women's rights.[44] And non-governmental groups in Afghanistan report that Afghan women and girls have begun killing themselves in record numbers, burning themselves alive in order to escape widespread domestic abuse or forced marriages.[45]

Having gender quotas alone doesn't necessarily ensure that women's rights will be broadened, says Hoodfar of Concordia University. It depends on the type of quota a government implements, she argues, pointing out that in Jordan, for example, the government has set aside parliamentary seats for the six women who garner the most votes of any other female candidates in their districts — even if they do not win more votes than male candidates.[46] Many small, conservative tribes that cannot garner enough votes for a male in a countrywide victory are now nominating their sisters and wives in the hope that the lower number of votes needed to elect a woman will get them one of the reserved seats. As a result, many of the women moving into the reserved seats are extremely conservative and actively oppose providing women greater rights and freedoms.

And another kind of quota has been used against women in her home country of Iran, Hoodfar points out. Currently, 64 percent of university students in Iran are women. But the government recently mandated that at least 40 percent of university enrollees be male, forcing many female students out of school, Hoodfar said.

"Before, women didn't want to use quotas for politics because of concern the government may try to use it against women," she says. "But women are beginning to look into it and talk about maybe developing a good system."

Quotas can be enacted by constitutional requirements, such as those enacted in Rwanda, by statute or voluntarily by political parties. Quotas also can vary in their requirements: They can mandate the number of women each party must nominate, how many women must appear on the ballot (and the order in which they appear, so women are not relegated to the bottom of the list), or the number of women who must hold government office. About 40 countries now use gender quotas in national parliamentary elections, while another 50 have major political parties that voluntarily use quotas to determine candidates.

Aside from questions about the effectiveness of quotas, others worry about the fairness of establishing quotas based on gender. "That's something feminists have traditionally opposed," says Harcourt.

"It's true, but it's also not fair the way it is now," says former Ambassador Hunt. "We are where we are today through all kinds of social structures that are not fair. Quotas are the lesser of two evils."

Stockholm University's Dahlerup says quotas are not "discrimination against men but compensation for discrimination against women." Yet quotas are not a panacea for women in politics, she contends. "It's a mistake to think this is a kind of tool that will solve all

Women Still Far from Reaching Political Parity

Although they have made strides in the past decade, women hold only a small minority of the world's leadership and legislative posts (right). Nordic parliaments have the highest rates of female representation — 41.4 percent — compared with only 9 percent in Arab countries (below). However, Arab legislatures have nearly tripled their female representation since 1997, and some countries in Africa have dramatically increased theirs as well: Rwanda, at 48.8 percent, now has the world's highest percentage of women in parliament of any country. The U.S. Congress ranks 70th in the world, with 89 women serving in the 535-member body — or 16.6 percent.

Women in Government

	Elected to Parliament	Serving as Ministers*	Elected Heads of Government/State
1997	11.7%	N/A	5.8%
2008	17.8%	20.6%	7.3%

Women in Parliament
(Percentage by region, 1997 and 2008)

	Nordic countries	Americas (including U.S.)	Europe, non-Nordic countries	Sub-Saharan Africa	Asia	United States	Pacific Countries	Arab States
1997	36%	13%	14%	10%	13%	11.2%	10%	3%
2008	41.4%	21.3%	18.8%	17.8%	16.7%	16.6%	15%	9.1%

* Includes deputy prime ministers, ministers and prime ministers who hold ministerial portfolios.

Sources: Interparliamentarian Union, www.ipu.org/wmn-e/world.htm; State of the World's Children 2007, UNICEF, www.unicef.org/sowc07/; "Worldwide Guide to Women in Leadership" database, www.un.org/womenwatch/daw/csw/41sess.htm.

problems. It doesn't solve problems about financing campaigns, caring for families while being in politics or removing patriarchal attitudes. It would be nice if it wasn't necessary, and hopefully sometime in the future it won't be."

Until that time, however, quotas are a "necessary evil," she says.

Women's Work: From Hauling and Churning . . .

Women's work is often back-breaking and monotonous, such as hauling firewood in the western Indian state of Maharashtra (top) and churning yogurt into butter beside Lake Motsobunnyi in Tibet (bottom). Women labor two-thirds of the total hours worked around the globe each year but earn only 10 percent of the income.

Do international treaties improve women's rights?

In recent decades, a variety of international agreements have been signed by countries pledging to improve women's lives, from the 1979 Convention for the Elimination of All Forms of Discrimination Against Women to the Beijing Platform of 1995 to the Millennium Development Goals (MDGs) adopted in 2000. The agreements aimed to provide women with greater access to health, political representation, economic stability and social status. They also focused attention on some of the biggest obstacles facing women.

But despite the fanfare surrounding the launch of those agreements, many experts on women's issues say on-the-ground action has yet to match the rhetoric. "The report is mixed," says Haleh Afshar, a professor of politics and women's studies at the University of York in the United Kingdom and a nonpartisan, appointed member of the House of Lords, known as a crossbench peer. "The biggest problem with Beijing is all these things were stated, but none were funded. Unfortunately, I don't see any money. You don't get the pay, you don't get the job done."

The Beijing Platform for Action, among other things, called on governments to "adjust budgets to ensure equality of access to public sector expenditures" and even to "reduce, as appropriate, excessive military expenditure" in order to achieve the Platform goals.

But adequate funding has yet to be provided, say women's groups.[47] In a report entitled "Beijing Betrayed," the Women's Environment & Development Organization says female HIV cases outnumber male cases in many parts of the world, gender-related violence remains a pandemic and women still make up the majority of the world's poor — despite pledges in Beijing to reverse these trends.[48]

And funding is not the only obstacle. A 2004 U.N. survey revealed that while many countries have enacted laws in recent years to help protect women from violence and discrimination, long-standing social and cultural traditions block progress. "While constitutions provided for equality between women and men on the one hand, [several countries] recognized and gave precedent to customary law and practice in a number of areas . . . resulting in discrimination against women," the report said. "Several countries noted that statutory, customary and religious law coexist, especially in regard to family, personal status and inheritance and land rights. This perpetuated discrimination against women."[49]

While she worries about the lack of progress on the Beijing Platform, WEDO Executive Director Zeitlin says international agreements are nevertheless critical in raising global awareness on women's issues. "They have a major impact on setting norms and standards," she says. "In many countries, norms and standards are very important in setting goals for women to advocate for. We complain about lack of implementation, but if we didn't have the norms and standards we couldn't complain about a lack of implementation."

Like the Beijing Platform, the MDGs have been criticized for not achieving more. While the U.N. says promoting women's rights is essential to achieving the millenium goals — which aim to improve the lives of all the world's populations by 2015 — only two of the eight specifically address women's issues.[50]

One of the goals calls for countries to "Promote gender equality and empower women." But it sets only one measurable target: "Eliminate gender disparity in primary and secondary education, preferably by 2005, and in all levels of education" by 2015.[51] Some 62 countries failed to reach the 2005 deadline, and many are likely to miss the 2015 deadline as well.[52]

Another MDG calls for a 75 percent reduction in maternal mortality compared to 1990 levels. But according to the human-rights group ActionAid, this goal is the "most off track of all the MDGs." Rates are declining at less than 1 percent a year, and in some countries — such as Sierra Leone, Pakistan and Guatemala — maternal mortality has increased since 1990. If that trend continues, no region in the developing world is expected to reach the goal by 2015.[53]

Activist Peggy Antrobus of Development Alternatives with Women for a New Era (DAWN) — a network of feminists from the Southern Hemisphere, based currently in Calabar, Cross River State, Nigeria — has lambasted the MDGs, quipping that the acronym stands for the "Most Distracting Gimmick."[54] Many feminists argue that the goals are too broad to have any real impact and that the MDGs should have given more attention to women's issues.

But other women say international agreements — and the public debate surrounding them — are vital in promoting gender equality. "It's easy to get disheartened, but Beijing is still the blueprint of where we need to be," says Mollmann of Human Rights Watch. "They are part of a political process, the creation of an international culture. If systematically everyone says [discrimination against women] is a bad thing, states don't want to be hauled out as systematic violators."

In particular, Mollmann said, CEDAW has made real progress in overcoming discrimination against women. Unlike the Beijing Platform and the MDGs, CEDAW legally obliges countries to comply. Each of the 185 ratifying countries must submit regular reports to the U.N. outlining their progress under the convention. Several

AP Photo/Sergei Grits

AFP/Getty Images/Ali Burafi

. . . to Gathering and Herding

While many women have gotten factory jobs thanks to globalization of trade, women still comprise 70 percent of the planet's inhabitants living on less than a dollar a day. Women perform a variety of tasks around the world, ranging from gathering flax in Belarus (top) to shepherding goats in central Argentina (bottom).

countries — including Brazil, Uganda, South Africa and Australia — also have incorporated CEDAW provisions into their constitutions and legal systems.[55]

Still, dozens of ratifying countries have filed official "reservations" against the convention, including Bahrain, Egypt, Kuwait, Morocco and the United Arab Emirates, all of whom say they will comply only within the bounds of Islamic sharia law.[56] And the United States has refused to ratify CEDAW, with or without reservations, largely because of conservatives who say it would, among other things, promote abortion and require the government to pay for such things as child care and maternity leave.

Indian women harvest wheat near Bhopal. Women produce half of the food used domestically worldwide and 60 to 80 percent of the household food grown in developing countries.

BACKGROUND

'Structural Defects'

Numerous prehistoric relics suggest that at one time matriarchal societies existed on Earth in which women were in the upper echelons of power. Because early societies did not understand the connection between sexual relations and conception, they believed women were solely responsible for reproduction — which led to the worship of female goddesses.[57]

In more modern times, however, women have generally faced prejudice and discrimination at the hands of a patriarchal society. In about the eighth century B.C. creation stories emerged describing the fall of man due to the weakness of women. The Greeks recounted the story of Pandora who, through her opening of a sealed jar, unleashed death and pain on all of mankind. Meanwhile, similar tales in Judea eventually were recounted in Genesis, with Eve as the culprit.[58]

In ancient Greece, women were treated as children and denied basic rights. They could not leave their houses unchaperoned, were prohibited from being educated or buying or selling land. A father could sell his unmarried daughter into slavery if she lost her virginity before marriage. If a woman was raped, she was outcast and forbidden from participating in public ceremonies or wearing jewelry.[59]

The status of women in early Rome was not much better, although over time women began to assert their voices and slowly gained greater freedoms. Eventually, they were able to own property and divorce their husbands. But early Christian leaders later denounced the legal and social freedom enjoyed by Roman women as a sign of moral decay. In the view of the early church, women were dependent on and subordinate to men.

In the 13th century, the Catholic priest and theologian St. Thomas Aquinas helped set the tone for the subjugation of women in Western society. He said women were created solely to be "man's helpmate" and advocated that men should make use of "a necessary object, woman, who is needed to preserve the species or to provide food and drink."[60]

From the 14th to 17th centuries, misogyny and oppression of women took a step further. As European societies struggled against the Black Plague, the 100 Years War and turmoil between Catholics and Reformers, religious leaders began to blame tragedies, illnesses and other problems on witches. As witch hysteria spread across Europe — instituted by both the religious and non-religious — an estimated 30,000 to 60,000 people were executed for allegedly practicing witchcraft. About 80 percent were females, some as young as 8 years old.[61]

"All wickedness is but little to the wickedness of a woman," Catholic inquisitors wrote in the 1480s. "What else is woman but a foe to friendship, an unescapable punishment, a necessary evil, a natural temptation, a desirable calamity. . . . Women are . . . instruments of Satan, . . . a structural defect rooted in the original creation."[62]

Push for Protections

The Age of Enlightenment and the Industrial Revolution in the 18th and 19th centuries opened up job opportunities for women, released them from domestic confines and provided them with new social freedoms.

In 1792 Mary Wollstonecraft published *A Vindication of the Rights of Women*, which has been hailed as "the feminist declaration of independence." Although the book had been heavily influenced by the French Revolution's notions of equality and universal brotherhood, French revolutionary leaders, ironically, were not sympathetic to feminist causes.[63] In 1789 they had refused to accept a Declaration of the Rights of Women when it was presented at the National Assembly. And Jean Jacques Rousseau, one of the philosophical founders of the revolution, had written in 1762:

"The whole education of women ought to be relative to men. To please them, to be useful to them, to make themselves loved and honored by them, to educate them when young, to care for them when grown, to counsel them, to make life sweet and agreeable to them — these are the duties of women at all times, and what should be taught them from their infancy."[64]

As more and more women began taking jobs outside the home during the 19th century, governments began to pass laws to "protect" them in the workforce and expand their legal rights. The British Mines Act of 1842, for instance, prohibited women from working underground.[65] In 1867, John Stuart Mill, a supporter of women's rights and author of the book *Subjection of Women*, introduced language in the British House of Commons calling for women to be granted the right to vote. It failed.[66]

But by that time governments around the globe had begun enacting laws giving women rights they had been denied for centuries. As a result of the Married Women's Property Act of 1870 and a series of other measures, wives in Britain were finally allowed to own property. In 1893, New Zealand became the first nation to grant full suffrage rights to women, followed over the next two decades by Finland, Norway, Denmark and Iceland. The United States granted women suffrage in 1920.[67]

One of the first international labor conventions, formulated at Berne, Switzerland, in 1906, applied exclusively to women — prohibiting night work for women in industrial occupations. Twelve nations signed on to it. During the second Berne conference in 1913, language was proposed limiting the number of hours women and children could work in industrial jobs, but the outbreak of World War I prevented it from being enacted.[68] In 1924 the U.S. Supreme Court upheld a night-work law for women.[69]

In 1946, public attention to women's issues received a major boost when the United Nations created the Commission on the Status of Women to address urgent problems facing women around the world.[70] During the 1950s, the U.N. adopted several conventions aimed at improving women's lives, including the Convention on the Political Rights of Women, adopted in 1952 to ensure women the right to vote, which has been ratified by 120 countries, and the Convention on the Nationality of Married Women, approved in 1957 to ensure that marriage to an alien does not automatically affect the nationality of the woman.[71] That convention has been ratified by only 73 countries; the United States is not among them.[72]

In 1951 The International Labor Organization (ILO), an agency of the United Nations, adopted the Convention on Equal Remuneration for Men and Women Workers for Work of Equal Value, to promote equal pay for equal work. It has since been ratified by 164 countries, but again, not by the United States.[73] Seven years later, the ILO adopted the Convention on Discrimination in Employment and Occupation to ensure equal opportunity and treatment in employment. It is currently ratified by 166 countries, but not the United States.[74] U.S. opponents to the conventions claim there is no real pay gap between men and women performing the same jobs and that the conventions would impose "comparable worth" requirements, forcing companies to pay equal wages to men and women even if the jobs they performed were different.[75]

In 1965, the Commission on the Status of Women began drafting international standards articulating equal rights for men and women. Two years later, the panel completed the Declaration on the Elimination of Discrimination Against Women, which was adopted by the General Assembly but carried no enforcement power.

The commission later began to discuss language that would hold countries responsible for enforcing the declaration. At the U.N.'s first World Conference on Women in Mexico City in 1975, women from around the world called for creation of such a treaty, and the commission soon began drafting the text.[76]

Women's 'Bill of Rights'

Finally in 1979, after many years of often rancorous debate, the Convention on the Elimination of All Forms of Discrimination Against Women (CEDAW) was adopted by the General Assembly — 130 to none, with 10 abstentions. After the vote, however, several countries said their "yes" votes did not commit the support of their governments. Brazil's U.N. representative told the assembly, "The signatures and ratifications necessary to make this effective will not come easily."[77]

Despite the prediction, it took less than two years for CEDAW to receive the required number of ratifications to enter it into force — faster than any human-rights convention had ever done before.[78]

CHRONOLOGY

1700s-1800s *Age of Enlightenment and Industrial Revolution lead to greater freedoms for women.*

1792 Mary Wollstonecraft publishes *A Vindication of the Rights of Women,* later hailed as "the feminist declaration of independence."

1893 New Zealand becomes first nation to grant women full suffrage.

1920 Tennessee is the 36th state to ratify the 19th Amendment, giving American women the right to vote.

1940s-1980s *International conventions endorse equal rights for women. Global conferences highlight need to improve women's rights.*

1946 U.N. creates Commission on the Status of Women.

1951 U.N. International Labor Organization adopts convention promoting equal pay for equal work, which has been ratified by 164 countries; the United States is not among them.

1952 U.N. adopts convention calling for full women's suffrage.

1960 Sri Lanka elects the world's first female prime minister.

1974 Maria Estela Martínez de Perón of Argentina becomes the world's first woman president, replacing her ailing husband.

1975 U.N. holds first World Conference on Women, in Mexico City, followed by similar conferences every five years. U.N. launches the Decade for Women.

1979 U.N. adopts Convention on the Elimination of All Forms of Discrimination against Women (CEDAW), dubbed the "international bill of rights for women."

1981 CEDAW is ratified — faster than any other human-rights convention.

1990s *Women's rights win historic legal recognition.*

1993 U.N. World Conference on Human Rights in Vienna, Austria, calls for ending all violence, sexual harassment and trafficking of women.

1995 Fourth World Conference on Women in Beijing draws 30,000 people, making it the largest in U.N. history. Beijing Platform outlining steps to grant women equal rights is signed by 189 governments.

1996 International Criminal Tribunal convicts eight Bosnian Serb police and military officers for rape during the Bosnian conflict — the first time sexual assault is prosecuted as a war crime.

1998 International Criminal Tribunal for Rwanda recognizes rape and other forms of sexual violence as genocide.

2000s *Women make political gains, but sexual violence against women increases.*

2000 U.N. calls on governments to include women in peace negotiations.

2006 Ellen Johnson Sirleaf of Liberia, Michelle Bachelet of Chile and Portia Simpson Miller of Jamaica become their countries' first elected female heads of state. . . . Women in Kuwait are allowed to run for parliament, winning two seats.

2007 A woman in Saudi Arabia who was sentenced to 200 lashes after being gang-raped by seven men is pardoned by King Abdullah. Her rapists received sentences ranging from 10 months to five years in prison, and 80 to 1,000 lashes. . . . After failing to recognize any gender-based crimes in its first case involving the Democratic Republic of the Congo, the International Criminal Court hands down charges of "sexual slavery" in its second case involving war crimes in Congo. More than 250,000 women are estimated to have been raped and sexually abused during the country's war.

2008 Turkey lifts 80-year-old ban on women's headscarves in public universities, signaling a drift toward religious fundamentalism. . . . Former housing minister Carme Chacón — 37 and pregnant — is named defense minister of Spain, bringing to nine the number of female cabinet ministers in the Socialist government. . . . Sen. Hillary Rodham Clinton becomes the first U.S. woman to be in a tight race for a major party's presidential nomination.

Often described as an international bill of rights for women, CEDAW defines discrimination against women as "any distinction, exclusion or restriction made on the basis of sex which has the effect or purpose of impairing or nullifying the recognition, enjoyment or exercise by women, irrespective of their marital status, on a basis of equality of men and women, of human rights and fundamental freedoms in the political, economic, social, cultural, civil or any other field."

Ratifying countries are legally bound to end discrimination against women by incorporating sexual equality into their legal systems, abolishing discriminatory laws against women, taking steps to end trafficking of women and ensuring women equal access to political and public life. Countries must also submit reports at least every four years outlining the steps they have taken to comply with the convention.[79]

CEDAW also grants women reproductive choice — one of the main reasons the United States has not ratified it. The convention requires signatories to guarantee women's rights "to decide freely and responsibly on the number and spacing of their children and to have access to the information, education and means to enable them to exercise these rights."[80]

While CEDAW is seen as a significant tool to stop violence against women, it actually does not directly mention violence. To rectify this, the CEDAW committee charged with monitoring countries' compliance in 1992 specified gender-based violence as a form of discrimination prohibited under the convention.[81]

In 1993 the U.N. took further steps to combat violence against women during the World Conference on Human Rights in Vienna, Austria. The conference called on countries to stop all forms of violence, sexual harassment, exploitation and trafficking of women. It also declared that "violations of the human rights of women in situations of armed conflicts are violations of the fundamental principles of international human rights and humanitarian law."[82]

Shortly afterwards, as fighting broke out in the former Yugoslavia and Rwanda, new legal precedents were set to protect women against violence — and particularly rape — during war. In 1996, the International Criminal Tribunal in the Hague, Netherlands, indicted eight Bosnian Serb police officers in connection with the mass rape of Muslim women during the Bosnian war, marking the first time sexual assault had ever been prosecuted as a war crime.[83]

Two years later, the U.N.'s International Criminal Tribunal for Rwanda convicted a former Rwandan mayor for genocide, crimes against humanity, rape and sexual violence — the first time rape and sexual violence were recognized as acts of genocide.[84]

"Rape is a serious war crime like any other," said Regan Ralph, then executive director of Human Rights Watch's Women's Rights Division, shortly after the conviction. "That's always been true on paper, but now international courts are finally acting on it."[85]

Today, the International Criminal Court has filed charges against several Sudanese officials for rape and other crimes committed in the Darfur region.[86] But others are demanding that the court also prosecute those responsible for the rapes in the Eastern Congo, where women are being targeted as a means of destroying communities in the war-torn country.[87]

Beijing and Beyond

The U.N. World Conference on Women in Mexico City in 1975 produced a 44-page plan of action calling for a decade of special measures to give women equal status and opportunities in law, education, employment, politics and society.[88] The conference also kicked off the U.N.'s Decade for Women and led to creation of the U.N. Development Fund for Women (UNIFEM).[89]

Five years later, the U.N. held its second World Conference on Women in Copenhagen and then celebrated the end of the Decade for Women with the third World Conference in Nairobi in 1985. More than 10,000 representatives from government agencies and NGOs attended the Nairobi event, believed to be the largest gathering on women's issues at the time.[90]

Upon reviewing the progress made on women's issues during the previous 10 years, the U.N. representatives in Nairobi concluded that advances had been extremely limited due to failing economies in developing countries, particularly those in Africa struggling against drought, famine and crippling debt. The conference developed a set of steps needed to improve the status of women during the final 15 years of the 20th century.[91]

Ten years later, women gathered in Beijing in 1995 for the Fourth World Conference, vowing to turn the rhetoric of the earlier women's conferences into action. Delegates from 189 governments and 2,600

Women Suffer Most in Natural Disasters

Climate change will make matters worse.

In natural disasters, women suffer death, disease and hunger at higher rates then men. During the devastating 2004 tsunami in Asia, 70 to 80 percent of the dead were women.[1] During cyclone-triggered flooding in Bangladesh that killed 140,000 people in 1991, nearly five times more women between the ages of 20 and 44 died than men.[2]

Gender discrimination, cultural biases and lack of awareness of women's needs are part of the problem. For instance, during the 1991 cyclone, Bangladeshi women and their children died in higher numbers because they waited at home for their husbands to return and make evacuation decisions.[3] In addition, flood warnings were conveyed by men to men in public spaces but were rarely communicated to women and children at home.[4]

And during the tsunami, many Indonesian women died because they stayed behind to look for children and other family members. Women clinging to children in floodwaters also tired more quickly and drowned, since most women in the region were never taught to swim or climb trees.[5] In Sri Lanka, many women died because the tsunami hit early on a Sunday morning when they were inside preparing breakfast for their families. Men were generally outside where they had earlier warning of the oncoming floods so they were better able to escape.[6]

Experts now predict global climate change — which is expected to increase the number of natural disasters around the world — will put women in far greater danger than men because natural disasters generally have a disproportionate impact on the world's poor. Since women comprise 70 percent of those living on less than $1 a day, they will be hardest hit by climate changes, according to the Intergovernmental Panel on Climate Change.[7]

"Climate change is not gender-neutral," said Gro Harlem Brundtland, former prime minister of Norway and now special envoy to the U.N. secretary-general on climate change. "[Women are] more dependent for their livelihood on natural resources that are threatened by climate change…. With changes in climate, traditional food sources become more unpredictable and scarce. This exposes women to loss of harvests, often their sole sources of food and income."[8]

Women produce 60 to 80 percent of the food for household consumption in developing countries.[9] As drought, flooding and desertification increase, experts say women and their families will be pushed further into poverty and famine.

Women also suffer more hardship in the aftermath of natural disasters, and their needs are often ignored during relief efforts.

In many Third World countries, for instance, women have no property rights, so when a husband dies during a natural disaster his family frequently confiscates the land from his widow, leaving her homeless and destitute.[10] And because men usually dominate emergency relief and response agencies, women's specific needs, such as contraceptives and sanitary napkins, are often overlooked. After floods in Bangladesh in 1998, adolescent girls reported high rates of rashes and urinary tract infections because they had

NGOs attended. More than 30,000 women and men gathered at a parallel forum organized by NGOs, also in Beijing.[92]

The so-called Beijing Platform that emerged from the conference addressed 12 critical areas facing women, from poverty to inequality in education to inadequate health care to violence. It brought unprecedented attention to women's issues and is still considered by many as the blueprint for true gender equality.

The Beijing Conference also came at the center of a decade that produced historic political gains for women around the world — gains that have continued, albeit at a slow pace, into the new century. The 1990s saw more women entering top political positions than ever before. A record 10 countries elected or appointed women as presidents between 1990 and 2000, including Haiti, Nicaragua, Switzerland and Latvia. Another 17 countries chose women prime ministers.[93]

In 2006 Ellen Johnson Sirleaf of Liberia became Africa's first elected woman president.[94] That same year, Chile elected its first female president, Michelle Bachelet, and Jamaica elected Portia Simpson Miller as its

no clean water, could not wash their menstrual rags properly in private and had no place to hang them to dry.[11]

"In terms of reconstruction, people are not talking about women's needs versus men's needs," says June Zeitlin, executive director of the Women's Environment and Development Organization, a New York City-based international organization that works for women's equality in global policy. "There is a lack of attention to health care after disasters, issues about bearing children, contraception, rape and vulnerability, menstrual needs — things a male programmer is not thinking about. There is broad recognition that disasters have a disproportionate impact on women. But it stops there. They see women as victims, but they don't see women as agents of change."

Women must be brought into discussions on climate change and emergency relief, say Zeitlin and others. Interestingly, she points out, while women are disproportionately affected by environmental changes, they do more than men to protect the environment. Studies show women emit less climate-changing carbon dioxide than men because they recycle more, use resources more efficiently and drive less than men.[12]

"Women's involvement in climate-change decision-making is a human right," said Gerd Johnson-Latham, deputy director of the Swedish Ministry for Foreign Affairs. "If we get more women in decision-making

The smell of death hangs over Banda Aceh, Indonesia, which was virtually destroyed by a tsunami on Dec. 28, 2004. From 70 to 80 percent of the victims were women.

positions, we will have different priorities, and less risk of climate change."[13]

[1] "Tsunami death toll," CNN, Feb. 22, 2005. Also see "Report of High-level Roundtable: How a Changing Climate Impacts Women," Council of Women World Leaders, Women's Environment and Development Organization and Heinrich Boll Foundation, Sept. 21, 2007, p. 21, www.wedo.org/files/Round table%20Final%20Report%206%20 Nov.pdf.

[2] *Ibid.*

[3] "Cyclone Jelawat bears down on Japan's Okinawa island," CNN.com, Aug. 7, 2000, http://archives .cnn.com/2000/ASIANOW/east/08/07/asia.weather/index.html.

[4] "Gender and Health in Disasters," World Health Organization, July 2002, www.who.int/gender/other_health/en/genderdisasters.pdf.

[5] "The tsunami's impact on women," Oxfam briefing note, March 5, 2005, p. 2, www.oxfam.org/en/files/bn050326_tsunami_women/download.

[6] "Report of High-level Roundtable," *op. cit.*, p. 5.

[7] "Gender Equality" fact sheet, Oxfam, www.oxfam.org.uk/resources/ issues/gender/introduction.html. Also see *ibid.*

[8] *Ibid.*, p. 4.

[9] "Five years down the road from Beijing: Assessing progress," *News and Highlights*, Food and Agriculture Organization, June 2, 2000, www.fao .org/News/2000/000602-e.htm.

[10] "Gender and Health in Disasters," *op. cit.*

[11] *Ibid.*

[12] "Women and the Environment," U.N. Environment Program, 2004, p. 17, www.unep.org/Documents.Multilingual/Default.asp? DocumentID=468&ArticleID= 4488&l=en. Also see "Report of High-level Roundtable," *op. cit.*, p. 7.

[13] *Ibid.*

first female prime minister.[95] Also that year, women ran for election in Kuwait for the first time. In Bahrain, a woman was elected to the lower house of parliament for the first time.[96] And in 2007, Fernández de Kirchner became the first woman to be elected president of Argentina.

Earlier, a World Bank report had found that government corruption declines as more women are elected into office. The report also cited numerous studies that found women are more likely to exhibit "helping" behavior, vote based on social issues, score higher on "integrity tests," take stronger stances on ethical behavior and behave more generously when faced with economic decisions.[97]

"Increasing the presence of women in government may be valued for its own sake, for reasons of gender equality," the report concluded. "However, our results suggest that there may be extremely important spinoffs stemming from increasing female representation: If women are less likely than men to behave opportunistically, then bringing more women into government may have significant benefits for society in general."[98]

Honor Killings on the Rise

Women in Multan, Pakistan, demonstrate against "honor killings" in 2003 (top). Although Pakistan outlawed such killings years ago, its Human Rights Commission says 1,205 women were killed in the name of family honor in 2007 — a fourfold jump in two years. Nazir Ahmed Sheikh, a Punjabi laborer (bottom), unrepentantly told police in December 2005 how he slit the throats of his four daughters one night as they slept in order to salvage the family's honor. The eldest had married a man of her choice, and Ahmed feared the younger daughters would follow her example.

CURRENT SITUATION
Rise of Fundamentalism

Despite landmark political gains by women since the late 1990s, violence and repression of women continue to be daily occurrences — often linked to the global growth of religious fundamentalism.

In 2007, a 21-year-old woman in Saudi Arabia was sentenced to 200 lashes and ordered jailed for six months after being raped 14 times by a gang of seven men. The Saudi court sentenced the woman — who was 19 at the time of the attack — because she was alone in a car with her former boyfriend when the attack occurred. Under Saudi Arabia's strict Islamic law, it is a crime for a woman to meet in private with a man who is not her husband or relative.[99]

After public outcry from around the world, King Abdullah pardoned the woman in December. A government spokesperson, however, said the king fully supported the verdict but issued the pardon in the "interests of the people."[100]

Another Saudi woman still faces beheading after she was condemned to death for "witchcraft." Among her accusers is a man who claimed she rendered him impotent with her sorcery. Despite international protest, the king has yet to say if he will pardon her.[101]

In Iraq, the rise of religious fundamentalism since the U.S. invasion has led to a jump in the number of women being killed or beaten in so-called honor crimes. Honor killings typically occur when a woman is suspected of unsanctioned sexual behavior — which can range from flirting to "allowing" herself to be raped. Her relatives believe they must murder her to end the family's shame. In the Kurdish region of Iraq, the stoning death of 17-year-old Aswad is not an anomaly. A U.N. mission in October 2007 found that 255 women had been killed in Iraqi Kurdistan in the first six months of 2007 alone — most thought to have been murdered by their communities or families for allegedly committing adultery or entering into a relationship not sanctioned by their families.[102]

The rise of fundamentalism is also sparking a growing debate on the issue of women wearing head scarves, both in Iraq and across the Muslim world. Last August Turkey elected a conservative Muslim president whose wife wears a head scarf, signaling the emergence of a new ruling elite that is more willing to publicly display religious beliefs.[103] Then in February, Turkey's parliament voted to ease an

80-year ban on women wearing head scarves in universities, although a ban on head scarves in other public buildings remains in effect.

"This decision will bring further pressure on women," Nesrin Baytok, a member of parliament, said during debate over the ban. "It will ultimately bring us Hezbollah terror, al Qaeda terror and fundamentalism."[104]

But others said lifting the ban was actually a victory for women. Fatma Benli, a Turkish women's-rights activist and lawyer, said the ban on head scarves in public buildings has forced her to send law partners to argue her cases because she is prohibited from entering court wearing her head scarf. It also discourages religiously conservative women from becoming doctors, lawyers or teachers, she says.[105]

Many women activists are quick to say that it is unfair to condemn Islam for the growing abuse against women. "The problem women have with religion is not the religion but the ways men have interpreted it," says Afshar of the University of York. "What is highly negative is sharia law, which is made by men. Because it's human-made, women can unmake it. The battle now is fighting against unjust laws such as stoning."

She says abuses such as forced marriages and honor killings — usually linked in the Western media to Islamic law — actually go directly against the teachings of the *Koran*. And while the United Nations estimates that some 5,000 women and girls are victims of honor killings each year, millions more are abused and killed in violence unrelated to Islam. Between 10 and 50 percent of all women around the world have been physically abused by an intimate partner in their lifetime, studies show.[106]

"What about the rate of spousal or partner killings in the U.K. or the U.S. that are not called 'honor killings'?" asks Concordia University's Hoodfar. "Then it's only occasional 'crazy people' [committing violence]. But when it's present in Pakistan, Iran or Senegal, these are uncivilized people doing 'honor killings.' "

And Islamic fundamentalism is not the only brand of fundamentalism on the rise. Christian fundamentalism is also growing rapidly. A 2006 Pew Forum on Religion and Public Life poll found that nearly one-third of all Americans feel the Bible should be the basis of law across the United States.[107] Many women's-rights activists say Christian fundamentalism threatens women's rights, particularly with regard to reproductive issues. They also condemn the Vatican's opposition to the use of condoms, pointing

Pakistani acid attack survivors Saira Liaqat, right, and Sabra Sultana are among hundreds, and perhaps thousands, of women who are blinded and disfigured after being attacked with acid each year in Pakistan, Bangladesh, India, Cambodia, Malaysia, Uganda and other areas of Africa. Liaqat was attacked at age 18 during an argument over an arranged marriage. Sabra was 15 when she was burned after being married off to an older man who became unsatisfied with the relationship. Only a small percentage of the attacks — often perpetrated by spurned suitors while the women are asleep in their own beds — are prosecuted.

out that it prevents women from protecting themselves against HIV.

"If you look at all your religions, none will say it's a good thing to beat up or kill someone. They are all based on human dignity," says Mollmann of Human Rights Watch. "[Bad things] are carried out in the name of religion, but the actual belief system is not killing and maiming women."

In response to the growing number of honor-based killings, attacks and forced marriages in the U.K., Britain's Association of Chief Police Officers has created an honor-based violence unit, and the U.K.'s Home Office is drafting an action plan to improve the response of police and other agencies to such violence. Legislation going into effect later this year will also give U.K. courts greater guidance on dealing with forced marriages.[108]

Evolving Gender Policies

This past February, the U.N. Convention on the Elimination of All Forms of Discrimination Against Women issued a report criticizing Saudi Arabia for its repression of women. Among other things, the report attacked Saudi Arabia's ban on women drivers and its

Female farmworkers in Nova Lima, Brazil, protest against the impact of big corporations on the poor in March 2006, reflecting the increasing political activism of women around the globe.

system of male guardianship that denies women equal inheritance, child custody and divorce rights.[109] The criticism came during the panel's regular review of countries that have ratified CEDAW. Each government must submit reports every four years outlining steps taken to comply with the convention.

The United States is one of only eight countries — among them Iran, Sudan and Somalia — that have refused to ratify CEDAW.[110] Last year, 108 members of the U.S. House of Representatives signed on to a resolution calling for the Senate to ratify CEDAW, but it still has not voted on the measure.[111] During a U.N. vote last November on a resolution encouraging governments to meet their obligations under CEDAW, the United States was the lone nay vote against 173 yea votes.[112]

American opponents of CEDAW — largely pro-life Christians and Republicans — say it would enshrine the right to abortion in *Roe v. Wade* and be prohibitively expensive, potentially requiring the U.S. government to provide paid maternity leave and other child-care services to all women.[113] They also oppose requirements that the government modify "social and cultural patterns" to eliminate sexual prejudice and to delete any traces of gender stereotypes in textbooks — such as references to women's lives being primarily in the domestic sector.[114] Many Republicans in Congress also have argued that CEDAW would give too much control over U.S. laws to the United Nations and that it could even require the legalization of prostitution and the abolition of Mother's Day.[115]

The last time the Senate took action on CEDAW was in 2002, when the Senate Foreign Relations Committee, chaired by Democratic Sen. Joseph Biden of Delaware, voted to send the convention to the Senate floor for ratification. The full Senate, however, never took action. A Biden spokesperson says the senator "remains committed" to the treaty and is "looking for an opportune time" to bring it forward again. But Senate ratification requires 67 votes, and there do not appear to be that many votes for approval.

CEDAW proponents say the failure to ratify not only hurts women but also harms the U.S. image abroad. On this issue, "the United States is in the company of Sudan and the Vatican," says Bien-Aimé of Equality Now.

Meanwhile, several countries are enacting laws to comply with CEDAW and improve the status of women. In December, Turkmenistan passed its first national law guaranteeing women equal rights, even though its constitution had addressed women's equality.[116] A royal decree in Saudi Arabia in January ordered an end to a long-time ban on women checking into hotels or renting apartments without male guardians. Hotels can now book rooms to women who show identification, but the hotels must register the women's details with the police.[117] The Saudi government has also said it will lift the ban on women driving by the end of the year.[118]

And in an effort to improve relations with women in Afghanistan, the Canadian military, which has troops stationed in the region, has begun studying the role women play in Afghan society, how they are affected by military operations and how they can assist peacekeeping efforts. "Behind all of these men are women who can help eradicate the problems of the population," said Capt. Michel Larocque, who is working with the study. "Illiteracy, poverty, these things can be improved through women."[119]

In February, during the 52nd session of the Commission on the Status of Women, the United Nations kicked off a new seven-year campaign aimed at ending violence against women. The campaign will work with international agencies, governments and individuals to increase funding for anti-violence campaigns and pressure policy makers around the world to enact legislation to eliminate violence against women.[120]

But women's groups want increased U.N. spending on women's programs and the creation of a single unified

Should sex-selective abortions be outlawed?

YES

Nicholas Eberstadt
*Henry Wendt Chair in Political
Economy, American Enterprise Institute
Member, President's Council on Bioethics*

Written for *CQ Global Researcher*, April 2008

The practice of sex-selective abortion to permit parents to destroy unwanted female fetuses has become so widespread in the modern world that it is disfiguring the profile of entire countries — transforming (and indeed deforming) the whole human species.

This abomination is now rampant in China, where the latest census reports six boys for every five girls. But it is also prevalent in the Far East, South Korea, Hong Kong, Taiwan and Vietnam, all of which report biologically impossible "sex ratios at birth" (well above the 103-106 baby boys for every 100 girls ordinarily observed in human populations). In the Caucasus, gruesome imbalances exist now in Armenia, Georgia and Azerbaijan; and in India, the state of Punjab tallies 126 little boys for every 100 girls. Even in the United States, the boy-girl sex ratio at birth for Asian-Americans is now several unnatural percentage points above the national average. So sex-selective abortion is taking place under America's nose.

How can we rid the world of this barbaric form of sexism? Simply outlawing sex-selective abortions will be little more than a symbolic gesture, as South Korea's experience has shown: Its sex ratio at birth continued a steady climb for a full decade after just such a national law was passed. As long as abortion is basically available on demand, any legislation to abolish sex-selective abortion will have no impact.

What about more general restrictions on abortion, then? Poll data consistently demonstrate that most Americans do not favor the post-*Roe* regimen of unconditional abortion. But a return to the pre-*Roe* status quo, where each state made its own abortion laws, would probably have very little effect on sex-selective abortion in our country. After all, the ethnic communities most tempted by it are concentrated in states where abortion rights would likely be strongest, such as California and New York.

In the final analysis, the extirpation of this scourge will require nothing less than a struggle for the conscience of nations. Here again, South Korea may be illustrative: Its gender imbalances began to decline when the public was shocked into facing this stain on their society by a spontaneous, homegrown civil rights movement.

To eradicate sex-selective abortion, we must convince the world that destroying female fetuses is horribly wrong. We need something akin to the abolitionist movement: a moral campaign waged globally, with victories declared one conscience at a time.

NO

Marianne Mollmann
*Advocacy Director, Women's Rights
Division, Human Rights Watch*

Written for *CQ Global Researcher*, April 2008

Medical technology today allows parents to test early in pregnancy for fetal abnormalities, hereditary illnesses and even the sex of the fetus, raising horrifying questions about eugenics and population control. In some countries, a growing number of women apparently are terminating pregnancies when they learn the fetus is female. The resulting sex imbalance in countries like China and India is not only disturbing but also leads to further injustices, such as the abduction of girls for forced marriages.

One response has been to criminalize sex-selective abortions. While it is tempting to hope that this could safeguard the gender balance of future generations, criminalization of abortion for whatever reason has led in the past only to underground and unsafe practices. Thus, the criminalization of sex-selective abortion would put the full burden of righting a fundamental wrong — the devaluing of women's lives — on women.

Many women who choose to abort a female fetus face violence and exclusion if they don't produce a boy. Some see the financial burden of raising a girl as detrimental to the survival of the rest of their family. These considerations will not be lessened by banning sex-selective abortion. Unless one addresses the motivation for the practice, it will continue — underground.

So what is the motivation for aborting female fetuses? At the most basic level, it is a financial decision. In no country in the world does women's earning power equal men's. In marginalized communities in developing countries, this is directly linked to survival: Boys may provide more income than girls.

Severe gaps between women's and men's earning power are generally accompanied by severe forms of gender-based discrimination and rigid gender roles. For example, in China, boys are expected to stay in their parental home as they grow up, adding their manpower (and that of a later wife) to the family home. Girls, on the other hand, are expected to join the husbands' parental home. Thus, raising a girl is a net loss, especially if you are only allowed one child.

The solution is to remove the motivation behind sex-selective abortion by advancing women's rights and their economic and social equality. Choosing the blunt instrument of criminal law over promoting the value of women's lives and rights will only serve to place further burdens on marginalized and often vulnerable women.

agency addressing women's issues, led by an under-secretary general.[121] Currently, four different U.N. agencies address women's issues: the United Nations Development Fund for Women, the International Research and Training Institute for the Advancement of Women (INSTRAW), the Secretary-General's Special Advisor on Gender Issues (OSAGI) and the Division for the Advancement of Women. In 2006, the four agencies received only $65 million — a fraction of the more than $2 billion budget that the U.N.'s children's fund (UNICEF) received that year.[122]

"The four entities that focus on women's rights at the U.N. are greatly under-resourced," says Zeitlin of the Women's Environment & Development Organization. "If the rhetoric everyone is using is true — that investing in women is investing in development — it's a matter of putting your money where your mouth is."

Political Prospects

While the number of women leading world governments is still miniscule compared to their male counterparts, women are achieving political gains that just a few years ago would have been unthinkable.

While for the first time in U.S. history a woman is in a tight race for a major party's nomination as its candidate for president, South America — with two sitting female heads of state — leads the world in woman-led governments. In Brazil, Dilma Rousseff, the female chief of staff to President Luiz Inacio Lula da Silva, is the top contender to take over the presidency when da Silva's term ends in 2010.[123] In Paraguay, Blanca Ovelar was this year's presidential nominee for the country's ruling conservative Colorado Party, but she was defeated on April 20.[124]

And in Europe, Carme Chacón was named defense minister of Spain this past April. She was not only the first woman ever to head the country's armed forces but also was pregnant at the time of her appointment. In all, nine of Spain's 17 cabinet ministers are women.

In March, Pakistan's National Assembly overwhelmingly elected its first female speaker, Fahmida Mirza.[125] And in India, where Patil has become the first woman president, the two major political parties this year pledged to set aside one-third of their parliamentary nominations for women. But many fear the parties will either not keep their pledges or will run women only in contests they are unlikely to win.[126]

There was also disappointment in Iran, where nearly 600 of the 7,000 candidates running for parliament in March were women.[127] Only three won seats in the 290-member house, and they were conservatives who are not expected to promote women's rights. Several of the tallies are being contested. Twelve other women won enough votes to face run-off elections on April 25; five won.[128]

But in some countries, women running for office face more than just tough campaigns. They are specifically targeted for violence. In Kenya, the greatest campaign expense for female candidates is the round-the-clock security required to protect them against rape, according to Phoebe Asiyo, who served in the Kenyan parliament for more than two decades.[129] During the three months before Kenya's elections last December, an emergency helpdesk established by the Education Centre for Women in Democracy, a nongovernmental organization (NGO) in Nairobi, received 258 reports of attacks against female candidates.[130]

The helpdesk reported the attacks to police, worked with the press to ensure the cases were documented and helped victims obtain medical and emotional support. Attacks included rape, stabbings, threats and physical assaults.[131]

"Women are being attacked because they are women and because it is seen as though they are not fit to bear flags of the popular parties," according to the center's Web site. "Women are also viewed as guilty for invading 'the male territory' and without a license to do so!"[132]

"All women candidates feel threatened," said Nazlin Umar, the sole female presidential candidate last year. "When a case of violence against a woman is reported, we women on the ground think we are next. I think if the government assigned all women candidates with guns...we will at least have an item to protect ourselves when we face danger."[133]

Impunity for Violence

Some African feminists blame women themselves, as well as men, for not doing enough to end traditional attitudes that perpetuate violence against women.

"Women are also to blame for the violence because they are the gatekeepers of patriarchy, because whether educated or not they have different standards for their sons and husbands [than for] their daughters," said Njoki Wainaina, founder of the African Women Development

Communication Network (FEMNET). "How do you start telling a boy whose mother trained him only disrespect for girls to honor women in adulthood?"[134]

Indeed, violence against women is widely accepted in many regions of the world and often goes unpunished. A study by the World Health Organization found that 80 percent of women surveyed in rural Egypt believe that a man is justified in beating a woman if she refuses to have sex with him. In Ghana, more women than men — 50 percent compared to 43 percent — felt that a man was justified in beating his wife if she used contraception without his consent.[135] (*See survey results, p. 56.*)

Such attitudes have led to many crimes against women going unpunished, and not just violence committed during wartime. In Guatemala, no one knows why an estimated 3,000 women have been killed over the past seven years — many of them beheaded, sexually mutilated or raped — but theories range from domestic violence to gang activity.[136] Meanwhile, the government in 2006 overturned a law allowing rapists to escape charges if they offered to marry their victims. But Guatemalan law still does not prescribe prison sentences for domestic abuse and prohibits abusers from being charged with assault unless the bruises are still visible after 10 days.[137]

In the Mexican cities of Chihuahua and Juárez, more than 400 women have been murdered over the past 14 years, with many of the bodies mutilated and dumped in the desert. But the crimes are still unsolved, and many human-rights groups, including Amnesty International, blame indifference by Mexican authorities. Now the country's 14-year statute of limitations on murder is forcing prosecutors to close many of the unsolved cases.[138]

Feminists around the world have been working to end dismissive cultural attitudes about domestic violence and other forms of violence against women, such as forced marriage, dowry-related violence, marital rape, sexual harassment and forced abortion, sterilization and prostitution. But it's often an uphill battle.

After a Kenyan police officer beat his wife so badly she was paralyzed and brain damaged — and eventually died — media coverage of the murder spurred a nationwide debate on domestic violence. But it took five years of protests, demonstrations and lobbying by both women's advocates and outraged men to get a family protection bill enacted criminalizing domestic violence. And the bill passed only after legislators removed a provision outlawing

marital rape. Similar laws have languished for decades in other African legislatures.[139]

But in Rwanda, where nearly 49 percent of the elected representatives in the lower house are female, gender desks have been established at local police stations, staffed mostly by women trained to help victims of sexual and other violence. In 2006, as a result of improved reporting, investigation and response to rape cases, police referred 1,777 cases for prosecution and convicted 803 men. "What we need now is to expand this approach to more countries," said UNIFEM's director for Central Africa Josephine Odera.[140]

Besides criticizing governments for failing to prosecute gender-based violence, many women's groups also criticize the International Criminal Court (ICC) for not doing enough to bring abusers to justice.

"We have yet to see the investigative approach needed to ensure the prosecution of gender-based crimes," said Brigid Inder, executive director of Women's Initiatives for Gender Justice, a Hague-based group that promotes and monitors women's rights in the international court.[141] Inder's group released a study last November showing that of the 500 victims seeking to participate in ICC proceedings, only 38 percent were women. When the court handed down its first indictments for war crimes in the Democratic Republic of the Congo last year, no charges involving gender-based crimes were brought despite estimates that more than 250,000 women have been raped and sexually abused in the country. After an outcry from women's groups around the world, the ICC included "sexual slavery" among the charges handed down in its second case involving war crimes in Congo.[142]

The Gender Justice report also criticized the court for failing to reach out to female victims. It said the ICC has held only one consultation with women in the last four years (focusing on the Darfur conflict in Sudan) and has failed to develop any strategies to reach out to women victims in Congo.[143]

OUTLOOK
Economic Integration

Women's organizations do not expect — or want — another international conference on the scale of Beijing. Instead, they say, the resources needed to launch such a

Seaweed farmer Asia Mohammed Makungu in Zanzibar, Tanzania, grows the sea plants for export to European companies that produce food and cosmetics. Globalized trade has helped women entrepreneurs in many developing countries improve their lives, but critics say it also has created many low-wage, dangerous jobs for women in poor countries that ignore safety and labor protections in order to attract foreign investors.

conference would be better used to improve U.N. oversight of women's issues and to implement the promises made at Beijing.

They also fear that the growth of religious fundamentalism and neo-liberal economic policies around the globe have created a political atmosphere that could actually set back women's progress.

"If a Beijing conference happened now, we would not get the type of language or the scope we got 10 years ago," says Bien-Aimé of Equity Now. "There is a conservative movement, a growth in fundamentalists governments — and not just in Muslim countries. We would be very concerned about opening up debate on the principles that have already been established."

Dahlerup of Stockholm University agrees. "It was easier in the 1990s. Many people are afraid of having big conferences now, because there may be a backlash because fundamentalism is so strong," she says. "Neo-liberal trends are also moving the discourse about women toward economics — women have to benefit for the sake of the economic good. That could be very good, but it's a more narrow discourse when every issue needs to be adapted into the economic discourse of a cost-benefit analysis."

For women to continue making gains, most groups say, gender can no longer be treated separately from broader economic, environmental, health or other political issues. While efforts to improve the status of women have historically been addressed in gender-specific legislation or international treaties, women's groups now say women's well-being must now be considered an integral part of all policies.

Women's groups are working to ensure that gender is incorporated into two major international conferences coming up this fall. In September, the Third High-Level Forum on Aid Effectiveness will be hosted in Accra, Ghana, bringing together governments, financial institutions, civil society organizations and others to assess whether assistance provided to poor nations is being put to good use. World leaders will also gather in November in Doha, Qatar, for the International Conference on Financing for Development to discuss how trade, debt relief and financial aid can promote global development.

"Women's groups are pushing for gender to be on the agenda for both conferences," says Zeitlin of WEDO. "It's important because . . . world leaders need to realize that it really does make a difference to invest in women. When it comes to women's rights it's all micro, but the big decisions are made on the macro level."

Despite decades of economic-development strategies promoted by Western nations and global financial institutions such as the World Bank, women in many regions are getting poorer. In Malawi, for example, the percentage of women living in poverty increased by 5 percent between 1995 and 2003.[144] Women and girls make up 70 percent of the world's poorest people, and their wages rise more slowly than men's. They also have fewer property rights around the world.[145] With the growing global food shortage, women — who are the primary family caregivers and produce the majority of crops for home consumption in developing countries — will be especially hard hit.

To help women escape poverty, gain legal rights and improve their social status, developed nations must rethink their broader strategies of engagement with developing countries. And, conversely, female activists say, any efforts aimed at eradicating poverty around the world must specifically address women's issues.

In Africa, for instance, activists have successfully demanded that women's economic and security concerns be addressed as part of the continent-wide development plan known as the New Partnership for Africa's Development (NEPAD). As a result, countries participating in NEPAD's peer review process must now show they are taking measures to promote and protect women's rights. But, according to Augustin Wambo, an agricultural specialist at the NEPAD secretariat, lawmakers now need to back up their pledges with "resources from national budgets" and the "necessary policies and means to support women."[146]

"We have made a lot of progress and will continue making progress," says Zeitlin. "But women's progress doesn't happen in isolation to what's happening in the rest of the world. The environment, the global economy, war, peace — they will all have a major impact on women. Women all over world will not stop making demands and fighting for their rights."

NOTES

1. http://ballyblog.wordpress.com/2007/05/04/warning-uncensored-video-iraqis-stone-girl-to-death-over-loving-wrong-boy/.

2. Abdulhamid Zebari, "Video of Iraqi girl's stoning shown on Internet," Agence France Presse, May 5, 2007.

3. *State of the World Population 2000*, United Nations Population Fund, Sept. 20, 2000, Chapter 3, "Ending Violence against Women and Girls," www.unfpa.org/swp/2000/english/ch03.html.

4. Brian Brady, "A Question of Honour," *The Independent on Sunday*, Feb. 10, 2008, p. 8, www.independent.co.uk/news/uk/home-news/a-question-of-honour-police-say-17000-women-are-victims-every-year-780522.html.

5. Correspondance with Karen Musalo, Clinical Professor of Law and Director of the Center for Gender & Refugee Studies at the University of California Hastings School of Law, April 11, 2008.

6. "Broken Bodies, Broken Dreams: Violence Against Women Exposed," United Nations, July 2006, http://brokendreams.wordpress.com/2006/12/17/dowry-crimes-and-bride-price-abuse/.

7. Various sources: www.womankind.org.uk, www.unfpa.org/gender/docs/studies/summaries/reg_exe_summary.pdf, www.oxfam.org.uk. Also see "Child rape in Kano on the increase," IRIN Humanitarian News and Analysis, United Nations, www.irinnews.org/report.aspx?ReportId=76087.

8. "UNICEF slams 'licence to rape' in African crisis," Agence France-Press, Feb. 12, 2008.

9. "Film Documents Rape of Women in Congo," "All Things Considered," National Public Radio, April 8, 2008, www.npr.org/templates/story/story.php?storyId=89476111.

10. Jeffrey Gettleman, "Rape Epidemic Raises Trauma Of Congo War," *The New York Times*, Oct. 7, 2007, p. A1.

11. Dan McDougall, "Fareeda's fate: rape, prison and 25 lashes," *The Observer*, Sept. 17, 2006, www.guardian.co.uk/world/2006/sep/17/pakistan.theobserver.

12. Zarar Khan, "Thousands rally in Pakistan to demand government withdraw rape law changes," The Associated Press, Dec. 10, 2006.

13. *State of the World Population 2000, op. cit.*

14. Laura Turquet, Patrick Watt, Tom Sharman, "Hit or Miss?" ActionAid, March 7, 2008, p. 10.

15. *Ibid.*, p. 12.

16. "Women in Politics: 2008" map, International Parliamentary Union and United Nations Division for the Advancement of Women, February 2008, www.ipu.org/pdf/publications/wmnmap08_en.pdf.

17. Gavin Rabinowitz, "India's first female president sworn in, promises to empower women," The Associated Press, July 25, 2007. Note: India's first female prime minister was Indira Ghandi in 1966.

18. Monte Reel, "South America Ushers In The Era of La Presidenta; Women Could Soon Lead a Majority of Continent's Population," *The Washington Post*, Oct. 31, 2007, p. A12. For background, see Roland Flamini, "The New Latin America," *CQ Global Researcher*, March 2008, pp. 57-84.

19. Marcela Valente, "Cristina Fernandes Dons Presidential Sash," Inter Press Service, Dec. 10, 2007.

20. "Women in Politics: 2008" map, *op. cit.*

21. *Ibid.*; Global Database of Quotas for Women, International Institute for Democracy and Electoral Assistance and Stockholm University, www.quotaproject.org/country.cfm?SortOrder=Country.

22. "Beijing Betrayed," Women's Environment and Development Organization, March 2005, p. 10, www.wedo.org/files/gmr_pdfs/gmr2005.pdf.

23. "Women in Politics: 2008" map, *op. cit.*

24. Gertrude Mongella, address by the Secretary-General of the 4th World Conference on Women, Sept. 4, 1995, www.un.org/esa/gopher-data/conf/fwcw/conf/una/950904201423.txt. Also see Steven Mufson, "Women's Forum Sets Accord; Dispute on Sexual Freedom Resolved," *The Washington Post*, Sept. 15, 1995, p. A1.

25. "Closing statement," Gertrude Mongella, U.N. Division for the Advancement of Women, Fourth World Conference on Women, www.un.org/esa/gopher-data/conf/fwcw/conf/una/closing.txt.

26. "Trading Away Our Rights," Oxfam International, 2004, p. 9, www.oxfam.org.uk/resources/policy/trade/downloads/trading_rights.pdf.

27. "Trafficking in Persons Report," U.S. Department of State, June 2007, p. 7, www.state.gov/g/tip/rls/tiprpt/2007/.

28. Turquet, *et al.*, *op. cit.*, p. 4.

29. United Nations Division for the Advancement of Women, www.un.org/womenwatch/daw/cedaw/.

30. Geraldine Terry, *Women's Rights* (2007), p. 30.

31. United Nations Division for the Advancement of Women, www.un.org/womenwatch/daw/cedaw/.

32. "The impact of international trade on gender equality," The World Bank PREM notes, May 2004, http://siteresources.worldbank.org/INTGENDER/Resources/premnote86.pdf.

33. Thalia Kidder and Kate Raworth, " 'Good Jobs' and hidden costs: women workers documenting the price of precarious employment," *Gender and Development*, July 2004, p. 13.

34. "Trading Away Our Rights," *op. cit.*

35. Martha Chen, *et al.*, "Progress of the World's Women 2005: Women, Work and Poverty," UNIFEM, p. 17, www.unifem.org/attachments/products/PoWW2005_eng.pdf.

36. Eric Neumayer and Indra de Soys, "Globalization, Women's Economic Rights and Forced Labor," London School of Economics and Norwegian University of Science and Technology, February 2007, p. 8, http://papers.ssrn.com/sol3/papers.cfm?abstract_id=813831. Also see "Five years down

the road from Beijing — assessing progress," *News and Highlights*, Food and Agriculture Organization, June 2, 2000, www.fao.org/News/2000/000602-e.htm.

37. "Trafficking in Persons Report," *op. cit.*, p. 13.

38. "World Survey on the Role of Women in Development," United Nations, 2006, p. 1, www.un.org/womenwatch/daw/public/WorldSurvey2004-Women&Migration.pdf.

39. Julie Ballington and Azza Karam, eds., "Women in Parliament: Beyond the Numbers," International Institute for Democracy and Electoral Assistance, 2005, p. 155, www.idea.int/publications/wip2/upload/WiP_inlay.pdf.

40. "Women in Politics: 2008," *op. cit.*

41. Ballington and Karam, *op. cit.*, p. 158.

42. *Ibid.*, p. 161.

43. Global Database of Quotas for Women, *op. cit.*

44. Jerome Starkey, "Afghan government official says that student will not be executed," *The Independent*, Feb. 6, 2008, www.independent.co.uk/news/world/asia/afghan-government-official-says-that-student-will-not-be-executed-778686.html?r=RSS.

45. "Afghan women seek death by fire," BBC, Nov. 15, 2006, http://news.bbc.co.uk/1/hi/world/south_asia/6149144.stm.

46. Global Database for Quotas for Women, *op. cit.*

47. "Beijing Declaration," Fourth World Conference on Women, www.un.org/womenwatch/daw/beijing/beijingdeclaration.html.

48. "Beijing Betrayed," *op. cit.*, pp. 28, 15, 18.

49. "Review of the implementation of the Beijing Platform for Action and the outcome documents of the special session of the General Assembly entitled 'Women 2000: gender equality, development and peace for the twenty-first century,' " United Nations, Dec. 6, 2004, p. 74.

50. "Gender Equality and the Millennium Development Goals," fact sheet, www.mdgender.net/upload/tools/MDGender_leaflet.pdf.

51. *Ibid.*

52. Turquet, *et al.*, *op. cit.*, p. 16.

53. *Ibid.*, pp. 22-24.

54. Terry, *op. cit.*, p. 6.

55. "Inclusive Security, Sustainable Peace: A Toolkit for Advocacy and Action," International Alert and Women Waging Peace, 2004, p. 12, www.huntalternatives .org/download/35_introduction.pdf.

56. "Declarations, Reservations and Objections to CEDAW," www.un.org/womenwatch/daw/cedaw/ reservations-country.htm.

57. Merlin Stone, *When God Was a Woman* (1976), pp. 18, 11.

58. Jack Holland, *Misogyny* (2006), p. 12.

59. *Ibid.*, pp. 21-23.

60. Holland, *op. cit.*, p. 112.

61. "Dispelling the myths about so-called witches" press release, Johns Hopkins University, Oct. 7, 2002, www.jhu.edu/news_info/news/home02/ oct02/witch.html.

62. The quote is from the *Malleus maleficarum* (*The Hammer of Witches*), and was cited in "Case Study: The European Witch Hunts, c. 1450-1750," *Gendercide Watch*, www.gendercide.org/case witch-hunts.html.

63. Holland, *op. cit.*, p. 179.

64. Cathy J. Cohen, Kathleen B. Jones and Joan C. Tronto, *Women Transforming Politics: An Alternative Reader* (1997), p. 530.

65. *Ibid.*

66. Holland, *op. cit*, p. 201.

67. "Men and Women in Politics: Democracy Still in the Making," IPU Study No. 28, 1997, http:// archive.idea.int/women/parl/ch6_table8.htm.

68. "Sex, Equality and Protective Laws," *CQ Researcher*, July 13, 1926.

69. The case was *Radice v. People of State of New York*, 264 U. S. 292. For background, see F. Brewer, "Equal Rights Amendment," *Editorial Research Reports*, April 4, 1946, available at *CQ Researcher Plus Archive*, www.cqpress.com.

70. "Short History of the CEDAW Convention," U.N. Division for the Advancement of Women, www .un.org/womenwatch/daw/cedaw/history.htm.

71. U.N. Women's Watch, www.un.org/womenwatch/ asp/user/list.asp-ParentID=11047.htm.

72. United Nations, http://untreaty.un.org/ENGLISH/ bible/englishinternetbible/partI/chapterXVI/ treaty2.asp.

73. International Labor Organization, www.ilo.org/ public/english/support/lib/resource/subject/ gender.htm.

74. *Ibid.*

75. For background, see "Gender Pay Gap," *CQ Researcher*, March 14, 2008, pp. 241-264.

76. "Short History of the CEDAW Convention" *op. cit.*

77. "International News," The Associated Press, Dec. 19, 1979.

78. "Short History of the CEDAW Convention" *op. cit.*

79. "Text of the Convention," U.N. Division for the Advancement of Women, www.un.org/women-watch/daw/cedaw/cedaw.htm.

80. Convention on the Elimination of All Forms of Discrimination against Women, Article 16, www .un.org/womenwatch/daw/cedaw/text/econvention .htm.

81. General Recommendation made by the Committee on the Elimination of Discrimination against Women No. 19, 11th session, 1992, www.un.org/women watch/daw/cedaw/recommendations/recomm .htm#recom19.

82. See www.unhchr.ch/huridocda/huridoca.nsf/ (Symbol)/A.CONF.157.23.En.

83. Marlise Simons, "For First Time, Court Defines Rape as War Crime," *The New York Times*, June 28, 1996, www.nytimes.com/specials/bosnia/ context/0628warcrimes-tribunal.html.

84. Ann Simmons, "U.N. Tribunal Convicts Rwandan Ex-Mayor of Genocide in Slaughter," *Los Angeles Times*, Sept. 3, 1998, p. 20.

85. "Human Rights Watch Applauds Rwanda Rape Verdict," press release, Human Rights Watch, Sept. 2, 1998, http://hrw.org/english/docs/1998/09/02/ rwanda1311.htm.

86. Frederic Bichon, "ICC vows to bring Darfur war criminals to justice," Agence France-Presse, Feb. 24, 2008.

87. Rebecca Feeley and Colin Thomas-Jensen, "Getting Serious about Ending Conflict and Sexual Violence in Congo," Enough Project, www.enoughproject.org/reports/congoserious.

88. "Women; Deceived Again?" *The Economist*, July 5, 1975.

89. "International Women's Day — March 8: Points of Interest and Links with UNIFEM," UNIFEM New Zealand Web site, www.unifem.org.nz/IWDPointsofinterest.htm.

90. Joseph Gambardello, "Reporter's Notebook: Women's Conference in Kenya," United Press International, July 13, 1985.

91. "Report of the World Conference to Review and Appraise the Achievements of the United Nations Decade for Women: Equality Development and Peace," United Nations, 1986, paragraph 8, www.un.org/womenwatch/confer/nfls/Nairobi1985report.txt.

92. U.N. Division for the Advancement of Women, www.un.org/womenwatch/daw/followup/background.htm.

93. "Women in Politics," Inter-Parliamentary Union, 2005, pp. 16-17, www.ipu.org/PDF/publications/wmn45-05_en.pdf.

94. "Liberian becomes Africa's first female president," Associated Press, Jan. 16, 2006, www.msnbc.msn.com/id/10865705/.

95. "Women in the Americas: Paths to Political Power," *op. cit.*, p. 2.

96. "The Millennium Development Goals Report 2007," United Nations, 2007, p. 12, www.un.org/millenniumgoals/pdf/mdg2007.pdf.

97. David Dollar, Raymond Fisman, Roberta Gatti, "Are Women Really the 'Fairer' Sex? Corruption and Women in Government," The World Bank, October 1999, p. 1, http://siteresources.worldbank.org/INTGENDER/Resources/wp4.pdf.

98. *Ibid.*

99. Vicky Baker, "Rape victim sentenced to 200 lashes and six months in jail; Saudi woman punished for being alone with a man," *The Guardian*, Nov. 17, 2007, www.guardian.co.uk/world/2007/nov/17/saudiarabia.international.

100. Katherine Zoepf, "Saudi King Pardons Rape Victim Sentenced to Be Lashed, Saudi Paper Reports," *The New York Times*, Dec. 18, 2007, www.nytimes.com/2007/12/18/world/ middleeast/18saudi.html.

101. Sonia Verma, "King Abdullah urged to spare Saudi 'witchcraft' woman's life," *The Times* (Of London), Feb. 16, 2008.

102. Mark Lattimer, "Freedom lost," *The Guardian*, Dec. 13, 2007, p. 6.

103. For background, see Brian Beary, "Future of Turkey," *CQ Global Researcher*, December, 2007, pp. 295-322.

104. Tracy Clark-Flory, "Does freedom to veil hurt women?" *Salon.com*, Feb. 11, 2008.

105. Sabrina Tavernise, "Under a Scarf, a Turkish Lawyer Fighting to Wear It," *The New York Times*, Feb. 9, 2008, www.nytimes.com/2008/02/09/world/europe/09benli.html?pagewanted=1&sq=women&st=nyt&scp=96.

106. Terry, *op. cit.*, p. 122.

107. "Many Americans Uneasy with Mix of Religion and Politics," The Pew Forum on Religion and Public Life, Aug. 24, 2006, http://pewforum.org/docs/index.php?DocID=153.

108. Brady, *op. cit.*

109. "Concluding Observations of the Committee on the Elimination of Discrimination against Women: Saudi Arabia," Committee on the Elimination of Discrimination against Women, 40th Session, Jan. 14-Feb. 1, 2008, p. 3, www2.ohchr.org/english/bodies/cedaw/docs/co/CEDAW. C.SAU.CO.2.pdf.

110. Kambiz Fattahi, "Women's bill 'unites' Iran and US," BBC, July 31, 2007, http://news.bbc.co.uk/2/hi/middle_east/6922749.stm.

111. H. Res. 101, Rep. Lynn Woolsey, http://thomas.loc.gov/cgi-bin/bdquery/z?d110:h.res.00101.

112. "General Assembly Adopts Landmark Text Calling for Moratorium on Death Penalty," States News Service, Dec. 18, 2007, www.un.org/News/Press/docs//2007/ga10678.doc.htm.

113. Mary H. Cooper, "Women and Human Rights," *CQ Researcher*, April 30, 1999, p. 356.

114. Christina Hoff Sommers, "The Case against Ratifying the United Nations Convention on the Elimination of All Forms of Discrimination against Women," testimony before the Senate Foreign Relations Committee, June 13, 2002, www.aei.org/publications/filter.all,pubID.15557/pub_detail.asp.

115. "CEDAW: Pro-United Nations, Not Pro-Woman" press release, U.S. Senate Republican Policy Committee, Sept. 16, 2002, http://rpc.senate.gov/_files/FOREIGNje091602.pdf.

116. "Turkmenistan adopts gender equality law," BBC Worldwide Monitoring, Dec. 19, 2007.

117. Faiza Saleh Ambah, "Saudi Women See a Brighter Road on Rights," *The Washington Post*, Jan. 31, 2008, p. A15, www.washingtonpost.com/wp-dyn/content/article/2008/01/30/AR2008013003805.html.

118. Damien McElroy, "Saudi Arabia to lift ban on women drivers," *The Telegraph*, Jan. 1, 2008.

119. Stephanie Levitz, "Lifting the veils of Afghan women," *The Hamilton Spectator* (Ontario, Canada), Feb. 28, 2008, p. A11.

120. "U.N. Secretary-General Ban Ki-moon Launches Campaign to End Violence against Women," U.N. press release, Feb. 25, 2008, http://endviolence.un.org/press.shtml.

121. "Gender Equality Architecture and U.N. Reforms," the Center for Women's Global Leadership and the Women's Environment and Development Organization, July 17, 2006, www.wedo.org/files/Gender%20Equality%20Architecture%20and%20UN%20Reform0606.pdf.

122. Bojana Stoparic, "New-Improved Women's Agency Vies for U.N. Priority," Women's eNews, March 6, 2008, www.womensenews.org/article.cfm?aid=3517.

123. Reel, *op. cit.*

124. Eliana Raszewski and Bill Faries, "Lugo, Ex Bishop, Wins Paraguay Presidential Election," Bloomberg, April 20, 2008.

125. Zahid Hussain, "Pakistan gets its first woman Speaker," *The Times* (of London), March 20, p. 52.

126. Bhaskar Roy, "Finally, women set to get 33% quota," *Times of India*, Jan. 29, 2008.

127. Massoumeh Torfeh, "Iranian women crucial in Majlis election," BBC, Jan. 30, 2008, http://news.bbc.co.uk/1/hi/world/middle_east/7215272.stm.

128. "Iran women win few seats in parliament," Agence-France Presse, March 18, 2008.

129. Swanee Hunt, "Let Women Rule," *Foreign Affairs*, May-June 2007, p. 109.

130. Kwamboka Oyaro, "A Call to Arm Women Candidates With More Than Speeches," Inter Press Service, Dec. 21, 2007, http://ipsnews.net/news.asp?idnews=40569.

131. Education Centre for Women in Democracy, www.ecwd.org.

132. *Ibid.*

133. Oyaro, *op. cit.*

134. *Ibid.*

135. Mary Kimani, "Taking on violence against women in Africa," *AfricaRenewal*, U.N. Dept. of Public Information, July 2007, p. 4, www.un.org/ecosocdev/geninfo/afrec/vol21no2/212-violence-aganist-women.html.

136. Correspondence with Karen Musalo, Clinical Professor of Law and Director of the Center for Gender & Refugee Studies, University of California Hastings School of Law, April 11, 2008.

137. "Mexico and Guatemala: Stop the Killings of Women," Amnesty International USA Issue Brief, January 2007, www.amnestyusa.org/document.php?lang=e&id=engusa20070130001.

138. Manuel Roig-Franzia, "Waning Hopes in Juarez," *The Washington Post*, May 14, 2007, p. A10.

139. Kimani, *op. cit.*

140. *Ibid.*

141. "Justice slow for female war victims," *The Toronto Star*, March 3, 2008, www.thestar.com/News/GlobalVoices/article/308784p.

142. Speech by Brigid Inder on the Launch of the "Gender Report Card on the International Criminal Court," Dec. 12, 2007, www.iccwomen.org/news/docs/Launch_GRC_2007.pdf

143. "Gender Report Card on the International Criminal Court," Women's Initiatives for Gender Justice,

November 2007, p. 32, www.iccwomen.org/ publications/resources/docs/GENDER_04-01- 2008_FINAL_TO_PRINT.pdf.

144. Turquet, *et al.*, *op. cit.*, p. 8.

145. Oxfam Gender Equality Fact Sheet, www.oxfam .org.uk/resources/issues/gender/introduction .html.

146. Itai Madamombe, "Women push onto Africa's agenda," *AfricaRenewal*, U.N. Dept. of Public Information, July 2007, pp. 8-9.

BIBLIOGRAPHY

Books

Holland, Jack, *Misogyny: The World's Oldest Prejudice, Constable & Robinson*, **2006.**
The late Irish journalist provides vivid details and anecdotes about women's oppression throughout history.

Stone, Merlin, *When God Was a Woman, Harcourt Brace Jovanovich*, **1976.**
The book contends that before the rise of Judeo-Christian patriarchies women headed the first societies and religions.

Terry, Geraldine, *Women's Rights, Pluto Press*, **2007.**
A feminist who has worked for Oxfam and other nongovernmental organizations outlines major issues facing women today — from violence to globalization to AIDS.

Women and the Environment, UNEP, **2004.**
The United Nations Environment Programme shows the integral link between women in the developing world and the changing environment.

Articles

Brady, Brian, "A Question of Honour," *The Independent on Sunday*, **Feb. 10, 2008, p. 8.**
"Honor killings" and related violence against women are on the rise in the United Kingdom.

Kidder, Thalia, and Kate Raworth, " 'Good Jobs' and hidden costs: women workers documenting the price of precarious employment," *Gender and Development*, **Vol. 12, No. 2, p. 12, July 2004.**
Two trade and gender experts describe the precarious working conditions and job security experienced by food and garment workers.

Reports and Studies

"Beijing Betrayed," *Women's Environment and Development Organization*, **March 2005, www.wedo .org/files/gmr_pdfs/gmr2005.pdf.**
A women's-rights organization reviews the progress and shortcomings of governments in implementing the commitments made during the Fifth World Congress on Women in Beijing in 1995.

"The Millennium Development Goals Report 2007," *United Nations*, **2007, www.un.org/millenniumgoals/ pdf/mdg2007.pdf.**
International organizations demonstrate the progress governments have made — or not — in reaching the Millennium Development Goals.

"Trafficking in Persons Report," *U.S. Department of State*, **June 2007, www.state.gov/documents/ organization/82902.pdf.**
This seventh annual report discusses the growing problems of human trafficking around the world.

"The tsunami's impact on women," *Oxfam briefing note*, **March 5, 2005, www.oxfam.org/en/files/ bn050326_tsunami_women/download.**
Looking at how the 2004 tsunami affected women in Indonesia, India and Sri Lanka, Oxfam International suggests how governments can better address women's issues during future natural disasters.

"Women in Politics," *Inter-Parliamentary Union*, **2005, www.ipu.org/PDF/publications/wmn45-05_en.pdf.**
The report provides detailed databases of the history of female political representation in governments around the world.

Ballington, Julie, and Azza Karam, "Women in Parliament: Beyond the Numbers," *International Institute for Democracy and Electoral Assistance*, **2005, www.idea.int/publications/wip2/upload/WiP_ inlay.pdf.**
The handbook provides female politicians and candidates information and case studies on how women have overcome obstacles to elected office.

Chen, Martha, Joann Vanek, Francie Lund, James Heintz, Renana Jhabvala and Christine Bonner, "Women, Work and Poverty," *UNIFEM*, 2005, www .unifem.org/attachments/products/PoWW2005_eng .pdf.
The report argues that greater work protection and security is needed to promote women's rights and reduce global poverty.

Larserud, Stina, and Rita Taphorn, "Designing for Equality," *International Institute for Democracy and Electoral Assistance*, 2007, www.idea.int/publications/designing_for_equality/upload/Idea_Design_low.pdf.

The report describes the impact that gender quota systems have on women's representation in elected office.

Raworth, Kate, and Claire Harvey, "Trading Away Our Rights," *Oxfam International*, 2004, www .oxfam.org.uk/resources/policy/trade/downloads/ trading_rights.pdf.
Through exhaustive statistics, case studies and interviews, the report paints a grim picture of how trade globalization is affecting women.

Turquet, Laura, Patrick Watt and Tom Sharman, "Hit or Miss?" *ActionAid*, March 7, 2008.
The report reviews how governments are doing in achieving the U.N.'s Millennium Development Goals.

For More Information

Equality Now, P.O. Box 20646, Columbus Circle Station, New York, NY 10023; www.equalitynow.org. An international organization working to protect women against violence and promote women's human rights.

Global Database of Quotas for Women; www.quotaproject.org. A joint project of the International Institute for Democracy and Electoral Assistance and Stockholm University providing country-by-country data on electoral quotas for women.

Human Rights Watch, 350 Fifth Ave., 34th floor, New York, NY 10118-3299; (212) 290-4700; www.hrw.org. Investigates and exposes human-rights abuses around the world.

Hunt Alternatives Fund, 625 Mount Auburn St., Cambridge, MA 02138; (617) 995-1900; www.huntalternatives.org. A private foundation that provides grants and technical assistance to promote positive social change; its Initiative for Inclusive Security promotes women in peacekeeping.

Inter-Parliamentary Union, 5, Chemin du Pommier, Case Postale 330, CH-1218 Le Grand-Saconnex, Geneva, Switzerland; +(4122) 919 41 50; www.ipu.org. An organization of parliaments of sovereign states that

maintains an extensive database on women serving in parliaments.

Oxfam International, 1100 15th St., N.W., Suite 600, Washington, DC 20005; (202) 496-1170; www.oxfam.org. Confederation of 13 independent nongovernmental organizations working to fight poverty and related social injustice.

U.N. Development Fund for Women (UNIFEM), 304 East 45th St., 15th Floor, New York, NY 10017; (212) 906-6400; www.unifem.org. Provides financial aid and technical support for empowering women and promoting gender equality.

U.N. Division for the Advancement of Women (DAW), 2 UN Plaza, DC2-12th Floor, New York, NY 10017; www .un.org/womenwatch/daw. Formulates policy on gender equality, implements international agreements on women's issues and promotes gender mainstreaming in government activities.

Women's Environment & Development Organization (WEDO), 355 Lexington Ave., 3rd Floor, New York, NY 10017; (212) 973-0325; www.wedo.org. An international organization that works to promote women's equality in global policy.

4

Rapid Urbanization

Can Cities Cope With Rampant Growth?

Jennifer Weeks

AFP/Getty Images/Rob Elliott

Children scavenge for recyclables amid rubbish in the Dharavi slum in Mumbai, India. About a billion people worldwide live in slums — where sewer, water and garbage-collection services are often nonexistent. If impoverished rural residents continue streaming into cities at current rates, the world's slum population is expected to double to 2 billion within the next two decades, according to the United Nations.

From *CQ Researcher*,
April 2009.

India's most infamous slum lives up to its reputation. Located in the middle of vast Mumbai, Dharavi is home to as many as 1 million people densely packed into thousands of tiny shacks fashioned from scrap metal, plastic sheeting and other scrounged materials. Narrow, muddy alleys crisscross the 600-acre site, open sewers carry human waste and vacant lots serve as garbage dumps. There is electricity, but running water is available for only an hour or so a day. Amid the squalor, barefoot children sing for money, beg from drivers in nearby traffic or work in garment and leather shops, recycling operations and other lightly regulated businesses.

Moviegoers around the globe got a glimpse of life inside Dharavi in last year's phenomenally popular Oscar-winning film "Slumdog Millionaire," about plucky Jamal Malik, a fictional Dharavi teenager who improbably wins a TV quiz-show jackpot. The no-holds-barred portrayal of slum life may have been shocking to affluent Westerners, but Dharavi is only one of Asia's innumerable slums. In fact, about a billion people worldwide live in urban slums — the ugly underbelly of the rapid and haphazard urbanization that has occurred in many parts of the world in recent decades. And if soaring urban growth rates continue unabated, the world's slum population is expected to double to 2 billion by 2030, according to the U.N.[1]

But all city dwellers don't live in slums. Indeed, other fast-growing cities presented cheerier faces to the world last year, from Dubai's glittering luxury skyscrapers to Beijing's breathtaking, high-tech pre-Olympic cultural spectacle.

World Will Have 26 Megacities by 2025

The number of megacities — urban areas with at least 10 million residents — will increase from 19 to 26 worldwide by the year 2025, according to the United Nations. The seven new megacities will be in Asia and sub-Saharan Africa. Most megacities are in coastal areas, making them highly vulnerable to massive loss of life and property damage caused by rising sea levels that experts predict will result from climate change in the 21st century.

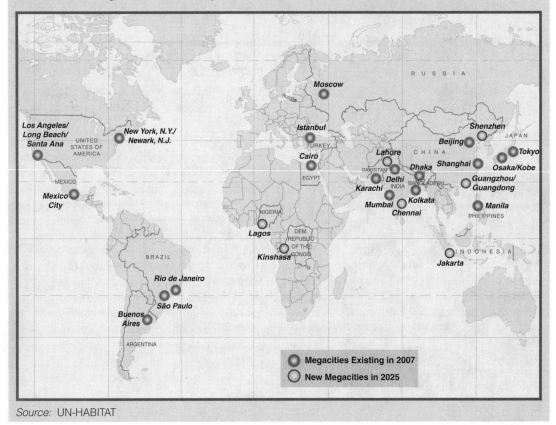

Source: UN-HABITAT

Today, 3.3 billion people live in cities — half the world's population — and urbanites are projected to total nearly 5 billion (out of 8.1 billion) worldwide by 2030.[2] About 95 percent of that growth is occurring in the developing world, especially in Africa and Asia.[3]

These regions are going through the same threefold evolution that transformed Europe and North America over a 200-year period between 1750 and 1950: the industrialization of agriculture, followed by rural migration to cities and declining population growth as life expectancy improves. But today's developing countries are modernizing much faster — typically in less than 100 years — and their cities are expanding at dizzying rates: On average, 5 million people in developing countries move to cities every month. As urban areas struggle to absorb this growth, the new residents often end up crowded into already teeming slums. For instance, 62 percent of city dwellers in sub-Saharan Africa live in slums, 43 percent in southern Asia, 37 percent in East Asia and 27 percent in Latin America and the Caribbean, according to UN-HABITAT, the United Nations agency for human settlements.[4]

UN-HABITAT defines a slum as an urban area without at least one of the following features:

- Durable housing,
- Adequate living space (no more than three people per room),
- Access to clean drinking water,
- Access to improved sanitation (toilets or latrines that separate human waste from contact with water sources), or
- Secure property rights.[5]

But all slums are not the same. Some lack only one basic necessity, while others lack several. And conditions can be harsh in non-slum neighborhoods as well. Thus, experts say, policies should focus on specific local problems in order to make a difference in the lives of poor city dwellers.[6]

Cities "are potent instruments for national economic and social development. They attract investment and create wealth," said HABITAT Executive Director Anna Tibaijuka last April. But, she warned, cities also concentrate poverty and deprivation, especially in developing countries. "Rapid and chaotic urbanization is being accompanied by increasing inequalities, which pose enormous challenges to human security and safety."[7]

Today, improving urban life is an important international development priority.[8] One of the eight U.N. Millennium Development Goals (MDGs) — broad objectives intended to end poverty worldwide by 2015 — endorsed by world leaders in 2000 was environmental sustainability. Among other things, it aims to cut in half the portion of the world's people without access to safe drinking water and achieve "significant improvement" in the lives of at least 100 million slum dwellers.[9]

Tokyo Is by Far the World's Biggest City

With more than 35 million residents, Tokyo is nearly twice as big as the next-biggest metropolises. Tokyo is projected to remain the world's largest city in 2025, when there will be seven new megacities — urban areas with at least 10 million residents. Two Indian cities, Mumbai and Delhi, will overtake Mexico City and New York as the world's second- and third-largest cities. The two largest newcomers in 2025 will be in Africa: Kinshasa and Lagos.

Population of Megacities, 2007 and 2025
(in millions)

2007		2025 (projected)	
Tokyo, Japan	35.68	Tokyo, Japan	36.40
New York, NY/Newark, NJ	19.04	Mumbai, India	26.39
Mexico City, Mexico	19.03	Delhi, India	22.50
Mumbai, India	18.98	Dhaka, Bangladesh	22.02
São Paulo, Brazil	18.85	São Paulo, Brazil	21.43
Delhi, India	15.93	Mexico City, Mexico	21.01
Shanghai, China	14.99	New York, NY/Newark, NJ	20.63
Kolkata, India	14.79	Kolkata, India	20.56
Dhaka, Bangladesh	13.49	Shanghai, China	19.41
Buenos Aires, Argentina	12.80	Karachi, Pakistan	19.10
Los Angeles/Long Beach/ Santa Ana (CA)	12.50	Kinshasa, Dem. Rep. Congo	16.76
Karachi, Pakistan	12.13	Lagos, Nigeria	15.80
Cairo, Egypt	11.89	Cairo, Egypt	15.56
Rio de Janeiro, Brazil	11.75	Manila, Philippines	14.81
Osaka/Kobe, Japan	11.29	Beijing, China	14.55
Beijing, China	11.11	Buenos Aires, Argentina	13.77
Manila, Philippines	11.10	Los Angeles/Long Beach/ Santa Ana (CA)	13.67
Moscow, Russia	10.45	Rio de Janeiro, Brazil	13.41
Istanbul, Turkey	10.06	Jakarta, Indonesia	12.36
		Istanbul, Turkey	12.10
		Guangzhou/Guangdong, China	11.84
		Osaka/Kobe, Japan	11.37
		Moscow, Russia	10.53
		Lahore, Pakistan	10.51
		Shenzhen, China	10.20
		Chennai, India	10.13

New megacities in 2025

Source: UN-HABITAT

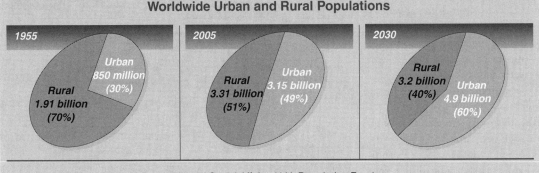

Global Population Is Shifting to Cities

Half a century ago, less than a third of the world's population lived in cities. By 2005, nearly half inhabited urban areas, and in 2030, at least 60 percent of the world's population will be living in cities, reflecting an unprecedented scale of urban growth in the developing world. This will be particularly notable in Africa and Asia, where the urban population will double between 2000 and 2030.

Worldwide Urban and Rural Populations

1955
Urban 850 million (30%)
Rural 1.91 billion (70%)

2005
Rural 3.31 billion (51%)
Urban 3.15 billion (49%)

2030
Rural 3.2 billion (40%)
Urban 4.9 billion (60%)

Source: U.N. Department of Economic and Social Affairs; U.N. Population Fund

Delivering even the most basic city services is an enormous challenge in many of the world's 19 megacities — metropolises with more than 10 million residents. And smaller cities with fewer than 1 million inhabitants are growing even faster in both size and number than larger ones.[10]

Many fast-growing cities struggle with choking air pollution, congested traffic, polluted water supplies and inadequate sanitation services. The lack of services can contribute to larger social and economic problems. For example, slum dwellers without permanent housing or access to mass transit have trouble finding and holding jobs. And when poverty becomes entrenched it reinforces the gulf between rich and poor, which can promote crime and social unrest.

"A city is a system of systems. It has biological, social and technical parts, and they all interact," says George Bugliarello, president emeritus of Polytechnic University in New York and foreign secretary of the National Academy of Engineering. "It's what engineers call a complex system because it has features that are more than the sum of its parts. You have to understand how all of the components interact to guide them."

Improving life for the urban poor begins with providing shelter, sanitation and basic social services like health care and education. But more is needed to make cities truly inclusive, such as guaranteeing slum dwellers' property rights so they cannot be ejected from their homes.[11]

Access to information and communications technology (ICT) is also crucial. In some developing countries, ICT has been adopted widely, particularly cell phones, but high-speed Internet access and computer use still lag behind levels in rich nations. Technology advocates say this "digital divide" slows economic growth in developing nations and increases income inequality both within and between countries. Others say the problem has been exaggerated and that there is no critical link between ICTs and poverty reduction.

Managing urban growth and preventing the creation of new slums are keys to both improving the quality of life and better protecting cities from natural disasters. Many large cities are in areas at risk from earthquakes, wildfires or floods. Squatter neighborhoods are often built on flood plains, steep slopes or other vulnerable areas, and poor people usually have fewer resources to escape or relocate.

For example, heavy rains in northern Venezuela in 1999 caused mudslides and debris flows that demolished many hillside shantytowns around the capital city of Caracas, killing some 30,000 people. In 2005 Hurricane Katrina killed more people in New Orleans' lower-income neighborhoods, which were located in a flood plain, than in wealthier neighbor-hoods of the Louisiana port city that were built on higher ground. As global warming raises sea levels, many of the world's largest cities are expected to be increasingly at risk from flooding.

Paradoxically, economic growth also can pose a risk for some cities. Large cities can be attractive targets for terrorist attacks, especially if they are symbols of national prosperity and modernity, such as New York City, site of the Sept. 11, 2001, attack on the World Trade Center. Last November's coordinated Islamic ter-rorist attacks in Mumbai followed a similar strategy: Landmark properties frequented by foreigners were targeted in order to draw worldwide media coverage, damage India's economy and send a message that nowhere in India was safe.[12]

Today the global economic reces-sion is creating a new problem for city dwellers: Entry-level jobs are disappearing as trade con-tracts evaporate and factories shut down. Unable to find other jobs, many recent migrants to cities are returning to rural areas that are ill-prepared to receive them, and laborers who remain in cities have less money to send to families back home.[13]

As national leaders, development experts and city officials debate how to manage urban growth, here are some issues they are considering:

Does urbanization make people better off?

With a billion city dwellers worldwide trapped in slums, why do people keep moving to cities? Demographic experts say that newcomers hope to earn higher incomes and find more opportunities than rural areas can offer.

"Often people are fleeing desperate economic condi-tions," says David Bloom, a professor of economics and demography at Harvard University's School of Public Health. "And the social attractions of a city — opportu-nities to meet more people, escape from isolation or in some cases to be anonymous — trump fears about

Most African City Dwellers Live in Slums

Most of the world's slum dwellers are in developing countries, with nearly two-thirds of sub-Saharan Africa's city dwellers living in slums.

Percentage of Urban Populations Living in Slums, by Region

☐ sub-Saharan Africa	☐ Eastern Asia	☐ Latin America/ Caribbean	☐ Western Asia
☐ Southern Asia	☐ Southeastern Asia	☐ Oceania	☐ Northern Africa

Source: UN-HABITAT, State of the World's Cities 2008-2009

difficult urban conditions. If they have relatives or friends living in cities already, that reduces some of the risk."

When nations attract foreign investment, it creates new jobs. In the 1990s both China and India instituted broad economic reforms designed to encourage foreign invest-ment, paving the way for rapid economic growth. That growth accelerated as information technology advances like the Internet, fiber-optic networks and e-mail made it faster and cheaper to communicate worldwide in real time.[14] As a result, thousands of manufacturing and white-collar jobs were "outsourced" from the United States to India, China and other low-wage countries over the past decade.[15]

These jobs spurred major growth in some cities, especially in areas with educated, English-speaking work forces. The large southern Indian city of Bangalore became a center for information technology — dubbed "India's Silicon Valley." Other cities in India, Singapore and the Philippines now host English-language call cen-ters that manage everything from computer technical support to lost-baggage complaints for airlines. In a

Packed buses in Dhaka take residents in the Bangladeshi capital to their homes in outlying villages on the eve of the Muslim holiday Eid al-Adha — the "Festival of Sacrifice." Rapidly growing cities have trouble keeping up with the transportation needs of residents.

twist on this model, the Chinese city of Dalian — which was controlled by Japan from 1895 through World War II and still has many Japanese speakers — has become a major outsourcing center for Japanese companies.[16]

Some observers say an increasingly networked world allows people to compete for global "knowledge work" from anywhere in the world instead of having to emigrate to developed countries. In his best-seller *The World Is Flat*, author and *New York Times* columnist Thomas Friedman cites Asian call centers as an example of this shift, since educated Indians can work at the centers and prosper at home rather than seeking opportunity abroad. While he acknowledges that millions of people in developing countries are poor, sick and disempowered, Friedman argues that things improve when people move from rural to urban areas.

"[E]xcess labor gets trained and educated, it begins working in services and industry; that leads to innovation and better education and universities, freer markets, economic growth and development, better infrastructure, fewer diseases and slower population growth," Friedman writes. "It is that dynamic that is going on in parts of urban India and urban China today, enabling people to compete on a level playing field and attracting investment dollars by the billions."[17]

But others say it's not always so simple. Educated newcomers may be able to find good jobs, but migrants without skills or training often end up working in the "informal economy" — activities that are not taxed, regulated or monitored by the government, such as selling goods on the street or collecting garbage for recycling. These jobs are easy to get but come without minimum wages or labor standards, and few workers can get credit to grow their businesses. Members of ethnic minorities and other underprivileged groups, such as lower castes in India, often are stuck with the dirtiest and most dangerous and difficult tasks.[18]

And some countries have experienced urban growth without job growth. Through the late 1980s, many Latin American countries tried to grow their economies by producing manufactured goods at home instead of importing them from abroad.

"Years of government protection insulated these industries from outside competition, so they did not feel pressure to become more productive. Then they went under when economies opened up to trade," says Steven Poelhekke, a researcher with DNB, the national bank of the Netherlands. "In Africa, industrialization has never really taken off. And without job creation governments cannot deliver benefits for new urbanites."[19]

Meanwhile, when cities grow too quickly, competition for land, space, light and services increases faster than government can respond. Real estate prices rise, driving poor residents into squatter neighborhoods, where crowding and pollution spread disease. "When cities get too big, the downsides to city life are bigger than the benefits for vulnerable inhabitants," says Poelhekke.

Broadly, however, urbanization has reduced the total number of people in poverty in recent years. According to a 2007 World Bank study, about three-quarters of the world's poor still live in rural areas. Poor people are urbanizing faster than the population as a whole, so some poverty is shifting to cities. Yet, clearly, many of those new urbanites are finding higher incomes — even if they end up living in city slums — because overall poverty rates (urban plus rural) fall as countries urbanize. While the persistence of urban poverty is a serious concern, the authors concluded, if people moved to the cities faster, overall poverty rates would decline sooner.[20]

Many development advocates say policy makers must accept urbanization as inevitable and strive to make it more beneficial. "We need to stop seeing migration to cities as a problem," says Priya Deshingkar, a researcher at the Overseas Development Institute in Hyderabad, India. "These people were already vulnerable because they can't make a living in rural areas. Countries need to rethink their development strategies. The world is urbanizing, and we have to make more provisions for people moving to urban areas. They can't depend on agriculture alone."

Should governments limit migration to cities?

Many governments have tried to limit urban problems by discouraging migration to cities or regulating the pace of urban growth. Some countries use household registration policies, while others direct aid and economic development funds to rural areas. Political leaders say limiting migration reduces strains on city systems, slows the growth of slums and keeps villages from languishing as their most enterprising residents leave.

China's *hukou* system, for example, requires households to register with the government and classifies individuals as rural or urban residents. Children inherit their *hukou* status from their parents. Established in the 1950s, the system was tightly controlled to limit migration from agricultural areas to cities and to monitor criminals, government critics and other suspect citizens and groups.[21]

In the late 1970s China began privatizing farming and opened its economy to international trade, creating a rural labor surplus and greater demand for city workers. The government offered rural workers temporary residence permits in cities and allowed wealthy, educated citizens to buy urban *hukou* designations. Many rural Chinese also moved to cities without changing their registration. According to recent government estimates, at least 120 million migrant workers have moved to Chinese cities since the early 1980s.[22] Today *hukou* rules are enforced inconsistently in different Chinese cities, where many rural migrants cannot get access to health care, education, affordable housing or other urban services because they are there illegally.

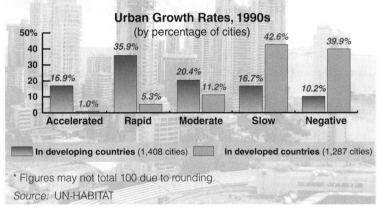

Cities in Developing World Growing Rapidly

More than half the developing world's cities experienced fast annual growth in the 1990s, compared to just 6.3 percent of those in wealthier countries. Conversely, more than 80 percent of cities in the wealthier countries had slow or negative growth, compared to about a quarter of those in developing countries.

Urban Growth Rates, 1990s
(by percentage of cities)

	Accelerated	Rapid	Moderate	Slow	Negative
In developing countries (1,408 cities)	16.9%	35.9%	20.4%	16.7%	10.2%
In developed countries (1,287 cities)	1.0%	5.3%	11.2%	42.6%	39.9%

* Figures may not total 100 due to rounding.
Source: UN-HABITAT

Chinese officials say they must manage growth so all areas of the country will benefit. In a 2007 report to the 17th Communist Party Congress, President Hu Jintao promised to promote "a path of urbanization with Chinese characteristics" that emphasized "balanced development of large, medium-sized and small cities and towns."[23]

But critics say the *hukou* system has created an urban underclass and should be scrapped. When the municipality of Chongqing (which omits an estimated 4.5 million migrant workers from its official population figures) established November 4 as Migrant Workers' Day in 2007, the *Asia Times* commented, "By not changing the [*hukou*] system and instead giving the migrant workers a special holiday, it's a bit like showing starving people menus instead of feeding them."[24]

India and Vietnam also control migration to urban areas by requiring people to register or show local identity cards to access social services. "They're both trying to promote rural development and keep from overburdening urban areas," says Deshingkar at the Overseas Development Institute. "But it doesn't work. People move despite these regulations. It just makes it harder for them, and if they can access services it's at a price."

Many experts say governments should not try to halt rural-to-city migration because when migrant workers send large shares of their wages home to their families in the country it helps reduce rural poverty and inequality. In Dhaka, Bangladesh, for example, remittances from city workers provide up to 80 percent of rural households' budgets, according to the Coalition for the Urban Poor.[25]

Urban growth also helps rural economies by creating larger markets for agricultural products — including high-value products like meat, chicken and fish that people tend to add to their diets as their incomes rise. Cities can promote economic growth in surrounding areas by creating a demand for local farmers' products. For instance, South Africa's Johannesburg Fresh Produce Market offers vendors stalls, overnight storage space, business-skills training and financing; it also requires market agents to buy at least 10 percent of their produce from small, low-income farms.[26]

However, the rootless lifestyle adopted by so-called circular migrants — those who move back and forth between the city and the country — makes people vulnerable, Deshingkar points out. "There are roughly 100 million circular migrants in India now, and they're completely missed by official statistics because the government only counts permanent migrants," she says. "They can't get any insurance or social services, so they carry all the risk themselves."

Beyond the fact that anti-migration policies usually fail, experts say the biggest factor driving population increase in many fast-growing cities is not new residents moving in but "natural increase" — the rate at which people already living there have children. Natural increase accounts for about 60 percent of urban growth worldwide, while 20 percent comes from domestic and international migration and 20 percent results from reclassification of rural areas as urban.[27]

Family-planning programs helped reduce poverty rates in several developing Asian countries — including South Korea, Taiwan, Thailand, Singapore, Indonesia and Malaysia — where having smaller families increased household savings and reduced national education costs.[28] In contrast, artificial birth control is difficult to obtain in the Philippines, where the population is 80 percent Catholic and the government supports only "natural" family planning. Several professors at the University of the Philippines have calculated that if Filipinos had

followed Thailand's example on family planning in the 1970s, the Philippines would have at least 4 million fewer people in poverty and would be exporting rice rather than importing it. Instead, the Philippine government's opposition to family planning "contributed to the country's degeneration into Southeast Asia's basket case," said economist Arsenio Balisacan.[29]

Can we make large cities greener?

Many fast-growing cities are unhealthy places to live because of dirty air, polluted water supplies and sprawling waste dumps. City governments worldwide are increasingly interested in making their cities greener and more sustainable.

Greening cities has many up-front costs but can provide big payoffs. For example, energy-efficient buildings cost less to operate and give cities cachet as centers for advanced technology and design.

Green policies also may help cities achieve broader social goals. When Enrique Peñalosa was elected mayor of Bogotá, Colombia, in 1998, the city was overrun with traffic and crime. Wealthy residents lived in walled-off neighborhoods, while workers were squeezed into shanties on the city's outskirts. Under Peñalosa's rule, the city built hundreds of new parks and a rapid-transit bus system, limited automobile use, banned sidewalk parking and constructed a 14-mile-long street for bicyclists and pedestrians that runs through some of the city's poorest neighborhoods. The underlying goal of the programs: Make Bogotá more people-friendly for poor residents as well as the rich.

"[A]nything that you do in order to increase pedestrian space constructs equality" said Peñalosa, who now consults with city officials in other developing countries. "It's a powerful symbol showing that citizens who walk are equally important to those who have a car."[30] His administration also invested funds that might otherwise have been spent building highways in social services like schools and libraries. Air pollution decreased as more residents shifted to mass transit. Crime rates also fell, partly because more people were out on the streets.[31]

"Mobility and land use may be the most important issues that a mayor can address, because to unlock the economic potential of cities people have to be able to move from one area to another," says Polytechnic University's Bugliarello. "You also have to take care of water supplies and sanitation, because cities concentrate people and pathologies. Appropriate technologies aren't always the most expensive options, especially if cities get together and form markets for them."

For example, bus rapid transit (BRT) systems, which create networks of dedicated lanes for high-speed buses, are much cheaper than subways but faster than conventional buses that move in city traffic. By 2007 some 40 cities worldwide had developed BRT systems, including Bogotá; Jakarta, Indonesia; and Guayaquil, Ecuador. Many others are planned or under construction.[32]

Some developing countries are planning entire green cities with walkable neighborhoods, efficient mass transit and renewable-energy systems. Abu Dhabi, part of the United Arab Emirates on the Persian Gulf, is designing a $20 billion project called Masdar City, which it bills as the world's first carbon-neutral, zero-waste city. Located on the coast next to Abu Dhabi's airport, Masdar City will be a mixed-use community with about 40,000 residents and 50,000 commuters traveling in to work at high-tech companies. Plans call for the city to be car-free and powered mainly by solar energy.[33]

Abu Dhabi wants to become a global hub for clean technologies, according to Khaled Awad, property development director for the Masdar initiative. "It lets us leverage our energy knowledge [from oil and gas production] and our research and development skills and adapt them to new energy markets," he said.

"If we can do it there, we can do it anywhere," said Matthias Schuler, an engineer with the German climate-engineering firm Transsolar and a member of the international Masdar City design and planning team.[34] He points out that average daytime summer temperatures in Abu Dhabi are well over 100 degrees Fahrenheit, and coastal zones are very humid. "You can't find a harsher climate."

In China, meanwhile, green urban design is gaining support as a way to attract foreign investment and demonstrate environmental awareness. But some showpiece projects are falling short of expectations.

Huangbaiyu was supposed to be a sustainable "green village" that would provide new homes for a farming town of more than 1,400 in rural northeast China. But the master plan, produced by a high-profile U.S. green architecture firm, called for 400 densely clustered bungalows without enough yard space for livestock. This meant that villagers would lose their existing income from

backyard gardens, sheep flocks and trout ponds. The plan also proposed to use corncobs and stalks to fuel a biogas plant for heat, but villagers needed these crop wastes as winter feed for their goats.

By December 2008 the Chinese builder had constructed 42 houses, but only a few were occupied. The designer blamed the builder for putting up low-quality houses, but others said the plan did not reflect what villagers wanted or needed.[35] Planners "inadvertently designed an ecologically sound plan — from the perspectives of both birds and the green movement — that would devastate the local economy and bankrupt the households whose lives were to be improved," wrote Shannon May, an American graduate student who lived in the old village of Huangbaiyu for two years and wrote her dissertation on the project.[36]

Dongtan, a larger Chinese city designed as a green project with zero-carbon-emission buildings and transit systems, has also been sidetracked. Groundbreaking on the model city of 500,000 on a Manhattan-sized island near Shanghai is more than a year behind schedule. Highrise towers are sprouting up around the site, leading some observers to call the project expensive "greenwashing" — attempting to make lavish development acceptable by tacking on environmentally friendly features.

" 'Zero-emission' city is pure commercial hype," said Dai Xingyi, a professor at Fudan University in Shanghai. "You can't expect some technology to both offer you a luxurious and comfortable life and save energy at the same time. That's just a dream."[37]

Construction is also under way on a new green city southeast of Beijing for 350,000 residents, co-developed by China and Singapore. Tianjin's features include renewable-energy sources, efficient water use and green building standards. Premier Wen Jiabao attended the 2008 groundbreaking.[38]

Although China's green development projects have a mixed record so far, "The government is starting to recognize that it has responsibility for environmental impacts beyond its borders, mainly by promoting renewable energy," says Alastair MacGregor, associate vice president of AECOM, an international design firm with large building projects in China. "Chinese culture is playing catch-up on sustainability."

More than 130 buildings designed to LEED (Leadership in Energy and Environmental Design)

China Aggressively Tackles Air Pollution

"No country in developing Asia takes those challenges more seriously"

China's large cities have some of the world's worst air pollution, thanks to rapid industrial growth, heavy use of coal and growing demand for cars.

The capital, Beijing, lost its 1993 bid to host the 2000 Summer Olympic Games partly because the city was so polluted. A chronic grey haze not only sullied Beijing's international image but also threatened to cause health problems for athletes and impair their performances.

When Beijing was chosen in 2001 to host the 2008 Summer Games, it pledged to put on a "green Olympics," which was widely understood to include clearing the air.

Between 2001 and 2007, however, China's economy grew beyond all predictions, with its gross domestic product expanding by up to 13 percent a year.[1] Beijing's air pollution worsened as new factories, power plants and cars crowded into the city. Winds carried in more pollutants from other burgeoning cities, including nitrogen oxides and sulfur dioxide — which contribute to acid rain and smog — and fine particulates, which can cause or worsen heart and lung problems.

With the Olympic deadline looming, many observers predicted Beijing would not meet its targets even if it relied heavily on authoritarian measures like shutting down factories and limiting auto use.[2] International Olympic Committee President Jacques Rogge said some outdoor endurance sports might have to be postponed if they occurred on high-pollution days — an embarrassing prospect for Chinese leaders.[3]

But China met its promised target, keeping Beijing's daily air pollution index — based on combined measurements of sulfur dioxide, nitrogen dioxide and fine particulates — below 100 during the month the Olympics took place. A 100 index score means air quality will not affect daily activities, compared to a maximum score of 500, when officials warn residents to stay indoors. In fact, during the Olympics in August 2008 Beijing's daily air pollution reached the lowest August measurements since 2000, sometimes even dropping into the 20s.[4]

"No country in Asia has bigger air quality challenges than China, but no country in developing Asia takes those challenges more seriously," says Cornie Huizenga, executive director of the Clean Air Initiative for Asian Cities (CAI-Asia), an international network based in the Philippines and founded by the Asian Development Bank, the World Bank and the U.S. Agency for International Development. "China has taken a whole series of long-term structural measures to address air pollution. The Olympics put a

standards — which measure energy efficiency and healthy indoor working conditions — are planned or under construction in Beijing, Shanghai, Chongqing, Wuhan and other Chinese cities.[39] Chinese investors see LEED buildings as premium products, not as an everyday model, said MacGregor.

Some Chinese cities are developing their own green standards. About half of worldwide new construction between 2008 through 2015 is projected to occur in China, so even greening a modest share of that development would be significant.

"China could end up being a sustainability leader just by virtue of its size," MacGregor predicted.[40]

BACKGROUND

From Farm to Factory

At the beginning of the 19th century only 3 percent of the world's population lived in cities, and only Beijing had more than a million inhabitants.[41] Then new technologies like the steam engine and railroads began to transform society. As the Industrial Revolution unfolded, people streamed from rural areas to manufacturing centers in Europe and the United States seeking a better income and life. This first great wave of urbanization established cities like London, Paris and New York as centers of global commerce.

magnifying glass on Beijing and made them focus there, but its programs are much bigger."

For instance, China continuously monitors air quality in more than 100 cities, requires high-polluting provinces and companies to close small, inefficient emission sources and install pollution-control equipment and has new-car emissions standards roughly equivalent to U.S. and Western European laws.

"For the Olympics China took temporary measures on top of those policies, like closing down large facilities and keeping cars off the roads. All of this plus good weather let Beijing deliver what it promised for the Games," says Huizenga.

Now China is further expanding air pollution regulations. During the Olympics, the Ministry of Environment announced that in 2009 it would start monitoring ultrafine particle and ozone pollution — persistent problems in many developed countries. And Beijing officials plan to increase spending on public transportation.

Local pollution sources, weather patterns and geography influence air pollution, so China's policies for cleaning up Beijing's air might not work in other large cities. Mexico City, for instance, also has tried to reduce its severe air pollution but is hampered by the city's high altitude (7,200 feet). Car engines burn fuel inefficiently at high altitudes, so they pollute more than at sea level. And while automobiles are the biggest emission sources, scientists also found that leaking liquefied petroleum gas (LPG) — which most Mexican households burn for cooking and heating — also contributes to Mexico City's air pollution.[5]

"We need better-harmonized air quality monitoring in developing countries before we can compare them," says Huizenga. "But other cities should be able to make progress on a large scale like Beijing. There's a lot of low-hanging fruit, such as switching to cleaner transportation fuels, getting rid of vehicles with [high-polluting] two-stroke engines, managing dust at construction sites and cutting pollution from coal-fired power plants. But to make them work, you also need effective agencies with enough people and money to carry [out] policies."

[1] Michael Yang, "China's GDP (2003-2007)," forum.china.org.cn, Nov. 10, 2008; "China Revises 2007 GDP Growth Rate to 13%," Jan. 15, 2009, http://english.dbw.cn.

[2] Edward Russell, "Beijing's 'Green Olympics' Test Run Fizzles," *Asia Times*, Aug. 10, 2007; Jim Yardley, "Beijing's Olympic Quest: Turn Smoggy Sky Blue," *The New York Times*, Dec. 29, 2007; David G. Streets, *et al.*, "Air Quality during the 2008 Beijing Olympic Games," *Atmospheric Environment*, vol. 41 (2007).

[3] "IOC President: Beijing Air Pollution Could Cause Events to Be Delayed During 2008 Olympics," The Associated Press, Aug. 7, 2007.

[4] "Summary: AQ in Beijing During the 2008 Summer Olympics," Clean Air Initiative for Asian Cities, www.cleanairnet.org/caiasia/1412/article-72991.html. Weather conditions are important factors in air pollution levels — for example, summer heat and humidity promote the formation of ground-level ozone, a major ingredient of smog — so to put conditions during the Olympics in context, scientists compared them to readings taken in August of previous years.

[5] Tim Weiner, "Terrific News in Mexico City: Air Is Sometimes Breathable," *The New York Times*, Jan. 5, 2001.

It also spawned horrific slums in factory towns and large cities. Tenement houses became a feature of working-class neighborhoods, with little access to fresh air or clean drinking water. Often whole neighborhoods shared a single water pump or toilet, and trash was usually thrown into the streets.[42]

German social scientist and a co-founder of communist theory Friedrich Engels graphically described urban workers' living conditions in cities like London and Manchester in 1844: "[T]hey are penned in dozens into single rooms. . . . They are given damp dwellings, cellar dens that are not waterproof from below or garrets that leak from above. . . . They are supplied bad, tattered or rotten clothing, adulterated or indigestible food. . . . Thus are the workers cast out and ignored by the class in power, morally as well as physically and mentally."[43]

Engels and his collaborator Karl Marx later predicted in *The Communist Manifesto* that oppression of the working class would lead to revolution in industrialized countries. Instead, public health movements began to develop in Europe and the United States in mid-century. Seeking to curb repeated cholera and typhoid epidemics, cities began collecting garbage and improving water-supply systems. A new medical specialty, epidemiology (the study of how infections are spread) developed as scientists worked to track and contain illnesses. Cities built

CHRONOLOGY

1700s-1800s *Industrial Revolution spurs rapid urban growth in Europe and the U.S. Expanding slums trigger reforms and public health laws.*

1804 World population reaches 1 billion.

1854 British doctor John Snow discovers the connection between contaminated drinking water and a cholera outbreak in London.

1897 Brazil's first *favela* (shanty town), is established outside Rio de Janeiro.

1900-1960s *Europe and the United States are the most urbanized. Africa and Asia begin gaining independence and struggle to develop healthy economies.*

1906 An earthquake and subsequent fire destroy much of San Francisco, killing more than 3,000 people.

1927 World population reaches 2 billion.

1949 Chinese communists defeat nationalists, establishing the People's Republic of China, which aggressively promotes industrial development.

1960 World population hits 3 billion.

1964 Tokyo becomes first Asian city to host the Olympic Games and soon after that displaces New York as the world's largest city.

1970s-1990s *Urbanization accelerates in Asia and Africa. Many U.S. and European cities shrink as residents move to suburbs.*

1971 East Pakistan secedes from West Pakistan and becomes the independent nation of Bangladesh; populations in Dhaka and other cities grow rapidly.

1974 World population reaches 4 billion.

1979 China initiates broad economic reforms, opens diplomatic and trade relations with the United States and starts to ease limits on migration to cities.

1985 An earthquake in Mexico City kills some 10,000 people and damages water-supply and transit systems.

1987 World population reaches 5 billion.

1991 India institutes sweeping market reforms to attract foreign investors and spur rapid economic growth.

1999 World population reaches 6 billion.

2000s *Most industrialized countries stabilize at 70-80 percent urban. Cities continue to grow in Asia and Africa.*

2000 International community endorses the U.N. Millennium Development Goals designed to end poverty by 2015, including improving the lives of slum dwellers.

2001 Many international companies shift production to China after it joins the World Trade Organization; migration from rural areas accelerates. . . . Terrorists destroy World Trade Center towers in New York City, killing thousands. . . . Taiwan completes Taipei 101, the world's tallest skyscraper (1,671 feet), superseding the Petronas Towers in Kuala Lumpur, Malaysia (1,483 feet).

2005 United Nations condemns Zimbabwe for slum-clearance operations that leave 700,000 people homeless.

2007 The nonprofit group One Laptop Per Child unveils a prototype $100 laptop computer designed for children in developing countries to help close the "digital divide" between cities and rural areas.

2008 More than half of the world's population lives in cities. . . . Beijing hosts Summer Olympic Games. . . . Coordinated terrorist attacks in Mumbai kill nearly 170 people and injure more than 300.

2009 A global recession leaves millions of urban workers jobless, forcing many to return to their home villages.

2030 World's urban population is expected to reach 5 billion, and its slum population could top 2 billion.

2070 About 150 million city dwellers — primarily in India, Bangladesh, China, Vietnam, Thailand, Myanmar and Florida — could be in danger due to climate change, according to a 2008 study.

green spaces like New York's Central Park to provide fresh air and access to nature. To help residents navigate around town, electric streetcars and subway trains were built in underground tunnels or on elevated tracks above the streets.

Many problems persisted, however. Homes and factories burned coal for heat and power, blanketing many large cities in smoky haze. Horse-drawn vehicles remained in wide use until the early-20th century, so urban streets were choked with animal waste. Wealthy city dwellers, seeking havens from the noise, dirt and crowding of inner cities, moved out to cleaner suburban neighborhoods.

Despite harsh conditions, people continued to pour into cities. Economic growth in industrialized countries had ripple effects in developing countries. As wealthier countries imported more and more raw materials, commercial "gateway cities" in developing countries grew as well, including Buenos Aires, Rio de Janeiro and Calcutta (now Kolkata). By 1900, nearly 14 percent of the world's population lived in cities.[44]

End of Empires

Worldwide migration from country to city accelerated in the early-20th century as automation spread and fewer people were needed to grow food. But growth was not uniform. Wars devastated some of Europe's major cities while industrial production swelled others. And when colonial empires dissolved after World War II, many people were displaced in newly independent nations.

Much of the fighting during World War I occurred in fields and trenches, so few of Europe's great cities were seriously damaged. By the late 1930s, however, long-range bombers could attack cities hundreds of miles away. Madrid and Barcelona were bombed during the Spanish Civil War, a prelude to intensive air attacks on London, Vienna, Berlin, Tokyo and elsewhere during World War II. In 1945 the United States dropped atomic bombs on the Japanese cities of Hiroshima and Nagasaki, destroying each. For centuries cities had walled themselves off against outside threats, but now they were vulnerable to air attacks from thousands of miles away.

After 1945, even victorious nations like Britain and France were greatly weakened and unable to manage overseas colonies, where independence movements were underway. As European countries withdrew from their holdings in the Middle East, Asia and Africa over the next 25 years, a wave of countries gained independence, including Indonesia, India, Pakistan, the Philippines, Syria, Vietnam and most of colonial Africa. Wealthy countries began providing aid to the new developing countries, especially in Asia and Latin America. But some nations, especially in Africa, received little focused support.

By mid-century most industrialized countries were heavily urbanized, and their populations were no longer growing rapidly. By 1950 three of the world's largest cities — Shanghai, Buenos Aires and Calcutta — were in developing countries. Populations in developing countries continued to rise through the late 1960s even as those nations struggled to industrialize. Many rural residents moved to cities, seeking work and educational opportunities.

In the 1950s and '60s U.S. urban planners heatedly debated competing approaches to city planning. The top-down, centralized philosophy was espoused by Robert Moses, the hard-charging parks commissioner and head of New York City's highway agency from 1934 to 1968. Moses pushed through numerous bridge, highway, park and slum-clearance projects that remade New York but earned him an image as arrogant and uncaring.[45] His most famous critic, writer and activist Jane Jacobs, advocated preserving dense, mixed-use neighborhoods, like New York's Greenwich Village, and consulting with residents to build support for development plans.[46] Similar controversies would arise later in developing countries.

By the 1960s car-centered growth characterized many of the world's large cities. "Circle over London, Buenos Aires, Chicago, Sydney, in an airplane," wrote American historian Lewis Mumford in 1961. "The original container has completely disappeared: the sharp division between city and country no longer exists." City officials, Mumford argued, only measured improvements in quantities, such as wider streets and bigger parking lots.

"[T]hey would multiply bridges, highways [and] tunnels, making it ever easier to get in and out of the city but constricting the amount of space available within the city for any other purpose than transportation itself," Mumford charged.[47]

Population Boom

In the 1970s and '80s, as populations in developing countries continued to grow and improved agricultural

Cities Need to Plan for Disasters and Attacks

Concentrated populations and wealth magnify impact

Flash floods in 1999 caused landslides in the hills around Caracas, Venezuela, that washed away hundreds of hillside shanties and killed an estimated 30,000 people — more than 10 times the number of victims of the Sept. 11, 2001, terrorist attacks in the United States.

Because cities concentrate populations and wealth, natural disasters in urban areas can kill or displace thousands of people and cause massive damage to property and infrastructure. Many cities are located on earthquake faults, flood plains, fire-prone areas and other locations that make them vulnerable. The impacts are magnified when high-density slums and squatter neighborhoods are built in marginal areas. Political instability or terrorism can also cause widespread destruction.

Protecting cities requires both "hard" investments, such as flood-control systems or earthquake-resistant buildings, and "soft" approaches, such as emergency warning systems and special training for police and emergency-response forces. Cities also can improve their forecasting capacity and train officials to assess different types of risk.[1] Although preventive strategies are expensive, time-consuming and often politically controversial, failing to prepare for outside threats can be far more costly and dangerous.

Global climate change is exacerbating flooding and heat waves, which are special concerns for cities because they absorb more heat than surrounding rural areas and have higher average temperatures — a phenomenon known as the urban heat island effect. According to a study by the Organization for Economic Cooperation and Development (OECD), about 40 million people living in coastal areas around the world in 2005 were exposed to so-called 100-year floods — or major floods likely to occur only once every 100 years. By the 2070s, the OECD said, the population at risk from such flooding could rise to 150 million as more people move to cities, and climate change causes more frequent and ferocious storms and rising sea levels.

Cities with the greatest population exposure in the 2070 forecast include Kolkata and Mumbai in India, Dhaka (Bangladesh), Guangzhou and Shanghai in China, Ho Chi Minh City and Hai Phong in Vietnam, Bangkok (Thailand), Rangoon (Myanmar) and Miami, Florida. Cities in developed countries tend to be better protected, but there are exceptions. For example, London has about the same amount of flooding protection as Shanghai, according to the OECD.[2]

"All cities need to look at their critical infrastructure systems and try to understand where they're exposed to natural hazards," says Jim Hall, leader of urban research at England's Tyndall Centre for Climate Change Research. For example, he says, London's Underground subway system is vulnerable to flooding and overheating. Fast-growing cities planning for climate change, he adds, might want to control growth in flood-prone areas, improve water systems to ensure supply during droughts or build new parks to help cool urban neighborhoods. "Risks now and in the future depend on what we do to protect cities," says Hall.

In some cities, residents can literally see the ocean rising. Coastal erosion has destroyed 47 homes and more than 400 fields in recent years in Cotonou, the capital city of the West African nation of Benin, according to a local non-profit called Front United Against Coastal Erosion. "The sea was far from us two years ago. But now, here it is. We are scared," said Kofi Ayao, a local fisherman. "If we do not find a solution soon, we may simply drown in our sleep one day."[3]

methods made farmers more productive, people moved to the cities in ever-increasing numbers. Some national economies boomed, notably the so-called Asian tigers — Hong Kong, Singapore, Taiwan and South Korea — by focusing on manufacturing exports for industrialized markets and improving their education systems to create productive work forces.

Indonesia, Malaysia, the Philippines and Thailand — the "tiger cubs" — went through a similar growth phase in the late 1980s and early '90s.

After China and India opened up their economies in the 1980s and '90s, both countries became magnets for foreign investment and created free-trade areas and special economic zones to attract business activity. Cities in

Social violence can arise from within a city or come as an attack from outside. For example, in 2007 up to 600 people were killed when urban riots erupted in Kenya after a disputed national election.[4]

Urban leaders often justify slum-clearance programs by claiming that poor neighborhoods are breeding grounds for unrest. Others say slums are fertile recruiting grounds for terrorist groups. Slums certainly contain many who feel ill-treated, and extreme conditions may spur them

A Bangladeshi boy helps slum residents cross floodwaters in Dhaka. Rising waters caused by global warming pose a significant potential threat to Dhaka and other low-lying cities worldwide.

foreigners and local elites) and had a heavy media presence that guaranteed international coverage.[5]

But serendipity can also make one city a target over another, says Parachini. "Attackers may know one city better or have family links or contacts there. Those local ties matter for small groups planning a one-time attack," he says.

Developing strong core services, such as police forces and public health systems, can be the first step in strengthening most cities against terror-

into action. Overall, however, experts say most slum dwellers are too busy trying to eke out a living to riot or join terrorist campaigns.

"Poverty alone isn't a sufficient cause [for unrest]," says John Parachini, director of the Intelligence Policy Center at the RAND Corp., a U.S. think tank. "You need a combination of things — people with a profound sense of grievance, impoverishment and leaders who offer the prospect of change. Often the presence of an enemy nearby, such as an occupying foreign power or a rival tribal group or religious sect, helps galvanize people."

Last November's terrorist attacks in Mumbai, in which 10 gunmen took dozens of Indian and foreign hostages and killed at least 164 people, showed an ironic downside of globalization: Wealth, clout and international ties can make cities terrorist targets.

"Mumbai is India's commercial and entertainment center — India's Wall Street, its Hollywood, its Milan. It is a prosperous symbol of modern India," a RAND analysis noted. Mumbai also was accessible from the sea, offered prominent landmark targets (historic hotels frequented by

ism, he says, rather than creating specialized units to handle terrorist strikes.

"Basic governance functions like policing maintain order, build confidence in government and can pick up a lot of information about what's going on in neighborhoods," he says. "They make it harder to do bad things."

---

[1] George Bugliarello, "The Engineering Challenges of Urban Sustainability," *Journal of Urban Technology*, vol. 15, no. 1 (2008), pp. 64-65.

[2] R. J. Nicholls, *et al.*, "Ranking Port Cities with High Exposure and Vulnerability to Climate Extremes: Exposure Estimates," *Environment Working Papers No. 1*, Organization for Economic Cooperation and Development, Nov. 19, 2008, pp. 7-8, www.olis.oecd.org/olis/2007doc .nsf/LinkTo/NT000058 8E/$FILE/JT03255617.PDF.

[3] "Rising Tides Threaten to Engulf Parts of Cotonou," U.N. Integrated Regional Information Network, Sept. 2, 2008.

[4] "Chronology: Kenya in Crisis After Elections," Reuters, Dec. 31, 2007; "The Ten Deadliest World Catastrophes 2007," Insurance Information Institute, www.iii.org.

[5] Angel Rabasa, *et al.*, "The Lessons of Mumbai," *RAND Occasional Paper*, January 2009.

---

those areas expanded, particularly along China's southeast coast where such zones were clustered.

As incomes rose, many Asian cities aspired to global roles: Seoul hosted the 1988 Summer Olympics, and Malaysia built the world's tallest skyscrapers — the Petronas Twin Towers, completed in 1998, only to be superseded by the Taipei 101 building in Taiwan a few years later.

Some Asian countries — including Malaysia, Sri Lanka and Indonesia — implemented programs to improve living standards for the urban poor and helped reduce poverty. However, poverty remained high in Thailand and the Philippines and increased in China and Vietnam.[48]

Cities in South America and Africa also expanded rapidly between 1970 and 2000, although South America

AP Photo

Security officers forcibly remove a woman from her home during land confiscations in Changchun, a city of 7.5 million residents in northeast China, so buildings can be demolished to make way for new construction. Some rapidly urbanizing governments use heavy-handed methods — such as land confiscation, eviction or slum clearance — so redevelopment projects can proceed.

was farther ahead. By 1965 Latin America was already 50 percent urbanized and had three cities with populations over 5 million (Buenos Aires, São Paulo and Rio de Janeiro) — a marker sub-Saharan Africa would not achieve for several decades.[49] Urban growth on both continents followed the "primacy" pattern, in which one city is far more populous and economically and politically powerful than all the others in the nation. The presence of so-called primate cities like Lima (Peru), Caracas (Venezuela) or Lagos (Nigeria) can distort development if the dominant city consumes most public investments and grows to a size that is difficult to govern.

Latin America's growth gradually leveled out in the 1980s: Population increases slowed in major urban centers, and more people moved to small and medium-sized cities.[50] On average the region's economy grew more slowly and unevenly than Asia's, often in boom-and-bust cycles.[51] Benefits accrued mostly to small ruling classes who were hostile to new migrants, and income inequality became deeply entrenched in many Latin American cities.

Africa urbanized quickly after independence in the 1950s and '60s. But from the mid-1970s forward most countries' incomes stagnated or contracted. Such "urbanization without growth" in sub-Saharan Africa created the world's highest rates of urban poverty and income inequality. Corruption and poor management reinforced wealth gaps that dated back to colonial

times. Natural disasters, wars and the spread of HIV/AIDS further undercut poverty-reduction efforts in both rural and urban areas.[52]

New Solutions

As the 21st century began, calls for new antipoverty efforts led to an international conference at which 189 nations endorsed the Millennium Development Goals, designed to end poverty by 2015. Experts also focused on bottom-up strategies that gave poor people resources to help themselves.

An influential proponent of the bottom-up approach, Peruvian economist Hernando de Soto, stirred debate in 2000 with his book *The Mystery of Capital: Why Capitalism Triumphs in the West and Fails Everywhere Else.* Capitalist economies did not fail in developing nations because those countries lacked skills or enterprising spirit, de Soto argued. Rather, the poor in those countries had plenty of assets but no legal rights, so they could not prove ownership or use their assets as capital.

"They have houses but not titles; crops but not deeds; businesses but not statutes of incorporation," de Soto wrote. "It is the unavailability of these essential representations that explains why people who have adapted every other Western invention, from the paper clip to the nuclear reactor, have not been able to produce sufficient capital to make their domestic capitalism work." But, he asserted, urbanization in the developing world had spawned "a huge industrial-commercial revolution" which clearly showed that poor people could contribute to economic development if their countries developed fair and inclusive legal systems.[53]

Not all experts agreed with de Soto, but his argument coincided with growing interest in approaches like microfinance (small-scale loans and credit programs for traditionally neglected customers) that helped poor people build businesses and transition from the "extra-legal" economy into the formal economy. Early microcredit programs in the 1980s and '90s had targeted mainly the rural poor, but donors began expanding into cities around 2000.[54]

The "digital divide" — the gap between rich and poor people's access to information and communications technologies (ICTs) — also began to attract the attention of development experts. During his second term (1997-2001), U.S. President Bill Clinton highlighted the issue as an obstacle to reducing poverty both domestically and at the global level. "To maximize potential, we must turn the digital divide among and within our nations into digital opportunities," Clinton said at the Asia Pacific Economic Cooperation Forum in 2000, urging Asian nations to expand Internet access and train citizens to use computers.[55] The Millennium Development Goals called for making ICTs more widely available in poor countries.

Some ICTs, such as mobile phones, were rapidly adopted in developing countries, which had small or unreliable landline networks. By 2008, industry observers predicted, more than half of the world's population would own a mobile phone, with Africa and the Middle East leading the way.[56]

Internet penetration moved much more slowly. In 2006 some 58 percent of the population in industrial countries used the Internet, compared to 11 percent in developing countries and only 1 percent in the least developed countries. Access to high-speed Internet service was unavailable in many developing regions or was too expensive for most users.[57] Some antipoverty advocates questioned whether ICTs should be a high priority for poor countries, but others said the issue was not whether but when and how to get more of the world's poor wired.

"The more the better, especially broadband," says Polytechnic University's Bugliarello.

While development experts worked to empower the urban poor, building lives in fast-growing cities remained difficult and dangerous in many places. Some governments still pushed approaches like slum clearance, especially when it served other purposes.

Notoriously, in 2005 President Robert Mugabe of Zimbabwe launched a slum-clearance initiative called Operation Murambatsvina, a Shona phrase translated by some as "restore order" and others as "drive out the trash." Thousands of shacks in Zimbabwe's capital, Harare, and other cities across the nation were destroyed, allegedly to crack down on illegal settlements and businesses.

"The current chaotic state of affairs, where small-to-medium enterprises operated outside of the regulatory framework and in undesignated and crime-ridden areas, could not be countenanced much longer," said Mugabe.[58]

But critics said Mugabe was using slum clearance as an excuse to intimidate and displace neighborhoods that supported his opponents. In the end, some 700,000 people were left homeless or jobless by the action, which the United Nations later said violated international law.[59]

Over the next several years Mugabe's government failed to carry out its pledges to build new houses for the displaced families.[60]

CURRENT SITUATION

Economic Shadow

The current global economic recession is casting a dark cloud over worldwide economic development prospects. Capital flows to developing countries have declined sharply, and falling export demand is triggering layoffs and factory shutdowns in countries that produce for Western markets. But experts say even though the overall picture is sobering, many factors will determine how severely the recession affects cities.

In March the World Bank projected that developing countries would face budget shortfalls of $270 billion to $700 billion in 2009 and the world economy would shrink for the first time since World War II. According to the bank, 94 out of 116 developing countries were already experiencing an economic slowdown, and about half of them already had high poverty levels. Urban-based exporters and manufacturers were among the sectors hit hardest by the recession.[61]

These trends, along with an international shortage of investment capital, will make many developing countries increasingly dependent on foreign aid at a time when donor countries are experiencing their own budget crises. As workers shift out of export-oriented sectors in the cities and return to rural areas, poverty may increase, the bank projected.

The recession could mean failure to meet the Millennium Development Goals, especially if donor countries pull back on development aid. The bank urged nations to increase their foreign aid commitments and recommended that national governments:

- Increase government spending where possible to stimulate economies;
- Protect core programs to create social safety nets for the poor;
- Invest in infrastructure such as roads, sewage systems and slum upgrades; and
- Help small- and medium-size businesses get financing to create opportunities for growth and employment.[62]

Getty Images/Daniel Berehulak

AFP/Getty Images/Pal Pillai

Slum Redevelopment Plan Stirs Controversy

Conditions for the 60,000 families living in Mumbai's Dharavi neighborhood (top) — one of Asia's largest slums — are typical for a billion slum dwellers around the globe. Slums often lack paved roads, water-distribution systems, sanitation and garbage collection — spawning cholera, diarrhea and other illnesses. Electric power and telephone service are usually poached from available lines. Mumbai's plans to redevelop Dharavi, located on 600 prime acres in the heart of the city, triggered strong protests from residents, who demanded that their needs be considered before the redevelopment proceeds (bottom). The project has stalled recently due to the global economic crisis.

President Barack Obama's economic stimulus package, signed into law on Feb. 17, takes some of these steps and contains at least $51 billion for programs to help U.S. cities. (Other funds are allocated by states and may provide more aid to cities depending on each state's priority list.) Stimulus programs that benefit cities include $2.8 billion for energy conservation and energy efficiency, $8.4 billion for public transportation investments, $8 billion for

high-speed rail and intercity passenger rail service, $1.5 billion for emergency shelter grants, $4 billion for job training and $8.8 billion for modernizing schools.[63]

Governments in developing countries with enough capital may follow suit. At the World Economic Forum in Davos, Switzerland, in January, Chinese Premier Wen Jibao announced a 4 trillion yuan stimulus package (equivalent to about 16 percent of China's GDP over two years), including money for housing, railways and infrastructure and environmental protection. " 'The harsh winter will be gone, and spring is around the corner,' " he said, predicting that China's economy would rebound this year.[64]

But according to government figures released just a few days later, more than 20 million rural migrant workers had already lost their jobs in coastal manufacturing areas and moved back to their home towns.[65] In March the World Bank cut its forecast for China's 2009 economic growth from 7.5 percent to 6.5 percent, although it said China was still doing well compared to many other countries.[66]

In India "circular migration" is becoming more prevalent, according to the Overseas Development Institute's Deshingkar. "Employment is becoming more temporary — employers like to hire temporary workers whom they can hire and fire at will, so the proportion of temporary workers and circular migrants is going up," she says. "In some Indian villages 95 percent of migrants are circular. Permanent migration is too expensive and risky — rents are high, [people are] harassed by the police, slums are razed and they're evicted. Keeping one foot in the village is their social insurance."

Meanwhile, international development aid is likely to decline as donor countries cut spending and focus on their own domestic needs. "By rights the financial crisis shouldn't undercut development funding, because the total amounts given now are tiny compared to the national economic bailouts that are under way or being debated in developed countries," says Harvard economist Bloom. "Politically, however, it may be hard to maintain aid budgets."

At the World Economic Forum billionaire philanthropist Bill Gates urged world leaders and organizations to keep up their commitments to foreign aid despite the global financial crisis. "If we lose sight of our long-term priority to expand opportunity for the world's poor and abandon our commitments and partnerships to reduce inequality, we run the risk of emerging from the current economic downturn in a world with even greater disparities in health and education and fewer opportunities for people to improve their lives," said Gates, whose Bill and Melinda Gates Foundation supports efforts to address both rural and urban poverty in developing nations.[67]

In fact, at a summit meeting in London in early April, leaders of the world's 20 largest economies pledged $1.1 trillion in new aid to help developing countries weather the global recession. Most of the money will be channeled through the International Monetary Fund.

"This is the day the world came together to fight against the global recession," said British Prime Minister Gordon Brown.[68]

Slum Solutions

As slums expand in many cities, debate continues over the best way to alleviate poverty. Large-scale slum-clearance operations have long been controversial in both developed and developing countries: Officials typically call the slums eyesores and public health hazards, but often new homes turn out to be unaffordable for the displaced residents. Today development institutions like the World Bank speak of "urban upgrading" — improving services in slums instead of bulldozing them.[69]

This approach focuses on improving basic infrastructure systems like water distribution, sanitation and electric power; cleaning up environmental hazards and building schools and clinics. The strategy is cheaper than massive demolition and construction projects and provides incentives for residents to invest in improving their own homes, advocates say.[70]

To do so, however, slum dwellers need money. Many do not have the basic prerequisites even to open bank accounts, such as fixed addresses and minimum balances, let alone access to credit. Over the past 10 to 15 years, however, banks have come to recognize slum dwellers as potential customers and have begun creating microcredit programs to help them obtain small loans and credit cards that often start with very low limits. A related concept, micro-insurance, offers low-cost protection in case of illness, accidents and property damage.

Now advocates for the urban poor are working to give slum dwellers more financial power. The advocacy group, Shack/Slum Dwellers International (SDI), for example, has created Urban Poor Funds that help attract direct

Reflecting China's stunningly rapid urbanization, Shanghai's dramatic skyline rises beside the Huangpu River. Shanghai is the world's seventh-largest city today but will drop to ninth-place by 2025, as two south Asian megacities, Dhaka and Kolkata, surpass Shanghai in population.

investments from banks, government agencies and international donor groups.[71] In 2007 SDI received a $10 million grant from the Gates foundation to create a Global Finance Facility for Federations of the Urban Poor.

The funds will give SDI leverage in negotiating with governments for land, housing and infrastructure, according to Joel Bolnick, an SDI director in Cape Town, South Africa. If a government agency resists, said Bolnick, SDI can reply, " 'If you can't help us here, we'll take the money and put it on the table for a deal in Zambia instead.' "[72]

And UN-HABITAT is working with lenders to promote more mortgage lending to low-income borrowers in developing countries. "Slum dwellers have access to resources and are resources in themselves. To maximize the value of slums for those who live in them and for a city, slums must be upgraded and improved," UN-HABITAT Executive Director Tibaijuka said in mid-2008.[73]

Nevertheless, some governments still push slum clearance. Beijing demolished hundreds of blocks of old city neighborhoods and culturally significant buildings in its preparations to host the 2008 Olympic Games. Some of these "urban corners" (a negative term for high-density neighborhoods with narrow streets) had also been designated for protection as historic areas.[74] Developers posted messages urging residents to take government resettlement fees and move, saying, "Living in the Front Gate's courtyards is ancient history; moving to an apartment makes

Two-thirds of sub-Saharan Africa's city dwellers live in slums, like this one in Lagos, Nigeria, which has open sewers and no clean water, electric power or garbage collection. About 95 percent of today's rapid urbanization is occurring in the developing world, primarily in sub-Saharan Africa and Asia.

you a good neighbor," and "Cherish the chance; grab the good fortune; say farewell to dangerous housing."[75]

Beijing's actions were not unique. Other cities hosting international "mega-events" have demolished slums. Like Beijing, Seoul, South Korea, and Santo Domingo in the Dominican Republic were already urbanizing and had slum-clearance programs under way, but as their moments in the spotlight grew nearer, eviction operations accelerated, according to a Yale study. Ultimately, the study concluded, the benefits from hosting big events did not trickle down to poor residents and squatter communities who were "systematically removed or concealed from high-profile areas in order to construct the appearance of development."[76]

Now the debate over slum clearance has arrived in Dharavi. Developers are circling the site, which sits on a square mile of prime real estate near Mumbai's downtown and airport. The local government has accepted a $3 billion redevelopment proposal from Mukesh Mehta, a wealthy architect who made his fortune in Long Island, N.Y., to raze Dharavi's shanties and replace them with high-rise condominiums, shops, parks and offices. Slum dwellers who can prove they have lived in Dharavi since 1995 would receive free 300-square-foot apartments, equivalent to two small rooms, in the new buildings. Other units would be sold at market rates that could reach several thousand dollars per square foot.[77]

Mehta contends his plan will benefit slum residents because they will receive new homes on the same site. "Give me a better solution. Until then you might want to accept this one," he said last summer.[78] But many Dharavi residents say they will not be able to keep small businesses like tanneries, potteries and tailoring shops if they move into modern high-rises, and would rather stay put. (*See "At Issue," p. 107.*)

"I've never been inside a tall building. I prefer a place like this where I can work and live," said Usman Ghani, a potter born and raised in Dharavi who has demonstrated against the redevelopment proposals. He is not optimistic about the future. "The poor and the working class won't be able to stay in Mumbai," he said. "Many years ago, corrupt leaders sold this country to the East India Company. Now they're selling it to multinationals."[79]

OUTLOOK
Going Global

In an urbanizing world, cities will become increasingly important as centers of government, commerce and culture, but some will be more influential than others. Although it doesn't have a precise definition, the term "global city" is used by city-watchers to describe metropolises like New York and London that have a disproportionate impact on world affairs. Many urban leaders around the world aspire to take their cities to that level.

The 2008 *Global Cities Index* — compiled by *Foreign Policy* magazine, the Chicago Council on Global Affairs and the A. T. Kearney management consulting firm — ranks 60 cities on five broad criteria that measure their international influence, including:

- Business activity,
- Human capital (attracting diverse groups of people and talent),
- Information exchange,
- Cultural attractions and experiences, and
- Political engagement (influence on world policy making and dialogue).[80]

The scorecard is topped by Western cities like New York, London and Paris but also includes developing-country cities such as Beijing, Shanghai, Bangkok, Mexico

Will redevelopment of the Dharavi slum improve residents' lives?

YES
Mukesh Mehta
Chairman, MM Project Consultants

Written for *CQ Global Researcher*, April 2009

Slum rehabilitation is a challenge that has moved beyond the realm of charity or meager governmental budgets. It requires a pragmatic and robust financial model and a holistic approach to achieve sustainability.

Dharavi — the largest slum pocket in Mumbai, India, and one of the largest in the world — houses 57,000 families, businesses and industries on 600 acres. Alarmingly, this accounts for only 4 percent of Mumbai's slums, which house about 7.5 million people, or 55 percent of the city's population.

Mumbai's Slum Rehabilitation Authority (SRA) has undertaken the rehabilitation of all the eligible residents and commercial and industrial enterprises in a sustainable manner through the Dharavi Redevelopment Project (DRP), following an extensive consultative process that included Dharavi's slum dwellers. The quality of life for those residents is expected to dramatically improve, and they could integrate into mainstream Mumbai over a period of time. Each family would receive a 300-square-foot home plus adequate workspace, along with excellent infrastructure, such as water supply and roads. A public-private partnership between the real estate developers and the SRA also would provide amenities for improving health, income, knowledge, the environment and socio-cultural activities. The land encroached by the slum dwellers would be used as equity in the partnership.

The primary focus — besides housing and infrastructure — would be on income generation. Dharavi has a vibrant economy of $600 million per annum, despite an appalling working environment. But the redevelopment project would boost the local gross domestic product to more than $3 billion, with the average family income estimated to increase to at least $3,000 per year from the current average of $1,200. To achieve this, a hierarchy of workspaces will be provided, including community spaces equivalent to 6 percent of the built-up area, plus individual workspaces in specialized commercial and industrial complexes for leather goods, earthenware, food products, recycling and other enterprises.

The greatest failure in slum redevelopment has been to treat it purely as a housing problem. Improving the infrastructure to enable the local economy to grow is absolutely essential for sustainable development. We believe this project will treat Dharavi residents as vital human resources and allow them to act as engines for economic growth. Thus, the DRP will act as a torchbearer for the slums of Mumbai as well as the rest of the developing world.

NO
Kalpana Sharma
Author, Rediscovering Dharavi:
Stories from Asia's Largest Slum

Written for *CQ Global Researcher*, April 2009

The controversy over the redevelopment of Dharavi, a slum in India's largest city of Mumbai, centers on the future of the estimated 60,000 families who live and work there.

Dharavi is a slum because its residents do not own the land on which they live. But it is much more than that. The settlement — more than 100 years old — grew up around one of the six fishing villages that coalesced over time to become Bombay, as Mumbai originally was called. People from all parts of India live and work here making terra-cotta pots, leather goods, garments, food items and jewelry and recycling everything from plastic to metal. The annual turnover from this vast spread of informal enterprises, much of it conducted inside people's tiny houses, is an estimated $700 million a year.

The Dharavi Redevelopment Plan — conceived by consultant Mukesh Mehta and being implemented by the Government of Maharashtra state — envisages leveling this energetic and productive part of Mumbai and converting it into a collection of high-rise buildings, where some of the current residents will be given free apartments. The remaining land will be used for high-end commercial and residential buildings.

On paper, the plan looks beautiful. But people in Dharavi are not convinced. They believe the plan has not understood the nature and real value of Dharavi and its residents. It has only considered the value of the land and decided it is too valuable to be wasted on poor people.

Dharavi residents have been left with no choice but to adapt to an unfamiliar lifestyle. If this meant a small adjustment, one could justify it. But the new form of living in a 20-story high-rise will force them to pay more each month, since the maintenance costs of high-rises exceed what residents currently spend on housing. These costs become unbearable when people earn just enough to survive in a big city.

Even worse, this new, imposed lifestyle will kill all the enterprises that flourish today in Dharavi. Currently, people live and work in the same space. In the new housing, this will not be possible.

The alternatives envisaged are spaces appropriate for formal, organized industry. But enterprises in Dharavi are informal and small, working on tiny margins. Such enterprises cannot survive formalization.

The real alternative is to give residents security of tenure and let them redevelop Dharavi. They have ideas. It can happen only if people are valued more than real estate.

In addition to Dubai's glittering, new downtown area filled with towering skyscrapers, the city's manmade, palm-tree-shaped islands of Jumeirah sport hundreds of multi-million-dollar second homes for international jetsetters. Development has skidded to a temporary halt in the Arab city-state, much as it has in some other rapidly urbanizing cities around the globe, due to the global economic downturn.

City and São Paulo. Many of these cities, the authors noted, are taking a different route to global stature than their predecessors followed — a shorter, often state-led path with less public input than citizens of Western democracies expect to have.

"Rulers in closed or formerly closed societies have the power to decide that their capitol is going to be a world-class city, put up private funds and spell out what the city should look like," says Simon O'Rourke, executive director of the Global Chicago Center at the Chicago Council on Global Affairs. "That's not necessarily a bad path, but it's a different path than the routes that New York or London have taken. New global cities can get things done quickly — if the money is there."

Abu Dhabi's Masdar Initiative, for example, remains on track despite the global recession, directors said this spring. The project is part of a strategic plan to make Abu Dhabi a world leader in clean-energy technology. "There is no question of any rollback or slowing down of any of our projects in the renewable-energy sector," said Sultan Ahmed Al Jaber, chief executive officer of the initiative, on March 16.[81] Last year the crown prince of Abu Dhabi created a $15 billion fund for clean-energy investments, which included funds for Masdar City.

Money is the front-burner issue during today's global recession. "Unless a country's overall economic progress is solid, it is very unlikely that a high proportion of city dwellers will see big improvements in their standard of living," says Harvard's Bloom. In the next several years, cities that ride out the global economic slowdown successfully will be best positioned to prosper when world markets recover.

In the longer term, however, creating wealth is not enough, as evidenced by conditions in Abu Dhabi's neighboring emirate, Dubai. Until recently Dubai was a booming city-state with an economy built on real estate, tourism and trade — part of the government's plan to make the city a world-class business and tourism hub. It quickly became a showcase for wealth and rapid urbanization: Dozens of high-rise, luxury apartment buildings and office towers sprouted up seemingly overnight, and man-made islands shaped like palm trees rose from the sea, crowded with multi-million-dollar second homes for jetsetters.

But the global recession has brought development to a halt. The real estate collapse was so sudden that jobless expatriate employees have been fleeing the country, literally abandoning their cars in the Dubai airport parking lot.[82]

Truly global cities are excellent in a variety of ways, says O'Rourke. "To be great, cities have to be places where people want to live and work." They need intellectual and cultural attractions as well as conventional features like parks and efficient mass transit, he says, and, ultimately, they must give residents at least some role in decisionmaking.

"It will be very interesting to see over the next 20 years which cities can increase their global power without opening up locally to more participation," says O'Rourke. "If people don't have a say in how systems are built, they won't use them."

Finally, great cities need creative leaders who can adapt to changing circumstances. Mumbai's recovery after last November's terrorist attacks showed such resilience. Within a week stores and restaurants were open again in neighborhoods that had been raked by gunfire, and international travelers were returning to the city.[83]

The Taj Mahal Palace & Tower was one of the main attack targets. Afterwards, Ratan Tata, grand-nephew of the Indian industrialist who built the five-star hotel, said, "We can be hurt, but we can't be knocked down."[84]

NOTES

1. Ben Sutherland, "Slum Dwellers 'to top 2 billion,'" *BBC News*, June 20, 2006, http://news.bbc.co.uk/2/hi/in_depth/5099038.stm.

2. United Nations Population Fund, *State of World Population 2007: Unleashing the Potential of Urban Growth* (2007), p. 6.

3. UN-HABITAT, *State of the World's Cities 2008/2009* (2008), p. xi.

4. UN-HABITAT, *op cit.*, p. 90.

5. *Ibid.*, p. 92.

6. *Ibid.*, pp. 90-105.

7. Anna Tibaijuka, "The Challenge of Urbanisation and the Role of UN-HABITAT," lecture at the Warsaw School of Economics, April 18, 2008, p. 2, www.unhabitat.org/downloads/docs/5683_16536_ed_warsaw_version12_1804.pdf.

8. For background see Peter Katel, "Ending Poverty," *CQ Researcher*, Sept. 9, 2005, p. 733-760.

9. For details, see www.endpoverty2015.org. For background, see Peter Behr, "Looming Water Crisis," *CQ Global Researcher*, February 2008, pp. 27-56.

10. Tobias Just, "Megacities: Boundless Growth?" Deutsche Bank Research, March 12, 2008, pp. 4-5.

11. Commission on Legal Empowerment of the Poor, *Making the Law Work for Everyone* (2008), pp. 5-9, www.undp.org/legalempowerment/report/Making_the_Law_Work_for_Everyone.pdf.

12. Angel Rabasa, *et al.*, "The Lessons of Mumbai," *RAND Occasional Paper*, 2009, pp. 1-2, www.rand.org/pubs/occasional_papers/2009/RAND_OP249.pdf.

13. Wieland Wagner, "As Orders Dry Up, Factory Workers Head Home," *Der Spiegel*, Jan. 8, 2009, www.spiegel.de/international/world/0,1518,600188,00.html; Malcolm Beith, "Reverse Migration Rocks Mexico," *Foreign Policy.com*, February 2009, www.foreignpolicy.com/story/cms.php?story_id=4731; Anthony Faiola, "A Global Retreat As Economies Dry Up," *The Washington Post*, March 5, 2009, www.washington-post.com/wp-dyn/content/story/2009/03/04/ST2009030404264.html.

14. For background, see David Masci, "Emerging India, *CQ Researcher*, April 19, 2002, pp. 329-360; and Peter Katel, "Emerging China," *CQ Researcher*, Nov. 11, 2005, pp. 957-980.

15. For background, see Mary H. Cooper, "Exporting Jobs," *CQ Researcher*, Feb. 20, 2004, pp. 149-172.

16. Ji Yongqing, "Dalian Becomes the New Outsourcing Destination," *China Business Feature*, Sept. 17, 2008, www.cbfeature.com/industry_spotlight/news/dalian_becomes_the_new_outsourcing_destination.

17. Thomas L. Friedman, *The World Is Flat: A Brief History of the Twenty-First Century*, updated edition (2006), pp. 24-28, 463-464.

18. Priya Deshingkar and Claudia Natali, "Internal Migration," in *World Migration 2008* (2008), p. 183.

19. Views expressed here are the speaker's own and do not represent those of his employer.

20. Martin Ravallion, Shaohua Chen and Prem Sangraula, "New Evidence on the Urbanization of Global Poverty," World Bank Policy Research Working Paper 4199, April 2007, http://siteresources.worldbank.org/INTWDR2008/Resources/2795087-1191427986785/RavallionMEtAl_UrbanizationOfGlobalPoverty.pdf.

21. For background on the *hukou* system, see Congressional-Executive Commission on China, "China's Household Registration System: Sustained Reform Needed to Protect China's Rural Migrants," Oct. 7, 2005, www.cecc.gov/pages/news/hukou.pdf; and Hayden Windrow and Anik Guha, "The Hukou System, Migrant Workers, and State Power in the People's Republic of China," *Northwestern University Journal of International Human Rights*, spring 2005, pp. 1-18.

22. Wu Zhong, "How the Hukou System Distorts Reality," *Asia Times*, April 11, 2007, www.atimes.com/atimes/China/ID11Ad01.html; Rong Jiaojiao, "Hukou 'An Obstacle to Market Economy,'" *China Daily*, May 21, 2007, www.chinadaily.com.cn/china/2007-05/21/content_876699.htm.

23. "Scientific Outlook on Development," "Full text of Hu Jintao's report at 17th Party Congress," section V.5, Oct. 24, 2007, http://news.xinhuanet.com/english/2007-10/24/content_6938749.htm.

24. Wu Zhong, "Working-Class Heroes Get Their Day," *Asia Times*, Oct. 24, 2007, www.atimes.com/atimes/China_Business/IJ24Cb01.html.

25. "Internal Migration, Poverty and Development in Asia," *Briefing Paper no. 11*, Overseas Development Council, October 2006, p. 3.

26. Clare T. Romanik, "An Urban-Rural Focus on Food Markets in Africa," The Urban Institute, Nov. 15, 2007, p. 30, www.urban.org/publications/411604.html.

27. UN-HABITAT, *op. cit.*, pp. 24-26.

28. "How Shifts to Smaller Family Sizes Contributed to the Asian Miracle," *Population Action International*, July 2006, www.popact.org/Publications/Fact_Sheets/FS4/Asian_Miracle.pdf.

29. Edson C. Tandoc, Jr., "Says UP Economist: Lack of Family Planning Worsens Poverty," *Philippine Daily Inquirer*, Nov. 11, 2008, http://newsinfo.inquirer.net/breakingnews/nation/view/20081111-171604/Lack-of-family-planning-worsens-poverty; Blaine Harden, "Birthrates Help Keep Filipinos in Poverty," *The Washington Post*, April 21, 2008, www.washingtonpost.com/wp-dyn/content/story/2008/04/21/ST2008042100778.html.

30. Kenneth Fletcher, "Colombia Dispatch 11: Former Bogotá Mayor Enrique Peñalosa," Smithsonian.com, Oct. 29, 2008, www.smithsonianmag.com/travel/Colombia-Dispatch-11-Former-Bogota-mayor-Enrique-Penalosa.html.

31. Charles Montgomery, "Bogota's Urban Happiness Movement," *Globe and Mail*, June 25, 2007, www.theglobeandmail.com/servlet/story/RTGAM.20070622.whappyurbanmain0623/BNStory/lifeMain/home.

32. Bus Rapid Transit Planning Guide, 3rd edition, Institute for Transportation & Development Policy, June 2007, p. 1, www.itdp.org/documents/Bus%20Rapid%20Transit%20Guide%20%20complete%20guide.pdf.

33. Project details at www.masdaruae.com/en/home/index.aspx.

34. Awad and Schuler remarks at Greenbuild 2008 conference, Boston, Mass., Nov. 20, 2008.

35. "Green Dreams," Frontline/World, www.pbs.org/frontlineworld/fellows/green_dreams/; Danielle Sacks, "Green Guru Gone Wrong: William McDonough," *Fast Company*, Oct. 13, 2008, www.fastcompany.com/magazine/130/the-mortal-messiah.html; Timothy Lesle, "Cradle and All," *California Magazine*, September/October 2008, www.alumni.berkeley.edu/California/200809/lesle.asp.

36. Shannon May, "Ecological Crisis and Eco-Villages in China," *Counterpunch*, Nov. 21-23, 2008, www.counterpunch.org/may11212008.html.

37. Rujun Shen, "Eco-city seen as Expensive 'Green-Wash,'" *The Standard* (Hong Kong), June 24, 2008, www.thestandard.com.hk/news_detail.asp?we_cat=9&art_id=67641&sid=19488136&con_type=1&d_str=20080624&fc=8; see also Douglas McGray, "Pop-Up Cities: China Builds a Bright Green Metropolis," *Wired*, April 24, 2007, www.wired.com/wired/archive/15.05/feat_popup.html; Malcolm Moore, "China's Pioneering Eco-City of Dongtan Stalls," *Telegraph*, Oct. 19, 2008, www.telegraph.co.uk/news/worldnews/asia/china/3223969/Chinas-pioneering-eco-city-of-Dongtan-stalls.html; "City of Dreams," *Economist*, March 19, 2009, www.economist.com/world/asia/displaystory.cfm?story_id=13330904.

38. Details at www.tianjinecocity.gov.sg/.

39. "LEED Projects and Case Studies Directory," U.S. Green Building Council, www.usgbc.org/LEED/Project/RegisteredProjectList.aspx.

40. Remarks at Greenbuild 2008 conference, Boston, Mass., Nov. 20, 2008.

41. Population Reference Bureau, "Urbanization," www.prb.org; Tertius Chandler, *Four Thousand Years of Urban Growth: An Historical Census* (1987).

42. Lewis Mumford, *The City In History: Its Origins, Its Transformations, and Its Prospects* (1961), pp. 417-418.

43. Frederick Engels, *The Condition of the Working Class in England* (1854), Chapter 7 ("Results"), online at Marx/Engels Internet Archive, www.marxists.org/archive/marx/works/1845/condition-working-class/ch07.htm.

44. Population Reference Bureau, *op. cit.*

45. Robert A. Caro, *The Power Broker: Robert Moses and the Fall of New York* (1975).

46. Jane Jacobs, *The Death and Life of Great American Cities* (1961).

47. Mumford, *op. cit.*, pp. 454-455.

48. Joshua Kurlantzick, "The Big Mango Bounces Back," *World Policy Journal*, spring 2000, www.worldpolicy.org/journal/articles/kurlant.html; UN-HABITAT, *op. cit.*, pp. 74-76.

49. BBC News, "Interactive Map: Urban Growth," http://news.bbc.co.uk/2/shared/spl/hi/world/06/urbanisation/html/urbanisation.stm.

50. Licia Valladares and Magda Prates Coelho, "Urban Research in Latin America: Towards a Research Agenda," MOST Discussion Paper Series No. 4 (undated), www.unesco.org/most/valleng.htm#trends.

51. Jose de Gregorie, "Sustained Growth in Latin America," Economic Policy Papers, Central Bank of Chile, May 2005, www.bcentral.cl/eng/studies/economic-policy-papers/pdf/dpe13eng.pdf.

52. UN-HABITAT, *op cit.*, pp. 70-74.

53. Hernando de Soto, *The Mystery of Capital: Why Capitalism Triumphs in the West and Fails Everywhere Else* (2000), excerpted at http://ild.org.pe/en/mystery/english?page=0%2C0.

54. Deepak Kindo, "Microfinance Services to the Urban Poor," *Microfinance Insights*, March 2007; World Bank, "10 Years of World Bank Support for Microcredit in Bangladesh," Nov. 5, 2007; "Micro Finance Gaining in Popularity," *The Hindu*, Aug. 25, 2008, www.hindu.com/biz/2008/08/25/stories/2008082550121600.htm.

55. Michael Richardson, "Clinton Warns APEC of 'Digital Divide,'" *International Herald Tribune*, Nov. 16, 2000, www.iht.com/articles/2000/11/16/apec.2.t_2.php.

56. Abigail Keene-Babcock, "Study Shows Half the World's Population With Mobile Phones by 2008," Dec. 4, 2007, www.nextbillion.net/news/study-shows-half-the-worlds-population-with-mobile-phones-by-200.

57. "Millennium Development Goals Report 2008," United Nations, p. 48, www.un.org/millenniumgoals/pdf/The%20Millennium%20Development%20Goals%20Report%202008.pdf.

58. Robyn Dixon, "Zimbabwe Slum Dwellers Are Left With Only Dust," *Los Angeles Times*, June 21, 2005, http://articles.latimes.com/2005/jun/21/world/fg-nohomes21.

59. Ewen MacAskill, "UN Report Damns Mugabe Slum Clearance as Catastrophic," *Guardian*, July 23, 2005, www.guardian.co.uk/world/2005/jul/23/zimbabwe.ewenmacaskill.

60. Freedom House, "Freedom in the World 2008: Zimbabwe," www.freedomhouse.org/uploads/press_release/Zimbabwe_FIW_08.pdf.

61. "Crisis Reveals Growing Finance Gaps for Developing Countries," World Bank, March 8, 2009, http://web.worldbank.org/WBSITE/EXTERNAL/NEWS/0,,contentMDK:22093316~menuPK:34463~pagePK:34370~piPK:34424~theSitePK:4607,00.html.

62. "Swimming Against the Tide: How Developing Countries Are Coping with the Global Crisis," World Bank, background paper prepared for the G20 finance Ministers meeting, March 13-14, 2009, http://siteresources.worldbank.org/NEWS/Resources/swimmingagainstthetide-march2009.pdf.

63. "Major Victories for City Priorities in American Recovery and Reinvestment Act," U.S. Conference of Mayors, Feb. 23, 2009, www.usmayors.org/usmayornewspaper/documents/02_23_09/pg1_major_victories.asp.

64. Carter Dougherty, "Chinese Premier Injects Note of Optimism at Davos," *The New York Times*, Jan. 29, 2009, www.nytimes.com/2009/01/29/business/29econ.html?partner=rss.

65. Jamil Anderlini and Geoff Dyer, "Downturn Causes 20m Job Losses in China," *Financial Times*, Feb. 2, 2009, www.ft.com/cms/s/0/19c25aea-f0f5-11dd-8790-0000779fd2ac.html.

66. Joe McDonald, "World Bank Cuts China's 2009 Growth Forecast," The Associated Press, March 18, 2009.

67. "Bill and Melinda Gates Urge Global Leaders to Maintain Foreign Aid," Bill and Melinda Gates Foundation, Jan. 30, 2009, www.gatesfoundation.org/press-releases/Pages/2009-world-economic-forum-090130.aspx.

68. Mark Landler and David E. Sanger, "World Leaders Pledge $1.1 Trillion to Tackle Crisis," *The New York*

Times, April 4, 2009, www.nytimes.com/2009/04/03/world/europe/03summit.html?_r=1&hp.

69. "Is Demolition the Way to Go?" World Bank, www.worldbank.org/urban/upgrading/demolition.html.

70. "What Is Urban Upgrading?" World Bank, www.worldbank.org/urban/upgrading/what.html.

71. For more information, see "Urban Poor Fund," *Shack/Slum Dwellers International*, www.sdinet.co.za/ritual/urban_poor_fund/.

72. Neal R. Peirce, "Gates Millions, Slum-Dwellers: Thanksgiving Miracle?" *Houston Chronicle*, Nov. 22, 2007, www.sdinet.co.za/static/pdf/sdi_gates_iupf_neal_peirce.pdf.

73. "Statement at the African Ministerial Conference on Housing and Urban Development," UN-HABITAT, Abuja, Nigeria, July 28, 2008, www.unhabitat.org/content.asp?cid=5830&catid=14&typeid=8&subMenuId=0.

74. Michael Meyer, *The Last Days of Old Beijing* (2008), pp. 54-55; Richard Spencer, "History is Erased as Beijing Makes Way for Olympics," *Telegraph* (London), June 19, 2006, www.telegraph.co.uk/news/worldnews/asia/china/1521709/History-is-erased-as-Beijing-makes-way-for-Olympics.html; Michael Sheridan, "Old Beijing Falls to Olympics Bulldozer," *Sunday Times* (London), April 29, 2007, www.timesonline.co.uk/tol/news/world/asia/china/article1719945.ece.

75. Meyer, *op. cit.*, pp. 45, 52.

76. Solomon J. Greene, "Staged Cities: Mega-Events, Slum Clearance, and Global Capital," *Yale Human Rights & Development Law Journal*, vol. 6, 2003, http://islandia.law.yale.edu/yhrdlj/PDF/Vol%206/greene.pdf.

77. Slum Rehabilitation Authority, "Dharavi Development Project," www.sra.gov.in/htmlpages/Dharavi.htm; Porus P. Cooper, "In India, Slum May Get Housing," *Philadelphia Inquirer*, Sept. 22, 2008.

78. Mukul Devichand, "Mumbai's Slum Solution?" BBC News, Aug. 14, 2008, http://news.bbc.co.uk/2/hi/south_asia/7558102.stm.

79. Henry Chu, "Dharavi, India's Largest Slum, Eyed By Mumbai Developers," *Los Angeles Times*, Sept. 8, 2008, www.latimes.com/news/nationworld/world/la-fg-dharavi8-2008sep08,0,1830588.story; see also Dominic Whiting, "Dharavi Dwellers Face Ruin in Development Blitz," Reuters, June 6, 2008, http://in.reuters.com/article/topNews/idINIndia-33958520080608; and Mark Tutton, "Real Life 'Slumdog' Slum To Be Demolished," CNN.com, Feb. 23, 2009, www.cnn.com/2009/TRAVEL/02/23/dharavi.mumbai.slums/.

80. Unless otherwise cited, this section is based on "The 2008 Global Cities Index," *Foreign Policy*, November/December 2008, www.foreignpolicy.com/story/cms.php?story_id=4509.

81. T. Ramavarman, "Masdar To Proceed with $15 Billion Investment Plan," *Khaleej Times Online*, March 16, 2009, www.khaleejtimes.com/biz/inside.asp?xfile=/data/business/2009/March/business_March638.xml&section=business&col=; Stefan Nicola, "Green Oasis Rises From Desert Sands," *Washington Times*, Feb. 2, 2009, www.washingtontimes.com/themes/places/abu-dhabi/; Elisabeth Rosenthal, "Gulf Oil States Seeking a Lead in Clean Energy," *The New York Times*, Jan. 13, 2009, www.nytimes.com/2009/01/13/world/middleeast/13greengulf.html.

82. David Teather and Richard Wachman, "The Emirate That Used to Spend It Like Beckham," *The Guardian*, Jan. 31, 2009, www.guardian.co.uk/world/2009/jan/31/dubai-global-recession; Robert F. Worth, "Laid-Off Foreigners Flee as Dubai Spirals Down," *The New York Times*, Feb. 12, 2009, www.nytimes.com/2009/02/12/world/middleeast/12dubai.html; Elizabeth Farrelly, "Dubai's Darkening Sky: The Crane Gods are Still," *Brisbane Times*, Feb. 26, 2009, www.brisbanetimes.com.au/news/opinion/dubais-darkening-sky-the-crane-gods-are-still/2009/02/25/1235237781806.html.

83. Raja Murthy, "Taj Mahal Leads India's Recovery," *Asia Times*, Dec. 3, 2008, www.atimes.com/atimes/South_Asia/JL03Df01.html.

84. Joe Nocera, "Mumbai Finds Its Resiliency," *The New York Times*, Jan. 4, 2009, http://travel.nytimes.com/2009/01/04/travel/04journeys.html.

BIBLIOGRAPHY

Books

Meyer, Michael, *The Last Days of Old Beijing: Life in the Vanishing Backstreets of a City Transformed*, *Walker & Co.*, 2008.
An English teacher and travel writer traces Beijing's history and describes life in one of its oldest neighborhoods as the city prepared to host the 2008 Olympic Games.

Silver, Christopher, *Planning the Megacity: Jakarta in the Twentieth Century*, *Routledge*, 2007.
An urban scholar describes how Indonesia's largest city grew from a colonial capital of 150,000 in 1900 into a megacity of 12-13 million in 2000, and concludes that overall the process was well-planned.

2007. State of the World: Our Urban Future, *Worldwatch Institute*, Norton, 2007.
Published by an environmental think tank, a collection of articles on issues such as sanitation, urban farming and strengthening local economies examines how cities can be healthier and greener.

Articles

"The 2008 Global Cities Index," *Foreign Policy*, November/December 2008, www.foreignpolicy.com/story/cms.php?story_id=4509.
Foreign Policy magazine, the Chicago Council on World Affairs and the A.T. Kearney management consulting firm rank the world's most "global" cities in both industrialized and developing countries, based on economic activity, human capital, information exchange, cultural experience and political engagement.

"Mexico City Bikers Preach Pedal Power in Megacity," *The Associated Press*, Dec. 28, 2008.
Bicycle activists are campaigning for respect in a city with more than 6 million cars, taxis and buses.

Albright, Madeleine, and Hernando De Soto, "Out From the Underground," *Time*, July 16, 2007.
A former U.S. Secretary of State and a prominent Peruvian economist contend that giving poor people basic legal rights can help them move from squatter communities and the shadow economy to more secure lives.

Bloom, David E., and Tarun Khanna, "The Urban Revolution," *Finance & Development*, September 2007, pp. 9-14.
Rapid urbanization is inevitable and could be beneficial if leaders plan for it and develop innovative ways to make cities livable.

Chamberlain, Gethin, "The Beating Heart of Mumbai," *The Observer*, Dec. 21, 2008, www.guardian.co.uk/world/2008/dec/21/dharavi-india-slums-slumdog-millionaire-poverty.
Eight boys growing up in Dharavi, Asia's largest slum, talk about life in their neighborhood.

Osnos, Evan, "Letter From China: The Promised Land," *The New Yorker*, Feb. 9, 2009, www.newyorker.com/reporting/2009/02/09/090209fa_fact_osnos.
Traders from at least 19 countries have set up shop in the Chinese coastal city of Guangzhou to make money in the export-import business.

Packer, George, "The Megacity," *The New Yorker*, Nov. 13, 2006, www.newyorker.com/archive/2006/11/13/061113fa_fact_packer.
Lagos, Nigeria, offers a grim picture of urban life.

Schwartz, Michael, "For Russia's Migrants, Economic Despair Douses Flickers of Hope," *The New York Times*, Feb. 9, 2009, www.nytimes.com/2009/02/10/world/europe/10migrants.html?n=Top/Reference/Times%20Topics/People/P/Putin,%20Vladimir%20V.
Russia has an estimated 10 million migrant workers, mainly from former Soviet republics in Central Asia — some living in shanty towns.

Reports and Studies

"Ranking of the World's Cities Most Exposed to Coastal Flooding Today and in the Future," *Organization for Economic Cooperation and Development*, 2007, www.rms.com/Publications/OECD_Cities_Coastal_Flooding.pdf.
As a result of urbanization and global climate change, up to 150 million people in major cities around the world could be threatened by flooding by 2070.

"State of World Population 2007," *U.N. Population Fund*, 2007, www.unfpa.org/upload/lib_pub_file/695_filename_sowp2007_eng.pdf.

A U.N. agency outlines the challenges and opportunities presented by urbanization and calls on policy makers to help cities improve residents' lives.

"State of the World's Cities 2008/2009: Harmonious Cities," UN-HABITAT, 2008.

The biennial report from the U.N. Human Settlements Programme surveys urban growth patterns and social, economic and environmental conditions in cities worldwide.

For More Information

Chicago Council on Global Affairs, 332 South Michigan Ave., Suite 1100, Chicago, IL 60604; (312) 726-3860; www.thechicagocouncil.org. A nonprofit research and public education group; runs the Global Chicago Center, an initiative to strengthen Chicago's international connections, and co-authors the Global Cities Index.

Clean Air Initiative for Asian Cities, CAI-Asia Center, 3510 Robinsons Equitable Tower, ADB Avenue, Ortigas Center, Pasig City, Philippines 1605; (632) 395-2843; www.cleanairnet.org/caiasia. A nonprofit network that promotes and demonstrates innovative ways to improve air quality in Asian cities.

Institute for Liberty and Democracy, Las Begonias 441, Oficina 901, San Isidro, Lima 27, Peru; (51-1) 616-6100; http://ild.org.pe. Think tank headed by economist Hernando de Soto that promotes legal tools to help the world's poor move from the extralegal economy into an inclusive market economy.

Overseas Development Institute, 111 Westminster Bridge Road, London SE1 7JD, United Kingdom; (44) (0)20 7922

0300; www.odi.org.uk. An independent British think tank focusing on international development and humanitarian issues.

Shack/Slum Dwellers International; (+27) 21 689 9408; www.sdinet.co.za. The Web site for the South Africa-based secretariat of an international network of organizations of the urban poor in 23 developing countries.

UN-HABITAT, P.O. Box 30030 GPO, Nairobi, 00100, Kenya; (254-20) 7621234; www.unhabitat.org. The United Nations Human Settlements Programme; works to promote socially and environmentally sustainable cities and towns.

World Bank, 1818 H Street, N.W., Washington, DC 20433, USA; (202) 473-1000; http://web.worldbank.org. Two development institutions with 185 member countries, which provide loans, credits and grants to middle-income developing countries (International Bank for Reconstruction and Development) and the poorest developing countries (International Development Association)

Residents struggle to maintain normalcy in Kenya's Eldoret camp, home to 14,000 Kenyans who fled their homes during post-election rioting in December 2007. But they are the lucky ones. Many of the world's 26 million internally displaced people (IDPs) receive no aid at all or live in crude huts made of sticks and plastic sheeting, without reliable access to food or clean water. The U.N. High Commissioner for Refugees provided aid to some 13.7 million IDPs in 2007.

From *CQ Researcher*,
March 2009

5

Aiding Refugees

Should the U.N. Help More Displaced People?

John Felton

For more than two decades, the guerrilla group known as the Lord's Resistance Army (LRA) has been terrorizing villagers in Uganda — forcibly recruiting child soldiers and brutally attacking civilians. In recent years, the dreaded group has crossed the border into the Democratic Republic of Congo.

Last October, LRA marauders attacked Tambohe's village in northeastern Congo. They shot and killed her brother-in-law and two others, then torched the houses, even those with people inside.

Tambohe and her surviving family members — five adults and 10 children — fled into the forest, briefly returning five days later to bury the bodies after the raiders had left. The family then walked north for three days until they found safety in a village just across the border in southern Sudan, living with several hundred other Congolese displaced by the LRA.

"We have built a hut, and we live there," the 38-year-old Tambohe later told the medical aid group Doctors Without Borders. "The children sleep badly due to the mosquitoes and because we sleep on the ground. I sleep badly because I dream of the stench of burnt flesh. I dream they [the LRA] come and . . . take us to their camp."[1]

LRA violence is only one aspect of ongoing conflict in Congo that has killed 5 million people in the past decade and forced millions from their homes — including more than 400,000 last year, according to Human Rights Watch.[2]

Many, like Tambohe, fled their homes and crossed into another country, making them legally refugees. Under international law, she and her family should be able to remain in Sudan and receive

Most Displaced People Are in Africa and the Middle East

The U.N. High Commissioner for Refugees (UNHCR) monitors nearly 32 million people around the world who have been uprooted for a variety of reasons, including 25 million who fled their homes to escape war or conflict, mostly in Africa and the Middle East. Among those are 11 million refugees — those who have crossed borders and thus are protected by international law — and nearly 14 million internally displaced people (IDPs) who remain in their home countries. Some critics want the UNHCR to monitor and assist the world's other 12.3 million IDPs now being aided by other agencies.

Displaced Populations Monitored by the UNHCR

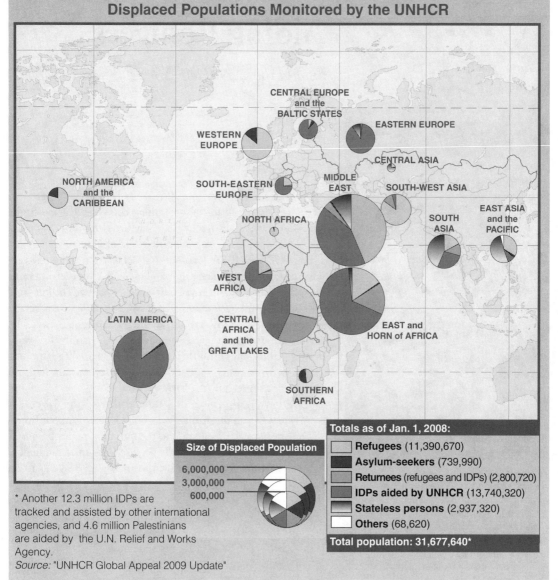

Size of Displaced Population
- 6,000,000
- 3,000,000
- 600,000

Totals as of Jan. 1, 2008:
- Refugees (11,390,670)
- Asylum-seekers (739,990)
- Returnees (refugees and IDPs) (2,800,720)
- IDPs aided by UNHCR (13,740,320)
- Stateless persons (2,937,320)
- Others (68,620)

Total population: 31,677,640*

* Another 12.3 million IDPs are tracked and assisted by other international agencies, and 4.6 million Palestinians are aided by the U.N. Relief and Works Agency.
Source: "UNHCR Global Appeal 2009 Update"

humanitarian aid, shelter and protection because they have a "well-founded fear" of persecution if they return home.[3]

If Tambohe had fled her home but remained in Congo, she would have been considered an "internally displaced person" (IDP), and the Congolese government would be legally responsible for aiding and protecting her. But in the Democratic Republic of the Congo and many other countries, international law is little more than a theory. The Kinshasa government is weak, and the army itself has been accused of abusing civilians.[4] So helping the Tambohes of the world falls primarily to the United Nations (U.N.) and nongovernmental aid agencies.

Today, there are more than 90 million refugees, displaced persons and disaster victims around the world. More than 40 million have fled conflict or violence, according to Antonio Guterres, U.N. High Commissioner for Refugees (UNHCR), who leads international efforts to aid the displaced.[5] Of those, about 16 million are refugees (including 4.6 million Palestinians) and 26 million are IDPs. (*See map, p. 116.*) Up to 50 million more people are victims of natural disaster, according to the U.N.'s Office for the Coordination of Humanitarian Affairs. In China's Sichuan Province, for example, many of the 5 million people who lost their homes last May in an earthquake remain homeless, and thousands of Americans are still displaced from Hurricane Katrina, which struck New Orleans in 2005.[6]

Millions of displaced people overseas live in sprawling camps or settlements established by governments or the United Nations, often in harsh desert or jungle environments. A large but unknown number of others, like Tambohe, find their own temporary

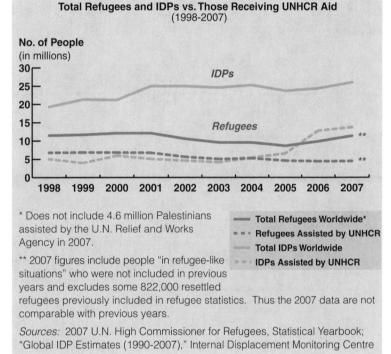

U.N. Serves About Half the World's Displaced

The U.N. High Commissioner for Refugees (UNHCR) has provided aid to an average of about 5.7 million of the globe's 11 million refugees each year — mostly in developing countries — over the past decade (dark gray lines). Meanwhile, the world's population of internally displaced persons (IDPs) has risen from 19 million in 1998 to 26 million in 2007. Individual governments are responsible for IDPs. But since 2005 the UNHCR has more than doubled the number of IDPs it serves each year — from 6.6 million in 2005 to 13.7 million in 2007 (light gray lines).

Total Refugees and IDPs vs. Those Receiving UNHCR Aid
(1998-2007)

No. of People
(in millions)

IDPs

Refugees

Total Refugees Worldwide*
Refugees Assisted by UNHCR
Total IDPs Worldwide
IDPs Assisted by UNHCR

* Does not include 4.6 million Palestinians assisted by the U.N. Relief and Works Agency in 2007.

** 2007 figures include people "in refugee-like situations" who were not included in previous years and excludes some 822,000 resettled refugees previously included in refugee statistics. Thus the 2007 data are not comparable with previous years.

Sources: 2007 U.N. High Commissioner for Refugees, Statistical Yearbook; "Global IDP Estimates (1990-2007)," Internal Displacement Monitoring Centre

shelter — sometimes living with friends or relatives but more often building makeshift tents and huts or moving into crowded rental housing in urban slums.

Food insecurity — or even starvation — rank among the most serious consequences of displacement. In Kenya, for example, last year's post-election bloodshed caused so many farmers from key food-producing areas to flee their homes — leaving crops unplanted or unharvested — that an estimated 10 million Kenyans now face starvation.[7]

Sudan Hosts Most Displaced People

Of the millions of refugees and internally displaced persons (IDPs) monitored by the U.N. High Commissioner for Refugees, Sudan houses nearly 4 million — more than any other country. Four of the top 10 host countries are in Africa. Most refugees and IDPs come from Iraq, Afghanistan, Colombia and five African countries.

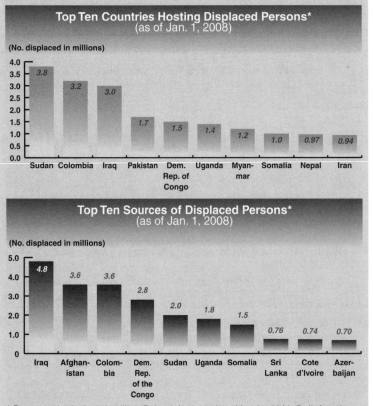

Top Ten Countries Hosting Displaced Persons*
(as of Jan. 1, 2008)

(No. displaced in millions)

Sudan 3.8 / Colombia 3.2 / Iraq 3.0 / Pakistan 1.7 / Dem. Rep. of Congo 1.5 / Uganda 1.4 / Myanmar 1.2 / Somalia 1.0 / Nepal 0.97 / Iran 0.94

Top Ten Sources of Displaced Persons*
(as of Jan. 1, 2008)

(No. displaced in millions)

Iraq 4.8 / Afghanistan 3.6 / Colombia 3.6 / Dem. Rep. of Congo 2.8 / Sudan 2.0 / Uganda 1.8 / Somalia 1.5 / Sri Lanka 0.76 / Cote d'Ivoire 0.74 / Azerbaijan 0.70

* Does not include 4.6 million Palestinians assisted by the U.N. Relief and Works Agency.

Source: "UNHCR Global Appeal, 2009 Update," U.N. High Commissioner for Refugees, January 2009

Some experts predict the world increasingly will be forced to deal with massive displacements — potentially involving hundreds of millions of people — caused by natural disasters intensified by climate change. Elisabeth Rasmusson, secretary general of the Norwegian Refugee Council, which aids and advocates for the displaced, warned last December that the world faces a potential vicious cycle: As climate change degrades the environment, it triggers more civil conflicts as people fight for access to water and other resources, further damaging the environment — displacing more people at each stage.[8]

Long before concern about climate change, however, international agencies were overwhelmed by the magnitude of conflict-caused displacements, which have been rising dramatically over the past decade.[9] And while the UNHCR's budget has nearly doubled since 2000 — from under $1 billion to $1.8 billion this year — the agency struggles to protect and care for refugees and IDPs in 116 countries around the world. As of Jan. 1, 2008, the agency was aiding 4.5 million of the world's 11.4 million refugees and 13.7 million of the world's 26 million IDPs. (*See graph on p. 117.*) Because the UNHCR and other aid agencies often operate in or near conflict zones, the delivery of humanitarian relief can be dangerous and, at times, impossible. In the Darfur region of western Sudan, for example, aid groups repeatedly have been forced to halt aid shipments because of attacks on relief convoys.[10]

But the lack of security is only one of a daunting litany of challenges faced by the UNHCR and its dozens of partner agencies, including chronic shortages of funds and reliance on "emergency" appeals to wealthy countries, the hostility of local governments, bureaucratic turf battles and indifference among world leaders.

And, despite promises to the contrary, the U.N. Security Council often has been unable or unwilling to take effective action — such as in Rwanda in 1994 and in Darfur since 2003 — to halt horrific death and displacement tolls. In both situations, ill-equipped and undermanned U.N. peacekeepers were unable to prevent what some have called the genocidal slaughter of hundreds of thousands of people. Yet some critics question whether the U.N. is trying to do either too much or too

Refugees Fall into Eight Categories

When people flee their homes and seek aid, they can be assigned to one of eight classifications, each of which conveys unique legal rights or restrictions. For instance, some are entitled under international law to receive humanitarian aid, shelter and protection because they have a "well-founded fear" of persecution if they return home. Here are the key definitions under international law and commonly accepted practice of the various categories of people who are seeking, or in need of, assistance:

Asylum-seeker: A person who has applied (either individually or as part of a group) for legal refugee status under national and international laws. If refugee status is denied, the asylum-seeker must leave the country (and could face expulsion) unless he or she is given permission to stay on humanitarian grounds.

Internally displaced person (IDP): Someone who has been forced to flee his home due to armed conflict, generalized violence, human-rights violations or natural or man-made disasters but has not crossed an international border.

Migrants: In the absence of a universally accepted definition of a migrant, the International Organization on Migration says the term is "usually understood" to cover all cases in which "the decision to migrate is taken freely by the individual concerned for reasons of 'personal convenience' and without intervention of an external compelling factor. An "economic migrant" is someone who leaves his home country in search of better economic opportunities elsewhere.

Persons in "IDP-like" situations: This relatively new term developed by the U.N. High Commissioner for Refugees (UNHCR) describes "groups of persons who are inside their country of nationality or habitual residence and who face protection risks similar to those of IDPs, but who, for practical or other reasons, could not be reported as such." For example, the UNHCR has used the term to describe displaced people in Georgia (including former residents of the breakaway provinces of Abkhazia and South Ossetia) and Russia.

Persons in "refugee-like" situations: Another relatively recent term used by the UNHCR to describe people who are outside their country or territory of origin "who face protection risks similar to those of refugees, but for whom refugee status has, for practical or other reasons, not been ascertained." In many cases, these are refugees who have settled more or less permanently in another country on an informal basis. The largest single population in this group is the estimated 1.1 million Afghans living outside formal refugee camps in Pakistan.

Refugee: Under the 1951 Refugee Convention (as amended in 1967), a refugee is someone who, due to a "well-founded fear of being persecuted for reasons of race, religion, nationality, membership of a particular social group or political opinions," has left his home country and is unable or, owing to fear, "unwilling to avail himself of the protection of that country." A person becomes a refugee by meeting the standards of the Refugee Convention, even before being granted asylum (*see above*), which legally confirms his or her refugee status.

Returnee: A refugee or IDP who has returned to his home — or home country or region.

Stateless person: Anyone who is not recognized as a citizen of any country. Stateless persons lack national or international legal protections and cannot legally cross international borders because they don't have and cannot obtain a valid passport or other identity papers. Between 3 million and 12 million people worldwide are stateless; the wide range results from a lack of information in some countries and conflicting assessments about which groups actually are stateless.

Sources: "Glossary on Migration," International Migration Law, International Organization for Migration, Geneva, Switzerland, www .iom.int/jahia/webdav/site/myjahiasite/shared/shared/mainsite/ published_docs/serial_publications/Glossary_eng.pdf; and "Glossary," U.N. High Commissioner for Refugees, Geneva, Switzerland, www .unhcr.org/publ/PUBL/4922d4390.pdf

little, and others say international refugee law needs to be updated to take into account recent trends, such as the rapid increase in IDPs.

Those living in refugee and IDP camps have more immediate concerns, including overcrowded conditions;

inadequate housing, food and medical care; and the refusal of local governments to allow them to work (or even to leave the camps). Negash, an Ethiopian who has lived in Kenya's sprawling Kakuma refugee camp for nearly four years, says aid officials often don't understand how their

IRIN/Manoocher Deghati (both)

Camp Life

Tents patched together from scraps of cloth house Afghans living in a camp near Kabul, Afghanistan (top). The government helps Afghans uprooted by decades of war, but many face overcrowded conditions and inadequate housing, food and medical care. Typically, internally displaced persons cannot work for wages in order to preserve jobs for local residents, so some set up their own small businesses inside the camps, such as a Kenyan seamstress at the Eldoret camp in Kenya (bottom).

decisions affect the camp's 50,000 residents every day. "There are people who work for agencies here that don't know what is happening in the camp," he says. "They live in their own compounds and don't really communicate with the refugees to find out what is happening to them."

The United Nations began reforming its humanitarian system in 2005, partly to address concerns about its inability to deliver timely and effective aid to internally displaced people. Jeff Crisp, director of policy and evaluations for UNHCR, says the U.N.'s reforms are having "a solid and positive impact" on the lives of displaced people even though revamping such a large-scale system of delivering aid "clearly is a work in progress."

The rise in refugees and IDPs is the direct result of dozens of small wars between rebels and government soldiers during the last 50 years, particularly in Africa and Asia. Some have dragged on for decades, creating generations of displaced families. For instance, Sudan's 20-year-long civil war displaced 400,000 people, but at least 130,000 remain in neighboring countries, according to the U.N.[11] Colombia's ongoing civil conflict has displaced nearly 10 percent of the country's population.[12]

Even when the wars end, civilians often remain displaced because they fear returning home, their homes have been destroyed or they have become settled elsewhere. In Afghanistan, for example, more than 5 million Afghan refugees have returned home since the United States ousted the Taliban regime seven years ago, but some 3 million remain in neighboring Pakistan and Iran — a large number of whom probably never will go back.[13]

The Afghan refugees represent what experts call a "protracted situation," which is defined as when at least 25,000 people are displaced from their homes for five years or more. (*See sidebar, p. 130.*) More than 30 protracted situations exist around the world, according to Elizabeth Ferris, director of the Brookings-Bern Project on Internal Displacement, run by the Brookings Institution in Washington, D.C., and the University of Bern (Switzerland) School of Law.

As governments, international agencies and specialists in the field seek better ways to protect and aid refugees and internally displaced people, here are some of the questions being debated:

Is the U.N. meeting refugees' needs?

Since its founding in 1951, the UNHCR has been the world's frontline agency for aiding and protecting refugees. Working with other U.N. agencies and nongovernmental agencies — such as CARE and the International Federation of Red Cross and Red Crescent Societies — the Geneva, Switzerland-based agency is spending $1.8 billion this year to provide housing, food, medical care and protection for millions of refugees and displaced persons in 116 countries.[14] The agency also decides the legal status of refugees in 75 countries that can't, or won't, make those determinations themselves. In 2007, the UNHCR determined the status of 48,745 people.[15]

Both critics and its defenders, however, say the agency often falls short of its official mandate to safeguard "the rights and well-being of refugees."[16] Barbara Harrell-Bond, the founder and former director of the Refugee Studies Center at Oxford University and a harsh critic of the UNHCR, says one of her biggest concerns is how aid programs are funded.

"The funds . . . always come from emergency budgets and are allocated to UNHCR by governments at their discretion," she says. As a result, agency programs are "at the mercy of the whims of international politics."

If world leaders become fixated on a particular crisis that is making headlines in Western countries — such as the situation in Sudan's Darfur region — refugees elsewhere suffer, Harrell-Bond says. In addition, education and job training programs designed to help refugees lead dignified lives once they leave the camps are considered "development" programs, she says, which "come from a completely different budget . . . and never the twain shall meet."

Moreover, local governments rarely receive international aid for hosting refugees and usually are anxious for refugees to go home, she says, so they have little incentive to improve camp conditions. As a consequence, refugees are "just warehoused" in camps for years and years. Furthermore, she adds, the UNHCR and its partner agencies routinely deny refugees' basic rights, including the right to leave the camps. Most host governments want refugees to be contained in camps, and the U.N. complies "by putting them in what amounts to gigantic cages," Harrell-Bond says.

In her 2005 book, *Rights in Exile: Janus Faced Humanitarianism*, Harrell-Bond and a co-author argue that "the rights of refugees cannot be protected in camps and settlements." They harshly criticize the UNHCR for not protecting refugees' rights, based on extensive research into the treatment of Kenyan and Ugandan refugees during the late 1990s — treatment the authors say continues today in many refugee camps.

For instance, refugees usually are not allowed to leave the camps and are not allowed to work. Harrell-Bond says the UNHCR should push governments harder to accept refugees into the local community. "Refugees can contribute to the societies where they have taken refuge and not simply live on handouts from the U.N.," she

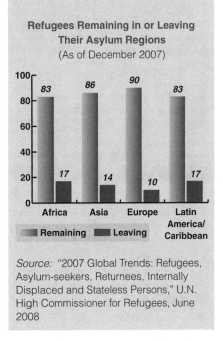

Most Refugees Flee to Neighboring Countries

Contrary to the perception that refugees are flooding into developed countries in Europe and other regions, most find asylum in neighboring countries and remain there. Only between 10 percent and 17 percent leave the countries where they were granted asylum.

Refugees Remaining in or Leaving Their Asylum Regions
(As of December 2007)

Africa — Remaining 83, Leaving 17
Asia — Remaining 86, Leaving 14
Europe — Remaining 90, Leaving 10
Latin America/Caribbean — Remaining 83, Leaving 17

Source: "2007 Global Trends: Refugees, Asylum-seekers, Returnees, Internally Displaced and Stateless Persons," U.N. High Commissioner for Refugees, June 2008

says, citing examples in Uganda and Zambia where so-called "local integration" has worked.

UNHCR Policy Director Crisp acknowledges the agency sometimes fails to meet refugees' needs but says decisions to "warehouse" refugees are made by the host countries. "In many cases, refugees are admitted to countries on strict condition that they be accommodated in camps and provided with their basic needs by UNHCR and other agencies," he says. UNHCR tries to get governments to improve refugees' situations, "but this is not always possible."

Despite such constraints, Crisp says the UNHCR is trying new approaches, particularly for those trapped in

Chaos in Somalia Puts Nation at Risk

Humanitarian aid feeds nearly half the population

Mohamed Abdi, his wife, and five children fled the never-ending violence in Somalia's capital city of Mogadishu last October, finding safety — but not much more — in the breakaway region of Somaliland to the north. The trip took nine days, and all along the way they feared being attacked by the opposing sides in the most recent round of conflict in Somalia.

Once they reached Somaliland, Abdi and his family found very little in the way of services, but the local government welcomed them as refugees. "We don't have much, and we depend on the kindness of these people; some days we eat, some we don't," he told the United Nations' IRIN news service in October. "But at least we have peace and security. That is what we want and the chance to make a living for our families without being afraid of being killed."[1]

Displaced people like Abdi never have it easy, often living in crude shelters and on starvation rations. But the situation is especially grave in Somalia — the only country in the world that for nearly two decades has been without even a functioning government — where a fatal combination of internal conflict and natural disaster has generated hundreds of thousands of refugees, migrants and internally displaced people (IDPs).

Ever since the last real government — a harsh dictatorship — was overthrown in 1991, hundreds of thousands of refugees settled in Kenya and other neighboring countries. Thousands of others have crossed the dangerous Gulf of Aden to equally impoverished Yemen.

Meanwhile, an estimated 1.3 million Somalis have become IDPs — displaced but living within their own country.[2] Most had fled Mogadishu, decimated by years of fighting among warlords, rebel groups, failed temporary governments and the Ethiopian army, which invaded in late 2006 and withdrew in January.

But IDPs escaping violence are not the only Somalis suffering. The U.N. Food and Agriculture Organization reported in October 2008 that 3.2 million people — 43 percent of the population — regularly need humanitarian assistance to survive.[3] While armed conflict has created most of the dislocations among Somalis, frequent droughts and floods have also caused recurrent famines that sent rural families fleeing to urban areas, often to be displaced by fighting.

Waves of conflict and displacement have swept over Somalia ever since the military dictatorship of Major General Mohamed Siad Barre was pushed from power in 1991. The most severe recent displacement occurred in August 2007, just eight months after Ethiopia invaded Somalia to oust a short-lived Islamist regime. Some 400,000 people were displaced by fighting in Mogadishu; most of them ended up in one of 200 camps that cropped up along a nine-mile stretch of the main road outside of the capital — "the most congested IDP nexus in the world," according to a refugee official.[4]

The U.N. High Commissioner for Refugees (UNHCR) and other aid groups provide limited food and medical aid to the camps, but little in the way of shelter. Patrick Duplat, an advocate for Refugees International who visited the camps twice in 2008, describes them as "mostly a sprawl of makeshift shelters — twigs and cloth, and sometimes plastic sheeting, whatever people are able to find."

Since Ethiopia withdrew its army in January, some 40,000 IDPs have returned to several Mogadishu neighborhoods, apparently with the intention of staying, according to the UNHCR.[5] Even so, continued fighting in the city has displaced an unknown number of others. The UNHCR said on Feb. 27 it is still discouraging IDPs from returning to what would be "ruined homes and livelihoods."[6]

In recent years nearly 500,000 people have fled Somalia to neighboring countries, but they have encountered daunting hazards along the way, including bandits, security forces

protracted situations. For instance, in 2008 the high commissioner set deadlines for getting people out of five specific protracted situations:

- Afghan refugees in Iran and Pakistan;
- Bosnian and Croatian refugees in Serbia;
- Eritrean refugees in eastern Sudan;

- Burundians in Tanzania; and
- Members of Myanmar's Rohingya minority who fled to Bangladesh.[17]

More broadly, as part of its 2005 reform program, the U.N. established clear guidelines for which U.N. agency should provide services in specific situations.[18] The

demanding bribes and even possible death on the high seas.[7] Those who avoid violence and persecution may be eligible for refugee status and entitled to return home someday; others probably would be considered migrants because they are searching for economic opportunities overseas.

Thousands of Somalis have risked crossing the Gulf of Aden or the Red Sea by boat to reach Yemen. On Feb. 28, 45 Somalis drowned when their boat capsized as they were crossing the gulf. Those who arrive safely generally are given *de jure* refugee status, even

An estimated 1.3 million people have been uprooted by the ongoing conflict in Somalia but are still living inside the country. Persistent violence, drought and flooding have created one of the world's longest ongoing humanitarian crises.

they had tried to register as refugees but had given up because of the lack of space in the camps. "After risking their lives to flee appalling violence in Somalia and make it to the relative safety of Kenya, they end up with nothing: no food, no shelter, and incredibly difficult access to water and health care," Simpson said.[12]

though many might be considered migrants because they never plan to return to their homes. About 82,000 Somalis were registered as refugees in Yemen in late 2008, but the UNHCR said the total could be closer to 150,000.[8]

Most Somali refugees, however, have fled into neighboring Kenya, even though it closed its borders to Somalis in 2007. According to the U.N., some 250,000 Somali refugees are in Kenya, including at least 45,000 who entered in 2008.[9]

At the border, would-be refugees often set out on foot to the U.N.'s official transit camps at Dadaab, 50 miles inside Kenya, frequently traveling at night to evade Kenyan police. As of late January the camps held 244,127 people — nearly triple their capacity. "Trying to squeeze 200,000-plus people into an area intended for 90,000 is inviting trouble," said Craig Johnstone, deputy U.N. high commissioner for refugees, after visiting on Feb. 5.[10] The UNHCR has been trying to raise $92 million from international donors to build two new camps for 60,000 more refugees.[11]

Human Rights Watch researcher Gerry Simpson, who visited the camps in late 2008, said many people told him

[1] "Fleeing from the frying pan into the fire," IRIN news service, Oct. 29, 2008, www.irinnews.org/Report .aspx?ReportId=81164.

[2] "Displaced Populations Report," U.N. Office for the Coordination of Humanitarian Affairs, Regional Office for Central and East Africa, July-December 2008, p. 5.

[3] "Poor rains intensify human suffering and deprivation — report," IRIN news service, Oct. 17, 2008, www.irinnews.org/Report .aspx?ReportId=80971.

[4] "Somalia: To Move Beyond the Failed State," International Crisis Group, Dec. 23, 2008, pp. 12, 18.

[5] "Thousands of Somalis Return to Mogadishu Despite Renewed Fighting," U.N. High Commissioner for Refugees, Feb. 27, 2009, www.unhcr.org/news/NEWS/49a7d8bb2.html.

[6] *Ibid.*

[7] "Somalia Complex Emergency: Situation Report," Jan. 15, 2009, U.S. Agency for International Development, www.usaid.gov/our_work/ humanitarian_assistance/disaster_assistance/countries/somalia/ template/fs_sr/fy2009/somalia _ce_sr04_01-15-2009.pdf.

[8] "2009 Global Update for Yemen," U.N. High Commissioner for Refugees, p. 1, www.unhcr.org/publ/PUBL/4922d4240.pdf.

[9] "Displaced Populations Report," *op. cit.*, p. 6.

[10] "Camp resources stretched by influx of Somali refugees," IRIN news service, Feb. 6, 2009, www.irinnews.org/Report.spx?ReportId=82792.

[11] "Somali refugees suffer as Dadaab camp populations swell to 230,000," UNHCR, www.unhcr.org/news/NEWS/4950ef401.html.

[12] "Kenya: Protect Somali Refugees. Government and Donors Should Urgently Address Refugee Crisis," Human Rights Watch, Nov. 13, 2008, www.hrw.org/en/news/2008/11/13/kenya-protect-somali-refugees.

so-called cluster approach made the UNHCR responsible for managing camps for IDPs displaced by natural disasters and providing emergency shelter and protection for IDPs displaced by conflict.[19]

A 2007 evaluation found the new approach had improved humanitarian responses in Chad, the Democratic Republic of the Congo, Somalia and

Uganda.[20] Ramesh Rajasingham, head of the Displacement and Protection Support Section for the U.N.'s humanitarian affairs office, says giving UNHCR a "clear leadership" role in managing displacement camps and emergency shelters has fostered "an improved IDP response."

But some non-U.N. experts say the bureaucratic changes have produced only modest benefits. Implementation has

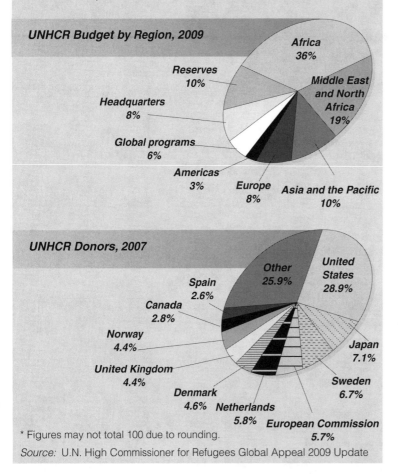

Most Funds Go to Africa, Come From U.S.

More than one-third of U.N. refugee aid in 2009 will go to programs in Africa, more than any other region. In 2007, the United States contributed nearly one-third of the funds for the Office of the U.N. High Commissioner for Refugees (UNHCR) — four times more than No. 2-donor Japan.

UNHCR Budget by Region, 2009

- Africa 36%
- Middle East and North Africa 19%
- Asia and the Pacific 10%
- Europe 8%
- Americas 3%
- Global programs 6%
- Headquarters 8%
- Reserves 10%

UNHCR Donors, 2007

- United States 28.9%
- Other 25.9%
- Japan 7.1%
- Sweden 6.7%
- European Commission 5.7%
- Netherlands 5.8%
- Denmark 4.6%
- United Kingdom 4.4%
- Norway 4.4%
- Canada 2.8%
- Spain 2.6%

* Figures may not total 100 due to rounding.

Source: U.N. High Commissioner for Refugees Global Appeal 2009 Update

recommends a rewards structure that would give agencies and individuals an incentive to better aid and protect displaced persons.

"Agencies need to internalize their work with IDPs and not see it as something separate from their missions or a burden they have to carry," she says.

James Milner, a refugee policy analyst at Carleton University in Ottawa, Ontario, Canada, and former UNHCR consultant, says the agency "does a good job in some places and a bad job in some places." While it has saved millions of lives during civil wars, the agency also ends up "warehousing" refugees for long periods, he says, causing them to abandon hope for better lives and become totally dependent on aid.

Like Harrell-Bond, Milner — who coauthored a 2008 book sympathetic to the agency's successes and failures — traces most of UNHCR's problems to its funding procedures. In effect, he says, industrialized countries that provide the bulk of UNHCR's money "earmark" where they want the money to go.[21]

"The United States, for example, gives funding to emergencies it considers important" but gives less to other situations, Milner says. "When I worked in Cameroon, each October we simply ran out of funding to provide health care for nursing mothers, because that was not a priority for the people in Washington. You can criticize UNHCR for not being more aggressive in some of these situations, but when you recognize the constraints placed on UNHCR, it places the challenges in a broader context."

Should the Refugee Convention be updated?

The 1951 Convention Relating to the Status of Refugees — known as the Refugee Convention — is the

been "half-hearted," especially in protecting IDPs, says Roberta Cohen, a senior fellow at the Brookings Institution and prominent IDP advocate. The UNHCR is not "playing the robust leadership role" she had hoped for in protecting IDPs.

Likewise, Joel Charny, vice president for policy at Refugees International, says the UNHCR's protection of IDPs remains "problematic." Ferris, Cohen's successor at the Brookings-Bern Project on Displacement,

basic underpinning of refugee law. Created to protect European refugees during and after World War II, the treaty was amended in 1967 to apply worldwide.

The treaty grants "asylum" to refugees, or groups of them, who can demonstrate a "well-founded fear of being persecuted" because of race, nationality, religion or political beliefs. Those who flee their country because of such a fear are considered refugees. The process of demonstrating that fear and seeking permission to stay in the country of refuge is called seeking asylum. However, in many places — including the United States — asylum seekers may be imprisoned for months or even years while their cases are reviewed. Once asylum is granted, refugees can stay in the host country until it is safe to return home. Refugees who are denied asylum often are deported, usually back to their home countries.

Even with the 1967 amendment, the convention does not apply to the vast majority of people who flee from their homes. For example, IDPs do not have legal protection because they do not cross international borders, nor do those who flee across borders to escape natural disasters.[22] Being covered by the treaty might have little significance for people forced from their homes by violent groups like the Lord's Resistance Army. Even so, some advocates say applying the treaty to IDPs might, in some cases, pressure the governments involved to take better care of their citizens.

The treaty has critics across the ideological spectrum. Some refugee advocates, including Harrell-Bond, complain that it lacks universal standards for granting asylum, so Western countries, in particular, "are free to turn away asylum-seekers on no basis whatsoever."

Some Western officials say the treaty is being misused by "economic migrants" — would-be immigrants from poor countries simply seeking a better life — who claim to be refugees but do not qualify for asylum on the basis of a fear of persecution.

The treaty "is no longer working as its framers intended," then British Home Secretary Jack Straw said in 2001, citing the large increase in displaced people worldwide. "Too much effort and resources are being expended on dealing with unfounded claims for asylum, and not enough on helping those in need of protection."[23] He called for "radical thinking" on a better way to determine who is a refugee and who is not.

Despite such concerns, many experts say the convention will not be amended or updated any time soon. The U.N.

More than 250,000 Sri Lankans have been forced from their homes, often repeatedly, in the latest — and possibly final — round of the 26-year war between government forces and separatist Tamil Tiger guerrillas. Above, internally displaced Tamil civilians wait to enter a government shelter near Colombo.

treaty-making process is cumbersome and takes years to complete. Moreover, global interest in new treaties has dwindled in recent years, and even IDP advocates aren't willing to risk having the treaty watered down instead of strengthened.

Carleton University's Milner notes the current treaty was negotiated shortly after World War II, "when notions of human justice were quite powerful because of what happened during the war, particularly in Nazi Germany." Nearly six decades later, Western countries — the desired destination for many refugees — are increasingly reluctant to open their borders. "If we reopened the Refugee Convention, we likely would see a race to the lowest common denominator — protecting borders — rather than refugees," Milner says. "That's a risk I'm not willing to take."

Khalid Koser, an analyst specializing in refugee affairs at the Geneva Center for Security Policy, agrees. "At least the current convention has 150-odd signatories, most of whom abide by it," Koser says.

The UNHCR has expressed similar concerns. In a recent paper exploring whether those fleeing natural disasters should be given legal status under the treaty, the agency warned that any attempt to modify the convention could lower refugee-protection standards "and even undermine the international refugee-protection regime altogether."[24]

Meanwhile, Europe is engaged in a spirited debate over implementation of the treaty; since 2001 the European Union (EU) has been developing a common system for granting asylum among its 27 member countries. The European Pact on Immigration and Asylum, adopted by EU leaders on Oct. 16, 2008, promises that EU countries will speed up asylum determinations, eliminating delays that often stretch into months or years.[25] Refugee rights advocates, however, worry the EU is trying to close its doors to legitimate refugees, not just economic migrants who are not entitled to asylum under the treaty.

At Human Rights Watch, refugee policy Director Bill Frelick says the new European pact also does little to relieve unequal burden-sharing. Most migrants and refugees from Africa and the Middle East enter Europe through the poorest countries in southeastern Europe, which have been rejecting refugees at very high rates. For instance, since 2004 Greece has granted asylum to fewer than 1 percent of the refugees from Iraq, Afghanistan and other countries, according to the European Council on Refugees and Exiles, a coalition of 69 nongovernmental organizations.[26] By contrast, some other European countries, particularly in Scandinavia, accept upwards of 90 percent of asylum-seekers, Frelick notes.

"There has been an utter failure to share the refugee burdens," Frelick says. "The richer countries have done an effective job of deflecting the burden off onto the poor countries, which are responding by turning people away, even those who are legitimate refugees."

Should the United States admit more Iraqi refugees?

Fearing that some could be terrorists, the United States has been slow to accept Iraqis who have fled to neighboring countries — notably Syria and Jordan — since the U.S. invasion in 2003.

Through the middle of 2008, the Bush administration accepted only about 10,000 Iraqi refugees out of the 1-2 million who have fled, according to Refugees International and other nongovernmental organizations.[27] But under pressure from Congress and advocacy groups, it stepped up Iraqi admissions last year and admitted more than 13,800 Iraqis as permanent residents — slightly more than the administration's

12,000 annual goal for fiscal 2008, which ended on Oct. 1. The administration's 2009 goal is 17,000 Iraqi admissions.[28]

Several major refugee and human-rights groups want the U.S. quota raised to 105,000 Iraqis in 2009. Among the Iraqi refugees in Syria and Jordan are thousands who worked directly with the U.S. military and other government agencies, American contractors and the news media. Some served as translators or even intelligence operatives, while others filled jobs such as drivers and cooks.

"Their stay in neighboring states remains extremely precarious, and many live in fear of being forcibly returned to Iraq, where they face death threats and further persecution," said a joint statement by Refugees International and a dozen other organizations on July 31, 2008. Helping these Iraqis resettle in the United States "will demonstrate America's dedication to protecting the most vulnerable and our commitment to peace and security in the region."[29]

The U.S. Department of Homeland Security said in September it was "committed to streamlining the process for admitting Iraqi refugees to the U.S. while ensuring the highest level of security."[30] However, the Obama administration has not announced plans for a dramatic increase in admissions. A State Department spokesman said in early February a decision was pending.

A report released in January by the Center for American Progress, a liberal think tank in Washington, D.C., said 30,000 to 100,000 Iraqis have been "affiliated" with the United States in one way or another during the war, and many would be "in imminent danger" of assassination if they returned home.[31]

The group advocates bringing up to 25,000 of those Iraqis and their families to the United States over the next five years. Natalie Ondiak, lead author of the proposal, says the United States "has a moral obligation to the Iraqis who have worked for the government, were loyal to us and now fear for their lives because of the stigma of having been associated with the United States."

However, Ann Corcoran — a Maryland blogger who runs the Refugee Resettlement Watch blog — is a vocal critic of such proposals. She cites cases in which church groups and other agencies bring refugees to the United States but fail to help them adjust to their new lives.

"These organizations are not taking very good care of the refugees who are already here, and they say they don't have the resources to do the job," she says. "So, if we are talking about another 25,000 or 100,000 refugees, where do they think these people will be cared for? Who is going to make sure they have housing and jobs and education for their children? It's just insane."[32]

A better alternative, she says "is to keep them in the region, to keep them comfortable and proceeding with their lives in the Middle East until the situation in Iraq is safe enough for them to return."

Congress in 2006 created a program to speed up admissions for up to 500 Iraqi and Afghan translators per year. In 2008 Congress added another program allowing up to 5,000 Iraqis who worked in various capacities for the U.S. government or contractors to enter the United States in each of the five fiscal years, beginning in 2008. However, Ondiak says only about 600 translators gained admission in 2008.

BACKGROUND

Refugee Rights and Needs

Although the forced displacement of people from their homes is as old as human history, the idea that society has a moral obligation to come to their aid is relatively new.

After World War I, the newly formed League of Nations created the post of High Commissioner for Refugees but gave the office little authority and few resources. The league (the forerunner of the U.N.) also adopted two treaties in the 1930s offering limited legal protection to refugees, but only a handful of countries ratified them.[33]

The displacement of millions of people during World War II finally brought significant action on refugees. As the war was winding down, the United States and its allies created the United Nations Relief and Rehabilitation Agency, which gave emergency aid to 7 million displaced people. After the war, a successor organization, the International Refugee Organization, helped some 1 million dislocated Europeans find new homes.[34]

The modern era of international aid to refugees began in 1950-51, when the United Nations created the office of the U.N. High Commissioner for Refugees and held a special conference in Geneva to draft the treaty that became known as the Refugee Convention. Both the UNHCR and the treaty were aimed at aiding European war refugees or those who fled Eastern Europe after the Soviet Union imposed communist rule across the region. In fact, the treaty applied only to those who had become refugees before Jan. 1, 1951, and the text made clear the drafters had Europeans in mind. Moreover, the U.N. General Assembly gave the UNHCR only a three-year mandate, assuming the refugee problem would be quickly solved.[35]

In 1949, before the UNHCR started work, the U.N. Relief and Works Agency for Palestine Refugees in the Near East (known as UNRWA) was created to assist the 700,000 Palestinians who fled or were driven from their homes in what is now Israel during the 1948 Arab-Israeli war.[36] The UNRWA also was considered short-lived. But nearly 60 years later the ultimate status of the Palestinians remains unresolved, and the UNRWA is still providing food, medical care and other aid to a Palestinian population that has grown to 4.6 million. About 1.4 million Palestinians live in UNRWA camps in Jordan, Lebanon, Syria, the West Bank and Gaza Strip; the rest live on their own.[37]

Conflicts continued across the globe after World War II, some of them widely seen as proxy wars among governments and rebel groups backed by the two Cold War superpowers, the Soviet Union and the United States. In each case, dislocated civilians crossed international borders and created a new generation of refugees.

The U.N. General Assembly officially recognized the new refugee trend in 1967, adopting an amendment, or protocol, to the refugee convention. The Protocol Relating to the Status of Refugees dropped the pre-1951 limitation, giving legal protection to refugees worldwide, not just in Europe.[38] The convention and its protocol are now among the most widely adopted U.N. treaties; each has been ratified by 144 countries.[39]

The collapse of the Soviet Union in 1991 brought new hope for peace. But bloody sectarian conflicts in the Balkans and Africa's Great Lakes region shattered such dreams. Some conflicts dislocated enormous populations, but many people, for one reason or another, stayed in their own countries, where as IDPs they were not covered by the international refugee treaties.

In the 1990s international agencies and human-rights advocates began demanding aid and legal protections for

CHRONOLOGY

1940s-1950s *Newly created United Nations (U.N.) aids refugees after World War II ends.*

1949 U.N. Relief and Works Agency is established to aid Palestinians pushed from their homes during the 1949 Arab-Israeli war.

1950 Office of U.N. High Commissioner for Refugees (UNHCR) is created.

1951 Special U.N. conference adopts Convention Relating to the Status of Refugees (the Refugee Convention) to protect those who fled their countries before Jan. 1, 1951, to escape persecution due to "race, religion, nationality or membership of a particular social group." Generally viewed as applying only to Europeans, the treaty goes into effect in 1954.

1960s-1980s *Cold War conflicts and upheavals create waves of new refugees.*

1967 U.N expands Refugee Convention to cover all refugees fleeing persecution as described in the treaty, not just Europeans who left their home countries before 1951.

1969 Organization of African Unity broadly defines a refugee in Africa as anyone who flees his country because of "external aggression, occupation, foreign domination or events seriously disturbing public order in either part or the whole of his country of origin."

1984 The Colloquium on the International Protection of Refugees in Central America, Mexico and Panama adopts the Cartagena Declaration, defining refugees as anyone fleeing their country because their "lives, safety or freedom" are threatened by "generalized violence, foreign aggression, internal conflicts, massive violation of human rights or other circumstances." Although not official policy, many regional governments adopt the declaration.

1990s-2000s *New wave of civil conflicts forces policy makers to pay more attention to the needs of people displaced within their own borders.*

1992-1995 Civil conflicts in the former Yugoslavia displace several hundred thousand people.

1994 Genocidal rampage in Rwanda kills 800,000 Hutus and Tutsis; hundreds of thousands of others flee their homes, many into neighboring countries.

1997 Government-backed rebels oust longtime dictator Mobutu Sese Seko of Zaire (later the Democratic Republic of the Congo), triggering years of civil war in Africa's Great Lakes region; an estimated 5 million people die, and thousands are displaced during fighting that continues today.

1998 The Guiding Principles on Internal Displacement establish rules for aiding and protecting internally displaced persons (IDPs); the guidelines eventually are incorporated into U.N procedures but are not legally binding.

2002 About 2 million Afghan refugees return home (mostly from Pakistan and Iran) after a U.S.-led invasion topples the Taliban government. Some 6 million had fled during three decades of war — the largest number of refugees generated by any conflict since World War II.

2004 In a landmark decision, Colombia's Constitutional Court orders the government to increase aid to about 2 million people displaced by conflict.

2005 U.N. adopts "responsibility to protect" doctrine, which holds every government responsible for protecting the rights of its citizens and says the international community has a responsibility to intervene if a government abuses its own citizens. . . . U.N. gives UNHCR more responsibility for helping IDPs.

2008 U.N. launches a year-long publicity campaign to focus international attention on the needs of IDPs. . . . UNHCR starts a campaign to help end long-term displacements of those forced from their homes in Afghanistan, the Balkans, Burundi, Eritrea and Myanmar.

2009 African Union is scheduled in April to adopt a treaty recognizing the rights of internally displaced people, based on the 1998 Guiding Principles.

these large groups. In 1992, U.N. Secretary-General Boutros Boutros-Ghali appointed Francis Deng, a former Sudanese diplomat, as the U.N.'s first special representative on internally displaced people.

Deng, who held the post until 2004, was largely responsible for drafting the Guiding Principles on Internal Displacement.[40] Although the document has never been put into international law, U.N. agencies and a dozen countries have incorporated its principles into their laws and policies. (*See box, p. 138.*)

However, says refugee specialist Koser at the Geneva Center for Security Policy, "there is very little political will to formalize [the principles] into a binding convention, and few states would ratify it."

Rising Displacements

U.N. officials and policy experts count more than four dozen countries — most in Africa and Asia — with significant populations displaced by civil wars or other violence. When the consequences of natural disasters are considered, however, the displacement problem becomes nearly universal. Thousands of Gulf Coast residents in the United States remain displaced by Hurricane Katrina in 2006, and millions in China's Sichuan Province are homeless nearly a year after a major earthquake.

Colombia has one of the world's largest IDP populations, and hundreds of thousands of people are still displaced in Chechnya and Georgia in the Caucuses and in Bosnia, Croatia, Kosovo and Serbia as a result of the Balkan wars. Thousands more have been displaced by ongoing conflict and instability in Somalia. (*See sidebar, p. 122.*)

Here are some of the displacements that are high on the international agenda:

Afghanistan — At least 6 million Afghans fled — mostly to Pakistan and Iran — between the Soviet Union's December 1979 invasion and the U.S. ousting of the Taliban government in late 2001. During periods of relative calm in the 1980s and '90s, hundreds of thousands of Afghan refugees returned home, but many fled again when fighting resumed.[41]

Shortly after a new Western-backed government took office in Kabul at the end of 2001, refugees began returning home in large numbers. Between 2002 and late 2008, about 5.6 million refugees returned, of whom nearly 4.4 million received UNHCR aid (the rest returned on their own).[42] Since 2007, thousands of refugees have returned because Pakistan closed some refugee camps, and Iran deported thousands of mostly undocumented Afghan men seeking work.[43]

By late 2008, the UNHCR estimated that about 2 million Afghan refugees were still in Pakistan and nearly 1 million in Iran.[44] Worried about its inability to provide housing, jobs and other services for returning refugees, the Afghan government in 2008 began discouraging large-scale returns. "We don't have the means to provide an encouraging environment for refugees to repatriate," Shir Mohammad Etibari, minister of refugees and returnees, said in September. The U.N. and other international agencies "only make promises but do little."[45]

Another 235,000 Afghans are displaced but still in Afghanistan. Some were forced to return to Afghanistan against their will, only to find that they had no place to live and could find no jobs. Among the most vulnerable are several thousand returnees who were forced out of Pakistan and now live at a camp in the Chemtala desert, about 15 miles west of Jalalabad. Last winter they struggled to survive in mud huts and tents provided by the UNHCR and the Norwegian Refugee Council. "I wish we hadn't left Pakistan," said elderly returnee Golam Shah. "Life was much better there."[46]

A similar complaint came from 18-year-old Wali, who grew up in Pakistan's Jalozai refugee village. Forced out last May, he now lives in a tent in Balkh Province in northern Afghanistan. "I didn't expect to face such problems or to end up in such a place," he said. "There is nothing here — no shelter, not enough water, no trees for firewood, no electricity and no work."[47]

Colombia — A long-running rebel insurgency and the government's aggressive, U.S.-backed war against narcotics cartels have created what the U.N. calls the worst humanitarian crisis in the Western Hemisphere. Up to half a million Colombians have fled to neighboring countries, and thousands have emigrated to the United States. At least 2.8 million mostly rural people are internally displaced in the nation of 45 million.[48]

Since the 1960s the military has brutally suppressed two leftist guerrilla groups claiming to be fighting for land reform and other social causes — the Revolutionary Armed Forces of Colombia (FARC) and the National Liberation Army (ELN). Right-wing paramilitary armies formed by major landowners and elements of the military aided the anti-insurgency campaign.

Millions Remain in Exile for Decades

"Whole generations of kids grow up in refugee camps."

Miljo and Milica Miljic grabbed their two children and fled Tuzla, Bosnia, in 1992, at the beginning of a nearly four-year civil war that tore their country apart. "We didn't take anything with us because we didn't have time," Miljo told a representative of the U.N. High Commissioner for Refugees (UNHCR) this past January. "We had to run for our lives. The only thing that comes to mind in such a situation is to save your children and your own life. You don't think about the photographs, about personal documents, clothes, whatever."[1]

The Miljics are among nearly 97,000 refugees from Bosnia and Croatia who have not returned to their homes, even though the war ended in late 1995. They are still in Serbia, where the refugee population has slowly dwindled down from more than 500,000 in 1996.[2]

The words "refugees" and "displaced persons" conjure up images of short-term emergencies: people fleeing their homes temporarily because of wars, hurricanes or earthquakes, only to return home a few weeks, or at most a few months, later. While many do return home once a crisis has passed, most refugees and internally displaced persons (IDPs) remain displaced long after the emergency is over.

In fact, refugees fleeing conflict end up staying away from their homes an average of 18 years, and many IDPs are displaced for comparable periods. James Milner, a refugee expert at Carleton University in Ottawa, Canada, says some situations last even longer: The Palestinians who fled Israel during the 1948-49 Arab-Israeli war have been in exile ever since.

In recent years experts have begun focusing on "protracted situations" involving refugees and IDPs displaced for at least five years, and numerous conferences have been held to discuss the problem of long-term displacements. U.N. High Commissioner Antonio Guterres said more than 30 situations around the world involve a total of about 6 million refugees who have been living in long-term exile.

"Many are effectively trapped in the camps and communities where they are accommodated," Guterres said. "Their home countries are caught in endless conflict or afflicted by political stalemate or human-rights violations, and most are not allowed to hold jobs, work the land where they live or integrate into the local communities."[3]

Most of the long-term displaced are children and youth, says Elizabeth Ferris, director of the Brookings-Bern Project on Internal Displacement. "You have whole generations of kids who grow up and live in refugee camps, where typically you have a breakdown of normal social institutions," she says.

From 11 million to 17 million people have been displaced for at least five years but are still living inside their own countries, Ferris says. "Unfortunately, the world has paid very little attention to these situations, which are allowed to fester for years and years," she says.

Aside from the Palestinians, perhaps the best-known protracted refugee situation involves the estimated 6 million people who have fled their homes during three decades of warfare in Afghanistan, which began with the Soviet Union's invasion in 1979. Most went to neighboring Iran or Pakistan, where they settled in formal camps or moved into cities. Millions of Afghan refugees returned home after the U.S. invasion in 2001, but nearly 3 million are still refugees.[4]

Many scholars and aid officials worry that another long-term refugee situation is developing among the 2 million or more Iraqis who have fled their homeland. Although the Baghdad government has encouraged some to return, the U.N. and private aid groups say it is still too unsafe, especially for Sunni Muslims or members of other minority groups.[5]

Other protracted refugee situations prioritized by the UNHCR include:

- **Myanmar/Bangladesh.** Some 200,000 Rohingya, a Muslim ethnic group in North Rakhine state in Myanmar, fled to neighboring Bangladesh in 1991 to escape persecution by the military junta in Myanmar. Thousands have since returned to Myanmar, but the majority remain in Bangladesh and are classified by the U.N. as "stateless" persons because Myanmar no longer considers them as citizens.[6]

- **Eritrea/Sudan.** Some 90,000 Eritreans are long-term refugees in eastern Sudan, many since the late 1960s when Eritrean rebels launched a 30-year-long war against Ethiopia. (Eritrea gained its independence in 1993, but the two countries fought another bloody war from 1998 until 2000.) Additional Eritrean refugees continue to arrive in Sudan, joined by refugees from Ethiopia and Somalia. Most live in camps and lack any rights or protections but have increasingly begun to move into Khartoum and other Sudanese cities, over the government's objection.[7]

- **The Balkans.** Like the Miljics, hundreds of thousands of people dislocated by war in the former Yugoslavia during the 1990s have not returned to their home regions. Some 200,000 refugees, mostly ethnic Serbs, became naturalized citizens in Serbia rather than return to Bosnia or Croatia, where Serbs are in the minority.[8]

- **Burundi/Tanzania.** Violent civil conflict in Burundi in 1972 forced thousands to flee into neighboring Tanzania, where the government created three settlements in central and western Tanzania and provided land and other services for them. In 2007, about 218,000 refugees were still in the settlements. Under an agreement that many experts consider historic, Burundi and Tanzania decided in 2008 to resolve the status of these so-called "old settlement" refugees from 1972. Tanzania agreed to grant citizenship to, and fully integrate into local communities, some 176,000 of the remaining refugees. Those wanting to return to Burundi were to be allowed to do so by September 2009.[9]

Protracted IDP Situations

Globally, about half of the estimated 26 million IDPs displaced by violence are stuck in protracted situations, according to Neill Wright, the UNHCR's senior coordinator for IDPs. And some who were forced from their homes by natural disasters also remain displaced after five years.

Both types of protracted situations exist in Kenya, where about 350,000 people have been displaced long-term by conflict, unresolved land disputes and natural disasters.[10] Post-election violence displaced another 500,000 Kenyans in late 2007 and early 2008, but about half of those had returned home by late 2008.[11]

Ferris, of the Brookings-Bern project, says at least three-dozen countries have long-term displacement situations, and people are still being displaced in about a dozen others, such as Colombia, the Democratic Republic of the Congo and Somalia. In most other countries, the fighting has ended, but thousands remain displaced because peace agreements were never negotiated or the IDPs there are afraid, or unwilling, to return to their homes for other reasons.

Experts say no single solution will solve the protracted-displacement problem. Even negotiating peace agreements does not guarantee that displaced people can or will return home.

But policy makers have identified several essential elements that would help create "durable solutions" for protracted situations. One element, they say, is recognizing that forcing or encouraging people to return to their original homes may not always be the best solution, particularly when people have been displaced for many years, and they no longer have reasons for returning home.

An alternative to repatriation is "local integration" — allowing displaced people to become part of the local communities where they have taken refuge. This route is often politically difficult because local communities usually don't

The U.N. Relief and Works Agency, which for 60 years has aided Palestinian refugees, was stretched thin during prolonged Israeli military strikes earlier this year. More than 1,000 Palestinians were killed and many homes were destroyed, such as this woman's house in the Jabalia refugee camp in northern Gaza.

AFP/Getty Images/Mohammed Abed

want to absorb large numbers of outsiders. Milner says he hopes Tanzania's willingness to accept Burundians displaced for nearly four decades as citizens will become a model for other countries.

"This creates a significant strategic opportunity for the international community to demonstrate that local integration can work," he says. "Now, the next step is for the donor community to meet its responsibilities to help countries, like Tanzania, that might be willing to resolve these situations."

The UNHCR also acknowledged in November 2008 that its policy of providing only short-term humanitarian aid to refugees in camps had failed to help them develop personal independence and job skills that would allow them to live on their own. Too often, a UNHCR report said, "refugees were left to live in camps indefinitely, often with restrictions placed on their rights, as well as their ability to support themselves by means of agriculture, trade or employment."[12]

Under the U.N.'s "humanitarian reform" program adopted in late 2005, the agency is changing its approach, says Jeff Crisp, director of UNHCR's policy and evaluation service.

[1] "The continuing struggle of Europe's forgotten refugees," U.N. High Commissioner for Refugees, Jan. 12, 2009, www.unhcr.org/news/NEWS/496b6ad12.html..

[2] *Ibid.*

[3] "Protracted Refugee Situations: High Commissioner's Initiative," U.N. High Commissioner for Refugees, December 2008, p. 2, www.unhcr.org/protect/PROTECTION/4937de6f2.pdf.

[4] "Protracted Refugee Situations: Revisiting The Problem," U.N. High Commissioner for Refugees, June 2, 2008, pp. 5-6, www.unhcr.org/excom/EXCOM/484514c12.pdf.

[5] "NGOs warn against encouraging large-scale refugee returns," IRIN news service, Nov. 3, 2008, www.irinnews.org/Report.aspx?ReportId=81258.

[6] "Protracted Refugee Situations: The High Commissioner's Initiative," *op. cit.*, pp. 9-11.

[7] *Ibid.*, p. 14.

[8] *Ibid.*, p. 32.

[9] *Ibid.*, pp. 25-29.

[10] "Frequently Asked Questions on IDPs," U.N. Office for the Coordination of Humanitarian Affairs, Dec. 4, 2008, p. 4.

[11] *Ibid.*, p. 2.

[12] "Protracted Refugee Situations: A discussion paper prepared for the High Commissioner's Dialogue on Protection Challenges," Nov. 20, 2008, p. 13, www.unhcr.org/protect/PROTECTION/492ad3782.pdf.

Colombia's long-running rebel insurgency and the government's aggressive, U.S.-backed war against narcotics cartels have created the worst humanitarian crisis in the Western Hemisphere, according to the U.N. This family living in a tent in a Bogotá park is among at least 2.8 million displaced Colombians.

Both the guerrillas and paramilitaries eventually became deeply involved in the drug trade, turning an ideological war over land reform and other social issues into a battle for control of illegal cocaine production. The government's war against cocaine — most of which is consumed in the United States — has been funded largely by Washington.

Colombia is now the hemisphere's major source of refugees, most of whom have fled to Ecuador and Venezuela; others sought refuge in Brazil, Panama and Costa Rica.[49] About 460,000 Colombians are in "refugee-like situations" — they've fled Colombia but are not officially considered refugees and receive little if any official aid.[50] The flow of refugees has worsened Colombia's relations with left-leaning Ecuador and Venezuela.

Colombia estimates it has 2.8 million registered IDPs — among the world's highest for an individual country.[51] But nongovernmental agencies say the real number is much higher. The Catholic Church-affiliated Consultancy for Human Rights and Displacement puts the number at more than 4.3 million.[52] Many displaced people do not register for fear of retaliation or being forced to return to unsafe areas. The displacement rate has escalated in recent years, according to both the government and private agencies: About 300,000 people were displaced in 2007, but 270,000 were displaced in just the first six months of 2008.[53]

Colombia's IDPs have received serious attention since the country's Constitutional Court in 2004 ordered the government to provide aid — one of the few instances where an activist court has significantly helped IDPs.

Andrea Lari, a senior advocate at Refugees International, says the government helps IDPs survive on a daily basis but does virtually nothing to enable them to escape from urban shantytowns. The government provides "too much social welfare and not enough . . . job training or education beyond primary schools — the help needed to sustain themselves where they now live," he says. Going home "is not a serious option" for most because they have lost their land and are afraid to return.

Democratic Republic of the Congo — Hundreds of thousands of civilians continue to suffer from fighting in the eastern provinces of Africa's second-largest country — a war that officially ended more than five years ago. At least 400,000 Congolese were displaced in 2008 and early this year by continuing violence, bringing the total displaced to about 1.25 million.[54]

Two major wars — involving five other African countries at one point — raged in Congo from 1997 until peace agreements hammered out in 2002-03 ended most of the fighting and led to elections in 2006. More than 5 million people may have died during the wars — the largest toll by far of any post-World War II conflict, according to the International Rescue Committee.[55]

Lingering conflicts still plague several areas, including North Kivu Province on the borders with Rwanda and Uganda. There, remnants of the Hutu extremist forces responsible for Rwanda's genocide in 1994 have battled a rebel force claiming to support the Congolese Tutsis, members of the same ethnic group targeted by the Hutus in the Rwandan genocide. Until recently, the Congolese army had not curbed either faction.

In January, however, the Congolese and Rwandan armies launched an unusual joint military operation targeting both the Hutu and Tutsi forces in North Kivu. And in a potential step toward peace, the Rwandan army on Jan. 22 arrested the self-styled Tutsi general Laurent Nkunda, whose rebels had wreaked havoc in the region.[56] The arrest — coming on the heels of a related international campaign against the Lord's Resistance Army — offered the first tangible hope in many years that the region's troubles might some day come to an end.[57]

Online Newspaper Fights for Refugees in Kenya

'We need to be able to help ourselves'

Problems with the water supply, inadequate health inspections of food suppliers, indifferent officials. Such issues would be the meat-and-potatoes of any local newspaper. But who draws attention to such concerns in a refugee camp as big as a mid-size city?

Most refugee camps have community organizations that present residents' concerns to camp officials, but they rarely receive wide attention locally. Since last December, however, the problems faced by the 50,000 refugees at the Kakuma camp in northwest Kenya have been exposed not only to local residents but to people around the world via the camp's Internet newspaper, *Kanere* (KAkuma NEws REflector).

The paper (http://kakuma.wordpress.com) is run by staff of volunteer journalists aided by Bethany Ojalehto, a 2008 Cornell University graduate who is studying the rights of refugees at the camp on a Fulbright research scholarship. She says several refugees interested in starting a newspaper approached her for help when she arrived at the camp last October, and she agreed because their interests and her research "blended seamlessly and have now been channeled into this project."

So far *Kanere* is published only in English, which is a common language for many of the camp's residents, who can read it at computer stations in several locations. The paper's editors say they hope to expand into other languages once they get more help.

Twenty-four-year-old Qabaata, one of the paper's editors, says he fled Ethiopia in 2003 after being targeted by government security forces for writing an article supporting a student strike. A journalism student at the time, he went with other students to Kakuma after being arrested and released by authorities in Addis Ababa, Ethiopia's capital. He is seeking asylum status from the UNHCR because he says he cannot return to Ethiopia. "It is not safe for me there," he says. He hopes to win a scholarship to finish his journalism studies but has no immediate prospects for attaining that goal.

Kakuma has one of the most diverse camp populations in Africa. Opened in 1992 to aid refugees from the long civil war in southern Sudan, Kakuma now houses about 25,000 Sudanese, 18,000 Somalis, 4,500 Ethiopians and 1,800 other Africans.[1] Since mid-2008 the U.N. High Commissioner for Refugees (UNHCR) has transferred thousands of Somali refugees to Kakuma from three overcrowded camps at Dadaab, Kenya, about 700 miles to the east. (*See Somalia box, p. 122.*)

Qabaata says *Kanere* provides a unique opportunity to share concerns across the camp's different ethnic and national communities and to voice grievances to camp officials. "The refugees here don't have access to the people who are governing them," he says. "They only have access through their community leaders, but even their leaders do not always have access."

Negash, another Ethiopian refugee who works on *Kanere*, notes that one crucial issue is water. All water for the camp comes from underground aquifers and is rationed at about 20 liters per refugee per day. And some refugees have to walk long distances to get it. The paper's first issue, in December 2008, pointed out that refugees in one section of the camp had recently gone without adequate water for three days while a broken pump was being fixed. Why is water rationed for refugees, the paper asked, while U.N. and other aid agencies' staff members living nearby "are given unlimited water?"

Kanere also deals with UNHCR budget cutbacks, long food-distribution lines, the lack of job opportunities, low pay for refugees compared to local Kenyans and the "poor performance" of the camp's 14 primary and two secondary schools.

Above all, say Qabaata and Negash, *Kanere* advocates on behalf of refugees' basic human rights. "As refugees, we are told we have rights, but in reality we have no rights here in the camp," Negash says. "We hope *Kanere* will empower the refugee community, help it to be self-reliant. As it is, the humanitarian community is just making us dependent, reliant on them. We need to be able to help ourselves."

---

[1] "Kenya: Population of Concern to UNHCR," November 2008, p. 6, www.unhcr.org/partners/PARTNERS/4951ef9d2.pdf.

Permanent Solutions Sought for the Displaced

Aid agencies turning away from short-term solutions

In the past, the U.N. High Commissioner for Refugees (UNHCR) and other aid agencies have focused primarily on short-term fixes — such as providing emergency food, medical care and other aid — for those displaced by war, conflict or natural disaster. They also generally assumed that displaced people wanted to return to their homes, and encouraging them to do so was easier than resettling them elsewhere.

But in recent years aid agencies have begun paying more attention to moving displaced people out of camps and makeshift shelters and back into normal lives.

Three so-called durable solutions have been proposed for refugees as well as internally displaced persons (IDPs), or those still living in their own countries:

- **Return or repatriation** — Returning either to their past residence or to their home neighborhood or region.
- **Local integration** — Settling permanently in the locality or country where the person has sought temporary refuge.
- **Resettlement elsewhere** — For refugees, moving to a willing third country; for IDPs, moving to a different part or region of their home countries.

In the absence of universally accepted standards for deciding when an IDP is no longer displaced, the Brookings-Bern Project on Internal Displacement in 2007 created a "Framework for Durable Solutions" for IDPs, which has been officially "welcomed" by the U.N.[1] It says IDPs' displacement should be considered ended when one of the three durable solutions occurs, and they "no longer have needs specifically related to their displacement." Although former IDPs may still have humanitarian needs, at this point "their needs are basically the same as other people in the local population, and it's the government's responsibility to help them," says project director Elizabeth Ferris.

In 2007, about 2 million IDPs and 731,000 refugees returned to their home countries, their actual homes or to their home regions, according to the UNHCR.[2] About half were in the Democratic Republic of the Congo, although conflict displaced another 500,000 Congolese that same year.[3] More than half of the returning refugees — some 374,000 — were Afghans.[4]

Barbara Harrell-Bond, a veteran advocate for refugees and leading critic of the UNHCR, faults the agency for continuing to focus on repatriation for refugees, because she says integration in asylum countries "often is the only solution." UNHCR officials, however, say local integration and resettlement are difficult because host countries are not inclined to accept refugees and displaced people on a per-manent basis.

But resettlement efforts are occurring, albeit on a small scale, say the UNHCR and refugee advocacy groups. In 2007, the UNHCR recommended 99,000 refugees for resettlement in third countries, nearly double the previous year, but only 70,000 were able to resettle — less than 1 percent of the total refugees.[5] Historically, the United States has accepted more refugees than any other country; in 2006, the last year for which comparative figures are

Iraq — The 1991 Persian Gulf War and sectarian violence following the 2003 U.S. invasion of Iraq have swelled the ranks of displaced Iraqis to between 3 million and 5 million — out of a total population of around 28 million. Most have remained in the country but fled their home regions, usually to escape sectarian violence.[58]

Many of the Iraqi IDPs live with friends or relatives and receive government food rations. For those who cannot get rations, the World Food Program on Jan. 3 announced a one-year program to aid about 750,000 Iraqis inside Iraq and 360,000 in Syria.[59]

Many IDPs live in informal camps inside Iraq. The Iraqi government early in 2008 had announced an ambitious plan to build IDP housing, but falling oil prices have forced budget cuts that endanger the effort.[60] Then in late 2008 the government moved to close some of the camps by giving families one-time $4,250 stipends to return to their homes or find new places to live.[61] The UNHCR plans to help about 400,000 Iraqi IDPs this year.[62]

Some 300,000 displaced Iraqis have returned home, and nearly two-thirds of those still displaced want to return to their original home regions, according to a

available, the United States accepted 41,300 refugees — more than half of the 71,700 resettlements that occurred that year.[6]

Local integration sometimes occurs informally, particularly when displaced people are not confined to official camps or settlements. For instance, in Pakistan, many of the estimated 1.8 million remaining Afghan refugees have established new lives in Peshawar, Quetta and other cities. Many had been refugees for more than 20 years, and more than half were born outside Afghanistan; a substantial number were ethnic Pashtuns, which also is the dominant ethnic group in the border areas of Pakistan. As a result, remaining in Pakistan has been a natural solution for them.[7]

In contrast, official agreements allowing large numbers of refugees or IDPs to move permanently from camps into local communities are rare. An exception is Tanzania, where more than 200,000 Burundians have been refugees since 1972. Seeking to resolve a situation that had dragged on so long, and with U.N. help that included limited financial aid, Burundi and Tanzania agreed in 2007 that 172,000 refugees could remain in Tanzania as citizens, while 46,000 would return to Burundi. The agreement is expected to be implemented by late 2009.[8]

James Milner, of Canada's Carleton University, says Tanzania's willingness to accept long-term refugees as permanent refugees "creates a strategic opportunity for the

Afghan refugees who have just returned from Pakistan wait to register at a transition center in Kabul in June 2008. Aid agencies have begun focusing on moving displaced people out of camps and back into normal lives, often by returning them to their home countries.

AFP/Getty Images/Jaime Reina

international community to show that there are alternatives to warehousing refugees forever in camps."

The only missing element, he says, is a willingness by the major donor nations to put their money and diplomatic leverage to work to encourage other countries to follow Tanzania's example. "The United States is the hegemon in the global refugee regime," he says. "If the United States were to support more of this kind of action, eventually we could see real solutions for refugees."

[1] "When Displacement Ends: A Framework for Durable Solutions," Brookings-Bern Project on Internal Displacement, June 2007, www.brookings.edu/reports/2007/09displacementends.aspx.

[2] "Note on International Protection," U.N. High Commissioner for Refugees, June 2008, p. 2, www.unhcr.org/publ/PUBL/484807202.pdf.

[3] *Ibid.*, p. 15.

[4] *Ibid.*

[5] *Ibid.*, p. 17.

[6] "Global Trends for 2006: Refugees, Asylum-seekers, Returnees, Internally Displaced and Stateless Persons," U.N. High Commissioner for Refugees, June 2007, p. 8, www.unhcr.org/statistics/STATISTICS/4676a71d4.pdf.

[7] "Afghanistan — The Challenges of Sustaining Returns," U.N. High Commissioner for Refugees, www.unhcr.org/cgi-bin/texis/vtx/afghan?page=intro.

[8] "Protracted Refugee Situations: The High Commissioner's Initiative," U.N. High Commissioner for Refugees, December 2008, pp. 25-29, www.unhcr.org/protect/PROTECTION/4937de6f2.pdf.

survey released on Feb. 22 by the International Organization for Migration.[63]

Since 2003 at least 2 million Iraqis have fled to several neighboring countries: Syria (1.2 million), Jordan (450,000), the Gulf states (150,000), Iran (58,000), Lebanon (50,000) and Egypt (40,000).[64]

Some experts question the government estimates. Amelia Templeton, an analyst at Human Rights First, suggests only about 1 million Iraqi refugees are living in neighboring countries, based on school registrations and the number of refugees receiving UNHCR aid.

In contrast to many other refugee situations, nearly all of the Iraqi refugees live in or near major cities, such as Damascus, Syria, and Amman, Jordan, because Iraq's neighbors don't permit refugee camps. A high proportion of Iraqi refugees are lawyers, doctors, professors and other well-educated professionals.

National Public Radio journalist Deborah Amos tells the stories of Iraqi refugees in Syria and Lebanon in a soon-to-be-published book. She says many of the professionals belonged to the Sunni elite or Christian minority groups (such as Chaldeans), who for centuries were tolerated in

Iraq but suddenly were targeted with violence. Many have spent their life savings during the years in exile and now rely on U.N. handouts. As in much of the world, local governments will not allow the refugees to work, forcing some female refugees in Damascus to turn to prostitution to support their families, Amos writes.

Myanmar — Cyclone Nargis struck on May 2, 2008, killing 140,000 people — mostly by drowning — and forcing up to 800,000 from their homes.[65] Humanitarian agencies pressed the government to allow international aid workers into the vast Irrawaddy Delta, but the secretive generals who run Myanmar resisted the appeals for several weeks until U.N. Secretary-General Ban Ki-moon finally persuaded the top general, Thwan Shwe, to accept outside aid.

Aid agencies and foreign governments donated emergency relief supplies and began helping rebuild homes and communities. But about 500,000 people remained displaced at year's end.[66] Many of those displaced by cyclone-caused floods have faced severe water shortages in recent months due to the recent onset of the dry season and water contamination caused by the cyclone.[67] Full recovery from the cyclone could take three to four years, a senior U.N. aid official said in January.[68]

Meanwhile, members of the Muslim Rohingya minority, from the northern state of Rakhine, are officially stateless. According to Amnesty International, thousands of Rohingyas flee Myanmar each year because of land confiscation, arbitrary taxation, forced eviction and denial of citizenship.[69] Since 1991, more than 250,000 have fled, mostly to neighboring Bangladesh, where the UNHCR runs two camps housing 28,000 refugees; another 200,000 unregistered Rohingyas live outside the camps.[70]

In early 2009, the Thai navy reportedly intercepted boats carrying hundreds of Rohingya trying to cross the Andaman Sea. The action generated international outrage after CNN published a photo purportedly showing armed forces towing refugee boats out to sea and leaving the occupants to die, but the Thai government denied the reports. Some were later rescued off the coasts of India and Indonesia, but many went missing.[71]

In early February actress and U.N. goodwill ambassador Angelina Jolie visited refugee camps in Thailand housing 110,000 Karen and Kareni ethnic refugees from Myanmar. She called on the Thai government to lift its ban on refugees working outside the camps and asked the government to extend hospitality to the Rohingyas.[72]

Prime Minister Abhisit Vejjajiva had said earlier that Thailand would not build a camp for the Rohingyas and will continue to expel them. "They are not refugees," he said. "Our policy is to push them out of the country because they are illegal migrants."[73]

Leaders of the Association of Southeast Asian Nations agreed on March 2 to discuss the status of the Rohingyas at a mid-April summit in Bali. Malaysian Prime Minister, Abdullah Ahmad Badawi said the Rohingya problem "is a regional issue that needs to be resolved regionally."[74]

Sudan — Two major internal conflicts plus other conflicts in central and eastern Africa have displaced millions of Sudanese in the past three decades. At the beginning of 2009, more than 3.5 million were still displaced, including about 130,000 in neighboring countries. Sudan hosts more than 250,000 refugees from nearby countries.[75]

Sudan's two-decade civil war between the government in Khartoum and a separatist army in south Sudan ended with an uneasy peace in January 2005. More than 300,000 refugees who had fled the violence have returned to their home regions, but UNHCR has estimated that about 130,000 remain in Egypt, Ethiopia, Kenya and Uganda.[76] And more conflict could erupt if, as expected, the southerners vote in 2011 for full independence.

Elsewhere in Sudan, a series of inter-related conflicts between the Khartoum government and rebel groups in western Darfur have displaced about 2.7 million people and killed an estimated 300,000.[77] Although Darfur has generally faded from world headlines, the conflict continues, with about 1,000 people fleeing their homes every day.[78] Complicating the refugee crisis, 243,000 Darfuris have fled into Chad, while some 45,000 Chadians have crossed into Darfur to escape a related conflict.[79]

More than 200,000 other refugees also are in Sudan, mostly from Eritrea, having fled the long war between Eritrea and Ethiopia.[80]

CURRENT SITUATION

'Responsibility to Protect'

Since last fall, 26-year-old Kandiah and his family have moved eight times to avoid the long-running civil war

Should the U.N. High Commissioner for Refugees help more displaced people?

YES

Joel R. Charny
Vice President for Policy
Refugees International

NO

Guglielmo Verdirame
Professor, International Human Rights
and Refugee Law, Cambridge University

Co-author, Rights in Exile: Janus-Faced
Humanitarianism

Written for *CQ Global Researcher*, February 2009

Current efforts to help displaced populations do not reflect the fact that twice as many people displaced by conflict remain inside their own borders rather than crossing an international one, thus failing to become refugees protected under international law. With the U.N. High Commissioner for Refugees (UNHCR) focusing primarily on legal protection for refugees, the current system is outmoded. A bold solution is needed to prevent further unnecessary suffering.

Internally displaced people (IDPs) suffer when their governments don't aid and protect their own citizens. They also suffer from the lack of a dedicated international agency mandated to respond to their needs when their states fail. With IDP numbers growing, expanding the UNHCR's mandate to include IDPs is the best option available to fill this gap.

A dedicated agency would be more effective than the current system, characterized by the "cluster leadership" approach, under which international agencies provide help by sectors, such as health, water and sanitation and shelter. For example, in the 1990s the U.N. secretary-general mandated that UNHCR respond to the needs of IDPs displaced by the civil war in Sri Lanka. Over the years, the agency effectively fulfilled this responsibility with donor support, and the entire U.N. country team — as well as the Sri Lankan government — benefited from the clarity of knowing that the agency was in charge. Moreover, carrying out this exceptional mandate did not undermine either the UNHCR's work with refugees in the region or the right of Tamil Sri Lankans to seek asylum in southern India.

Giving one agency responsibility for an especially vulnerable population is more effective than patching together a response system with multiple independent agencies. Because the circumstances and needs of IDPs are so similar to those of refugees, and because UNHCR has a proven capacity to respond holistically to displacement, it is best suited to take on this responsibility.

Having a formal mandate for IDPs would triple UNHCR's caseload and pose an immense challenge. The agency already has difficulty fulfilling its current mandate and perpetually lacks sufficient funds. Taking the lead on internal displacement would require new thinking, more advocacy work with governments and flexible approaches to programming outside of camp settings. But the alternative is worse: Maintain the status quo and perpetuate the gap in protection and assistance for some of the world's most vulnerable people.

Written for *CQ Global Researcher*, February 2009

Forced displacement is a human tragedy even when it occurs within the boundaries of a state. But the test for deciding whether it would be appropriate for the U.N. High Commissioner for Refugees (UNHCR) to add internally displaced people (IDPs) to its current mandate on a permanent basis is not one of comparability of suffering. Rather, the proper test is whether UNHCR is the right institution for dealing with this problem. I think it is not, for several reasons.

First, crossing an international boundary continues to make a difference in today's world. By virtue of being outside their country of nationality, refugees are in a different position than the internally displaced.

Second, the international legal regime for refugees was established as an exception to the sovereign prerogatives enjoyed by states over admission and expulsion of aliens in their territory. While most refugees were the victims of a human-rights violation in their home country, the focus of the refugee legal regime is not on the responsibility of the country of nationality but on the obligations of the country where they take refuge. Because internally displaced persons are still inside their home countries, protecting their rights will require different strategies and methods.

Third, human-rights bodies, including the office of the U.N. High Commissioner for Refugees, are better-placed to deal with what are, in essence, violations of human rights against citizens.

Finally, the rationale for getting the UNHCR involved with IDPs is premised on a distinctly problematic view of the organization as a provider of humanitarian relief rather than as the international protector of refugees. UNHCR's work with refugees has already greatly suffered from the sidelining of the agency's role as legal protector: The warehousing of refugees in camps is just one example. It would not help the internally displaced if the UNHCR's involvement resulted in their being warehoused in camps, as refugees already are.

In a world where asylum is under serious threat, the real challenge for UNHCR is to rediscover its protection mandate, to act as the advocate of refugees and as the institutional overseer of the obligations of states under the 1951 Refugee Convention. It is a difficult enough task as it is.

Legal Protections for Displaced Populations

A 1951 treaty gives refugees the most protection

International law protects some — but not all — refugees who cross international borders, while the non-binding Guiding Principles on Internal Displacement cover internally displaced people (IDPs), or those forcibly displaced within their home countries.

Here are the main laws protecting refugees and IDPs:

1951 Refugee Convention

The Convention Relating to the Status of Refugees — the basic international treaty concerning refugees — was adopted by a United Nations conference on July 28, 1951, and became effective on April 22, 1954. It defines a refugee as someone who, "owing to well-founded fear of being persecuted for reasons of race, religion, nationality, membership of a particular social group or political opinion, is outside the country of his nationality and is unable or, owing to such fear, is unwilling to avail himself of the protection of that country; or who, not having a nationality and being outside the country of his former habitual residence as a result of such events, is unable or, owing to such fear, is unwilling to return to it."

Excluded are those who flee their countries because of generalized violence (such as a civil war) in which they are not specifically targeted, or those who flee because of natural disasters or for economic reasons, such as a collapsing economy. The convention also prohibits a host country from expelling or returning refugees against their will to a territory where they have a "well-founded" fear of persecution.

The 1967 Protocol

Because the 1951 convention applied only to people who became refugees before Jan. 1, 1951, it was widely considered to apply only to European refugees from World War II. To aid those displaced by subsequent events, the United Nations adopted a new treaty, known as a Protocol, which eliminated the pre-1951 limitation. It took effect on Oct. 4, 1967.[1]

As of October 2008, 144 countries were parties to both the convention and the Protocol, though the two groups are not identical.[2]

Regional Treaties

Two regional documents expanded refugee protections of the convention and Protocol to Africa, Mexico and Central America. The 1969 Convention Governing the Specific

between the Sri Lankan army and rebels known as the Tamil Tigers. By late February they had joined several dozen people sleeping on a classroom floor in Vavuniya, in northern Sri Lanka.

At one point, Kandiah (not his real name) and his family stayed in an area that was supposed to be safe for civilians. For more than a week, he said, "We stayed in the open air with scores of other families . . . but the shelling was intense. There was shelling every day. We barely escaped with our lives."[81]

Kandiah and his family are among more than 250,000 people forced from their homes, often repeatedly, in the latest — and possibly final — round of the 26-year war. Claiming to represent the ethnic Tamil minority, the Tigers have been fighting for independence in the eastern and northern portions of the island.

Although the conflict has been among the world's most violent, international pressure to end it has been modest, at best. The U.N. Security Council, for example, considered it an "internal" affair to be resolved by Sri Lankans themselves, not by the international community and has never even adopted a resolution about it. Norway took the most significant action, mediating a cease-fire in 2002 that lasted nearly three years.

The plight of people like Kandiah illustrates the international community's failure to follow through on promises world leaders made in September 2005. At a summit marking the U.N.'s 60th anniversary, world leaders adopted the "responsibility to protect" philosophy, which holds every government responsible for protecting its own citizens.[82] Moreover, if a government fails to protect its citizens, it cannot prevent the international community

Aspects of Refugee Problems in Africa — adopted by what is now the African Union — defined refugees in Africa, while the 1984 Cartagena Declaration on Refugees is an informal statement of principles drafted by legal experts from Mexico and Central America.[3]

Guiding Principles on Internal Displacement

The U.N. has never adopted a treaty specifically aimed at establishing legal rights for IDPs. However, in 1998 the organization endorsed a set of 30 nonbinding guidelines intended to heighten international awareness of the internally displaced and offer them more legal protection. Known as the Guiding Principles on Internal Displacement, they have been presented to the various U.N. bodies but never formally adopted.

Based on the Universal Declaration of Human Rights and other treaties and agreements, the principles provide legal and practical standards for aiding and protecting displaced people. For example, the first principle states that displaced persons should enjoy "the same rights and freedoms under international and domestic law as do other persons in their country. They shall not be discriminated against . . . on the ground that they are internally displaced."

Regional bodies (including the European Union and the Organization of American States) and numerous nongovernmental organizations have endorsed the principles, and the UNHCR has treated them as official policy since world leaders — meeting at the U.N. in September 2005 — endorsed them. Nearly a dozen countries also have incorporated all or some of the principles into national legislation. In one case, the Colombian Constitutional Court in 2001 placed them into the country's "constitutional block," effectively making them a binding part of national law. Other countries that have adopted the principles into national laws or policies include the Maldives, Mozambique, Turkey and Uganda.

IDP advocates say the most significant potential use of the Guiding Principles is in Africa, where the African Union since 2006 has been working on a plan to incorporate a version of them into a binding regional treaty. This treaty — to be called the Convention for the Prevention of Internal Displacement and the Protection of and Assistance to Internally Displaced Persons in Africa — is expected to be adopted by African leaders at a summit meeting in Kampala, Uganda, in April.[4]

---

[1] Text of the Convention and Protocol is at www.unhcr.org/protect/PROTECTION/3b66c2aa10.pdf.

[2] "States Parties to the Refugee Convention," U.N. High Commissioner for Refugees, www.unhcr.org/protect/PROTECTION/3b73b0d63.pdf.

[3] Text of Refugee Convention in Africa is at www.unhcr.org/basics/BASICS/45dc1a682.pdf; Text of the Cartegena Declaration is at www.unhcr.org/basics/BASICS/45dc19084.pdf.

[4] Text of the Guiding Principles is at www3.brookings.edu/fp/projects/idp/resources/GPEnglish.pdf.

---

from intervening on their behalf. World leaders at the summit declared the U.N.'s right to take "collective action, in a decisive and timely manner," when governments failed to protect their own citizens.[83]

The U.N. has not followed through on that ringing declaration, however, usually because of dissension within the Security Council — the only U.N. body authorized to take forceful action. In addition, major countries with large, well-equipped armies — notably the United States and many European countries — have been unwilling to contribute sufficient troops to U.N. peacekeeping forces. The U.N.'s inability to protect displaced people has been most evident in eastern Congo and Darfur, where peacekeeping forces, mainly from African Union countries, are ill-equipped and undermanned.[84]

Early in February, for example, Doctors Without Borders bitterly denounced the U.N. peacekeeping mission in Congo for its "inaction" in response to the recent LRA attacks. Laurence Gaubert, head of mission in Congo for the group, said the U.N. peacekeepers "are just based in their camp, they don't go out of their camp, they don't know what is happening in the area."[85] Gaubert noted that the Security Council last Dec. 22 adopted Resolution 1856 demanding protection for civilians in Congo.[86] "This is something they have signed," she said, "but is not something you can see in the field that they have put in place."[87]

U.N. Under-Secretary-General for Humanitarian Affairs John Holmes acknowledged that the peacekeepers could do more to protect civilians but said the harsh criticism of them was "unreasonable and unjustified."

Serb refugees stage a demonstration along the Kosovo border in April 2007 to urge the U.N. to return them to their home provinces. Hundreds of thousands of people dislocated by war in the former Yugoslavia during the 1990s have not yet returned to their home regions.

Only 250-300 troops were in the area at the time, he said, and most were engineers, not combat forces.[88]

The U.N. has faced similar hurdles in trying to protect the millions of civilians displaced in Darfur since 2003. African Union peacekeepers began limited operations in Sudan in 2004 but lacked either the mandate or the resources to prevent government-backed militias or rebel groups from attacking civilians in camps and settlements. The Sudanese government agreed in 2006 and 2007 to allow beefed up U.N. peacekeeping missions, but — as in Congo — the U.N. has been unable to deploy adequate forces over such an enormous area. In Sudan, the government dragged its feet in following through on its agreement, and other countries have failed to provide the necessary money and manpower. The UNHCR operates in seven displaced-persons camps in Darfur (and in six camps in eastern Chad) but must rely on the peacekeeping mission for security.[89]

U.N. officials have repeatedly called for more forceful action to protect Darfuri civilians, only to be stymied by the Security Council — largely because of resistance from China, which has economic interests in Sudan — and delaying tactics by Sudan. The Khartoum government on Feb. 17 signed an agreement with the largest Darfur rebel group, the Justice and Equality Movement, calling for negotiation of a formal peace accord within three months.[90] The hurdles to such an accord were evident the very next day, when government forces reportedly bombed some of the rebel group's positions. The future of the peace agreement was further complicated by the International Criminal Court's (ICC) landmark decision on March 4 to issue an arrest warrant for Sudanese President Omar al-Bashir, charging him with directing the mass murder of tens of thousands of Darfuri civilians and "forcibly transferring large numbers of civilians, and pillaging their property." It was the first time the Hague-based court has accused a sitting head of state of war crimes. Unless he leaves Sudan, there is no international mechanism for arresting Bashir, who denies the accusations and does not recognize the court's jurisdiction. Some aid organizations fear the ICC ruling could trigger more violence — and thus more displacements.[91]

Focusing on IDPs

The number of people displaced by violence who remain within their own countries has been averaging more than 20 million per year, according to the Internal Displacement Monitoring Center, an arm of the Norwegian Refugee Council. More than a third of them are in just three countries: Colombia (up to 4.3 million), Sudan (3.5 million) and Iraq (up to 2.8 million).[92] Tens of millions more have been driven from their homes by natural disasters.

In December 2008, to give IDPs more international attention, the U.N.'s Office for the Coordination of Humanitarian Affairs launched a series of events focusing on IDPs, including workshops, panel discussions, a Web site and high-level conferences.

The agency is particularly concerned about displaced people who languish for years without help from their governments. "For millions of IDPs around the world, an end to their years of displacement, discrimination and poverty seems to be of little concern for those in power," said the U.N.'s Holmes. The U.N. also is encouraging governments to adopt the Guiding Principles on Internal

AFP/Getty Images/Sasa Maricic

Displacement for dealing with IDPs. And, it is pressing for "more predictable, timely and principled funding" for programs that help IDPs return home or find new homes, he said.[93]

In recent years, displaced people, usually from rural areas, have tended to head for cities. Experts say it is difficult to calculate the number of urban IDPs, but the monitoring center put the 2007 figure at 4 million, and the UNHCR estimated in 2008 that about half of the 11.4 million refugees were in cities.[94]

Urban IDPs and refugees pose logistical problems for local and international agencies charged with helping them. "In a camp, you have all these tents lined up in a row, and so it's easy to know how many people are there, and how much food and medicine you need every day," says Patrick Duplat, an advocate for Refugees International. "In an urban setting, it's much more complicated to reach people. Who is a refugee, who is an IDP and how are they different from the local population?"

U.N. High Commissioner Guterres acknowledged in a speech last October that global efforts to aid and protect urban refugees and IDPs have been "weak."[95] The approximately 2 million Iraqi refugees living in Damascus and Amman represent "a completely new and different challenge in relation to our usual activities in encampment situations," he told a conference in Norway.[96]

Last year the UNHCR tried handing out cash coupons and ATM cards to several thousand Iraqi refugees in Damascus, enabling them to buy food and other goods at local markets. The UNHCR and the World Food Program also gave food baskets or rice, vegetable oil and lentils to Iraqi refugees considered most in need, aiding about 177,000 Iraqis in 2008.[97] But some refugees reportedly were selling their rations to pay for housing and other needs.[98]

A major step toward legally protecting African IDPs could come in April at a planned special African Union (AU) summit meeting in Uganda. Experts have been working for nearly three years on a Convention for the Protection and Assistance of Internally Displaced Persons in Africa. This treaty would incorporate some, but not all, of the 1998 Guiding Principles on Internal Displacement, which sets nonbinding standards for protecting IDPs.[99]

If a treaty is produced, ratified and implemented, it could be an important step in protecting IDPs, because so many are in Africa, says Cohen from Brookings. But she is concerned that the final treaty, which already has been revised several times, might not be as strong in protecting human rights as the voluntary Guiding Principles. "We'll have to wait and see what the leaders agree to, and even if they adopt it," she says.

Guterres strongly endorses the AU's plan for a binding treaty. He also says that because the treaty has been developed by Africans, not imposed by outsiders, it "will not be subject to questions about the legitimacy of its objectives."[100]

OUTLOOK
Environmental Refugees

Environmental deterioration caused by climate change could force up to 1 billion people from their homes in coming decades, according to a paper presented to a high-level U.N. meeting last October.[101] Small island nations, notably the Maldives in the Indian Ocean and Kiribati and Tuvalu in the Pacific, could be inundated — causing mass evacuations — if sea levels rise to the extent predicted by many scientists.[102]

Rising seas also endanger several hundred million people in low-lying coastal regions. Many of these areas are in developing countries — such as Bangladesh and the Philippines — that already are prone to cyclones, floods, earthquakes or volcanic eruptions.[103] Many scientists believe that climate change will increase the severity and frequency of weather-linked disasters, particularly cyclones and floods, thus displacing even more people in the future.

L. Craig Johnstone, deputy U.N. High Commissioner for Refugees, said "conservative" estimates predict that up to 250 million people could be displaced by the middle of the 21st century due to climate change. The minority of scientists who doubt the impact of climate change dismiss such estimates as overblown.[104] But aid officials at the U.N. and other international agencies say they have no choice but to prepare for the worst.

Regardless of the impact of climate change on displacements, experts across the spectrum say it is becoming increasingly important for the international community to decide how long to provide humanitarian aid for displaced people. Decades-long displacements are difficult for both the IDPs and refugees as well as the aid groups and host countries involved. (*See sidebar, p. 134.*)

"When can they stop being vulnerable as a result of their displacement and simply be compared to any other poor person in their country?" asks Koser, at the Geneva Center for Security Policy. He cites the 4.6 million Palestinians still being aided by the United Nations six decades after their original displacement.

UNHCR officials acknowledge that international aid programs are not always equitable but say addressing the vulnerability of the world's poor and ending the causes of displacement depend on the political will of global leaders. In his annual remarks to the Security Council on Jan. 8, High Commissioner Guterres said global displacement issues won't be solved until the conflicts that force people from their homes are ended.

"While it is absolutely vital that the victims of armed conflict be provided with essential protection and assistance, we must also acknowledge the limitations of humanitarian action and its inability to resolve deep-rooted conflicts within and between states," he said. "The solution, as always, can only be political."[105]

NOTES

1. "Only after five days we dared to bury the bodies," Doctors Without Borders, Jan. 19, 2009, www.condition-critical.org/.

2. "Congo Crisis" fact sheet, International Rescue Committee, p. 1, www.theirc.org/resources/2007/congo_onesheet.pdf; also see "World Report 2009," Human Rights Watch, www.hrw.org/en/world-report/2009/democratic-republic-congo-drc.

3. "Convention and Protocol Relating to the Status of Refugees," U.N. High Commissioner for Refugees, www.unhcr.org/protect/PROTECTION/3b66c2aa10.pdf.

4. "World Report 2009," *op. cit.*

5. "Statement by Mr. Antonio Guterres, United Nations High Commissioner for Refugees, to the Security Council, New York," U.N. High Commissioner for Refugees, Jan. 8, 2009, www.unhcr.org/admin/ADMIN/496625484.html.

6. "Internally Displaced People: Exiled in their Homeland," U.N. Office for the Coordination of Humanitarian Affairs, http://ochaonline.un.org/News/InFocus/InternallyDisplacedPeopleIDPs/tabid/5132/language/en-US/Default.aspx; also see "China Earthquake: Facts and Figures," International Federation of Red Cross and Red Crescent Societies, Oct. 31, 2008, www.ifrc.org/Docs/pubs/disasters/sichuan-earthquake/ff311008.pdf.

7. Jeffrey Gettleman, "Starvation And Strife Menace Torn Kenya," *The New York Times*, March 1, 2009, p. 6.

8. "Top UNHCR official warns about displacement from climate change," U.N. High Commissioner for Refugees, Dec. 9, 2008, www.unhcr.org/news/NEWS/493e9bd94.html.

9. "2007 Statistical Yearbook," U.N. High Commissioner for Refugees, p. 23, www.unhcr.org/cgi-bin/texis/vtx/home/opendoc.pdf?id=4981c3252&tbl=STATISTICS; "Statement by Mr. Antonio Guterres," *op. cit.*

10. For background, see Karen Foerstel, "Crisis in Darfur," *CQ Global Researcher*, September 2008, pp. 243-270.

11. "2009 Global Update: Sudan," U.N. High Commissioner for Refugees, pp. 1-3, www.unhcr.org/publ/PUBL/4922d4130.pdf.

12. "Millions of Hectares of Land Secured for Internally Displaced," International Organization for Migration, Jan. 9, 2009, www.iom.int/jahia/Jahia/pbnAM/cache/offonce;jsessionid=29AD6E92A35F-DE971CDAB26007A67DB2.worker01?entryId=21044.

13. "Afghanistan — The Challenges of Sustaining Returns," U.N. High Commissioner for Refugees, www.unhcr.org/cgi-bin/texis/vtx/afghan?page=home.

14. See "UNHCR Global Appeal, 2009"; "2009 Global Update, Mission Statement," U.N. High Commissioner for Refugees, www.unhcr.org/publ/PUBL/4922d43f11.pdf; "Statement by Mr. Antonio Guterres," *op. cit.*; "2009 Global Update, Working with the Internally Displaced," U.N. High Commissioner for Refugees, www.unhcr.org/publ/PUBL/4922d44c0.pdf.

15. The Refugee Status Determination (RSD) Unit, U.N. High Commissioner for Refugees, www.unhcr.org/protect/3d3d26004.html.

16. "2009 Global Update, Mission Statement," *op. cit.*

17. "Protracted Refugee Situations: High Commissioner's Initiative," U.N. High Commissioner for Refugees, December 2008, www.unhcr.org/protect/PROTECTION/4937de6f2.pdf.

18. "Humanitarian Reform," United Nations, www.humanitarianreform.org.

19. "The Global Cluster Leads," U.N. Office for the Coordination of Humanitarian Affairs, http://ocha.unog.ch/humanitarianreform/Default.aspx?tabid=217.

20. "Cluster Approach Evaluation 2007," United Nations, www.humanitarianreform.org/Default.aspx?tabid=457.

21. The book Milner co-authored is *The United Nation's High Commissioner for Refugees (UNHCR): The Politics and Practice of Refugee Protection into the 21st Century* (2008).

22. "Convention and Protocol Relating to the Status of Refugees," *op. cit.*

23. "Full Text of Jack Straw's Speech," *The Guardian*, Feb. 6, 2001, www.guardian.co.uk/uk/2001/feb/06/immigration.immigrationandpublicservices3.

24. "Climate change, natural disasters and human displacement: a UNHCR perspective," www.unhcr.org/protect/PROTECTION/4901e81a4.pdf.

25. "European Pact on Immigration and Asylum," www.immigration.gouv.fr/IMG/pdf/Plaquette_EN.pdf.

26. "ECRE calls for suspension of Dublin transfers to Greece," European Council on Refugees and Exiles, April 3, 2008, www.ecre.org/resources/Press_releases/1065.

27. "NGO Statement Addressing the Iraqi Humanitarian Challenge," July 31, 2008, www.refugeesinternational.org/policy/letter/ngo-statement-addressing-iraqi-humanitarian-challenge.

28. "Fact Sheet: USCIS Makes Major Strides During 2008," U.S. Citizenship and Immigration Services, Nov. 6, 2008, www.uscis.gov/portal/site/uscis/menuitem.5af9bb95919f35e66f614176543f6d1a/?vgnextoid=2526ad6f16d6d110VgnVCM1000004718190aRCRD&vgnextchannel=68439c7755cb9010VgnVCM10000045f3d6a1RCRD.

29. "NGO Statement: Addressing the Iraqi Humanitarian Challenge," *op. cit.*

30. "Fact Sheet: Iraqi Refugee Processing," U.S. Citizenship and Immigration Services, Sept. 12, 2008, www.dhs.gov/xnews/releases/pr_1221249274808.shtm.

31. "Operation Safe Haven Iraq 2009," Center for American Progress, www.americanprogress.org/issues/2009/01/iraqi_airlift.html.

32. Her blog site is http://refugeeresettlementwatch.wordpress.com/.

33. "The 1951 Refugee Convention," U.N. High Commissioner for Refugees, www.unhcr.org/1951convention/dev-protect.html.

34. *Ibid.*

35. *Ibid.*

36. "Establishment of UNRWA," www.un.org/unrwa/overview/index.html.

37. "UNRWA Statistics," www.un.org/unrwa/publications/index.html.

38. "A 'Timeless' Treaty Under Attack: A New Phase," U.N. High Commissioner for Refugees, www.unhcr.org/1951convention/new-phase.html.

39. "States Parties to the Convention and the Protocol," U.N. High Commissioner for Refugees, www.unhcr.org/protect/PROTECTION/3b73b0d63.pdf.

40. "Guiding Principles on Internal Displacement," www3.brookings.edu/fp/projects/idp/resources/GPEnglish.pdf.

41. "FMO Research Guide: Afghanistan," Teresa Poppelwell, July 2007, pp. 17-19, www.forcedmigration.org/guides/fmo006/.

42. "Afghanistan — The Challenges of Sustaining Returns," U.N. High Commissioner for Refugees, www.unhcr.org/cgi-bin/texis/vtx/afghan?page=home.

43. "Jalozai camp closed, returnees face difficulties at home," IRIN news service, June 2, 2008, www.irinnews.org/Report.aspx?ReportId=78506; also see "Iran called upon to halt winter deportations," IRIN news service, Dec. 18, 2008, www.irinnews.org/PrintReport.aspx?ReportId=82007.

44. "Afghanistan — The Challenges of Sustaining Returns," *op. cit.*

45. "Minister disputes call to boost refugee returns," IRIN news service, Sept. 10, 2008, www.irinnews.org/Report.aspx?ReportId=80218.

46. "Cold tents for returnees in east," IRIN news service, Jan. 15, 2009, www.irinnews.org/Report.aspx?ReportId=82373.

47. "Afghanistan at the crossroads: Young Afghans return to a homeland they never knew," U.N. High Commissioner for Refugees, Nov. 14, 2008, www.unhcr.org/cgi-bin/texis/vtx/afghan?page=news&id=491d84c64.

48. "2009 Global Update, Colombia situation," U.N. High Commissioner for Refugees, www.unhcr.org/publ/PUBL/4922d43411.pdf.

49. "Colombia Situation," U.N. High Commissioner for Refugees 2008-09 Global Appeal for Colombia, p. 2, www.unhcr.org/home/PUBL/474ac8e814.pdf.

50. *Ibid.*

51. "Millions of Hectares of Land Secured for Internally Displaced," International Organization for Migration, Jan. 9, 2009, www.iom.int.

52. *Ibid.*

53. *Ibid.*

54. "2009 Global Update," Democratic Republic of the Congo, U.N. High Commissioner for Refugees, www.unhcr.org/publ/PUBL/4922d4100.pdf.

55. "Congo Crisis" fact sheet, *op. cit.*

56. "A Congolese Rebel Leader Who Once Seemed Untouchable Is Caught," *The New York Times*, Jan. 24, 2009, www.nytimes.com/2009/01/24/world/africa/24congo.html?_r=1.

57. "An arresting and hopeful surprise," *The Economist*, Jan. 29, 2009, www.economist.com/displayStory.cfm?story_id=13022113. For background, see David Masci, "Aiding Africa," *CQ Researcher*, Aug. 29, 2003, pp. 697-720; John Felton, "Child Soldiers," *CQ Global Researcher*, July 2008.

58. "2009 Global Update: Iraq," U.N. High Commissioner for Refugees, p. 2, www.unhcr.orgpubl/PUBL/4922d4230.pdf.

59. "WFP to help feed one million displaced Iraqis," World Food Program, Jan. 3, 2009, www.wfp.org/English/?ModuleID=137&Key=2732.

60. "Budget cuts threaten IDP housing projects," IRIN news service, Jan. 6, 2009, www.irinnews.org/Report.aspx?ReportId=82209.

61. "IDPs enticed to vacate southern camp," IRIN news service, Dec. 15, 2008, www.irinnews.org/Report.aspx?ReportId=81963.

62. "2009 Global Update: Iraq," *op. cit.*, p. 2.

63. "Three Years of Post-Samarra Displacement in Iraq," International Organization for Migration, Feb. 22, 2009, p. 1, www.iom.int/jahia/webdav/shared/shared/mainsite/published_docs/studies_and_reports/iom_displacement_report_post_samarra.pdf.

64. *Ibid.*

65. "Post-Nargis Periodic Review I," Tripartite Core Group, December 2008, p. 4, www.aseansec.org/22119.pdf.

66. "2009 Global Update: Myanmar," U.N. High Commissioner for Refugees, p. 2, www.unhcr.org/publ/PUBL/4922d42b0.pdf.

67. "Cyclone survivors face water shortages," IRIN news service, Dec. 29, 2008, www.irinnews.org/Report.aspx?ReportId=82129.

68. "Cyclone recovery 'will take up to four years,' " IRIN news service, Jan. 15, 2009, www.IRINnews.org/Report.aspx?ReportId=82383.

69. Michael Heath, "Angelina Jolie, U.N. Envoy, Asks Thailand to Aid Myanmar Refugees," Bloomberg News, www.bloomberg.com/apps/news?pid=20601080&sid=aL5VlfM46aAc&refer=asia#.

70. "2009 Global Update: Bangladesh," U.N. High Commissioner for Refugees, p. 1, www.unhcr.org/publ/PUBL/4922d42818.pdf.

71. "Myanmar Refugees Rescued at Sea," *The New York Times*, Feb. 3, 2009, www.nytimes.com/2009/02/04/world/asia/04indo.html?ref=world.

72. "Angelina Jolie voices support for Myanmar refugees in northern Thailand camps," U.N. High Commissioner for Refugees, Feb. 5, 2009, www.unhcr.org/news/NEWS/498ab65c2.html.

73. *Ibid.*

74. "ASIA: Regional approach to Rohingya boat people," IRIN news service, March 2, 2009, www.irinnews.org/Report.aspx?ReportId=83232.

75. "2009 Global Update: Sudan," U.N. High Commissioner for Refugees, pp. 1-3, www.unhcr.org/publ/PUBL/4922d4130.pdf.

76. "Number of returnees to South Sudan passes the 300,000 mark," U.N. High Commissioner for Refugees, Feb. 10, 2009, www.unhcr.org/news/NEWS/4991a8de2.html; "2009 Global Update," *op. cit.*, p. 1.

77. "Darfur remains tense after recent eruption of fighting, U.N. reports," IRIN news service, Jan. 28, 2009, www.un.org/apps/news/story.asp?NewsID=29699&Cr=darfur&Cr1=.

78. "Report of the Secretary-General on the deployment of the African Union-United Nations Hybrid Operation in Darfur," United Nations, Oct. 17, 2008, p. 11, http://daccessdds.un.org/doc/UNDOC/GEN/N08/553/95/PDF/N0855395.pdf?OpenElement.

79. "2009 Global Update: Sudan," *op. cit.*; "2009 Global Update: Chad," U.N. High Commissioner for Refugees, www.unhcr.org/publ/PUBL/4922d41214.pdf.

80. "2009 Global Update: Sudan," *op. cit.*, p. 3; "World Refugee Survey, 2008," Sudan chapter, U.S. Committee for Refugees and Immigrants, www.refugees.org/countryreports.aspx?id=2171.

81. "Kandiah: 'There was shelling every day. We barely escaped with our lives,'" IRIN news service, Feb. 19, 2009, www.IRINnews.org/Report.aspx?ReportId=83015.

82. For background, see Lee Michael Katz, "World Peacekeeping," *CQ Global Researcher*, April 2007, pp. 75-100.

83. "World Summit Outcome 2005," U.N. General Assembly, Resolution A/RES/60/1, paragraphs 138-139, September 2005, www.un.org/summit2005/documents.html.

84. See Foerstel, *op. cit.*

85. "DRC: MSF denounces the lack of protection for victims of LRA violence in Haut-Uélé," Doctors Without Borders, Feb. 4, 2009, www.msf.org.

86. Security Council Resolution 1856, Dec. 22, 2006, http://daccessdds.un.org/doc/UNDOC/GEN/N08/666/94/PDF/N0866694.pdf?OpenElement.

87. *Ibid.*

88. "Press Conference by Humanitarian Affairs Head on Recent Trip to Democratic Republic of Congo," U.N. Department of Public Information, Feb. 13, 2009, www.un.org/News/briefings/docs/2009/090213_DRC.doc.htm.

89. "2009 Global Update: Sudan," *op. cit.*

90. "Sudan and Darfur Rebel Group Agree to Peace Talks," *The New York Times*, Feb. 18, 2009, www.nytimes.com/2009/02/18/world/africa/18sudan.html?_r=1&ref=todayspaper.

91. "Sudan bombs rebels day after Darfur deal: rebels," Agence France-Presse, Feb. 18, 2009. See Mike Corder, "International court issues warrant for Sudan president on charges of war crimes in Darfur," The Associated Press, March 4, 2009.

92. "2009 Global Update," *op. cit.*; "Global Overview of Trends and Developments: 2007," Internal Displacement Monitoring Centre, Norwegian Refugee Council, p. 12, April 2008, www.internal-displacement.org/idmc/website/resources.nsf/(httpPublications)/0F926CFAF1EADE5EC125742E003B7067?OpenDocument.

93. "UN launches year-long campaign to highlight, and solve, plight of displaced," IRIN news service, Dec. 18, 2009, www.un.org/apps/news/story.asp?NewsID=29358&Cr=IDPs&Cr1.

94. "Addressing Urban Displacement: A Project Description," Internal Displacement Monitoring Centre, Norwegian Refugee Council, 2007, p. 2; also see "2007 Global Trends," U.N. High Commissioner for Refugees, June 2008, p. 2, www.unhcr.org/statistics/STATISTICS/4852366f2.pdf.

95. "Ten years of Guiding Principles on Internal Displacement: Achievements and Future Challenges," statement by Antonio Guterres, Oslo, Oct. 16, 2008, www.unhcr.org/admin/ADMIN/48ff45e12.html.

96. *Ibid.*

97. "WFP to help feed one million displaced Iraqis," World Food Program, Jan. 3, 2008, www.wfp.org/English/?ModuleID=137&Key=2732.

98. "Iraqi refugees selling some of their food rations," IRIN news service, Jan. 28, 2009, http://one.wfp.org/english/?ModuleID=137& Key=2732.

99. "From Voluntary Principles to Binding Standards," *IDP Action*, Jan. 9, 2009, www.idpaction.org/index.php/en/news/16-principles2 standards.

100. "Ten Years of Guiding Principles on Internal Displacement," *op. cit.*

101. "Climate Change, Migration and Displacement: Who will be affected?" Working paper submitted by the informal group on Migration/Displacement and Climate Change of the U.N. Inter-Agency Standing Committee, Oct. 31, 2008, http:// unfccc.int/resource/docs/2008/smsn/igo/022. pdf.

102. "Climate Change and Displacement," *Forced Migration Review*, p. 20, October 2008, www .fmreview.org/climatechange.htm; for background see Colin Woodard, "Curbing Climate Change," *CQ Global Researcher*, February 2007, pp. 27-50, and Marcia Clemmitt, "Climate Change," *CQ Researcher*, Jan. 27, 2006, pp. 73-96.

103. "Climate Resilient Cities: A Primer on Reducing Vulnerabilities to Disasters," World Bank, 2009, pp. 5-6.

104. "Top UNHCR official warns about displacement from climate change," *op. cit.*

105. "Statement by Mr. Antonio Guterres," *op. cit*

BIBLIOGRAPHY

Books

Evans, Gareth, *The Responsibility to Protect: Ending Mass Atrocity Crimes Once and For All,* **Brookings Institution Press, 2008.**
A former Australian foreign minister and current head of the International Crisis Group offers an impassioned plea for world leaders to follow through on their promises to protect civilians, even those abused by their own governments.

Loescher, Gil, Alexander Betts and James Milner, *The United Nations High Commissioner for Refugees (UNHCR): The Politics and Practice of Refugee Protection Into the 21st Century,* **Routledge, 2008.**
Academic experts on refugee issues offer a generally sympathetic but often critical assessment of the UNHCR's performance as the world's main protector of refugees.

Verdirame, Guglielmo, and Barbara Harrell-Bond, with Zachary Lomo and Hannah Garry, *Rights in Exile: Janus-Faced Humanitarianism,* **Berghahn Books, 2005.**
A former director of the Refugee Studies Center at Oxford University (Harrell-Bond) and an expert on refugee rights at Cambridge University offer a blistering critique of the U.N. and nongovernment agencies that protect refugees.

Articles

"Managing the Right of Return," *The Economist,* **Aug. 4, 2008.**
The practical implications of refugees' legal right to return to their home countries are examined.

Cohen, Roberta, and Francis Deng, "The Genesis and the Challenges," *Forced Migration Review,* **December 2008.**
This is the keystone article in an issue devoted to the Guiding Principles on Internal Displacement 10 years after their creation. Cohen and Deng were prime movers of the document.

Feyissa, Abebe, with Rebecca Horn, "Traveling Souls: Life in a Refugee Camp, Where Hearts Wander as Minds Deteriorate," *Utne Reader,* **September-October 2008, www.utne.com/2008-09-01/Great Writing/Traveling-Souls.aspx.**
An Ethiopian who has lived in northwestern Kenya's Kakuma refugee camp for 16 years writes about life in the camp.

Guterres, Antonio, "Millions Uprooted: Saving Refugees and the Displaced," *Foreign Affairs,* **September/October 2008.**
The U.N. High Commissioner for Refugees lays out an ambitious agenda of action to aid and protect the displaced.

Harr, Jonathan, "Lives of the Saints: International Hardship Duty in Chad," *The New Yorker,* **Jan. 5, 2009, www.newyorker.com/reporting/2009/01/05/ 090105fa_fact_harr.**
A frequent *New Yorker* contributor offers a sympathetic portrait of idealistic aid workers at refugee camps in Chad.

Stevens, Jacob, "Prison of the Stateless: The Derelictions of UNHCR," *New Left Review,* **November-December 2006, www.newleftreview.org/? page=article&view=2644.**

A review of the memoirs of former High Commissioner Sadako Ogata becomes a strongly worded critique of the U.N. refugee agency. A rebuttal by former UNHCR special envoy Nicholas Morris is at www.unhcr.org/research/RESEARCH/460d131d2.pdf.

Reports and Studies

"2009 Global Update," *U.N. High Commissioner for Refugees*, **November 2008, www.unhcr.org/ga09/index .html.**

Published in November, this is the most recent summary from the UNHCR of its operations, plans and budget for 2009.

"Future Floods of Refugees: A comment on climate change, conflict and forced migration," *Norwegian Refugee Council*, **April 2008, www.nrc.no/arch/_ img/9268480.pdf.**

The refugee council surveys the debate over whether climate change will worsen natural disasters and force untold millions of people from their homes.

"Protracted Refugee Situations: High Commissioner's Initiative," *U.N. High Commissioner for Refugees*, **December 2008, www.unhcr.org/protect/ PROTECTION/4937de6f2.pdf.**

The UNHCR offers a plan of action for resolving several long-term situations in which refugees have been trapped in camps or settlements for decades.

"When Displacement Ends: A Framework for Durable Solutions," *Brookings-Bern Project on Internal Displacement*, **June 2007, www.brookings.edu/ reports/2007/09displacementends.aspx.**

This detailed blueprint for how international agencies can help IDPs find "durable solutions" to their displacements is the product of conferences and other studies.

Cohen, Roberta, "Listening to the Voices of the Displaced: Lessons Learned," *Brookings-Bern Project on Internal Displacement*, **September 2008, www .brookings.edu/reports/2008/09_internal_displacement_ cohen.aspx.**

The author recommends better ways to aid and protect displaced people around the world, based on interviews with dozens of IDPs.

For More Information

Brookings-Bern Project on Internal Displacement, The Brookings Institution, 1775 Massachusetts Avenue, N.W., Washington, DC, 20036; (202) 797-6168; www.brookings .edu/projects/idp.aspx. A joint project of the Brookings Institution and the University of Bern (Switzerland) School of Law; conducts research and issues reports on policy questions related to internally displaced people (IDPs).

Institute for the Study of International Migration, Georgetown University, Harris Building, Third Floor, 3300 Whitehaven St. N.W., Washington, DC, 20007; (202) 687-2258; www12.georgetown.edu/sfs/isim/index.html. An academic research center focusing on all aspects of international migration, including refugees.

Internal Displacement Monitoring Centre, Chemin de Balexert, 7-9 1219 Chatelaine Geneva, Switzerland; 41-22-799-07 00; www.internal-displacement.org. Provides regular reports on IDPs globally; the major source of information about the numbers of people displaced by conflict.

International Organization for Migration, 17 Route des Morillons, CH-1211, Geneva 19, Switzerland; 41-22-717-9111; www .iom.int. A U.N. partner (not officially within the U.N. system) that aids refugees and migrants and studies migration trends.

Norwegian Refugee Council, P.O. Box 6758, St. Olavs Plass, 0130 Oslo, Norway; 47-23-10 9800; www.nrc.no. A prominent nongovernmental organization that provides aid programs for displaced persons and advocates on their behalf.

Refugee Studies Centre, Queen Elizabeth House, University of Oxford, Mansfield Road, Oxford OX1 3TB, United Kingdom; 44-1865-270-722; www.rsc.ox.ac.uk/index .html?main. A prominent research center on refugees and the displaced. Publishes the *Forced Migration Review,* a quarterly journal written by experts in the field.

Refugees International, 2001 S St., N.W., Suite 700, Washington, DC, 20009; (202) 828-0110; www.refugees international.org. Advocates on behalf of refugees and IDPs and publishes regular reports based on site visits to key countries.

U.N. High Commissioner for Refugees, Case Postale 2500, CH-1211, Geneva 2 Depot, Switzerland; 41-22-739-8111; www.unhcr.org/home.html. The U.N. agency with prime responsibility for aiding and protecting refugees; increasingly has taken on a similar role in regard to IDPs.

U.S. Committee for Refugees and Immigrants, 2231 Crystal Dr., Suite 350, Arlington VA 22202-3711; (703) 310-1130; www.refugees.org. An advocacy group that publishes reports focusing on human-rights abuses and other problems encountered by refugees and immigrants.

6

Disaster Preparedness

Is the U.S. Ready for Another Major Disaster?

Pamela M. Prah

Hundreds of shipping containers, recreational vehicles and motorboats litter a residential area of Gulfport, Miss., after Hurricane Katrina hit. The storm killed more than 1,300 people in Louisiana, Alabama and Mississippi and racked up $200 billion in property damage and relief expenses, making it the costliest storm in U.S. history.

AFP/Getty Images/Paul J. Richards

From *CQ Researcher*,
November 18, 2005

ix days before Hurricane Katrina tore through the Gulf Coast, Wal-Mart swung into action. As the deadly storm barreled toward New Orleans, the world's biggest retailer dispatched a fleet of tractor-trailer trucks loaded with generators, dry ice, thousands of cases of bottled water and other vitally needed supplies to nearby staging areas.[1]

Federal, state and local authorities also saw Katrina coming — but their delayed and deeply flawed response became a national scandal.

President Bush declared a state of emergency for Louisiana on Aug. 27, two days before the storm struck, making it eligible for federal assistance. When Katrina made landfall on Aug. 29, Bush issued a federal "declaration of emergency," activating the country's disaster plan. The $64,000 question is why it took so long for federal authorities to act.

Michael Brown, director of the Federal Emergency Management Agency (FEMA), was deemed so inept he was called back to Washington mid-disaster. Local officials were overwhelmed by the scope of the devastation and unsure who was in charge. More than 1,300 people died, and at one point more than 300,000 evacuees were housed in shelters in 40 states.[2] And politicians at all levels bickered openly about who was to blame for the horrific catastrophe that was unfolding on live TV for the world to see.

Critics charged that little thought had been given to helping people without the means to evacuate on their own — the elderly, disabled and poor.

Disaster Relief Soared in 2005

The busy 2004 and 2005 hurricane seasons caused record spending on federal disaster relief this year. Expenditures in 2002 ranked second due to the Sept. 11, 2001 terrorist attacks.

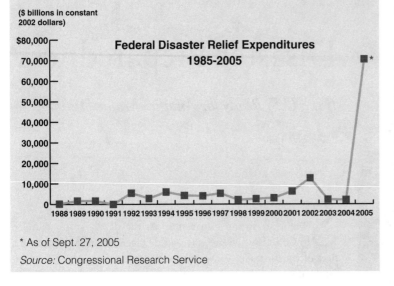

($ billions in constant 2002 dollars)

Federal Disaster Relief Expenditures 1985-2005

* As of Sept. 27, 2005

Source: Congressional Research Service

history," wrote Donald F. Kettl, director of the Fels Institute of Government at the University of Pennsylvania."[4]

The fabled Big Easy suffered such extensive damage that some officials questioned the wisdom of rebuilding. (*See sidebar, p. 160.*)

Disaster experts blame much of the flawed response to Katrina on inadequate communications technology. Emergency-phone systems in different jurisdictions were "interoperable." Nearly forty 911 centers were knocked out, leaving citizens no way to call for help. New Orleans Mayor Ray Nagin was stuck in a hotel without a phone for two days while Louisiana Gov. Kathleen Blanco, a Democrat, reportedly couldn't get through to President Bush for two crucial days.

While looting was extensive, wildly exaggerated reports of mayhem and murder added to the sense of an out-of-control city. Even the arrival of more than 50,000 National Guard and 20,000 active-duty troops turned controversial, because critics said they came too late or were ordered not to stop the looters.

When Hurricane Rita hit Texas and Louisiana three weeks later, the response was better. But the system again faltered in late October when Hurricane Wilma — as predicted — hit Key West and Fort Lauderdale, forcing thousands of Floridians to wait in lines for water, gas, ice and insurance help.

Emergency experts and administration critics were particularly concerned about the bungled 2005 storm responses because hurricanes come with plenty of advance warning, but terrorist attacks, tornadoes and earthquakes don't.

"If we can't get Katrina right, how on Earth are we going to get a dirty bomb right, a bioterrorist attack right, the avian flu right?" asks Kathleen Tierney, director of the Natural Hazards Center at the University of Colorado in Boulder.

And most homeland security experts say another terrorist attack on the United States is all but inevitable.

As for New Orleans, experts have long known the below-sea-level city was a catastrophe waiting to happen.

As a result, residents who had banked on government help were left to fend for themselves. In New Orleans, levees broke, and as floodwaters rose thousands of residents huddled on rooftops. The 20,000 people who took refuge in the Superdome found inadequate food and water, scant medical help and toilets that quickly were overwhelmed. Outside the disaster zone, government doctors stood by hundreds of empty cots, watching for patients who never arrived. Paltry resources were predeployed, or arrived late. Experts fear that sick and injured victims died for lack of timely care.

"If the federal government would have responded as quickly as Wal-Mart, we could have saved more lives," said Jefferson Parish Sheriff Harry Lee.[3]

Hurricane Katrina ranks as the most destructive storm in U.S. history. It destroyed some 200,000 homes in New Orleans alone and cost as much as $200 billion. Katrina directly affected more than a half-million people in Louisiana, Mississippi and Alabama. More than that, Katrina revealed what was widely seen as a shocking lack of readiness for another major catastrophe.

"The government's response to Katrina ranks as perhaps the biggest failure of public administration in the nation's

The federal government in 2001 ranked the potential damage to New Orleans from a hurricane as among the three likeliest, most catastrophic disasters facing this country.[5] Engineers said the city's levees would not withstand the strongest of hurricane winds. Indeed, when FEMA and Louisiana authorities practiced responding to a severe mock hurricane in July 2004, they anticipated conditions eerily similar to those wrought by Katrina: the evacuation of a million people, overflowing levees and the destruction of up to 600,000 buildings.[6]

Critics say the country should have been better prepared, particularly after the Sept. 11, 2001, terrorists attacks revealed that communications systems used by emergency workers from different jurisdictions often did not work with one another. Yet three years after the attacks, emergency equipment used in more than 80 percent of America's cities was still not interoperable with federal agencies, and 60 percent of the cities did not have communication systems that meshed with state emergency centers.[7]

The White House and Congress are both investigating the government's botched response to Katrina, but they had better act fast. Experts at the National Hurricane Center warn that the country has entered a new weather cycle that will produce more frequent "super-hurricanes" for the next 20 years, threatening cities even as far north as New York.[8]

"Houston, Galveston, Tampa Bay, southwest Florida, the Florida Keys, southeast Florida, New York City, Long Island and, believe it or not, New England, are all especially vulnerable," Max Mayfield, director of the National Hurricane Center's Tropical Prediction Center, told a Senate panel on Sept. 20.

The picture isn't much brighter for earthquakes, which threaten 75 million Americans in 39 states.[9] Experts say the United States has been lucky that recent earthquakes have occurred relatively far from populated areas, but that a major quake eventually is going to hit a big city like San Francisco.

Katrina Was Costliest U.S. Disaster

By far the most expensive disaster in the nation's history, Katrina is expected to cost at least three times more than the second-costliest U.S. disaster, the 1988 heat wave and drought.

Ten Costliest U.S. Natural Disasters
(1980-2005)

Year	Cost ($ in billions)	Disaster	Location
2005	$200 (est.)	Hurricane Katrina	Gulf Coast
1988	$61.6	Heat wave, drought	Central, Eastern U.S.
1980	$48.4	Heat wave, drought	Central, Eastern U.S.
1992	$35.6	Hurricane Andrew	South Florida, Louisiana
1993	$26.7	Floods	Midwest
1994	$25	Earthquake	Northridge/San Francisco, Calif.
2004	$14	Hurricane Charley	Florida, S.C., N.C.
1989	$13.9	Hurricane Hugo	S.C., N.C.
2004	$12	Hurricane Ivan	Florida, Alabama
1989	$10	Earthquake	Loma Prieta, Calif.

Sources: National Climatic Data Center, National Oceanic and Atmospheric Administration; Insurance Information Institute

FEMA has long been criticized as a dumping ground for White House political appointees. A report on the agency's blunders in responding to Hurricane Andrew in 1992 noted, "Currently, FEMA is like a patient in triage. The president and Congress must decide whether to treat it or let it die."[10]

But even FEMA critics concede that part of the problem is that many Americans mistakenly see the agency as a national fire-and-rescue squad, equipped with its own fire trucks, personnel and advanced technology. FEMA actually is a tiny agency — only 2,500 employees — charged with coordinating all the federal help available to states and localities.

"The federal government is never going to be the nation's first-responder. We shouldn't be, we don't have the capability to be, and we won't be," said White House homeland security adviser Frances Fragos Townsend, who is spearheading a review of the federal government's response to Katrina.[11]

Some, including President Bush and the U.S. Conference of Mayors, ask whether the military should take the lead in disaster response.[12] Others still champion FEMA but say that budget cuts and changes

Katrina flooded three-quarters of New Orleans and revealed gaping weaknesses in the nation's disaster-response system. Many experts question the government's ability to deal with future catastrophes.

following 9/11 — and the country's preoccupation with terrorism — have jeopardized FEMA's effectiveness. For example, nearly three out of every four grant dollars that the Department of Homeland Security (DHS) handed out to first-responders in 2005 were for terrorism-related activities.[13]

"It's like we've adopted the philosophy that if you are prepared for a terrorist event, then you are prepared for any event that could possibly affect the people of the United States," says Albert Ashwood, director of Oklahoma's Department of Emergency Management.

As politicians debate the effectiveness of FEMA and lessons learned from Katrina, here are some questions being discussed:

Is the United States prepared for another major disaster?

Many emergency-management experts say the country is ready for the next "disaster," but not for another "catastrophe" like Katrina. Others say the country falls woefully short on both counts.

In disasters, not everyone in the affected area is a victim, explains John R. Harrald, director of the Institute for Crisis, Disaster and Risk Management at George Washington University, in Washington, D.C. Typically roads, communications and medical systems are still in good enough shape for first-responders to get in and help. For example, three blocks from the collapsed Twin Towers on Sept. 11, New Yorkers still had electricity and phones.

In a "catastrophic event" like Katrina, however, all systems fail. Entire swaths of the Gulf Coast had no communications; city halls and police stations were destroyed; power, water and sewer systems ceased functioning. New Orleans lost virtually its entire infrastructure — transportation, telecommunications, energy and medical systems.

Disaster experts say preparedness depends on the locale. California is prepared for earthquakes, Florida for hurricanes (notwithstanding recent problems after Wilma); and the Northeast and Midwest for major snowstorms, experts say. These areas are prepared because they have learned from experience. "If you do something a number times, you get good at it," says David Aylward, secretary of the ComCARE Alliance, an organization of safety groups, first-responders and medical professionals.

But Tierney of the Natural Hazards Center worries that the country is not only unprepared for catastrophes but also ill-equipped for "ordinary" disasters, largely because of the latest reorganization of the country's disaster management system.

After the 2001 terrorist attacks, the federal government realized its response plan for "extreme events" needed to be revamped to deal with the terrorism threat. But Tierney wonders if local officials fully understand the revised 426-page National Response Plan — released in December 2004 — or their roles in it.[14] "We don't know the extent to which states and local governments have absorbed the new response philosophies under the national response plan," she says. "If Hurricane Katrina is any indication, we're in deep trouble."

Critics say the new plan focuses almost exclusively on terrorism rather than natural disasters. For instance, of the 15 emergency scenarios that the plan recommends states and localities train and prepare for — 13 are terrorist events.

Likewise, terrorism prevention now receives the lion's share of federal emergency-preparedness dollars. In 2005 some $180 million was allocated nationwide for state and local governments to fund emergency management, but it was in the form of 50-50 matching grants, which require local governments to supply a dollar for every federal dollar received. At the same time, the federal government dispersed $2.3 billion for anti-terrorism measures, with no matching funds required, explains Ashwood.

But supporters of the new federal plan point out that even before Sept. 11, FEMA had provided funds for "all-hazards" emergency preparedness. The Government Accountability Office (GAO) concluded this year that while most funding today is targeted at preventing terrorist attacks, the all-hazards approach is generally working, training first-responders for skills needed for both kinds of disasters.[15]

However, says Aylward, the country spends far too little on emergency medicine — only $3.5 million in 2005 for states to build up medical-trauma capacity. A flu pandemic, for example, could send 2.3 million Americans to hospitals, many in need of respirators — but there are only 105,000 respirators available in U.S. hospitals, and most are already in constant use.[16]

"We've pumped billions of dollars into preparedness since 9/11, but virtually none of that has gone to the one place where we know 80 percent of patients go first," said Rick Blum, president of the American College of Emergency Physicians.[17]

Most agree that the country falls particularly short in emergency communications. Many communities do not have technology that allows first-responders, government officials and others to stay in contact with each other. And local, state and federal officials also do not have systems in place enabling them to communicate with one another during an emergency.

In the aftermath of Katrina, some rescuers finally got a radio system that let them talk to one another — only after FedEx technical adviser Mike Mitchell of Memphis realized while watching Katrina TV coverage that a broken FedEx radio antenna in New Orleans could be adapted with some spare parts, a generator and radios. He made his way to the city, and atop a 54-story building near the convention center he installed a new nine-foot FedEx radio antenna that an Army helicopter lowered to him.[18]

The independent commission that investigated the 9/11 attacks recommended that more spectrum, or airwaves, be reserved for public-safety use, but Congress has yet to act. "We know, looking back at 9/11, that lives were lost because we didn't have interoperability and didn't have access to public radio spectrum," former Sen. Timothy J. Roemer, D-Ind., a 9/11 Commission member, told Congress.[19] "We know that lives were lost in New Orleans because we didn't have this capability."

The Homeland Security department's study on interoperability won't be finished until summer 2006, and a Federal Communications Commission (FCC) report on the need for additional spectrum is due in December.[20]

"If something knocks out phones, electricity, the Internet and radio towers, is there a backup so that responders can still communicate?" Aylward asks. "To my knowledge, no one has done that."

In addition to first-responders' radios, Katrina knocked out 40 call centers that provide 911 assistance, and more than 20 million telephone calls did not go through the day after the hurricane struck.[21] The hurricane also knocked 80 percent of the radio stations and 70 percent of the TV stations off the air.[22] Hundreds of thousands of hurricane victims were unable to receive news and emergency information, and emergency workers and public safety officials had difficulty coordinating their efforts. The New Orleans Police Department, for example, was severely crippled for three days following the storm.[23]

FCC Chairman Kevin Martin told Congress that Katrina made the commission realize that when 911 call centers go down, "there's not even a standard protocol" for rerouting the calls. So when Hurricane Rita followed shortly after, federal authorities made sure 911 centers knew to contact telephone companies with backup plans.

Satellite-phone companies did not lose service during Katrina and were able to provide phone and video links to police, emergency personnel and news outlets. Ironically, when the storm hit, New Orleans was one of 25 cities taking part in an "integrated wireless network" program spearheaded by the departments of Justice, Homeland Security and Treasury designed to usher in the next generation of radio systems for federal law enforcement.[24]

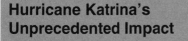

Hurricane Katrina's Unprecedented Impact

Katrina affected an area roughly the size of Great Britain and will cost an estimated $200 billion.

During the relief effort:

- 72,000 federal workers and 50,000 National Guard troops were deployed;

- 33,000 people were rescued by the Coast Guard;

- 300,000 evacuees were sheltered in more than 40 states;

- 717,000 households received $1.5 billion in federal aid;

- 27 million hot meals were served by the Red Cross; and

- 93 Disaster Recovery Centers were operated.

Source: Dept. of Homeland Security

Ashwood, of the National Emergency Management Association, says that while enabling responders to communicate with one another is extremely important, it pales in comparison to the need for first-responders to know each other and what each one does.

"If you want to talk about the big communications problem in this country, that's it," says Ashwood. "It has nothing to do with radios."

Should the military play the lead role in disaster response?

President Bush has asked Congress to consider allowing the military to take the lead in certain disaster responses. "It is now clear that a challenge on this scale requires greater federal authority and a broader role for the armed forces — the institution of our government most capable of massive logistical operations on a moment's notice," Bush said in a Sept. 15 televised speech from New Orleans.[25]

Indeed, after Katrina, the public saw the military as the only government entity that seemed able to restore order swiftly. Bush tapped Coast Guard Vice Adm. Thad W. Allen to temporarily head the government's response to Katrina. And no-nonsense Lt. Gen. Russel Honore, the military's task force commander, epitomized why the military should take the lead. Mayor Nagin called him a "John Wayne dude" who can "get some stuff done."[26]

But many officials vehemently oppose tapping the military to lead the federal response to disasters. Governors in particular don't want to lose control of their National Guard troops, whom they call up for natural disasters, crowd control and quelling civil violence. Moreover, active-duty soldiers are prohibited from enforcing civilian laws or providing police services by the 1878 *Posse Comitatus* Act.*

Of 38 governors asked by *USA Today* about Bush's idea, only Republicans Mitt Romney of Massachusetts and Tim Pawlenty of Minnesota supported it.[27] Even the president's brother, Gov. Jeb Bush, R-Fla., opposes more federal involvement. "Federalizing emergency response to catastrophic events would be a disaster as bad as Hurricane Katrina," Gov. Bush told Congress in October. "Just as all politics are local, so too are disasters. The most effective response is one that starts at the local level and grows with the support of surrounding communities, the state and then the federal government."[28]

Typically, active-duty soldiers are called in only if local, state and other federal resources are overwhelmed and the lead federal agency — typically FEMA — requests help. Under the Stafford Act, the president can declare a federal emergency or disaster and deploy troops, but only to help deliver aid.[29] Lt. Gen. Honore reminded his soldiers that New Orleans wasn't Iraq and to keep their guns pointed down.

To seize control of the Katrina mission, President Bush would have had to invoke the Insurrection Act, which allows federal troops to suppress a rebellion and enforce federal laws. Bush's father invoked the law in 1992 during riots in south-central Los Angeles following the acquittal of police officers charged in the beating of Rodney King.

Pentagon leaders are waiting for completion of a Defense Department review before making recommendations on

---

* Posse Comitatus ("power to the county" in Latin) was passed after the Civil War to end the use of federal troops in Southern states.

whether to amend current laws prohibiting the military from policing local communities. The Pentagon reportedly is considering creating new "rapid response" units trained to respond to domestic catastrophes. The units would be used rarely and would quickly transfer responsibilities to civilian authorities.[30]

Defense Secretary Donald H. Rumsfeld stressed in September that the current system "works pretty well" for dealing with most natural disasters, but that Hurricane Katrina was "distinctly different" because "the first-responders [were] victims themselves, and as such, somewhat overwhelmed by the catastrophic nature of Hurricane Katrina and the floods" that followed.[31]

The New Orleans Police Department was unable to account for 240 officers on its 1,450-member force following Hurricane Katrina and has since fired more than 50 officers for desertion.[32]

Actually, military officials began deploying ships and personnel before receiving specific requests from the DHS or FEMA. In fact, they began preparing responses a week before Katrina hit.[33]

A day after the hurricane struck, the DHS declared Katrina an "incident of national significance," which under the new National Response Plan should trigger a coordinated federal response. By the following day, the amphibious assault ship *USS Bataan* arrived with supplies off New Orleans, but not until Sept. 5 — a week after Katrina hit — did troops arrive.[34]

The governors of Louisiana and Mississippi had both declared states of emergency before Katrina made

Are You Prepared?

Disasters can wipe out basic services — water, gas, electricity or telephones. Often emergency personnel cannot reach everyone right away. Experts stress the importance of individuals being prepared to take care of themselves for at least three days or until basic services are restored or help arrives.

Create a Family Disaster Plan

- Establish two places to meet in the event your home is damaged or roads are blocked — one near the home and one outside of the immediate area.
- Arrange a way to contact each other should you be separated during a disaster. Since local phone calls may be impossible, designate an out-of-state person as the "family contact."
- Plan for an urgent evacuation. Keep a backpack or duffle bag packed in advance with:
  - First aid kit, prescription drugs for three days and extra eyeglasses (copies of the drug and eyeglass prescriptions).
  - Flashlight, batteries, battery-powered radio, bottled water.
  - A change of clothes, a sleeping bag or bedroll and pillow for each household member.
  - Car keys (and keys to where you are going if it is a friend's or relative's house).
  - Checkbook, cash, credit cards, driver's license or personal identification, Social Security card, proof of residence (deed or lease), insurance policies, birth and marriage certificates, stocks, bonds and other negotiable certificates, wills, deeds and copies of recent tax returns.

"Sheltering in Place"

Have an Emergency Preparedness Kit (preferably stored in waterproof containers) prepared in advance with sufficient supplies for your family to survive in your home for at least three days without power or municipal services, including:

- The same supplies you would take with you when evacuating. (*See above.*)
- Water (a gallon per person per day).
- Foods that do not require refrigeration or cooking.
- Special items or medical equipment for infants and family members.
- Sanitation supplies: toilet paper, towelettes, soap, hand sanitizer, toothbrush, contact lens supplies, feminine supplies, garbage bags.
- Tool kit with matches in waterproof container, pliers, paper/pencil, map of the area.
- Non-electronic entertainment, games, books.

For more information, contact www.prepare.org or www.redcross.org. Fact sheets and a 204-page guide from FEMA are available at www.fema.gov/areyouready/.

Sources: American Red Cross, FEMA

Ousted FEMA Director Michael Brown answers lawmakers' questions about the agency's response to Hurricane Katrina. Brown defended his agency's performance, blaming many of the problems in Louisiana on state and local authorities.

landfall, but many of their National Guard units were deployed overseas. Within 10 days of the hurricane hitting, National Guard personnel from all 50 states had joined in the relief operations, an unprecedented effort.[35]

Some wonder whether lives would have been saved in New Orleans if the military had been in charge from the beginning. "When you have a disaster that overwhelms state and local government and requires a federal response, the Department of Defense is the agency best positioned to do it," said Lawrence Korb, former assistant secretary of Defense for manpower and personnel during the Reagan administration.[36]

Sen. John W. Warner, R-Va., chairman of the Senate Armed Services Committee, supported an expanded military role in emergencies even before Katrina hit, calling for a change in the *Posse Comitatus* law.[37] "The current framework of law did not in any way render less

effective the inner working of the [National] Guard and active forces in this Katrina situation," Warner said in September. "But who knows about the next one?"[38]

Mayors also would like the military to take a more active role in relief — at least in the first few days after a disaster — and want to get military help without needing the state's approval.[39] But the military is already stretched thin with deployments in Iraq and Afghanistan, and many question whether adding more domestic tasks would undermine military readiness.[40] Plus, it would depart from the longstanding tradition of keeping the U.S. military out of civilian affairs.

"Putting full-time warriors into a civilian policing situation can result in serious collateral damage to American life and liberty," said Gene Healy, a defense expert at the libertarian Cato Institution.[41]

Expanding the military's role was also explored after Hurricane Andrew ripped through South Florida in 1992. At Congress' request, the National Academy of Public Administration studied the proposition and eventually opposed it. Essentially, the academy concluded the current structure allows the military to provide support to civilian authorities, such as logistics and humanitarian aid, but that ultimately civilians must maintain decision-making authority.[42]

States and localities should be able to turn to the military, but disaster response is "entirely a civilian function," says George Washington University's Harrald.

The key, according to state and local officials, is better coordination. "Hurricane Katrina, and to some extent Rita, revealed the need for improved intergovernmental response to catastrophic disasters," Audwin M. Samuel, mayor pro tem of Beaumont, Texas, told Congress.[43]

Robert W. Klein, director of the Center for Risk Management at Georgia State University, does not oppose a military-led response, but, he says, ideally a "properly staffed, properly charged and properly oriented" FEMA would take the lead role. But in either scenario, he says the military role should happen automatically. "The disaster czar or disaster general shouldn't be waiting for a phone call."

Does politics reduce FEMA's effectiveness?

Some experts say that structural changes were made at FEMA after Sept. 11 strictly for political reasons — and that the country's preparedness has suffered. Others contend that incompetence — not politics — is a bigger factor at FEMA.

Former FEMA Director Brown told the special House panel investigating Katrina he didn't want to make the problems surrounding the response partisan. But noting he didn't have problems evacuating Alabama and Mississippi, Brown added, "I can't help that Alabama and Mississippi are governed by Republican governors, and Louisiana is governed by a Democratic governor."[44]

Brown largely blamed post-Katrina missteps on strained relations between Gov. Blanco and Mayor Nagin — both Democrats. "I very strongly personally regret that I was unable to persuade [them] to sit down, deal with their differences and work together. I just couldn't pull that off," he said.[45]

For their part, neither Blanco nor Nagin had anything positive to say about FEMA or the White House. After the storm, Blanco reportedly was unable to reach either President Bush or his chief of staff and had to plead for help via a message left with a low-level adviser.[46] Nagin angrily complained on national television that federal officials "don't have a clue what's going on down here" and called on them to "get off your asses and do something."[47]

Some speculate that Bush was reluctant to step in and take control in a Southern state run by a Democrat, and a woman at that. "Can you imagine how it would have been perceived if a president of the United States of one party had pre-emptively taken from the female governor of another party the command and control of her forces?" a senior administration official told *The New York Times*.[48]

But in 17 years of emergency management, Ashwood says he has never seen politics enter into decisions. "It's after-the-fact finger-pointing," he says. "It's people saying, 'Well, I might have made mistakes, but I didn't make as many as that guy.'"

George Washington's Harrald agrees: "I don't think anyone intentionally, for political reasons, made bad decisions. Bad decisions and inaction were a matter of competence, not intent."

Some experts point out that in the mid-1990s — after its disastrous response to Hurricane Andrew — FEMA overcame its reputation for being slow and bureaucratic, but that post-9/11 changes have undermined the agency's ability to respond to natural disasters. "The system that exists today is nothing like the emergency-management system that had been built up over the last 30 years," says Tierney of the Natural Hazards Center in Colorado. "Those patterns were radically reversed after 9/11. All this talk about FEMA, FEMA, FEMA" misses the point. "We're operating under a homeland-security policy system now, not a comprehensive emergency-management system."

For example, when FEMA was incorporated into the new DHS after Sept. 11, it lost its status as an independent agency with direct access to the president. Instead, the agency and its 2,500 employees became one of 22 agencies folded into the 180,000-employee DHS.

"The driving force behind the creation of DHS was the need of elected officials to . . . be seen as responding to the attacks of Sept. 11, 2001," said Kettl at the University of Pennsylvania.[49] But in the process, he said, FEMA's role in disaster response was weakened.

Richard W. Krimm, a former senior FEMA official for several administrations, agreed. "It was a terrible mistake to take disaster response and recovery . . . and put them in Homeland Security," he said.[50]

Critics say it is now impossible for FEMA to implement the four steps that make up comprehensive emergency management. The first is mitigation, which is the ongoing effort to reduce the potential impact disasters can have on people and property, such as engineering bridges to withstand earthquakes and enforcing effective building codes to protect property from hurricanes. The other steps are preparedness, response and recovery.

"These four steps should be seamlessly integrated," says Tierney. But since Sept. 11, "The comprehensive emergency-management approach has been broken up."

Moreover, key FEMA posts were not filled by people experienced in emergency management. James Lee Witt, the Clinton administration FEMA director who was widely credited with turning FEMA around, previously had headed the Office of Emergency Services in Arkansas. Ousted FEMA Director Brown had little emergency-management experience, having joined the agency as legal counsel after several years at the International Arabian Horse Association.

"You get the impression that for higher-level appointments at FEMA, political connections weighed heavier than qualifications," says Klein of Georgia State University. Indeed, of the eight top officials at FEMA, only two had experience with fire and emergency services, and they were not used early on in the Katrina response, according to

William Killen, president of the International Association of Fire Chiefs. "The coordination would have been a lot better if there had been more people with operational experience in emergency response in position," Killen told a House panel.[51]

Brown also lacked the same access to the president that Witt had enjoyed under Clinton. "That direct relationship to the White House is crucial," former Gov. Bob Wise, D-W.Va., told Congress. "All the other federal agencies must know that the FEMA director and the president communicate directly and that there isn't anyone between them."[52]

The reorganization of FEMA required Brown to send budget and policy requests to the DHS secretary, who would then pitch FEMA's issues to the president. After being fired as FEMA director, Brown complained bitterly to the House panel that his budget requests had never made it to the president and that his budget and staff were cut.

Experts outside the agency agree that many competent FEMA officials left the agency out of frustration or were contracted out after the reorganization, leaving key posts without expertise. In fact, many of the DHS employees assigned to the Gulf Coast after Katrina had to first spend two to three days studying federal emergency-management rules, including the types of aid available to hurricane victims.[53]

"The organization just wasn't there. We lost that and didn't really realize it," says Harrald. "There was not an awareness that the system was collapsing."

The new emphasis on terrorism also undercut FEMA. "After Sept. 11, they got so focused on terrorism they effectively marginalized the capability of FEMA," said George D. Haddow, a former Clinton administration FEMA official.[54]

BACKGROUND

FEMA's Roots

The federal government hasn't always taken an active role in natural disasters.

The Congressional Act of 1803, considered the first piece of disaster legislation, provided federal assistance to Portsmouth, N.H., following a huge fire.

Over the next century, Congress passed more than 100 measures in response to hurricanes, earthquakes, floods and other natural disasters, but those actions were ad hoc, often

overlapping and disjointed.[55] Local communities, on the whole, were expected to handle disaster relief.

Even the 1900 hurricane that killed 6,000 people in Galveston, Texas — the most deadly U.S. natural disaster — triggered only a limited federal response. The Army Corps of Engineers helped build a new sea wall, but it was up to the locals to help survivors and rebuild the flattened city.[56]

The efforts of future President Herbert Hoover in Florida following two deadly hurricanes in the late 1920s probably helped the then-secretary of Commerce win the presidency in 1928.[57] In 1926, a hurricane hit South Florida, killing about 240 people. Two years later, less than two months before the election, another hurricane hit Lake Okeechobee, killing 2,500. Hoover visited the area following both storms and was instrumental in the push for new channels and levees. Since then, presidents have found that their own responses to natural disasters can affect the outcome of an election, with some historians dubbing the phenomenon as "The Photo-op Presidency."[58]

During the Depression, President Franklin D. Roosevelt initiated a more active federal role in disaster response. For instance, he authorized the Reconstruction Finance Corporation, established by Hoover in 1932 to bolster the banking industry, to make reconstruction loans for public facilities damaged by earthquakes, and later, other disasters. In 1934 the Bureau of Public Roads was given authority to provide funding for highways and bridges damaged by natural disasters. The Flood Control Act of 1936, which gave the Army Corps of Engineers greater authority to implement flood control projects, also became law during FDR's era.

This piecemeal approach lasted until the 1960s and early '70s, when a series of hurricanes and earthquakes spurred the federal government to become more involved. In 1961, the Kennedy administration created the Office of Emergency Preparedness inside the White House to deal with natural disasters. Then in 1968, Congress created the National Flood Insurance Program (NFIP), which offered new flood protection to homeowners. The insurance was available only to those in communities that adopted and enforced a federally approved-plan to reduce flood risks.

The Disaster Relief Act of 1974 laid out the formal process that permits a president to declare "disaster areas," which are eligible for federal assistance, including money for state and local governments to make repairs, clear debris and provide temporary housing and unemployment

CHRONOLOGY

1800-1950s *President Franklin D. Roosevelt increases federal government's role in disasters.*

1803 The first federal disaster relief law, the Congressional Act of 1803, provides assistance to Portsmouth, N.H., after an extensive fire.

May 31,1889 Johnstown, Pa., is devastated by the worst flood in the nation's history, killing more than 2,200 residents.

Sept. 8, 1900 Hurricane destroys Galveston, Texas, killing 6,000 residents.

Sept. 16, 1928 Hurricane kills 2,500 in South Florida.

1933-34 The Reconstruction Finance Corporation and Bureau of Public Roads are authorized to make disaster loans.

1936 Flood Control Act of 1936 gives Army Corps of Engineers greater authority to implement flood control projects.

1960s-1970s *Washington boosts federal role in disaster preparedness and response.*

1961 John F. Kennedy administration creates the Office of Emergency Preparedness inside the White House to deal with natural disasters.

1974 Disaster Relief Act permits president to declare "disaster areas," thus providing federal help to states.

Aug. 7, 1978 Carter declares a federal emergency at Love Canal, the neighborhood near Niagara Falls, N.Y., contaminated by hazardous wastes.

Sept. 16, 1978 President Jimmy Carter creates Federal Emergency Management Agency (FEMA).

1980s-1992 *FEMA comes under fire.*

1980 FEMA is accused of stretching its authority by responding to Cuban refugee crisis in Miami.

1985 FEMA director resigns amid charges of misusing government funds; the agency is lampooned in the comic strip "Doonesbury."

1989 FEMA's sluggish response to Hurricane Hugo prompts Sen. Ernest Hollings, D-S.C., to call the agency "the sorriest bunch of bureaucratic jackasses" he had ever seen.

1992 FEMA's response to Hurricane Andrew in Florida is bungled; Congress considers abolishing FEMA.

1993-2001 *FEMA is rehabilitated under Clinton.*

1993 President Bill Clinton picks James L. Witt, a 14-year veteran of Arkansas' emergency services, as FEMA director and makes him a Cabinet member.

1993-94 Witt streamlines disaster relief-and-recovery operations; FEMA wins praise for efforts in 1993 flooding in Midwest and the 1994 Northridge, Calif., earthquake.

1995 The Murrah Federal Building in Oklahoma City is bombed, killing 168 and raising questions about FEMA's role in responding to terrorist attacks.

Sept. 11, 2001 The World Trade Center and Pentagon are attacked; nearly 3,000 people are killed.

2001-Present *Budget cuts, reorganization and loss of experienced employees weaken FEMA's ability to respond to disasters.*

March 1, 2003 FEMA becomes part of the Department of Homeland Security, losing its independence and Cabinet status.

August-September 2004 Four hurricanes hit Florida, a pivotal state in the ongoing presidential campaign. President George W. Bush quickly declares the state a disaster area, making it eligible for federal assistance.

August-September, 2005 Numerous hurricanes are spawned in the Atlantic, including Katrina, which strikes the Gulf Coast on Aug. 29, causing massive flooding and destruction. FEMA's poor response prompts Congress and the White House to review the nation's preparedness.

Should New Orleans Be Rebuilt?

President Bush has vowed to rebuild New Orleans, and Congress has already started doling out reconstruction funds. But is that a good idea? Hurricane Katrina put 80 percent of the city under water, destroying some 200,000 homes.

House Speaker J. Dennis Hastert, R-Ill., came under withering criticism, particularly from Democratic lawmakers who represent New Orleans, when he said rebuilding "doesn't make sense," adding, it "looks like a lot of that place could be bulldozed." Hastert later said he was not "advocating that the city be abandoned or relocated."[1]

But some experts argue that rebuilding a city below sea level, on land that is sinking, near a large lake and in a hurricane-prone area is simply another disaster waiting to happen — and taxpayers shouldn't have to keep picking up the tab.

"Should we rebuild New Orleans . . . just so it can be wiped out again?" asked Klaus Jacob, a geophysicist and adjunct professor at Columbia University's School of International and Public Affairs. Even strengthening the levee system isn't the answer, Jacob said. "The higher the defenses, the deeper the floods that will inevitably follow," he wrote.[2]

"It is time to face up to some geological realities and start a carefully planned deconstruction of New Orleans," Jacob continued, "assessing what can or needs to be preserved, or vertically raised and, if affordable, by how much."

The city is nestled in a so-called bowl, sandwiched between levees holding back Lake Pontchartrain to the north and the Mississippi River to the south. Some places are up to 10 feet below sea level; areas nearer the river generally are higher in elevation.

Traditional homeowner insurance policies do not cover losses from floods, so homeowners, renters and businesses that want insurance must turn to the National Flood Insurance Program (NFIP) for coverage. Nationwide, about half of eligible properties are covered by flood insurance.[3]

Many people wrongly believe that the U.S. government will take care of their financial needs if they suffer damage due to flooding. In fact, federal disaster assistance is only available if the president formally declares a disaster, which he did for Katrina. But often, federal disaster-assistance loans must be repaid. That is on top of any mortgage loans that people may still owe on the damaged property.

Katrina was the largest and costliest flood disaster in U.S. history. FEMA estimates flood insurance payouts for 225,000 claims from hurricanes Katrina and Rita could hit $23 billion, far exceeding the $15 billion that has been paid out since the NFIP program began in 1968.[4]

While FEMA collects the premiums, it lacks reserves and must borrow from the U.S. Treasury to meet the

and cash assistance for individuals. The law was amended in 1988 and renamed the Robert T. Stafford Disaster Relief and Emergency Act, after its chief sponsor, a Republican senator from Vermont. It remains the main federal disaster law.

In the late 1970s, hazards associated with nuclear power plants and the transportation of hazardous substances were added to the list of potential disasters. Eventually, more than 100 federal agencies were authorized to deal with disasters, hazardous incidents and emergencies. Similar programs and policies existed at the state and local level, further complicating disaster-relief efforts.

Frustrated with the overlapping programs and confusing bureaucracy, the nation's governors urged President Jimmy Carter to centralize federal emergency functions.

Carter responded with a 1979 executive order that merged some 100 separate disaster-related responsibilities into a new agency — FEMA.[59]

For the first time, Carter said, "key emergency-management and assistance functions would be unified and made directly accountable to the president and Congress."[60] As the federal government's lead disaster agency, FEMA established official relationships with organizations such as Catholic Charities, the United Way, the Council of Jewish Federations and the American Red Cross.

The Red Cross is the only relief organization chartered by Congress "to maintain a system of domestic and international disaster relief." In fact, the National Response Plan specifically calls on the Red Cross to provide local relief. During Katrina, the Red Cross provided hurricane payouts. Congress in September temporarily increased the amount FEMA could borrow to $3.5 billion from $1.5 billion and is considering upping that to $8.5 billion under a measure pending in Congress.[5]

Private insurers are expected to pay about $40 billion in Katrina damage, according to Robert P. Hartwig, chief economist at the Insurance Information Institute.[6] The institute said the percentage of homes with flood insurance affected by Hurricane Katrina varied in Louisiana from nearly 58 percent in some areas down to 7 percent. In many areas, homeowners and business owners were not required, or even encouraged, by their banks or their insurance companies to purchase flood insurance, partly because outdated floodplain maps were used.

Critics say taxpayers are too often left holding the bag for those who continually build in flood-prone or other risky areas. "Are we going to continue to bail out people who will continue to build in very, very hazardous areas?" asked Sen. Richard Shelby, R-Ala., chairman of the Banking, Housing and Urban Affairs Committee, which examined the NFIP program in October.[7]

Congress in 2004 approved a pilot program that would impose higher insurance premiums for property owners at severe risk of suffering repeated flood damage.

Rather than allowing rebuilding in lowlying areas, some suggest more radical approaches: "Moving the city is clearly going to be an option," said John Copenhaver, a former FEMA Southeast regional director. "It would be an unbelievably expensive and difficult proposition, but it has to be on the table."[8]

And such a solution is not unprecedented. The government has helped move entire towns following disasters, including Soldiers Grove, Wis., after a 1979 flood. And businesses were moved in several communities — including Valmeyer, Ill., and Pattonsburg, Mo. — after floods in 1993.[9]

Hastert said undoubtedly New Orleans residents would rebuild, adding, however: "We ought to take a second look at it. But you know, we build Los Angeles and San Francisco on top of earthquake fissures, and they rebuild, too. Stubbornness."[10]

[1] The Associated Press, "Hastert: Rebuilding New Orleans 'doesn't make sense to me," Sept. 2, 2005.

[2] Klaus Jacob, "Time for a Tough Question: Why Rebuild?" *The Washington Post*, Sept. 6, 2005, p. A25.

[3] Testimony of William Jenkins, Government Accountability Office, before Senate Banking, Housing and Urban Affairs Committee on National Flood Insurance Program, Oct. 18, 2005.

[4] Testimony of David Maurstad, Acting Mitigation Division Director, FEMA, before U.S. Senate Banking Housing and Urban Affairs Committee on National Flood Insurance Program, Oct. 18, 2005.

[5] Liriel Higa, "FEMA Would Get Second Boost in Borrowing Authority Under House Bill," *CQ Weekly*, Oct. 31, 2005, p. 2925.

[6] Peter Whoriskey, "Risk Estimate Led to Few Flood Policies," *The Washington Post*, Oct. 17, 2005, p. A1.

[7] Transcript of hearing of Senate Banking, Housing and Urban Affairs Committee on National Flood Insurance Program, Oct. 18, 2005.

[8] Seth Borenstein and Pete Carey, "Experts debate rebuilding New Orleans," *The* [San Jose] *Mercury News*, Sept. 1, 2005.

[9] FEMA Region X press release, "New Planning Guide Helps Communities Become Disaster-Resistant," April 26, 1999.

[10] The Associated Press, *op. cit.*

survivors with nearly 3.42 million overnight stays in more than 1,000 shelters. And, in coordination with the Southern Baptist Convention, it served nearly 27 million hot meals to victims.

Political Storms

In addition to natural disasters, FEMA handled the 1970s cleanup of Love Canal, near Niagara Falls, N.Y., contaminated by buried toxic wastes; the 1979 accident at the Three Mile Island nuclear power plant, near Harrisburg, Pa., and the 1980 "Mariel boat lift" crisis, in which 125,000 Cuban refugees converged on South Florida. Carter declared all the affected regions disaster areas, although critics said the refugee crisis was not, technically, a disaster.

In the early and mid-1980s, FEMA also faced political and legal disasters. During the Reagan administration Congress, the Justice Department and a grand jury investigated senior FEMA political officials on a variety of charges, including misuse of government funds. FEMA Director Louis O. Guiffrida resigned in 1985, and the agency was repeatedly lampooned in the comic strip "Doonesbury."[61]

In its early years, FEMA was, like much of the federal government, preoccupied with protecting Americans from the threat of the Soviet Union. "When I entered this profession 17 years ago, FEMA and emergency management in general were quasi-military, [trying to] figure out where a nuclear attack was going to take place and how to relocate the nation's citizens," Oklahoma's Ashwood recently told Congress.[62]

But just as the Cold War was ending in the late 1980s and early '90s, a pair of hurricanes and an earthquake put FEMA — then plagued by morale problems, poor leadership and conflicts with its state and local partners — in a negative national spotlight.[63]

FEMA was widely criticized for its slow response to Hugo, the 1989 hurricane that devastated Charleston, S.C. Sen. Ernest Hollings, D-S.C., described FEMA as "the sorriest bunch of bureaucratic jackasses" he had ever encountered in the federal government.[64] Hugo caused $7 billion in damage in the United States, making it the costliest hurricane in U.S. history at that time.

Less than a month later, San Francisco was hit by the Loma Prieta earthquake — the largest quake along the San Andreas Fault since the 1906 San Francisco earthquake. Although FEMA was unprepared for the quake — which caused nearly $6 billion in damage and 63 deaths — California was ready, thanks to "good mitigation practices in building codes and construction . . . and some good luck," wrote former FEMA official Haddow.[65]

When Hurricane Andrew struck in 1992, it further devastated FEMA's credibility along with parts of South Florida and Louisiana. The agency's response to the disaster, which caused $25 billion in damage and left thousands without shelter and water for weeks, was blasted as disorganized.

"Where in the hell is the cavalry on this one?" asked Miami-Dade County Emergency Management Director Kate Hale.[66] "They keep saying we're going to get supplies. For God's sake, where are they?"

President George H. W. Bush, who was running for re-election, then dispatched federal troops, mobile kitchens and tents. Within a week, nearly 20,000 troops were in South Florida.[67] Nonetheless, many analysts say FEMA's poor performance cost Bush votes in the 1992 election, in which he was defeated by Democrat Bill Clinton.

Some three weeks after Andrew, one of the most powerful hurricanes in Hawaiian history hit Kauai. This time, FEMA sent disaster teams to Hawaii even before Iniki struck.

After Andrew and Iniki, some critics proposed abolishing FEMA and giving the military a bigger disaster role. The National Academy of Public Administration, however, recommended establishing a White House Domestic Crisis Monitoring Unit to ensure "timely, effective and well coordinated" federal responses to catastrophes.[68]

Reforming FEMA

President Clinton gave the agency a shot in the arm when he nominated Witt as FEMA director — the first with experience as a state emergency manager. Clinton elevated the post to Cabinet level, and Witt urged governors to similarly elevate their state emergency-management directors.[69]

Witt is credited with streamlining disaster relief and recovery operations and focusing workers on "customer service." When floods ravaged the Midwest in 1993 and an earthquake shook Los Angeles the next year, FEMA crisis-management teams quickly delivered aid to the injured. After the floods, Witt persuaded the federal government to buy flood-prone properties in the Midwest and relocate businesses and residents, saving taxpayers millions of dollars when floods struck again in 1995.[70]

FEMA also won praise for its response to a 1994 earthquake in Northridge, Calif., a modern urban environment generally designed to withstand earthquakes. Although $20 billion in damages resulted, few lives were lost.

The Oklahoma City bombing on April 19, 1995, raised questions about FEMA's role in responding to terrorist attacks. Debates raged among officials at FEMA and the Justice and Defense departments over who should be the first-responder — fire, police, emergency management or emergency medical services? Terrorism was part of FEMA's "all-hazards" approach to emergency management, but it lacked the resources and technologies to address specific terrorism issues such as weapons of mass destruction.[71]

When George W. Bush became president, like Clinton he appointed a close friend to head FEMA, Joe Allbaugh, Bush's former chief of staff as governor of Texas and his campaign manager during the 2000 presidential race. Allbaugh's lack of emergency-management experience was not an issue during his confirmation hearings.[72]

In a speech the day before the 9/11 attacks, Allbaugh outlined firefighting, disaster mitigation and catastrophic preparedness as his top priorities.[73] Ironically, on Sept. 11 Allbaugh and other FEMA senior leaders were in Montana, attending the annual meeting of the National Emergency Management Association, whose members are state emergency officials. FEMA immediately activated the Federal Response Plan.

Some elements of the response to 9/11 — particularly the communication problems — revealed major weaknesses in the country's ability to respond to terrorism and raised questions about the capabilities and appropriate role of states and localities in managing a massive disaster. Less than a week later, President Bush announced the formation of a Homeland Security Office, and a year later, on Nov. 25, 2002, Congress approved the Homeland Security Act, consolidating 22 federal agencies, including FEMA, into the new Department of Homeland Security — the largest government reorganization in 50 years.

When FEMA was officially transferred to DHS on March 1, 2003, it lost its Cabinet-level status and its independence. It also lost some of its personnel and funding to another new agency, the Office of Domestic Preparedness. In addition, $80 million was transferred from FEMA's coffers to help pay for DHS's overhead, and in 2003 and 2004 FEMA lost $169 million to DHS for other purposes, including funds FEMA was supposed to have saved from being folded into DHS.[74]

Since then, up to a third of the staff has been cut from FEMA's five Mobile Emergency Response Support detachments — teams that deploy quickly to set up communications gear, power generators and life-support equipment to help federal, state and local officials coordinate disaster response.[75]

"Over the past three-and-a-half years, FEMA has gone from being a model agency to being one where . . . employee morale has fallen, and our nation's emergency management capability is being eroded," veteran FEMA staffer Pleasant Mann told Congress in 2004.

The Bush administration also cut Corps of Engineers' flood control funds. "For the first time in 37 years, federal budget cuts have all but stopped major work on the New Orleans area's east bank hurricane levees," the New Orleans *Times-Picayune* reported in June 2004.[76]

Meanwhile, the natural disasters continued. Nine tropical systems affected the United States in 2004, causing some $42 billion in damage.[77] President Bush issued 68 major disaster declarations — the most for a single year in nearly a decade.[78]

In 2004 — as Bush was running for re-election — an unprecedented four hurricanes (Charley, Frances, Ivan and Jeanne) slammed into Florida, which had been a pivotal state in Bush's race for the White House in 2000. Careful to avoid his father's delays after Hurricane Andrew in 1992, Bush quickly declared the state a federal disaster

Hurricane victims slog past a police officer standing guard in flooded downtown New Orleans. Water was up to 12 feet high in some areas. The storm forced more than 300,000 people to evacuate their homes, mainly in Louisiana and Mississippi.

area, making it eligible for federal assistance. Less than two days later the president was touring hard-hit neighborhoods in southwest Florida.[79]

Bush handled the next storm, Frances, in a similar fashion, drawing partisan allegations that he was using the hurricane as a photo opportunity. The president was "touting a $2 billion aid package that has already been promised to Florida as a result of Hurricane Charley," complained Rep. Robert Wexler, a Democrat from West Palm Beach.[80] The aid package was not without controversy. At least 9,800 people from Miami-Dade County received more than $21 million in assistance even though Frances hit 100 miles away and inflicted little damage in the county.

Still, the 2004 hurricane destruction in Florida was unprecedented. An estimated one in five Florida homes was damaged, and 117 people died.[81]

Two months later, Bush won the state and the presidency.

CURRENT SITUATION

Katrina Aftershocks

In the wake of Hurricane Katrina, the DHS is "re-engineering" its disaster preparedness; Congress is trying to figure out what went wrong and how to pay for the damage; and states and localities are reviewing their emergency plans.

Katrina ignited weeks of contradictory testimony, finger-pointing and conflicting reports from federal, state and local officials. There's no argument, however, that all three levels of government were ill prepared for a deadly storm they all knew was coming.

"It turned out we were all wrong," said White House homeland security adviser Townsend. "We had not adequately anticipated."[82] The review of the disaster being spearheaded by Townsend is expected to make recommendations by the end of 2005.

Homeland Security Secretary Michael Chertoff also acknowledged to lawmakers that Katrina overwhelmed FEMA and promised to revamp the agency and hire more experienced staff.[83] "Dealing with this kind of an ultra-catastrophe . . . requires a lot of work beforehand, months beforehand," Chertoff said in October.[84]

Several Democrats, including Sen. Hillary Rodham Clinton, N.Y., say Chertoff's proposed changes don't go far enough and that the administration's changes in the agency have gutted it. "The bureaucracy created by moving FEMA under the Department of Homeland Security is clearly not working," she said in introducing legislation restoring FEMA to Cabinet-level rank.[85]

The Democrats have boycotted Congress' probe into the Katrina relief efforts and called for an independent commission similar to the panel that investigated the 9/11 attacks. But Senate Majority Leader Bill Frist, R-Tenn, noted in a letter to Democratic Minority Leader Harry Reid of Nevada that it took longer than a year for Congress to form an outside commission to investigate the federal government's handling of the Sept. 11 attacks. Such a delay now, Frist wrote, "would put more people at risk for a longer time than is necessary."[86]

The administration is pressing ahead with its own reforms. Chertoff, for example, said FEMA needs to learn from the military and private companies that were able to keep communication lines open. DHS is setting up "emergency reconnaissance teams" that will be deployed to catastrophes to provide up-to-the-minute reports to federal planners, who can then send the appropriate resources.[87]

Meanwhile, FEMA continues to come under fire for spending $236 million to temporarily house Katrina victims and emergency workers on cruise ships. FEMA also was criticized for handing out $2,000 checks to hurricane victims. In three Louisiana parishes, for example, FEMA issued more checks than there are households, at a cost of at least $70 million.[88]

Katrina-related contracts have also stirred controversy, including a $500 million debris-removal contract awarded to AshBritt Environmental, which has ties to Mississippi Gov. Haley Barbour, a former Republican National Committee chairman.[89] And former FEMA Director Allbaugh and his wife founded a company that has received federal contracts for Gulf Coast cleanup.[90] Homeland Security Inspector General Richard Skinner said in October he is investigating "all the contracting activities that took place immediately following this disaster from day one."[91]

Contracting questions aside, many emergency-management experts worry most about communication problems between federal, state and local authorities. Chertoff said his department is reviewing emergency-operations plans for every major urban area to ensure they are clear, detailed and up-to-date. "That includes a hard, realistic look at evacuation planning ranging from earthquakes to subway bombings," he said.

Local Reviews

Every city in the country is looking at its evacuation plan" in the aftermath of Katrina, says Aylward of the ComCare Alliance.

States and localities aren't always finding what they expected. A week before Hurricane Wilma hit, Gov. Bush touted Florida's hurricane readiness before a House panel. "Local and state governments that fail to prepare are preparing to fail," he said.[92]

The next week, however, when Wilma struck, "We did not perform to where we want to be," Bush said, noting that many residents failed to prepare and ended up overwhelming local government water-and-ice distribution sites. "People had ample time to prepare. It isn't that hard to get 72 hours' worth of food and water," he said, repeating the advice officials gave days before the storm.[93]

But enabling all levels of government to communicate with one another has been harder. "Since 9/11, enormous investments of time, effort and taxpayer money have been made to craft a system in which all levels of government can communicate and coordinate for the most effective response possible, whether to a natural disaster or a terrorist attack. That did not occur with Katrina," said Sen. Susan Collins, R-Maine, chairwoman of a Senate panel that examined FEMA's recovery efforts.[94]

Indeed, fire chiefs who responded to Katrina told Congress there was an "utter lack of structure and communication at any level of government in the first 10 days."[95] As for former FEMA Director Brown, he was in an area totally cut off from communications when the hurricane hit and "probably would have been better off staying in Washington," says Harrald of George Washington University.

Some relief may be on the way. The proposed budget savings package working through Congress would free up spectrum for emergency responders and provide between $500 million and $1 billion in grants to local government to buy "interoperable" communication equipment.[96]

Congress is considering creating a national alert office capable of disseminating warnings of natural disasters and terrorist attacks using a wide range of media, including cell phones, cable and satellite TV and radio and PDAs (personal digital assistants). A Senate panel on Oct. 20 approved a measure sponsored by Sen. Jim DeMint, R-S.C., chairman of the Commerce Subcommittee on Disaster Prevention and Prediction. "Without a proper way to alert those in danger, even the most accurate disaster prediction is useless," he said.[97] The House does not have a companion bill.

Congress has approved more than $62 billion in emergency aid following Katrina, but more than $40 billion remained unspent as of late October. The White House wants to shift $17 billion of the unspent portion to levee reconstruction, road repairs and other basic infrastructure work in the region.[98]

Lawmakers already have shifted $750 million from FEMA to a program that lends money to local governments to maintain essential services such as police and fire protection. The measure was signed shortly after New Orleans Mayor Nagin announced plans to lay off 3,000 city employees because of funding shortfalls.

Cleaning up after Katrina is expected to dwarf clean-up expenses of past disasters. For example, about 150 million cubic yards of debris will have to be removed from four Gulf Coast states — 10 times more than Hurricane Andrew left behind in Florida in 1992, which was several times greater than the amount hauled away (at a cost of $1.7 billion) after the World Trade Center Twin Towers collapsed.[99]

While Congress is debating how to pay this year's hurricane bill, some argue that now is the time to develop a more coherent disaster policy. "The response to the disaster has been to open up the wallet and dump it out," said U.S. Rep. Dennis Cardoza, D-Calif.[100]

Thousands wait for food, water and medical aid outside the New Orleans Convention Center on Sept. 1, 2005 — three days after Hurricane Katrina struck New Orleans.

David Moss, a Harvard Business School economist who studies disaster financing, agrees. "Right now we cover major disaster losses mainly on an ad hoc basis," he says. "We wait until the disaster strikes, and then we spend whatever seems necessary to relieve the victims."

Natural disasters also batter the insurance industry. It estimates Katrina alone is likely to cost at least $34.4 billion in insured property losses.[101]

Florida Insurance Commissioner Kevin McCarty has asked government officials nationwide to support a "national catastrophe fund." One of its supporters is Rep. Mark Foley, R-Fla., who has sponsored a bill to amend the federal tax code to allow insurance companies to voluntarily set aside, on a tax-deferred basis, reserves to pay for future catastrophic losses. And Sen. Kay Bailey Hutchinson, R-Texas, proposes setting up an emergency reserve fund for domestic disasters and emergencies.

Moss says insurers could also include a "catastrophe rider" on every insurance policy covering losses stemming from terrorism and natural disasters, and the federal government could also offer some sort of "backstop" covering losses above a certain level, such as $100 billion.

Homeowners' insurance policies do not cover flood damage caused by the storm surges that accompany hurricanes. Experts estimate that Katrina caused $44 billion in flood damage. Flood insurance is available through the National Flood Insurance Program, but it is expensive, and many homeowners do not buy it. In addition, the New Orleans maps used to

AT ISSUE

Did race play a role in the government's slow response to Hurricane Katrina?

 YES The Rev. Jesse L. Jackson, Sr.
Founder and President,
National Rainbow/PUSH Coalition

Written for the *CQ Researcher*, November 2005

Race played a role in who was left behind. Race seems to be a factor in who will get back in. Class played a role in who was left behind. Class may play a role in who is let back in.

Incompetence and cronyism played a role, especially in the slowness of the response. No-bid contracts to out-of-state corporations suggest that role has not yet ended.

The hurricane hit the whole region, without concern for skin color or wealth — but Katrina's impact was multiplied if you were African-American or poor — and so many facing the worst flooding were both.

We can't forget that years of neglect and disinvestment in public goods and services — after years of politically motivated attacks on the role of government in our society — left the people of New Orleans defenseless. Some had the individual resources to escape; many did not. And race and class are heavily correlated with those who did not.

Then there is the war. Tax money spent on invading Iraq, rather than for needed goods and services at home, such as levees. National Guard troops stuck in Baghdad, not saving lives in Biloxi.

The whole world watched in horror as helpless people were stranded and neglected in the wealthiest, most powerful nation ever to exist. It must never happen again.

Let's rebuild New Orleans. Instead of experimenting on real people in trouble with an agenda based on right-wing economic ideology, we should rebuild, reinvest in and revitalize all of New Orleans.

The rescue is not over yet. People continue to need relief, shelter, food. They want jobs, living wages and the chance to come back home. Small businesses and contractors want to help do the rebuilding. New housing must be built in Louisiana, and affordable housing provided in the meantime, near people's jobs and neighborhoods. Families and communities must be reunified.

Reconstruction must be bottom-up, not top-down, and include everyone. Reconstruction should emphasize public investment to rebuild levees, construct mass transit and sewers, open up new schools and parks. I have suggested a Civilian Reconstruction Corps to provide former residents with work, training and a chance to be part of rebuilding their homes and their city.

Too many people were abandoned during Katrina. Surely we will not abandon them again, by not bringing them home and helping them participate in the rebirth of their own beloved New Orleans.

 NO John McWhorter
Senior Fellow, Manhattan Institute

Written for the *CQ Researcher*, November 2005

The almost all-black crowds sweltering, starving and dying in the Convention Center after Hurricane Katrina showed us that in New Orleans, as in so many other places, by and large to be poor is to be black. This is the legacy of racism, although opinions will differ as to whether that racism is in the past or the present.

But to claim that racism is why the rescue effort was so slow is not a matter of debate. It is, in fact, absurd.

To say "George Bush doesn't care about black people" is to honestly believe that if it were the white poor of Louisiana who happened to live closest to the levees, then barely anyone would have even gotten wet, and 50,000 troops would have been standing at the ready as soon as Katrina popped up on meteorologists' radar screens. The National Guard would have magically lifted the long-entrenched bureaucratic restrictions that only allow states to assign troops when it is proven that they are needed. Suddenly, against all historical precedent, just for that week, the Federal Emergency Management Agency would have morphed into a well-organized and dependable outfit.

But what about the hurricane that Katrina displaced as the third strongest on record to hit America — Andrew in 1992 — which left 250,000 people homeless? Ground zero for this one was Homestead, Fla., where whites were a big majority. So help was pouring in as soon as the rain stopped, right?

Well, not exactly. "Where in the hell is the cavalry on this one?" asked Kate Hale, Miami-Dade County emergency-management director, on national television. People went without electricity or food and dealt with looters for five days, just like in New Orleans. FEMA was raked over the coals for the same bureaucratic incompetence that is making headlines now.

Is it so far-fetched to admit that the problem after Katrina as well was the general ineptness of America's defenses against unforeseen disasters? A little event called 9/11 comes to mind. Two presidential administrations neglected increasingly clear signs that Osama bin Laden was planning to attack us on our shores. In general, bureaucracies are notoriously bad at foresight and long-term planning, and FEMA has never exactly been a counter-example.

Of course, there will be those who will insist, no matter what the evidence, that racism slowed down the rescue effort. But this is essentially the way a certain kind of person affirms their sense of importance when they lack healthier ones.

determine if a home is in a floodplain were apparently out of date, and many homeowners whose homes flooded had been told that they were not in danger of being flooded.

OUTLOOK

Just Talk?

While there is a lot of talk about improving disaster preparedness and response, few experts expect radical changes any time soon.

"The investigations are focusing on individual blame, rather than system failures," says George Washington University's Harrald. "The hubris in Washington is that we can solve everything by passing a law or reorganizing something inside the Beltway. It's a little more complicated."

Ashwood, director of emergency management in Oklahoma, agrees. "All we are doing right now is just talking. Nobody is doing anything else." He adds that while it's all good that people in Washington want answers, some of the scrutiny is misdirected. He notes that 90 auditors have been sent to monitor the 72 full-time FEMA employees who work on disaster recovery. "Ninety auditors covering 72 people," he says. "That's ridiculous."

Meanwhile, on Capitol Hill, many lawmakers — particularly Democrats —feel the Katrina investigations are losing steam. "In the case of 9/11, it took a while to develop, and only after intense political pressure from the families," said former Rep. Lee Hamilton, D-Ill., who co-chaired the 9/11 Commission. "I don't see anything comparable" happening for the Katrina disaster.[102]

The fact that FEMA reacted quicker to hurricanes Rita and Wilma also may dampen the urgency for action, experts say. Others worry that the attention on Katrina may give short shrift to future floods, earthquakes and other disasters. "That is part of the human experience. We react to the last disaster," Harrald says.

While homeland security adviser Townsend admits that a "failure of communication" within the federal

Worst-Case Scenarios

Scientists and storm chasers always have their sights on the next disaster. Experts at the National Hurricane Center, for example, say Katrina won't be the last major hurricane to strike a big city, forecasting that even New York City is vulnerable. Other catastrophes that scientists think could occur include:

- Gulf Coast tsunami (generated by a fault line in the Caribbean)
- East Coast tsunami (caused by asteroid falling into the Atlantic Ocean)
- Heat waves (as the population ages, urban areas get hotter and electricity systems are strained)
- Midwest earthquake
- Colossal volcanic eruption at Yellowstone National Park could destroy life for hundreds of miles and bury half the country in ash up to 3 feet deep
- Los Angeles tsunami (generated by an earthquake fault off Southern California)
- Asteroid impact
- New York City hurricane
- Pacific Northwest megathrust earthquake (could cause a tsunami like the 2004 tsunami in South Asia)

Source: Live Science, http://livescience.com

government and with state and local officials was the "single most important" contributor to the Katrina breakdown, some disaster experts aren't optimistic that even that situation will change.[103]

"The federal government needs to take a leadership role to pull the agencies together," said Priscilla Nelson, a former National Science Foundation executive. "That really hasn't happened yet . . . [and] I don't have a reasonable expectation it will. People are organized in a way that doesn't promote integration or accountability or authority."[104]

The University of Pennsylvania's Kettl says the federal government's "lack of imagination" — cited by the 9/11 Commission as a reason for the government's failure in 2001 — contributed to its poor performance after Katrina. The United States has failed to "build the capacity to deal with costly, wicked problems that leave little time to react," he wrote, and instead is "trying to solve the most important challenges of the 21st century by retreating back to models from the past."[105]

Aylward of ComCare says the discussions sparked by Hurricane Katrina miss a key point. "There's a real mistaken idea that disasters are somehow different from day-to-day events. But these are the same firemen, the same police, all the same people on the ground using the same radios, same computers," he says. "We ought to be focusing on improving the day-to-day response of emergency agencies."

For her part, the University of Colorado's Tierney hopes individual citizens will become more prepared. "The ultimate first-responders in any disaster are members of the public," she says. "If we want to be prepared for the future terrorist attack, for the future disasters in this country, we have to build within neighborhoods and through local community organizations to help people to be self-sufficient, to help others when disaster strikes. Katrina certainly taught us that."

NOTES

1. Devin Leonard, "The Only Lifeline Was the Wal-Mart," *Fortune*, Oct. 3, 2005, p. 74.

2. Testimony of David Paulison, acting under secretary for emergency preparedness, before Senate Homeland Security and Governmental Affairs Committee, Oct. 6, 2005.

3. Leonard, *op. cit.*

4. Donald F. Kettl, "The Worst is Yet to Come: Lessons from September 11 and Hurricane Katrina," University of Pennsylvania, Fels Institute of Government, September 2005.

5. Eric Berger, "The foretelling of a deadly disaster in New Orleans," *The Houston Chronicle*, Dec. 1, 2001. See also Dean E. Murphy, "Storm Puts Focus on Other Disasters in Waiting," *The New York Times*, Nov. 13, 2005, p. A1.

6. FEMA press release, "Hurricane Pam Exercise Concludes," July 23, 2004. See also Joel K. Bourne, Jr. "Gone with the Water," *National Geographic*, October 2004.

7. U.S. Conference of Mayors, "Report on Interoperability," June 28, 2004.

8. Prepared testimony of Max Mayfield, director, National Hurricane Center, before Senate Commerce Committee's Disaster Prediction and Prevention Subcommittee, Sept. 20, 2005.

9. Fact sheet, U.S. Geological Survey, Earthquake Hazards Program.

10. National Academy of Public Administration, "Coping With Catastrophe: Building an Emergency Management System to Meet People's Needs in Natural and Manmade Disaster," February 1993.

11. White House transcript, "Press Briefing by Homeland Security and Counterterrorism Adviser Frances Fragos Townsend," Oct. 21, 2005.

12. White House transcript, "President's Remarks During Hurricane Rita Briefing in Texas," Sept. 25, 2005.

13. U.S. Government Accountability Office, "Homeland Security: DHS' Efforts to Enhance First Responders' All Hazards Capabilities Continue to Evolve," July 2005.

14. The National Response Plan is available at www.dhs .gov/interweb/assetlibrary/NRP_FullText.pdf.

15. *Ibid.*

16. Jerry Adler, "The Fight Against the Flu," *Newsweek*, Oct. 31, 2005, p. 39.

17. *Ibid.*

18. Ellen Florian Kratz, "For FedEx, It Was Time To Deliver," *Fortune*, Oct. 3, 2005, p. 83.

19. Testimony before House Energy and Commerce Subcommittee on Telecommunications and the Internet, Sept. 29, 2005.

20. Testimony of David Boyd, director of SAFECOM Program, Department of Homeland Security, before House Energy and Commerce Subcommittee on Telecommunications and the Internet, Sept. 29, 2005.

21. Testimony of Kevin Martin, chairman, Federal Communications Commission, before House Subcommittee on Telecommunications and the Internet, Sept. 29, 2005.

22. *Ibid.*

23. Testimony of Chuck Canterbury, National President, Fraternal Order of Police, before House Homeland Security Subcommittee on Emergency Preparedness, Science and Technology, Sept. 29, 2005.

24. Transcript of House Energy and Commerce Subcommittee on Telecommunications and the Internet, Sept. 29, 2005.

25. White House transcript, "President Discusses Hurricane Relief in Address to the Nation," Sept. 15, 2005

26. CNN, "Lt. Gen. Honore a 'John Wayne dude,' " Sept. 3, 2005.

27. Bill Nichols and Richard Benedetto, "Govs to Bush: Relief our job," *USA Today*, Oct. 3, 2005.

28. Prepared testimony of Gov. Jeb Bush before U.S. House Committee on Homeland Security, Oct. 19, 2005.

29. Congressional Research Service, "Hurricane Katrina: DOD Disaster Response," Sept. 19, 2005.

30. Barbara Starr, "Military ponders disaster response unit," CNN, Oct. 11, 2005 and Ann Scott Tyson, "Pentagon Plans to Beef Up Domestic Rapid-Response Forces," *The Washington Post*, Oct. 13, 2004, p. A4.

31. The Associated Press, "NOPD Fires 51 for Desertion," CBS News, Oct. 28, 2005.

32. Department of Defense news briefing, Sept. 27, 2005.

33. Congressional Research Service, *op. cit.*

34. *Ibid.*

35. *Ibid.*

36. "NewsHour with Jim Lehrer," "Using the Military at Home," Sept. 27, 2005.

37. Congressional Research Service, "The Posse Comitatus Act and Related Matters: A Sketch," June 6, 2005.

38. Anne Plummer, "Change in 'Posse' Law Unwise, Say Critics," *CQ Weekly*, Sept. 26, 2005, pp. 2550-2551.

39. U.S. Conference of Mayors, "The U.S. Conference of Mayors Hold Special Meeting on Emergency Response and Homeland Security," Oct. 24, 2005.

40. For background see Pamela M. Prah, "War in Iraq," *CQ Researcher*, Oct. 21, 2005, pp. 881-908, and Pamela Prah, "Draft Debates," *CQ Researcher*, Aug. 19, 2005, pp. 661-684.

41. Gene Healy, "What of 'Posse Comitatus'?" *Akron Beacon Journal*, Oct. 7, 2005, reprinted on Cato Institute Web site, www.cato.org/pub_display.php?pub_id=5115.

42. National Academy of Public Administration," *op. cit.*

43. Testimony before U.S. House Committee on Homeland Security, Oct. 19, 2005.

44. Transcript of House Select Katrina Response Investigation Committee, Sept. 27, 2005.

45. *Ibid.*

46. *Time*, "4 places Where the System Broke Down," Sept. 18, 2005, p. 38.

47. CNN, "Mayor to Feds: Get Off Your Asses," Sept. 2, 2005, www.cnn.com/2005/US/09/02/nagin.transcript/.

48. Eric Lipton, Eric Schmitt and Thom Shanker, "Political Issues Snarled Plans for Troop Aid," *The New York Times*, Sept. 9, 2005, p. A1.

49. Kettl, *op. cit.*

50. Peter G. Gosselin and Alan C. Miler, "Why FEMA was Missing in Action," *Los Angeles Times*, Sept. 5, 2005.

51. Testimony before Homeland Security Subcommittee on Emergency Preparedness, Science and Technology, Sept. 29, 2005.

52. Transcript, House Transportation and Infrastructure Subcommittee on Development, Public Buildings and Emergency Management, Oct. 6, 2005.

53. Rebecca Adams, "FEMA Failure a Perfect Storm of Bureaucracy, *CQ Weekly*, Sept. 12, 2005, p. 2378.

54. Frank James and Andrew Martin, "Slow response bewilders former FEMA officials," *Chicago Tribune*, Sept. 3, 2005, p. A1.

55. "FEMA History," www.fema.gov/about/history.shtm.

56. James O'Toole, "U.S. help for disaster victims goes from nothing to billions," *Pittsburgh Post-Gazette*, Oct. 2, 2005.

57. Ken Rudin, National Public Radio, "The Hurricane and the President (Hoover, That Is)," Oct. 5, 2005.

58. Aaron Schroeder and Gary Wamsley Robert Ward, "The Evolution of Emergency Management in America: From a Painful Past to a Promising but Uncertain Future," in *Handbook of Crisis and Emergency Management* (2001), p. 364.

59. "FEMA History," *op. cit.*

60. White House statement, June 19, 1978.

61. George D. Haddow and Jane A. Bullock, *Introduction to Emergency Management* (2003), p. 8.

62. Testimony before House Transportation and Infrastructure Subcommittee on Economic Development, Public Buildings and Emergency Management, Oct. 6, 2005.

63. Haddow and Bullock, *op. cit.*

64. *Ibid.*

65. http://seismo.berkeley.edu/faq/1989_0.html

66. *CQ Historic Documents 1993*, "President George Bush on Disaster Relief for Florida and Louisiana After Hurricane Andrew," Aug. 24, 1992.

67. Ali Farazmand, *Handbook of Crisis and Emergency Management* (2001), p. 379.

68. National Academy of Public Administration," *op. cit.*

69. Haddow and Bullock, *op. cit.*

70. Adams, *op. cit.*

71. Haddow and Bullock, *op. cit.*, p. 12.

72. Haddow and Bullock, *op. cit.*, p. 12.

73. *Ibid*, p. 13.

74. Justin Rood, "FEMA's decline: an agency's slow slide from grace," www.govexec.com, Sept .28, 2005.

75. *Ibid.*

76. Dick Polman, "A possible sea change on federal spending," *The Philadelphia Inquirer*, Sept. 7, 2005.

77. www.ncdc.noaa.gov/oa/climate/research/2004/hurricanes04.html.

78. www.fema.gov/news/newsrelease_print.fema?id=15967.

79. Charles Mahtesian, "How FEMA delivered Florida for Bush," Govexec.com, *National Journal*, Nov. 3, 2004.

80. Adam C. Smith, "Hurricanes roil the political waters," *St. Petersburg Times*, Sept. 8, 2004.

81. www.ncdc.noaa.gov/oa/climate/research/2004/hurricanes04.html.

82. White House transcript, "Press Briefing by Homeland Security and Counterterrorism Advisor Fran Townsend," Oct. 21, 2005

83. Transcript, House Select Katrina Response Investigation Committee, Oct. 19, 2005.

84. *Ibid.*

85. Statement, Sept. 6, 2005 http://clinton.senate.gov/news/statements/details.cfm?id=24526&&.

86. Susan Ferrechio and Martin Kady II, "Little Headway on Compromise for Select Panel to Examine Katrina Response," *CQ Today*, Sept. 20, 2005.

87. *Ibid.*, transcript, Oct. 19, 2005.

88. Sally Kestin, Megan O'Matz and John Maines, "FEMA's waste continues as millions in extra payments given out for Katrina," *Sun-Sentinel*, Oct. 20, 2005.

89. Eamon Javers, "Anatomy of a Katrina Cleanup Contract," *Business Week*, Oct. 27, 2005.

90. Leslie Wayne and Glen Justice, "FEMA Director Under Clinton Profits From Experience," *The New York Times*, Oct. 10, 2005 and Jonathan E. Kaplan, "Former FEMA chief Albaugh in the middle," *The Hill*, Sept. 30, 2005. See also "Profiting from Katrina: The contracts," Center for Public Integrity, www.publicintegrity.org/katrina.

91. Transcript, House Transportation and Infrastructure Subcommittee on Economic Development, Public Buildings and Emergency Management Hearing on FEMA After Katrina, Oct. 6, 2005.

92. Testimony before House Committee on Homeland Security, Oct. 19, 2005.

93. The Associated Press, "Gov. Bush Criticizes State's Storm Effort," Oct. 27, 2005.

94. Transcript of Senate Homeland Security and Governmental Affairs Committee Hearing on Status Report on FEMA Recovery Efforts, Oct. 6, 2005.

95. Killen, *op. cit.*

96. Amol Sharma, "Senate Panel Approves Bill That Would Create A National Alert Office, *CQ Weekly*, Oct. 20, 2005.

97. Tim Starks, "Unpromising Prospects for First Responders," *CQ Weekly*, Nov. 14, 2005, p. 3034.

98. Liriel Higa and Stephen J. Norton, "Louisiana Senators Remain Disappointed with Bush's Rebuilding plan," *CQ Today*, Oct. 28, 2005.

99. Spencer S. Hsu and Ceci Connolly, "La. Wants FEMA to Pay for Majority of Damage to State Property," *The Washington Post*, Oct. 28, 2005, p. A14.

100. Edmund L. Andrews, "Emergency Spending as a Way of Life," *The New York Times*, Oct. 2, 2005, p. A4.

101. Insurance Information Institute, "Catastrophes: Insurance Issues," November 2005.

102. Tim Starks, "Critics Expecting Little from Hurricane Probes," *CQ Today*, Oct. 18, 2005.

103. White House transcript, Townsend briefing, Oct. 21, 2005.

104. Brain Friel and Paul Singer, "Gaps remain in government strategy for handling natural disasters," *National Journal*, Govexec.com, Oct. 28, 2005.

105. Kettl, *op. cit.*

BIBLIOGRAPHY

Books

Bea, Keith, *Federal Disaster Polices After Terrorists Strike, Nova Science Publishers,* **2003.**
Prepared at the request of members of Congress, this book is primarily about terrorism, but it provides a good introduction to the Robert T. Stafford Disaster Relief and Emergency Assistance Act, the country's main federal disaster-assistance law.

Farazmand, Ali, (ed.), *Handbook of Crisis and Emergency Management, Marcel Dekker,* **2001.**
A professor of public administration at Florida Atlantic University has compiled essays and case studies of crisis and emergency management, as well as a good primer on Federal Emergency Management Agency history.

Haddow, George D., and Jane A. Bullock, *Introduction to Emergency Management, Butterworth-Heinemann,* **2003.**
Two former FEMA officials provide background on the history of disaster response and preparedness and strategies for improving planning and mitigation.

Articles

"FEMA: A Legacy of Waste," *South Florida Sun-Sentinel,* **Sept. 18, 2005, p. A1.**
A team of *Sun-Sentinel* reporters examined 20 disasters nationwide and found a pattern of mismanagement and fraud at FEMA.

"4 Places Where the System Broke Down," *Time,* **Sept. 19, 2005, pp. 28-42.**
A team of *Time* reporters shows how confusion, incompetence and fear of making mistakes hobbled the government at all levels in the New Orleans relief efforts, laying blame on the mayor, governor, FEMA director and secretary of Homeland Security.

Adams, Rebecca, "FEMA Failure a Perfect Storm of Bureaucracy," *CQ Weekly,* **Sept. 12, 2005.**
The reporter provides an overview of FEMA's challenges and pending proposals in Congress in the wake of the agency's sluggish response to Hurricane Katrina.

O'Toole, James, "U.S. help for disaster victims goes from nothing to billions," *Pittsburgh Post-Gazette,* **Oct. 2, 2005.**
The federal government has been assuming an increasing role in trying to make individuals, businesses and local governments whole after natural disasters, but there is no plan to budget for natural disasters.

Rood, Justin, "FEMA's decline: an agency's slow slide from grace," **www.govexec.com, Sept. 28, 2005.**
This article from a magazine for government executives discusses the budget and staffing cuts that FEMA has experienced in recent years and concludes that FEMA "was not the agency it once was" when Katrina struck.

Sappenfield, Mark, "Military wary of disaster role," *The Christian Science Monitor,* **Sept. 29, 2005.**
In some respects, the greatest opponent of giving the military more authority in U.S. disaster relief is the military itself.

Reports

Government Accountability Office, **"Hurricane Katrina: Providing Oversight of the Nation's Preparedness, Response and Recovery Activities," Sept. 28, 2005.**
This report to Congress includes a 10-page list of past GAO studies related to hurricanes and other natural disasters, including preparedness, the military's role and insurance.

Insurance Information Institute, **"Catastrophes: Insurance Issues," November 2005.**
A leading insurance industry group explains in simple language how catastrophes affect the insurance industry and how Katrina is prompting a re-examination of how the country pays for natural disasters.

Kettl, Donald, "The Worst is Yet to Come: Lesson from September 11 and Hurricane Katrina," *University of Pennsylvania Fels Institute of Government*, **September 2005.** A professor of public policy specializing in state issues and homeland security concludes that policymakers need to pull FEMA out of the Department of Homeland Security and establish better communications systems.

***National Academy of Public Administration,* "Coping with Catastrophe: Building an Emergency Management System to Meet People's Needs in Natural and Manmade Disasters," February 1993.**

A panel of experts that convened in the wake of the slow federal response to Hurricane Andrew in 1992 recommends that the military not take the lead in disaster responses.

***National Academy of Public Administration,* "Review of Actions Taken to Strengthen the Nation's Emergency Management System," March 1994.** This follow-up report, requested by FEMA Director James L. Witt, concluded that progress was being made but that FEMA needed fewer political appointees in leadership positions and that the president should establish a Domestic Crisis Monitoring Unit.

For More Information

American Red Cross, 2025 E St., N.W., Washington, DC 20006; (202) 303-4498; www.redcross.org. The congressionally chartered nonprofit provides disaster relief nationwide. Its Web site tells how to prepare for disasters.

Centers for Disease Control and Prevention, 1600 Clifton Road, Atlanta, GA 30333; (404) 639-3311; www.bt.cdc.gov. Provides information on emergency preparedness for bioterrorism, chemical and radiation emergencies, natural disasters and contagious diseases.

Department of Homeland Security, Washington, DC 20528; (202) 282-8000; www.dhs.gov. The principal agency charged with preventing terrorist attacks within the United States and minimizing the damage from attacks and natural disasters.

Federal Emergency Management Agency, 500 C St., S.W., Washington, DC 20472; (202) 566-1600; www.fema.gov. Provides information on preparedness, emergency response, the National Flood Insurance Program, how to apply for disaster relief, latest details on Katrina and a copy of the National Response Plan. A list of all 50 state emergency-management offices is at www.fema.gov/fema/statedr.shtm.

National Emergency Management Association, P.O. Box 11910, Lexington, KY 40578; (859) 244-8000; www.nemaweb.org. Represents state emergency-management directors.

National Hurricane Center, Tropical Prediction Center, 11691 S.W. 17th St, Miami, FL 33165-2149; (305) 229-4470; www.nhc.noaa.gov. Tracks and forecasts hurricanes.

Insurance Information Institute, 110 William St., New York, NY 10038; (212) 346-5500; www.iii.org. Represents the insurance industry and tracks the impact of catastrophes, floods and terrorist acts on the industry.

International Association of Emergency Managers, 201 Park Washington Court, Falls Church, Va. 22046-4527; (703) 538-1795; www.iaem.com. Represents local emergency managers and tracks federal homeland security grants and policies that affect local emergency officials.

U.S. Geological Survey's Earthquake Hazards Program, 12201 Sunrise Valley Dr., MS 905, Reston, VA 20192; 1-888-275-8747; http://earthquake.usgs.gov/. Provides information on worldwide earthquake activity and hazard-reduction. Web site lists the largest U.S. earthquakes.

7

Wounded Veterans

Is America Shortchanging Vets on Health Care?

Peter Katel

AP Photo/The (Yuma) Daily Sun/Terry Ketron

U.S. Army Sgt. Frank Sandoval, 27, died in June after struggling for nearly two years to recover from a massive head injury. Traumatic brain injury (TBI) has been called the signature wound of the Iraq War because of the numerous roadside bombs and rocket-propelled grenades used against U.S. troops. Critics have blasted the Veterans Affairs Department for being unprepared to deal with the large number of TBI patients and their families.

From *CQ Researcher*,
August 31, 2007.

S gt. Garrett Anderson of the Illinois National Guard lost his right arm in Iraq. But after coming home, he faced another battle — with the Department of Veterans Affairs (VA).

Anderson also suffers from traumatic brain injury and is riddled with shrapnel, but the VA rated him 90 percent disabled, although VA guidelines call for a 100 percent disability rating. Incredibly, his evaluation report said, "Shrapnel injury not related to combat."

Anderson laughed at first. Then he got angry. "After everything I went through, this is the last thing I wanted to happen," he says. The 90 percent rating meant disability payments of $1,600 a month instead of $2,600 (plus relief from paying property taxes).

Clearly, Anderson hadn't joined the Guard with a body full of shrapnel. But the VA said shrapnel wasn't mentioned in his battle-care records.

Well, no wonder, says L. Tammy Duckworth, director of Illinois' Department of Veterans Affairs, "They were too busy saving his life!"

Anderson finally got his 100 percent rating after he, his wife and top Illinois politicians spent nearly a year appealing the VA. (*See sidebar, p. 188.*)

Anderson is one of many veterans forced to run a benefits obstacle course through the VA bureaucracy. But in early 2007, a devastating exposé in *The Washington Post* revealed new problems being faced by wounded veterans of the fighting in Iraq and Afghanistan.[1] At Walter Reed Army Medical Center, just a few miles from the Capitol, recovering outpatient vets were coping with moldy, vermin-infested outpatient housing and overworked, sometimes incompetent, staff.[2]

Record Number of Troops Wounded in Iraq

An unprecedented number of American soldiers have been injured in the fighting in Iraq and Afghanistan compared with the number killed — by far the highest killed-to-wounded ratio in U.S. military history. More than 50,500 soldiers suffered non-mortal wounds and more than 3,000 were killed — a ratio of 16 wounded for every fatality. The high number of wounded reflects the effectiveness of military medicine as well as the widespread use of IEDs (improvised explosive devices) and similar anti-personnel weapons.

Number of Wounded Soldiers Per Fatality in Major American Wars

War	Number of wounded
Iraq and Afghanistan	16.0*
Desert Storm/Desert Shield	1.2
Vietnam War	2.6
Korean War	2.8
World War II	1.6
World War I	1.8
Civil War (Union)	0.7
War of 1812	0.5
Revolutionary War	0.7

* Using the Pentagon's narrower definition of wounded personnel, the ratio is 8 wounded per fatality.

Source: Linda Bilmes, "Soldiers Returning from Iraq and Afghanistan: The Long-term Costs of Providing Veterans Medical Care and Disability Benefits," John F. Kennedy School of Government, Harvard University, January 2007

In the glare of TV news cameras, the Pentagon rushed repair crews to the center, and new Defense Secretary Robert Gates cleaned house, too, firing the secretary of the Army, Walter Reed's commander and the Army's surgeon general. In July, President George W. Bush accepted the resignation of the Veterans Affairs secretary.[3]

But Walter Reed was just the beginning. ABC News reported soon afterward that the Pentagon and VA weren't coping with a surge in traumatic brain injury (TBI), the signature wound of the Iraq and Afghanistan wars because of the large number of IEDs (improvised explosive devices) and rocket-propelled grenades aimed at U.S. troops.[4]

"In prior conflicts, TBI was present in at least 14-20 percent of surviving combat casualties," according to the Pentagon's Defense and Veterans Brain Injury Center. "Preliminary information from the current conflict in the

Middle East suggests that this number is now much higher."[5]

In 2006, the VA's own Inspector General's Office had blasted the agency's long-term management of TBI patients and their families.[6] "We've got a lot of work to do" on TBI, new Army Secretary Preston "Pete" Geren told a Senate confirmation hearing in June 2007.[7]

"The system is breaking at the seams and cries out for real, radical change," says House Veterans Affairs Chairman Bob Filner, D-Calif. "We have increasing needs for Vietnam veterans, but we are still treating World War II vets, plus we have an incredible onslaught from Iraq and Afghanistan with injuries never foreseen."[8]

Congressional Republicans charge critics with trying to transform problems into catastrophe. "It's part of political gamesmanship by Democrats to say that the administration has failed veterans," Sen. Larry E. Craig, R-Idaho, said shortly before his resignation from the Senate Veterans' Affairs Committee, where he was the ranking Republican. "They want to cause a confidence crisis in the country for their personal, political gain."*

As of Aug. 7, the government said 13,163 service members had been wounded in Iraq and Afghanistan badly enough not to be returned to duty within 72 hours; another 15,588 were wounded and returned to duty.[9]

Some experts say, however, that the toll is far greater. Linda Bilmes, a professor of budgeting and public finance at Harvard's Kennedy School of Government, cites Pentagon reports showing about 63,000 casualties, once non-combat injuries and wounds that didn't require medical air transport are included. The Defense Department, saying it didn't want to mislead the public

---

* On Aug. 29, Craig resigned all his committee leadership posts following news he had pleaded guilty to a disorderly conduct charge stemming from his arrest during a sex sting in a men's room at the Minneapolis-St. Paul International Airport.

about the war's toll, changed its main casualty Web site in January 2007 to show only combat injuries.[10]

In March President Bush named a blue-ribbon commission* to study the care system for wounded military personnel, chaired by former Sen. Bob Dole, R-Kan., a wounded World War II veteran, and Donna Shalala, president of the University of Miami and a former secretary of Health and Human Services.[11] Among its six major recommendations:

- Simplify the disability-ratings system;
- Assign a care coordinator to each seriously wounded service member;
- Improve care for post-traumatic stress disorder (PTSD) and TBI; and
- Increase support for relatives to care for wounded service members, including expansion of the Family Medical Leave Act.[12]

More Than 3,000 Soldiers Seriously Wounded

Of the 1.5 million service members who have served in either Iraq or Afghanistan, more than 3,000 have been seriously injured, including more than 2,700 with traumatic brain injury (TBI).

Number of service members deployed	1,500,000
Air evacuated for illness or injuries	37,851
Wounded in action	28,000
Treated and returned to duty within 72 hours	23,270
Seriously injured	3,082*
Traumatic brain injuries	2,726
Amputations	644
Serious burns	598
Polytrauma	391
Spinal cord injuries	94
Blindness	48

* Recipients of Traumatic Servicemembers' Group Life Insurance

Note: A wounded service member can appear in more than one category.

Source: President's Commission on Care for America's Returning Wounded Warriors, "Serve, Support, Simplify," July 2007

Bush ordered the Defense and Veterans Affairs secretaries to carry out the recommendations "so that we can say with certainty that any soldier who has been hurt will get the best possible care and treatment that this government can offer."[13]

But Rep. Filner rebukes the commission for not going further. "Now is the time to shake up the system," he says, arguing for automatic VA coverage for all veterans. Presently, they get two years of automatic health coverage after discharge; afterwards, vets must prove their medical conditions resulted from their service.

In principle, all of the nation's 24.5 million veterans are eligible for lifetime VA medical treatment. In reality, the agency has to ration care based on its annual appropriations and only provides care to about 5 million vets.

Veterans' organizations have long demanded "mandatory" funding of the agency so that all veterans could get care.[14]

But commission co-chair Shalala says panel members focused on immediately achievable results. "We wanted to make recommendations that would actually affect the people who were injured in those wars," she says. "We were focused on what the system could absorb."

Trends both on the battlefield and at home underlie the clash over veterans' care. Medical advances have cut the fatality rate among wounded soldiers to 9 percent, compared to almost double that during Vietnam and 23 percent in World War II.[15]

Moreover, many veterans are coming home with multiple amputations and severe brain injuries. "We have survivors now who come to us with medical conditions, rehab needs, multiple impairments that we've not seen before," Lucille "Lu" Beck, chief consultant to the VA for rehabilitative services, told *USA Today.*[16]

The psychological toll is also heavy. More than one-third of Army and Marine troops have consulted mental-health professionals on return from Iraq, according to a

---

* The nine-member commission included two wounded Iraq vets: Marc Giammateo, now a Harvard Business School student; and Jose Ramos, a student at George Mason University in Fairfax, Va.; and Tammy Edwards of Cibolo, Texas, the wife of an Army sergeant severely burned in a car bombing.

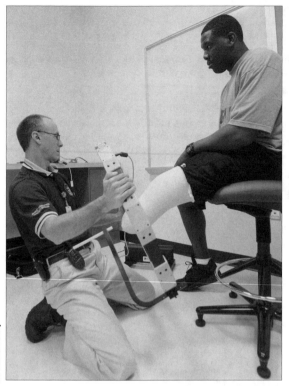

Sgt. Tawan Williamson gets fitted for a prosthetic leg at Brooke Army Medical Center in San Antonio in March. Williamson was wounded by a bomb that blew up his Humvee in June 2006. This fall he expects to become an Army job counselor and affirmative action officer. In a new policy, the military is putting many more amputees back on active duty.

AP Photo/Eric Gay

recent study, and 19 percent "screened positive for a mental health concern."[17]

Indeed, a Pentagon task force acknowledged in June that as many as one-half of active duty and Reserve fighters deployed to combat zones reported various mental health symptoms, including possible PTSD. "But most report they have not yet sought help for these problems," the task force said.[18]

A major reason for the non-reporting may lie in the negative responses soldiers receive from their superiors. Army Spec. Alex Lotero of Fort Carson, Colo., said in May he was cursed at and accused of insubordination when doctors' appointments for treatment of nightmares forced him to miss training.

"They belittled my condition," he said.[19]

"I'm one of the few — of the people I served with — who's gone and got help for it," says Army National Guard Sgt. Patrick Campbell, legislative director of Iraq and Afghanistan Veterans of America, and a former medic in Baghdad. If everyone who needed help all of a sudden asked for help, the system would break under the pressure."

Another sign of post-combat problems is suicide. Neither the VA nor the Pentagon tracks suicide among veterans, though news accounts report several. However, the Defense Department does keep figures on active-duty suicides. A Pentagon report in August disclosed 99 suicides among active-duty Army troops, mostly in Iraq, in 2006, up from 88 in 2005.[20]

The VA supports pending legislation that would focus new attention on preventing suicide among vets suffering post-traumatic stress (*see p. 187*). And Defense and VA officials say they're adding resources to meet the demand for PTSD treatment.

But veterans filing claims for disability payments from the VA — based on PTSD and all other injuries — face waiting periods that average 127 days; and those who appeal the initial rulings spend an average of nearly two years — 657 days — waiting for a decision. "That is absolutely unacceptable," says Paul Sullivan, a former VA staffer who is director of Veterans for Common Sense, an advocacy organization that filed a class-action lawsuit in July in federal district court in California challenging treatment of veterans.[21]

Former Spec. Luis Calderon, 22, of Puerto Rico, became a quadriplegic after a wall fell on him in Baghdad; he had to wait months for his VA benefits and now feels abandoned by the military.[22] National Guard Staff Sgt. Jim Sparks, 43, a police detective in Fairfax, Va., says he had to wait a year for hearing aids after he was injured in an IED attack in Ramadi on Jan. 17, 2006.

"The VA said I didn't need hearing aids. I called back," says Sparks, whose age and experience as a policeman may have equipped him to deal with red tape.

"Care for the wounded is strapped right now," he says. "I've heard lots of talk [of improvement] but not seen a lot of action. I'm not so worried about me, but the 18- and 19-year-old guys I serve with — having them lose a leg or arm or eye and having to deal with insufficient care."

As debate about veterans' care continues, here are some of the questions being asked:

Does the Dole-Shalala commission have the best plan for improving veterans' care?

"The United States has a very spotty record in terms of looking after veterans," says sociologist David Segal, who heads the University of Maryland's Center for Research on Military Organization. "Vietnam veterans did not do well. Veterans are doing badly again because the government, not having anticipated the size of duration of the current engagement, grossly underestimated the number of veterans it was going to have to deal with, and did not understand what we are going to face in terms of experiences — psychiatric and physical."

But Rep. Steve Buyer, R-Ind., the top Republican on the House Veterans' Affairs Committee, notes that today there is no hostility toward Iraq veterans.

"That's a change," he says, attributing the shift in part to bad consciences of Vietnam War protesters — "who in later years feel pretty guilty about their behavior in their youth. I compliment them."

But skeptics say that good feelings alone won't provide the care veterans need.

After the Dole-Shalala commission issued its report on July 25, White House Press Secretary Tony Snow said flatly that President Bush is "not going to be making recommendations; he's not going to be issuing calls for actions," But the following day, Bush said he stood behind the report's recommendations.[23]

The commission reported problems in:

- Coordinating care and patient information by the Defense and Veterans Affairs departments, whose procedures now often leave veterans in limbo between the two agencies.
- Reconciling the differing Defense and Veterans Affairs standards for evaluating veterans' disabilities.
- Treating post-traumatic stress disorder (PTSD) and traumatic brain injury (TBI), due to a lack of staff specialists.
- Supporting family members of wounded soldiers, even as relatives are uprooting themselves for months at a time to help loved ones recover.
- Transferring patient information from the military to the VA.

The report also urged that Walter Reed Medical Center — scheduled for closing in 2012 — be maintained in top shape, with first-rate staff, until then.

Above all, the commission advocated focusing the military- and veterans-care system squarely on the patient: "The tendency to make systems too complex and rule-bound must be countered . . . [Patients'] needs and aspirations should inform the medical care and disability systems."

The commission's conclusions reflected testimony and reports by numerous veterans-advocacy organizations and news media. "It represents very much a consensus view," says Thomas Donnelly, an expert on military affairs at the conservative American Enterprise Institute. "I can't imagine that it's going to cause a whole lot of controversy."

Yet some influential experts argue that the commission didn't seize the moment. "What they are doing is letting the two biggest bureaucracies in the federal government, Defense and Veterans Affairs, continue with some improvements — but not enough to meet what is an emergency situation," says House Veterans Affairs Chairman Filner.

The commission's recommendations aren't bad, Filner says, just too cautious. "I wish they would have issued a clarion call that this is a disaster — a Katrina-like disaster."

Republican Rep. Buyer scoffs at the notion of a system in crisis. "The use of that language indicates someone who is ignorant of the present health system," he says. "Someone saying that is not credible. That's someone who would be from the outside and does not know, or from inside who hasn't invested time" in understanding the system.

Buyer says the Dole-Shalala commission did zero in on some of the top problems in veterans' care — above all the call for a patient-centered philosophy. The Defense and Veterans Affairs departments tend to use budgetary justifications for limiting veterans' options he says. "We take that wounded warrior, and in sub-acute care, we send them back to their homes — and home may be two or three or four hours from a military medical facility. And when they're so distant, we ought to be able to contract for that care," Buyer says. "Sometimes the green-eyeshade guys start making decisions based on dollars, not on patients."

Still, Buyer says, the notion of a system in disaster obscures progress that is being made. "The cooperation

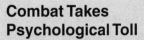

Combat Takes Psychological Toll

Nearly half of all National Guard members suffer psychological symptom within 120 days of returning from combat.

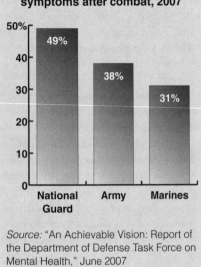

Percentage of service members reporting psychological symptoms after combat, 2007

Source: "An Achievable Vision: Report of the Department of Defense Task Force on Mental Health," June 2007

between DoD and VA improves every day," he says. "Has it achieved satisfaction? I don't know if we can get there. That's Valhalla. But there's not a society that invests more in caring for wounded warriors. That doesn't mean there aren't hiccups along the way."

But Stephen L. Robinson, a former Army Airborne Ranger and Ranger instructor who is one of the nation's most active veterans' advocates, argues that veterans are facing more than hiccups. The commission "missed an opportunity to put out a charge to the nation and create a bipartisan movement that everyone can get behind," he says. "It was an opportunity to bring the nation together for a common cause." Robinson now serves on the staff of ONE Freedom, a Boulder, Colo.-based non-profit that has developed stress-reduction programs for returning veterans.

Senate Veterans Affairs Committee Chairman Daniel K. Akaka, D-Hawaii, however, argues the Dole-Shalala panel "was given far too little time, but they made the best of it." The recommendation for cutting through the red tape that clogs ex-soldiers' transitions from the military to the Veterans Affairs Department is on target, and so are the commission's other proposals, he says.

Are veterans being shortchanged by DoD and VA to save money?

Dozens of hours of House and Senate committee hearings held this year on treatment of wounded soldiers and veterans featured exchanges on an explosive topic — whether care was being withheld in order to save money.

James Terry Scott, a retired Army lieutenant general, told a joint hearing of the Senate Veterans Affairs and Armed Services committees on April 12 that Department of Defense (DoD) standards for evaluating the extent of a service member's disabilities apparently vary according to what the Pentagon can afford. "It is apparent that DoD has a strong incentive to rate [disability] less than 30 percent so that only severance pay is awarded," said Scott, who heads the Veterans Disability Benefits Commission, which Congress created in 2004 to recommend changes in the compensation system for wounded veterans.[24]

Army Secretary Geren responded that no such incentive existed. "Any government program, the more people who avail themselves of the benefits . . . it's going to cause that program to cost more," he said. "But I don't think there's any evidence to show that the people who make the decision on those evaluation boards are influenced by that at all."[25]

But Deputy Defense Secretary Gordon England added that he wasn't certain about financial constraints. "So, yes, it's probably appropriate to step back and make absolutely certain that that is the case, that we are not unduly constraining the system because of funding."[26]

Medical treatment for serious wounds gets virtually unanimous praise.

But a string of official studies have concluded that the Defense and Veterans Affairs departments haven't been able to meet the demand for mental health services for Iraq and Afghanistan veterans.

The Government Accountability Office (GAO) in 2006 concluded that only 22 percent of the troops who served in Afghanistan or Iraq and seemed at risk for PTSD were referred for more detailed evaluations: "DoD cannot provide reasonable assurance that . . . service members who need referrals receive them."[27]

Similarly for the VA, the GAO in 2005 questioned "VA's capacity to meet veterans' needs for PTSD services."[28]

Moreover, hundreds of service members have been discharged for "personality disorder" after seeking PTSD treatment. Army veteran Jonathan Town told the House Veterans Affairs Committee in July that after suffering PTSD symptoms following a rocket attack in 2004, he was discharged with a "personality disorder," which left him ineligible for benefits, including treatment, although the doctor who made the diagnosis told him he would be covered. "I never realized everything that was said to me during that day were all lies," Town said.[29]

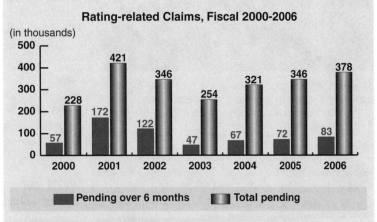

Backlog of Disability Ratings Claims Grew

The number of pending rating-related claims handled by the Department of Veterans Affairs has increased by 66 percent since 2000, to 378,000 claims in 2006. Claims pending for over six months rose 45 percent, from 57,000 in 2000 to 83,000 last year. Resolution of claims appeals "remains a lengthy process," according to the Government Accountability Office, taking an average of 657 days in fiscal 2006.

Rating-related Claims, Fiscal 2000-2006

Source: "Veterans' Disability Benefits: Long-Standing Claims Processing Challenges Persist," Government Accountability Office, March 7, 2007

Pentagon officials at the hearing didn't challenge Town's account. Bruce Crow, the psychology consultant to Army Surgeon General Gale Pollock, is reviewing the records of the 295 service members discharged for personality disorder last year after serving in a combat zone. "To the uniformed, civilian and contract health-care professionals that care for these soldiers," he said, "the thought of even one soldier being inappropriately discharged for personality disorder is disturbing."[30]

Meanwhile, a pending amendment to the National Defense Authorization Act sponsored by Sen. Patty Murray, D-Wash., and five colleagues would block personality-disorder discharges until an independent discharge review board is established. "We need to ensure these discharges are medically accurate and that service members are not being denied the treatment or benefits they deserve," Murray said.[31]

The Dole-Shalala commission also explored concerns about payments of promised bonuses. "We learned that service members' remaining enlistment bonuses were not

being paid when they were injured and medically retired or separated from active duty," the commission said. After the commission stepped in, withheld bonuses were paid retroactive to 2001.[32]

With the PTSD issue getting growing attention, Antoinette Zeiss, the VA's deputy chief consultant for mental health, told the House Oversight and Government Reform Committee in May that the department had "improved capacity and access, supporting hiring, so far, of over 1,000 new mental health professionals, with more in the pipeline."[33]

The following month, however, the DoD's Task Force on Mental Health reported that some veterans who needed attention may have been left waiting indefinitely. The panel cited the frequency with which PTSD symptoms appear after expiration of the two-year period in which vets are automatically eligible for treatment. Consequently, "Someone may enter the system without special eligibility, be assigned low priority and not be able to access mental health care while waiting for the outcome" of the evaluation process.[34]

AP Photo/Jeff Chiu

Army Staff Sgt. Eric Cagle, 27, lost an eye and suffered partial paralysis and brain damage when a bomb destroyed his Humvee in Iraq. Here he works on a computer at the veterans' hospital in Palo Alto, Calif., in July 2006.

There's no question the demand on the VA is considerable. Some 399,000 veterans are awaiting decisions on how their disabilities are rated. Overall, the backlog stands at about 629,000 cases, if simple requests are included, such as changes in benefits because a child has been born.

Former Army First Lt. Brady van Engelen, who served a tour in Iraq in 2003-2004 in the 1st Armored Division, says he received no follow-up medical attention after he was treated at Walter Reed for a bullet wound from a sniper that tore through the side of his head under the lip of his helmet. "They just didn't account for the number of walking wounded that would walk out of this war," he says. "Maybe they just didn't think about it."

Testifying before the House committee last March, he called veterans care a "broken system."[35]

While the system's defenders acknowledge rules and procedures can complicate veterans' lives, they reject talk of a financial emergency. "When I hear these complaints about a shortage of funds for VA, I just shake my head in astonishment," said Sen. Craig in an e-mail. "We are on our way to spending at least $86 billion next year — increasing spending on veterans by more than 77 percent since 2001."

Yet, Craig adds, "What do we hear from our friends on the other side of the aisle: 'VA funding is woefully inadequate.' It's an easy sell that just doesn't jibe with reality." So far, he says, citing the Dole-Shalala report, there

are about 6,000 seriously wounded U.S. Iraq-Afghanistan veterans. A cohort of that size "should not be overwhelming the VA system," Craig says. "And they aren't."

Indeed, Michael Kussman, acting VA undersecretary for health, testified in March there will be an estimated 263,000 Iraq and Afghanistan veteran patients next fiscal year (including the 6,000 seriously wounded) out of a total population of 5.8 million veterans receiving VA treatment. "So it's a relatively small number . . . We are ideally poised to be able to take care of the patients as they transition out" of the full-time military.[36]

"I think we're doing a good job with the physical injuries that we can see," Veterans advocate Robinson says. "Where we're falling down is the unseen wounds of war — both in traumatic brain injury as a result of the blasts, and the psychological toll of the war. It's very clear; every commission, every report has said that we do not have the capacity to deliver the kind of mental health care that people are demanding."

Would more money solve most of the problems with veterans' care?

Those who say there's a crisis in veterans' care as well as those who argue there is certainly a problem — just not a crisis — agree more money is needed.

But agreement ends at how the money should be allocated — and whether it would solve *most* of the problems.

"Most" is the key word. Uwe E. Reinhardt, a professor of political economy at Princeton University and a leading expert on health-care finance, told the Senate Veterans Affairs Committee in July that economic inequities in the larger society show up in the veterans-care debate as well. Referring to his son, a Marine captain who was wounded in Afghanistan, Reinhardt said: "When we went to [the military hospital in] Landstuhl [Germany] to visit our son, I asked myself, 'How easy is it actually for people from the lower economic strata to fly to Landstuhl?' My wife and I just jumped on the plane and flew there and stayed in a hotel . . . Those visits are crucial to the healing. So it is a real problem." No one on the committee responded.[37]

Conservative military-affairs analyst Donnelly, for his part, has no doubt that funding is the issue. "There are bureaucratic snafus, no doubt," he says. "But in general terms, this is a case of, 'You get what you pay for.'"

A supporter of the war in Iraq, Donnelly blames some of the veterans' problems on the initial planners and strategists of the war. "It's pretty clear that, for whatever reason, nobody really anticipated that there would be so many casualties. Nobody intended or thought or imagined that serious fighting was going to go on as long as it has. There was a sense of denial."

As a result, says Segal at the University of Maryland's Center for Research on Military Organization, "There has to be a change in our thinking about what is going in Afghanistan and Iraq. There has been an unwillingness to admit the number of psychological casualties coming out of this war."

The unique conditions that troops are encountering in both countries are behind the upsurge in PTSD claims, Segal argues. "In past conflicts, there were tremendous differences in exposure to psychological trauma between combat troops and support troops. Now, it doesn't matter. Now people in logistics and other support functions are seeing more combat than in past wars. Basically, once you put boots on the ground in Iraq, you're in a combat zone."

Nonetheless, money still seems to be the solution, according to Senate Veterans Affairs Committee Chairman Akaka. "There are larger concerns about how DoD and VA cooperate," he acknowledges. "But funding is at the heart of many of the known shortcomings. In recent years, the administration has not requested sufficient funding for VA health care.

"Veterans are coming home with PTSD and other invisible wounds like TBI, and the VA should have been prepared for them, but they are not."

A World War II veteran, Akaka advocates so-called "mandatory" funding for VA health care, or funding independent of annual appropriations from Congress. Other Democrats active in veterans' affairs urge the same approach.

"They don't have money to take care of every veteran," says Duckworth, who lost both legs when the Black Hawk helicopter she was piloting in Iraq as a major in the Illinois National Guard was shot down. "If funding were mandatory, every veteran who has a service-connected disability would have the care that this country promised them. That is what the American people think they're getting."

Rep. Buyer, the senior Republican on House Veterans Affairs, calls the mandatory approach irresponsible. "If

you put me on a mandatory-funding glide path, what incentives do I have for improvement? Why do I have to create efficiencies? I think it would be very bad judgment and bad policy to take advantage of the American people's compassion toward our wounded warriors."

But Chairman Filner argues that mandatory funding would bring a welcome simplicity to the regulation-filled world of veterans' care. "I would like to break through the system and say, 'Give me your discharge papers and you're in,'" Filner says. "We'd be saving so much on bureaucracy. All the issues that Vietnam veterans and World War II veterans have — a guy claims his Parkinson's disease is a result of Agent Orange. Just accept the claim. They fought for us, they're ill, let's treat them."

Sen. Craig dismisses such talk as facile, given the enormous demands on the budget created by other "mandatory" funding arrangements. "We already have three very large programs that are considered to be funded by 'mandatory spending' — namely Social Security, Medicare and Medicaid," he says by e-mail. "And notable economic experts . . . have been warning us that unless we make changes to those systems soon [they] will crowd out every other federal program — including defense and homeland security."

BACKGROUND

The 'Great War'

Many of the 4 million American veterans of the American Expeditionary Force who came home from the World War I battlefields of France, Belgium and Germany — and the 3 million more who never saw action — re-entered civilian life with high expectations.[38]

It was a bittersweet homecoming for many. Not only were jobs scarce, but corruption in the Veterans Bureau diverted most of the money that Congress allocated for wounded and disabled ex-soldiers. For example, Congress authorized $33 million for veterans' hospitals, but only 200 new beds were produced.

Shortchanging the wounded was especially grievous due to the devastating after-effects of a frightening new weapon — poison gas. About 27 percent of all fatal and non-fatal casualties were caused by gas, a modern military historian calculates.[39]

CHRONOLOGY

1918-1950 *Treatment of veterans evolves from limited benefits and care after World War I to society-changing benefits after the second global conflict.*

1921 President Warren G. Harding forms the Veterans Bureau, which soon becomes notorious for limited accomplishments and widespread corruption.

1924 Congress enacts bonus to compensate veterans for the higher pay that civilian defense factory workers received.

1932 Army veterans demanding an early payout of the bonus to help them weather the Depression march on Washington and set up "Hooverville" encampment. . . . Repression of the "bonus army" on orders from Republican President Herbert Hoover helps Democrat Franklin D. Roosevelt win the presidency.

1945 Roosevelt and Congress, determined to avoid a repeat of the "bonus march" debacle, create the GI Bill. . . . Millions of veterans take advantage of its benefits to attend college and buy homes, vastly expanding the nation's middle class.

1950s-1980s *The atmosphere toward veterans chills slightly after the Korean War and more so after the Vietnam War, leaving a lasting bitterness among the vets.*

1953 Veterans returning from the three-year Korean conflict get a new, less generous GI Bill but are not welcomed as warmly as World War II vets.

1960s-1984 Returning Vietnam vets encounter attitudes ranging from indifference to hostility. . . . Thousands begin developing symptoms linked to exposure to the defoliant Agent Orange.

1967 Vietnam Veterans Against the War (VVAW) is founded.

1970 Following an article in *The New Yorker,* Senate Subcommittee on the Environment holds hearings on Agent Orange. . . . Soon after, Defense Department bans use of dioxin, the chemical used in the defoliant.

April 1971 Veterans at VVAW demonstration in Washington — including future Sen. John Kerry, D-Mass. — protest the war by tossing their medals onto the Capitol steps.

Nov. 13, 1982 Vietnam Veterans Memorial — "The Wall" — opens on the National Mall bearing the names of 58,249 dead or missing servicemen and women.

1984 Veterans claiming serious illness from dioxin sue the government.

1990s-Present

1992 Veterans of the 1990-91 Persian Gulf War begin reporting ailments collectively dubbed "Gulf War syndrome" and attributed to possible chemical exposure.

1997 Medical researchers report in the *Journal of the American Medical Association* "Gulf War syndrome" results from exposure to combinations of pesticide and nerve gas.

2003 Improvised explosive devices (IEDs) begin wreaking havoc on American troops — including multiple loss of limbs.

Dec. 22, 2005 Army Reserve Spc. Joshua Omvig, 22, of Grundy Center, Iowa, commits suicide after an 11-month tour in Iraq; his parents say he was suffering from post-traumatic stress disorder (PTSD).

2006 Government Accountability Office says military efforts to treat PTSD symptoms fall short. . . . Joshua Omvig Veterans Suicide Prevention Act introduced in House in July, charges VA with setting up a program to screen and monitor for suicide risk.

2007 *Washington Post* series reports shocking conditions for outpatients at Walter Reed Army Medical Center. . . . Army secretary and two top medical officers are forced out. . . . Presidential panel recommends simplification of disability-rating process and other changes in veterans'-care system. . . . Congress takes up raft of legislation on veterans' benefits. . . . Bush administration and Congress move toward possible showdown over veterans'-care spending.

Veterans also noticed that the $60 they got when mustering out added up to little compared with bonuses of up to $14 a day that wartime defense-factory workers had received. In 1924, Congress created a bonus-pay system to compensate vets for the higher civilian incentives they'd missed out on. The bonus was calculated at $1.25 for each day served overseas, and $1 a day for those who stayed stateside.

But there was a catch. The money would be paid out in bonds that would mature in 1945. And after the stock market crash of 1929 launched the Great Depression, vets desperately needed their bonus money immediately.

In 1932, groups of struggling ex-soldiers, along with their wives and children, began gathering in Washington. Eventually numbering as many as 40,000 men, women and children, the Bonus Expeditionary Force (BEF) camped across the Anacostia River from the Capitol. They called their shantytown "Hooverville," in a sarcastic salute to President Herbert Hoover, who rejected their bonus demands.

In July, troops led by Gen. Douglas MacArthur destroyed the encampment and routed the protesters. The ugly spectacle of mounted American troops charging into unarmed veterans and their families helped Democrat Franklin D. Roosevelt defeat Hoover in the 1932 presidential election.

GI Bill Benefits

World War II marked the beginning of a change in views about war and its effects on fighters. Early in the war, in 1942, anti-aircraft artillery crews were told, for example, "if a soldier was a man he would not permit his self-respect to admit an anxiety neurosis or to show fear," a military historian has written. Yet, as the fighting ground on in Europe and the Pacific, commanders and physicians came to accept that combat could cause psychiatric casualties.[40]

By the time the war ended, there was greater acceptance of the strains that fighting could place on the spirit, not to mention the political lessons learned from the "bonus marchers" debacle. Even before the final victory, the Roosevelt administration and Congress had created one of the most far-reaching pieces of social legislation ever enacted: the GI Bill of Rights.

The 1944 law provided funding for veterans to attend college or trade school and buy homes with no down payments and low-interest loans. The postwar economic boom and the simultaneous expansion of

the college-educated middle class grew directly out of the "GI Bill," as it was widely known. By 1947, just two years after the war's end, 1 million vets had purchased homes, giving rise to the suburbs. By 1949, average annual income reached double the 1939 level.

The GI Bill even addressed the likelihood that many veterans would need to readjust gradually to civilian life, providing $20 a week for unemployment compensation for up to 52 weeks — a provision promptly dubbed the "52/20 club."

"If it wasn't for the GI Bill I wouldn't be here," says Sen. Akaka, who graduated from the University of Hawaii in 1952 after serving in the Army from 1945-1947. He adds that his fellow Hawaiian senator, Daniel K. Inouye, who lost an arm during combat in Italy, also went on to college and law school on the GI Bill. "We need to add that back as a program," Akaka says.

But even the nation's warm embrace of World War II vets couldn't banish the strains that fighting had placed on them. In the 1990s, a team of researchers predicted in the *American Journal of Psychiatry* that 15 years after combat, "a subject would experience physical decline or death." In some veterans, they hypothesized, physical symptoms may have resulted from inability to talk about what they went through.[41]

Korea to Vietnam

None of the wars that followed saw veterans greeted as warmly as those coming back from World War II.

The first to note the chill were veterans of the much less popular Korean War, a brutal, 1950-1953 conflict in which the United States beat back an invasion of South Korea by communist North Korea, aided by China.

Although Korea veterans did receive benefits, they were less generous than those provided by the original GI Bill. Korea vets also had to cope with a perceived blot on their collective reputation. Some of the 4,000 Americans held captive in grim prison camps succumbed to North Korean torture and allowed themselves to be put on display in propaganda films or broadcasts.

Seeing civilians neither sympathetic nor well-informed about the war, Korean War vets tried their best to fade into society. But during and after America's next big conflict — in Vietnam — veterans stayed vocal and visible enough to keep their generation of ex-soldiers on the sociopolitical radar screen for decades.

Recruiters Turn to Fail-Safe Approach

Big cash bonuses help reach quotas.

Times are tough for military recruiters. A steady stream of stories of veterans coming home with limbs missing, brains injured or nerves shattered — and government bungling in vets' care — have left the Defense Department reaching for a traditional tool of companies with hard-to-fill jobs: cold, hard cash.

In July, after missing its combined May and June recruitment goal of 13,900 by 10 percent — 1,400 enlistees — the Army started offering "quick ship" bonuses of $20,000 each to recruits who agree to report for combat training by the end of September, which is also the end of the federal fiscal year.[1]

The incentive worked. Recruiters signed up 9,972 young men and women in July, exceeding their 9,750-recruit goal for the month and reversing a worrisome trend in which the Army failed to meet its targets for the previous two months.

The extent to which veterans' problems are playing a role in discouraging enlistment and re-enlistment, however, hasn't been established.

"I don't think it's possible to make a really clear connection," says Thomas Donnelly, a military-affairs specialist at the conservative American Enterprise Institute. But the realities of the war itself are clearly weighing more heavily on America's youth, says Donnelly, citing talks about the war with his 19- and 21-year-old sons, both in college — "the

kind a lot of families are having with their kids," says Donnelly, who did not serve in the military.

Some veterans' activists go further, arguing that the public focus on mishandled treatment of veterans inevitably is making itself felt in the military's manpower problems.

"There have been plenty of stories about veterans," says Stephen L. Robinson, a former Army Airborne Ranger and Ranger instructor. "The best way to make sure that we always have an all-volunteer Army is to keep our promises that we will use them judiciously and appropriately, give them the things they need to succeed — and take care of them should they become injured in war. It's the best recruiting tool there is. When we fail, we see results in recruiting and retention."

As Maj. Gen. Thomas P. Bostick, who heads the Army Recruiting Command at Fort Knox, Ky., told the House Armed Services Committee in August: "We are recruiting during a period of protracted combat. Today's recruiting environment is incredibly challenging."[2]

Still, the Army is doing better in keeping those already in uniform — meeting 101 percent of the retention goal for the active-duty force, 119 percent for the Army Reserve, and 107 percent for the Army National Guard.

"I still think there are lots of young guys who are passionate about serving," says Army National Guard Staff Sgt. Jim Sparks, who is training for his third combat deployment.

Like the rest of American society in the 1960s and '70s, veterans split into pro- and anti-war camps. Vietnam Veterans Against the War (VVAW), founded in 1967, soon formed part of a movement whose biggest constituency was college students who had avoided the draft. For all of its visibility, though, VVAW clearly occupied a minority position among the 3.4 million Americans who served in Southeast Asia during the war.[42]

Most Vietnam veterans didn't get tickertape parades welcoming them home. But the amount of hostility they encountered is still hotly debated. As recently as this year, the dispute has come to center on what is seen as the signature insult of the times: spitting.

Richard H. Taylor, a Vietnam vet, writes in a new book of a vet who reported trying to enroll in a California

college. "A young woman and two young men approached him. . . . She screamed at him, calling him a baby-killer; one of the guys with her spit on him."[43]

Although such accounts are plentiful, Jack Shafer, a media columnist for *Slate*, an online magazine, provoked a series of angry replies when he described the frequent accounts of returning veterans being spat upon as an "urban myth."

"I've yet to locate a news account that documents a specific spit altercation or a police or court paper trail that would back the accusations," Shafer wrote.[44]

The division between pro-war and anti-war Vietnam vets faded somewhat as veterans ran into issues that affected them both.

One was the level of care provided by the VA. "Veterans considered VA hospitals the last resort for medical care,"

"You see them wearing baggy pants and listening to gangsta rap — but their [dedicated] service gives you faith in youth, it really gives you back that feelgood sensation about the younger crowd, the new generation."

And Sparks himself, an ex-Marine, volunteered for service even though it costs him the overtime pay that makes up an appreciable part of his family's income. He is a detective in Fairfax County, Va. "I really consider it an honor to wear the uniform; I really enjoy serving."

Enthusiasm aside, money is playing a role for at least some service members opting to stay in uniform. "I only re-enlisted this time for college," Marine Cpl. Cara Tighe told *Army Times*, referring to the $10,000 bonus she got for re-upping. She has no plans to do so again.[3]

Defense experts note the cost of such sweeteners is skyrocketing. "Spending on enlistment and recruitment bonuses tripled from $328 million before the war in Iraq to over $1 billion in 2006," Lawrence J. Korb, military strategy director at the Center for American Progress, a liberal think tank, told the House Armed Services Committee in July. Korb is a Vietnam-era Navy veteran and former Defense official in the Reagan administration.[4]

Nor is the retention picture uniformly bright. Retention among West Point graduates has reached its lowest point in

Gunnery Sgt. Brian Bensen, a Marine recruiter in Belle Vernon, Pa., has a quota of two recruits per month.

30 years, Korb said. And he cited indications that the strain of repeated combat deployments is provoking an increase in post-traumatic stress disorder symptoms among service members deployed repeatedly to Iraq and Afghanistan.

Veterans' issues aside, the realities of the war itself are looming large for potential recruits and their families, says Donnelly. "Everybody knows that if you join the military now you're going to war," he says. "It's a more sobering proposition. You're not joining so much for career development."

---

[1] See Josh White, "Many Take Army's 'Quick Ship' Bonus," *The Washington Post*, Aug. 27, 2007, p. A1; Thom Shanker, "Army, Shedding a Slump, Met July Recruiting Goal," *The New York Times*, Aug. 11, 2007, p. A8.

[2] See "Army Recruiting and Retention," House Armed Services Committee, Committee testimony, Aug. 1, 2007.

[3] Quoted in Rick Maze and William H. McMichael, "Here today . . . gone tomorrow?; Turning tide of war may drain bonus pool," *Army Times*, July 30, 2007, p. A14. Also, "Retention Remains High Military-Wide, Including in Combat Zone," *CQ Federal Department and Agency Documents*, July 11, 2007.

[4] See "Troop Deployment Policy," House Armed Services Committee, Committee testimony (written), July 27, 2007.

Taylor writes. "Medical care in combat was crude, but fast, effective and always there. But at VA hospitals they could die in a waiting room, and no one would notice."[45]

The second unifying issue was the chemical defoliant dioxin — Agent Orange — which had been sprayed from U.S. aircraft to destroy jungle canopy that gave cover to the enemy. In 1970, Thomas Whiteside reported in *The New Yorker* that scientific evidence linked Agent Orange to cancer.[46]

The article led to hearings by the Senate Subcommittee on the Environment, after which the Pentagon quit using Agent Orange.[47] But the ban didn't help those already exposed. Starting in the late 1970s, a wave of diseases including leukemia began striking Vietnam veterans. Some medical experts traced the origins to dioxin. Veterans filed

the first class-action lawsuit arising from dioxin exposure in 1984. Veterans have largely prevailed in court, but the Veterans Affairs Department has been fighting to limit benefits.

As recently as July, the 9th U.S. Circuit Court of Appeals in San Francisco threw out the government's appeal of a decision ordering retroactive disability payments to veterans suffering from leukemia linked to dioxin exposure.

"What is difficult for us to comprehend is why the Department of Veterans Affairs, having entered into a settlement agreement and agreed to a consent order some 16 years ago, continues to resist its implementation so vigorously, as well as to resist equally vigorously the payment of desperately needed benefits to Vietnam War veterans who fought for their country and suffered grievous

Getty Images/Alex Wong

The scandal over conditions at Walter Reed Army Medical Center led Defense Secretary Robert M. Gates to fire Maj. Gen. George Weightman, commander of the center, right, and Army Surgeon General Lt. General Kevin C. Kiley. Above, they testify before a House Government Reform and Oversight subcommittee on March 5, 2007.

injury as a result of our government's own conduct," Judge Stephen Reinhardt wrote in the decision.[48]

Along with Agent Orange, homelessness also is often associated with Vietnam veterans. The nation's homeless population seemed to grow during the 1970s and '80s, and many homeless men were believed to be vets suffering from the effects of combat. Recent studies suggest the link between Vietnam and homelessness is weaker than popularly believed. "Vietnam era veterans, who are often thought to be the most overrepresented group of homeless veterans, were barely more likely to be homeless than non-veterans (1.01 times)," the Congressional Research Service reported in May, citing a 1994 study using 1980s data.[49]

Gulf War and Beyond

The 1990-1991 Persian Gulf War, pitting a U.S.-assembled coalition against the forces of Iraqi leader Saddam Hussein, was the shortest of all major post-Vietnam conflicts, with the ground war lasting just 100 hours.

A relatively small number of troops — 382 — died in the war zone. But soon after returning stateside about 100,000 of the 694,000 troops who served in the Gulf began reporting symptoms such as joint pain, chronic fatigue, aches and fevers.[50]

As with Agent Orange, Veterans department officials resisted compensating veterans suffering from what came to be collectively defined as Gulf War Syndrome.

Veterans and some scientists speculated the cause was exposure to destroyed Iraqi supplies of sarin nerve gas, to insect repellents or to the nerve-gas antidote pyridostigmine bromide — separately or together.

In 2004, a government-sponsored committee gave credence to the chemical-exposure hypothesis and to the theory that the ailments reflected neurological damage. A "probable link" exists between the exposure and the damage to vets' brains, the panel said.[51]

But two years later, a committee appointed by the non-governmental Institute of Medicine reached a different conclusion. "We can't identify a Gulf War syndrome," said Lynn R. Goldman, a physician and epidemiologist who headed the committee. The committee did find that Gulf War vets suffered PTSD and depression two to three times more frequently than ex-soldiers from other conflicts. The panel noted researchers were hampered by a lack of hard data on Gulf War troops' chemical exposure.[52]

Less than a month after the 9/11 terrorist attacks, the United States launched Operation Enduring Freedom to chase the Taliban regime from Afghanistan. On March 19, 2003, the Bush administration launched Operation Iraqi Freedom to oust Saddam.

By August 2003, American commanders in Iraq realized that the deadliest weapon they faced was the improvised explosive device (IED) — "the insurgents' weapon of choice," the *Los Angeles Times* reported. Generally made with artillery shells, IEDs were hidden under or alongside roads and highways. Set off by remote control, the biggest IEDs could even immobilize tanks, to say nothing of the destruction they could wreak on the ubiquitous unarmored Humvees.[53]

As the war ground on, National Guard and Reserve troops were thrown into battle. Along with active-duty troops, they found themselves deployed to Iraq and Afghanistan two and even three times.

For Army troops, war-zone deployments lasted 12 months (the Marine Corps mostly keeps to its standard seven-month combat tours). In April, Defense Secretary Gates ordered that Army tours be lengthened to 15 months, and some commanders warned troops to expect 18-month deployments.[54]

As reports mounted of the growing number of veterans with severe physical and psychological injuries, and of strains on families' lives, the series of articles on failures in veterans' services *The Washington Post* began on Feb. 18, 2007, prompted a round of hearings, formation of a blue-ribbon commission and more widespread journalistic probing. Among other disclosures, journalists highlighted complaints by Guardsmen and Reservists that they were forced to wait months for medical care and benefits.[55]

CURRENT SITUATION

Congress Reacts

Lawmakers are responding to a cascade of studies, news reports and committee testimony with bills that would change virtually every aspect of the veterans-care system. House Veterans Affairs Chairman Filner says he's considering side-by-side bills separately embodying the recommendations of the Dole-Shalala commission and the sweeping changes he advocates, including guaranteed health care for all veterans.

Congress' single biggest move is a spending bill — still awaiting final action — on veterans and military construction. The House passed its version of the legislation on June 15, the day after the Senate Appropriations Committee approved a similar measure. Details differ from bill to bill, but both call for spending about $4 billion more than the Bush administration requested for VA benefits and medical care. A full Senate vote — followed by reconciliation of differences with the House legislation — was pending as Congress prepared to go back into session after Labor Day. Bush has threatened to veto other spending bills to make room for the higher spending levels the veterans' legislation calls for — unless lawmakers themselves do the cutting.[56]

Meanwhile, the Senate already has passed legislation initially sparked by *The Post's* Walter Reed exposé. Shortly before taking its summer recess, the Senate passed the "Wounded Warrior Act," which would set up a hotline for reporting deficient conditions, improve training of caregivers and step up congressional oversight.

The Senate bill contains some departures from the version that originated in the House, including the addition of a military pay raise. A conference to resolve differences in the two versions has yet to be scheduled.[57]

Other legislation growing directly out of the present wars would step up efforts at suicide prevention. The Joshua Omvig Veterans Suicide Prevention Act, named after a 22-year-old Iowa veteran who killed himself in 2005 on return from Iraq, would require screening of all patients at VA centers for suicide potential, and the monitoring of those at risk. The bill has passed the House, where its sponsor was Rep. Leonard Boswell, D-Iowa; it is pending in the Senate, where Tom Harkin, also an Iowa Democrat, is the sponsor.[58]

"The VA endorses the bill," Ira Katz, the agency's mental health director, testified. "We are already implementing almost all of that bill with existing legislative authority. We're committed to doing everything possible to prevent veteran suicide."[59]

Meanwhile, proposed legislation would protect veterans who interrupted their educations to serve in the armed forces from being penalized by schools and school lenders. The bills were introduced in late June in the Senate by Sherrod Brown, D-Ohio, and in the House by Susan Davis, D-Calif. Campbell, of the Iraq and Afghanistan Veterans of America, drafted the bill based on his own experience. Returning to law school, he found that he'd used up his repayment grace period while serving in Iraq. The bill would extend the repayment period to 13 months. And schools would be required to refund unused tuition and to guarantee re-entry to returning veterans.[60]

Other bills pending in the Senate include a proposal by Senate Veterans Affairs Chairman Akaka to increase services to veterans with TBI. The bill would authorize $48 million for VA programs to improve the quality of life for veterans who are too impaired to manage daily life on their own.

"There must be new approaches to best meet the health-care needs of these veterans," Akaka said.[61]

The legislation also includes a measure calling for restoration of VA health care to so-called "Priority 8" veterans, those whose relatively high incomes and lack of service-connected disabilities led the VA to cut them off from care in 2003.[62]

The health care-restoration provision sparked a partisan fight in the Senate Veterans' Affairs Committee, as the panel prepared final versions of legislation. "I was elected to change the priorities of this country," Sen. Bernard Sanders, I-Vt., said in support of the measure, adding that he opposed the Bush administration tax cuts that benefited

A Wounded Vet Comes Home

"I expected better treatment."

Coming home from Iraq has been difficult for Sgt. Garrett Anderson, a 30-year-old National Guardsman from Champaign, Ill. The wounds bothered him, of course, but it was the red tape that really hurt.

A sniper for the Army's 130th Infantry, Anderson was wounded in Abu Ghraib province in October 2005 after an IED exploded next to his armored Humvee. He lost part of his right arm in the explosion, which also shattered his jaw and eye socket and left him with traumatic brain injury (TBI) and shrapnel throughout his body.

He arrived at Washington's Walter Reed Army Medical Center three days later and remained there for seven months. He has nothing but praise for the nurses and doctors in his amputee ward. His encounter with the VA would be another matter.

After Anderson retired from the Army in June 2006, he immediately filed a disability claim with the VA. That was when the battle on the home front began.

"The VA officers who were assigned to help me were completely helpless," Anderson recalls. "They did nothing for me. The paperwork they filled out for me wasn't thorough enough." As a result, six months would pass until his first VA medical appointment.

More bad news followed. Last March, the VA declined to give Anderson a 100 percent disability rating, although he appeared eligible under VA regulations. "Shrapnel injury not related to combat," the VA letter said. His claim on his brain injury was denied as well. He later learned the shrapnel injuries were disallowed because they were not officially documented in his care report.

Instead, he was given a 90 percent disability rating, which entitled him to $1,600 from the government every month, significantly less than the $2,600 for a 100 percent rating.

Anderson was appalled. "Oh, I laughed to the point of anger when I saw that letter," he recalls. "After everything I had to go through, this was the last thing I wanted to happen. I expected better treatment."

The 10 percent difference would burden his wife, Samantha, and baby daughter as well. Anderson, who is now working with Sen. Richard J. Durbin, D-Ill., on improving veterans' health care, hopes to attend college by using the educational benefits given to veterans. His wife,

---

the wealthy. "Tax breaks to Paris Hilton's parents" is one of those priorities in need of change, Sanders said.[63]

Idaho Republican Craig says the legislation would flood the VA system with 17 million new patients — the now-excluded Priority 8 vets — endangering care for veterans in greater need. "This is the wrong focus at the wrong time," he said. His attempt to eliminate the provision failed.[64]

Calling All Civilians

As the Bush administration and Congress respond to calls to improve the veterans-care system, a growing number of veterans' advocates are urging citizens to mobilize to help veterans rejoin the civilian world.

House Veterans' Affairs Chairman Filner argues that the Bush administration is resisting making sweeping changes. "They're trying to low-key it," he says. "The president has sort of walled off the war from our national consciousness. We don't see the injuries, the caskets."

Idaho Republican Craig contends veterans are getting the help they need. "Citizens' groups have cropped up around the country to help veterans, and their efforts have been highlighted by the Department of Defense." He cites a Pentagon Web site, "America Supports You," that provides links to organizations aimed at boosting the morale of troops overseas and their families. The site also includes links to organizations that help veterans meet potential employers and that build or remodel homes for disabled veterans.[65]

But Sparks, the Army sergeant training for his third deployment to a war zone since the 9/11 terrorist attacks, says he sees little sign that the public at large is engaged in the struggle that the troops on the ground are waging. "People are getting a little weary of the war," he says. "The general populace isn't affected by it. We forget 9/11 and all the U.N. resolutions that were in place on Saddam."

Some veterans' advocates also argue that efforts such as the Pentagon's Web-based outreach program haven't

however, was not entitled to spousal educational benefits, which are only available to spouses of vets with a 100 percent disability rating.

After some lobbying from Sen. Durbin and Rep. Timothy V. Johnson, R-Ill., plus extensive media coverage and research on the disability process by his wife, the VA in June reclassified Anderson as 100 percent disabled — a year after his initial claim.

"Sgt. Garrett Anderson's 100 percent rating is well deserved and long overdue," says Durbin. "It is unacceptable that an American soldier who fought [and] came home wounded had to spend the next year of his life fighting for proper care and compensation."

The Andersons are relieved, but not everything has been resolved. Mrs. Anderson, who is attending law school, has submitted a request for spousal educational reimbursement going back to June 2006 — when disability was claimed — but she has yet to receive any compensation.

Back home in Champaign, Ill., Sgt. Garrett Anderson and his wife and child visit with Sen. Ricahrd J. Durbin, who helped with his benefits appeal.

Office of Sen. Richard J. Durbin

"An injury [forces] the uninjured spouse to seek employment that can financially support the family," she says in an e-mail. . . . "This cannot be done without some sort of post high school education, and unless the veteran has received a 100 percent rating from the VA, the family will suffer great difficulty in trying to recover financially after an injury."

Thanks to the new disability rating, she is eligible to receive an additional $800 per month in educational assistance.

Anderson joined the Army for its sense of brotherhood and camaraderie. And, bureaucratic obstacles with the VA notwithstanding, he has no regrets.

"No question. I still feel my duty to my country was worth it," he says. "I would definitely do it all over again.

"My problem is simply with the bureaucratic system."

— *Darrell Dela Rosa*

penetrated the national consciousness. "Unless you know a soldier who's been injured, you do not understand the depth of their need," says Robinson of ONE Freedom. Like many others in the veterans' community, he observes that the 1.5 million military personnel who have served or are serving in Iraq and Afghanistan don't even amount to 1 percent of a nation of 300 million people. "Most of America assumes they go to war, they come home, go to the VA to get what they need and we've done what we're supposed to do."

But, he argues, only the civilian world can provide the depth of support that returning veterans need. "I don't think that any program that DoD or VA has can be as complete as a community that wraps its arms around you. We need to engage the nation in the communities where the soldiers live to help them return from war and help them reintegrate into society in a meaningful way."

In Los Angeles, the director of a residential program for homeless veterans — many of them Vietnam veterans

with drug problems, PTSD and other psychological war wounds — speaks in almost identical terms. "I just don't think the VA is capable of the kind of extreme reform that is needed to address this population," says Toni Reinis, executive director of New Directions, which operates on government contracts, private grants and its own enterprises — including a diner that residents operate.[66]

"We need to make sure that, when they are released from the military, they're not just dumped — as our Vietnam vets were — on the streets of America," Reinis says. "We need to make sure that there's a strong connection with families, and that families know what to expect — what the symptoms are of depression and PTSD."

Whether civilians reach out now, or leave veterans' care to the government, the non-military majority will be involved in veterans' matters in any case. Testifying about psychological effects of the present wars on those fighting them, Thomas Insel, director of the National Institute of

Do today's veterans face a health-care crisis?

YES
Rep. Bob Filner, D-Calif.
Chairman, House Committee on Veterans' Affairs

Written for *CQ Researcher*, August 2007

The nation's veterans' health-care system is strained to the breaking point. America has a moral and legal obligation to provide care for our nation's veterans. Veterans have kept their promise to serve our nation, and we must keep our promises to our veterans.

As chairman of the House Veterans' Affairs Committee, I have met with individual veterans, heard the testimony of veterans' service organizations and held town hall meetings across the country, and I am told that veterans are falling through the cracks and that more funding is needed to provide care to our veterans.

This administration does not understand that treating our veterans is part of the cost of war. The reality is that this administration did not ask for enough funding to begin addressing the problems faced by veterans. Any planned military surge must be accompanied by a funding surge for health care for veterans.

Our troops come back with post-traumatic stress disorder and can get no services. They come back with dental problems and have to wait a year for an appointment. The average wait for veterans to receive their earned benefits is 177 days.

Today, many of our service members return from Afghanistan and Iraq without legs and arms. They return with many and varied physical and mental health-care needs. Today, many of our veterans live longer and need long-term care — and we should be prepared to provide for them. Today, we have people that have died while waiting for their veterans' benefit claim to be adjudicated. People have lost their homes because they could not afford them. The backlog of claims is a disgrace.

The VA is meant to be an advocate for veterans but is too often seen as an adversary of veterans.

In June, the House of Representatives passed a bill that provides for the largest increase in funding for veterans' health care in the 77-year history of the VA. This bill provides the resources and support to the VA so that veterans can receive the treatment they have been promised. This bill provides the necessary resources to improve health care and expand mental health services. This bill invests in the hiring and training of new claims processors to reduce the VA benefits backlog. This bill will mean increased funding to address the repair and maintenance needs of VA facilities.

The work of this Congress can only begin to address the crisis faced by our veterans. It is our moral obligation to do more — and we must keep our promises to the men and women who have defended our country.

NO
Rep. Steve Buyer, R-Ind.
Ranking Member, House Committee on Veterans' Affairs

Written for *CQ Researcher*, August 2007

The Department of Veterans Affairs provides health care to 5.5 million patients. As of July 2007, Iraq and Afghanistan veterans made up about 5 percent of the total, 96 percent of whom were seen by the VA on an outpatient basis.

Since eligibility reform in 1996, Congress and two administrations have worked effectively to provide quality care for veterans who need it most. Eligibility reform was designed to strike a balance, maintaining a patient base large and varied enough to keep clinicians in practice, without straining the system and compromising quality with excessive enrollments by those who need VA care least.

The nation can be proud of an aging VA workforce, whose men and women have dedicated their lives to care for all veterans. The health-care system they helped build provides excellent care to a well-defined population, but it is not designed to handle a huge influx of non-service-connected patients. That is why former VA Secretary Anthony Principi, to prevent this type of potential crisis in a time of war, suspended enrollment of new "Priority 8" veterans.

We must preserve quality care for VA's core constituency — veterans with service-connected disabilities and illnesses, those with catastrophic disabilities such as blindness and paralysis and the poor. While veterans of Iraq and Afghanistan seeking VA care represent a small percentage of the department's patient base, they do present new challenges — not problems. Responding to the increase of traumatic brain injury (TBI), Congress created four VA polytrauma rehabilitation centers in 2004. These centers have so far treated just over 400 TBI patients. Mental health will continue to receive increased funding to improve access and care. Each war brings its unique challenges, but our obligation to the veterans who have served us in every generation does not vary.

Fulfilling that obligation requires us to remain cognizant of the pressures on the system and sensitive to the influence of patient flow on quality. We will be vigilant in improving transitions, electronic medical records, sub-acute care, administrative support, disability evaluations and medical modernization and research.

The VA has earned its reputation for providing excellent care to our nation's veterans who need it most. If anything will put VA health care into crisis, it would be enrolling millions of non-service-connected patients — who already have access to other health-care options — into a system that is not prepared to receive them.

Mental Health, told the House Oversight and Government Reform Committee in May, "This is not simply a problem for the VA or for DoD. . . . Much of the burden of illness will spill over to the public sector to mental health care in the civilian sector."[67]

OUTLOOK

More Money?

Some observers say that widespread support — at least on the political level — for improved veterans' care bodes well for the future.

"There's no constituency for treating these wounded warriors badly," says Shalala, co-chair of the president's commission on veterans' care. "With all the fussing that's going on, the bureaucracy doesn't want that, Congress doesn't want it, the American people don't want it. Everybody wants to make certain we've done our best. I'm quite optimistic."

Former First Lt. van Engelen, who was treated for a sniper wound at Walter Reed, agrees. "It doesn't matter which organization I speak to, no matter how far left or how far right, regardless of their views of the war, none of them are going to turn down services for a veteran, especially a wounded veteran."

However, double-amputee Tammy Duckworth, at the Illinois' veterans' affairs department, sounds a downbeat note. "I think we're going to forget about the vets," she says. Only two possibilities exist to counter that trend, she says.

One would be veterans putting more pressure on the system to pay attention to their needs. As a state veterans' official, she feels pressure to get things done quickly. "I feel that I have two or three years, if that, to set up programs to make sure that we take care of veterans into the future," she says. "If that doesn't happen now, I can't see that anyone will be going back in 10 years to take action."

Sullivan of Veterans for Common Sense, which filed a class-action suit in California on behalf of veterans, agrees that now is the time to expand or initiate programs. "We have to increase capacity so that veterans see the doctor right away and get their disability payments right away. If we don't fix that now, there will be a social catastrophe — alcohol abuse, drug abuse, DUIs, homelessness."

Army Capt. Ian Perry tries out a one-handed keyboard at a career fair at Walter Reed Army Medical Center in June 2007. Perry was injured in April in a rocket attack while patrolling in Mahmoudiyah, Iraq.

Getty Images/Chip Somodevilla

Worries over the future hinge in large part on whether more money will be available. The Kennedy School's Bilmes, who is forecasting the possible financial consequences of the fighting in Iraq and Afghanistan, calculates a low-end cost of $350 billion in lifetime medical and disability expenses for all wounded veterans. The underlying assumption is that no more troops are deployed and that the pattern of claims matches that of Gulf War veterans. At the high end, if 200,000 to 500,000 more troops are sent into the field, the lifetime costs could rise to $663 billion.[68]

Democratic supporters of mandatory funding cite Bilmes' study to make their case. At a Senate Veterans' Affairs hearing in July, however, Republican Sen. Craig warned that mandatory funding inevitably would raise taxes. "But there have been incredible improvements over the past 10 years in VA's health-care delivery system," Craig explained in an e-mail. "To suggest that the system is broken and therefore we need to change the funding model is simply, in my opinion, an exaggeration of the reality at hand."

Princeton health-care economist Reinhardt agreed that taxes will go up whether or not mandatory funding is enacted. In any event, he told the committee, prospects for the new generation of veterans appear dim, if recent history is any guide. His physician daughter, he noted, treats homeless men, many of them Vietnam veterans.

And Reinhardt recounted what he told his son when he was considering enlisting in the Marine Corps: "My experience has been that soldiers are usually not well-treated by their society."[69]

NOTES

1. For the number of military personnel deployed in Iraq and Afghanistan, see "Serve, Support, Simplify: Report of the President's Commission on Care for America's Returning Wounded Warriors," July 2007, p. 2, www.pccww.gov/docs/Kit/Main_Book_CC%5BJULY 26%5D.pdf.

2. See Dana Priest and Anne Hull, "Soldiers Face Neglect, Frustration at Army's Top Medical Facility," *The Washington Post*, Feb. 18, 2007, p. A1.

3. See Thom Shanker and David Stout, "Chief Army Medical Officer Ousted in Walter Reed Furor," *The New York Times*, March 13, 2007, p. A13. For Nicholson resignation, see Christopher Lee, "VA Secretary is Ending a Trying Tenure," *The Washington Post*, July 17, 2007, p. A3.

4. See Nancy Chandross, "Bob Woodruff: Turning Personal Injury Into Public Inquiry," ABC News, Feb. 26, 2007 (site provides links to Web video of Woodruff's reports), http://abcnews.go.com/WNT/Story?id=2904214&page=1.

5. See "Blast Injury" in "Defense and Veterans Brain Injury Center," undated, www.dvbic.org.

6. See "Health Status of and Services for Operation Enduring Freedom/Operation Iraqi Freedom Veterans after Traumatic Brain Injury Rehabilitation," Department of Veterans Affairs, Office of the Inspector General, July 12, 2006, www.va.gov/oig/54/reports/VAOIG-05-01818-165.pdf.

7. See "Senate Armed Services Committee Holds Hearing on the Nomination of Preston Geren to be Secretary of the Army," *Congressional Transcripts*, June 19, 2007.

8. Other commissions that reported on veterans care-related matters include the Department of Defense Task Force on Mental Health; the Institute of Medicine; the President's Task Force on Returning Global War on Terror Heroes; the Independent Review Group (examining Walter Reed Army Medical Center and National Naval Medical Center). All are listed in "Serve, Support, Simplify," *op. cit.*, p. 29.

9. See the Pentagon Web site, www.defenselink.mil/news/casualty.pdf.

10. See Denise Grady, "U.S. Reconfigures the Way Casualty Totals Are Given," *The New York Times*, Feb. 2, 2007, p. A17. Also see "Operation Iraqi Freedom U.S. Casualty Status, Operation Enduring Freedom Casualty Status," (updated weekly), www.defenselink.mil/news/casualty.pdf; "Global War on Terrorism — Operation Iraqi Freedom, By Casualty Category Within Service," (updated weekly), http://siadapp.dmdc.osd.mil/personnel/CASUALTY/OIF-Total.pdf; "Global War on Terrorism — Operation Enduring Freedom," siadapp.dmdc.osd.mil/personnel/CASUALTY/WOTSUM.pdf.

11. See "Serve, Support, Simplify," *op. cit.*, pp. 5-11.

12. See "Commissioners," in President's Commission on Care for America's Returning Wounded Warriors," 2007, www.pccww.gov/Commissioners.html.

13. Quoted in James Gerstenzang, "Panel urges better care for war vets," *Los Angeles Times*, July 26, p. A10.

14. See Sidath Viranga Panangala, "Veterans' Health Care Issues in the 109th Congress," Congressional Research Service, updated Oct. 26, 2006, pp. 25-27, www.fas.org/sgp/crs/misc/RL32 961.pdf.

15. See Brian J. Eastridge M.D., *et al.*, "Trauma System Development in a Theater of War: Experiences From Operation Iraqi Freedom and Operation Enduring Freedom," *The Journal of Trauma*, December 2006, www.usaisr.amedd.army.mil/gwot/Combat%20Trauma%20System.pdf.

16. Quoted in Gregg Zoroya, "Families bear catastrophic war wounds," *USA Today*, Sept. 25, 2006, p. A8.

17. See Charles W. Hoge M.D., *et al.*, "Mental Health Problems, Use of Mental Health Services, and Attrition From Military Service After Returning From Deployment to Iraq or Afghanistan," *Journal of the American Medical Association*, March 1, 2006, p. 1023.

18. See "An Achievable Vision: Report of the Department of Defense Task Force on Mental Health," June 2007, p. 5, www.ha.osd.mil/dhb/mhtf/MHTF-Report-Final.pdf.

19. Quoted in Dan Frosch, "Fighting the Terror of Battles That Rage in Soldiers' Heads," *The New York Times*, May 13, 2007, p. A18.

20. See "High Rate of Suicide Seen in Soldiers," *Los Angeles Times* (The Associated Press), Aug. 11, 2007, p. A13. "Global War on Terrorism — Operation Iraqi Freedom . . ." and ". . . Operation Enduring Freedom," *op. cit.* See also, Jennifer C. Kerr, "The battle within: Iraq vet suicides," *Marine Corps Times* (The Associated Press), May 28, 2007.

21. For statistics on claims handling, see Daniel Bertoni, "Veterans Disability Benefits: Long-Standing Claims Processing Challenges Persist," Government Accountability Office, testimony before Senate Veterans' Affairs Committee, March 7, 2007, www.gao.gov/new.items/d07512t.pdf. The complaint, *Veterans for Common Sense, et al., v. R. James Nicholson,* et al., C 07 3758, is available at www.mofo.com/docs/pdf/PTSD070723.pdf.

22. Holland Carter, "Words Unspoken Are Rendered on War's Faces," *The New York Times*, Aug. 22, 2007, p. B1.

23. Quoted in Steve Vogel, "Overhaul Urged in Care for Soldiers," *The Washington Post*, July 26, 2007, p. A1.

24. See "Senate Armed Services and Veterans' Affairs Committees Hold Joint Hearing on Disabled Veterans," *Congressional Transcripts*, April 12, 2007.

25. *Ibid.*

26. *Ibid.*

27. See "Post-Traumatic Stress Disorder: DoD Needs to Identify the Factors Its Providers Use to Make Mental Health Evaluation Referrals for Servicemembers," Government Accountability Office, May 2006, p. 21.

28. See "VA Health Care: VA Should Expedite the Implementation of Recommendations Needed to Improve Post-Traumatic Stress Disorder Services," Government Accountability Office, February 2005, p. 5.

29. See "Post-Traumatic Stress Disorder," House Veterans' Affairs Committee, written committee testimony, July 25, 2007.

30. *Ibid.*

31. "Sens. Murray, Obama, Bond, Boxer, McCaskill Introduce Amendment to Temporarily Decrease Military Personality Disorder Discharges," *US Fed News*, July 12, 2007.

32. See "Final Report Draft — The President's Commission on Care for America's Returning Wounded Warriors," July 24, 2007, p. 24, www.usatoday.com/news/pdf/07%2025%202007%20wounded%20warriors.pdf.

33. See "House Oversight and Government Reform Committee Holds Hearing on U.S. Military Mental Health," *Congressional Transcripts*, May 24, 2007.

34. "An Achievable Vision," *op. cit.*, p. 30.

35. "Veterans Affairs Claims Process," House Veterans' Affairs Committee, written committee testimony, March 13, 2007.

36. See House Veterans' Affairs Committee, "Subcommittee on Oversight and Investigations Holds Hearing on Impact of Poor Conditions on Soldiers Leaving Service," *Congressional Transcripts*, March 8, 2007.

37. See "Senate Veterans' Affairs Committee Holds Hearing on Veterans' Affairs Health Care Funding," *Congressional Transcripts*, July 25, 2007.

38. Unless otherwise noted, this section is drawn from Richard H. Taylor, "Homeward Bound: American Veterans Return From War," 2007. See also William Triplett, "Treatment of Veterans," *CQ Researcher*, Nov. 19, 2004, pp. 973-996.

39. See Maj. Charles E. Heller, "Chemical Warfare in World War I: The American Experience, 1917 — 1918," Combat Studies Institute, U.S. Army Command and General Staff College, Fort Leavenworth, Kansas, September 1984, www-cgsc.army.mil/carl/resources/csi/Heller/HELLER.asp#5.%20The%20Quick%20and%20the%20Dead:%20The%20AEF%20on%20the%20Chemical%20Battlefield.

40. Roger J. Spiller, "Shellshock," *American Heritage*, May-June 1990, www.americanheritage.com/articles/magazine/ah/1990/4/1990_4_74.shtml.

41. See Glen H. Elder Jr., Ph.D, *et al.*, "Linking Combat and Physical Health: The Legacy of World War II in Men's Lives," *American Journal of Psychiatry*, March 1997, p. 330, http://ajp.psychiatryonline.org/cgi/reprint/154/3/330.

42. For statistics on military service during the Vietnam era, see "Fact Sheet: America's Wars," Department of Veterans Affairs, November 2006, www1.va.gov/opa/fact/amwars.asp.

43. See Taylor, *op. cit.*, p. 134.

44. See Jack Shafer, "Spitfire," *Slate*, Feb. 5, 2007, www.slate.com/id/2159099/.

45. See Taylor, *op. cit.*, p. 135.

46. See Thomas Whiteside, "Defoliation," *The New Yorker*, Feb. 7, 1970, www.vietnam.ttu.edu/star/images/225/2250209003.pdf.

47. See Douglas Martin, "Thomas Whiteside, 79, Dies," *The New York Times*, Oct. 12, 1997, p. A44.

48. Quoted in Henry Weinstein, "VA rebuked for balking on Agent Orange care," *Los Angeles Times*, July 20, 2007, p. B1. For full text of the decision, see *Nehmer*, et al., *v. Department of Veterans Affairs*, United States Court of Appeal for the 9th Circuit, July 19, 2007, www.ca9.uscourts.gov/ca9/newopinions.nsf/28D4FD1ECE6EEC3B8825731D0057D6DD/$file/0615179.pdf?openelement.

49. See Libby Perl, "Veterans and Homelessness," Congressional Research Service, May 31, 2007, p. 7, www.fas.org/sgp/crs/misc/RL34024.pdf.

50. See "Fact Sheet: America's Wars," *op. cit.*

51. Quoted in Scott Shane, "Chemicals Sickened Gulf War Veterans, Latest Study Finds," *The New York Times*, Oct. 15, 2004, p. A1.

52. Quoted in David Brown, "Panel Discounts Existence of Unique Gulf War Syndrome," *The Washington Post*, Sept. 13, 2006, p. A10.

53. See Edwin Chen, Chris Kraul and Patrick J. McDonnell, "Bush Pledges 'No Retreat' From Iraq," *Los Angeles Times*, Aug. 27, 2003, p. A1; Tom Squiteri, "Army Late with Orders for Armored Humvees," *USA Today*, March 28, 2005, p. A1.

54. See Ann Scott Tyson and Josh White, "Strained Army Extends Tours to 15 Months," *The Washington Post*, April 12, 2007, p. A1; Kimberly Johnson, "Conway: Corps sticking to 7-month tours," *Marine Corps Times*, July 12, 2007.

55. See Rone Tempest, "Injured Vet Faces Battle of Red Tape," *Los Angeles Times*, March 21, 2007, p. A1.

56. See John M. Donnelly and Josh Rogin, "Appropriators Call Bush's Bluff on VA," *CQ Weekly*, June 18, 2007, p. 1860; Josh Rogin, "Spending Measures Reflect Growing Need for Veterans' Health Care," *CQ Today*, June 15, 2007.

57. See John M. Donnelly and Kathleen Hunter, "Senate Passes Military Health Care Overhaul, Pay Raise," *CQ Today*, July 25, 2007.

58. See Patrick Yoest, "House Expected to Pass Trio of Bills Aimed at Improving Veterans' Benefits," *CQ Today*, March 20, 2007; "Bill at a Glance," March 21, 2007.

59. See House Veterans' Affairs Committee, March 8, 2007, *op. cit.*

60. See Rep. Susan Davis, *Congressional Record*, p. E1548, June 29, 2007.

61. Quoted in *Congressional Record*, Senate, April 26, 2007, p. S5211.

62. See Sara Lubbes, "Senate Committee Approves Five Veterans Measures," CQ Committee Coverage, June 27, 2007; Edward Walsh, "VA Cuts Some Veterans' Access to Health Care," *The Washington Post*, Jan. 17, 2003, p. A21.

63. Quoted in Lubbes, *op. cit.*

64. *Ibid.*

65. See "America Supports You," www.americasupportsyou.mil/americasupportsyou/.

66. See the organization's Web site at www.newdirections.org.

67. See "House Oversight and Government Reform Committee Holds Hearing on U.S. Military Mental Health," *Congressional Transcripts*, May 24, 2007.

68. See Linda Bilmes, "Soldiers Returning from Iraq and Afghanistan: The Long-term Costs of Providing Veterans Medical Care and Disability Benefits," Harvard University, John F. Kennedy School of Government, Faculty Research Working Papers Series, January 2007, pp. 16-17, http://ksgnotes1.harvard.edu/Research/wpaper.nsf/rwp/RWP07-001/$File/rwp_07_001_bilmes.pdf.

69. See Senate Veterans' Affairs Committee, July 25, 2007, *op. cit.*

BIBLIOGRAPHY

Books

Rieckhoff, Paul, *Chasing Ghosts — Failures and Faces in Iraq: A Soldier's Perspective, NAL Caliber,* 2006.
The founder of Iraq and Afghanistan Veterans of America chronicles his wartime experiences as a National Guard infantry lieutenant and his transformation into an anti-war activist.

Taylor, Richard H., with Sandra Wright Taylor, *Homeward Bound: American Veterans from War, Praeger Security International,* 2007.
A veteran of the Vietnam War traces the experiences of vets returning home from war, including those suffering from post-traumatic stress disorder (PTSD) after fighting in Iraq and Afghanistan.

Wood, Trish, *What Was Asked of Us: An Oral History of the Iraq War by the Soldiers Who Fought It, Little, Brown and Co.,* 2006.
An investigative reporter recounts veterans' combat experiences and examines life after war — including the account of helicopter pilot Tammy Duckworth, who was shot down and lost both legs.

Articles

The Associated Press, "Home from Iraq a Shattered Man," *Los Angeles Times,* July 1, 2007, p. A18.
A VA physician examines the injuries of Iraq veteran Joseph Briseno Jr., whom some consider the most severely injured American soldier in the war.

Glasser, Ronald, "A Shock Wave of Brain Injuries," *The Washington Post,* April 8, 2007, p. B1.
A physician who treated medically evacuated troops in Vietnam reports on the extent and effects of traumatic brain injury in the war in Iraq.

Kraul, Chris, "Veteran Medics Help Reduce Iraq Fatalities," *Los Angeles Times,* Feb. 12, 2006, p. A15.
An on-scene report from a combat hospital in Baghdad describes how surgeons are helping to vastly improve the odds of survival for severely wounded soldiers.

Perry, Tony, "War Injuries Strain Hospitals," *Los Angeles Times,* March 19, 2007, p. B3.
Military and VA hospitals in the San Diego area near major Navy and Marine bases are trying to cope with a growing number of patients.

Priest, Dana, and Anne Hull, "Soldiers Face Neglect, Frustration at Army's Top Medical Facility," *The Washington Post,* Feb. 18, 2007, p. A1.
Two reporters spent several months visiting recovering soldiers in a dilapidated outpatient residence at Walter Reed Army Medical Center to produce this dramatic series.

Priest, Dana, and Anne Hull, "The War Inside," *The Washington Post,* June 17, 2007, p. A1.
Priest and Hull examine the hardships of veterans trying to deal with post-traumatic stress disorder (PTSD) — often with little help from the VA.

Tempest, Rone, "Troops Get Help Battling Stress," *Los Angeles Times,* April 22, 2007, p. B1.
A pilot program embeds psychologists and social workers with Iraq National Guard veterans in an effort to detect and deal with PTSD.

Zucchino, David, "Injured in Iraq, a Soldier Reclaims His Independence," *Los Angeles Times,* July 4, 2006, p. A1.
A lengthy profile of a veteran who lost three limbs in Iraq provides a window into the life-long cost of war.

Reports and Studies

"An Achievable Vision: Report of the Department of Defense Task Force on Mental Health," June 2007, www.openminds.com/indres/070907mhtfreport.pdf.
A Pentagon panel takes a self-critical look at the availability of services for treating the psychological wounds of war.

"Serve, Support, Simplify," *Report of the President's Commission on Care for America's Returning Wounded Warriors,* July 2007, www.pccww.gov/docs/Kit/Main_ Book_CC%5BJULY26%5D.pdf.
The Dole-Shalala commission proposes six recommendations designed to produce immediate improvements in the veterans' care system.

"Veterans' Disability Benefits: Claims Processing Challenges Persist," *Government Accountability Office,* March 2007, www.gao.gov/new.items/d07512t.pdf.

Daniel Bertoni, the Government Accountability Office's acting director for education, workforce and income security, tells lawmakers that the VA system has failed to meet its own goals for faster responses to veterans' applications in disability ratings-related matters.

Panangala, Sidath Viranga, "Veterans' Health Care Issues in the 109th Congress," *Congressional Research Service*, **Updated Oct. 26, 2006, www.fas.org/sgp/crs/misc/RL32961.pdf.**

A detailed explanation of the disability-ratings system and the ongoing debate over mandatory funding keep this report relevant even past the close of the 109th Congress.

For More Information

America Supports You, www.americasupportsyou.mil/americasupportsyou/index. A Defense Department-created program aimed at citizens and organizations who want to mount projects supporting troops and veterans.

Defense & Veterans Brain Injury Center, Building 1, Room B209, Walter Reed Army Medical Center, 6900 Georgia Ave., N.W., Washington, DC 20307; (202) 782-6345; www.dvbic.org. A Defense Department program for active-duty personnel and veterans that provides medical care, sponsors research and publishes information.

Iraq War Veterans Organization — Long War Veterans Organization, P.O. Box 571, Yucaipa, CA 92399; www.iraqwarveterans.org. Service organization for veterans of the present wars as well as those now serving.

National Veterans Legal Services Program, P.O. Box 65762, Washington, DC 20035; (202) 265-8305; www.nvlsp.org. Nonprofit organization that sues the government to obtain benefits for veterans and trains non-lawyer advocates to represent veterans before government agencies.

ONE Freedom, P.O. Box 7418, Boulder, CO 80306; (888) 334-8387; www.onefreedom.org. Nonprofit developer of programs aimed at helping veterans and their families manage post-combat stress.

Veterans for America, 1025 Vermont Ave., N.W., 7th Floor, Washington, DC 20005; (202) 483-9222; www.veteransforamerica.org. Advocacy organization whose purposes go beyond traditional veterans' issues, to include campaigning for humanitarian relief in war-ravaged countries.

Veterans for Common Sense, 1101 Pennsylvania Ave., S.E., Suite 203, Washington, DC 20003; www.veteransforcommonsense.org. Critically evaluates government programs.

Veterans of Foreign Wars, 406 West 34th St., Kansas City, MO 64111; (816) 756-3390; www.vfw.org. A longtime leader in veterans' affairs.

Veterans' Disability Benefits Commission, 1101 Pennsylvania Ave., N.W., 5th Floor, Washington, DC 20004; (202) 756-7729; www.vetscommission.org. Created by law to study the entire veterans' benefits system.

8

Religious Fundamentalism

Does It Lead to Intolerance and Violence?

Brian Beary

Burqas enshroud women in Kabul, Afghanistan's capital, reflecting life under strict Islamic regimes like the Taliban. Overthrown in 2001, the radically fundamentalist Taliban has regained control in some parts of the country. In addition to requiring the burqa, it restricts women's movements, prevents men from shaving or girls from being educated and prohibits singing and dancing.

From *CQ Researcher*, February 2009.

L ife is far from idyllic in Swat, a lush valley once known as "the Switzerland of Pakistan." Far from Islamabad, the capital, a local leader of the Taliban — the extremist Islamic group that controls parts of the country — uses radio broadcasts to coerce residents into adhering to the Taliban's strict edicts.

"Un-Islamic" activities that are now forbidden — on pain of a lashing or public execution — range from singing and dancing to watching television or sending girls to school. "They control everything through the radio," said one frightened Swat resident who would not give his name. "Everyone waits for the broadcast." And in case any listeners in the once-secular region are considering ignoring Shah Duran's harsh dictates, periodic public assassinations — 70 police officers beheaded in 2008 alone — provide a bone-chilling deterrent.[1]

While the vast majority of the world's religious fundamentalists do not espouse violence as a means of imposing their beliefs, religious fundamentalism — in both its benign and more violent forms — is growing throughout much of the world. Scholars attribute the rise to various factors, including a backlash against perceived Western consumerism and permissiveness. And fundamentalism — the belief in a literal interpretation of holy texts and the rejection of modernism — is rising not only in Muslim societies but also among Christians, Hindus and Jews in certain countries. (*See graph, p. 198.*)

Religious Fundamentalism Spans the Globe

Fundamentalists from a variety of world religions are playing an increasingly important role in political and social life in countries on nearly every continent. Generally defined as the belief in a literal interpretation of holy texts and a rejection of modernism, fundamentalism is strongest in the Middle East and in the overwhelmingly Christian United States.

Where Fundamentalism Influences Social and Political Life

Role of Fundamentalism
- ☐ Plays a role
- ■ Plays a dominant role
- Ⓜ Muslim
- Ⓒ Christian
- (M, C) Muslim, Christian
- Ⓙ Jewish
- (H, M, S) Hindu, Muslim, Sikh

* The ultra-conservative Taliban ruled from 1996-2001 and are fighting to regain control.

Sources: U.S. National Counter Terrorism Center, Worldwide Incidents Tracking System, http://wits.nctc.gov; David Cingranelli and David Richards, Cingranelli-Richards (CIRI) Human Rights Dataset, CIRI Human Rights Project, 2007, www.humanrightsdata.org; The Association of Religious Data Archives at Pennsylvania State University, www.thearda.com; Office of the Coordinator for Counterterrorism, Country Reports on Terrorism, United States Department of State, April 2008, www.state.gov/documents/organization/105904.pdf; Peter Katel, "Global Jihad," CQ Researcher, Oct. 14, 2005

Islamic fundamentalism is on the rise in Pakistan, Afghanistan, the Palestinian territories and European nations with large, often discontented Muslim immigrant populations — notably the United Kingdom, Germany, Denmark, Spain and France, according to Maajid Nawaz, director of the London-based Quilliam Foundation think tank.

In the United States — the birthplace of Christian fundamentalism and the world's most populous predominantly Christian nation — 90 percent of Americans say they believe in God, and a third believe in a literal interpretation of the Bible.[2] Perhaps the most extreme wing of U.S. Christian fundamentalism are the Christian nationalists, who believe the scriptures "must govern every aspect of public and private life," including government, science, history, culture and relationships, according to author Michelle Goldberg, who has studied the splinter group.[3] She says Christian nationalists are "a significant and highly mobilized minority" of U.S. evangelicals that is gaining influence.[4] TV evangelist Pat Robertson is a leading Christian nationalist and "helped put dominionism — the idea that Christians have a God-given right to rule — at the center of the movement to bring evangelicals into politics," she says.[5]

Although the number of the world's Christians who are fundamentalists is not known, about 20 percent of the 2 billion Christians are conservative evangelicals, according to the World Evangelical Alliance (WEA).[6] Evangelicals reject the "fundamentalist" label, and most do not advocate creating a Christian theocracy, but they are the socially conservative wing of the Christian community, championing "family values" and opposing abortion and gay marriage. In recent decades they have exercised considerable political power on social issues in the United States.

Many Religions Have Fundamentalist Groups

Religious fundamentalism comes in many forms around the globe, and many different groups have emerged to push their own type of fundamentalism — a handful through violence. The term "Islamist" is often used to describe fundamentalist Muslims who believe in a literal interpretation of the Koran and want to implement a strict form of Islam in all aspects of life. Some also want to have Islamic law, or sharia, imposed on their societies.

Christian Fundamentalists

- Lord's Resistance Army (LRA), a rebel group in Uganda that wants to establish a Christian nation — **violent**
- Various strands within the evangelical movement worldwide, including the U.S.-based Christian nationalists, who insist the United States was founded as a Christian nation and believe that all aspects of life (including family, religion, education, government, media, entertainment and business) should be taken over by fundamentalist Christians — **rarely violent**
- Society of St. Pius X, followers of Catholic Archbishop Marcel Lefebvre, who reject the Vatican II modernizing reforms — **nonviolent**

Islamic Fundamentalists

- Jihadists, like al Qaeda and its allies across the Muslim world — **violent***
- Locally focused Islamist groups Hezbollah (Lebanon) and Hamas (Gaza) — **violent**
- Revolutionary Islamists, like Hizb-ut-Tahrir (HT), a pan-Islamic Sunni political movement that wants all Muslim countries combined into a unitary Islamic state or caliphate, ruled by Islamic law; has been involved in some coup attempts in Muslim countries and is banned in some states — **sometimes violent**
- Political Islamists, dedicated to the "social and political revivification of Islam" through nonviolent, democratic means. Some factions of the Muslim Brotherhood — the world's largest and oldest international Islamist movement — espouse using peaceful political and educational means to convert Muslim countries into sharia-ruled states, re-establishing the Muslim caliphate. Other factions of the group have endorsed violence from time to time.
- Post-Islamists, such as the AKP, the ruling party in Turkey, which has Islamist roots but has moderated its fundamentalist impulses — **nonviolent**

Judaism

- Haredi, ultra-orthodox Jews — **mostly nonviolent**
- Gush Emunim, aim to reoccupy the biblical Jewish land including Palestinian territories — **sometimes violent**
- Chabad missionaries, who support Jewish communities across the globe — **nonviolent**

Indian subcontinent

- Sikh separatists — **sometimes violent**
- Hindu extremists, anti-Christian/Muslim — **sometimes violent**

* For an extensive list of global jihadist groups, see "Inside the Global Jihadist Network," pp. 860-861, in Peter Katel, "Global Jihad," CQ Researcher, Oct. 14, 2005, pp. 857-880.

Sources: Encyclopedia of Fundamentalism; "Foreign Terrorist Organizations," U.S. Department of State

Christians Are a Third of the World's Population

About 20 percent of the world's 2 billion Christians are evangelicals or Pentecostals — many of whom are fundamentalists. But statistics on the number of other fundamentalists are not available. Christians and Muslims together make up more than half the world's population.

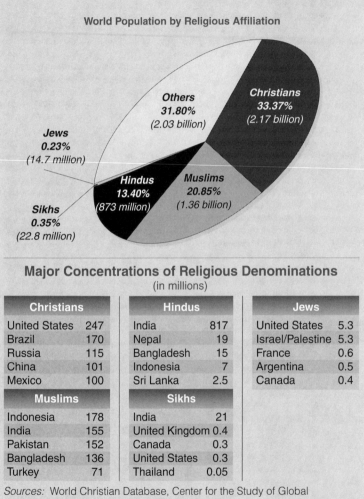

World Population by Religious Affiliation

Others 31.80% (2.03 billion)

Christians 33.37% (2.17 billion)

Jews 0.23% (14.7 million)

Hindus 13.40% (873 million)

Muslims 20.85% (1.36 billion)

Sikhs 0.35% (22.8 million)

Major Concentrations of Religious Denominations
(in millions)

Christians		Hindus		Jews	
United States	247	India	817	United States	5.3
Brazil	170	Nepal	19	Israel/Palestine	5.3
Russia	115	Bangladesh	15	France	0.6
China	101	Indonesia	7	Argentina	0.5
Mexico	100	Sri Lanka	2.5	Canada	0.4

Muslims		Sikhs	
Indonesia	178	India	21
India	155	United Kingdom	0.4
Pakistan	152	Canada	0.3
Bangladesh	136	United States	0.3
Turkey	71	Thailand	0.05

Sources: World Christian Database, Center for the Study of Global Christianity, Gordon-Conwell Theological Seminary, www.worldchristiandatabase.org/wcd/home.asp; John L. Allen Jr., "McCain's choice a nod not only to women, but post-denominationalists," National Catholic Reporter, Aug. 30, 2008, http://ncrcafe.org/node/2073

Anglicans and Baptists — very active in evangelizing," says James Nkansah, a Ghanaian-born Baptist minister who teaches at the Nairobi Evangelical Graduate School of Theology in Kenya. "Even the Catholics are doing it, although they do not call themselves evangelists." A similar trend is occurring in Latin America, especially in Brazil, Guatemala and Peru among the Pentecostals, who stress the importance of the Holy Spirit, faith healing and "speak in tongues" during services.

Both evangelicals and Catholics in Latin America have adopted the basic tenets of U.S.-style evangelicalism, according to Valdir Steuernagel, a Brazilian evangelical Lutheran pastor who is vice president at World Vision International, a Christian humanitarian agency. Like U.S. evangelicals, South American evangelicals passionately oppose gay marriage and abortion, but they do not use the term "fundamentalist," says Steuernagel, because the word "does not help us to reach out to the grassroots."

South Korea also has a thriving evangelical community. A visiting U.S. journalist describes a recent service for about 1,000 people at a popular Korean evangelical church: "It was part rock concert and part revival meeting," with the lead guitarist, "sometimes jumping up and down on the altar platform" like Mick Jagger, recalls Michael Mosettig.[8] Elsewhere in Asia — the world's most religiously diverse continent — Christian missionaries in China have grown their flocks from fewer than 2 million

Christian evangelicalism is booming in Africa — especially in Anglophone countries like Kenya, Uganda, Nigeria, Ghana and South Africa.[7] "We are all — Pentecostals, Christians in 1979 to more than 16 million Protestants alone in 2008.[9] It is unknown how many of those are fundamentalists.

Among the world's 15 million Jews, about 750,000 are ultra-Orthodox "Haredi" Jews who live in strict accordance with Jewish law. Half of them live in Israel, most of the rest in the United States, while there are small pockets in France, Belgium, the United Kingdom, Canada and Australia. About 80,000 live in the Palestinian territories on Israel's West Bank because they believe it is God's will.[10] The flourishing fundamentalist Chabad movement — whose adherents would prefer to live in a Jewish theocracy governed by religious laws — sends missionaries to support isolated Jewish communities in 80 countries.

"We accept the Israeli state, but we would have liked the Torah to be its constitution," says Belgian-based Rabbi Avi Tawil, an Argentine Chabad missionary. "But we are not Zionists, because we do not encourage every Jew to go to Israel. Our philosophy is, 'Don't run away from your own place — make it better.' "

In India, Hindu fundamentalists insist their vast country should be for Hindus only. In late 2008, a sudden upsurge in fundamentalist Hindu attacks against Christian minorities in the state of Orissa in eastern India ended with 60 Christians killed and 50,000 driven from their homes.[11] (See p. 221.)

Besides their rejection of Western culture, the faithful embrace fundamentalism out of fear of globalization and consumerism and anger about U.S. action — or inaction — in the Middle East, experts say. Some also believe a strict, religiously oriented government will provide better services than the corrupt, unstable, secular regimes governing their countries. Religious fundamentalism also thrives in societies formerly run by repressive governments. Both Christian and Muslim fundamentalism are spreading in Central Asian republics — particularly Uzbekistan, Kyrgyzstan and Tajikistan — that were once part of the repressive, anti-religious Soviet Union. (See sidebar, p. 212.)

Many fundamentalists — such as the Quakers, Amish and Jehovah's Witnesses — oppose violence for any reason. And fundamentalists who call themselves "political Islamists" pursue their goal of the "social and political revivification of Islam" through nonviolent, democratic means, according to Loren Lybarger, an assistant professor of classics and world religions at Ohio University and author of a recent book on Islamism in the Palestinian territories.[12]

In recent years radical Islamic extremists have perpetrated most violence committed by fundamentalists. From January 2004 to July 2008, for instance, Muslim militants killed 20,182 people, while Christian, Jewish and Hindu extremists together killed only 925, according to a U.S. government database.[13] Most of the Muslim attacks were between Sunni and Shia Muslims fighting for political control of Iraq. (See chart, p. 203.)[14]

Asmaa Abdol-Hamiz, a Muslim Danish politician and social worker, questions the State Department's statistics. "When Muslims are violent, you always see them identified as Muslims," she points out. "When Christians are violent, you look at the social and psychological reasons."

In addition, according to Radwan Masmoudi, president of the Center for the study of Islam and Democracy, such statistics do not address the "more than one million innocent people" killed in the U.S.-led wars in Iraq and Afghanistan, which, in his view, were instigated due to pressure from Christian fundamentalists in the United States. (See "At Issue," p. 219.)

Nevertheless, some radical Islamists see violence as the only way to replace secular governments with theocracies. The world's only Muslim theocracy is in Iran. While conservative Shia clerics exert ultimate control, Iranians do have some political voice, electing a parliament and president. In neighboring Saudi Arabia, the ruling royal family is not clerical but supports the ultra-conservative Sunni Wahhabi sect as the state-sponsored religion. Meanwhile, in the Palestinian territories, "there has been a striking migration from more nationalist groups to more self-consciously religious-nationalist groups," wrote Lybarger.[15]

Experts say Muslim militants recently have set their sights on troubled countries like Somalia and nuclear-armed Pakistan as fertile ground for establishing other Islamic states. Some extremist groups, such as Hizb-ut-Tahrir, want to establish a single Islamic theocracy — or caliphate — across the Muslim world, stretching from Indonesia to Morocco.

Still other Muslim fundamentalists living in secular countries such as Britain want their governments to allow Muslims to settle legal disputes in Islamic courts. Islamic law, called sharia, already has been introduced in some areas in Africa, such as northern Nigeria's predominantly Muslim Kano region.[16]

AP Photo/Sunday Alamba

AP Photo/Gurinder Osan

In the Wake of Fundamentalist Violence

Two days of fighting between Christians and fundamentalist Muslims in December destroyed numerous buildings in Jos, Nigeria, (top) and killed more than 300 people. In India's Orissa state, a Christian woman (bottom) searches through the remains of her house, destroyed during attacks by fundamentalist Hindus last October. Sixty Christians were killed and 50,000 driven from their homes.

Muslim extremists are not the only fundamentalists wanting to establish theocracies in their countries. The Jewish Israeli group Kach, for instance, seeks to restore the biblical state of Israel, according to the U.S. State Department's list of foreign terrorist organizations. Hindu fundamentalists want to make India — a secular country with a majority Hindu population that also has many Muslims and Christians — more "Hindu" by promoting traditional Hindu beliefs and customs.

While militant Christian fundamentalist groups are relatively rare, the Lord's Resistance Army (LRA) has led a 20-year campaign to establish a theocracy based on the Ten Commandments in Uganda. The group has abducted hundreds of children and forced them to commit atrocities as soldiers. The group has been blamed for killing hundreds of Ugandans and displacing 2 million people.[17]

In the United States, most Christian fundamentalists are nonviolent, although some have been responsible for sporadic incidents, primarily bombings of abortion clinics. "The irony," says John Green, a senior fellow at the Washington-based Pew Forum on Religion and Public Policy, "is that America is a very violent country where the 'regular' crime rates are actually higher than they are in countries where global jihad is being waged."

Support for violence by Islamic extremists has been declining in the Muslim world in the wake of al Qaeda's bloody anti-Western campaigns, which have killed more Muslims than non-Muslims. U.S. intelligence agencies concluded in November 2008 that al Qaeda "may decay sooner" than previously assumed because of "undeliverable strategic objectives, inability to attract broad-based support and self-destructive actions."[18]

But fundamentalist violence, especially Islamist-inspired, remains a serious threat to world peace. In Iraq, fighting between Sunni and Shia Muslims has killed tens of thousands since 2003 and forced more than 4 million Iraqis to flee their homes. And 20 of the 42 groups on the State Department's list of terrorist organizations are Islamic fundamentalist groups.[19] No Christian or Hindu fundamentalists are included on the terrorist list.

However, Somali-born writer Ayaan Hirsi Ali — herself a target of threats from Islamic fundamentalists — says that while "Christian and Jewish fundamentalists are just as crazy as the Islamists . . . the Islamists are more violent because 99 percent of Muslims think Mohammad is perfect. Christians do not see Jesus in as absolute a way."

As religious fundamentalism continues to thrive around the world, here are some of the key questions experts are grappling with:

Is religious fundamentalism on the rise?

Religious fundamentalism has been on the rise worldwide for 30 years and "remains strong," says Pew's Green.

Fundamentalism is growing throughout the Muslim and Hindu worlds but not in the United States, where its growth has slowed down in recent years, says Martin Marty, a religious history professor at the University of Chicago, who authored a multivolume series on fundamentalism.[20] Christian fundamentalism is strong in Africa and Latin America and is even being exported to industrialized countries. Brazilian Pastor Steuernagel says "evangelical missionaries are going from Brazil, Colombia and Argentina to Northern Hemisphere countries like Spain, Portugal and the United Kingdom. They are going to Asia and Africa too, but there they must combine their missionary activities with aid work."

Islamic fundamentalism, meanwhile, has been growing for decades in the Middle East and Africa. For example, in Egypt the Muslim Brotherhood — which seeks to make all aspects of life in Muslim countries more Islamic, such as by applying sharia law — won 20 percent of the seats in 2005 parliamentary elections — 10 times more than it got in the early 1980s.[21] In Somalia, the Islamist al-Shabaab militia threatens the fragile government.

More moderate Muslims who want to "reform" Islam into a more tolerant, modern religion face an uphill battle, says Iranian-born Shireen Hunter, author of a recent book on reformist voices within Islam. Reformers' Achilles' heel is the fact that "they are often secular and do not understand the Islamic texts as well as the fundamentalists so they cannot compete on the same level," she says.

In Europe, secularism is growing in countries like France and the Netherlands as Christian worship rates plummet, but Turkey has been ruled since 2002 by the Justice and Development Party, which is rooted in political Islam. Though it has vowed to uphold the country's secular constitution, critics say the party harbors a secret fundamentalist agenda, citing as evidence the

Radical Muslims Caused Most Terror Attacks

More than 6,000 religiously motivated terrorist attacks in recent years were perpetrated by radical Muslims — far more than any other group. The attacks by Christians were mostly carried out by the Lord's Resistance Army (LRA) in Uganda.

Religious Attacks, Jan. 1, 2004-June 30, 2008

	Killed	Injured	Incidents
Christian	917	371	101
Muslim*	20,182	43,852	6,180
Jewish	5	28	5
Hindu**	3	7	6
Total	**21,107**	**44,258**	**6,292**

* More than 90 percent of the reported attacks on civilians by Sunni and Shia terrorists were by Sunnis. Does not include the Muslim attacks in Mumbai, India, in December 2008, allegedly carried out by Muslim extremists from Pakistan.

** Uncounted are the Hindu extremist attacks on Christian minorities in late 2008 in India, which left more than 60 Christians dead.

Note: Perpetrators do not always claim responsibility, so attributing blame is sometimes impossible. Also, it is often unclear whether the attackers' motivation is purely political or is, in part, the result of criminality.

Sources: National Counter Terrorism Center's Worldwide Incidents Tracking System, http://wits.nctc.gov; Human Security Research Center, School for International Studies, Simon Fraser University, Vancouver, www.hsrgroup.org.

government's recent relaxation of restrictions on women wearing headscarves at universities.[22]

In Israel, the ultra-Orthodox Jewish population is growing thanks to an extremely high birthrate. Haredi Jews average 7.6 children per woman compared to an average Israeli woman's 2.5 children.[23] And ultra-Orthodox political parties have gained 15 seats in the 120-member Knesset (parliament) since the 1980s, when they had only five.[24] Secularists in the United States saw Christian fundamentalists grow increasingly powerful during the presidency of George W. Bush (2001-2009). Government policies limited access to birth control and abortions, and conservative religious elements in the military began to engage in coercive proselytizing. "From about 2005, I noticed a lot of religious activity: Bible study weeks, a multitude of religious services linked to public holidays that I felt were excessive," says U.S. Army Reserve intelligence officer Laure Williams. In February 2008, she

Moderate Islamist cleric Sheik Sharif Ahmed became Somalia's new president on Jan. 31, raising hope that the country's long war between religious extremists and moderates would soon end. But the hard-line Islamist al-Shabaab militia later took over the central Somali town of Baidoa and began imposing its harsh brand of Islamic law.

recalls, she was sent by her superiors to a religious conference called "Strong Bonds," where fundamentalist books advocating sexual abstinence, including one called *Thrill of the Chaste*, were distributed. Williams complained to her superiors but did not get a satisfactory response, she says.

In the battle for believers among Christian denominations, "Conservative evangelicals are doing better than denominations like Methodists and Lutherans, whose liberal ideology is poisonous and causing them to implode," says Tennessee-based Southern Baptist preacher Richard Land. "When you make the Ten Commandments the 'Ten Suggestions,' you've got a problem."

However, the tide may be turning, at least in some quarters, in part because the next generation appears to be less religious than its elders. Some see the November 2008 election of President Barack Obama — who got a lot of his support from young voters in states with large evangelical populations where the leaders had endorsed Obama's opponent — as evidence that the reign of the Christian right is over in the United States.

"The sun may be setting on the political influence of fundamentalist churches," wrote *Salon.com* journalist Mike Madden.[25] In fact, the fastest-growing demographic group in the United States is those who claim no religious affiliation; they make up 16 percent of Americans today, compared to 8 percent in the 1980s.[26]

And in Iran, while the Islamic theocracy is still in charge, "the younger generation is far less religious than the older," says Ahmad Dallal, a professor of Arab and Islamic studies at Georgetown University in Washington, D.C.

Moreover, support for fundamentalist violence — specifically by al Qaeda's global terrorist network — has been declining since 2004.[27] For example, 40 percent of Pakistanis supported suicide bombings in 2004 compared to 5 percent in 2007.[28] Nigeria is an exception: 58 percent of Nigerians in 2007 said they still had confidence in al Qaeda leader Osama bin Laden, who ordered the Sept. 11, 2001, terrorist attacks on the United States. Notably, al Qaeda has not carried out any terrorist attacks in Nigeria. Support for al Qaeda has plummeted in virtually all countries affected by its attacks.[29]

And while the Muslim terrorist group Jemaah Islamiyah remains active in Indonesia — the world's most populous Muslim-majority country — claims of rampant fundamentalism there are overstated, according to a report by the Australian Strategic Policy Institute. The study found that 85 percent of Indonesians oppose the idea of their country becoming an Islamic republic.[30]

Although there has been a "conspicuous cultural flowering of Islam in Indonesia," the report continued, other religions are booming, too. In September 2008, for example, authorities overrode Muslim objections and approved an application for a Christian megachurch that seats more than 4,500 people.[31]

Is religious fundamentalism a reaction to Western permissiveness?

Religious experts disagree about what attracts people to religious fundamentalism, but many say it is a response to rapid modernization and the spread of Western multiculturalism and permissiveness.

"Fundamentalism is a modern reaction against modernity," says Jerusalem-based journalist Gershom Gorenberg. "They react against the idea that the truth is not certain. It's like a new bottle of wine with a label saying 'ancient bottle of wine.'"

Peter Berger, director of the Institute on Culture, Religion and World Affairs at Boston University, says fundamentalism is "an attempt to restore the taken-for-grantedness that has been lost as a result of modernization. We are constantly surrounded by people with other views, other norms, other lifestyles. . . . Some people live with this quite well, but others find it oppressive, and they want to be liberated from the liberation."[32]

Sayyid Qutb, founder of Egypt's Muslim Brotherhood, was repulsed by the sexual permissiveness and consumerism he found in the United States during a visit in 1948.[33] He railed against "this behavior, like animals, which you call 'Free mixing of the sexes'; at this vulgarity which you call 'emancipation of women'; at these unfair and cumbersome laws of marriage and divorce, which are contrary to the demands of practical life. . . . These were the realities of Western life which we encountered."[34]

A similar sentiment was felt by Mujahida, a Palestinian Islamic jihadist who told author Lybarger she worried that her people were losing their soul after the 1993 peace agreement with Israel. "There were bars, nightclubs, loud restaurants serving alcohol, satellite TV beaming American sitcoms, steamy Latin American soap operas [and] casinos in Jericho" to generate tax and employment.[35]

And opposition to abortion and gay rights remain the primary rallying call for U.S. evangelicals. In fact, the late American fundamentalist Baptist preacher Jerry Falwell blamed the 9/11 Islamic terrorist attacks in the United States on pagans, abortionists, feminists and homosexuals who promote an "alternative lifestyle" and want to "secularize America."[36]

In her account of the rise of Christian nationalism, journalist Goldberg said the things Islamic fundamentalists hate most about the West — "its sexual openness, its art, the possibilities for escaping the bonds of family and religion, for inventing one's own life — are what Christian nationalists hate as well."[37]

Pew's Green agrees fundamentalists are irritated by permissive Western culture. "There has always been sin in the world," he says, "but now it seems glorified."

But others say the U.S.-led invasion of Iraq in March 2003 triggered the global surge in violent Islamic militancy. The average annual global death toll between March 2003 to September 2006 from Muslim terrorist attacks jumped 237 percent from the toll between September 2001 to March 2003, according to a study published by Simon Fraser University in Canada.[38]

Moreover, when bin Laden declared war on the United States in a 1998 fatwa, he never mentioned Western culture. Instead, he objected to U.S. military bases in Saudi Arabia, the site of some of Islam's holiest shrines. "The Arabian Peninsula has never — since God made it flat, created its desert and encircled it with seas — been stormed by any forces like the crusader armies now spreading in it like locusts, consuming its riches and destroying its plantations." Bin Laden also railed against Israel — "the Jew's petty state" — and "its occupation of Jerusalem and murder of Muslims there."[39]

Some believe former President George W. Bush's habit of couching the "war on terror" in religious terms helped radical Islamic groups recruit jihadists. *An-Nuur* — a Tanzanian weekly Islamic magazine — noted: "Let us remember President Bush is a saved Christian. He is one of those who believe Islam should be destroyed."[40]

Nawaz, a former member of the revolutionary Islamist Hizb ut-Tahrir political movement, says fundamentalists' motivation varies depending on where they come from. "Some political Islamists are relatively liberal," says the English-born Nawaz. "It's the Saudis that are religiously conservative. The problem is their vision is being exported elsewhere."

Indeed, since oil prices first skyrocketed in the 1970s, the Saudi regime has used its growing oil wealth to build conservative Islamic schools (madrassas) and mosques around the world. As *New York Times* reporter Barbara Crossette noted, "from the austere Faisal mosque in Islamabad, Pakistan — a gift of the Saudis — to the stark Istiqlal mosque of Jakarta, Indonesia, silhouettes of domes and minarets reminiscent of Arab architecture are replacing Asia's once-eclectic mosques, which came in all shapes and sizes."[41]

Pew Forum surveys have found no single, predominant factor motivating people to turn to Islamic fundamentalism. Thirty five percent of Indonesians blame immorality for the growth in Islamic extremism; 40 percent of Lebanese blame U.S. policies and

What Is a Fundamentalist?

Few claim the tarnished label

With the word fundamentalism today conjuring up images of cold-blooded suicide bombers as well as anti-abortion zealots, it is hardly surprising that many religious people don't want to be tarred with the fundamentalist brush.

Yet there was a time when traditionalist-minded Christianity wore it as a badge of honor. Baptist clergyman Curtis Lee Laws coined the term in 1910 in his weekly newspaper *Watchman-Examiner*, when he said fundamentalists were those "who still cling to the great fundamentals and who mean to do battle royal for the faith."[1] Several years earlier, Christian theologians had published a series of pamphlets called "The Fundamentals," which defended traditional belief in the Bible's literal truth against modern ideas such as Charles Darwin's theory of evolution.

Essentially a branch within the larger evangelical movement, the fundamentalists felt that the Christian faith would be strengthened if its fundamental tenets were clearly spelled out. Today, while one in three U.S. Christians considers himself an evangelical, "a small and declining percentage would describe themselves as fundamentalist," says Southern Baptist minister Richard Land of Nashville, Tenn. "While most evangelicals support fundamentalist principles, it is unfair to compare them to the Islamists who take up arms and kill people," he says.

Although some may see the label "fundamentalist" as synonymous with radical Islamic extremists, Ahmad Dallal, a professor of Arab and Islamic Studies at Georgetown University in Washington, D.C., notes that the Arabic word for fundamental — *usul* — was never used in this context historically. "There is some logic to applying the word 'fundamental' in an Islamic context, however," he says, because "both the Muslim and Christian fundamentalists emphasize a literal interpretation of the holy texts."

Traditionalist Catholics do not call themselves fundamentalists either. But Professor Martin Marty, a religious history professor at the University of Chicago and author of a multivolume series on fundamentalism, says Catholic followers of French Archbishop Marcel Lefebvre are fundamentalists because they refuse to accept reforms introduced by the Second Vatican Council in 1965. But "theocons" — a group of conservative U.S. Catholic intellectuals — are

influence; 39 percent of Moroccans blame poverty and 34 percent of Turks blame a lack of education.[42]

Then there are those who just want to regain their lost power, notes Iranian-born author Hunter. "In Iran, Turkey, Tunisia and Egypt, there was a forced secularization of society," she says. "Religious people lost power — sometimes their jobs, too. They had to develop a new discourse to restore their standing."

Religious fundamentalists in Nigeria are largely motivated by anger at the government for frittering away the country's vast oil supplies through corruption and mismanagement. "When a government fails its people, they turn elsewhere to safeguard themselves and their futures, and in Nigeria . . . they have turned to religion," asserted American religion writer Eliza Griswold.[43]

Many Christian and Muslim leaders preach the "Gospel of prosperity," which encourages Nigerians to better themselves economically. But Kenyan-based Baptist preacher Nkansah says that "while the Gospel brings good health and prosperity," the message can be taken too far. "There are some people in the Christian movement who are too materialistic."

Nkansah argues that evangelism is growing in Africa because "as human beings we all have needs. When people hear Christ came onto this planet to save them, they tend to respond."

But a journalist in Tajikistan says poverty drives Central Asians to radical groups like the Hizb ut-Tahrir (HT). "In the poor regions, especially the Ferghana Valley on the Kyrgyz-Tajik-Uzbek border, HT is very active," says the journalist, who asks to remain unnamed for fear of reprisals. "Unemployment pushes people to find consolation in something else, and they find it in religion."

Should religious fundamentalists have a greater voice in government?

Religious fundamentalists who have taken the reins of government — in Iran (since 1979), Afghanistan

not fundamentalists, he says, because they accept the so-called Vatican II changes. Theocon George Weigel, a fellow at the Ethics and Public Policy Center in Washington, eschews the word "fundamentalist" because he says it is "a term used by secular people with prejudices, which doesn't illuminate very much."

Neither are religious Jews keen on the term. Rabbi Avi Tawil, director of the Brussels office of the Chabad Jewish missionary movement, says "fundamentalism is about forcing people. We don't do that. We strictly respect Jewish law, which says if someone would like to convert then you have to help them."

Jerusalem-based writer Gershom Gorenberg notes that unlike Christians and Muslims, fundamentalist Jews do not typically advocate reading holy texts literally because their tradition has always been to have multiple interpretations. The

Al Qaeda leader Osama bin Laden hails the economic losses suffered by the United States after the Sept. 11, 2001, terrorist attacks. "God ordered us to terrorize the infidels, and we terrorized the infidels," bin Laden's spokesman Suleiman Abu Ghaith said in the same video, which was broadcast soon after the attacks that killed nearly 3,000 people.

term is even harder to apply to Hinduism because — unlike Christianity, Judaism and Islam — whose "fundaments" are their holy texts, Hinduism's origins are shrouded in ancient history, and its core elements are difficult to define.[2]

Yet fundamentalists are united in their aversion to modernism.

As Seyyed Hossein Nasr, an Islamic studies professor at George Washington University, noted: "When I was a young boy in Iran, 50 or 60 years ago . . . the word fundamentalism hadn't been invented. Modernism was just coming into the country."[3]

---

[1] Brenda E. Brasher, *Encyclopedia of Fundamentalism* (2001), p. 50.
[2] *Ibid.*, p. 222.

[3] His comments were made at a Pew Forum discussion, "Between Relativism and Fundamentalism: Is There a Middle Ground?" March 4, 2008, in Washington, D.C., http://pewforum.org/events/?EventID=172.

(1996-2001) and the Gaza Strip (since 2007) — have either supported terrorism or have instituted repressive regimes. Grave human rights abuses have been documented, dissenters tortured, homosexuals hanged, adulterers stoned, music banned and education denied for girls.

Ayaan Hirsi Ali — a Somali-born feminist writer, a former Dutch politician and a fellow at the conservative American Enterprise Institute who has denounced her family's Muslim faith — says fundamentalists should be able to compete for the chance to govern. "But we must tell them a system based on Islamic theology is bad," she says. "The problem is that Muslims cannot criticize their moral guide. Mohammad is more than a pope, he is a king. As a classical liberal, I say not even God is beyond criticism."

However, Danish politician Abdol-Hamid, whose parents are Palestinian, argues that because most countries won't talk to Hamas, the ruling party in the Gaza Strip, because of its terrorist activities, "we failed the Palestinians

by never giving Hamas a chance." In Denmark, she continues, "We have Christian extremists, and I have to accept them." For instance, she explains, the far-right Danish Peoples Party (DPP) wants to ban the wearing of Muslim headscarves in the Danish parliament, and DPP member of parliament Soren Krarup, a Lutheran priest, says the hijab and the Nazi swastika are both symbols of totalitarianism. Abdol-Hamid hopes to become the first hijab-wearing woman elected to the parliament.

After interviewing Hamas' founding father, Sheikh Ahmed Yassin, Lebanese-born journalist Zaki Chebab wrote that Yassin "was confident that . . . Israel would disappear off the map within three decades," a belief he said came from the Koran.[44]

A Christian fundamentalist came to power in Northern Ireland without dire consequences after the Rev. Ian Paisley — the longtime leader of Ulster's Protestants, who established his own church stressing biblical literalism and once called the pope the "antichrist" — ultimately

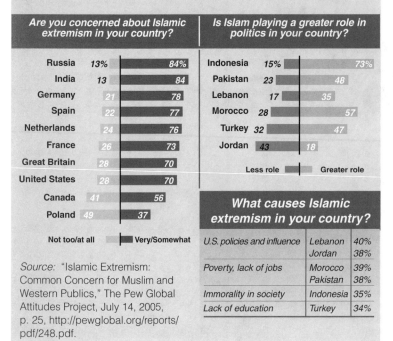

Many Voice Concern About Islamic Extremism

A majority of respondents in nine out of 10 Western countries were "very" or "somewhat" concerned about Islamic extremism in a 2005 poll. Islam was playing a greater role in politics in five out of six Muslim nations, according to the respondents, and most blamed U.S. policies and poverty for the rise in Islamic extremism.

Are you concerned about Islamic extremism in your country?

Country	Not too/at all	Very/Somewhat
Russia	13%	84%
India	13	84
Germany	21	78
Spain	22	77
Netherlands	24	76
France	26	73
Great Britain	28	70
United States	28	70
Canada	41	56
Poland	49	37

Is Islam playing a greater role in politics in your country?

Country	Less role	Greater role
Indonesia	15%	73%
Pakistan	23	48
Lebanon	17	35
Morocco	28	57
Turkey	32	47
Jordan	43	18

What causes Islamic extremism in your country?

U.S. policies and influence	Lebanon	40%
	Jordan	38%
Poverty, lack of jobs	Morocco	39%
	Pakistan	38%
Immorality in society	Indonesia	35%
Lack of education	Turkey	34%

Source: "Islamic Extremism: Common Concern for Muslim and Western Publics," The Pew Global Attitudes Project, July 14, 2005, p. 25, http://pewglobal.org/reports/pdf/248.pdf.

"It is a delicate game," says fundamentalism expert Marty. "If you have a republican system with a secular constitution, then, yes [fundamentalists must be allowed to have a voice], because they have to respect that constitution. But it's very much a case of 'handle with care.'"

Conservative Catholic theologian George Weigel, a senior fellow at the Ethics and Public Policy Center in Washington, says religious people are entitled to be involved in politics, but "they should translate their religiously informed moral convictions into concepts and words that those who don't share their theological commitments can engage and debate. This is called 'democratic courtesy.' It's also political common sense."

Indeed, religious Muslims not only have the right but also the duty to participate in government, according to Rachid Ghannouchi, a Tunisian-born Islamic thinker. Denouncing countries like Tunisia and Algeria that repress Islamic fundamentalism, Ghannouchi said, "the real problem lies in convincing the ruling regimes...of the right of Islamists — just like other political groups — to form political parties, engage in political activities and compete for power or share in power through democratic means."[46]

But ex-Islamist Nawaz warns: "We should not be encouraging Islamists, because every terrorist group has grown out of a nonviolent Islamist group."

Israeli journalist Gorenberg also notes that radical Jewish fundamentalists have repeatedly resorted to violence, citing the case of Baruch Goldstein, a U.S.-born Israeli doctor and supporter of the Kach party who killed 29 Muslims at the tomb of Abraham in Hebron in 1994.

Washington-based Turkish journalist Tulin Daloglu is anxious about her country's future under the ruling Justice and Development Party. "Women are starting to cover their hair in order to get jobs in government," she claims. "The case is not at all proven that Islam and

reconciled his lifelong differences with Northern Irish Catholic leaders and has served amicably with them in government after they offered him political power.[45]

Kenyan-based evangelical Nkansah says "politics is part of life." If a religious person is called into politics in Kenya, he explains, "they should go because that is their vocation." He supports Kenya's model, in which many clergy members, including bishops, enter politics, even though the constitution bans parties based on religion. But evangelical pastor Steuernagel says that in Brazil, religious leaders are increasingly going into politics. "I do not think it is healthy," he says, "but it is happening."

In Central Asia, Islamic parties are only allowed in Tajikistan. But while the Islamic Revival Party has become a significant force there, the party "is neither dangerous nor radical," according to the Tajik journalist, and "does not dream about having a state like Iran."

democracy can live in harmony. Turkey is a swing state" in that regard.

Meanwhile, in some Asian and African countries where the rule of law is weak — Pakistan and Somalia for example — many are clamoring for Islamic law. Often the existing government is so dysfunctional that the quick, decisive administration of Islamic law, or sharia, is attractive. In Pakistan, says British journalist Jason Burke, "the choice between slow, corrupt and expensive state legal systems and the religious alternative — rough and ready though it may be — is not hard." Even educated, relatively wealthy women are demanding sharia, he said.[47]

For example, the Taliban has been able to seize control in Pakistan's Swat region because of "an ineffectual and unresponsive civilian government, coupled with military and security forces that, in the view of furious residents, have willingly allowed the militants to spread terror deep into Pakistan."[48]

BACKGROUND

'Great Awakening'

Christian fundamentalist movements trace their origins to the emergence of Protestantism in 16th-century Europe, when the German monk Martin Luther (1483-1546) urged people to return to the basics of studying the Bible.[49] In 1620 a group of fundamentalist Protestants known as the Pilgrims fleeing persecution in England settled in North America and, along with the Puritans who arrived shortly afterwards, greatly influenced the course of Christianity in New England.

In the 1700s, as science began to threaten religion's preeminence, North Americans launched a Protestant revival known as the "Great Awakening," from which the evangelical movement was born. Revivals held throughout the American colonies between 1739 and 1743, offered evangelical, emotionally charged sermons — often in open-air services before large groups — that stressed the need to forge a personal relationship with Jesus Christ. Leaders in the movement included preachers George Whitfield, Gilbert Tennent and Jonathan Edwards.[50]

A similar revival movement — the Sunday school movement — began in the late 18th century, becoming a

AFP/Getty Images/Walter Astrada

Evangelicals from Uganda's Born Again Church are spiritually moved last August while listening to a sermon by Pastor Robert Kayanja, one of Uganda's most prominent evangelical preachers. While Uganda has long been heavily Christian, many churchgoers have switched from mainstream to Pentecostal sects in recent years.

primary vehicle for evangelism.[51] The term "fundamentalist" originated in the United States when the first of a 12-volume collection of essays called *The Fundamentals* was published in 1910, outlining the core tenets of Christianity.[52] In 1925 fundamentalists were the driving force in the trial of Tennessee schoolteacher John Scopes, who was convicted of breaking a Tennessee law that forbade the teaching of evolution instead of the Bible's version of how the world was created. Even though the fundamentalists won the case, they were lampooned in the popular press, and their credibility and esteem suffered. They withdrew from the limelight and formed their own subculture of churches, Bible colleges, camps and seminaries.

By 1950, the charismatic American Baptist preacher Billy Graham had begun to broaden the fundamentalists' base, and they became masters at harnessing the mass media, especially radio and television. The 1973 U.S. Supreme Court's *Roe v. Wade* ruling legalizing abortion further galvanized evangelicals, leading Baptist preacher Falwell in 1979 to establish the Moral Majority — a conservative political advocacy group.

After his unsuccessful run for president of the United States in 1988, television evangelist and Christian nationalist Robertson formed the Christian Coalition to fight for "family-friendly" policies — specifically policies against homosexuality and abortion. By the mid-1990s

CHRONOLOGY

A.D. 70-1700s *The three great, monotheistic, text-based religions — Christianity, Islam and Judaism — spread worldwide.*

70 Romans destroy the second Jewish temple in Jerusalem, causing Jews to scatter across the globe.

319 Christianity becomes the official religion of the Roman Empire; pagan sacrifices are outlawed.

632 Mohammad dies in Medina, Arabia. . . . Islam begins to spread to the Middle East, Africa, India, Indonesia and Southern Europe.

1730s-40s Evangelical movement is born in the United States in a religious revival known as the "Great Awakening."

1800s-1920s *Fundamentalist impulses are triggered in reaction to scientific developments, modernization and — in the case of Islam — Western colonization.*

1859 British biologist Charles Darwin presents theory of evolution in *On the Origin of Species*, casting doubt on the Bible's account of creation.

1906 African-American evangelist William J. Seymour launches the Azusa Street revival in Los Angeles, sparking the worldwide Pentecostal movement.

1910 American Christian oil magnates Lyman and Milton Stewart commission The Fundamentals, promoting fundamentalist Protestant beliefs that the Bible contains no errors.

1921 Jailed Hindu nationalist Vinayak Damodar Savarkar writes *Hindutva: Who is a Hindu?* — laying the foundation for movements promoting Hindu identity, including the radical Bajrang Dal.

1928 Hasan al-Banna, a schoolteacher in Cairo, Egypt, establishes the Muslim Brotherhood, which calls for all Muslims to make their societies more Islamic.

1940s-1970s *Fundamentalism becomes a significant force in politics and society.*

1948 Israel declares independence, causing millions of Jews — both secular and religious — to return to their spiritual homeland.

1967 Fundamentalist Jews settle in Palestinian territories occupied after the Six-day War, triggering an explosion in Islamic fundamentalism among disgruntled Arabs.

1973 U.S. Supreme Court's *Roe v. Wade* ruling legalizes abortion, galvanizing Christian fundamentalists into political activism.

1979 Islamists overthrow the Shah of Iran and install the world's first Islamic theocracy in modern times.

1980s-2000s *Fundamentalists increasingly endorse violence to further their goals — especially in the Muslim world.*

1984 Indian government storms a Sikh temple, which Sikh militants had occupied, leading two of Prime Minister Indira Gandhi's Sikh bodyguards to murder her.

1994 American Jewish fundamentalist Baruch Goldstein kills 29 Muslims praying at a mosque in the Palestinian city of Hebron.

Sept. 11, 2001 Al Qaeda Islamists kill nearly 3,000 people by flying hijacked planes into the World Trade Center and Pentagon; a third hijacked plane crashes in Pennsylvania.

2002 Sectarian fighting between Hindus and Muslims in Gujarat, India, kills more than 800 people — mostly Muslims.

2006 Palestinians elect Hamas, a radical Islamic party, to lead the government.

2008 Sixty Christians die after outbreak of fundamentalist Hindu violence against Christians in India. . . . Pakistan-based Islamists launch coordinated attacks in Mumbai, India, killing 164 people. . . . Troops from Congo, Uganda and South Sudan launch ongoing joint offensive to crush Uganda's fundamentalist Lord's Resistance Army. . . . Israel launches major attack on Gaza in effort to weaken Hamas, resulting in 1,300 Palestinian deaths.

the coalition became the most prominent voice in the Christian movement, largely by publishing voter guides on how local politicians voted on specific social issues important to Christian fundamentalists. Many credit the coalition with helping the Republican Party, which had embraced their platform on social issues, to take majority control of the U.S. Congress in the 1994 midterm elections.[53]

Some U.S. fundamentalists segregated themselves from mainstream society — which they saw as immoral — and educated their children at home.[54] A strand of race-based fundamentalism also emerged, called the Christian Identity movement, which claimed the Bible was the history of the white race and that Jews were the biological descendants of Satan. A Christian Reconstructionist movement, led by preacher Mark Rushdoony, emerged as well, advocating local theocracies that would impose biblical law.[55] The reconstructionists oppose government schools and demand that civil disputes be settled in church courts and that taxes be limited to 10 percent of income (based on the tithe). Through its books, the movement has had a significant influence on other Christian political organizations.[56]

Meanwhile, a fundamentalist Catholic movement emerged in Europe after French Archbishop Marcel Lefebvre refused to accept changes introduced by the Vatican in the 1960s, notably saying Mass in languages other than Latin.[57] Other conservative Catholic movements include Opus Dei, founded by Spanish priest Josemaria Escriva in 1928. Today it is based in Rome, has 75,000 members in 50 countries and appeals to well-educated lay Catholics.[58] In the United States, a group of Catholic intellectuals — including Michael Novak, Weigel and Richard John Neuhaus — became known as the "theocons" and allied themselves with Protestant evangelicals in opposing abortion and gay rights.[59]

Bush's presidency was a high point for U.S. evangelicals. Bush announced during the 2000 campaign that he was a "born again" Christian whose favorite philosopher was Jesus Christ — "because he changed my heart." He also told a Texas evangelist that he felt God had chosen him to run for president, and he was accused of "creeping Christianization" of the federal government by establishing an Office for Faith-Based Initiatives, which critics claimed was just a vehicle for channeling tax dollars to conservative Christian groups.[60]

Bush liberally used religious rhetoric — declaring, for example, after the 9/11 attacks that his mission was "to rid the world of evil."[61] He named Missouri Sen. John Ashcroft, a fellow evangelist, as attorney general and filled his administration with Christian conservatives, such as Monica Goodling, a young Justice Department official who vetted candidates for executive appointments by checking their views on moral issues like abortion.[62]

Christian missionaries have been evangelizing — spreading their faith — since the 16th century, but fundamentalist strands have grown increasingly prominent in recent decades. Pentecostalism — which began in 1901 when a Kansas Bible studies student, Agnes Ozman, began "speaking in tongues" — is the dominant form of Protestantism in Latin America.[63] In Guatemala, evangelicalism began to overtake the Roman Catholic Church in the 1980s after Catholicism was seen as too European and elitist.[64] Although Pentecostals usually distinguish themselves from run-of-the-mill fundamentalists, both are part of the evangelical family.

In Africa, Christian fundamentalism developed its strongest base in sub-Saharan regions — particularly Nigeria, triggering rising tensions and sporadic violence between the country's Christian and Muslim populations. U.S. Christian fundamentalists have helped to spread an extreme brand of Christianity to Africa, according to Cedric Mayson, director of the African National Congress' Commission for Religious Affairs, in South Africa. "We are extremely concerned about the support given by the U.S. to the proliferation of right-wing Christian fundamentalist groups in Africa," Mayson wrote, as "they are the major threat to peace and stability in Africa."[65]

Uganda became home to the militant Christian fundamentalist Lord's Resistance Army. Its leader Joseph Kony — known as the "altar boy who grew up to be a guerrilla leader" — has transformed an internal Ugandan power struggle into an international conflict by roaming across Sudan and the Democratic Republic of Congo, kidnapping children en route for use as soldiers after slaughtering their parents.[66]

Patrick Makasi, the LRA's former director of operations, called Kony "a religious man" who "all the time...is talking about God. Every time he keeps calling many people to teach them about the legends and about God. That is how he leads people."[67]

Officials in the 'Stans' Uneasy About Islamization

Education is a key battleground

"The crowd in the airport parking lot was jubilant despite the cold, with squealing children, busy concession stands and a tangle of idling cars giving the impression of an eager audience before a rock concert," wrote journalist Sabrina Tavernise of a scene in Dushanbe, the capital of Tajikistan.[1]

"But it was religion, not rock 'n roll, that had drawn so many people," she wrote. The families were there to meet relatives returning from the Hajj — the pilgrimage to Mecca that Muslims strive to undertake at least once in their lifetime. Last year, 5,200 Tajiks participated — 10 times more than in 2000.

Since gaining independence from the anti-religious Soviet Union, Tajikistan has been re-embracing its Islamic roots, and a Westerner in the country — who asked to remain unnamed — worries the nation of 7.2 million people may adopt an extreme form of Islam. "Every day you can see on our streets more women wearing the veil and more men with beards," he says.

But while many women in Central Asia today do cover themselves from head to toe, it is "extremely rare" for them to cover their faces as well, which was not unusual in pre-Soviet Tajikistan and Uzbekistan, says Martha Brill Olcott, a senior associate at the Carnegie Endowment for International Peace in Washington, who has traveled there frequently since 1975.

The region is undergoing a wide mix of outside influences, not all of them Islamic, Olcott notes. For example, some women have begun wearing the hijab (a headscarf pinned tightly around the face so as to cover the hair) worn by modern Islamic women in the West, while others, notably in Uzbekistan, imitate secular Western fashions such as short skirts and visible belly piercing.

The Westerner in Tajikistan fears that the government's efforts to block the growing Islamization may be having the opposite effect. Government policies "are too severe," he says. "They give long prison sentences to young men and shut down unregistered mosques. This just strengthens people's resolution to resist an unfair system."

Further, he suggests, "If they developed local economies more, people would not think about radical Islam." Without economic development, "Tajikistan could become another Afghanistan or Iran."

Tajikistan, one of the poorer countries in the region, is in the midst of reverse urbanization due to economic decline, with

The refurbished Juma Mosque in Tashkent, Uzbekistan, reflects Islam's resurgence in Central Asia, where 18 years after the breakup of the former Soviet Union neighboring Iran and Saudi Arabia are exerting their influence on the vast region.

Getty Images/Uriel Sinai

77 percent of the population now living in rural areas compared to 63 percent in the mid-1980s.[2] A million Tajiks work in Russia.

In neighboring Uzbekistan, the picture is similar. Olcott likens the California-sized nation of 27 million people to an "ineffective police state. There are restrictions, but people can get around them and — more important — they are not afraid to get around them." She says the government's response is erratic: "If you do not draw attention to yourself, you can be an Islamist. But if you preach and open schools or wear very Islamic dress, you can get into trouble."

Christian missionaries are also active in Central Asia. Russian-dubbed broadcasts from U.S. televangelist Pat Robertson are aired throughout the region. According to the Tajikistan-based Westerner, after the 1991 fall of the Soviet Union "Jehovah's Witnesses, Baptists and Adventists came from Russia, Western Europe, South Korea and the United States. The locals were friendly to them because they provided humanitarian aid to poor people." However, authorities in the region have recently clamped down — especially on the Jehovah's Witnesses, he says.[3]

In Kazakhstan authorities have cracked down on Protestants and repressed the Hindu-based Hare Krishnas, while in Kyrgyzstan a new law makes it harder to register religious organizations.[4]

In Kyrgyzstan, the authorities are in a quandary about whether to allow a new political movement, the Union of Muslims, to be set up because bringing Islam into politics violates the constitution. Yet union co-founder Tursunbay Bakir Uulu argues that a moderately Islamic party would help stabilize the country. "Currently Hizb-ut-Tahrir is conquering the Issyk-Kul region," he warned. "Religious sects are stepping up their activities. We want moderate Islam, which has nothing to do with anti-religious teaching and which respects values of other world religions, to fill this niche."[5]

The Islamization began in the 1980s, when Soviet President Mikhail Gorbachev eased restrictions on religious worship that had been enforced by the communists for decades. After the Soviet Union's collapse, the relaxation accelerated as the Central Asian republics became independent nations. Muslim missionaries flocked to the region, and conservative Islamic schools, universities and mosques quickly sprang up, many financed by foundations in oil-rich Arab states like Saudi Arabia, where the ultra-fundamentalist Wahhabi Muslim sect is the state-sponsored religion.[6]

Many Central Asians see embracing conservative Islam as a way to define themselves and reject their Russian-dominated communist past. Curiously, their increasing exposure to secular culture through Russia-based migrant Tajik workers appears to be having a Westernizing influence on the society even as Islam is growing: "Five years ago, I could not wear shorts on the street," said the Westerner in Tajikistan. "Now in summer you can see a lot of Tajik men and even girls wearing shorts in the cities, although not in the villages."

The rise of Islam is strongest in Uzbekistan, Tajikistan and Kyrgyzstan, while Turkmenistan and Kazakhstan have stronger secular traditions. Uzbek authorities initially encouraged Islamization, believing it would help strengthen national identity. But by the late 1990s, they were afraid of losing control to radical elements and began repressing militant groups like the Islamic Movement of Uzbekistan and Hizb-ut-Tahrir.[7] A jailbreak by Islamists in Andijan, the Uzbek capital, in May 2005 triggered violent clashes between government forces and anti-corruption protesters — whom the government claimed were Islamic extremists — resulting in 187 deaths.[8]

Meanwhile, the Saudis are sending Islamic textbooks that promote their own conservative brand of Islam to schools in the region.[9] Saudi-Uzbek ties stretch back to the 1920s, when some Uzbeks fled to Saudi Arabia, according to Olcott.

But Saudi-inspired fundamentalism "is not a major factor" in Turkmenistan yet, says Victoria Clement, an assistant professor of Islamic world history at Western Carolina University, who has lived in Turkmenistan. "There are maybe a few individuals, but the government has not allowed madrasas [Islamic religious schools] since 2003." Even so, she notes, "when I went to the mosques, I saw clerics instructing the kids in the Koran, which technically they should not have been doing [under Turkmen law], but I do not think it was harmful."

Nevertheless, the Turkmen education system is growing more Islamic, Clement says, as new schools follow the model devised by Turkish preacher Fethullah Gulen. "They do not have classes in religion, but they teach a conservative moral code — no drinking, smoking, staying out late at night. I think it is a great alternative to the Islamic madrasas," she says.

Olcott says while the quality of education in the Gulen schools may be good, it is "still very Islamic." Gulen himself now lives in the United States, having left Turkey after being accused of undermining secularism.

The Westerner in Tajikistan notes, however, that in their efforts to stem the growth of radical Islam authorities have a bit of a blind spot when it comes to education. "In most Tajik villages, the children's only teacher is the person who can read the Koran in Arabic, and that is dangerous. The government makes demands about how students look — ties and suits for example — but does not care about what they have in their minds."

Islam Booming in the "Stans"

Several of the nations in Central Asia dubbed "the Stans" are rediscovering their Islamic roots, including Tajikistan and Uzbekistan. The Islamization began in the 1980s, when then Soviet President Mikhail Gorbachev eased restrictions on religious worship.

[1] Sabrina Tavernise, "Independent, Tajiks Revel in Their Faith," *The New York Times*, Jan. 3, 2009, www.nytimes.com/2009/01/04/world/asia/04tajik.html?emc=tnt&tntemail0=y.

[2] *Ibid.*

[3] Felix Corley, "Tajikistan: Jehovah's Witnesses Banned," Forum 18 News Service (Oslo, Norway), Oct. 18, 2007, www.forum18.org/Archive.php?article_id=1036; Felix Corley, "Turkmenistan: Fines, beatings, threats of rape and psychiatric incarceration," Forum 18 News Service (Oslo, Norway), Nov. 25, 2008, www.forum18.org/Archive.php?article_id=1221.

[4] Mushfig Bayram, "Kazakhstan: Police Struggle against Extremism, Separatism and Terrorism — and restaurant meals," Forum 18 News Service, Nov. 21, 2008, www.forum18.org/Archive.php?article_id=1220; and Mushfig Bayram, "Kyrgyzstan: Restrictive Religion Law passes Parliament Unanimously," Forum 18 News Service (Oslo, Norway), Nov. 6, 2008, www.forum18.org/Archive.php?article_id=1215.

[5] "Kyrgyz Experts Say Newly Set Up Union of Muslims Aims for Power," *Delo No* (Kyrgyzstan), BBC Monitoring International Reports, Dec. 9, 2008.

[6] See Martha Brill Olcott and Diora Ziyaeva, "Islam in Uzbekistan: Religious Education and State Ideology," Carnegie Endowment for International Peace, July 2008, www.carnegieendowment.org/publications/index.cfm?fa=view &id=21980&prog=zru.

[7] *Ibid.*, p. 2.

[8] For background, see Kenneth Jost, "Russia and the Former Soviet Republics," *CQ Researcher*, June 17, 2005, pp. 541-564.

[9] *Ibid.*, p. 19.

Anti-abortion demonstrators carry a statue of the Virgin Mary during the March for Life in Washington, D.C., on Jan. 22, 2009. The rally marked the 35th anniversary of the Supreme Court's landmark Roe v. Wade decision legalizing abortion in the United States. Fundamentalist Christians continue to exert significant influence on U.S. policies governing abortion, birth control and gay rights.

Islamic Fundamentalism

Originating in the 7th century with the Prophet Mohammad, Islam considers the Koran sacred both in content and form — meaning it should be read in the original language, Arabic. Muslims also follow the Hadith, Mohammad's more specific instructions on how to live, which were written down after he died. Though Islamic scholars have interpreted both texts for centuries, fundamentalists use the original texts.

The concept of a militant Islamic struggle was developed by scholar Taqi ad-Din Ahmad Ibn Taymiyyah (1263-1328), who called for "holy war" against the conquering, non-Muslim Mongols.[68] The Saudi-born Islamic scholar Muhammed Ibn Abd-al-Wahhab (1703-1792) criticized the Ottoman Empire for corrupting the purity of Islam. The descendants of one of Wahhab's followers, Muhammed Ibn Saud, rule Saudi Arabia today.[69]

Responding to the dominating influence of Western powers that were colonizing the Islamic world at the time, Egyptian schoolteacher Hasan Al-Banna set up the Muslim Brotherhood in 1928 to re-Islamize Egypt. The organization later expanded to other Arab countries and to Sudan.[70] "They copied what the Christian missionaries were doing in Africa by doing social work," notes Islamic studies Professor Dallal. "But they had no

vision for 'the state,' and they paid a price for this because the state ultimately suppressed them."

In the 1950s the extremist group Hizb-ut-Tahrir, which advocates a single Islamic state encompassing all predominantly Muslim countries, emerged and spread across the Islamic world. In the mid-1950s, while imprisoned in Egypt by the secular government, the U.S.-educated Egyptian scholar and social reformer Qutb (1906-1966) wrote *Milestones*, his diatribe against the permissiveness of the West, which persuaded many Muslims they needed to get more involved in politics in order to get their governments to make their societies more Islamic. In Pakistan, the politician Sayyid Abul A'la Mawdudi (1903-1979) urged Islamists to restore Islamic law by forming political parties and getting elected to political office, according to Dallal.

The 1973 oil crisis helped to spread conservative Islam by further enriching Saudi Arabia, which set up schools, universities and charities around the world advocating ultraconservative wahhabi Islam. And the 1979 Iranian Revolution — in which the pro-Western Shah Mohammad Reza Pahlavi was deposed in a conservative Shia Muslim revolt led by Ayatollah Ruhollah Khomeini — installed the first Islamic theocracy in the modern era.

In 1991 Islamists were voted into power in Algeria, but the military refused to let them govern, triggering a bloody civil war that the secularists eventually won. In Afghanistan, the ultraconservative Pakistan-sponsored Taliban seized power in 1996 and imposed their strict version of Islamic law — outlawing music, forbidding girls from going to school or leaving their homes without a male relative, forcing women to completely cover their bodies — even their eyes — in public, requiring men to grow beards and destroying all books except the Koran.[71] After the al Qaeda terrorist attacks of 9/11, the United States ousted the Taliban, which had been sheltering bin Laden.

Al Qaeda, a Sunni Muslim group that originated in Saudi Arabia, had been based in Afghanistan since the 1980s, when it helped eject Soviet occupiers, with U.S. aid. But in the 1990s bin Laden redirected his energies against the United States after American troops were stationed in his native Saudi Arabia, home to several sacred Muslim shrines.

After the U.S.-led invasion of Iraq in 2003, al Qaeda urged its followers to switch their attentions to Iraq, which became a magnet for Islamist jihadists. In 2007 al Qaeda attacks in Iraq escalated to such a level of violence — including attacking Shia mosques and repressing local Sunnis — that other Islamic groups like the Muslim Brotherhood repudiated them.[72]

In Europe, meanwhile, beginning in the 1980s the growing Muslim immigrant population began to attach greater importance to its religious identity, and some turned to violence. Algerian extremists set off bombs in Paris subways and trains in 1995-1996; Moroccan-born Islamic terrorists killed 191 people in train bombings in Madrid in 2004; and British-based al Qaeda operatives of mainly Pakistani origin killed 52 people in suicide train and bus bombings in London in 2005.[73] And an al Qaeda cell based in Hamburg, Germany, plotted the 9/11 attacks on the World Trade Center towers and the Pentagon.

The estimated 5 million Muslims in the United States — who are a mix of immigrants and African-Americans — are more moderate than their Western European counterparts.[74] Poverty is likely to have played a role in making European Muslims more radical: Whereas the average income of American Muslims is close to the national average, Muslims' average income lags well behind the national average in Spain, France, Britain and Germany.[75]

Meanwhile, the creation of Israel in 1948 — fiercely opposed by all of its Arab neighbors — and its successive expansions in the Gaza Strip and West Bank have helped to spur Islamic fundamentalism in the region. To Israel's north, the Shia-Muslim Hezbollah group emerged in the 1980s in Lebanon with the goal of destroying Israel and making Lebanon an Islamic state. The Sunni-Muslim group Hamas — an offshoot of the Muslim Brotherhood — won elections in the Palestinian territories in 2006. Hamas, which was launched during the Palestinian uprising against Israel of 1987, has forged strong links with Islamic fundamentalists in Iran and Saudi Arabia.[76]

Fundamentalist Jews

Predating both Islam and Christianity, Judaism takes the Torah and Talmud as its two holy texts and believes that the Prophet Moses received the Ten Commandments — inscribed on stone tablets — from God on Mount Sinai.[77] Fundamentalist Jews believe they are God's chosen people and that God gave them modern-day Israel as their homeland. A defining moment in this narrative is

AFP/Getty Images/Jack Guez

Members of the ultra-Orthodox Chabad-Lubavitch Jewish fundamentalist movement attend the funeral in Israel of two members of the missionary sect killed last fall during Islamist militant attacks in Mumbai, India.

the destruction of the second Jewish Temple in Jerusalem in 70 A.D., which triggered the scattering of Jews throughout the world for nearly 2,000 years.

Jews began returning to their spiritual homeland in significant numbers in the early 1900s with the advent of Zionism — a predominantly secular political movement to establish a Jewish homeland, founded by the Austro-Hungarian journalist Theodor Herzl in the late 19th century in response to rising anti-Semitism in Europe. The migration was accelerated after Nazi Germany began persecuting the Jewish people in the 1930s in a racially motivated campaign that resulted in the Holocaust and the murder of 6 million Jews and millions of others.[78] Today, a third the world's 15 million Jews live in Israel; most of the rest live in the United States, with substantial Jewish communities in France, Argentina and Canada.

Fundamentalist Jews regret that Israel was established as a secular democracy rather than a theocracy. While most Israelis support the secular model, there is a growing minority of ultra-Orthodox (Haredi) Jews for whom the Torah and Talmud form the core of their identity. They try to observe 613 commandments and wear distinctive garb: long black caftans, side curls and hats for men and long-sleeve dresses, hats, wigs and scarves for women.[79] The Haredim dream of building a new Jewish temple in Jerusalem where the old ones stood, which also happens to be the site of the Dome on the Rock — one of Islam's most revered shrines. The fundamentalist

Islamic Fundamentalism Limits Women's Rights

But Muslim women disagree on the religion's impact

As a high official in Saudi Arabia, Ahmed Zaki Yamani crafted many of the kingdom's laws, basing them on Wahhabism, the strict form of Islam that is Saudi Arabia's state religion. Under those laws, Muslim judges "have affirmed women's competence in all civil matters," he has written, but "many of them have reservations regarding her political competence." In fact, he added, one of Islam's holiest texts, the Hadith, "considered deficiency a corollary of femaleness."[1]

Since the 1970s, the Saudis have used their vast oil wealth to spread their ultra-conservative form of Islam throughout the Middle East, North Africa and South and Central Asia, including its controversial view of women as unequal to men. Under Saudi Wahhabism, women cannot vote, drive cars or mix freely with men. They also must have a male guardian make many critical decisions on their behalf, which Human Rights Watch called "the most significant impediment to the realization of women's rights in the kingdom."[2]

The advocacy group added that "the religious establishment has consistently paralyzed any efforts to advance women's rights by applying only the most restrictive provisions of Islamic law, while disregarding more progressive interpretations."[3]

In her autobiography, *Infidel*, Somali-born writer and former Dutch politician Ayaan Hirsi Ali writes about how shocked she was as a young girl when her family moved from Somalia's less conservative Islamic society to Saudi Arabia, where females' lives were much more restricted. "Any girl who goes out unaccompanied is up for grabs," she says.

Raised a Muslim but today an outspoken critic of Islam, Hirsi Ali says Saudi Arabia has had a "horrific" influence on the Muslim world — especially on women. In Africa, she says, religious strictures against women going out in public can have dire consequences, because many women must work outside the home for economic reasons.

While Wahhabism is perhaps the most extreme form of Islam, Hirsi Ali doubts any form of Islam is compatible with women's rights. "Islamic feminism is a contradiction in terms," she says. "Islam means 'submission.' This is double for women: She must appeal to God before anyone else. Yet this same God tells your man he can beat you."

In 2004, Dutch filmmaker Theo Van Gogh was murdered by a Muslim man angered by a film he made portraying violence against women in Islamic societies. Hirsi Ali, then a member of the Dutch parliament, had written the script for the movie, and the assassin left a note on Van Gogh's body threatening her.

She believes the entire philosophical underpinnings of Islam are flawed. For example, she says, she had been taught that Muslim women must wear the veil so they will not corrupt men, yet, "when I came to Europe I could not understand how women were not covered, and yet the men were not jumping on them. Then I saw all it took was to educate boys to exercise self-control. They don't do that in Saudi Arabia, Iran and Pakistan."

But forcing women to cover themselves is not the only way conservative Muslim societies infringe on women's rights. Until recently in Pakistan, rape cases could not be prosecuted unless four pious Muslim men were willing to testify that they had witnessed the attack. Without their testimony the victim could be prosecuted for fornication and alleging a false crime, punishable by stoning, lashing or prison.[4]

Ali's views are not shared by Asmaa Abdol-Hamid, a young, Danish Muslim politician of Palestinian parentage who lived in the United Arab Emirates before moving to Denmark at age 6. Covering oneself, she says, "makes women more equal because there is less focus on her body.... When you watch an ad on television, it is always women in bikinis selling the car."

A social worker, local council member representing a left-wing party and former television-show host, Abdol-Hamid is a controversial figure in Denmark. She wears a hijab and refuses to shake hands with men. "I prefer to put my hand on my heart," she explains. "That's just my way of greeting them. It's not that shaking hands is un-Islamic."

She has her own view of Islam's emphasis on female submission. "If women want to obey their husbands, it's up to them." However, "I could not live the Arab lifestyle, where the men beat the women. That's not Islam — it's Arab." In a global study of women's rights, Arab states accounted for 10 of the 19 countries with the lowest ranking for women's equality.[5]

Many fundamentalist Muslims say the freedoms advocated by secular women's-rights advocates disrupt the complementary nature of male and female roles that have been the basis of social unity since the rise of Islam. A Palestinian Islamic jihadist, known only as Mujahida, said women should "return to their natural and [Koran-based] functions as child-bearers, home-keepers and educators of the next generation." She rejects women's-rights advocates who urge women to take their abusive husbands to secular courts.

Muslim "family mediators," she said, were best placed to resolve such disputes.[6]

According to the Washington-based Pew Research Center, more than a third of Jordanians and Egyptians oppose allowing women to choose whether or not to veil, although the percentage is falling.[7] Also on the decline: the number of those who support restrictions prohibiting men and women from working in the same workplace.[8] In Saudi Arabia, such restrictions limit womens' employment, because employers must provide separate offices for women.[9]

Ayaan Hirsi Ali (right), a Somali-born former member of the Dutch parliament, has been threatened with death for her outspoken criticism of Islam's treatment of women in Islam. But Danish Muslim politician and social worker Asmaa Abdol-Hamid (left) attributes repressive gender-based policies in Muslim countries to local culture, not the Koran.

In Iran, an Islamic theocracy since 1979, a debate is raging over whether to allow women to inherit real estate, notes Shireen Hunter, an Iranian-born author and visiting scholar at Georgetown University in Washington. "Reformers are also trying to have the age of [marriage] consent raised from 9 to 16 years. This will take time," she says, because "trying to blend Islam and modernity is hard. It is easier to just say, 'Let's go back to fundamentalism.' "

Yet Abdol-Hamid argues that "fundamentalism does not have to be a bad thing. In Islam, going back to the Koran and Hadith would be good."

However, Pew found considerable support in Muslim nations for restricting a woman's right to choose her husband. For example, 55 percent of Pakistanis felt the family, not the woman, should decide.[10]

In Nigeria, Islamic fundamentalism has hurt women's rights, according to Nigerian activist Husseini Abdu. "Although it is difficult separating the Hausa [Nigerian tribe] and Islam patriarchal structure, the reintroduction or politicization of sharia [Islamic law] in northern Nigeria has contributed in reinforcing traditional, religious and cultural prejudices against women," Abdu says.[11] This includes, among other things, the absence of women in the judiciary, discrimination in the standards of evidence in court cases (especially involving adultery) and restrictions in the freedom of association.[12]

Christian countries are not immune from criticism for limiting women's rights. Human Rights Watch found that in Argentina the Catholic Church has had a hand in establishing government policies that restrict women's access to modern contraception, sex education and abortion.[13] And fundamentalist Christian groups have played a significant role in restricting sex education and the availability of birth control and abortion services in the United States.

But while Islamic countries are often criticized for their treatment of women, the world's two most populous Muslim nations, Pakistan and Indonesia, have both elected female leaders in the past — the late Benazir Bhutto in Pakistan and Megawati Sukarnoputri in Indonesia. The world's largest Christian country, the United States, has never had a female president.

Does Hirsi Ali see anything positive about a woman's life in Islamic societies? "I have never seen Muslim women doubt their femininity or sensuality," she says. "Western women question this more. They are less secure. They are always thinking, 'Am I really equal?' "

[1] Ahmed Zaki Yamani, "The Political Competence of Women in Islamic Law," pp. 170-177, in John J. Donohue and John L. Esposito, *Islam in Transition: Muslim Perspectives* (2007).

[2] "Perpetual Minors — Human Rights Abuses Stemming from Male Guardianship and Sex Segregation in Saudi Arabia," Human Rights Watch, April 19, 2008, p. 2, www.hrw.org/en/node/62251/section/1.

[3] *Ibid.*

[4] Karen Foerstel, "Women's Rights," *CQ Global Researcher*, May 2008, p. 118.

[5] *Ibid.*

[6] Loren D. Lybarger, *Identity and Religion in Palestine: The Struggle between Islamism and Secularism in the Occupied Territories* (2007), p. 105.

[7] In Jordan, 37 percent of respondents opposed women being allowed to choose whether to veil, compared to 33 percent in Egypt.

[8] The Pew Global Attitudes Project, "World Publics Welcome Global Trade — But Not Immigration," Pew Research Center, Oct. 4, 2007, p. 51, http://pewglobal.org/reports/pdf/258.pdf.

[9] "Perpetual Minors — Human Rights Abuses Stemming from Male Guardianship and Sex Segregation in Saudi Arabia," *op. cit.*, p. 3.

[10] Pew, *op. cit.*, p. 50.

[11] Carina Tertsakian, "Political Shari'a? Human Rights and Islamic Law in Northern Nigeria," Human Rights Watch, Sept. 21, 2004, p. 63, www.hrw.org/en/reports/2004/09/21/political-shari.

[12] *Ibid.*

[13] See Marianne Mollmann, "Decisions Denied: Women's Access to Contraceptives and Abortion in Argentina," Human Rights Watch, June 14, 2005, www.hrw.org/en/node/11694/section/1.

AFP/Getty Images/Kristian Brasen/Martin Bureau

Haredim are represented by several different political parties in Israel — each with a distinct ideology.

A newer strain of Jewish fundamentalism, the Gush Eminum movement, grew out of the 1967 Israeli-Arab War, in which Israel captured large swathes of Syrian, Egyptian and Jordanian territory. Founded by Rabbi Zvi Yehuda Kook, it believes Israel's victory in that war was a sign that God wanted Jews to settle the captured territories. Israeli authorities initially opposed such actions but did a U-turn in 1977, setting up settlements to create a buffer to protect Israel from hostile Arab neighbors. There now are some 500,000 settlers, and they have become a security headache for the Israeli government, which protects them from attacks from Palestinians who believe they have stolen their land.[80]

Meanwhile the Chabad movement — founded in the 18th century in Lubavitch, Russia, by Rabbi Schoeur Zalman — operates outside of Israel.[81] "They are very religious communities that have become missionaries, even though Jews are not supposed to convert non-Jews, and conversion is very difficult and mostly refused," says Anne Eckstein, a Belgian Jewish journalist. "They are especially active in ex-Soviet countries where the Holocaust and Soviet power wiped out the Jewish community or reduced it to a bare minimum."

Fundamentalism in India

Unlike Christianity, Islam and Judaism, which are monotheistic, Hinduism has thousands of deities representing an absolute power. In addition, it is based not on a single text but the belief that the universe is impersonal and dominated by cosmic energy.[82] Hindu fundamentalism emerged in the early 20th century, partly in reaction to proselytizing by Muslim and Christian missionaries. Some Hindus came to believe that their country needed to be made more Hindu, and that only Hindus could be loyal Indians.

Indian politician Vinayak Damodar Savarkar wrote the book *Hindutva*, the philosophical basis for Hindu fundamentalism.[83] Its cultural pillar is an organization called Vishva Hindu Parishad, founded in 1964, which has had a political wing since the 1980 establishment of the Bharatiya Janata Party, whose leader, Atal Bihari Vajpayee, was prime minister from 1998-2004.

The assertion of Hindu religious identity provoked unease among some of India's 20 million Sikhs, who worship one God and revere the *Adi Granth*, their holy book.[84] Indian Prime Minister Indira Gandhi was murdered in 1984 by two of her Sikh bodyguards in revenge for sending troops to storm the Sikhs' holiest shrine, the Golden Temple, which had been occupied by militant Sikh separatists. Hundreds of people were killed in the botched government operation.[85]

CURRENT SITUATION

Political Battles

Christian conservatives remain a potent force in American political life, even though they appear to have lost some of their political clout with the election of a liberal, pro-choice president and a decidedly more liberal Congress.

In the 2008 U.S. presidential election, evangelicals were briefly buoyed by the nomination of a Christian conservative, Alaska Gov. Sarah Palin, as the Republican vice presidential candidate. But their hopes of having another evangelical in high office were dashed when Palin and her running mate, Sen. John McCain, R-Ariz., were comfortably beaten by their Democratic rivals in November.

Palin was raised as a Pentecostal and regularly attended the Assemblies of God church in Wasilla, Alaska. In a Republican National Convention speech, she stressed the need to govern with a "servant's heart" — which in the evangelical world means Christian humility.[86]

But as details of her religious and political views were revealed, secular Americans began to question her candidacy. Video footage surfaced of her being blessed by a Kenyan pastor in 2005 who prayed for her to be protected from "every form of witchcraft" and for God to "bring finances her way" and to "use her to turn this nation the other way around."[87] Palin was also videotaped speaking at the same church in June 2008, calling a $30 billion gas pipeline project in Alaska "God's will" and the war in Iraq "a task that is from God."[88]

While Palin ultimately may have hurt the Republican ticket more than helping, the passage on Election Day of referenda banning gay marriage in several states — including California — shows that Christian conservatism remains a significant force. And across the American South and heartland, religious conservatives have pressured state and local governments to pass a variety of "family" and faith-based measures, ranging from

Is Islamic fundamentalism more dangerous than Christian fundamentalism?

YES

Maajid Nawaz
Director, Quilliam Foundation, London, England

Written for *CQ Global Researcher,* February 2009

While not all Muslim fundamentalists are a threat, certain strands of Muslim fundamentalism are more dangerous than Christian fundamentalism. This is simply a truth we must face up to as Muslims. The first stage of healing is to accept and recognize the sickness within. Until such recognition comes, we are lost.

But if Muslim fundamentalism is only a problem in certain contexts, this is not true of political Islam, or Islamism. Often confused with fundamentalism, political Islamism is a modernist project to politicize religion, rooted in the totalitarian political climate of post-World War I Egypt. But this ideology didn't restrict itself to political goals. Instead, its adherents aspired to create a modern, totalitarian state that was illiberal but not necessarily fundamentalist.

In the 1960s, the Muslim Brotherhood — Egypt's largest Islamist group — failed to impose their non-fundamentalist brand of Islam in Egypt. Instead, they fled to religiously ultraconservative Saudi Arabia. Here they allied with reactionary fundamentalists. It is from this mix of modernist Islamism and fundamentalism that al Qaeda and jihadist terrorism emerged. It was in Saudi Arabia that Osama bin Laden was taught by Muslim Brotherhood exiles. It was from Saudi Arabia that streams of Muslim fundamentalists traveled to Afghanistan and Pakistan where they fell under the spell of the Egyptian Islamist Abdullah Azzam, another inspiration for bin Laden. The root of the present terrorist danger is the alliance between modernist political Islamists and Muslim fundamentalists.

This global jihadist terrorism — modern in its political ideals and tactics yet medieval in both its religious jurisprudence and justification for violence — is more dangerous than Christian fundamentalism. I believe that such terrorism, far from representing the fundamentals of Islam, is actually un-Islamic. However, a Christian may similarly argue that attacking abortion clinics is un-Christian. We both need to acknowledge the role that religion plays in motivating such individuals.

So, having recognized this problem, how can Muslims tackle it? It is not enough for Muslims to merely take a stand against terrorism and the killing of innocent civilians. This is the very least that should be expected of any decent human being. Muslims must also challenge both conservative fundamentalism and the modern Islamist ideology behind jihadist terrorism. Islamism is to blame, alongside Western support for dictatorships, for the situation we face today.

NO

Radwan Masmoudi
President, Center for the Study of Islam and Democracy, Washington, D.C.

Written for *CQ Global Researcher,* February 2009

The term "fundamentalism" can be misleading, because the overwhelming majority of Muslims believe the Koran is the literal word of God and a guide for the individual, the family and society to follow on everything social, political and economic. In a recent Gallup Poll, more than 75 percent of Muslims — from Morocco to Indonesia — said they believe Islamic laws should be either the only source or one of the main sources of laws in their countries. Under a U.S. definition of "fundamentalism," these people would all be considered "fundamentalists."

However, the overwhelming majority of Muslims are peaceful and reject violence and extremism. In the same poll, more than 85 percent of Muslims surveyed said they believe democracy is the best form of government. Thus, they are not interested in imposing their views on others but wish to live according to the teachings of their religion while respecting people of other religions or opinions. Democracy and respect for human rights — including minority rights and women's rights — are essential in any society that respects and practices Islamic values.

It would be a terrible mistake to consider all fundamentalist Muslims a threat to the United States or to mankind. Radical and violent Muslim extremist groups such as al Qaeda and the Taliban represent a tiny minority of all Muslims and a fringe minority of religious (or fundamentalist) Muslims. These extremist groups are a threat both to their own societies and to the West. But they do not represent the majority opinion among religious-based groups that are struggling to build more Islamic societies through peaceful means.

Many Christian fundamentalist groups have resorted to violence, specifically attacks against abortion clinics in the United States. In addition, prominent Christian fundamentalist leaders, such as John Hagee, Pat Robertson and others say Islam is the enemy and have called for the United States to invade Muslim countries like Iraq, Afghanistan and even Iran. These wars have cost the lives of more than 1 million innocent people in these countries and could still cause further deaths and destruction around the world. The devout of all faiths should condemn the killing of innocents and the self-serving labeling of any religion as the "enemy" against which war should be waged. Surely, one — whether Muslim or Christian — can be extremely devout and religious without calling for violence or hoping for Armageddon.

AFP/Getty Images/Yehuda Raizner

AFP/Getty Images/Gali Tibbon

Jewish Settlements Stir Outrage and Support

Left-wing Israelis criticize Israel last December for allowing fundamentalist Jews to build settlements in the Palestinian territories (top). Evangelicals from the U.S.-based Christians United for Israel movement (bottom) support the settlements during a rally in Jerusalem last April. Many analysts say pressure from American fundamentalist Christians led former President George W. Bush, a born-again Christian, to offer unqualified support for Israel and to invade Iraq — policies that have exacerbated U.S.-Muslim relations.

restrictions on access to birth control and abortion to requirements that "intelligent design" be taught in place of or alongside evolution in schools. The laws have triggered ire — and a slew of lawsuits — on the part of groups intent on retaining the Constitution's separation of church and state.[89]

Meanwhile, thousands of conservative Episcopalians in the United States have abandoned their church because of the hierarchy's tolerance of homosexuality and are teaming up with Anglican Protestants in Africa who share their conservative views.[90]

In Latin America, evangelical television preachers are using their fame to launch themselves into politics, notes Dennis Smith, a U.S.-born Presbyterian mission worker who has lived in Guatemala since 1977. He says that in Brazil, Pentecostal preacher Edir Macedo cut a deal with President Luiz Inacio Lula de Silva in which Macedo got to hand-pick the country's vice president. In Guatemala Harold Caballeros, a Pentecostal who preaches that the Mayan Indians there have made a pact with the devil by clinging to their traditional beliefs, is trying to become president, Smith adds.

In Africa, the Somali parliament on Jan. 31 elected a moderate Islamist cleric, Sheik Sharif Ahmed, as the country's new president. The election occurred just as the hard-line Islamist al-Shabaab militia took control of the central Somali town of Baidoa and began imposing its harsh brand of Islamic law there.[91]

Rising Violence

Attacks on Christian minorities in Iraq and India — and efforts to forcibly convert them — have escalated in recent months.

In November militants said to be from the Pakistan-based Lashkar-e-Taiba carried out a meticulously planned attack in Mumbai, India, killing 164 people in a shooting spree that targeted hotels frequented by Western tourists.[92] Ex-Islamist Nawaz says of the group: "I know them well. They want to reconquer India. They see it as being under Hindu occupation now because it was once ruled by Muslim emperors of Turko-Mongol descent. They use the territorial dispute between India and Pakistan over the sovereignty of Kashmir as a pretext for pursuing their global jihad agenda."

Lisa Curtis, a research fellow for South Asia at the Heritage Foundation in Washington, believes that Pakistan is playing a sinister role here. "The Pakistan military's years of support for jihadist groups fighting in Afghanistan and India," she says, is "intensifying linkages between Pakistani homegrown terrorists and al Qaeda."

India's suspicion that forces within the Pakistani government have given Lashkar-e-Taiba a free rein is further straining an already tense relationship between the two nations.

The Lashkar attackers also killed two young Jewish missionaries, Rabbi Gavriel Holtzberg and his wife Rivkah, in an assault on the Chabad center in Mumbai, where they had been based since 2003. While some accuse the Chabad of proselytizing, Rabbi Avi Tawil, who studied with U.S.-born Gavriel Holtzberg for two years in Argentina, insists, "He did not force anyone to accept his philosophy. He was doing social work — working with prisoners for example."

But the Mumbai attacks were not the only violence perpetrated by religious extremists in India last year. Between August and December, members of the paramilitary, right-wing Hindu group Bajrang Dal — using the rallying cry "kill Christians and destroy their institutions" — murdered dozens of Christians, including missionaries and priests, burned 3,000 homes and destroyed more than 130 churches in Orissa state.[93] The attackers were angered at proselytizing by Pentecostal missionaries in the region and tried to force Christians to convert back to Hinduism.[94]

Martha Nussbaum, a professor of law and ethics at the University of Chicago and author of the recent book *The Clash Within: Democracy, Religious Violence and India's Future*, writes that no one should be surprised right-wing Hindus "have embraced ethno-religious cleansing." Since the 1930s, "their movement has insisted that India is for Hindus, and that both Muslims and Christians are foreigners who should have second-class status in the nation."[95]

India's bloodiest religiously based violence in recent years was the slaughter of up to 2,000 Muslim civilians by Hindu mobs in Gujarat state in 2002.[96] A Bajrang Dal leader boasted: "There was this pregnant woman, I slit her open. . . . They shouldn't even be allowed to breed. . . . Whoever they are, women, children, whoever . . . thrash them, slash them, burn the bastards. . . . The idea is, don't keep them alive at all; after that, everything is ours."[97]

In Iraq last fall, in the northern city of Mosul, some 400 Christian families were forced to flee their homes after attacks by Sunni Muslim extremists.[98]

In Nigeria, sectarian violence between Christians and Muslims in the city of Jos spiked again in late November, leaving at least 300 dead in the worst clashes since 2004, when 700 people died. Religious violence in Nigeria tends to break out in the "middle belt" between the Muslim north and the predominantly Christian south.[99]

Then in December Israel launched a massive offensive against the Islamist Hamas government in the Gaza Strip, in response to Hamas' continuous rocket attacks into Israel; at least 1,300 Palestinians died during the 22-day assault. An uneasy truce now exists, but Hamas remains defiant, refusing to accept Israel's right to exist and vowing to fight for the creation of an Islamic Palestinian state in its place.[100]

While most commentators focus on the political dimension of the conflict, Belgian Jewish journalist Anne Eckstein is as concerned about Hamas' religious extremism. "I see nothing in them apart from hatred and death to all who are not Muslims. . . . Jews first but then Christians and everybody else. And those who believe that this is not a war of civilization are very mistaken."

Also in December, troops from, Uganda, southern Sudan and the Democratic Republic of Congo launched a joint offensive to catch Lord's Resistance Army (LRA) leader Kony.[101] The LRA retaliated, massacring hundreds. Kenya-based evangelical Professor Nkansah insists the LRA is "not really religious — no one has ever seen them praying. They are just playing to the Christian communities in Uganda. If they were true Christians, they would not be destroying human life like they are."

Even in areas where religious violence has not broken out, a certain fundamentalist-secular tension exists. In the United Kingdom, for example, a debate has broken out over whether Muslim communities should be allowed to handle family matters — such as divorce and domestic violence cases — in Muslim courts that apply Islamic law. These increasingly common tribunals, despite having no standing under British law, have "become magnets for Muslim women seeking to escape loveless marriages."[102] In Africa, the Tanzanian parliament is having a similar debate, with proponents noting that Kenya, Rwanda and Uganda have had such courts for decades.[103]

In Israel, the majority-secular Jewish population has begun to resent ultra-Orthodox Jewish men who subsist on welfare while immersing themselves in perpetual study of the holy texts. "They claim this is what Jews did in the past, but this is nonsense," says Jerusalem-based journalist Gorenberg, who notes that ultra-Orthodox wives often work outside the home in order to support their very large families. The Haredim are trying to restore ancient Judaism by weaving priestly garments in the traditional way, producing a red heifer using genetic engineering and raising boys in a special compound kept ritually pure for 13 years, says Gorenberg, a fierce critic of fundamentalist Jews.[104]

Many secular Israelis also resent the religious Jews that have settled in the Palestinian territories, arguing they make Muslims hate Israel even more and thus threaten Israel's very security.

OUTLOOK

More of the Same?

Al Qaeda's Egyptian-born chief strategist, Ayman Al-Zawihiri, is very clear about his goal. "The victory of Islam will never take place until a Muslim state is established in the heart of the Islamic world, specifically in the Levant [Eastern Mediterranean], Egypt and the neighboring states of the [Arabian] Peninsula and Iraq."[105]

Former-Islamist Nawaz says such a state would not, as fundamentalists claim, be a return to the past but a modernist creation, having more in common with the totalitarian regimes of 20th-century Europe than with the tolerant Islamic caliphates in the Middle Ages. He thinks Islamists have the greatest chance of seizing power in Egypt and Uzbekistan.

Given the Islamization that she has observed on numerous visits to Uzbekistan, Martha Brill Olcott, a senior associate at the Carnegie Endowment for International Peace in Washington, predicts the country will not remain secular. Because the Muslims there are Sunni, she thinks they will follow an Egyptian or Pakistani model of government.

Georgetown Professor Dallal predicts Iran will remain the world's only theocracy. "I do not think the Iranian model will be replicated," he says. "The religious elite is more institutionalized and entrenched there than elsewhere."

And although young Iranians are more secular than their parents and have been disenchanted with the religious rulers, "We should not assume this is a deep-rooted trend," warns Iranian-born author Hunter. "Look at Arab countries: Forty years ago we thought they were going secular, but not now."

As for Islamist militancy, the signs are mixed. While a Pew survey showed a drop in support for global jihad among Muslims overall, it also found that young Muslims in the United States were more likely to support radical Islam than their parents. Fifteen percent of 18-29-year-olds thought suicide bombing could be justified compared to just 6 percent of those over 30.[106]

And even if, as some analysts suggest, al Qaeda is faltering, other Islamist groups may thrive, such as Hezbollah in Lebanon, Hamas in Gaza and Pakistan's Lashkar-e-Taiba. They attract popular support because they also provide social services, unlike al Qaeda, whose bloody campaigns have alienated most Muslims.[107]

The Israel-Palestine conflict, intractable as ever, will continue to be grist for the Islamist mill. Bin Laden has urged Muslims to "kill the Americans and their allies [and] to liberate the Al-Aqsa Mosque," which is located on the Temple Mount in Jerusalem that Israel has controlled since 1967.[108]

In the Palestinian territories, "Islamist symbols, discourses and practices have become widely disseminated across the factional spectrum," according to Ohio State's Lybarger, but whether it continues depends on the actions of Israel, the United States and other Arab states toward Palestine, he says.[109] Many observers hope President Obama and his newly-appointed Middle East envoy George Mitchell will be able to broker a peace deal, given Obama's aggressive outreach to the Muslim world.

In the United States, the Christian right is likely to remain strong, even as Obama moves to overhaul Bush's faith-based initiatives. Secularists may ask Obama to prohibit groups receiving government funds from discriminating in hiring based on religious beliefs. "Hiring based on religious affiliation is justified," says Stanley Carlson-Thies, director of the Center for Public Justice in Washington, D.C. "Would you ask a senator not to ask about political ideology when selecting staff? A ban would [be] a sweeping change."[110]

Looking farther afield, Baptist minister Land says "by 2025 the majority of Christians . . . will be African, Latin American and Asian. That is where evangelical Christianity is growing fastest." The fastest-growing Christian denominations are in Nigeria, Sudan, Angola, South Africa, India, China and the Philippines, according to the World Christian Database.[111]

But Kenya's Nkansah doubts that Christian-based political parties will emerge in sub-Saharan Africa. "In North Africa almost everyone is Muslim, so it is easier to have Islamic parties. But here, there is more of a mix, and politicians do not want to create unnecessary tensions."

In Guatemala, American Presbyterian missionary Smith says, "Since neither modernity nor democracy has been able to bring security, the rule of law, social tolerance or broad-based economic development" evangelical television preachers will "continue to have great power for the foreseeable future."

Meanwhile, a glimpse of Asia's future might be found in South Korea. "As dusk turns to dark in this capital city," journalist Mosettig wrote, "the skyline glitters with more than the urban lights of office towers and apartment blocks. From the hills that define Seoul's topography and neighborhoods, it is easy to spot lighted electric crosses. They are among the most visible reminders of just how deeply Christianity shapes South Korea."[112]

NOTES

1. Richard A. Oppel Jr. and Pir Zubair Shah, "In Pakistan, Radio Amplifies Terror of Taliban," *The New York Times*, Jan. 24, 2009, www.nytimes.com/2009/01/25/world/asia/25swat.html?_r=1&scp=1&sq=Taliban%20Pakistan&st=cse.

2. "The U.S. Religious Landscape Survey," Pew Forum on Religion and Public Life, Feb. 25, 2008, p. 170, http://religions.pewforum.org.

3. Michelle Goldberg, *Kingdom Coming: The Rise of Christian Nationalism* (2007), p. 7.

4. *Ibid.*, p. 8.

5. Dominionism, Goldberg notes, is derived from a theocratic sect called Christian Reconstructionism, which advocates replacing American civil law with Old Testament biblical law.

6. See World Evangelical Alliance Web site, www.worldevangelicals.org. For background, see David Masci, "Evangelical Christians," *CQ Researcher*, Sept. 14, 2001, pp. 713-736.

7. Quoted in Eliza Griswold, "God's Country," *The Atlantic*, March 2008, www.theatlantic.com/doc/200803/nigeria.

8. Michael Mossetig, "Among Sea of Glittery Crosses, Christianity Makes Its Mark in South Korea," PBS, Nov. 5, 2007, www.pbs.org/newshour/indepth_coverage/asia/koreas/2007/report_11-05.html. For background, see Alan Greenblatt and Tracey Powell,

"Rise of Megachurches," *CQ Researcher*, Sept. 21, 2007, pp. 769-792.

9. Presentation by Wang Zuoan, China's deputy administrator of religious affairs, Sept. 11, 2008, at the Brookings Institution, Washington, D.C.

10. Estimates provided by Samuel Heilman, Sociology Professor and expert on Jewish fundamentalism at City University of New York.

11. "Christians Attacked in Two States of India" World Evangelical Alliance Web site, Dec. 15, 2008, www.worldevangelicals.org/news/view.htm?id=2277.

12. Loren D. Lybarger, *Identity and Religion in Palestine: The Struggle between Islamism and Secularism in the Occupied Territories* (2007), p. 73.

13. See National Counter Terrorism Center's Worldwide Incidents Tracking System, http://wits.nctc.gov.

14. The Shia, who make up 15 percent of the world's 1.4 billion Muslims, believe only the prophet Mohammad's family and descendants should serve as Muslim leaders (imams). Sunnis — who make up the other 85 percent — believe any Muslim can be an imam. Iran is the world's most Shia-dominated country, while there are also significant Shia communities in Iraq, Turkey, Lebanon, Syria, Kuwait, Bahrain, Saudi Arabia, Yemen, Pakistan and Azerbaijan.

15. Lybarger, *op. cit.*

16. "Sharia stoning for Nigeria man," BBC News, May 17, 2007, http://news.bbc.co.uk/2/hi/africa/6666673.stm.

17. For background, see John Felton, "Child Soldiers," *CQ Global Researcher*, July, 2008.

18. Scott Shane, "Global Forecast by American Intelligence Expects Al Qaeda's Appeal to Falter," *The New York Times*, Nov. 20, 2008, www.nytimes.com/2008/11/21/world/21intel.html?_r=1&emc=tnt&tntemail0=y.

19. "Country Reports on Terrorism," Office of the Coordinator for Counterterrorism, U.S. Department of State, April 2008, www.state.gov/documents/organization/105904.pdf.

20. Martin Marty and R. Scott Appleby, eds., *Fundamentalisms Comprehended* (The Fundamentalism Project), 2004, University of Chicago Press.

21. Source: Talk by Egyptian scholar and human rights activist Saad Eddin Ibrahim, at Woodrow Wilson International Center for Scholars, Washington, D.C., Sept. 8, 2008.

22. For background, see Brian Beary, "Future of Turkey," *CQ Global Researcher*, December 2007.

23. Raja Kamal, "Israel's fundamentalist Jews are multiplying," *The Japan Times*, Aug. 21, 2008, http://search.japantimes.co.jp/cgi-bin/eo20080821a1.html.

24. *Ibid.*

25. Mike Madden, "Sundown on Colorado fundamentalists," *Salon.com*, Nov. 2, 2008, www.salon.com/news/feature/2008/11/03/newlifechurch/index.html?source=rss&aim=/news/feature.

26. Susan Jacoby, "Religion remains fundamental to US politics," *The Times* (London), Oct. 31, 2008, www.timesonline.co.uk/tol/comment/columnists/guest_contributors/article5050685.ece.

27. "Human Security Brief 2007," Human Security Report Project, Simon Fraser University, Canada, May 21, 2008, www.humansecuritybrief.info.

28. "Unfavorable views of Jews and Muslims on the Increase in Europe," Pew Research Center, Sept. 17, 2008, p. 4, http://pewglobal.org/reports/pdf/262.pdf.

29. *Ibid.*

30. Andrew MacIntyre and Douglas E. Ramage, "Seeing Indonesia as a normal country: Implications for Australia," Australian Strategic Policy Institute, May 2008, www.aspi.org.au/publications/publication_details.aspx?ContentID=169&pubtype=5.

31. Michael Sullivan, "Megachurch Symbolizes Indonesia's Tolerance," National Public Radio, Oct. 19, 2008, www.npr.org/templates/story/story.php?storyId=95847081.

32. Comments from Pew Forum on Religion and Public Life discussion, "Between Relativism and Fundamentalism: Is There a Middle Ground?" March 4, 2008, Washington, D.C., http://pewforum.org/events/?EventID=172.

33. Sarah Glazer, "Radical Islam in Europe," *CQ Global Researcher*, November 2007.

34. Sayyid Qutb, *Milestones*, SIME (Studies in Islam and the Middle East) *Journal*, 2005, p. 125, http://majalla.org/books/2005/qutb-nilestone.pdf.

35. Lybarger, *op. cit.*

36. See Goldberg, *op. cit.*, p. 8.

37. *Ibid.*, p. 208.

38. "Human Security Brief 2007," *op. cit.*, p. 19.

39. Osama Bin Laden, "Text of Fatwa Urging Jihad Against Americans," Feb. 23, 1998, in John J. Donohue and John L. Esposito, *Islam in Transition: Muslim Perspectives* (2007), pp. 430-432.

40. "Tanzania: Muslim paper says war on terror guise to fight Islam," BBC Worldwide Monitoring, Aug. 24, 2008 (translation from Swahili of article in Tanzanian weekly Islamic newspaper *An-Nuur*, Aug. 15, 2008).

41. Barbara Crossette, "The World: (Mid) East Meets (Far) East; A Challenge to Asia's Own Style of Islam," *The New York Times*, Dec. 30, 2001.

42. Pew Global Attitudes Project, "Islamic Extremism: Common Concern for Muslim and Western Publics," July 14, 2005, p. 25, http://pewglobal.org/reports/pdf/248.pdf.

43. Griswold, *op. cit.*

44. Zaki Chehab, *Inside Hamas — The Untold Story of the Militant Islamic Movement* (2007), p. 104.

45. Gabriel Almond, Scott Appleby and Emmanuel Sivan, *Strong Religion: The Rise of Fundamentalisms Around the World* (The Fundamentalism Project), The University of Chicago Press, 2003, p. 110.

46. Rachid Ghannouchi, "The Participation of Islamists in a Non-Islamic Government," in Donohue and Esposito, *op. cit.*, pp. 271-278.

47. Jason Burke, "Don't believe myths about sharia law," *The Guardian* (United Kingdom), Feb. 10, 2008, www.guardian.co.uk/world/2008/feb/10/religion.law1. For background, see Robert Kiener, "Crisis in Pakistan" *CQ Global Researcher*, December 2008, pp. 321-348.

48. Oppel and Shah, *op. cit.*

49. Brenda E. Brasher, *Encyclopedia of Fundamentalism* (2001), p. 397.

50. *Ibid.*, pp. 202-204.

51. *Ibid.*, pp. 465-467.

52. *Ibid.*, p. 186.

53. For background, see the following *CQ Researchers*: Kenneth Jost, "Religion and Politics," Oct. 14, 1994,

pp. 889-912; and David Masci, "Religion and Politics," July 30, 2004, pp. 637-660.

54. For background, see Rachel S. Cox, "Home Schooling Debate," *CQ Researcher*, Jan. 17, 2003, pp. 25-48.

55. David Holthouse, "Casting Stones: An Army of radical Christian Reconstructionists is preparing a campaign to convert conservative fundamentalist churches," Southern Law Poverty Center, winter 2005, www.splcenter.org/intel/intelreport/article.jsp?aid=591.

56. Brasher, *op. cit.*, pp. 407-409.

57. *Ibid.*, p. 86.

58. *Ibid.*

59. Adrian Wooldridge, "The Theocons: Secular America Under Siege," *International Herald Tribune*, Sept. 26, 2006, www.iht.com/articles/2006/09/25/opinion/booktue.php.

60. See Paul Harris, "Bush says God chose him to lead his nation," *The Guardian*, Nov. 2, 2003, www.guardian.co.uk/world/2003/nov/02/usa.religion; and Melissa Rogers and E. J. Dionne Jr., "Serving People in Need, Safeguarding Religious Freedom: Recommendations for the New Administration on Partnerships with Faith-Based Organizations," The Brookings Institution, December 2008, www.brookings.edu/papers/2008/12_religion_dionne.aspx. For background, see Sarah Glazer, "Faith-based Initiatives," *CQ Researcher*, May 4, 2001, pp. 377-400.

61. James Carroll, "Religious comfort for bin Laden," *The Boston Globe*, Sept. 15, 2008, www.boston.com/news/nation/articles/2008/09/15/religious_comfort_for_bin_laden.

62. For background, see Dan Eggen and Paul Kane, "Goodling Says She 'Crossed the Line'; Ex-Justice Aide Criticizes Gonzales While Admitting to Basing Hires on Politics," *The Washington Post*, May 24, 2007, p. A1.

63. Brasher, *op. cit.*, p. 154.

64. Almond, Appleby and Sivan, *op. cit.*, p. 171.

65. Cedric Mayson, "Religious Fundamentalism in South Africa," African National Congress Commission for Religious Affairs, January 2007, http://thebrenthurstfoundation.co.za/Files/terror_talks/Religious%20Fundamentalism%20in%20SA.pdf.

66. Rob Crilly, "Lord's Resistance Army uses truce to rearm and spread its gospel of fear," *The Times* (London), Dec. 16, 2008, www.timesonline.co.uk/tol/news/world/africa/article5348890.ece.

67. *Ibid.*

68. Brasher, *op. cit.*, p. 37.

69. For background, see Peter Katel, "Global Jihad," *CQ Researcher*, Oct. 14, 2005, pp. 857-880.

70. Almond, Appleby and Sivan, *op. cit.*, pp. 177-79.

71. Brasher, *op. cit.*, p. 37.

72. "Human Security Brief 2007," *op. cit.*

73. For background, see Glazer, "Radical Islam in Europe," *op. cit.*

74. "World Christian Database," Center for the Study of Global Christianity, Gordon-Conwell Theological Seminary, www.worldchristiandatabase.org/wcd/home.asp.

75. "Muslim Americans: Middle Class and Mostly Mainstream," Pew Forum on Religion and Public Life, May 22, 2007, p. 4, http://pewforum.org/surveys/muslim-american.

76. Chehab, *op. cit.*, pp. 134-150.

77. Brasher, *op. cit.*, p. 255.

78. "World Christian Database," *op. cit.*

79. Brasher, *op. cit.*, p. 255.

80. *Ibid.*, p. 204.

81. See American Friends of Lubavitch Washington, D.C., www.afldc.org.

82. Brasher, *op. cit.*, p. 222.

83. Almond, Appleby and Sivan, *op. cit.*, pp. 136-139.

84. *Ibid.*, pp. 157-159.

85. *Ibid.*

86. John L. Allen Jr., "McCain's choice a nod not only to women, but post-denominationalists," *National Catholic Reporter*, Aug. 30, 2008, http://ncrcafe.org/node/2073.

87. Garance Burke, "Palin once blessed to be free from witchcraft," The Associated Press, Sept. 25, 2008, http://abcnews.go.com/Politics/wireStory?id=5881256. Video footage at www.youtube.com/watch?v=QIOD5X68lIs.

88. Alexander Schwabe, "Sarah Palin's Religion: God and the Vice-Presidential Candidate," *Spiegel* online, Sept. 10, 2008, www.spiegel.de/international/world/0,1518,577440,00.html. Video footage at www.youtube.com/watch?v=QG1vPYbRB7k.

89. For background see the following *CQ Researchers*: Marcia Clemmitt, "Intelligent Design," July 29, 2005, pp. 637-660; Kenneth Jost and Kathy Koch, "Abortion Showdowns," Sept. 22, 2006, pp. 769-792; Kenneth Jost, "Abortion Debates," March 21, 2003, pp. 249-272; and Marcia Clemmitt, "Birth-control Debate," June 24, 2005, pp. 565-588.

90. See Karla Adam, "Gay Bishop Dispute Dominates Conference; Anglican Event Ends With Leader's Plea," *The Washington Post*, Aug. 4, 2008, p. A8.

91. Jeffrey Gettleman and Mohammed Ibrahim, "Somalis cheer the selection of a moderate Islamist cleric as President," *The New York Times*, Feb. 1, 2009, www.nytimes.com/2009/02/01/world/africa/01somalia.html.

92. Ramola Talwar Badam, "Official: India received intel on Mumbai attacks," The Associated Press, *Denver Post*, Dec. 1, 2008, www.denverpost.com/business/ci_11111305.

93. Somini Sengupta, "Hindu Threat to Christians: Convert or Flee," *The New York Times*, Oct. 12, 2008, www.nytimes.com/2008/10/13/world/asia/13india.html?pagewanted=1&_r=1&sq=Christianspercent20India&st=cse&scp=1.

94. "Indian Christians Petition PM for Peace in Orissa at Christmas," World Evangelical Alliance Web site, Dec. 14, 2008, www.worldevangelicals.org/news/view.htm?id=2276.

95. Martha Nussbaum, "Terrorism in India has many faces," *Los Angeles Times*, Nov. 30, 2008, p. A35.

96. For background, see David Masci, "Emerging India," *CQ Researcher*, April 19, 2002, pp. 329-360.

97. Quoted in Nussbaum, *op. cit.*

98. "Iraq: Christians trickling back to their homes in Mosul," IRIN (humanitarian news and analysis service of the U.N. Office for the Coordination of Humanitarian Affairs), Nov. 6, 2008, www.irinnews.org/Report.aspx?ReportId=81317.

99. Ahmed Saka, "Death toll over 300 in Nigerian sectarian violence, The Associated Press, Nov. 29, 2008," www.denverpost.com/breakingnews/ci_11101598.

100. Gilad Shalit, "Hamas rejects Israel's Gaza cease-fire conditions," *Haaretz*, Jan. 28, 2009, www.haaretz.com/hasen/spages/1059593.html.

101. Scott Baldauf, "Africans join forces to fight the LRA," *The Christian Science Monitor*, Dec. 16, 2008, www.csmonitor.com/2008/1217/p06s01-woaf.html.

102. Elaine Sciolino, "Britain Grapples With Role for Islamic Justice," *The New York Times*, Nov. 18, 2008, www.nytimes.com/2008/11/19/world/europe/19shariah.html?_r=1&emc=tnt&tntemail0=y.

103. "Tanzania: Islamic Courts Debate Splits Legislators," *The Citizen* (newsletter, source: Africa News), Aug. 14, 2008.

104. Gershom Gorenberg, "The Temple Institute of Doom, or Hegel Unzipped," *South Jerusalem* (Blog), July 8, 2008, http://southjerusalem.com/2008/07/the-temple-institute-of-doom-or-hegel-unzipped.

105. See Katel, *op. cit.*, p. 859.

106. "Muslim Americans: Middle Class and Mostly Mainstream," *op. cit.*

107. Scott Shane, "Global Forecast by American Intelligence Expects Al Qaeda's Appeal to Falter," *The New York Times*, Nov. 20, 2008, www.nytimes.com/2008/11/21/world/21intel.html?_r1&emc=tnt&tntemail0=y.

108. Bin Laden, *op. cit.*

109. Lybarger, *op. cit.*, p. 244.

110. Carlson-Thies was speaking at a discussion on faith-based initiatives organized by the Brookings Institution in Washington, D.C. on Dec. 5, 2008.

111. See 'fastest growing denominations' category in "World Christian Database," *op. cit.*

112. Michael Mosettig, "Among Sea of Glittery Crosses, Christianity Makes its Mark in South Korea," Nov. 5, 2007, Public Broadcasting Service, www.pbs.org/newshour/indepth_coverage/asia/koreas/2007/report_11-05.html.

BIBLIOGRAPHY

Books

Almond, Gabriel A., Scott Appleby and Emmanuel Sivan, *Strong Religion: The Rise of Fundamentalisms Around the World, University of Chicago Press*, 2003.
Three history professors synthesize the findings of a five-volume project that looks at 75 forms of religious fundamentalism around the world.

Brasher, Brenda E., ed., *Encyclopedia of Fundamentalism, Routledge*, 2001.
Academics provide an A-Z on Christian fundamentalism — from its origins in the United States to its spread to other countries and religions.

Donohue, John J., and John L. Esposito, *Islam in Transition: Muslim Perspectives, Oxford University Press*, 2007.
Essays by Muslim thinkers address key questions, such as the role of women in Islam, the relationship between Islam and democracy and the clash between Islam and the West.

Lybarger, Loren D., *Identity and Religion in Palestine: The Struggle between Islamism and Secularism in the Occupied Territories, Princeton University Press*, 2007.
A U.S. sociologist who spent several years in the Palestinian territories explores how groups promoting fundamentalist Islam have gradually eclipsed secular nationalism as the dominant political force.

Thomas, Pradip Ninan, *Strong Religion, Zealous Media: Christian Fundamentalism and Communication in India, SAGE Publications*, 2008.
An associate professor of journalism at the University of Queensland, Australia, examines the influence of U.S televangelists in India and the battle for cultural power between Hindu, Muslim and Christian fundamentalists. SAGE is the publisher of *CQ Global Researcher.*

Articles

"The Palestinians: Split by geography and by politics," *The Economist*, Feb. 23, 2008, www.economist.com/world/mideast-africa/displaystory.cfm?story_id=10740648.
The secular organization Fatah controls the West Bank while the Islamist group Hamas is in charge in Gaza.

Crilly, Rob, "Lord's Resistance Army uses truce to rearm and spread its gospel of fear," *The Times* (London), Dec. 16, 2008, www.timesonline.co.uk/tol/news/world/africa/article 5348890.ece.
A violent military campaign led by Ugandan Christian fundamentalists threatens to destabilize the neighboring region.

Griswold, Eliza, "God's Country," *The Atlantic*, March 2008, pp. 40-56, www.theatlantic.com/doc/200803/nigeria.
An author recounts her visit to Nigeria, a deeply religious country where Christian and Muslim clerics compete to grow their flocks, and religious tensions often spill over into violence.

Tavernise, Sabrina, "Independent, Tajiks Revel in Their Faith," *The New York Times*, Jan. 3, 2009, www.nytimes.com/2009/01/04/world/asia/04tajik.html?emc=tnt&tntemail0=y.
The Central Asian republic has become increasingly Islamic since its independence from the Soviet Union, with strong influence from Saudi Arabia.

Traynor, Ian, "Denmark's political provocateur: Feminist, socialist, Muslim?" *The Guardian*, May 16, 2008, www.guardian.co.uk/world/2007/may/16/religion.uk.
The controversial Danish politician Asmaa Abdol-Hamid, a devout Muslim, hopes to become the first person elected to the Danish parliament to wear the Islamic headscarf.

Reports and Studies

"Islamic Extremism: Common Concern for Muslim and Western Publics," *The Pew Global Attitudes Project*, July 14, 2005, http://pewglobal.org/reports/pdf/248.pdf.
A U.S.-based research center surveys public opinion in 17 countries on why Islamic extremism is growing.

MacIntyre, Andrew and Douglas E. Ramage, "Seeing Indonesia as a normal country: Implications for Australia," *Australian Strategic Policy Institute*, May 2008, www.aspi.org.au/publications/publication_details.aspx?ContentID=169&pubtype=5.
Two Australian academics argue that claims of rampant Islamic fundamentalism in Indonesia — the world's most populous Muslim country — are exaggerated.

Mayson, Cedric, "Religious Fundamentalism in South Africa," *African National Congress, Commission for Religious Affairs,* January 2007, http://the-brenthurstfoundation.co.za/Files/terror_talks/Religious%20Fundamentalism%20in%20SA.pdf. A South African activist blames growing fundamentalism in South Africa on U.S. Christian fundamentalists.

Olcott, Martha Brill and Diora Ziyaeva, "Islam in Uzbekistan: Religious Education and State Ideology," *Carnegie Endowment for International Peace,* July 2008, www.carnegieendowment.org/publications/index.cfm?fa=view&id=21980&prog=zru. Two academics chart the growth of Islam in the Central Asian republic.

For More Information

Association of Evangelicals in Africa, www.aeafrica.org. A continent-wide coalition of 33 national evangelical alliances and 34 mission agencies that aims to "mobilize and unite" evangelicals in Africa for a "total transformation of our communities."

European Jewish Community Centre, 109 Rue Froissart, 1040 Brussels, Belgium; (32) 2-233-1828; www.ejcc.eu. Office of the Chabad Jewish missionary movement's delegation to the European Union.

Evangelical Graduate School of Theology, N.E.G.S.T., P.O. Box 24686, Karen 00502, Nairobi, Kenya; (254) 020-3002415; www.negst.edu. An Evangelical Christian institution devoted to the study of religion in Africa.

Forum 18 News Service, Postboks 6603, Rodeløkka, N-0502 Oslo, Norway; www.forum18.org. News agency reporting on government-sponsored repression of religion in Central Asia.

Organisation of the Islamic Conference, P.O. Box 178, Jeddah 21411, Saudi Arabia; (966) 690-0001; www.oic-oci.org. Intergovernmental organization with 57 member states, which promotes the interests of the Muslim world.

The Oxford Centre for Hindu Studies, 15 Magdalen St., Oxford OX1 3AE, United Kingdom; (44) (0)1865-304-300; www.ochs.org.uk. Experts in Hindu culture, religion, languages, literature, philosophy, history, arts and society.

Pew Forum on Religion and Public Life, 1615 L St., N.W., Suite 700, Washington, DC 20036-5610; (202) 202-419-4550; http://pewforum.org. Publishes surveys on religiosity, including fundamentalist beliefs, conducted around the world.

World Christian Database, BRILL, P.O. Box 9000, 2300 PA Leiden, The Netherlands; (31) (0)71-53-53-566; www.worldchristiandatabase.org. Provides detailed statistical data on numbers of believers, by religious affiliation; linked to U.S.-based Center for the Study of Global Christianity, Gordon-Conwell Theological Seminary.

World Evangelical Alliance, Suite 1153, 13351 Commerce Parkway, Richmond, BC V6V 2X7 Canada; (1) 604-214-8620; www.worldevangelicals.org. Network for evangelical Christian churches around the world.

Worldwide Incidents Tracking System, National Counter Terrorism Center, University of Maryland, College Park, MD 20742; (301) 405-1000; http://wits.nctc.gov. Provides detailed statistics on religiously inspired terrorist attacks across the world from 2004-2008.

9

Energy Nationalism

Do Petrostates Threaten Global Energy Security?

Peter Behr

The Caspian Sea oil town of Neft Dashlari ("Oil Rocks") produces more than half of Azerbaijan's crude oil. Built in 1947 on a chain of artificial islands, the facility contains 124 miles of streets, schools, libraries and eight-story apartments housing some 5,000 oil workers. Energy companies are targeting the Caspian Sea and other areas in the search for non-Persian Gulf oil sources.

From *CQ Researcher*, July 2007.

Getty Images/Reza

esterners saw the Soviet Union's 1991 collapse as a defining triumph of democracy, but Russian President Vladimir Putin has called it "the greatest geopolitical catastrophe of the century."[1] Today, to the growing unease of leaders in Washington and Europe, Putin is bent on erasing the wounds of what some Russian leaders call the "16 lost years" since the break-up and reclaiming Russia's position as a superpower. His weapon: the country's considerable energy resources.

With $500 million pouring into its coffers daily from oil and gas exports, Moscow is raising its voice — and using its elbows — in international business negotiations. During the winter of 2005-06, Russia temporarily cut off natural gas deliveries to Ukraine and Western Europe over a pricing dispute.[2] Putin also jailed Russian oil tycoon Mikhail Khodorkovsky after he challenged government energy plans and political control. And to the dismay of Washington, Moscow is considering energy investments in increasingly bellicose Iran and enticing former Soviet states Turkmenistan and Kazakhstan to channel new Caspian Sea natural gas production through Russia's existing and planned pipelines — supplies that will be vital to Europe.

"The truth is that Russia, having first scared its neighbors into [joining] NATO by its bullying behavior, is currently outmaneuvering a divided and indecisive West on almost every front, and especially on energy," said *The Economist*, the respected British newsweekly.[3]

Oil and politics have always made a volatile blend — particularly in the Middle East. But Russia's recent in-your-face actions represent a new strain of energy nationalism being practiced by Russia and a

'Hot Spots' to Supply Most of World's Energy

To reduce dependence on the unstable Persian Gulf, an oil-hungry world is turning to sources in Central Asia, Africa and Russia. But most of these "emerging" producers have either nationalized their oil industries or are considered vulnerable to terrorists or dissidents. By 2010, according to the U.S. Energy Information Agency, 58 percent of global daily oil production will be at risk because it originates or passes through one of the world's oil "hot spots," including Saudi Arabia, Russia, Iraq, Nigeria, the Caspian region, Venezuela and the straits of Hormuz and Malacca.

Source: U.S. Department of Energy

handful of emerging petrostates in Africa, Central Asia and Latin America that are nationalizing or taking greater control over their oil resources. Moreover, the leaders of some petrostates are imposing new political agendas on their oil sectors, notably Putin and Venezuela's combative socialist president Hugo Chávez.

"Everywhere there is a return to oil nationalism," says Jean-Marie Chevalier, director of the energy geopolitics center at Paris-Dauphine University.[4]

In the three decades since the world's first great oil shock in 1973, oil prices have periodically climbed and

crashed as shortages were followed by surpluses. But this time around, the high prices are likely to stay high, many experts warn. To be sure, the war in Iraq and a looming confrontation over Iran's nuclear program are feeding the high prices. And escalating global markets, led by booming China and India, also intensify demand.

But rising energy nationalism is also triggering anxiety in global oil markets. A dramatic shift has occurred in world oil supplies since 30 years ago, when roughly three-quarters of the world's oil production was managed by private multinational oil companies — the so-called

Seven Sisters — and the rest belonged to a handful of state-owned oil companies. "Today, that is about reversed," Former CIA Director John M. Deutch succinctly told the House Foreign Affairs Committee.[5]

As of 2005, 12 of the world's top 20 petroleum companies were state-owned or state-controlled, according to *Petroleum Intelligence Weekly* (*PIW*).[6] (*See chart, p. 236.*) "There has been a very significant change in the balance of power between international oil companies, and it's clear today that it is the national companies that have the upper hand," said Olivier Appert, president of the French Oil Institute.[7]

"One of the favorites of headline writers is 'Big Oil,' " says Daniel Yergin, author of *The Prize: The Epic Quest for Oil, Money & Power*. "But it's the wrong Big Oil. 'Big Oil' today means the national oil companies."

The nationalization of foreign oil company interests in Venezuela and Bolivia in the past two years is the hard edge of this new chapter in oil politics, echoing the same raging denunciations of Western governments and oil companies that accompanied Iran and Libya's nationalizations of foreign oil interests in the 1950s and '60s.[8] "The nationalization of Venezuela's oil is now for real," said Chávez at a ceremony in May marking the takeover of the country's last foreign-run oil fields. "Down with the U.S. empire!" he shouted as newly purchased Russian jet fighters roared overhead.[9]

Oil-production arrangements vary widely among the dozen leading national oil companies. In Nigeria and Brazil, the government invites foreign companies to develop their oil regions, while Kuwait keeps them out. Ecuadorian President Rafael Correa, a Chávez ally who took office in January, has demanded a higher share of revenues from foreign oil companies but needs outside help to expand refining facilities.[10] Russia is forcing Shell and BP to give up majority positions in oil and gas joint ventures but hasn't thrown them out. And neither have Chávez and Correa.

Kazakhstan, after becoming independent in 1991, combined existing state firms into KazMunaiGaz — a new company that it intends to take public — while maintaining government influence through a parent company. The China National Offshore Oil Corp. is publicly traded but state-controlled.

Pipeline Politics Play Pivotal Role

New and proposed oil and gas pipelines from fields in Russia, the Caspian region and Africa will likely play crucial roles in meeting the world's future energy needs. But global politics will influence when, where and whether the pipelines will be built. For instance, China covets oil and gas from eastern Siberia, but Russia's leaders have delayed building a proposed pipeline into Daqing, China. They want the pipeline to go to Russia's Pacific coast, to serve competing customers in Asia and the United States.

Source: U.S. Department of Energy

But whatever model a petrostate adopts, *PIW* says the trend is largely the same: Major oil companies are finding their interests "increasingly subordinated to the nationalistic political agendas of key reserve-holding host countries."[11]

The new oil nationalism has been fed by energy prices at or near peak levels — when adjusted for inflation — reached after the 1970s oil shocks. (*See "Background," p. 242, and chart, p. 232.*)[12]

Rising energy prices also have produced a vast shift in wealth — over $970 billion in 2006 — from consuming nations to producing countries, a $670 billion jump in four years, and most has gone to a handful of countries, according to the Federal Reserve Bank of New York.[13]

Some industry experts say new sources of oil coming online — often from politically unstable hot spots in Africa and Central Asia — could mean lower consumer prices if Russia and the Central Asian petrostates remain independent of the Organization of Petroleum Exporting Countries (OPEC), which seeks to set international oil prices. On the

World Oil Prices Respond to Events

Oil prices reached an all-time high of $78* a barrel in 1981, two years after the U.S.-Iran hostage crisis began. Prices dropped for the next 17 years as new non-OPEC (Organization of Petroleum Exporting Countries) supplies came online and demand declined. After bottoming out at $15.50 a barrel in 1998, prices have risen, largely due to increased demand from India and China, Middle East conflicts and the growing state control of oil operations around the world.

World Crude Oil Prices, 1973-2006
(in $U.S. per barrel, adjusted for inflation)

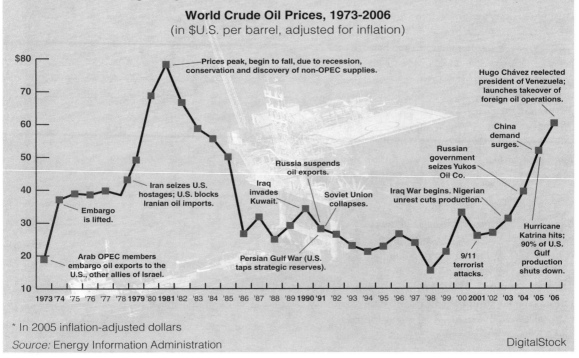

Prices peak, begin to fall, due to recession, conservation and discovery of non-OPEC supplies.

Hugo Chávez reelected president of Venezuela; launches takeover of foreign oil operations.

China demand surges.

Russian government seizes Yukos Oil Co.

Iran seizes U.S. hostages; U.S. blocks Iranian oil imports.

Russia suspends oil exports.

Iraq invades Kuwait.

Soviet Union collapses.

Iraq War begins. Nigerian unrest cuts production.

Embargo is lifted.

Persian Gulf War (U.S. taps strategic reserves).

9/11 terrorist attacks.

Hurricane Katrina hits; 90% of U.S. Gulf production shuts down.

Arab OPEC members embargo oil exports to the U.S., other allies of Israel.

1973 '74 '75 '76 '77 '78 1979 '80 1981 '82 '83 '84 '85 '86 '87 '88 '89 1990 '91 '92 '93 '94 '95 '96 '97 '98 '99 '00 2001 '02 '03 '04 '05 '06

* In 2005 inflation-adjusted dollars

Source: Energy Information Administration

DigitalStock

other hand, the dramatic changes occurring in the industry could boost prices and — eventually — lead to declining supplies if state-run companies reduce exploration investments or botch operations, as some have done.

The International Energy Agency estimates that at least $2.2 trillion will need to be invested in the global oil sector over the next 30 years to meet rising demand for oil, but oil nationalism "is slowing or even discouraging this needed investment," according to the James A. Baker III Institute for Public Policy at Rice University.[14]

Consolidation of the world's oil supplies into government hands also raises questions about whether the new oil producers will break the historic "curse of oil" pattern, in which petrostate leaders used oil profits to line their pockets and buy arms rather than lift indigent populations out of poverty. Still others worry that intensified competition for energy between nations will sow new conflicts around the globe.

In addition to oil shortages and high prices, the International Energy Agency says Earth is facing "twin energy-related threats" — inadequate and insecure supplies of affordable oil and, paradoxically, environmental harm caused by excessive oil consumption.[15]

High prices and dangerous climate-changing energy emissions are fostering conservation-oriented responses similar to those prompted by skyrocketing oil prices in the 1970s, including the use of smaller cars and investments in energy-efficient manufacturing, construction and appliances.[16]

But short supplies also can trigger intense competition between consuming nations, and experts are closely watching the political fallout as major powers vie for control over oil and gas resources. The construction of new pipelines to carry oil and gas from Central Asia to Asia and Europe has already sparked disputes among Russia, China and the United States, and more could follow.[17]

China's worldwide search for oil is causing particular concern because its aggressive attempts to secure important new reserves in countries such as Sudan and Myanmar (formerly Burma) have ignored human rights abuses in those countries that the international community is trying to halt, critics say.[18]

Trends in oil discoveries and price moves have long defied accurate forecasting. An escalation of Persian Gulf conflicts, a terrorist attack on Saudi Arabian oil facilities or congested sea channels could shoot oil prices past $100 a barrel.[19]

For the moment, the world is consuming oil faster than it is finding new supplies, and the historic trend of gradual increases in the world's hydrocarbon reserves has shifted to one of "stagnation and modest decline." Global oil reserves were down by nearly 1 percent in 2006, according to the *PIW's* latest reserves survey.[20]

As increased oil nationalism and global conditions trigger tight supplies, high prices, nervous markets and potential conflict, here are some questions being asked by the oil industry, its investors and critics:

Will emerging petrostates undermine OPEC's control over oil prices, benefiting consumers?

The first Arab oil embargo, in 1973, established oil as a pivotal political and economic lever. Since then, the OPEC cartel has sought to keep world oil prices high enough to maximize producers' returns without tipping global economies into recession.

It is widely assumed that OPEC's continued control over prices depends on whether emerging African, Caspian and Latin American producers reject OPEC membership and create excess global supply.

Of course, a widespread economic recession or financial crisis could slash oil demand, generating a surplus and a collapse in oil prices. In the past, OPEC has responded by cutting production to shore up prices, with mixed results.

So far, Russia has rejected OPEC requests to limit production. Neither Russia nor its Caspian neighbors are strong candidates to join OPEC, says Robert E. Ebel, senior adviser at the Center for Strategic and International Studies (CSIS). "Why would they want to join? Why would they want other people telling them what they can produce and export? They can derive all the benefits [of OPEC's pricing strategies] without being a member."

But experts disagree over whether Russia might support creation of an OPEC-style cartel for natural gas — of

A banner at a natural gas plant in Tarija, Bolivia, proclaims: "Nationalized: Property of the Bolivians," after President Evo Morales nationalized foreign oil and gas operations in May 2006. "The looting by the foreign companies has ended," he declared.

AFP/Getty Images/Presidencia

which it has the world's largest supply. In November 2006, a confidential NATO economic study warned Russia may be seeking to assemble a gas cartel with Algeria, Qatar, Libya, the countries of Central Asia and perhaps Iran.[21]

But Dmitry Peskov, deputy Kremlin spokesman, has denied the suggestion. "Our main thesis is interdependence of producers and consumers. Only a madman could think that Russia would start to blackmail Europe using gas, because we depend to the same extent on European customers."[22]

Whatever Russia does, the supply-demand balance is running tight for oil and gas, even with new petrostate supplies coming online, and new conflicts in oil-rich "hot spots" would only worsen conditions. "Many of the world's major oil-producing regions are also locations of geopolitical tension," said Daniel S. Sullivan, assistant secretary of State for economic, energy and business affairs. "Instability in producing countries is the biggest challenge we face, and it adds a significant premium to world oil prices."[23]

When supplies are tight, consumers lose. And tight supplies could persist since government-controlled energy operations may not develop new reserves or build pipelines as aggressively as the international oil companies. Instead, national oil companies tend to use more of their profits to fund social improvements and provide cheap, subsidized energy for citizens.[24]

To make matters worse, demand for more energy — led by booming China and India — is accelerating.

Have the World's Oil Supplies Peaked?

After 50 years, the debate continues

It's called the "peak oil" theory, and ever since American geologist M. King Hubbert developed it in 1956, oil experts have been divided into two camps — those who believe Earth's oil supplies have peaked, and those who don't.

If proponents of the theory are correct — that the world has used up half of the planet's oil stocks and the remaining supplies will face rapid depletion — the future promises even higher prices and more energy shocks. But critics of the theory say the high point in oil production is still 20 or 30 years away, that oil production is not likely to decline precipitously thereafter and that political events and energy prices — not hydrocarbon shortages — will dictate the industry's course until near the mid-century mark.

According to industry estimates, world oil reserves increased by 24 billion barrels during 2006 to 1.3 trillion barrels — a gain of about 2 percent over 2005.[1] Reserve estimates are periodically recalculated based on new geological and engineering data and new discoveries. But the 2006 increase cannot be documented because two of the countries reporting the greatest increases were Iran and Saudi Arabia, and their governments don't let outsiders check their figures.

"No one knows the amount of oil really contained in reservoirs," says Leonardo Maugeri, an economist and oil industry analyst with the Italian oil and gas company ENI. Such knowledge evolves over time after new wells are drilled and more sophisticated technology is developed.

"In fact," he adds, "countries such as Saudi Arabia or Iraq (which together hold about 35 percent of the world's proven reserves of oil) produce petroleum only from a few old fields, although they have discovered, but not developed, more than 50 new fields each."[2]

The peak oil argument begins with the controversial 1956 prediction by Hubbert that oil production from the lower U.S. 48 states would top out in 1968. The actual peak occurred two to four years later, depending on which measure of oil production is used. As a result of Hubbert's controversial prediction, "He found himself being harassed and vilified," says one of Hubbert's champions, Chris Skrebowski, editor of the monthly magazine *Petroleum Review*, published by the Energy Institute in London.[3]

But Peter M. Jackson, a director of the international research firm Cambridge Energy Research Associates (CERA), argues Hubbert erred in not considering how new drilling technologies could increase output from older fields or how energy prices affect exploration and production.[4]

He is even more critical of Hubbert's present-day disciples who say an oil field peaks when half of its available oil has been extracted. Their model is illustrated with a simple, smoothly rising and falling bell-shape curve.

Jackson says Hubbert's curve ignores the typical expansion of oil field dimensions as more exploration and development occurs. Oil production from the lower 48 states since 1970 has been 66 percent higher and 15 billion barrels greater that Hubbert predicted, Jackson writes, citing U.S. Geological Survey findings and his company's oil field analysis.

When admitted high-priced, "unconventional" sources such as shale and tar sands or Arctic fields are counted, the

Assuming their growth bubbles don't burst, experts predict China's energy use would have to grow by 150 percent by 2020 and India's to double to maintain current economic expansion.[25]

However, China's continued growth is not a certainty, according to a study from the Stanley Foundation, in Muscatine, Iowa.[26] "China faces immense problems, including pollution, disease, poverty, inequality, corruption, abuses of power, an aging population and a shrinking labor force," contend authors Michael Schiffer, a foundation program officer, and Gary Schmitt, director of the American Enterprise Institute's advanced-strategic

studies program. "China's leaders today are, thus, holding a tiger by the tail. They have built the legitimacy of their continued rule largely on meeting the rising expectations of a billion-plus people, but to meet those expectations they eventually have to release the reins of economic and political power they are clutching so tightly."[27]

Some experts hope China and India — which are eyeing Persian Gulf oil — could eventually add their considerable consumer weight to efforts by others to restrain OPEC's pricing strategies. "Much of the recent discussion in Washington about the growing oil demand of China — and to a lesser extent India — has focused

world's total supply of oil is 4.8 trillion barrels, Jackson stated. That is enough, at current growth rates, to delay a peak until 2030 or later, and even then, the peak will not be followed by a sharp decline, he said.

BP chief economist Peter Davies complains that Hubbert's theory also ignores the impact of increased conservation and the switching to alterative fuels that occurs as oil prices rise, which tend to extend oil supplies. Since 1980, for instance, the world's economic output has doubled while oil consumption has only increased by a third, he noted in a June 14, 2006, speech in London. "Year by year, a combination of exploration, investment and the application of technology is ensuring that every unit of oil and gas that is produced is replaced by new proved reserves," he said.[5]

Jackson likened peak oil advocates to sidewalk doomsayers who predict the end of the world. "Peakists continue to criticize those who disagree, but their projections of the date of the peak continue to come and go," he said in his CERA report. "One of the most recent peak oil dates was supposed to have occurred just after the U.S. Thanksgiving Day 2005, and we still wait for the evidence."

Skrebowski replied furiously that Jackson and the anti-peak oil crowd were either Polyannas or paid shills for an oil industry that must persuade investors that untapped oil abounds.[6]

But, when one gets beyond the name calling, the two sides appear less far apart. Skrebowski says Jackson's 4.8 trillion barrels may be technically available "but is only of interest if it can be discovered, mobilised and marketed within a reasonable time period. "This," he says, "is the entire debate: Can all the unfound and unproven resources be exploited quickly enough to more than offset the peaking and decline of the known and proven reserves?"

A leading peak oil advocate, Dallas energy financier Matthew R. Simmons, argues that Saudi Arabia's reserves are being greatly overestimated.[7] But he also says more than half the world's conventional oil and a larger share of its unconventional oil remain to be extracted. "What the world is running out of is cheap oil — the $20 oil we built our civilization around," he writes.[8]

That sounds close to the views of CERA chairman Daniel Yergin. However, he asks, will economics and government decisions in a politicized oil world permit enough new exploration and production to keep pipelines full?

Although energy companies will be prospecting in more difficult environments, he says, "the major obstacle to the development of new supplies is not geology but what happens above ground: namely, international affairs, politics, decision-making by governments and energy investment and new technological development."[9]

[1] "World Proved Reserves of Oil and Natural Gas," Energy Information Administration, Jan. 9, 2007; www.eia.doe.gov/emeu/international/reserves.html.

[2] "The Cheap Oil Era is Far from Over," *Alexander's Oil and Gas Connections*, June 2, 2004; www.gasandoil.com/goc/features/fex42299.htm.

[3] Chris Skrebowski, "Open letter to Peter Jackson of CERA," *Energy Bulletin*, Dec. 21, 2006; www.energybulletin.net/23977.html.

[4] Peter M. Jackson, "Why the 'Peak Oil' Theory Falls Down," Cambridge Energy Research Associates, Inc., Nov. 10, 2006; http://cera.ecnext.com/coms2/summary_0236-821_ITM.

[5] Peter Davies, "BP Statistical Review of World Energy 2005," presentation, London, June 14, 2006, p. 9.

[6] Skrebowski, *op. cit.*

[7] "Twilight in the Desert," *The Oil Drum*, June 13, 2005; www.theoildrum.com/classic/2005/06/twilight-in-desert.html.

[8] Randy Udall and Matthew R. Simmons, "CERA's Rosy Oil Forecast — Pabulum to the People," *ASPO-USA's Peak Oil Review/Energy Bulletin*, Aug. 21, 2006.

[9] Daniel Yergin, "Ensuring Energy Security," *Foreign Affairs*, March/April 2006, p. 75; www.foreignaffairs.org/20060301faessay85206/daniel-yergin/ensuring-energy-security.html.

on the threats posed to the U.S. economy and foreign policy, but that often obscures the fact that the oil interests of China, India and the United States are also broadly aligned," writes Xuecheng Liu, a senior fellow at China's Institute of International Studies.[28]

Will nationalizing oil wealth help the poor?

In May 2006, newly elected President Evo Morales ordered troops to occupy Bolivia's oil and gas fields and gave foreign companies 180 days to renegotiate their energy leases or leave the country. "The looting by the foreign companies has ended," he declared.[29]

Morales was elected partly on a populist platform to take over energy resources in Bolivia, which has Latin America's second-largest gas reserves after Venezuela. "We are the owners of this noble land," he said during the campaign, "and it is not possible that [natural resources] be in the hands of the transnationals."[30]

Echoing former Mexican President Lazaro Cardenas, who nationalized 17 foreign oil companies in 1938, leaders of Bolivia, Ecuador and Venezuela have called their energy reserves a critical tool for helping poor, indigenous populations.

Since the oil age began more than a century ago, governments in the developing world — on both the right

Saudi Arabia and Russia Have Biggest Reserves

Saudi Arabia and Canada lead the world in oil reserves, with nearly 450 billion barrels — more than half as much as the next 10 nations combined. Russia has the most natural gas reserves with 1.68 quadrillion cubic feet — almost three-quarters more than Iran.

Oil Reserves*			Natural Gas Reserves*		
Rank	Country	Barrels (in billions)	Rank	Country	Cubic ft. (in trillions)
1.	Saudi Arabia	262.3	1.	Russia	1,680.0
2.	Canada	179.2	2.	Iran	974.0
3.	Iran	136.3	3.	Qatar	910.5
4.	Iraq	115.0	4.	Saudi Arabia	240.0
5.	Kuwait	101.5	5.	United Arab Emirates	214.4
6.	United Arab Emirates	97.8	6.	United States	204.4
7.	Venezuela	80.0	7.	Nigeria	181.9
8.	Russia	60.0	8.	Algeria	161.7
9.	Libya	41.5	9.	Venezuela	152.4
10.	Nigeria	36.2	10.	Iraq	112.0
11.	Kazakhstan	30.0	11.	Kazakhstan (tie)	100.0
12.	United States	21.8	12.	Turkmenistan (tie)	100.0

* As of Jan. 1, 2007

Source: "World Proved Reserves of Oil and Natural Gas, Most Recent Estimates," Energy Information Administration, Jan. 9, 2007

and left — have promised their people a fair share of the wealth created by geological forces. But few leaders have followed through. Instead, "black gold" has spawned corruption, economic hardship, vast class differences and civil war.

"Look what oil is doing to us, to the oil-exporting countries," said OPEC founder Juan Pablo Pérez Alfonzo, a Venezuelan, nearly 30 years ago.[31] "It is the excrement of the devil."

Oil bonanzas often leave developing economies worse off — a phenomenon economists call the "resource curse."[32] PEMEX, Mexico's state-run oil company, pays an estimated 60 percent of oil earnings to fund government programs. But Mexico has overborrowed to keep production going and has more than $30 billion in pension liabilities, leaving it with a huge longstanding debt and too little money for maintaining old oil fields or finding new ones.[33] And Mexico's biggest field is in decline, raising fears that a chronic

slippage in oil revenues could trigger a budget disaster.[34]

Similarly, OPEC members had an average gain of 1.3 percent in per capita gross domestic product (GDP) between 1965 and 1980, while the rest of the world saw GDP grow 2.2 percent annually.[35]

Sudden oil windfalls have also triggered what economists call the "Dutch disease" — skyrocketing currency values that depress local manufacturers' exports and trigger huge jumps in imports. The economic paradox got its nickname from a drastic decline in economic growth in the Netherlands after natural gas was discovered there in the 1960s.[36]

Oil's easy money also often ends up filling government officials' Swiss bank accounts rather than benefiting public health or education. Some of the most egregious excesses are in Africa. Since oil was discovered in Nigeria's Niger Delta in 1956, for example, the country's infamous kleptocracy has used oil billions to enrich elites, leaving delta residents trapped in pollution and poverty. "Everything looked possible — but everything went wrong," *National Geographic's* Tom O'Neill reports.[37]

Now the situation "has gone from bad to worse to disastrous," said Senan Murray of BBC News.[38] The Movement for the Emancipation of the Niger Delta (MEND) has stepped up attacks on foreign oil facilities and the police who protect them, including an oil rig 40 miles offshore. In May, six Chevron employees were kidnapped and released after a month, but other kidnappings followed.[39] The oil companies — in conjunction with the Nigerian government — have pledged to support rural education, environmental cleanup and other social programs, but armed rebels in the delta say improvements aren't being implemented fast enough.[40]

In Venezuela, Chávez has kept his promises to channel petrodollars to health care, roads and housing. The percentage of Venezuelans living in poverty has shrunk from 42.8 percent to 30.4 percent under Chávez, according to government statistics. Researchers at Catholic University, near Caracas, estimate that about 45 percent of the population lives in poverty, less than in 1999.[41]

Chávez also uses oil money to promote his anti-capitalism ideology by investing in social programs in other Latin American countries. But he hasn't made a dent in Venezuela's chronic corruption, according to Transparency International. The Berlin-based nonprofit puts Venezuela in the bottom quarter of its 2002 and 2006 rankings.[42]

At the same time, the Washington-based advocacy group Freedom House says Chávez has presided over the "deterioration of the country's democratic institutions," replacing the Supreme Court, filling civilian government posts with military personnel, blacklisting political opponents from government positions and shutting down a leading opposition television station.[43]

Russia, China, Mexico and Iran also provide cheap, subsidized energy to their populations, in a tradeoff that carries a stiff economic price. The policy has backfired in Iran, where the government imposed gasoline rationing in June 2007, triggering violent protests that led to more than a dozen gas stations being set on fire.[44] Iran's subsidized gasoline prices are among the lowest in the world, so Iranian motor fuel consumption has been climbing fast. But the government was forced to ration gasoline because it has not used its oil profits to build enough refinery capacity, and gasoline imports have not kept up with demand.

Oil wealth has generated violence and even civil war in many developing countries. For instance, factions from northern and southern Sudan, where oil was discovered in 1978, fought a civil war in the 1980s over the nation's oil revenue. Although a peace accord was signed in 2005, the largely Arab and Islamist ruling party in the north has dragged its feet on sharing the oil wealth with the largely black, Christian southerners.

Meanwhile, some analysts say oil has played a key role in the international community's failure to stop the rape, murder and wholesale destruction of villages in western Sudan's Darfur region, where the Coalition for Darfur says as of 2005 Sudanese militia reportedly had killed 140,000 villagers, 250,000 have perished from disease, famine or exposure and 2 million more are homeless. The Sudanese government disputes the figures.[45]

Until recently, U.N. Security Council efforts to sanction Sudan have been hampered by China, which buys

A forest of oil derricks lines the Caspian shore just outside of Azerbaijan's capital Baku. The oil-rich Caucasus republic is expected to be a significant source of the world's oil in the future, some of it delivered via new pipelines.

AFP/Getty Images/Mladen Antonov

two-thirds of Sudan's oil and has invested more than $8 billion in its oil sector.[46] "Business is business," said Deputy Foreign Minister Zhou Wenzhong in 2004. "We try to separate politics from business."[47]

But this year, after critics threatened to make Darfur an issue during China's preparations to host the 2008 Summer Olympic Games, China shifted course. It now supports a combined U.N.-African Union peacekeeping force in Sudan, which Sudan agreed to accept in June. However, skeptics doubt the agreement will be fully carried out.[48]

In an effort to buffer the negative impact of oil wealth on developing countries, industrialized nations have launched the Extractive Industries Transparency Initiative, announced by then British Prime Minister Tony Blair in October 2002. By requiring oil, gas and other "extractive" companies to report what they pay foreign governments for their natural resources, the initiative aims to expose corruption and foster accurate reporting of oil revenues and spending.

"Knowing what companies pay and what governments receive is a critical first step" to creating accountability in the handling of oil wealth, says the initiative's statement of purpose.[49] Members include industrialized countries as well as the World Bank, major oil companies and about 20 oil-producing developing nations.

However, transparency efforts are still hampered by national oil companies that keep their energy books closed and ignore international accountability guidelines.

Nevertheless, BP chief economist Peter Davies is optimistic about the initiative. "There is still a broad tendency toward transparency," he says. "There are forces that counteract this from time to time, [but] the forces for progress are there."

Will the growing competition for energy trigger new international conflicts?

The Cold War that dominated the last half of the 20th century was about ideology. As a new century begins, a widely shared concern is that energy will become a new arena for superpower or regional confrontations.

Conflicts over oil historically have centered in the Middle East. Now, because of the new petrostates, other hot spots claim attention in Central Asia, Africa and Latin America. The risks are magnified by the recent escalation of energy prices, which have made oil and natural gas resources an even bigger prize for rulers seeking to take or keep power.

New York Times columnist Thomas L. Friedman recently described a perverse relationship between oil prices and democracy: The higher oil prices go, the more democracy suffers and authoritarianism grows in the countries with oil. "Not only will some of the worst regimes in the world have extra cash for longer than ever to do the worst things," Friedman wrote, "but decent, democratic countries — India and Japan, for instance — will be forced to kowtow or turn a blind eye to the behavior of petro-authoritarians, such as Iran or Sudan, because of their heavy dependence on them for oil. That cannot be good for global stability."[50]

Japan and China see themselves competing for access to natural gas reserves in eastern Russia. Poland fears that Russia's construction of a new "North Stream" natural gas pipeline to Germany, now under way, will enable Russia to cut gas deliveries to Poland if tensions between those two countries erupt.[51] (A large portion of Russia's lucrative gas sales to Germany now transit through Poland, but that route could be bypassed by the North Stream project, Polish leaders fear.)

In Latin America, Bolivia's seizure of majority control over its natural gas industry in 2006 was a direct challenge to Brazil, which needs Bolivia's gas and whose state energy company Petrobras is a major gas producer in Bolivia.[52]

Some experts especially worry about the possibility of conflicts over energy between the United States and China, which is on a path to challenge U.S. economic and military leadership within two decades unless its hyper-growth spins out of control. Maureen S. Crandall,

a professor of economics at the Industrial College of the Armed Forces, says that while China badly wants to import oil and natural gas from eastern Russia, it is not clear that pipelines will be built to deliver those resources. So China is looking hard at Caspian gas production and at the prospects for a pipeline through Iran to bring gas to seaports for export in liquefied form aboard tankers.[53]

That puts China in opposition to the Bush administration's top-priority campaign to isolate Iran to prevent it from developing nuclear weapons — a goal Iran denies it is seeking. The Iran issue headed America's agenda for the U.S.-China Senior Dialogue between top diplomats from both nations in June 2007, while China pushed for assurances the United States was not boosting its support for China's rival, Taiwan.[54]

The two nations are not consciously pointed toward conflict, says the National Intelligence Council's 2020 Project report — the most recent public forecast by the CIA's research arm. "[T]he growing dependence on global financial and trade networks increasingly will act as a deterrent to conflict among the great powers — the U.S., Europe, China, India, Japan and Russia," says the report.[55]

But, the report adds, inadvertent conflicts could erupt as a result of growing oil nationalism, the lack of effective international conflict-resolution processes or raw emotions exploding over key issues. For instance, a naval arms race could develop between China, intent on protecting vital seaborne oil shipments, and the United States, determined to maintain strategic leverage in Asian waters. While China's interest "lies with a peaceful and stable regional and international order," write Schiffer and Schmitt, China's ambitions or internal political conflicts could take it in a different direction.[56] Prudence favors maintaining a credible U.S. military posture in Asia, they argue, but if U.S. actions are seen as a bid for supremacy or a check on China's rightful regional role, "it might fuel further resentments and incite precisely the reaction we don't seek, a redoubling of countervailing military, economic and diplomatic strategies."

"The United States and China are not seeking to make war on one another," agrees Michael Klare, a political science professor at Hampshire College. "But they are inadvertently contributing to the risk of conflict in Africa and Central Asia by using arms transfers as an instrument of influence."

China, for instance, has sent troops to Sudan to protect its energy investment there, he points out, and the U.S. military maintains a presence in Central Asia. In

CHRONOLOGY

1951-1979 *Oil surpluses keep crude prices low; U.S. restricts oil production to maintain prices.*

1951 Soviet Union builds first deep-sea oil platform.

1956 Geologist M. King Hubbert's "peak oil" theory contends half of U.S. oil stocks would be depleted by the 1960s, and the remaining supplies face rapid depletion.

1960 Iran, Iraq, Kuwait, Saudi Arabia and Venezuela form the Organization of Petroleum Exporting Countries (OPEC) to stabilize world oil prices.

1970s *OPEC gains control of global oil pricing; Arab countries begin using oil as a political weapon.*

1972 Oil production from Lower 48 states peaks; limits on U.S. production are lifted.

1973 Major Arab oil producers impose embargo on oil exports to United States and several allies in retaliation for their support of Israel in Yon Kippur War; oil prices quadruple.

1979 Shah flees Iran; Iranian students seize hostages at U.S. Embassy, triggering more price shocks.

1980s *Oil from non-OPEC sources breaks the cartel's market hold, helping to create an oil glut.*

1980 Iraq attacks Iran, triggering an eight-year war.

1981 Global oil prices drop after a severe recession.

1983 Production from the North Sea and Alaska's North Slope swells global oil supply.

1985 Saudis boost output; prices plummet.

1988 Iran-Iraq War ends.

1990s *Breakup of Soviet Union raises hope for development of Caspian Sea oil and gas; oil production increases in Africa; global warming emerges as environmental issue.*

1990 Iraq invades Kuwait.

1991 U.S.-led coalition drives Iraq from Kuwait; Soviet Union collapses.

1993 Crude prices drop to $15 a barrel.

1996 Giant Sakhalin oil project announced in Russian Far East.

1997 Violence, protests disrupt Nigerian and Colombian production; Caspian pipeline consortium formed to deliver Caspian Sea oil to Black Sea ports; Kyoto global warming protocol drafted.

1999 Oil production flattens; prices rise.

2000s *Terrorist attacks in U.S. lead to new Iraq war; China becomes fastest-growing oil importer; oil prices climb.*

Sept. 11, 2001 Arab terrorists attack World Trade Center, Pentagon; oil prices surge.

2002 Oil workers strike in Venezuela.

2003 Iraq War begins; attacks close some oil platforms in Nigeria. . . . Major Iraq pipeline is sabotaged; violence escalates.

2004 Oil production in Russia, former Soviet states continues to recover, surpassing 1991 Soviet Union totals.

2005 China's oil demand soars. . . . Hurricane Katrina strikes the U.S. Gulf Coast, shutting down nearly 90 percent of oil and gas production in federal waters.

2006 Venezuelan President Hugo Chávez reelected, launches takeover of foreign-run oil operations. . . . Bolivian President Evo Morales announces the nationalization of all remaining natural gas reserves in the country. . . . Baku-Tblisi-Ceyhan pipeline opens, bypassing the Bosporus Strait.

2007 In a tariff dispute with Belarus, Russia's state-owned Transneft oil company shuts down a pipeline supplying oil to several European countries. . . . Dissidents attack three major pipelines in Nigeria's Niger Delta. . . . On May 1, Chávez takes control of the last remaining privately run oil operations in Venezuela.

World Crude Supplies Remain Vulnerable

Oil 'hot spots' are most at risk

On Feb. 24, 2006, a small band of al Qaeda gunmen attacked Saudi Arabia's giant oil processing facility at Abqaiq — the first such attack since terrorist leader Osama bin Laden publicly targeted Saudi oil installations in a 2004 audio message.

Although the Saudis repulsed the assault, the incident was a wake-up call as to what terrorists' intentions were concerning oil supplies, warned Simon Henderson, director of the Gulf and Energy Policy Program at the Washington Institute for Near East Policy. "Saudi oil production remains extremely vulnerable to sabotage," he wrote shortly after the attack, and the kingdom's estimated 12,000 miles of pipelines are also "at particular risk." A Saudi police raid on a terrorist hideout the previous year had reportedly uncovered copies of maps and plans of the new Shaybah oil field, he pointed out.[1]

Had the terrorists succeeded in destroying the sulfur-clearing towers at Abqaiq — through which about two-thirds of Saudi crude passes — it would have driven the price of crude to more than $100 a barrel for months, perhaps even up to bin Laden's goal of $200 a barrel, according to R. James Woolsey, a former CIA director.[2]

World leaders have been warning since the onset of the Industrial Age that the key to energy security lies in diversification of supplies. When Winston Churchill — then the First Lord of the Admiralty — shifted the Royal Navy from coal to oil on the eve of the First World War, he presciently warned, "Safety and certainty in oil lie in variety and variety alone."[3]

The conflicts and crises that have periodically disrupted Middle East oil supplies — from the oil shocks of the 1970s to Saddam Hussein's invasion of Kuwait in 1990 — have repeatedly reinforced the wisdom of Churchill's advice: find more sources of oil outside the Persian Gulf.

Today, the world is once again seeking to diversify its energy supplies, turning to sources in Central Asia, Africa and Russia. But while the emergence of these rising petrostates has increased the diversity of energy supplies, it has not increased energy security. Many of those new producers appear along with Saudi Arabia on the U.S. Energy Information Administration (EIA) list of various "hot spots" in world oil markets.

Saudi Arabia tops the list, but it is followed by other "emerging" oil producing states: Russia, Iran, Iraq, Nigeria, the Caspian region, Sudan, Venezuela and seven other countries where energy facilities are considered at risk from saboteurs or unstable domestic policies.[4] The EIA projects that by 2010 at least 50 million barrels of oil per day — 58 percent of worldwide daily production — will be in jeopardy because it originates or passes through oil hot spots.

"The security of the energy infrastructure is becoming progressively in doubt," says Massachusetts Institute of Technology Professor John Deutch, also a former CIA director. "Oil facilities, pipelines [and] control systems for the energy distribution systems are all very much more vulnerable to terrorist attack and national disaster."[5]

The choke points for seaborne oil — and, increasingly, natural gas — create some of the worst risks. According to Daniel Yergin, author of *The Prize: The Epic Quest for Oil, Money & Power*, those ocean chokepoints include the:

- Strait of Hormuz, at the entrance to the Persian Gulf;
- Suez Canal, which connects the Red Sea and the Mediterranean;
- Bab el Mandeb Strait at the Red Sea's entrance;
- Bosporus Strait, a major transit channel for Russian and Caspian oil; and
- Strait of Malacca between Malaysia and Indonesia, a conduit for 80 percent of the oil used by Japan and South Korea and about half of China's oil.[6]

the same vein, former Chinese deputy chief of staff Gen. Xiong Guangkai told an international conference on energy security last December that "the strategic race for the world's energy may result in regional tension and even trigger a military clash."[57]

The recent deterioration of U.S.-Russian relations is a case study of what should not be allowed to happen between the United States and China, say some experts. The dialogue has grown raw, escalated by Russia's sharp swing toward an aggressive nationalism. But the division

The Malacca strait is only 1.5 miles wide at its narrowest point, and if terrorists or pirates scuttled a ship at that choke point it could disrupt supplies for a long time, Yergin warns.

"It may take only one asymmetric or conventional attack on a Ghawar [Saudi oil field] or tankers in the Strait of Hormuz to throw the market into a spiral, warns Anthony H. Cordesman, a scholar at the Center for Strategic and International Studies in Washington.[7]

"Assuring the security of global energy markets will require coordination on both an international and a national basis among companies and governments, including energy, environmental, military, law enforcement and intelligence agencies," Yergin writes. "But in the United States, as in other countries, the lines of responsibility — and the sources of funding — for protecting critical infrastructures, such as energy, are far from clear."

Countries are trying a wide range of policies and practices to increase security of energy production and delivery, experts say. Colombia has military units — trained and partly supplied by the United States — tasked with combating rebel attacks on oil pipelines. The natural gas networks of Qatar and the United Arab Emirates are being connected to shipping terminals in Oman that lie outside the vulnerable Strait of Hormuz.[8] China is expanding its naval forces in order to protect oil shipments through Asian sea lanes where piracy is a threat.

But Gal Luft, executive director of the Institute for the Analysis of Global Security in Washington, says security efforts have been hampered by uncertainty over whether

AFP Photo/Dave Clark

Separatist rebels show their firepower in Nigeria's oil-rich Niger Delta in February 2006. Insurgents have kidnapped foreign oil workers and sabotaged oil facilities to protest the slow pace of economic development in the delta.

private companies or governments should pay for the additional security.

"NATO is looking into defining the roles of industry and government," Luft says. "Each wants the other to do more. In places where you can introduce technology or more manpower economically, you do it. But on the ground not a lot is happening."

Building in redundancy and the availability of alternative sources are also popular strategies for assuring energy deliveries, says Mariano Gurfinkel, associate head of the Center for Energy Economics at the University of Texas. "Since it is very hard to avoid all incidents on all elements of the energy infrastructure, efforts are made to minimize the consequences."

[1] Simon Henderson, "Al-Qaeda Attack on Abqaiq: The Vulnerability of Saudi Oil," Washington Institute for Near East Policy, www.washingtoninstitute.org/templateC05.php?CID=2446.

[2] R. James Woolsey, "Global implications of Rising Oil Dependence and Global Warming," testimony before the House Select Committee on Energy Independence and Global Warming, April 18, 2007, p. 2.

[3] Daniel Yergin, "Ensuring Energy Security," *Foreign Affairs*, March/April 2006, p. 69.

[4] "World Energy Hotspots," Energy Information Administration, Sept. 2005, www.eia.doe.gov/emeu/cabs/World_Energy_Hotspots/Full.html.

[5] John M. Deutch, testimony before the House Foreign Affairs Committee, March 22, 2007.

[6] Yergin, *op. cit.*, p. 79.

[7] Anthony H. Cordesman, "Global Oil Security," Center for Strategic and International Studies, Nov. 13, 2006, p. 14.

[8] Energy Information Administration, "Oman" country analysis, April 2007, www.eia.doe.gov/emeu/cabs/Oman/NaturalGas.html.

also has been fostered by arrogant and short-sighted U.S. moves over the past 15 years that treated Russia as a defeated world power and dictated terms to them instead of seeking a working relationship, says Blair Ruble, director of the Kennan Institute in Washington.

"It has been a bipartisan failure," adds Ruble's colleague, program associate F. Joseph Dresen. After the Soviet Union's collapse, the United States "had tons of leverage" but "we needed more influence. It starts with diplomacy."

A win-win relationship with China that minimizes potential for conflict "will take far more sophistication than U.S. policymakers from either political party have previously shown," Schiffer and Schmitt conclude.[58]

BACKGROUND

OPEC Is Born

In 1960, representatives of Iran, Iraq, Kuwait, Saudi Arabia and Venezuela met in Baghdad to form a cartel designed to stabilize world oil markets. Today the 12-member Organization of Petroleum Exporting Countries — now based in Vienna, Austria — also includes Qatar, Indonesia, Libya, the United Arab Emirates, Algeria, Nigeria and Angola. Ecuador and Gabon joined in the '70s but dropped out in the '90s.[59]

Despite the cartel's promise of stability, oil markets have been chaotic since the 1970s, characterized by four distinct periods.

Two oil shocks hit world energy markets in the 1970s. Resentful of U.S. efforts to suppress oil prices and angered by U.S. support for Israel in the 1973 Yom Kippur War, several Arab OPEC members on Oct. 17, 1973, imposed an oil embargo on the United States and other countries aiding Israel, followed by a production cut.[60] The world suddenly faced a crude-oil shortage of 4 million barrels a day, 7 percent below demand. Prices shot up from $3 a barrel to $12.[61] Long lines formed at gasoline pumps in the United States and some European countries.

To limit the impact on American consumers, President Richard M. Nixon imposed price controls on the U.S. economy, and President Gerald Ford created the U.S. Strategic Petroleum Reserve, which today holds more than 688 million barrels of crude oil in underground caverns.[62]

The embargo ended five months later — in March 1974 — after Arab-Israeli tensions eased. Egyptian President Anwar el-Sadat, intent on moving toward a peace agreement, argued successfully that the "oil weapon had served its purpose."[63]

But memories of the embargo continued to drive a search for new energy policies. On April 18, 1977, shortly after being inaugurated, President Jimmy Carter warned about America's overdependence on foreign oil supplies, calling the energy crisis "the moral equivalent of war." With the exception of preventing war, Carter said, "this is the greatest challenge our country will face during our lifetimes."[64]

Then in early 1979, after a year of paralyzing strikes and demonstrations by supporters of militant Iranian Shia Muslim cleric Ayatollah Ruhollah Khomeini, Iran's Shah Mohammad Reza Pahlavi fled Tehran, opening the door to the founding of an Islamic republic.

As the impact of the Iranian Revolution on world oil prices began to be felt, Carter in July 1979 unveiled a comprehensive energy plan to help America combat its overdependence on unstable Middle Eastern oil, promoting conservation, alternative fuels and higher taxes on gasoline and gas-guzzling cars.[65]

Four months later, on Nov. 4, Islamist zealots and students took over the U.S. Embassy in Tehran, holding 52 hostages for 444 days — until Ronald Reagan replaced Carter.[66] During the crisis, oil prices nearly doubled.[67] World oil markets got even tighter in 1980, when Iran's oil production nearly dried up after Iraq invaded — beginning an eight-year-long conflict. Panic purchases by governments, companies and consumers made the shortage worse, and, once again, motorists in industrialized countries queued up at gas stations.

The 1970s price shocks triggered a determined campaign to reduce energy dependence. Congress in 1975 directed U.S. auto manufacturers to double the efficiency of their cars within a decade, and businesses made serious efforts to shrink energy use.[68]

But the pendulum would soon be reversed. A sharp recession stunted energy demand, the search for oil outside the Persian Gulf intensified and the balance between supply and demand was set to shift again.

Oil Glut

Discoveries and exploitation of vast oil and gas reserves in the North Sea, Mexico and Alaska's North Slope in the early 1980s led to a tide of new production, tipping events in consumers' favor.

North Sea development, called "one of the greatest investment projects in the world," required intrepid drilling crews, path-breaking technology and platforms able to withstand crushing waves and 130-mile-per-hour winds.[69] By the early 1980s, daily North Sea production had reached 3.5 million barrels — more than Kuwait and Libya combined — and a new 800-mile pipeline to the port of Valdez from Alaska's landlocked North Slope was supplying up to 2 million barrels of oil a day to the Lower 48 states — a quarter of U.S. production.[70] In 1985, non-OPEC production had increased by 10 million barrels a day over 1974 levels, more than double the cartel's daily output.[71]

Moreover, by 1983 energy conservation was working. Americans were consuming less gasoline than in 1973, even with more cars on the road, and the U.S. economy had become 25 percent more energy efficient. Conservation efforts in Europe and Japan also were cutting consumption.[72] The two trends sent energy prices into a nosedive. By 1985 crude was below $10 a barrel ($20 in inflation-adjusted, 2006 prices), prompting Saudi Arabia to abandon efforts to control cartel production and boost its own output. Analysts have since interpreted the Saudis' decision as a strategic move to hamper the ability of Iran and Iraq to continue their war, raging just across the Saudi border. Others say the move hastened the demise of communism — by draining the Soviet Union's treasury at a time when it was facing rising internal pressures and fighting a war in Afghanistan.

But the lower oil prices also knocked the wind out of the conservation movement. The push to continue raising vehicle performance stalled in Congress, and gas-slurping minivans and SUVs became wildly popular.[73]

New Petrostates

Oil prices spiked briefly in 1991 after Saddam Hussein invaded Kuwait, and the U.S.-led coalition counterattacked, knocking out 3 percent of world oil output. After Iraq's defeat, the oil industry focused on the rising petrostates in Africa and Central Asia and on the collapse — and stunning recovery — of Russia's oil production.[74]

The Caspian Sea — about the size of California — holds one of the world's oldest-known concentrations of petroleum. The Caspian has long triggered fears that its oil, known since Alexander the Great's day, would become a conflict flashpoint. "It will be sad to see how the

Majority of Oil Companies Are State-Owned

Thirteen of the world's 25-largest oil companies are entirely owned or controlled by national governments, including all the companies in the Middle East; three other oil firms are partially state-owned. In 1973, by comparison, roughly three-quarters of the world's oil production was managed by the privately owned "Seven Sisters" — the seven major Western oil companies.*

World's Largest Oil Companies

Rank (2005)	Company	Country of origin	Percentage of firm owned by state
1	Saudi Aramco	Saudi Arabia	100
2	Exxon Mobil	United States	0
3	NIOC	Iran	100
4	PDVSA	Venezuela	100
5	BP	United Kingdom	0
6	Royal Dutch Shell	United Kingdom/Netherlands	0
7	PetroChina	China	90
8	Chevron	United States	0
8	Total	France	0
10	Pemex	Mexico	100
11	ConocoPhillips	United States	0
12	Sonatrach	Algeria	100
13	KPC	Kuwait	100
14	Petrobras	Brazil	32
15	Gazprom	Russia	50.002
16	Lukoil	Russia	0
17	Adnoc	United Arab Emirates	100
18	Eni	Italy	0
19	Petronas	Malaysia	100
20	NNPC	Nigeria	100
21	Repsol YPF	Spain	0
22	Libya NOC	Libya	100
23	INOC	Iraq	100
24	EGPC	Egypt	100
24	QP	Qatar	100

* The Seven Sisters were: Exxon, Mobil, Chevron, Texaco, Gulf, Shell, British Petroleum

Source: Petroleum Intelligence Weekly

magnet of oil draws great armies to the Caucasus," wrote journalist Louis Fischer in 1926.[75]

The Caspian is bordered by Russia on the northwest, Kazakhstan on the north and east, Turkmenistan to the east, Iran to the south and Azerbaijan in the west. (*See map, p. 231.*) The rise of the independent former Soviet

Motorists in London queue up for petrol in 1973. The world's first oil shock was caused by an Arab oil embargo, which established oil as a pivotal political and economic lever.

satellites triggered extravagant hopes that the Caspian could become "the Middle East of the next millennium." The State Department fanned the hyperbole, estimating Caspian oil reserves at 200 billion barrels, or 10 percent of the world's total potential reserves.[76]

Then developers began hitting dry holes, and war and separatist violence spread through the region. Caspian countries disagreed over how to divide the Caspian's energy reserves and whether the Caspian is, in fact, a "sea" or a "lake" — a definition that could affect the ultimate distribution. "The dreams have faded as the hard realities of energy development and politics have set in," says economist Crandall at the Industrial College of the Armed Forces, who predicts Caspian reserves will top out at 33-48 billion barrels, or 3 percent of the world's total.[77]

But even with the lower estimates, the Caspian reserves still are larger than Alaska's North Slope, big enough to attract not only Russia and Iran but also Europe and China. By 2010, the Energy Information Agency projects the Caspian region will be producing 2.9-3.8 million barrels a day — more than Venezuela.[78]

Dreams for a birth of democracy in the region also have faded. Most of the region's governments have become more authoritarian and corrupt since the demise of the

Soviet Union, says Martha Brill Olcott, a senior associate at the Carnegie Endowment for International Peace.[79] Indeed, says Crandall, most Central Asian states are "one-bullet regimes" that would fall into chaos if current leaders were deposed.[80]

In Africa, the discovery of oil in Algeria in 1955 — and later in the Niger Delta and Libya — seemed like gifts from the gods for the planet's poorest continent. The riches lured flocks of petroleum companies.

As exploration expanded, Africa's proven reserves more than doubled from 1980 to 2005, to 114.3 billion barrels, far ahead of overall reserve gains worldwide. In 2004, Nigeria ranked eighth among the world's biggest oil exporters, followed by No. 10 Algeria and 12th-place Libya.[81] Angola soon joined Africa's oil club: In the past 10 years, Angola's estimated oil reserves have nearly tripled and its crude oil production doubled.[82]

Oil also was found in Sudan, where production has been climbing since completion in 1999 of an oil pipeline for exports, despite years of civil war. In 2006, estimates of proven reserves topped 5 billion barrels, a 10-fold increase over the year before.[83]

Africa also has abundant natural gas. Nigeria has the continent's largest reserves and the world's seventh-biggest, while Algeria's reserves rank eighth.[84] Both are on a par with Saudi Arabia and the United States. Algeria in 1964 became the first nation to ship liquified natural gas (LNG) aboard tankers. But Nigeria, convulsed by tribal wars and coups, has been unable to capitalize on its gas deposits until recently. It still "flares," or burns away, 40 percent of the natural gas produced with its oil, although Nigeria is beginning to expand LNG production.[85]

The New Nationalism

China's staggering expansion and modernization have overtaken its energy resources. Twenty years ago, China was the largest oil exporter in East Asia. Now it is the world's second-largest oil purchaser, accounting for nearly one-third of the global increase in oil demand, note David Zweig and Bi Jianhai of the Hong Kong University of Science.[86] Similarly, India's oil consumption doubled between 1990 and 2004, and other industrializing Asian nations nearly matched that pace.[87]

Fortunately for the world's consumers, the explosive growth of China's oil demand was matched by a remarkable recovery in Russia's oil output. The fall of the

Soviet Union and a financial credit crisis had devastated Russia's oil industry. Starved for capital and leadership, it was producing only 6 million barrels a day in 1995. But oil output had rebounded to average 9.4 million barrels a day this year, making Russia currently the world's largest oil producer, ahead of Saudi Arabia, which has trimmed its output. With the world's largest production and reserves of natural gas, it is poised to be Europe's prime supplier while developing its immense Far East gas reserves for eventual use by China, the rest of Asia and North America.

Russia's energy wealth also has transformed its self-image and ambitions, as it pulls away from the West. "In the late 19th century, Russia's success was said to rest on its army and its navy; today, its success rests on its oil and gas," writes Dmitri Trenin, deputy director of the Carnegie Moscow Center.[88]

Today, says Leonid Grigoriev, president of the Institute for Energy and Finance in Moscow, "We see ourselves as a great power."[89]

That power has frightened Russia's neighbors, especially after the Putin government took control of major petroleum reserves and energy pipelines, forcing Western energy companies to surrender equity positions in the country's largest new gas fields. Putin "has a very traditional Soviet view of the nature of power," says the Kennan Institute's Ruble. "He views oil and gas as strategic playing cards to reassert Russia in the world scene."

Now Europe anxiously faces growing dependence on Russia for its energy. "Russia is a natural, reliable and stable supplier" for Europe, insists Grigoriev.

"They see things strictly through the eyes of Russia: What is in their national interest?" responds CSIS's Ebel.

"The issue of security of supply is critical for European consumers," says BP economist Davies. "That debate is continuing."

Like Putin, Venezuela's Chávez is an architect of oil's rising nationalism. Following in the footsteps of Argentinean strongman Juan Perón and Cuba's Fidel Castro, Chávez is using Venezuela's oil and gas reserves — the Western Hemisphere's largest — to promote his socialist "Bolivarian Revolution."[90] While Chávez delights in confronting U.S. policy goals in Latin America, he also finds willing listeners in the Middle East and Asia. Having survived a coup attempt and an oil-workers' strike that stunted output in the winter of 2002-03, the former rebel paratrooper is firmly in control.

Corbis Images/Ed Kashi

Pollution and poverty abound in the swampy Niger Delta region of Nigeria, where international oil companies are drilling for the country's rich oil resources. Shanties reflect the slow rate of development, which has sparked violent protests in recent years.

At home, Chávez has steered energy export earnings toward the three-quarters of the population that comprise Venezuela's poor. Their plight worsened in the 1980s and '90s despite market reforms recommended by globalization advocates at the International Monetary Fund (IMF) and World Bank. Chávez rejects free-market, capitalist economic approaches and vows to establish a socialist, classless society.[91] Social spending by Petróleos de Venezuela S.A. (PDVSA), the state-run oil and natural gas company, has increased 10-fold since 1997.

Abroad, Chávez seeks a coalition of allies who will help him parry opposition from the United States and pursue his agenda. He has offered low-priced oil to Latin America. (He also has donated heating oil to the poor in the United States.) PDVSA has forced major oil companies to give up majority holdings in Venezuela's oil fields and has signed oil deals with China, Iran, Vietnam, Brazil and Belarus.[92]

But Venezuela now spends more on social programs than on maintaining and expanding its oil production capacity, according to the Baker Institute. The current production rate of 2.4 million barrels a day is down from 3.1 million barrels when Chávez took office in 1999.[93]

"He is good at giving oil away, but he's not good at producing oil," says Chávez opponent Luis Giusti, who headed PDVSA in the 1990s.

While Chávez is a thorn in the side to the U.S. government and international oil companies, his overtures to

In the shadow of Istanbul's historic Blue Mosque (left), the Hagia Sophia Museum (center) and Topkapi Palace (right), an oil tanker enters the Bosporus Strait. The 21-mile-long waterway is the sole route for Caspian oil shipped through pipelines to the Black Sea, where it is then loaded onto tankers for the trip through the strait to the Mediterranean. Turkey fears increased tanker traffic could bring an environmental catastrophe to the already busy Bosporus, so it has encouraged development of an overland pipeline that would bypass the strait.

China and Iran and his willingness to slow future development in favor of higher returns today represent a new reality in the world's energy story.[94]

CURRENT SITUATION

Majors Shut Out

Government-owned or controlled petroleum companies today control a majority of the world's hydrocarbon reserves and production. By 2005, nationalized oil companies had taken over 77 percent of the world's 1.1 trillion barrels of oil reserves. And, while Western oil companies have absorbed their share of the short-term windfall created by recent higher prices, their long-term future does not look particularly rosy. Major oil firms now control only 10 percent of global petroleum reserves.[95]

"International majors have been relegated to second-tier status," concluded the Baker Institute. In the 1970s and '80s, Western companies were invited to explore the new fields in the North Sea, Alaska and the Gulf of Mexico, but today key future resources in Russia and Central Asia are government-controlled.

"The bulk of the resources remain in a number of key countries, which are dominated by states, and we have to be dependent on governments and state companies to deliver the capacity," says BP's Davies.

"Access really is a consideration," adds Cambridge Energy Research Associates chairman Yergin. "Where can you go to invest money, apply technology and develop resources and bring them to market? Terms get very tough. The decision-making slows down, if you can get there at all."

China's strategy for feeding its oil appetite is a major source of concern, says former CIA Director Deutch. Its oil companies scour the world seeking access to oil and gas resources, effectively reducing supplies on the world market.

"China — and now India — are making extensive efforts in Africa and elsewhere in the world to lock up oil supplies," says Deutch. These state-to-state deals typically are not based solely on market terms but include sweeteners such as political incentives, military assistance, economic aid or trade concessions, he explains.

International oil companies, while banking record profits, are facing higher taxes or demands to surrender parts of their stakes in projects. For instance, say Western analysts, Putin's government has shown its knuckles to Royal Dutch Shell and Exxon Mobil in disputes over control of two huge projects on Sakhalin Island, off Russia's Pacific coast. Shell had to give up controlling interest in the Sakhalin-2 pipeline project to Russia's natural gas monopoly Gazprom after suffering cost overruns. Russia wants to determine where the gas goes, says its oil minister.[96]

Emboldened by rising oil prices, Russia and nations in South America and West Africa that once relied on Western oil companies are now "increasingly calling the shots," said *The Wall Street Journal*.[97]

Producer Windfalls

Oil prices have more than tripled since 2002, sparking an unprecedented transfer of wealth from consuming to producing nations. The amount energy-importing nations must spend for oil has leaped from $300 billion in 2002 to nearly $1 trillion in 2006 (roughly the gross domestic product of Spain or South Korea).[98] The higher prices, of course, affect not only oil production but also the current value of oil in the ground. The IMF reports the value of energy exporters' oil reserves increased by more than $40 trillion between 1999 and 2005. Thus if prices stay at current levels, it would translate into an enormous increase in future wealth for the exporting nations, concentrated in the Middle East, Russia, Central Asia and Africa.[99]

Higher oil prices leave all consumers with less to spend and save, but the impact is harshest in poor countries with no oil. Without oil or other high-value exports to offset increased energy costs, poor countries go deeper in debt.

"Debt is the central inhibitor of economic development," says former CIA Director R. James Woolsey Jr. "Importing expensive oil is helping bind hundreds of millions of the world's poor more firmly into poverty."[100]

The flow of petrodollars also is profoundly affecting the United States — the world's richest nation but also its largest oil consumer. When the U.S. buys oil from abroad, dollars pile up in the exporting nations' coffers. The oil-dollar outflow has added enormously to the U.S. "current account" deficit, or the dollar difference between U.S. imports and exports and international financial transactions. The United States is the only major nation that pays for its oil imports by borrowing heavily from the rest of the world.[101]

"The U.S. now borrows from its creditors — such as China and Saudi Arabia — over $300 billion per year, approaching a billion dollars a day of national IOU-writing, to import oil," according to Woolsey.[102]

A consequence of the increasing role of national oil companies is that most U.S. dollars paid for oil go into accounts controlled by foreign governments, according to the Federal Reserve Bank of New York. A crucial question is what those governments will do with their petrodollars, bank experts said.[103]

The outward tide of U.S. petrodollars has been matched by purchases of U.S. securities and properties by exporting countries, providing crucial support for U.S. stock and bond markets, the Federal Reserve report notes. In a dramatic example, China recently purchased $3 billion in stock of the Blackstone Group, a prominent U.S. equity firm that buys and turns around distressed companies.

"Officials in Beijing have $1.2 trillion of reserves they want to invest more profitably than in U.S. Treasuries. They lack the expertise to do it themselves and don't want to pay money managers millions in fees," said financial columnist William Pesek.[104]

For its part, Blackstone will get the increased access to China's surging economy that it covets.[105]

But such purchases are full of complexities, the Federal Reserve report notes. The Blackstone stock purchase was made by China's new state-owned investment fund, and other oil

President Vladimir Putin addresses executives of Russia's Rosneft oil company in September 2005 after visiting the Tuapse oil terminal, pictured behind him. Putin is attempting to reclaim Russia's position as a superpower by harnessing its considerable energy resources.

AP Photo/Vladimir Rodionov

exporters have set up similar "sovereign wealth funds" to make direct investments in the United States and other oil-buying countries, writes columnist Sebastian Mallaby. "Chunks of corporate America could be bought by Beijing's government — or, for that matter, by the Kremlin." The economic and political fallout could be seismic, he adds.[106]

If events make oil exporters less willing to put dollars back into the United States, U.S. interest rates could increase to keep the foreign investment coming. Otherwise, U.S. consumers would have to cut their spending to reduce the outflow of dollars. A big shift of petrodollars away from the United States would pull a vital prop out from under stock markets.[107]

The flow of untraceable petrodollars also affects world security. Because so much oil revenue goes into the Middle East and from there into untraceable channels, some of it is being used to finance terrorist organizations opposed to the United States. "Thus . . . when we pay for Middle Eastern oil today, this long war in which we are engaged becomes the only war the U.S. has ever fought in which we pay for both sides," Woolsey says.[108]

AT ISSUE

Has a new cold war begun over oil that could lead to conflict?

YES Michael T. Klare
Five College Professor of Peace and World Security Studies (Amherst, Hampshire, Mount Holyoke and Smith colleges and the University of Massachusetts, Amherst)

Written for *CQ Global Researcher*, June 2007

Two simultaneous developments are likely to intensify future conflicts over oil. On one hand, increasing competition for a finite resource will become more intense in the years ahead. With China and India leading the growth in demand, competition is going to soar, and supply isn't likely to expand nearly as fast as demand. In addition, oil supplies increasingly will be located in areas of tension and inherent friction — the Middle East, Africa, Central Asia and other unstable places.

During the Cold War, the superpowers competed for influence by providing arms for various proxies in Africa, the Middle East and Asia. We are seeing the same thing happening in the oil cold war.

The United States, Russia and China, in their pursuit of oil allies, are again providing arms to proxies and suppliers, which is intensifying the risk of internal conflicts. It is an exceedingly dangerous development. The United States and China are not seeking to make war on one another. But they are inadvertently contributing to the risk of conflict in Africa and Central Asia by using arms transfers as an instrument of influence.

Ultimately, the only solution will be to reduce our craving for imported oil. That is easier said than done. It is a craving, and cravings lead to irrational behavior. For China, its close embrace of the Sudanese government — including supplying arms — is bringing the Chinese terrible criticism. The United States, for its part, engages in equally irrational behavior in creating close ties with — for example — the leaders of Kazakhstan and Azerbaijan — alienating the pro-democracy movements in those countries.

Ultimately, the most dangerous piece in all of this is the U.S.-China competition for energy. We have a cold war today, but it could become a hot war, although not through a deliberate act over oil. But we are engaged in competitive arms competition in Africa and Asia, and this could lead to inadvertent local conflicts and an accidental clash between the United States and China, much the way World War I began.

Neither side would choose such a conflict, but it would arise from a clash of proxies, eventually involving U.S. and Chinese advisers and troops.

Such an outcome may not be highly probable, but it is an exceedingly dangerous possibility.

NO Amy Myers Jaffe
Wallace S. Wilson Fellow in Energy Studies, James A. Baker III Institute for Public Policy; Associate Director, Rice University Energy Program

Written for *CQ Global Researcher*, June 2007

Competition over energy may contribute to fundamental global conflicts, but the conflicts would have happened with or without the energy situation. North Korea is not an oil issue. Kosovo was not about oil. The Iran confrontation is not an oil issue.

The Persian Gulf remains a special case. Saudi Arabia controls most of the world's excess oil production. In the case of the Iraq War in 1991 — which followed Iraq's invasion of oil-rich Kuwait — the United States was not going to let Saddam Hussein control 40-50 percent of the world's oil reserves. Saudi oil facilities have been targeted by terrorists, and Iran has threatened in the past to use military force to interfere with oil shipments through the Strait of Hormuz.

A future confrontation with Iran would greatly increase the risk to essential oil exports through the Persian Gulf. On the other hand, Iran is critically dependent upon revenues from its own oil sales and must import gasoline from foreign refiners to meet its population's requirements.

The overriding concern, however, is that the sudden loss of the Saudi oil network would paralyze the global economy. The United States — and the rest of the world — has a concrete interest in preventing that. But most conflicts facing the United States today, like North Korea or Afghanistan, are not going to change whether the price of oil is $50 a barrel or $70 a barrel.

Nor is Central Asia likely to become a flash point. We have been watching a revival of the so-called Great Game competition over Caspian oil for a decade. Why? Because the leaders in those countries have chosen to delay, trying to get the best economic and geopolitical deals they can. The Russians play the Japanese off the Chinese. The Chinese are trying to take care of their needs. Their motivations vary from country to country, but it is a dynamic that is very unlikely to lead to conflict. We are not likely to go to war with Russia over a pipeline in Kazakhstan.

The United States and China, as the world's largest oil importers, are economic partners by virtue of their trade and, consequently, potential political rivals. But both share a common interest in reasonable oil prices.

If the United States and China ever go to war over Taiwan, oil will not be the trigger.

Pipeline Politics

Over the next quarter-century, the world will rely on new oil and gas fields in Russia, Central Asia and Africa for a critical part of its energy needs. But uncertainty over when, where and if new pipelines will be built to access those new fields is heightening political tensions among the central players in the global competition for energy.

China covets oil and gas from eastern Siberia, but Russia's leaders have delayed building a pipeline into China, unwilling to hinge such a costly project on a single customer. Instead, Russia wants to channel those resources to its Pacific coast, where they can be shipped to competing customers not only in China but also in Japan, the rest of Asia and the United States.

Europe depends on Russian natural gas delivered over a Soviet-era pipeline network, which must be expanded to handle future growth. But Russia itself needs more gas and thus wants to build new pipelines into Central Asia to transport gas from Caspian fields — at market prices — to Europe.

Many Russian pipelines carrying Caspian oil terminate at the Black Sea. But Turkey opposes plans to expand that route because it fears a catastrophic oil spill from tanker traffic through the Bosporus Strait.

The most direct export route for Caspian oil is southward, by pipeline through Iran — a project China would welcome. But the United States opposes the route because it seeks to block Tehran's suspected nuclear-weapons development.[109]

Pipeline infighting is further reflected in BP's controversial $4 billion, 1,100-mile BTC pipeline from Baku, Azerbaijan, past Tbilisi, Georgia, and on to the Mediterranean port of Ceyhan, Turkey. The world's second-longest pipeline threads through mountains and volcanic regions and had to withstand unrest in Georgia, environmental opposition and sabotage threats. Its completion in 2005 fulfilled a hardball strategy by the United States to keep the pipeline out of Russian territory and block a shorter, cheaper route through Iran.[110] Leaders in Moscow and Tehran were infuriated.

"We really put all our cards on the table on that one," said Ebel, of CSIS.

But Russia has high cards to play, too, in the current pipeline tug-of-war over the undeveloped natural gas riches on the Caspian's eastern coast. The only gas pipeline through

Nigerians work on a French gas-drilling installation in Nigeria's Niger Delta, aided by Chinese contractors. The Chinese are competing with other international oil companies for the delta's rich oil reserves.

Corbis Images/Ed Kashi

this region now leads north from Turkmenistan, through Kazakhstan into Russia, and Moscow controls it.[111]

The United States is pushing for a new pipeline across the Caspian seabed to carry Turkmenistan's gas westward to Baku.

From there it could travel into Turkey and connect with a new pipeline that the European Union wants to see built into Austria, (the "Nabucco" project), thus completing a pathway for Caspian gas to Europe without setting foot on Russian soil.

"We would love to see the Trans-Caspian Gas Pipeline put in place," Deputy Assistant Secretary of State for European and Eurasian Affairs Matthew Bryza said in January.[112]

Putin has other ideas. He is pressing Turkmenistan and Kazakhstan to support a Russian-built pipeline around the north end of the Caspian into Russia to move the gas into Europe over old and new Russian lines. Russia insists that no pipeline may cross the Caspian Sea unless all five adjoining nations agree — and Moscow is ready with its veto.

Speaking in Turkey recently, Bryza took a shot at Gazprom's natural gas pipeline monopoly, saying Russia uses its pipelines to intimidate governments in Europe that depend on them. "Europeans are finally waking up to the reality, I'm sorry to say, that Gazprom isn't always the most reliable partner for them. The more gas that moves from Central Asia and Azerbaijan to Europe via Turkey, the better."[113]

Getty Images/Stanton R. Winter

Uncertainty over the construction of new oil and gas pipelines is heightening political tensions among the central players in the global competition for energy. New pipelines will be increasingly vital in moving energy resources from new fields in Russia, Central Asia and Africa.

Russian officials contend the United States is still trying to throw its weight around, telling Moscow what to do.

In May, Moscow claimed the advantage after Putin and President Gurbanguly Berdymukhammedov of Turkmenistan agreed to the Russian plan for moving Caspian gas, but the United States says the door is still open for its favored route.[114] "These two pipelines are different," Bryza said in June, speaking of the Russian plan and trans-Caspian pipeline.

Meanwhile, Turkmenistan continues to talk with China about an eastward pipeline connection for its gas.

Currently, however, most of the pipeline-route disputes remain on paper. Soaring steel prices continue to inflate the costs of the billion-dollar pipeline networks. "The

watchword today is delay," says Yergin of Cambridge Energy Research Associates, "not only because of political issues, but also because construction costs are going through the roof."

OUTLOOK

Curbing Demand

The race for Earth's remaining energy resources increasingly is splitting the world into two camps: countries that sell oil and natural gas and those that buy them.

The buyers — led by the United States, Europe, China and India and Japan — have a clear imperative, according to the International Energy Agency (IEA) and other energy experts: Start curbing demand.[115]

Energy security is the primary reason. Two-thirds of the growth in oil supplies over the next quarter-century will likely come from the Middle East, Russia, the Caspian region, Africa and Venezuela — areas beset by conflict or political instability.[116]

Climate change is also driving the need to curb demand. Total world economic output is projected to more than double by 2030, accelerating the discharge of greenhouse gases into the atmosphere. Eighty percent of the growth will come from China, India, Brazil and other developing countries.[117]

To avert potentially catastrophic climate disasters before the end of this century, both industrial and developing countries must agree on strategies for conserving energy and reducing greenhouse gases without halting economic growth, says the Intergovernmental Panel on Climate Change.[118]

Both energy insecurity and climate threats demand greater international cooperation than in the past decade, experts say. The United States has, until now, mainly sought to deal with its energy challenges by producing more oil and gas outside its borders, said a 2004 report for the Baker Institute for Public Policy.

After the Sept. 11, 2001, terrorist attacks, influential members of the Bush administration saw regime change in Iraq as a way to shake OPEC's hold on oil production, the Baker Institute authors wrote. Instead of taking responsibility for reducing energy consumption, however, the U.S. addressed the challenge "by attempting to control the Middle East."[119] But the strategy "has fallen flat on its face," the authors have asserted.

No matter how the Iraq War ends, the authors continue, the United States must move more decisively to reduce its energy demands if it wants credibility in seeking cooperation from China. China is quickly catching up to the United States in energy production and greenhouse-gas emissions, according to a recent report by U.S. climate experts Jeffrey Logan, Joanna Lewis and Michael B. Cummings.[120]

China has been building on average one new electric power plant a week for the past few years, and its automobile sales are booming (though they're small by U.S. standards).[121] But by the end of the decade, China will have 90 times more motor vehicles than it had in 1990, and by 2030 — or sooner — there may be more cars in China than in the United States.[122]

This year China announced new climate goals, including a 10 percent reduction in carbon-dioxide emissions over five years. "[W]e have to take responsibility for lowering greenhouse emissions," said Zhang Zhang Guobao, vice chairman of the energy-policy-setting National Development and Reform Commission.[123]

But China has adopted a "wait-and-see" attitude toward international climate-change agreements, unwilling to make binding commitments until it is clear what the United States and the developed world will do, according to Logan, Lewis and Cummings. The United States must lead by example, they said.

"Thinking about how to alter our energy-consumption patterns to bring down the price of oil is no longer simply a hobby for high-minded environmentalists or some personal virtue," says *Times* columnist Friedman. "It is a national-security imperative."[124]

"It must be recognized," says Yergin of Cambridge Energy Research Associates, "that energy security does not stand by itself but is lodged in the larger relations among nations and how they interact with one another."[125]

NOTES

1. The Associated Press, "Putin: Soviet Collapse a 'Genuine Tragedy,'" MSNBC, April 25, 2005, www.msnbc.msn.com/id/7632057.

2. "Russia Cuts Ukraine Gas Supplies," BBC News, Jan. 1, 2006; http://news.bbc.co.uk/1/hi/world/europe/4572712.stm.

AFP/Getty Images/Behrouz Mehri

Gas stations in Tehran were torched and looted on June 26, 2007, after the Iranian government announced plans to begin fuel rationing. The state-controlled National Iranian Oil Co. has subsidized consumer fuel prices, sparking increased demand for oil.

3. "Russia and the West; No Divide, No Rule," *The Economist*, May 17, 2007, p. 12.

4. "Oil Nationalism Troubling Multinationals," *Iran Daily*, Oct. 23, 2006, p. 11, http://irandaily.ir/1385/2691/pdf/i11.pdf.

5. John M. Deutch, testimony before the House Foreign Affairs Committee, March 22, 2007.

6. "PIW Ranks the World's Top Oil Companies," *Energy Intelligence*, www.energyintel.com/DocumentDetail.asp?document_id=137158.

7. *Iran Daily*, op. cit.

8. Peter Katel, "Change in Latin America," *CQ Researcher*, July 21, 2006, pp. 601-624.

9. Natalie Obiko Pearson, "Chávez takes over Venezuela's last private oil fields," The Associated Press Worldstream, May 2, 2007.

10. Alexandra Valencia, "Ecuador says started review of oil contracts," Reuters, June 6, 2007; www.reuters.com/article/companyNewsAndPR/idUSN0645081020070607.

11. *Energy Intelligence*, op. cit.

12. U.S. motorists were paying over $1.42 a gallon for regular gasoline in March 1981. Adjusted at 2006 price levels to account for inflation, that cost would be $3.22 a gallon; www.eia.doe.gov/emeu/steo/pub/fsheets/petroleumprices.xls.

13. Matthew Higgins, Thomas Klitgaard and Robert Lerman, "Recycling Petrodollars: Current Issues in Economics and Finance," Federal Reserve Bank of New York, December 2006, p. 1; www.newyorkfed .org/research/current_issues/ci12-9.pdf.

14. "The Changing Role of National Oil Companies in International Energy Markets," James A. Baker III Institute for Public Policy, April 2007; http://baker-institute.org/Pubs/BI_Pol%20Rep_35.pdf, page 2; see all reports www.rice.edu/energy/publications/ nocs.html.

15. "World Energy Outlook 2006," International Energy Agency, p. 1; www.worldenergyoutlook.org/ summaries2006/English.pdf.

16. For background, see Colin Woodard, "Curbing Climate Change," *CQ Global Researcher*, February 2007, pp. 27-50; and the following *CQ Researchers*: Barbara Mantel, "Energy Efficiency," May 19, 2006, pp. 433-456; Marcia Clemmitt, "Climate Change," Jan. 27, 2006, pp. 73-96; Mary H. Cooper, "Energy Policy," May 25, 2001, pp. 441-464; Mary H. Cooper, "Global Warming Treaty," Jan. 26, 2001, pp. 41-64; Mary H. Cooper, "Global Warming Update," Nov. 1, 1996, pp. 961-984.

17. Maureen S. Crandall, *Energy, Economics and Politics in the Caspian Region: Dreams and Realities* (2006), pp. 23, 46.

18. Amy Myers Jaffe and Matthew E. Chen, James A. Baker III Institute for Public Policy, testimony before the U.S.-China Economic and Security Review Commission, hearing on China's Role in the World, Aug. 4, 2006; www.uscc.gov/hearings/2006hearings/ written_testimonies/06_08_3_4wrts/06_08_3_4_ jaffe_amy_statement.php.

19. R. James Woolsey, "Global implications of Rising Oil Dependence and Global Warming," testimony before the House Select Committee on Energy Independence and Global Warming, April 18, 2007, p. 2.

20. "PIW Survey: Oil Reserves Are Not Rising," *Petroleum Intelligence Weekly*, April 16, 2007; www .energyintel.com/DocumentDetail.asp?document_ id=199949. See also "Performance Profiles of Major Energy Producers 2005," Energy Information Agency, pp. 20-21; www.eia.doe.gov/emeu/perfpro/ 020605.pdf.

21. Michael Connolly, "Fragmented Market Would Hamper Russian-Iranian 'Gas OPEC'," *Wall Street Journal Online*, Feb. 2, 2007.

22. Daniel Dombey, Neil Buckley, Carola Hoyos, "NATO fears Russian plans for 'gas OPEC'," *Financial Times*, Nov. 13, 2006.

23. Daniel S. Sullivan addressed the Energy Council's Federal Energy & Environmental Matters Conference, March 9, 2007.

24. James A. Baker III Institute for Public Policy Report, *op. cit.*; also Baker Institute Report, "Introductions and Summary Conclusions," pp. 7-19; www.rice .edu/energy/publications/docs/NOCs/Presentations/ Hou-Jaffe-KeyFindings.pdf.

25. "Mapping the Global Future: Report of the National Intelligence Council's 2020 Project," National Intelligence Council, December 2004; www.dni .gov/nic/NIC_globaltrend2020.html.

26. Michael Schiffer and Gary Schmitt, "Keeping Tabs on China's Rise," The Stanley Foundation, May 2007, p. 1; www.stanleyfoundation.org/publications/ other/SchifferSchimitt07.pdf.

27. *Ibid.*, p. 9.

28. Xuecheng Liu, "China's Energy Security and Its Grand Strategy," The Stanley Foundation, September 2006, p. 13; www.stanleyfoundation.org/publications/pab/ pab06chinasenergy.pdf.

29. Quoted in Paulo Prada, "Bolivian Nationalizes the Oil and Gas Sector," *The New York Times*, May 2, 2006, p. A9.

30. Quoted in Juan Forero, "Presidential Vote Could Alter Bolivia, and Strain Ties With U.S.," *The New York Times*, Dec. 18, 2005, p. A13.

31. Alfonzo quoted by Stanford University's Terry Lynn Karl, Senior Fellow at the Institute for International Studies, Stanford University, in "The Oil Trap," Transparency International, September 2003; ww1 .transparency.org/newsletters/2003.3/tiq-Sept2003 .pdf.

32. Richard M. Auty, *Sustaining Development in Mineral Economies: The Resource Curse Thesis* (Routledge), 1993. Summarized in Richard M. Auty, "The 'Resource Curse' in Developing Countries Can Be Avoided," United Nations University, Helsinki;

www.wider.unu.edu/research/pr9899d2/pr9899d2s.htm.

33. "Country Analysis Briefs: Mexico," Energy Information Administration, January 2007; www.eia.doe.gov/emeu/cabs/Mexico/Oil.html; and "Major Non-OPEC Countries' Oil Revenues," www.eia.doe.gov/cabs/opecnon.html.

34. Robert Collier, "Mexico's Oil Bonanza Starts to Dry Up," *San Francisco Chronicle*; www.sfgate.com/cgi-bin/article.cgi?file=/c/a/2006/06/30/MNGAAJN9JG1.DTL.

35. Karl, Transparency International, *op. cit.*, p. 1.

36. See "The 'Dutch Disease': Theory and Evidence," *Poverty and Growth Blog*, The World Bank, http://pgpblog.worldbank.org/the_dutch_disease_theory_and_evidence.

37. Tom O'Neill, "Hope and Betrayal in the Niger Delta," *National Geographic*, February 2007, p. 97.

38. Senan Murray, "Tackling Nigeria's Violent Oil Swamps," BBC News, May 30, 2007; http://news.bbc.co.uk/2/hi/africa/6698433.stm.

39. Karl Maier, "Nigeria Militants Release Six Chevron Oil Workers," Bloomberg, June 2, 2007; www.bloomberg.com/apps/news?pid=20601087&sid=aXT6yOlwMVGY&refer=home.

40. Daniel Balint Kurti, "New Militia is a Potent Force," *The Christian Science Monitor*, March 7, 2007; www.csmonitor.com/2006/0307/p04s01-woaf.html.

41. Bernd Debusmann, "In Venezuela, obstacles to 21st Century socialism," Reuters, June 20, 2007.

42. Transparency International, Corruption Perceptions Index, 2006; www.transparency.org/policy_research/surveys_indices/cpi/2006.

43. Freedom House, "Countries at the Crossroads 2006; Country Report: Venezuela," www.freedomhouse.org/template.cfm?page=140&edition=7&ccrpage=31&ccrcountry=141.

44. "Iran fuel rations spark anger, pump stations burn," Reuters, June 27, 2007, www.reuters.com/article/worldNews/idUSDAH72595420070627.

45. "New Analysis Claims Darfur Deaths Near 400,000," Coalition for Darfur, April 25, 2005, http://coalitionfordarfur.blogspot.com/2005/04/new-analysis-claims-darfur-deaths-near.html.

46. Jaffe, *op. cit.*

47. David Zweig and Bi Jianhai, "China's Global Hunt for Energy," *Foreign Affairs*, Sept./Oct. 2005, p. 32.

48. Scott McDonald, "China Welcomes Darfur Agreement," The Associated Press, June 14, 2007; www.boston.com/news/world/asia/articles/2007/06/14/china_welcomes_darfur_agreement/.

49. "Fact Sheet," Extractive Industries Transparency Initiative, 2007; www.eitransparency.org/section/abouteiti.

50. Thomas L. Friedman, "The First Law of Petropolitics," *Foreign Policy*, May/June 2006, p. 4; www.foreignpolicy.com/story/cms.php?story_id=3426.

51. Ariel Cohen, the Heritage Foundation, "The North Eureopean Gas Pipeline Threatens Europe's Energy Security," Oct. 26, 2006; www.heritage.org/Research/Europe/bg1980.cfm.

52. Alexandre Rocha, "Burned by Bolivia, Brazil Goes to Africa and Middle East Looking for Gas," *Brazzil Magazine* (online), June 20, 2007; www.brazzilmag.com/content/view/8368/1/.

53. Crandall, *op. cit.*, p. 143.

54. Foster Klug, "U.S. Presses China on Iran in Latest Talks," The Associated Press, June 20, 2007.

55. "Mapping the Global Future," *op. cit.*

56. Schiffer and Schmitt, *op. cit.*, p 14.

57. Evan Osnos, "U.S., China vie for oil, allies on new Silk Road," *Chicago Tribune*, Dec. 19, 2006, p. 4.

58. Schiffer and Schmitt, *op. cit.*, p. 15.

59. "About Us," Organization of Petroleum Exporting Countries, www.opec.org/aboutus/history/history.htm.

60. Until 1972 production limits set by the Texas Railroad Commission effectively set a ceiling on oil prices in the United States and the rest of the world. But U.S. output peaked then, opening the way for OPEC's moves to control oil markets; http://tonto.eia.doe.gov/dnav/pet/hist/mcrfpus1m.htm.

61. For background, see Mary H. Cooper, "OPEC: Ten Years After the Arab Oil Boycott," *Editorial Research Reports*, Sept. 23, 1983; available in *CQ Researcher Plus Archive*, www.cqpress.com.

62. "U.S. Strategic Petroleum Reserve," Fact Sheet, U.S. Department of Energy, May 30, 2007; www.fossil .energy.gov/programs/reserves.

63. Daniel Yergin, *The Prize: The Epic Quest for Oil, Money & Power* (1991), p. 631.

64. "Carter Energy Program," *CQ Historic Documents Series Online Edition.* Originally published in *Historic Documents of 1977*, CQ Press (1978), CQ Electronic Library; http://library.cqpress.com/historicdocuments/ hsdc77-0000106610.

65. *Ibid.*

66. "Iranian Hostage Crisis, 1980 Special Report," *Congress and the Nation, 1977-1980* (Vol. 5); CQ Press; available at CQ Congress Collection, CQ Electronic Library, http://library.cqpress.com/ congress/catn77-0010173673.

67. "Real Gasoline Prices," Energy Information Administration; www.eia.doe.gov/emeu/steo/pub/ fsheets/real_prices.html.

68. For background, see R. Thompson, "Quest for Energy Independence," *Editorial Research Reports*, Dec. 23, 1983, available in *CQ Researcher Plus Archive*, CQ Electronic Library, http://library.cqpress.com.

69. Yergin, *op. cit.*, p. 669.

70. *Ibid.*, p. 666.

71. "Annual Energy Review 2005, World Crude Oil Production, 1960-2005," Energy Information Administration; www.eia.doe.gov/emeu/aer/pdf/ pages/sec11_11.pdf.

72. Yergin, *op. cit.*, p. 718.

73. Mary H. Cooper, "SUV Debate," *CQ Researcher*, May 16, 2003, pp. 449-472.

74. For background, see Kenneth Jost, "Russia and the Former Soviet Republics," *CQ Researcher*, June 17, 2005; pp. 541-564.

75. Louis Fischer, *Oil Imperialism* (1926), cited by Robert E. Ebel, Center for Strategic and International Studies, July 25, 2006.

76. Bruce W. Nelan, "The Rush for Caspian Oil," *Time*, May 4, 1998, p. 40.

77. Crandall, *op. cit.*, p. 1.

78. "Caspian Sea," Energy Information Administration, 2007; www.eia.doe.gov/emeu/cabs/Caspian/Full.html.

79. Martha Brill Olcott, "Will Central Asia Have Another 'Second Chance'?" speech, Carnegie Endowment for International Peace, Sept. 15, 2005.

80. Crandall, *op. cit.*, p. 3.

81. "Top World Oil Producers, Exporters, Consumers, and Importers 2004," Information Please Database, 2007; www.infoplease.com/ipa/A0922041.html.

82. "BP Statistical Review 2006," British Petroleum, p. 8; www.bp.com/sectiongenericarticle.do?category Id=9017903&contentId=7033469.

83. "Sudan," Energy Information Administration, April 2007; www.eia.doe.gov/emeu/cabs/Sudan/Back ground.html.

84. "Libya — Natural Gas," Energy Information Administration, March 2006; www.eia.doe.gov/ emeu/cabs/Libya/NaturalGas.html.

85. "Nigeria/Natural Gas," Energy Information Administration, April 2007, www.eia.doe.govemeu/ cabs/Nigeria/NaturalGas.html.

86. Zweig and Jianhai, *op. cit.*, p. 25.

87. "International Energy Outlook, 2007," Energy Information Administration, p. 83; www.eia.doe .gov/oiaf/ieo/pdf/ieorefcase.pdf.

88. Dmitri Trenin, Deputy Director, Carnegie Moscow Center, "Russia Leaves the West," *Foreign Affairs*, July/August 2006.

89. Leonid Grigoriev, speaking at the Kennan Institute, Feb. 5, 2007; www.wilsoncenter.org/index.cfm? topic_id=1424&fuseaction=topics.event_summary &event_id=215229.

90. *Oil and Gas Journal*, quoted in www.eia.doe.gov/ emeu/cabs/Venezuela/Oil.html.Conventional reserves do not include the extensive Canadian tar sands or Venezuela's extra-heavy oil and bitumen deposits.

91. Michael Shifter, "In search of Hugo Chávez," *Foreign Affairs*, May/June 2006, p. 47. For background, see Peter Katel, "Change in Latin America," *CQ Researcher*, July 21, 2006, pp. 601-624.

92. Baker Institute for Public Policy, *op. cit.*, p. 6.

93. "Venezuela," Energy Information Administration, September 2006; www.eia.doe.gov/emeu/cabs/ Venezuela/Oil.html.

94. Baker Institute, *op. cit.*, p. 5.

95. *Ibid.*, p. 1.

96. Gregory L. White and Jeffrey Ball, "Huge Sakhalin Project Is Mostly on Track, As Shell Feels Pinch," *The Wall Street Journal*, May 7, 2007, p. 1.

97. *Ibid.*, p. 1. Also see Amy Myers Jaffe, James A. Baker III Institute for Public Policy, "Russia: Back to the Future?" testimony before the Senate Committee on Foreign Relations, June 29, 2006, p. 1.

98. Higgins, Klitgaard and Lerman, *op. cit.*, p. 1.

99. "World Economic Outlook, April 2006," Chapter 2, p. 24, International Monetary Fund; www.imf .org/external/pubs/ft/weo/2006/01/pdf/c2.pdf.

100. Woolsey, *op. cit.*, p. 3.

101. Higgins, Klitgaard and Lerman, *op. cit.*, p. 6.

102. Woolsey, *op. cit.*, p. 3.

103. Higgins, Klitgaard and Lerman, *op. cit.*, pp. 3-4.

104. William Pesek, "Blackstone + China = Bubble," Bloomberg, May 23, 2007; www.bloomberg.com/ apps/news?pid=20601039&sid=aU7bs9CJazGI& refer=columnist_pesek.

105. Ransdell Pierson and Tamora Vidaillet, "China flexes FX muscle with $3 bln Blackstone deal," Reuters, May 21, 2007.

106. Sebastian Mallaby, "The Next Globalization Backlash," *The Washington Post*, June 25, 2007, p. A19.

107. Higgins, Klitgaard and Lerman, *op. cit.*, p. 6.

108. Woolsey, *op. cit.*, p. 4.

109. The United States has its own huge pipeline project on the table, a plan to transport natural gas from Alaska's North Slope into the U.S. Midwest, which would reduce some of the future need for natural gas imports by LNG tankers from Russia and the Middle East.

110. Robert E. Ebel, "Russian Energy Policy," Center for Strategic and International Studies, testimony before the U.S. Senate Committee on Foreign Relations, June 21, 2005; Crandall, *op. cit.*, p. 23.

111. "Central Asia," Energy Information Administration, September 2005; www.eia.doe.gov/emeu/cabs/ Centasia/NaturalGas.html.

112. "Washington Pushes for Trans-Caspian Pipeline," *New Europe*, Jan. 15, 2007; www.neurope.eu/view_ news.php?id=69019.

113. Press statement, State Department, Consulate General-Istanbul, Remarks by Matthew Bryza, deputy assistant secretary of State for European and Eurasian affairs, May 11, 2007; http://istanbul .usconsulate.gov/bryza_speech_051107.html.

114. "Turkmenistan open oil, gas to Russia," UPI, June 13, 2007.

115. "World Energy Outlook 2006," International Energy Agency, p. 3; www.worldenergyoutlook .org/summaries2006/English.pdf.

116. "International Energy Outlook 2007," Energy Information Administration, p. 187; www.eia.doe . gov/oiaf/ieo/pdf/ieopol.pdf.

117. "Fighting Climate Change Through Energy Efficiency," United Nations Environment Program, May 30, 2006; www.unep.org/Documents .Multilingual/Default.asp?DocumentID= 477& ArticleID=5276&l=en.

118. "Working Group III Report," Intergovernmental Panel on Climate Change, May 2007; www.mnp .nl/ipcc/pages_media/AR4-chapters. html.

119. Joe Barnes, Amy Myers Jaffe, Edward L. Morse, "The Energy Dimension in Russian Global Strategy," James A. Baker III Institute for Public Policy," 2004, p. 5; www.rice.edu/energy/publica- tions/docs/PEC_BarnesJaffeMorse _10_2004.pdf.

120. Jeffrey Logan, Joanna Lewis and Michael B. Cummings, "For China, the Shift to Climate-Friendly Energy Depends on International Collaboration," *Boston Review*, January/February 2007; www.pewclimate .org/press_room/discussions/jlbostonreview.cfm.

121. Logan, Lewis and Cummings, *op. cit.*

122. Global Insight Forecast, "Outlook Still Buoyant for Chinese Auto Market," March 2007; www .globalinsight.com/SDA/SDADetail9307.htm.

123. Catherine Brahic, "China to promise cuts in green- house gases," NewScientist.com news services, Feb. 14, 2007, http://environment.newscientist.com/ article/dn11184.

124. Friedman, *op. cit.*, p. 10.

125. Yergin, "Ensuring Energy Security," *op. cit*, p. 69.

BIBLIOGRAPHY

Books

Crandall, Maureen S., *Energy, Economics, and Politics in the Caspian Region: Dreams and Realities*, Praeger Security International, 2006.
An economics professor at the National Defense University argues that the Caspian region's oil development will accelerate global and regional military, ethnic and religious conflict.

Klare, Michael, *Resource Wars: The New Landscape of Global Conflict*, Henry Holt, 2001.
A political science professor describes how the demand for scarce resources among growing populations has led to wars over the past century.

Yergin, Daniel, *The Prize: The Epic Quest for Oil, Money & Power*, Simon & Schuster, 1991.
In a Pulitzer Prize-winning work, the chairman of Cambridge Energy Research Associates chronicles the political and economic history of the oil industry.

Articles

"PIW Ranks the World's Top Oil Companies," *Energy Intelligence*, www.energyintel.com.
Petroleum Intelligence Weekly, a leading industry publication, ranks Saudi Aramco of Saudi Arabia and Exxon Mobil of the United States as the world's top two oil companies.

O'Neill, Tom, "Curse of the Black Gold," *National Geographic*, February 2007, p. 88.
The writer examines the politics and corruption of multinational petroleum companies that critics claim have created poverty and violence in the wake of Nigeria's oil boom.

Schiffer, Michael and Gary Schmitt, "Keeping Tabs on China's Rise," *The Stanley Foundation*, May 2007, www.stanleyfoundation.org.
Two foreign policy experts encourage the West to continue diplomatic relations with the Beijing government amid China's rise as a global superpower.

Shifter, Michael, "In Search of Hugo Chávez," *Foreign Affairs*, May-June 2006, p. 45.
According to a vice president of the Inter-American Dialogue, the profits from nationalization of Venezuela's oil have yielded only modest gains for the country's poor.

Trenin, Dmitri, "Russia Leaves the West," *Foreign Affairs*, July-Aug. 2006, p. 87.
Russia's vast energy resources make it a potential threat to the United States and other Western nations, according to the deputy director of the Carnegie Moscow Center.

Udall, Randy, and Matthew R. Simmons, "CERA's Rosy Oil Forecast — Pabulum to the People," *ASPO-USA's Peak Oil Review/Energy Bulletin*, Aug. 21, 2006, www.energy bulletin.net.
Two energy experts refute a recent optimistic oil study by Cambridge Energy Research Associates, contending that in actuality oil will be in shorter supply and more expensive by 2015.

Yergin, Daniel, "Ensuring Energy Security," *Foreign Affairs*, March-April 2006, p. 69.
The chairman of Cambridge Energy Research Associates explores new tactics for safeguarding the world's energy supplies and alleviating energy-related conflicts.

Zweig, David, and Bi Jianhai, "China's Global Hunt for Energy," *Foreign Affairs*, Sept.-Oct. 2005, p. 25.
Two foreign policy professors at Hong Kong University argue that China must find new energy sources if it wants to maintain rapid economic growth.

Reports

"Challenge and Opportunity, Charting a New Energy Future," *Energy Future Coalition*, 2002, www.energyfuturecoalition.org.
A bipartisan energy research group advocates alternative energy strategies to reduce dependence on foreign oil.

"The Changing Role of National Oil Companies in International Markets," *James A. Baker III Institute for Public Policy, Rice University*, May 1, 2007, www.rice.edu.
Energy researchers provide case studies analyzing the problems of private petroleum companies amid the rise of oil nationalism.

Ebel, Robert E., "Russian Energy Policy," *testimony before Senate Foreign Relations Committee*, June 21, 2005.
A senior energy adviser at the Center for Strategic and International Studies stresses the United States' need for a diplomatic energy-policy dialogue with Russia.

Jaffe, Amy Myers, "Russia: Back to the Future?" *testimony before Senate Foreign Relations Committee*, June 29, 2006.

A noted energy analyst reviews Russia's increasingly nationalistic energy policies.

Woolsey, R. James, "Geopolitical Implications of Rising Oil Dependence and Global Warming," *testimony before Select Committee on Energy Independence and Global Warming*, April 18, 2007.

A former CIA director offers solutions for curbing the United States' dependence on oil and natural gas.

For More Information

American Enterprise Institute, 1150 17th St., N.W., Washington, DC 20036; (202) 862-5800; www.aei.org. Public-policy research group studying economic and social issues.

American Petroleum Institute, 1220 L St., N.W., Washington, DC 20005-4070; (202) 682-8000; www.api.org. Industry group representing oil and gas producers.

James A. Baker III Institute, 6100 Main St., Rice University, Baker Hall, Suite 120, Houston, TX 77005; (713) 348-4683; http://bakerinstitute.org. Academic research group specializing in energy.

Cambridge Energy Research Associates, 55 Cambridge Parkway, Cambridge, MA 02142; (617) 866-5000; www.cera.com. Renowned energy consultancy to international energy firms, financial institutions, foreign governments and technology providers.

Center for Strategic and International Studies, 800 K St., N.W., Washington, DC 20006; (202) 887-0200; www.csis.org. Public-policy research group specializing in defense, security and energy issues.

Council on Foreign Relations, 1779 Massachusetts Ave., N.W., Washington, DC 20036; (202) 518-3400; www.cfr.org. Think tank focusing on international issues; publishes *Foreign Affairs*.

Energy Future Coalition, 1800 Massachusetts Ave., N.W., Washington, DC 20036; (202) 463-1947; www.energyfuturecoalition.org. A bipartisan advocacy group for energy conservation and alternative fuels.

Energy Information Administration, 1000 Independence Ave., S.W., Washington, DC 20585; (202) 586-8800; www.eia.doe.gov. The primary source of federal data and analysis on energy.

Extractive Industries Transparency Initiative, Ruseløkkveien 26, 0251 Oslo, Norway; +47 22 24 2110; www.eitransparency.org. Advocates responsible energy use and public disclosure of energy-based revenues and expenditures on behalf of more than 20 nations.

Human Rights Watch, 350 Fifth Ave., 34th floor, New York, NY 10118-3299; (212) 290-4700; www.hrw.org. Advocates for human rights.

International Energy Agency, 9 rue de la Fédération, 75739 Paris Cedex 15, France; 33 1 40 57 65 00/01; www.iea.org. The principal international forum for global energy data and analysis.

Kennan Institute, Woodrow Wilson International Center for Scholars, Ronald Reagan Building and International Trade Center, One Woodrow Wilson Plaza, 1300 Pennsylvania Ave., N.W., Washington, DC 20004-3027; (202) 691-4000; www.wilsoncenter.org. Think tank specializing in social, political and economic developments in Russia and the former Soviet states.

Organization of the Petroleum Exporting Countries, Obere Donaustrasse 93, A-1020 Vienna, Austria; +43-1-21112-279; www.opec.org. Coordinates and unifies petroleum policies among its 12 oil-exporting member nations.

Transparency International, Alt-Moabit 96, 10559 Berlin, Germany; 49-30-34-38 20-0; www.transparency.org. Advocacy group that campaigns against corruption worldwide.

World Bank, 1818 H St., N.W., Washington, DC 20433; (202) 473-1000; www.worldbank.org. Provides financial and technical assistance to developing countries.

10

Oceans in Crisis

Can the Loss of Ocean Biodiversity Be Halted?

Colin Woodard

A Russian trawler hauls in a netful of red fish on the Grand Banks in the northwest Atlantic Ocean. The world's oceans have lost more than 90 percent of large predatory fish — such as tuna, swordfish and grouper — over the past half-century, prompting fishermen to hunt smaller species. Scientists and environmentalists blame the loss of ocean biodiversity on overfishing, pollution and climate change.

From *CQ Researcher*, October 2007.

all Samba has spent much of his adult life fishing for octopus from his home in Nouadhibou, Mauritania, on Africa's Atlantic coast. Fishing from a wooden canoe, he could bring home 160 pounds on a five-day trip — earning $600 a month in a country where the average wage is only $200. In 2004, he built a home and bought new canoes; times were good.

Not anymore. "You used to be able to catch fish right in the port," the 39-year-old told *The Wall Street Journal* recently. "Now the only thing you can catch is water."[1]

Today Samba and other fishermen must compete with huge industrial trawlers from Russia, China and Spain. But while Samba pulls his catch out of the sea by hand in plastic traps, a single Spanish vessel dragging a massive nylon net catches 260,000 pounds of octopus on a typical 45-day fishing trip.

Some 340 big foreign vessels fish Mauritanian waters because the government recently sold fishing rights to Asian and European nations that have overfished their own territorial waters. Stocks of octopus, which account for half of Mauritania's fish exports, are declining, and Samba has seen his monthly income fall by two-thirds.

Samba's experience is rapidly becoming universal in the world's coastal regions. According to the U.N. Food and Agriculture Organization (FAO), a quarter of the world's commercial fish stocks have been overexploited or depleted, and about half are fully exploited — meaning fishermen are taking as much as can be reliably replenished by the ecosystem.[2] (*See graphic, p. 261.*)

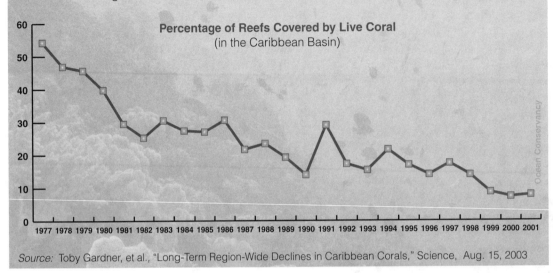

Caribbean Corals Are Disappearing

Only 10 percent of the coral reefs in the Caribbean are alive, compared with more than 50 percent three decades ago. Experts say corals are dying due to global warming, pollution, sedimentation and over-harvesting of fish and other reef resources — sometimes using dynamite or poison.

Percentage of Reefs Covered by Live Coral
(in the Caribbean Basin)

Ocean Conservancy

Source: Toby Gardner, et al., "Long-Term Region-Wide Declines in Caribbean Corals," Science, Aug. 15, 2003

Moreover, 90 percent of the world's large, predatory fish have been harvested since 1950, prompting fishermen to progressively move to smaller, less valuable species further down the food chain.[3] The shift has triggered the rapid depletion of marine species previously considered unmarketable — such as dogfish, urchins and basking sharks — which in turn has reduced the food available to the surviving stocks of larger species. Small, lower-valued schooling fish like anchovies now dominate world fishery landings.

"We're eating bait and moving on to jellyfish and plankton," says Daniel Pauly, director of the Fisheries Centre at the University of British Columbia, who predicts future generations will associate seafood not with tuna or cod but with simple, gelatinous creatures. "My kids will tell their children: 'Eat your jellyfish.' "[4]

The decimation of global fisheries is blamed largely on powerful, new technologies that allow fishermen to capture fish faster than the ocean can produce them. Radar, fish finders, satellite tracking and navigation systems, onboard processing plants and flash freezers are put aboard ever faster vessels capable of fishing far from shore for long periods.

In addition, most fishing gear is indiscriminate: The vast nets used by trawlers typically kill huge quantities of unmarketable marine life. Each year 7 million metric tons of seabirds, juvenile fish, sea turtles, dolphins, sharks, crabs, starfish, anemones, sponges and other creatures are caught, killed and discarded by mechanized fishing. On average, this "bycatch" accounts for 8 percent of fishermen's catches; but among shrimp fishermen in the tropics, bycatch represents 56 percent of the haul.[5]

Trawl nets and gear dragged along the sea bottom are said to cause lasting damage to the seafloor habitat and, thus, to the ability of marine ecosystems to sustain themselves. The heavy nets plow away the bottom plants, sponges and corals that animals use for cover, while killing large numbers of the invertebrates they feed on.

In the Gulf of Maine, for instance, the average seafloor section is trawled once a year; on the Georges Bank off Massachusetts, it's plowed three to four times a year. The trawls also create muddy clouds thought to reduce the survival of small fish by clogging their gills.[6] Elliott Norse, president of the Marine Conservation Biology Institute in Bellevue, Wash., calls sea bottom trawling "clear cutting the seafloor." Trawling companies contend there's no proof their activities damage the ocean floor and that trawling actually may benefit seafloor species.

It's not just fish that are in crisis, however. Coral reefs, the foundation of most tropical marine life, are declining at an alarming rate. The latest international assessment found that one-fifth of the world's coral reefs "have been effectively destroyed and show no immediate prospects of recovery," while another 24 percent are "under imminent risk of collapse." Live coral cover on Caribbean reefs has declined by 80 percent over the past 30 years.[7] (*See graph above.*)

Without corals, tropical oceans would become biological wastelands, because they don't support the growth of phytoplankton, the microscopic plants that form the base of the marine food chain. Reefs are colonies of coral polyps — anemone-like organisms that build limestone shells around themselves. They filter food particles from the water and capture the sun's energy through photosynthetic micro-organisms inside their tissue. Corals support the profusion of fish associated with tropical reefs.[8]

Reefs are being damaged in a variety of ways. Clearing coastal mangroves for development dooms reef creatures that feed there and triggers erosion that smothers the coral polyps under plumes of sand and soil. Overfishing results in the harvesting of increasing numbers of ever-smaller fish, lobsters and conch. Fishermen in the Philippines, Micronesia, Jamaica and Indonesia use dynamite and other explosives to stun and kill marine life over a wide area — a one-time bonanza that destroys the reef. Sewage and fertilizer run-off from towns, resorts, fish farms and golf courses trigger the

Most Fish Stocks Are Overexploited

Three-quarters of the world's fisheries were either fully exploited — at or near their maximum sustainable limits — overexploited or depleted in 2005. Fisheries biologists say the stocks cannot recover quickly and are in danger of further decline.

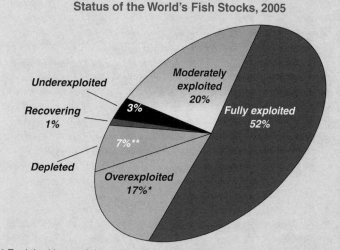

Status of the World's Fish Stocks, 2005

* Exploited beyond the ability of the system to sustain itself over the long term.

** Current catches fall far below historic levels.

China and Peru Catch the Most

China and Peru haul in nearly 27 million tons of fish a year — almost as much as the next eight countries combined.

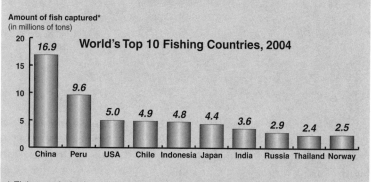

World's Top 10 Fishing Countries, 2004

Amount of fish captured*
(in millions of tons)

* Fish caught in the wild, excluding those grown by aquaculture.

Source: "The State of the World Fisheries and Aquaculture 2006," U.N. Food and Agriculture Organization, www.fao.org/docrep/009/A0699e/A0699E04.htm

Beach Litter Can Be Lethal

Nearly 7.7 million pieces of beach litter were collected in 2006 by some 350,000 Ocean Conservancy coastal cleanup volunteers around the world. About two-thirds of the items were food containers and plastic bags; the rest were smoking related. Experts say 1 million seabirds and 100,000 marine mammals and sea turtles die each year after ingesting or becoming entangled in ocean debris.

Top 10 Ocean Debris Items Worldwide

Debris Items	Number of Items	Percent of Total
Cigarette debris	1,901,519	24.7%
Food wrappers, containers	768,115	10.0%
Caps/lids	704,085	9.1%
Bags	691,048	9.0%
Beverage bottles (Plastic) 2 liters or less	570,299	7.4%
Beverage bottles (Glass)	420,800	5.5%
Cups/plates/forks/knives/spoons	353,217	4.6%
Straw/stirrers	349,653	4.5%
Beverage cans	327,494	4.3%
Cigar tips	186,258	2.4%

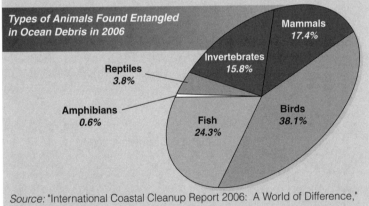

Types of Animals Found Entangled in Ocean Debris in 2006

Mammals 17.4%
Invertebrates 15.8%
Reptiles 3.8%
Amphibians 0.6%
Fish 24.3%
Birds 38.1%

Source: "International Coastal Cleanup Report 2006: A World of Difference," Ocean Conservancy

growth of seaweed, kelp and other plants that can smother and eventually kill the reefs. Even far from human activity, reefs are dying from disease and overly warm water temperatures linked to climate change.[9]

Colder waters are affected, too. In the High Arctic, Inuit mothers' breast milk is dangerous to their babies' health because the polar bears, seals, walruses, fish and whales they eat are contaminated by heavy metals, PCBs and other industrial compounds now found in seawater and stored in the animals' fat. Many Inuit have concentrations of certain pesticides in their bodies that exceed safe levels 20-fold. Beached whales often must be treated as hazardous waste because of the high concentrations toxic substances in their bodies.[10] Both wild and farm-raised salmon have also been shown to have potentially significant contaminant levels.[11]

Fertilizers, sewage and other nutrient pollution have triggered massive algal blooms that can strip the ocean of dissolved oxygen, dooming animals that cannot escape the area. Such oxygen-starved "dead zones" have spread from harbors and river mouths to suffocate entire seas. (*See sidebar, p. 266.*) Each summer, fertilizer runoff from 31 states and parts of Canada flows into the Mississippi River and then to the Gulf of Mexico, creating a New Jersey-size dead zone south of New Orleans where few species can survive.[12]

Non-native, or "invasive," species also can damage marine ecosystems.[13] The species are carried around the globe in the ballast tanks of ocean-going vessels, which pump water in and out of the tanks to maintain seaworthiness. This ballast can contain the eggs, larvae or adult forms of hundreds of species, some of which become established in waters that contains no natural predators.

"Once an exotic species is established, trying to remove it is like trying to put the toothpaste back in the tube," says James T. Carlton, professor of marine sciences at Williams College in Massachusetts. In the early 1990s, a comb jelly snuffed out much of the life in the Black Sea (*see p. 266*), while a mutant form of a tropical seaweed, *Caulerpa taxifolia*, has smothered vast stretches of the Mediterranean shore since it was accidentally released into the sea by a Monaco aquarium.[14]

Some scientists worry that in many marine ecosystems the more advanced organisms are disappearing while the populations of the most primitive ecosystems are exploding. "Dead zones aren't dead; they are just full of jellyfish and bacteria," notes Jeremy B. C. Jackson, director of the Geosciences Research Division at the Scripps Institution of Oceanography in San Diego, who calls the process "the rise of slime."

In Sweden, summer blooms of *cyanobacteria* turn the surface of the Baltic Sea into a yellow-brown slurry that kills fish, burns people's eyes and makes breathing difficult. Hawaiian condo owners have had to use tractors to remove piles of algae piling up on their beaches, while toxic algal blooms are believed responsible for mass die-offs of sea lions, whales, manatees and dolphins. Red tides — algal blooms that make shellfish poisonous to humans — are 10 times more common than they were 50 years ago, owing in part to increases in sewage and fertilizer run-off. "We're pushing the oceans back to the dawn of evolution, a half-billion years ago when the oceans were ruled by jellyfish and bacteria," says Pauly at the University of British Columbia.[15]

Experts argue that adopting ecosystem-based approaches to regulating human activity on the seas would help ensure the system as a whole is healthy, rather than just focusing on a particular species. Some fishing interests resist such an approach — which would involve creation of marine reserves and other protected areas — but its greatest opponent is public and political apathy.

As scientists and governments try to determine how best to protect the world's oceans, here are some of the questions being debated:

Are humans destroying the oceans?

Yes, according to numerous recent scientific studies including a June 2007 assessment of Europe's seas by 100 scientists from 15 countries.

"In every sea, we found serious damage related to the accelerated pace of coastal development, the way we transport our goods and the way we produce our food on land as well as the sea," said Laurence Mee, director of the Marine Institute at the University of Plymouth (in England), who coordinated the project. "Without a concerted effort to integrate protection of the sea into Europe's development plans, its biodiversity and resources will be lost."[16]

Ocean Conservancy

Plastic bottles, food containers and grocery bags make up a large portion of the refuse that ends up in the ocean and washes ashore. More than 100,000 marine mammals alone are killed each year by either ingesting or becoming entangled in debris.

A four-year analysis released in November 2006 by an international group of ecologists and economists concluded that if current trends continue, every seafood species currently fished will be commercially extinct by 2050. The study found that every species lost increases the speed at which the larger ecosystem unravels.

"Whether we looked at tide pools or studies over the entire world's oceans, we saw the same picture emerging," said the study's lead author, Boris Worm, assistant professor of biology at Dalhousie University in Halifax, Nova Scotia. "I was shocked and disturbed by how consistent these trends are — beyond anything we expected."[17]

Likewise, two independent, bipartisan U.S. commissions — the Pew Oceans Commission and the U.S. Commission on Ocean Policy (USCOP) — concluded in 2003 and 2004, respectively, that pollution, habitat destruction and overfishing are endangering the world's oceans.[18]

"There is overwhelming scientific evidence that our ocean ecosystems are in serious trouble, serious enough that it really is endangering the future of ocean life itself," says Leon Panetta, former chief of staff in the Clinton White House, who chaired the Pew Commission. "The biggest challenge is to get people to pay attention, because if they do, then we can make our case."

"What is the state of our oceans? Unfortunately we have to report to you that the state is not good, and it is getting worse," Admiral James D. Watkins, chair of USCOP told Congress. Furthermore, the harm humans are inflicting on the oceans, the USCOP report concluded, has "serious consequences for the entire planet."[19]

Marine scientists have been aware of the situation for more than a decade. In 1998 — the U.N. International Year of the Ocean — more than 1,600 marine scientists and conservation biologists from 65 nations issued a joint warning that the seas were in peril and that immediate action was needed to prevent further damage.

"Getting scientists to agree on anything is like herding cats, so having 1,600 experts voice their concerns publicly highlights just how seriously the sea is threatened," said Norse, of the Marine Conservation Biology Institute, who organized the effort. "We must change what we're doing now to prevent further irreversible decline."[20]

However, some researchers and fishing industry groups deny there is a problem, claiming the situation is exaggerated by environmentalists to further fundraising opportunities. "Are we running out of fish? No," said Dan Furlong, executive director of the U.S. Mid-Atlantic Fishery Management Council. Furlong cites U.S. National Marine Fisheries Service assessments showing that of the 230 stocks the agency manages, only 44 are known to be overfished, 136 "are not subject to overfishing," while the status of the remaining 50 are unknown. "In other words, the glass is more than half full for those stocks," he says. The public, he says, has been duped by environmentalists who pushed Congress to require that stocks be rebuilt. As a result, he says, "despite significant improvements across a broad range of fisheries, we are cast in the role of doing poorly because we will likely fail to meet . . . the arbitrary, capricious deadline to maximize stocks all at the same time."[21]

Bjorn Lomborg, associate professor of statistics at the University of Aarhus in Denmark, argues in his controversial book *The Skeptical Environmentalist* that while there are problems, the oceans are doing fine.

"The oceans are so incredibly big that our impact on them has been astoundingly insignificant," he argues, citing U.N. data suggesting that in the open oceans, far from land, the U.N. has found the seas to be relatively clean. He acknowledges that fertilizer is creating dead zones in places like the Gulf of Mexico and the Black Sea but says the disruptions are worth it when compared to the improved crop yields.[22]

"Our oceans have not been defiled . . . and although the nutrient influx has increased in many coastal waters like the Gulf of Mexico," he continues. "This does not constitute a major problem — in fact, the benefits generally outweigh the costs."[23]

Critics accuse Lomborg of cherry-picking facts that support his arguments and ignoring evidence to the contrary. For instance, Lomborg's book fails to address the crisis in the fisheries, the decline of the coral reefs, the problems caused by alien species and other issues.

And even some fishermen don't share Lomborg's view. "The combination of modern electronics with large fishing vessels has created a technology too powerful for fish stocks to withstand," said Ted Ames, a fisherman from Stonington, Maine, who won a McArthur Genius Grant for his research into the decline of Gulf of Maine fish stocks.[24]

Is ecosystem-based management the solution?

The destruction of life in the oceans presents humans with perhaps the greatest marine policy challenge in history: figuring out how to manage human activities so they don't damage marine biodiversity, critical habitat and overall ecosystem function. Known as "ecosystem-based management," the approach has wide support, including both USCOP and the Pew Commission.

"You're not going to have any fish to catch — or healthy fishing communities — unless there is a healthy marine ecosystem to provide the fish," says Jane Lubchenco, a professor of marine biology at Oregon State University, a former Pew Commissioner and past president of the American Association for the Advancement of Science. "We need mechanisms to better understand how ocean ecosystems work and how we're changing them if we are going to do a better job managing them."

And many scientists say they don't yet have that understanding.

For the past two years, dozens of scientists in New England and Canada's maritime provinces have been working to develop enough knowledge to undertake ecosystem-based management in the Gulf of Maine by 2010. Scientists working on the Gulf of Maine Census of Marine Life — part of the world's first pilot project for this type of management — are fanning out across the ecosystem examining sea life, ocean currents and the relationship between habitat, predators and prey. A series of ocean buoys is collecting long-term oceanographic data, and other researchers are using sonar technology to map the ocean bottom in unprecedented detail.

"We need to know the big picture of how it happens," says Gerhard Pohle, acting executive director of the Huntsman Marine Science Centre in St. Andrews, New Brunswick, Canada. "If we take one rivet out of the airplane, will it crash? If so, which rivet?"[25]

"We're just beginning to understand how to do the biology on both the super-tiny and the super-large scales," says Lubchenco, who is studying the California Current ecosystem off the U.S. West Coast. "You have to marry oceanography and ecology and genetics and microchemistry in a very interdisciplinary fashion to better understand the processes driving these ecosystems."

But other scientists — many of them government fisheries managers — say sufficient knowledge already exists to start ecosystem-wide management. "Make no mistake, we currently have sufficient scientific information to move forward with an ecosystem-based approach to management," said Andrew Rosenberg, dean of the College of Life Sciences at the University of New Hampshire, a USCOP commissioner and former deputy director of the U.S. National Marine Fisheries Service. "The nation's ocean policy should recognize these principles and seek to integrate management within regional ecosystems."[26]

Some scientists and environmentalists challenge the notion that humans can or should try to manage ecosystems. In the long term, they say, how could one manage a constantly changing ecosystem, when ideas about what is "healthy" or "desirable" are often based on present conditions or a theoretical, idyllic state. Others point out that an ecosystem means different things to different people, making them difficult to adequately define.[27]

Proponents are careful to point out that ecosystem-based management does not seek to manage the ecosystem — which would be scientific hubris in their opinion — but rather human activity affecting the ecosystem. "One of the reasons ecosystem-based management was pooh-poohed for many years was that there was this naïve assumption [that] you just learn everything you need to know about the ecosystem and then you manage it," says Lew Incze, director of the Aquatic Systems Group at the University of Southern Maine in Portland. "Now we know that we will never know everything — you can even have 100 years of good data, but the ocean is always changing.

"The question is," he continues, "what type of knowledge would allow you to pursue the idea?"

The Gulf of Maine Census of Marine Life is attempting to develop a basic framework by testing ideas about what factors control the number of upper-level predators like Atlantic cod or humpback whales; what indicators would best track the health and diversity of the entire system and how currents, tides and natural oceanographic cycles shape life there. "We're just now developing the tools to come to grips with this," says Pohle.

David Benton, executive director of the Marine Conservation Alliance, a coalition of Alaskan fishing interests, says ecosystem-based management is potentially very good for commercial fishermen.

"It's very clear to most of our membership that it is in their long-term interest to make sure that we have healthy oceans and fish stocks and that all the associated components of the ecosystem around those stocks are in good shape," he says. "A lot of these companies are looking at how these fisheries are going to support their business — not two years from now but a decade from now or longer."

Should ocean-floor trawling be restricted?

Concerns about the damage caused by shellfish dredges and trawl nets have prompted many scientists, environmentalists and governmental agencies to call for a ban on trawling where it is likely to cause lasting harm.

A 2002 study by the National Academy of Sciences' National Research Council recommended that the U.S. government reduce the impact and extent of bottom trawling to reduce its impact on undersea life. Trawls scrape away cold-water corals, sponges, plants, sea anemones, starfish and other creatures, the report found, and repeated passes can cause a 93 percent reduction in these and other bottom-dwelling animals.

The Black Sea's Cautionary Tale

Ecosystem collapse shows signs of recovery.

From ancient times, humans have been drawn to the Black Sea, a kidney-shaped basin the size of California nestled between Eastern Europe and Asia Minor. Its anchovy and sturgeon stocks sustained Ancient Greece, medieval Byzantium, the Ottoman Empire and Imperial Russia.

In the 20th century, millions of tourists flocked each summer to its beaches in Turkey and on the "Communist Riviera," which stretched from Bulgaria and Romania to Soviet Russia. They swam, feasted on fish and basked in the sunshine, recuperating from winter months in the factories of Budapest and Birmingham.[1]

Then, with astonishing suddenness, the ecosystem collapsed in the early 1990s due to a combination of fertilizer and sewage pollution runoff, destruction of wetlands and the introduction of an aggressive, non-native, jellyfish-like species. Given the plethora of critical ocean ecosystems now in jeopardy, the Black Sea collapse provides a cautionary tale about the fragility of marine ecosystems, say marine scientists.

"The Black Sea is a microcosm of the environmental problems of the planet," warns Janet Lubchenco, a professor of marine biology at Oregon State University. "Solutions to the Black Sea crisis may enlighten, inform and inspire our global challenges."[2]

Few saw it coming. The Black Sea had been subject to pollution for decades: Industrial wastes, oil spills and radiation from the 1986 Chernobyl nuclear accident had been carried to the sea by its tributaries — apparently without dramatic effect. But it was the buildup of raw sewage and fertilizer runoff — coupled with the accidental introduction of an alien, plankton-devouring species, the comb jelly — that triggered the near-death of the sea.

The sea's largest tributary, the Danube River, drains half the European continent during its 2,000-mile journey from the Black Forest of Switzerland to Romania's Black Sea delta. The last half of that journey winds through Eastern Europe, where for decades every village, town and city flushed its untreated sewage into the river. Starting in the late 1960s, state-owned farms used huge quantities of subsidized chemical fertilizers on their fields, and much of it ran off into the streams feeding the Danube. Hydroelectric projects and navigational canals also damaged or bypassed wetlands that once acted as the river's natural filtering system. And Romania's dictator, Nicolae Ceausescu, waged all-out war on the Danube delta — Europe's greatest wetland — in an ill-conceived attempt to convert it to rice production.[3]

As a result, concentrations of nitrogen and phosphorous nutrients in the Black Sea's ecologically critical northwestern shelf dramatically increased between 1960 and 1980.[4] The nutrients fueled enormous algae blooms in the late 1980s, smothering bottom life by using up the oxygen it needed. As the microscopic plants decomposed, they consumed still more oxygen in vast stretches of the sea, suffocating most other creatures.[5]

Then in 1982, *Mnemiopsis leidyi*, an inch-long comb jelly native to North America, was introduced to the sea in the ballast water of a passing ship. The creature established itself amid the gathering chaos and proceeded to graze the waters clean of survivors. With no natural predators, it ultimately achieved a biomass of 1 billion tons — 10 times the weight of all the fish caught by all the world's fishermen in a year.[6]

"The biomass of other zooplankton dropped sharply, and the catches of commercial fish sharply decreased," noted Yuvenaly P. Zaitsev chief scientist at the Odessa office of the

"The more we understand about the ecology of fishes, the more we find that for the animals that live right above the seafloor, the integrity of these seafloors is critical to their survival," said Peter Auster, science director of the National Undersea Research Center at the University of Connecticut and a co-author of the report.[28]

Mark Butler, policy director at the Ecology Action Center in Halifax, Nova Scotia, argues there are other fishing methods that don't damage bottom habitats. "We are talking about protecting the ocean floor, which is often the nursery for young fish. You damage that in a major way, then you perhaps start to impair the health of the fishery itself."[29]

Of particular concern are the effects of trawling on seamounts — underwater mountain havens for life in the deep ocean. A 2006 U.N. study found that many seamount fisheries had been quickly depleted and

Ukrainian National Academy of Science. "*Mnemiopsis* . . . is usually held responsible for much of what happened."[7]

By the early 1990s, total fish landings had fallen to one-seventh of their previous level, and the signature anchovy catch fell by 95 percent. Slicks of ugly, stinking slime drove tourists from the beaches and prompted long closures at the height of summer. Hundreds of bathers became ill and several died from cholera and other infectious diseases that thrived in the algae-choked environment. In 1999 the World Bank estimated the economic damage to the fisheries sector at $300 million a year and $400 million to tourism.[8]

The past five years have seen considerable progress, however, as the European Union — with its strict environmental regulations — expanded to include 10 former communist countries, including Slovakia, Hungary, Romania, Bulgaria and other nations in the Danube's middle and lower basin.[9]

"When these countries joined the EU, they had to adopt new environmental policies and regulations, which has had the benefit of improving the overall water quality situation in the Danube basin," notes Ivan Zavadsky, program director of the Danube/Black Sea Regional Program in Vienna, a joint project of the United Nations and World Bank, which has pumped $70 million into cleanup projects in the region.

New sewage treatment plants have been built in recent years, and many of the most polluting factories and agricultural enterprises collapsed in the early 1990s. As a result, Zavadsky notes, concentrations of phosphorus and nitrogen — the nutrients that ravaged the Black Sea — have dropped 50 percent and 20 percent, respectively, since 1989. Meanwhile, the *Mnemiopsis'* population dropped precipitously after the arrival of the Beroe, another invading comb jelly that feeds exclusively on *Mnemiopsis*. Once the Beroe had eaten all the *Mnemiopsis*, its food source was depleted, so Black Sea populations of both species have now been decimated.[10]

"We're witnessing the first signs of a recovery of the Black Sea ecosystem," says Zavadsky, citing reduced algae blooms and an increase in some bottom plants and animals. "But the situation remains on a knife's edge."

But Janos Zlinszky, the government and public affairs manager of the Regional Environmental Center for Central and Eastern Europe in Szentendre, Hungary, is concerned that many of the gains could be lost if the region's economic recovery outpaces its environmental investments. "Romania and Bulgaria have just joined the EU," he says. "If they decide to focus on intensive agriculture rather than the organic market, we could see great increases in fertilizer and pesticide use."

"There's an extraordinary window of opportunity to take action," says Laurence Mee, director of the Marine Institute at the School of Earth, Ocean and Environmental Sciences at the University of Plymouth, in England. "But it can easily be lost."

---

[1] Colin Woodard, *Ocean's End: Travels Through Endangered Seas* (2000), pp. 1-25.

[2] From a speech in Trabzon, Turkey, Sept. 20, 1997.

[3] Woodard, *op. cit.*, pp. 13-23.

[4] Amhet Kideys, "Fall and Rise of the Black Sea Ecosystem," *Science*, Aug. 30, 2002, p. 1482.

[5] "Pollution and Problems of the Black Sea," a speech by Radu Mihnea, Romanian Research Institute, in Batumi, Georgia, Sept. 21, 1997.

[6] Kideys, *op. cit.*, p. 1482; Woodard, *op. cit.*, p. 22.

[7] "The Black Sea: Status and Challenges," a speech by Yuvenaly Zaitsev in Novorossiysk, Russia, Sept. 23, 1997.

[8] "Black Sea Transboundary Diagnostic Analysis," Global Environment Facility, August 1997, pp. ii, 15, 123, 125; Woodard, *op. cit.*, p. 22; Emilia Battaglini, "The GEF Strategic Partnership for the Danube/Black Sea," Presentation to World Bank, Bucharest, February 2007.

[9] For background, see Brian Beary, "The New Europe," *CQ Global Researcher*, August 2007.

[10] Kideys, *op. cit.*

estimated that some 95 percent of the ecological damage found on the undersea mountains was due to bottom-trawling. The study prompted New Zealand, the United States and other countries to push for a worldwide ban on bottom trawling on the high seas — international waters located more than 200 nautical miles from dry land. The measure was defeated when Canada, Iceland, Russia and China refused to back it.[30]

The Madrid-based environmental organization Oceana advocates limiting bottom trawlers and dredgers to areas where they already fish, excluding them from areas containing deep sea coral and sponge habitat, two species that recover poorly from trawling disruptions. Although the U.S. Commission on Ocean Policy didn't address the trawling issue specifically, the Pew Commission said it should be excluded wherever it will

Marine Conservation Biology Institute/Elliot A. Norse

More than 7 million metric tons of unwanted sea life — bycatch — is caught in the huge nets of commercial fishermen and discarded, including seabirds, stingrays, juvenile fish, sea turtles, dolphins, sharks, crabs, starfish, anemones, sponges and other creatures. Bycatch often dies before it gets thrown back into the sea. In the tropics, bycatch represents 56 percent of the haul.

reduce biodiversity or alter or destroy "a significant amount of habitat." "Sensitive habitats as well as areas not currently trawled or dredged should be closed to such use immediately," the report said.[31]

Federal fisheries managers in the United States banned bottom trawling from 300,000 square miles of such habitat off the U.S. West Coast. New Zealand, generally regarded as a leader in oceans policy, banned bottom trawling in 2006 in 30 percent of its waters.[32] Rosenberg of the University of New Hampshire contends trawling doesn't need to be universally banned. "You have to manage where trawling occurs and what level of impact we can sustain without reducing the resource productivity."[33]

Meanwhile, the European Union has been criticized for the "cash for access" deals it made with 12 West African states. Under the agreements — which include few, if any, conservation provisions — hundreds of European trawlers are operating in a "fundamentally unsustainable" manner, according to Milan Ilnyckyj, a doctoral student at Oxford University who has studied the problem.[34]

Si'd Ahmed Ould Abeid, president of Mauritania's National Fisheries Federation, said the fisheries agreements with the EU have been "a catastrophe for the fishermen whose catches are down and for the future of the fish in our waters. . . . The fish are just taken from our water, our fishermen lose their lives and we don't gain anything."[35]

Justin Brashares, an assistant professor of environmental science policy at the University of California-Berkeley, argues that the quickest way to increase the production and sustainability of West African domestic fisheries would be to limit the access of the foreign trawlers.

But EU Fisheries Commissioner Joe Borg argues deals such as the one the EU struck with Mauritania would benefit both parties in terms of "jobs, strengthened monitoring and control, conservation of resources in compliance with scientific assessment and environmental protection."[36]

Paul Molyneaux, author of *The Doryman's Reflection*, about his career as a commercial fisherman in Alaska, New Jersey and Maine, says the damage wrought by industrial-scale fishing is so great that it will be years before trawling will be ecologically appropriate in many areas. "In the short term, I think it should be banned," he says. "In many places they have destroyed the ecosystem foundations by dragging, taking too many fish, and disrupting the stock structure. They put everybody else out of business, and then they went out of business themselves."

But trawler owners argue that, far from damaging the environment, their gear actually improves marine productivity by plowing the seafloor and churning up nutrients. "A lot of fishermen feel that they are freshening the bottom, sort of turning over the soil, tending a garden, and that this helps certain species," says Bonnie Brady, executive director of the Long Island Commercial Fishermen's Association.

James Kendall, executive director of the New Bedford (Mass.) Seafood Coalition, argues nobody knows whether scallop dredges harm or hurt the fishery. "Does this activity oxygenate the sediment, release buried nutrients, damage herring-egg beds or adversely affect juvenile fish and scallops?" he asks, adding that more study is needed to answer those questions.[37]

"I am not suggesting that the act of scalloping on the ocean floor does not create an impact upon it, but that it may not be the adverse one so easily assumed," he continues, noting that the best scallop grounds have remained constant for decades, despite intensive dragging.

Some studies from the intensively trawled North Sea support the fishermen's contentions, at least in part. Scientists have observed 35 times as many fish gathered in areas that had recently been trawled compared to adjacent unfished areas, suggesting the fish were attracted to the disturbed bottom to feed. Bottom trawling appears at least partially responsible for increased growth rates in sole and plaice, two North Sea flat fish, presumably because the disturbances promote the growth of small invertebrates they like to eat. A third study suggested that two other North Sea species — gurnards and whiting — were drawn to trawl tracks to feed on tube worms dredged up by the fishing gear.[38]

Furlong, of the Mid-Atlantic Fishery Management Council, contends dragging and dredging can be appropriate in sandy, muddy bottoms like those off New Jersey, Delaware and Maryland. "There's nothing to clear cut down there," he said. "You can't clear cut sand." A 1989 bottom trawling assessment of a sandy area by the Massachusetts Division of Marine Fisheries found no damage to bottom-dwelling lobsters and negligible habitat impacts.[39]

BACKGROUND

Run on the Banks

Fishing has been an important activity since prehistoric times. Fishermen using hand nets, hand lines and open boats may have found the seas teeming, but even then — archaeologists have found — early people depleted seafood resources. Ancient garbage heaps show the size of fish and shellfish often became smaller over time.[40]

The advent of industrialized fishing in the 19th century greatly increased human impact on marine ecosystems. Instead of using baited hooks or traps, fishermen

Greenpeace/©Robert Visser

The Seattle-based factory trawler Northern Eagle can harvest 50-60 metric tons of pollock per day in the Bering Sea. The decimation of global fisheries is blamed largely on powerful new technologies — including radar, fish finders and satellite tracking and navigation systems — as well as onboard processing plants, flash freezers and nets that stretch for miles.

developed gear that could pursue and scoop up fish. In the early 1800s, the development of steam-powered ships allowed fishermen to drag larger net bags across the seafloor. At first it was a clumsy proposition: The bag was held open with wooden beams that often hung up on rocks and other obstructions. In the 1890s, however, British fishermen replaced the beam with a pair of small boards, rigged in such a way that when pulled through water they flew apart like kites, holding the mouth of the net open; a heavy chain kept the net bottom dragging on the seafloor to prevent fish from escaping underneath. The so-called otter trawl was incredibly effective and quickly dominated the North Sea fleet. Starting in 1905, it was deployed in North America.[41]

The destructive potential of trawling was clear as early as 1912, when Congress demanded an investigation of fishermen's claims that it "is such an unduly destructive method that if generally adopted . . . the fishing grounds [will be] quickly rendered unproductive." Investigators recommended that trawls be restricted to a few areas in New England, but their advice was not acted upon.

In the 20th century the scale and power of fishing technology increased enormously. Diesel engines, introduced in the 1920s, were cheaper, safer and more reliable than steam; otter trawls were adapted to trap shrimp, clams, oysters and scallops. Processors invented a way to

C H R O N O L O G Y

1800s-Early 1900s *Fish stocks decline as fishing becomes more mechanized and new trawling methods are developed.*

1905 The steam-powered otter trawl is deployed in North America, making industrial fishing possible in previously unfished areas.

1920s-1940s *Diesel engines replace steam, triggering an expansion of offshore trawling. U.S. processors develop flash freezing. Norwegian fishermen begin dragging for shrimp.*

1936 New England halibut catch falls to 2 million pounds from 13.5 million in 1902; haddock falls by two-thirds.

1946 International Convention for the Regulation of Whaling is adopted.

1950s *The first factory trawlers come into use, mainly in North Atlantic. Pollution runoff from land-based development begins disrupting global ecosystems.*

1954 A Scottish firm builds the first freezer-equipped "factory" trawler, the *Fairtry*, which is four times the size of conventional trawlers.

1959 Antarctica Treaty is adopted, sparing the southern continent and surrounding oceans from hunting, industrial activity and fishing pressure.

1970s-1980s *Countries extend their territorial seas to prevent foreign overexploitation. Pollution disrupts ocean life. Fisheries decline sharply. Iceland fights "cod war" to extend its territorial waters.*

1972 Congress passes Coastal Zone Management, Clean Water and Marine Mammal Protection acts.

1975 U.N. adopts Convention on International Trade in Endangered Species, which helps reduce cross-border trade in marine animal products.

1977 U.S., Canada, others adopt 200-mile territorial limits. Trawlers move to Africa, Asia and the Caribbean.

1982 U.N. Convention on the Law of the Sea becomes the first international agreement to regulate ocean use. International Whaling Commission bans most commercial whaling beginning in 1986.

1989 Norway restricts cod fishing to protect declining stocks; cod recovers by 1992.

1990s-2000s *Black Sea ecosystem collapses. Coral reefs decline worldwide and climate change, pollution and chronic overfishing appear to be driving oceans into crisis.*

1990 Pollution, overfishing and the introduction of a non-native comb jelly species devastate the Black Sea.

1991 British North Sea cod stocks have declined by more than two-thirds in 10 years.

1992 Canada closes Grand Banks cod fishery; stock stands at 1 percent of 1965 levels.

1994 U.S. closes key New England fisheries; slow recovery begins.

1998 Bleaching destroys 16 percent of the world's coral reefs. Cause is unknown.

2002 European Union (EU) recommends member states adopt integrated coastal zone management.

2003 Pew Oceans Commission urges immediate action to protect the oceans; Canadian study says stocks of large predatory fish have fallen by 90 percent worldwide since 1950.

2004 U.S. Commission on Ocean Policy calls for ecosystem-based response to protecting oceans and coasts.

2006 Iceland breaks whaling ban. . . . Most EU members have adopted integrated coastal zone management plans. . . . Pro-whaling bloc gets whaling ban declared no longer necessary.

2007 Hundreds of marine species — including corals for the first time — are added to the World Conservation Union's "red list" of species facing the risk of extinction.

mass-produce fish fillets — which could be sold fresh, canned or smoked at processing plants — and commercial-scale flash freezing, which eventually led to fish "sticks." In the late 1920s, processors like General Foods began building their own trawler fleets, completing the industrialization of the industry.

But fish stocks could not stand up to the technology. In New England, the halibut catch fell from 13.5 million pounds in 1902 to 2 million in 1936; the haddock catch fell by two-thirds between 1929 and 1936, while winter flounder became so scarce fishermen began targeting the previously spurned yellowtail flounder. By World War II, the yellowtail had been depleted, and near-shore stocks of cod and haddock were driven into commercial extinction.[42]

In 1954, a Scottish whaling firm built the first factory trawler, modeled on the big processing ships that had wiped out Antarctica's whale stocks. *The Fairtry* weighed 2,600 tons, more than four times the size of the conventional trawlers of the day, and was equipped with an onboard processing and freezing plant and nets large enough to swallow the Statue of Liberty. It could operate 24 hours a day for weeks on end, allowing the ships to travel to fisheries thousands of miles from home. The design revolutionized distant-water fishing.

By the 1970s, the Soviet Union was operating more than 700 freezer trawlers, and the two Germanys, Poland, Spain, France and Japan each had dozens more.[43] So-called mid-water trawls were developed to target mackerel, herring and anchovies that lived in medium depths. The ships massed on fishing grounds off Newfoundland, New England, Antarctica and the Bering Sea and mined one fish stock after another into near-oblivion.

In 1977, following Iceland's lead, Canada, the United States and other nations extended their territorial waters from 12 to 200 nautical miles in order to push foreign factory trawlers off their banks and save the fish for themselves. Fish stocks had been damaged, but with proper regulation it was assumed they would recover.

Stocks Crash

After kicking foreign fleets out, the United States, Canada and other nations built their own modern trawler fleets. Though the vessels were much smaller, they carried the latest fish-finding gadgetry and were capable of fishing the offshore banks. Encouraged by government incentives, New England trawlers larger than 125 tons

grew by 144 percent between 1976 and 1979, while the number of medium-size trawlers nearly doubled. Other governments offered similar incentives, increasing the size of the world's fishing fleet by 322 percent from 1979 to 1989.[44]

In New England and Canada, the domestic fleets quickly wiped out many stocks, including the cod stocks that had attracted Europeans to colonize the region in the first place. Between 1965 and 1999, New England's haddock catch fell by 95 percent, halibut by 92 percent and cod by 40 percent, prompting managers to close many fishing grounds. On Newfoundland's Grand Banks, the greatest cod fishery in the world was reduced by 98.9 percent in the 30 years leading up to its 1992 closure.

The pain of the closures and other fishing restrictions eroded the economic and cultural foundations of many New England and Canadian communities, and fueled an exodus of young people from Newfoundland. "We are witnessing an entire generation without hope, enthusiasm and access to meaningful, steady employment," noted Michael Temelini, assistant professor of political science at the Memorial University of Newfoundland. "[Our] 500-year-old civilization is disappearing."[45]

Fifteen years after the closure, Newfoundland's cod appear unable to regain their place in the ecosystem, while depleted fish stocks on Georges Bank and in the Gulf of Maine are recovering slowly. Fish plants have closed throughout eastern North America, and large fishing vessels have vanished from harbors whose residents had fished offshore for centuries.[46]

Similar devastation has occurred from the North Sea to the Gulf of Thailand. "Ten years ago, we could catch anything we wanted," said Sophon Loseresakun, a fisherman in Talumphuk, Thailand. "Now we have almost nothing."[47]

Eventually, the large fishing vessels moved on to the developing world, buying access to fishing grounds that once supported small-scale local fishermen. "European and Russian distant-water fishing fleets shrank and their remnants turned south," recalled Carl Safina, president of the Blue Ocean Institute, a marine conservation advocacy group in East Norwich, N.Y., "under-paying their way into the fishing zones of countries too desperate for foreign cash to say no, lest the same bad offer be accepted by a neighboring country and the boats go there instead."[48]

Whaling Nations Want Hunting Ban Lifted

Japan, Iceland and Norway are leading the charge.

Great whales are up against a lot these days: Their food supply has diminished and is laced with PCBs and heavy metals, noise from sonar devices plagues their habitat and entangling fishing nets and passing ships are a constant threat. It's no surprise that most varieties — including blue, fin, humpback, sperm and right — remain on the endangered species list.

But in October 2006 Iceland announced it would resume hunting great whales, breaking the International Whaling Commission's (IWC) 21-year-old global moratorium on commercial whaling.*

Iceland's commercial whalers were permitted to kill nine endangered fin whales — the second-largest species after blue whales — and 30 smaller, more abundant minkes during the year ending Aug. 31, 2007, ostensibly for scientific research. By last November, however, they had already killed seven of the endangered fins, setting off a storm of international criticism.[1]

"It's outside all international norms to hunt an endangered species," says Susan Lieberman, director of the World Wildlife Fund's Global Species Program in Rome. "There is a commercial whaling moratorium in effect, so we're not saying it's fine and dandy to be hunting [the non-endangered] minkes. But targeting fin whales is a far more confrontational and aggressive act."

Whale meat is a delicacy in Iceland, Norway and Japan, particularly with older generations, and whaling nations say hunting and consuming whales is part of their cultural heritage. But critics point out that all three countries have difficulty disposing of whale blubber and other non-meat byproducts, leading conservationists to question why they continue the hunt.

Last November 25 countries — including the United States, Great Britain and Australia — demanded a halt to Iceland's hunt. Critics say it undermines the IWC by directly challenging its moratorium.[2]

"They are testing what the international reaction would be, and I think they've found it has been pretty harsh," says Sue Fisher, trade expert at Britain's Whale and Dolphin Conservation Society. "What they're doing is a violation of the ban."

In fact, the moratorium has been unraveling for years, largely because of Japan's diplomatic maneuvering. It used aid and trade measures to convince a small army of previously disinterested Caribbean and Pacific nations to join the IWC and vote with Japan. As a result, in 2006, the pro-whaling bloc achieved a simple majority and passed a symbolic measure declaring the ban no longer necessary. But the measure fell short of the three-quarters majority needed.

In retaliation, the United Kingdom and other anti-whaling nations have recently recruited five disinterested proxies of their own — Croatia, Cyprus, Ecuador, Greece and Slovenia — to help stave off the pro-whaling bloc.[3]

Norway, which is allowed to legally hunt whales commercially, focused exclusively on minkes, which are about an eighth the mass of fin whales. Operating from small vessels, Norwegian fishermen kill between 600 and 800 minkes each year out of an estimated North Atlantic population of over 170,000.

Norway's leading environmental groups support the hunt, arguing it is a sustainable fishery that produces organic

---

* The 1986 moratorium allowed nations to legally continue whale hunting if they filed official reservations prior to the adoption of the ban. Norway made such a reservation. Iceland and Japan did not, though Iceland tried to claim one after the fact, when it first resumed hunting minkes for "scientific purposes" in 2003. Japan conducts a "scientific" research hunt — also allowed under IWC rules — taking about 900 minkes in the Southern Ocean. Non-whaling nations consider the hunt a violation of the spirit of the treaty. Aboriginal hunters are exempt and permitted to hunt a limited number of whales for cultural and religious purposes.

Today, subsistence fishermen in canoes in Mauritania and other African nations compete with hundreds of government-subsidized Spanish, Russian and Chinese trawlers. West African fish stocks have declined by 50 percent over the past 30 years, and thousands of fishermen have been put out of work.[49] Likewise, South Pacific nations have sold tuna fishing rights to Russian, Chinese and Taiwanese companies, even though the valuable fish is one of their few natural resources.

Other vessels have turned to the high seas, beyond the reach of government, to fish for orange roughy, Patagonian toothfish and other long-lived, slow-to-reproduce species. According to a University of British Columbia study,

meat with fewer inputs than a corporate beef or pork farm. "We use small fishing vessels that consume few inputs and cause almost no pollution — it's very friendly eco-production," says Marius Holm, co-chairman of the Bellona Foundation environmental organization in Oslo. "Our principle is that we should harvest what nature provides, but in a sustainable way regarding the ecosystem as a whole and the specific stocks."

"The hunt we have had along our coast has always been sustainable," says Halvard Johansen, deputy director general of the Norwegian Ministry of Fisheries and Coastal Affairs. "We've been whaling on this coast since the 9th century, and we don't see that big a difference between aboriginal whaling in Alaska, Russia and Greenland and what we do here."

Stefan Asmundsson, Iceland's whaling commissioner, claims his country's hunts are also sustainable, despite targeting an endangered species. "The fin whale stocks being targeted by Iceland are not in any way endangered," he says. "There is no lineage between the stocks in the North Atlantic, which are abundant, and those in the Southern Hemisphere" that were decimated by factory whaling fleets in mid-20th century.

Indeed, many in the West fear a return to those dark days when Norway, Japan and other whaling nations drove many great whales to the brink of extinction to procure industrial oil and pet food. Recovery has been slow. In 2003, a study by Stanford University geneticist Stephen Palumbi suggested that the pre-whaling populations of

Japanese whalers butcher a Baird's beaked whale, a species not in danger of extinction. Despite a 1986 ban on commercial whaling, the International Whaling Commission allows Japan and Norway to hunt whales, and Iceland announced in October 2006 it would resume hunting great whales.

Getty Images/Koichi Kamoshida

North Atlantic humpback, fin and minke whales were far larger than previously thought and won't return to exploitable levels for many decades.[4]

Others say Japan and Iceland are defending whaling out of a sense of national pride rather than economic necessity, since their domestic markets have been unable to absorb the meat from their scientific minke hunts. As whale meat piles up in freezers — 4,400 tons according to Greenpeace — Japan has resorted to introducing it in school lunch programs.

"Almost all those who like whale meat are middle-aged and older," admits Kouji Shingru, owner of the only whale-meat retail shop in Tokyo. "Young people have no experience with eating whale. In fact, my shop is one of the only places where young people have a chance to eat it."[5]

"This is not driven by economics, it's just political, which makes it far more egregious," says Lieberman.

---

[1] Krista Mahr, "Defying global ban, Iceland to resume commercial whaling after almost 2 decades," The Associated Press, Oct. 17, 2006; Colin Woodard, "Thar She Blows," *E Magazine*, January 2007.

[2] Lewis Smith, "Iceland's whaling sinks tourism: Two dozen nations protest hunting," *Calgary Herald*, Nov. 2, 2006.

[3] Micheal McCarthy, "Pro-hunting Japanese seize control of whaling commission," *The Independent* (London), April 17, 2006, p. 2; Richard Lloyd Perry, "Japan may go it alone after defeat over whaling ban," *The Times* (London), June 2, 2007.

[4] Stephen Palumbi and Joe Roman, "Whales before whaling in the North Atlantic," *Science*, July 25, 2003, p. 508.

[5] Greenpeace International press release, Jan. 30, 2007; Leo Lewis, "Giant of the sea used as petfood," *The Times* (London), Feb. 10, 2006.

---

high-seas bottom trawlers receive $152 million a year in subsidies worldwide.

"Eliminating government subsidies would render the fleet economically unviable," said lead author Rashid Sumaila.[50]

"We are vacuuming the ocean of its content," said French environmentalist Jean-Michel Cousteau, son of

the late ocean explorer Jacques Cousteau. "If this continues, there will be nothing left."[51]

Shifting Baselines

Scientists now realize that the damage to the oceans is far worse than previously estimated. New forensic research using fishing logbooks, archaeological evidence and

A diver in the Great Barrier Reef Marine Park in Australia photographs masses of bleached staghorn coral, which occurs when sea temperatures rise and kill microbes that give coral its bright colors. Rising sea temperatures and other mostly man-made factors are said to be killing coral reefs at an alarming rate.

genetic tests reveals that ocean life was far more abundant in the pre-industrial era than anyone had assumed.

For instance, after witnessing the destruction of many of Jamaica's coral reefs, Jackson of the Scripps Institution used historical records to determine how the Caribbean might have looked in 1492. "Think about the wildebeests and lions and all that on the plains of Africa," he says. "Well, there was a world in which the biomass of big animals among the reefs was greater than the biomass of the big mammals of the Serengeti plains."[52]

Based on hunting records, adult green sea turtles — now rare — once numbered at least 35 million and may have exceeded 550 million. "Think about that: 35 million 220-pound turtles grazing on crustaceans, sea grass, starfish and mollusks," he says. "The productivity of those reefs must have been fantastic. The whole mind-set of scientists about what is a 'pristine' reef is completely wrong." His research suggests that by wiping out sea turtles — used for food in the 19th century — humans probably triggered the collapse of sea grass beds, which suffer infections when they are not grazed.[53]

Similarly, W. Jeffrey Bolster, a professor of maritime history at the University of New Hampshire, and colleagues used 19th-century logbooks to reconstruct the scale of the cod catch and the average size of the fish.

The results stunned fisheries experts. In 1861 alone, small-boat fishermen from several Maine towns — using small sailboats and baited hooks — caught more fish than all the U.S. and Canadian fishing fleets combined caught in the Gulf of Maine between 1996 and 1999. Today, there are virtually no cod in the area.

"Ask yourself, 'What were all those cod eating?' " Bolster says. "When you think about the copepods and krill, all the way up to the alewives and mackerel that had to be present in the inshore area to feed them, it's flabbergasting.

"The world we have today," he points out, was created by humans trying to "manage" the exploitation of fisheries resources. "In terms of engineered outcomes, it's been a disaster."

Climate Change

Global warming is already affecting polar marine ecosystems. On the Antarctic Peninsula, ice-dependent species like Adelie penguins and Weddell seals have moved southwards, replaced by the Gentoo penguins and elephant seals that prefer open water. Krill, the small marine crustaceans that form the basis of the Antarctic food chain, feed on algae that grow on the underside of winter sea ice. Experts fear less sea ice could mean less krill and, thus, less food to go around.

In the Arctic, reduced ice cover is causing starvation and reproductive failure among polar bears, prompting the United States to propose listing them as a threatened species.[54] Walruses and ringed seals also depend on floating ice as habitat.

Fishermen in Greenland have witnessed considerable changes in the composition of the continent's marine species in recent years. Cold-loving shrimp are becoming rarer on the south and west-central coasts, while cod are becoming more numerous. The fishing season is longer in areas where sea ice is failing to form, but polar bear and seal hunters cannot risk going out on the ice with their sled dogs.

"Hunters and fishermen have passed down detailed information about their environment for generations," says Lene Kielsen Holm, director for environment and sustainable development at the Greenland office of the Inuit Circumpolar Council, which represents the interests of the 160,000 Inuit, the indigenous people of the high arctic. "Now they tell us things are changing so quickly everything they have been taught by their elders is no longer accurate."

Scientists also worry that melting polar glaciers, ice caps and ice sheets could slow ocean circulation. Ocean currents normally act as a conveyor belt, moving warm surface waters toward the poles and cold bottom water from polar areas toward the equator. The release of fresh meltwater alters seawater density, which may slow or even stop circulation, with potentially devastating consequences for human and marine life.

A 2005 study indicated that the Gulf Stream, which keeps northern Europe's climate mild, may have slowed by 30 percent since 1992. "We don't want to say the circulation will shut down, but we are very nervous about our findings," said Harry L. Bryden, a specialist in the role of ocean heat and freshwater currents at the School of Ocean and Earth Science at the National Oceanography Centre in Southampton, England. "They have come as quite a surprise."[55]

Meanwhile, the increase in atmospheric carbon dioxide (CO_2) — one of the major causes of climate change — is making the ocean more acidic, with potentially catastrophic consequences. About 2 billion tons of atmospheric CO_2 ends up in the oceans each year — 10 times the natural rate — and the oceans have become 30 percent more acidic since the Industrial Revolution. That figure is expected to rise to 100 percent to 150 percent by the end of the century.

Increased acidity disrupts the ability of corals and other sea animals to build shells and skeletons. "There's a whole category of organisms that have been around for hundreds of millions of years that are at risk of extinction," says Ken Caldeira, a chemical oceanographer at the Carnegie Institution's Department of Global Ecology at Stanford University. The likely casualties include a range of microscopic creatures at the base of the food chain, including coccolithophores and pteropods; the polyps that build coral reefs; and starfish and sea cucumbers — popular food items for larger creatures. Oysters, scallops, mussels, barnacles and many other creatures may also be affected.

"This is a matter of the utmost importance," said reef expert Ove Hoegh-Guldberg of the University of Queensland in Australia. "I can't really stress it in words enough. It is a do-or-die situation."[56]

Governing the Seas

Historically, the seas were unregulated beyond three nautical miles from land, the effective range of shore-based

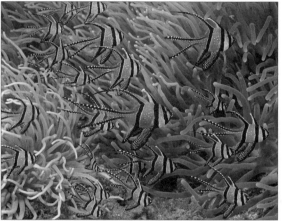

The Banggai cardinalfish, native to Indonesia, is among hundreds of marine animals and corals added to the World Conservation Union's 2007 "red list" of species in jeopardy or facing high risk of extinction. The group blames excessive and destructive fishing activities for the loss of ocean biodiversity.

Getty Images/Norbert Wu

cannon. But in the 20th century, fishery-dependent Iceland — in an effort to protect its fish from foreign fleets — extended its territorial waters first to four then to 12, 50 and, finally, to 200 nautical miles.

Initially, the world protested. Britain dispatched a fleet of warships to protect its trawlers, triggering three bloodless "cod wars" with Iceland's coast guard. Shots were fired, ships rammed and nets cut. Iceland barred British warplanes from landing at the NATO air base in Keflavik. Finally, in 1976, the world backed down, and soon nations around the world had declared their own 200-mile zones.[57]

The 200-mile limit was codified in the 1982 U.N. Convention on the Law of the Sea (UNCLOS), which has since been ratified by 155 nations. The United States — which had extended its own territorial waters to 200 miles in 1977 — has not yet ratified the treaty, but President George W. Bush has said it should be ratified.

Under UNCLOS, governments can regulate fishing and other economic activities within their 200-mile "exclusive economic zones" (EEZ) and are expected to take a precautionary approach in utilizing their EEZs "according to their capabilities." Legal scholars have said the conservation language is so weak as to be useless.

"Just as with bringing up children, a permissive approach to the law of the sea guarantees spoiling," writes John Charles Kunich, associate professor of law at the

Appalachian School of Law in Grundy, Va., and author of *Killing Our Oceans: Dealing with the Mass Extinction of Marine Life.* "It is all too predictable that nations often discover that other pressing needs prevent them . . . from doing anything to protect biodiversity in the oceans."[58]

Nations have cooperated in trying to regulate international exploitation of marine creatures that regularly cross borders through treaty organizations like the International Whaling Commission, the Northwest Atlantic Fisheries Organization and the International Commission for the Conservation of Atlantic Tuna. But the track record of most of these organizations is poor. In most cases, the populations of species they are supposed to protect have declined due to predation by humans. Even when member nations agree to tougher enforcement, unscrupulous vessel owners can simply re-register their ships in a "flag-of-convenience" nation that does not observe the relevant rules.

International cooperation has succeeded, however, in banning drift-net fishing — which indiscriminately kills any fish or mammals that come in contact with the massive nets — and the 1975 Convention on International Trade in Endangered Species helped reduce cross-border trade in hawksbill turtles, Caspian sturgeon roe and many whale products. The 1959 Antarctica Treaty has spared the southern continent and much of the surrounding ocean from continued hunting, industrial activity and fishing pressure.

But with most of the more ecologically productive parts of the ocean located within nations' EEZs, it will likely fall on national governments to protect them.

CURRENT SITUATION

Government Responses

World governments have been slow to address the ocean crisis, often stepping in only after a fishery has collapsed. And governments that have closed fishing grounds have had mixed results. While cod stocks on Canada's Grand Banks have failed to recover, for instance, New England's haddock, flounder and other species are slowly recovering. Scientists say New England stocks can recover completely if policy makers withstand industry pressure to allow more fishing.

Internationally, China, Iceland, Russia and other deep-sea fishing nations blocked a 2006 U.N. effort to ban high-seas bottom trawling. "There were several countries

that really didn't want any controls at all," said U.S. Assistant Secretary of State for Oceans, Environment and Science Claudia McMurray. "We're very disappointed."[59]

Many countries have considered privatizing fisheries by creating individual transferable quotas (ITQs). Under an ITQ system, scientists set quotas on the total allowable catch for a given season, species and fishing ground; shares of the quotas are bought and sold by private entities, and only those holding shares are allowed to fish.

Proponents say that creating "owners" of uncaught fish will encourage responsible stewardship. Opponents say an ITQ system represents a massive transfer of public resources to corporate control.

"Since quotas are bought and sold to the highest bidder, local fishermen — who can't compete with deep-pocketed corporations — are almost inevitably squeezed out," write Pietro Parravano, past president of the Pacific Coast Federation of Fishermen's Associations, and Lee Crockett, formerly of the Marine Fish Conservation Network and now federal fisheries policy director at the Pew Environment Group. "Moreover, because quotas are [initially] set on the number of fish historically caught by individual fishermen, those who tried to allow stocks to replenish by fishing responsibly [are] penalized, while those who fish rapaciously are rewarded."[60]

Others say ITQ rules can be written to prevent the concentration of ownership. Alaska's halibut and sablefish fisheries adopted ITQs in 1995, but the rules limited absentee ownership and consolidation of shares and allowed communities to buy blocks of shares to divvy up among individuals. A decade later, the fishery was safer and greener, according to Linda Behnken, executive director of the Alaska Longline Fishermen's Association.

"From a resource perspective, it's been an unqualified success," she said.[61]

Zoning the Sea

Some governments have tried to zone the ocean bottom just as cities use zoning rules to separate incompatible land uses and to establish parks and preserves. Environmentalists have long advocated a similar approach, as has the World Bank, the U.S. Commission on Ocean Policy and the Pew Oceans Commission. Sea-floor zoning — and establishing marine reserves where certain human activities are prohibited — is also a crucial part of ecosystem-based management.

"It's inevitable that once we developed methods to reach further and further into the sea, we would have to extend the regulatory framework we have on land to the sea," says Callum Roberts, an expert on marine zoning at the University of York in England.

To date, however, less than 2 percent of the oceans are within marine protected areas, and less than 0.2 percent are classified as no-take marine reserves where no disruptive activities are allowed.[62]

The Central American nation of Belize is leading the way on marine protected areas. With the help of the Global Environment Facility — a joint UN/World Bank environmental grant-making agency based in Washington — and scientists from the United States and Britain, Belize has created a surprisingly comprehensive array of fully protected parks, mixed-use reserves and specialized wildlife sanctuaries aimed at protecting biodiversity while enhancing the country's most important industries: fishing and eco-tourism.[63]

One of the reserves, Glover's Reef, a remote atoll 30 miles offshore, has been fully protected and carefully patrolled for nearly a decade. As a result, depleted commercial seafood species have rapidly rebounded: From 1998 to 2003, queen conch populations jumped by 350 percent and spiny lobster 250 percent. Similar results have been observed in New Zealand, where overall ecological productivity has jumped 50 percent in a reserve founded in 1977.[64]

"Right now, it's like we have a few oases in the desert," says Bill Ballantine, a marine biologist and former director of the University of Auckland's Leigh Marine Laboratory, who says the world needs many more.

To be effective, Belize's reserves must be "big enough so that a reasonable number of species can complete their life cycle within its borders, but small enough so the animals inside will produce larvae that wind up outside its borders and seed other fish populations," says Peter Sale, professor emeritus of biological sciences at the University of Windsor, Ontario.[65]

But there are problems, especially in cash-strapped developing countries like Belize. Running the reserves "is an enormously expensive undertaking," says Janet Gibson, former director of Belize's Coastal Zone Management Authority, "and there are really few ways to raise funds apart from charging entrance fees."

In Indonesia, the U.S.-based Nature Conservancy has provided funding for wardens at Komodo National Park,

Wastewater runoff from coastal developments is one of many threats to marine habitats. Each summer fertilizer runoff from 31 states in the United States flows into the Gulf of Mexico via the Mississippi River, creating a huge dead zone south of New Orleans where few species survive.

who have largely driven out the dynamite fishermen who blasted many of the area's reefs to rubble. Researchers have helped the reefs reestablish themselves by piling sandstone and limestone boulders on the sea floor. "Places that were just bare rock and rubble now have great coral growth and are surrounded by fish," says the World Wildlife Fund's senior marine conservation biologist Helen E. Fox, who worked on the project. The technique costs only about $5 per square meter, compared to between $550 and $10,000 to repair corals in the Florida Keys, she says.

In 2006, President Bush created the world's largest fully protected reserve, the 138,000-square-mile Papahanaumokuakea Marine National Monument in the northwestern Hawaiian Islands. The new reserve — 100 times the size of Yosemite National Park and larger than all other U.S. national parks combined — prohibits all exploitative activities except for limited ritualistic fishing by native Hawaiians. Environmentalists and ocean policy advocates widely praised the move, called by Fred Krupp, president of Environmental Defense, "as important as the establishment of Yellowstone."[66]

Some fishermen fear large areas could be declared reserves and closed to fishing. But proponents note that creating a reserve doesn't necessarily preclude fishing; it can, however, restrict fishing by method, times or places.

"What you zone for depends on what you are trying to protect," says Anthony Chatwin, director of the South American marine program at The Nature Conservancy. "Some areas will be reserved to protect marine biodiversity, others purely for fisheries management purposes, but they will be comprehensively put together."

Managing Better?

Some experts have identified examples of sustainable fisheries — those that work within the limits of what marine ecosystems can support. Most include community-based management, in which local communities develop their own rules for how, when and by whom the grounds can be fished.

In the Maine lobster fishery, for instance, catches remain at all-time highs despite an enormous increase in the number of fishermen and traps. Traditionally, lobster-men from each harbor controlled their own piece of the seafloor and defended it from intrusion by anyone without the community's permission. By controlling their own lobster pasture, the fishermen had an incentive to enforce or even enhance conservation laws, according to James Acheson, an anthropologist at the University of Maine. "The whole theory of common property resources like lobster assumes they're bound to be overexploited," he says. "That's nonsense."[67]

Numerous other successful fisheries have similar arrangements, from the coral reefs of Micronesia and Polynesia (where villages control fishing rights to nearby reefs) to the community fishing cooperatives that control inshore grounds in Japan's Ryukyu Islands. They have inspired others to advocate giving fishing communities proprietary rights to the resources they have long relied on in Atlantic Canada and elsewhere.[68]

Molyneaux, the author and former fisherman who received a Guggenheim Fellowship to study sustainable fisheries, points to Chile, where the government has blended privatization with community-based management. Small-scale fishermen are allowed to form unions, which are allocated a slot of ocean bottom. The government sets quotas on commercial species, but the union members decide how to manage the area.

"You don't get sole access to the fish but rather to the sedentary resources: shellfish, seaweed, abalone," says Molyneaux. "It's a form of privatization, but it's community based and intended to keep fishermen in their communities and not moving to shantytowns in the cities."

The unions pay for scientific assessments of the health of their stock but are left to work out the economic strategy for harvesting it. "They figured out how to give people the power to control and promote the resource, a reason for promoting sustainability," he says.

Some fishing gear is clearly less harmful than others. Maine lobstermen fish with baited traps that don't harm juvenile lobsters, oversized lobsters, non-target species or the ocean floor. New Brunswick weir fishermen capture herring in hand-built fish traps, with the rights to use a given location handed down in families. Some Icelandic fishermen combine high-tech with small-scale: fishing from small, locally built boats with hand-baited, computer-tended longlines, sophisticated electronic bottom maps and the capability to sell their catch electronically hours before they ever reach the dock.

Others say conventional gear and management can work, pointing to Alaska, where fisheries managers have prevented overfishing, reduced bycatch and protected habitats. By 2005, the North Pacific Fisheries Management Council — which includes fishing interests, scientists and public officials — had banned bottom trawling in nearly 40 percent of Alaska's federal waters and imposed fishing closures to protect the spawning and nursery grounds of herring, rockfish, crab and other commercial species.

Unlike its New England counterpart, the council never authorized catch quotas above those recommended by its scientific advisers. It also restricted fishing near Stellar sea lion rookeries. Federal managers also banned targeted fishing of key forage species like smelt, capelin and sand lance that feed seabirds and commercial fish.

"People in Alaska had been through some tough times in the past, and they created an ethic that puts protecting the resource first," said Benton of the Marine Conservation Alliance. "People around the world acknowledge Alaska as one of those places where you can look for positive lessons learned."[69]

Saving the Shore

Policy makers are paying considerable attention to calls to develop integrated coastal zone management plans that control human activities throughout an entire watershed and its associated coastline and estuaries.

Should the moratorium on commercial whaling be lifted?

 Rune Frøvik
CEO, High North Alliance, Norway

NO **Philippa Brakes**
*Senior Biologist, Whale and Dolphin
Conservation Society*

Written for *CQ Global Researcher*, September 2007

While fishing continues to enjoy almost universal acceptance as a means of food production, Western urban society has decided unilaterally to shut down whaling with complete disregard for any culture that still practices it.

Each culture has its own culinary idiosyncrasies. For many Asians, dog meat is a delicacy; the French like their frogs, snails and horse meat, and Australians have a taste for kangaroos. And there are just as many taboos — Indians forego the joy of beefsteak, while Jews and Muslims won't touch pork.

Beset with environmental challenges and yet respectful of cultural differences, the world community thankfully embraced Agenda 21's principle of striving for sustainable development — using renewable resources at rates that are within the resources' capacity for renewal.* Yet the West's cultural imperialists would have whales exempted from the sustainable-use principle — placing them above and apart from the animal kingdom to which they obviously belong.

For those who live close to nature, natural resources play vital roles, both nutritional and cultural, in their lives. Thus, coastal people will continue to harvest what nature provides — be it seals, fish, birds . . . or whales. And in the interest of self-preservation, they will strive to do so sustainably.

Sustainable whaling must be managed in accordance with agreed principles, not by launching destructive attacks on those who engage in exactly what we are striving for — sustainable use — just because one's cultural bias finds a particular harvest unpalatable.

In a world where trade depends on the exchange of money, there are commercial aspects to whalers' lives. In Greenland, Iceland, Japan and Norway whale meat is sold in supermarkets, and expensive whale souvenirs are sold to tourists in Alaska. Until whale meat is accepted as currency, whalers must do their shopping the same way as the rest of us — with cash.

Harvesting nature's surplus, including super-abundant whale resources, means biodiversity and habitat do not have to be destroyed and turned into agricultural land. True environmentalists are concerned not with appearances but with practicing the principles that they preach. In so doing, they have either reached the conclusion, or are getting there, that whaling should not only be continued but should even be increased to provide more people with ecological, healthy and nutritious food.

---

* Agenda 21 — adopted by more than 178 governments at the Earth Summit in June 1992 — is a 300-page plan for achieving sustainable development in the 21st century.

Written for *CQ Global Researcher*, September 2007

The unbridled ravages of commercial whaling — which brought several whale populations to the brink of extinction and significantly depleted many others — should serve as a grave warning to the dangers of the poorly regulated exploitation of marine mammals.

The moratorium was intended to allow whale populations to recover to pre-exploitation levels. Since the moratorium was implemented, however, we have learned what we know and what we don't know about whale populations. We have learned that it's difficult to accurately estimate whale populations and that whales now face new threats from noise and chemical pollution, ship strikes, loss of critical habitat, entanglement in fishing gear and, more recently, challenges due to climate change. All of these threats may influence recovery of whale populations.

Even if the threats to whale populations could be adequately mitigated, many question whether commercial whaling could ever, realistically, be well regulated. The lessons of history — and the burgeoning exploitation of the moratorium's loophole for "scientific" whaling — lead us to conclude that this is unlikely.

Moreover, grave concerns remain as to whether whaling could ever be conducted humanely. Since commercial whaling is conducted for profit, it is argued with good reason that whaling should be held accountable to the same standards for humane slaughter as other animals killed for commercial purposes. It is difficult — even, unpleasant — to imagine a situation in which an animal could escape and be lost during slaughter in an abattoir and be left to die of its injuries. Yet, whales that are injured and escape remain a permanent feature of all whaling practices.

In addition, there are also much broader ethical issues at stake: In the 21st century, many people, even some cultures, no longer view whales as a resource to be exploited but as social beings, with complex lives that should be afforded protection of their interests, not because of their potential value to humankind but because of their own value in and of themselves.

Perhaps rather than asking whether the moratorium should be lifted, the global community should now turn its attention to closing the legal loopholes that permit whaling under objection and whaling for "scientific" purposes, and we should instead ask how we can secure a brighter future for our seaborne cousins so they are protected from commercial hunting permanently.

Three-quarters of the ocean's pollution comes from land-based human activity, and the problem is getting worse. Half of the world's population lives within 62 miles of the coast; in Southeast Asia it's two-thirds. In the United States, 53 percent of the population lives in coastal counties that comprise only 17 percent of the country's landmass. Nine of the world's 10 largest cities are on the coast, and coastal population growth is expected to greatly exceed overall trends.[70] Already, 20th-century development activities have destroyed half of all coastal wetlands.[71]

Reengineering rivers compounds the problem with polluted watersheds. Egypt's Aswan High Dam cut off the flow of nutrients to the Nile Delta, causing the sardine catch to plummet from 18,000 to 600 tons in three years. In Louisiana, decades of levee- and channel-building by the Army Corps of Engineers has transformed the Mississippi River into a ditch that shunts fertilizers and sewage directly into the Gulf of Mexico. And by preventing the river from dropping silt in its delta, the levees are causing the Louisiana bayous to disappear into open water at the rate of 25-35 square miles a year.[72]

"The loss of Louisiana's marshes will incrementally destroy the economy, culture, ecology and infrastructure, not to mention the corresponding tax base of this state and this region," said banker King Milling, chairman of the state-appointed Committee on the Future of Coastal Louisiana.[73]

The U.S. Commission on Ocean Policy and the Pew Oceans Commission have called for integrated, watershed-wide planning in the United States. If implemented, the model might again draw on the experience of Belize, which found that protecting coral reefs required addressing problems far inland.

"To protect the reefs — or any other ecosystem for that matter — you have to take . . . an ecosystem approach," said Gibson, the former head of Belize's Coastal Zone Management Authority (CZMA). "You need to look at pollution in the watersheds, at coastal construction and urban expansion, at fisheries and forest loss, at the effects of tourism and air pollution.

"If there isn't coordination between economic sectors, your efforts to conserve an ecological system are not going to be successful," she continued. The CZMA has coordinated policies governing forestry, fisheries and water quality while sponsoring education programs to show people how rivers, mangroves, cays and reefs interact. Other countries have made advances in creating integrated coastal zone management plans. Australia created a national framework to integrate its state, territorial, regional and local government agencies to manage resources on a river-basin-by-river-basin level.[74] In 2002, the European Union recommended that member states move towards integrated management. A 2007 review found "a positive impact in stimulating progress" but acknowledged it would be a "slow and long-term process." Most member states hadn't adopted national strategies until 2006; six had not done so at all.[75]

OUTLOOK
Out of Mind

The oceans have never gotten the political attention they need, and after the Sept. 11, 2001, terrorist attacks, they seemed to sink even lower on the world's priority list.

"We are moving forward extremely slowly, and in fact we are actually retreating from some of the movement we had toward more concerted international action," says Mee of the University of Plymouth. "There's been concentration on other issues: terrorism, in particular, and security."

Ironically, the urgent attention being focused on climate change has further eclipsed the oceans' problems. "Action by celebrity figures like [former Vice President] Al Gore has managed to put climate change on the agenda and kept it there very effectively," says Mee. "We don't really have many champions for the marine environment. The oceans don't make it onto people's agenda, resulting in the feeling that action can be postponed."

The United States is a case in point. The chairmen of the Pew Oceans Commission and the U.S. Commission on Ocean Policy joined forces to press for implementation of their recommendations, including issuing "report cards" grading governments' progress The U.S. government got a D+ in 2005 and a C- in 2006, reflecting modest progress.

"The improvement is largely attributable to state action and a few notable federal accomplishments," explained Admiral Watkins and Panetta.[76]

States and regional organizations received an A- after 18 took steps to develop comprehensive strategies for protecting marine systems. But there was little progress in most areas. Even modest programs to establish ocean observation systems (which collect basic oceanographic information) or to monitor and protect the endangered North Atlantic right whale have seen drastic funding cuts in the past year. Getting attention for oceans issues will remain challenging due to the lack of public awareness of the problems, and other congressional priorities, such as the Iraq War.

Internationally, even problems that aren't that difficult to solve have been put on the backburner. For instance, many of the disruptions caused by alien species could be prevented if the shipping industry adopted a ballast water-exchange program in which ballast water is pumped to and from sterilized sources rather than into local harbors.

"It costs people money," notes Mee. "It's a tiny marginal cost on transportation, but it requires a greater sense of purpose to push it through."

In the future, the world community is expected to focus more attention on the negative impact China's burgeoning industrialization is having on the world's oceans. According to the World Wildlife Fund, China is now the largest polluter of the Pacific Ocean. Each year China releases about 2.8 billion tons of contaminated water into the Bo Hai — a sea along China's northern coast — and the heavy metal content of Bo Hai bottom mud is now 2,000 times as high as China's official safety standard. In 2006, heavily industrialized Guangdong and Fujian provinces discharged nearly 8.3 billion tons of untreated sewage into the ocean — up 60 percent since 2001. More than 80 percent of the East China Sea — one of the world's largest fisheries — is now rated unsuitable for fishing, and the Chinese prawn catch has plunged 90 percent over the past 15 years.[77]

Bill Wareham, acting director of the Marine Conservation Program at Canada's David Suzuki Foundation, is pessimistic international agencies will cooperate, citing the refusal in 2006 by China, Russia and other deep-sea fishing nations to support the U.N.'s measure to ban trawling.

If the world cannot depend on the U.N. to mandate the protection of fish habitat and to prevent the ongoing decline of high seas fish stocks, "then we are in a very sad state," he said. "The global governance system has failed to move past the stage of denial."[78]

NOTES

1. John W. Miller, "Global fishing trade depletes African waters," *The Wall Street Journal*, July 18, 2007, p. A1.

2. "State of World Fisheries and Aquaculture 2006," Food and Agriculture Organization, 2007.

3. Ransom A. Myers and Bruce Worm, "Rapid Worldwide Depletion of Predatory Fish Communities," *Nature*, May 15, 2003, p. 280.

4. Kenneth R. Weiss, "A primeval tide of toxins," *Los Angeles Times*, July 30, 2006, p. 1.

5. See Kieran Kelleher, "Discards in the world's marine fisheries: An update," Technical Paper 470, Food and Agriculture Organization, 2005, pp. xvi, 38.

6. Eleanor M. Dorsey and Judith Pederson, *Effects of Fishing Gear on the Sea Floor of New England*, Conservation Law Foundation (1998), pp. 1-6.

7. Clive Wilkinson (ed.), *Status of Coral Reefs of the World: 2004, Vol. 1*, Australian Institute for Marine Science, 2004, p. 7.

8. Colin Woodard, *Ocean's End: Travels Through Endangered Seas* (2000), pp. 144-160.

9. *Ibid.*, pp. 44-45, 156; "Research reveals virus link in deaths of reefs," *Evening Herald* [Plymouth, England], May 2, 2007, p. 13.

10. Anne Platt McGinn, "Safeguarding the Health of the Oceans," Worldwatch Institute, 1999, pp. 26-27.

11. For background, see Marcia Clemmitt, "Saving the Oceans," *CQ Researcher*, Nov. 4, 2005, pp. 933-956.

12. For a detailed discussion see Woodard, *op. cit.*, pp. 97-129.

13. For background, see David Hosansky, "Invasive Species," *CQ Researcher*, Oct. 5, 2001, pp. 785-816.

14. Colin Woodard, "Battling killer seaweed," *The Chronicle of Higher Education*, Aug. 2, 2002, p. 14.

15. Kenneth R. Weiss, "Dark tides, ill winds," *Los Angeles Times*, Aug. 1, 2006, p. 1; Weiss, *op. cit.*; Jeremy B. C. Jackson, "Habitat destruction and ecological extinction of marine invertebrates," 2006, http://cbc.amnh.org/symposia/archives/expandingthearc/speakers/transcripts/jackson-text.html; see also Frances M. Van Dolah, "Marine Algal Toxins: Origins, Health Effects,

and Their Increased Occurrence," *Environmental Health Perspectives Supplements*, March 2000, www .ehponline.org/members/2000/suppl-1/133-141 vandolah/vandolah-full.html.

16. "Major study predicts bleak future for Europe's seas," University of Plymouth press release, June 7, 2007.

17. "Current trends project collapse of currently fished seafoods by 2050," National Science Foundation press release, Nov. 2, 2006.

18. Clemmitt, *op. cit.*

19. Testimony of Admiral James D. Watkins before the U.S. Senate Committee on Commerce, Science and Transportation, April 22, 2004, p. xi, http://govinfo .library.unt.edu/oceancommission/newsnotices/ prelim_testimony.html.

20. "1,600+ scientists warn that the sea is in peril, call for action now," Marine Conservation Biology Institute press release, Jan. 6, 1998, www.gdrc.org/ oceans/troubled.html.

21. Quoted in Clemmitt, *op. cit.* Furlong was citing the "Fish Stocks Sustainability Index" of the National Oceanographic and Atmospheric Administration's Fisheries Service, April 1-June 30, 2007, www.nmfs .noaa.gov/sfa/domes_fish/StatusoFisheries/2006/ 3rdQuarter/Q3-2006-FSSIDescription.pdf.

22. Bjorn Lomborg, *The Skeptical Environmentalist* (2001), pp. 189, 201, 329.

23. *Ibid.*

24. Edie Clark, "Ted Ames and the Recovery of Maine Fisheries," *Yankee Magazine*, November 2006.

25. Colin Woodard, "Saving Maine," *On Earth*, Summer 2003.

26. Testimony before U.S. House Natural Resources Subcommittee on Fisheries, Wildlife and Oceans, April 26, 2007, www.jointoceancommission.org/images/ Rosenberg_testimony_H.R.21_04_26_07.pdf.

27. Wayne A. Morrisey, "Science Policy and Federal Ecosystem-based Management," *Ecological Applications*, August 2006, pp. 717-720; D. S. Slocombe, "Implementing ecosystem-based management," Bioscience, Vol. 43 (1993), pp. 612-622; U.S. Department of Commerce, *The Ecosystem Approach: Vol. I*, June 1995.

28. Kenneth R. Weiss, "Study urges trawling ban in fragile marine habitats," *Los Angeles Times*, March 19, 2002, p. 12; Joe Haberstroh, "The bottom of the trawling matter," *Newsday*, March 31, 2002, p. 31; Jeremy Collie, *et al.*, Effects of Trawling and Dredging on Sea Floor Habitat, National Research Council, March 2002.

29. Glen Whiffen, "Dragging technology hurts: advocate," *St. John's Telegram* [Newfoundland], May 4, 2005, p. A4.

30. U.N. General Assembly, "The Impacts of Fishing on Vulnerable Marine Ecosystems," July 14, 2006, www .un.org/Depts/los/general_assembly/documents/ impact_of_fishing.pdf; John Heilprin, "UN ban on bottom trawling fails," *Houston Chronicle*, Nov. 25, 2006, p. 2.

31. "America's Living Oceans: Charting a course for sea change," Pew Oceans Commission, May 2003, p. 47, www.pewtrusts.org/uploadedFiles/wwwpewtrustsorg/ Reports/Protecting_ocean_life/env_pew_oceans_ final_report.pdf.

32. "NZ to close 30pc of waters to trawling," New Zealand Press Association, Feb. 14, 2006.

33. Jeff Barnard, "Seafloors fished by trawlers hold fewer kinds of fish," The Associated Press, April 18, 2007.

34. Milan Ilnyckyj, "The legality and sustainability of European Union fisheries policy in West Africa," *MIT International Review*, Spring 2007, pp. 33-41, http:// web.mit.edu/mitir/2007/spring/fisheries.html.

35. Kim Willsheer, "Mauritanians rue EU fish deal with a catch," *The Guardian*, Feb. 9, 2001.

36. Stephen Castle, "EU Trawlers get fishing rights off Africa for pounds 350m," *The Independent*, July 24, 2006.

37. Haberstroh, *op. cit.*, p. A23; James Kendall, "Scallop dredge fishing," in Dorsey and Pederson, *op. cit.*, pp. 90-93.

38. M. J. Kaiser and B. E. Spencer, "The effects of beam-trawl disturbance on infaunal communities in different habitats," *Journal of Animal Ecology, Vol. 65* (1996), pp. 348-358; A.D. Rijnsdorp and P. I. Van Leewen, "Changes in growth of North Sea plaice

since 1950 in relation to density, eutrophication, beam trawl effort, and temperature," *ICES Journal Marine Science*, Vol. 53 (1996), pp. 1199-1213; R. S. Millner and C. L. Whiting, "Long-term changes in growth and population abundance of sole in North Sea from 1940 to present," *ICES Journal Marine Science*, Vol. 53 (1996), pp. 1185-1195.

39. Haberstroh, *op. cit.*, p. A23. Also see "The impact of bottom trawling on American lobsters off Duxbury Beach, MA," Massachusetts Division of Marine Fisheries, Oct. 1, 1989.

40. For background see Clemmitt, *op. cit.*, p. 946.

41. Colin Woodard, *The Lobster Coast* (2004), pp. 201-207; William Warner, *Distant Water* (1977), pp. 50-53.

42. Woodard, *ibid.*, p. 204.

43. Warner, *op. cit.*, pp. 52-53.

44. Marcus Gee, "Here's a fine kettle of . . . ," *Globe & Mail* [Toronto], May 16, 2003, p. A23; Woodard, *ibid.*, pp. 223-231.

45. Michael Temelini, "The Rock's newfound nationalism," [Toronto] *Globe & Mail*, June 29, 2007, p. A17.

46. For background, see Michael Harris, *Lament for an Ocean* (1998); Woodard, 2004, *op. cit.*, pp. 223-231.

47. "Fishers fear tough catch curbs again after cod-stocks claim," *Aberdeen Press and Journal*, Oct. 23, 2001, p. 19; John McQuaid, "Overfished waters running on empty," *New-Orleans Times-Picayune*, March 24, 1996, p. A39.

48. Carl Safina, "Fishing off the deep end — and back," *Multinational Monitor*, Sept. 1, 2003, p. 8.

49. Anne Platt McGinn, "Rocking the Boat," Worldwatch Institute, June 1998, pp. 43-44.

50. Margaret Munro, "Fuel subsidies keep trawlers 'strip-mining' sea," *Vancouver Sun*, Nov. 17, 2006, p. A3; see also U. R. Sumaila and D. Pauly, (eds.), "Catching more bait: a bottom-up re-estimation of global fisheries subsidies," Fisheries Centre Research Reports 14(6), p. 2. University of British Columbia, www.fisheries.ubc.ca/members/dpauly/chaptersInBooksReports/2006/ExecutiveSummaryCatchingMoreBait.pdf.

51. Patricia J. James, "Cousteau says lack of care impacts sea," *Telegram & Gazette* (Mass.), May 12, 2006, p. B1.

52. The Serengeti — a vast plain stretching from Kenya to northern Tanzania — is famous for its extensive wildlife.

53. Jeremy B. C. Jackson, "What was natural in the coastal oceans?" Proceedings of the National Academy of Sciences, May 8, 2001, pp. 5412-3; Woodard, 2000, *op. cit.*, pp. 160-161.

54. Woodard, *ibid.*, pp. 208-215; Juliet Eilperin, "US wants polar bears listed as threatened," *The Washington Post*, Dec. 27, 2006, p. 1.

55. Fred Pearce, "Failing ocean circulation raises fears of mini ice-age," NewScientist.com news service, Nov. 30, 2005, http://media.newscientist.com/article.ns?id=dn8398.

56. Elizabeth Kolbert, "The darkening sea," *The New Yorker*, Nov. 20, 2006, p. 67; Usha Lee McFarling, "A chemical imbalance," *Los Angeles Times*, Aug. 3, 2006, p. 1.

57. Woodard, 2004, *op. cit.*, pp. 212-213.

58. John Charles Kucinich, *Killing Our Oceans: Dealing with the Mass Extinction of Marine Life* (2006), pp. 56-57.

59. "World Digest," *The Capital* (Annapolis, Md.), Nov. 25, 2006, p. A2.

60. Petro Parravano and Lee Crockett, "Who should own the oceans?" *San Francisco Chronicle*, Sept. 25, 2000.

61. See Clemmitt, *op. cit.*, p. 941.

62. Jane Lubchenco, "Global changes for life in oceans," Conference presentation, *M/S Fram* off Greenland, Sept. 8, 2007; Jon Nevill, "Marine no-take areas: How large should marine protected area networks be?" white paper, Sept. 4, 2006, available from www.onlyoneplanet.com.au.

63. For background, see Rachel S. Cox, "Ecotourism," *CQ Researcher*, Oct. 20, 2006, pp. 865-888.

64. For background see Colin Woodard, "Belizean bonanza," *The Chronicle of Higher Education*, July 2, 2004, http://chronicle.com/subscribe/login?url=/weekly/v50/i43/43a01301.htm.

65. *Ibid.*

66. "U.S Ocean Policy Report Card," Joint Ocean Commission Initiative, February 2007, www

.jointoceancommission.org/images/report-card-06.pdf; Colin Woodard, "Faraway, natural and beautiful and it will stay that way," *Trust*, Fall 2006, pp. 2-11.

67. For a full discussion, see Woodard, *The Lobster Coast*, *op. cit.*, pp. 267-273.

68. John Cordell, ed., *Sea of Small Boats, Cultural Survival* (1989), pp. 337-367; R.E. Johannes, "Traditional Law of the Sea in Micronesia," *Micronesica*, December 1977, pp. 121-127; Janice Harvey and David Coon, "Beyond the Crisis in the Fisheries: A proposal for community-based ecological fisheries management," Conservation Council of New Brunswick, 1997.

69. Brad Warren, "Conserving Alaska's Oceans," Marine Conservation Alliance, 2006, www.marineconservationalliance.org/news/1359_MCA_Report_for_download.pdf.

70. "Population Trends Along the Coastal United States 1980-2003, National Oceanographic and Atmospheric Administration, March 2005.

71. Peter Weber, "Abandoned Seas: Reversing the Decline of the World's Oceans," Worldwatch Institute, November 1993, pp. 17-24, www.worldwatch.org/node/874; Woodard, 2000, *op. cit.*, p. 45.

72. Woodard, *ibid.*, p. 116.

73. Weber, *op. cit.*, p. 20; Pew Oceans Commission, *op. cit.*, p. 54.

74. "National Cooperative Approach to Integrated Coastal Zone Management," National Resource Management Ministerial Council, 2006, www.environment.gov.au/coasts/publications/framework/pubs/framework.pdf.

75. "Report to the European Parliament and Council: An evaluation of ICZM in Europe," European Commission, June 7, 2007, http://eurlex.europa.eu/LexUriServ/LexUriServ.do?uri=CELEX:52007DC0308:EN:NOT.

76. Leon Pannetta and James Watkins, "State's map for saving the oceans," *The Washington Post*, Feb. 3, 2007, p. A15.

77. See Elizabeth C. Economy, "The Great Leap Backward?" *Foreign Affairs*, September/October 2007, pp. 38-59.

78. James Vassallo, "Canada becoming a 'pariah' over trawling," *Prince Rupert Daily News* (BC), Nov. 28, 2006, p. 2.

BIBLIOGRAPHY

Books

Acheson, James M., *Capturing the Commons: Devising Institutions to Manage the Maine Lobster Industry, University Press of New England,* **2003.**
An anthropologist examines the successes of Maine's lobster fishery and state efforts to incorporate traditional lobster-fishing practices into law.

Barker, Rodney, *And the Waters Turned to Blood, Simon & Schuster,* **1997.**
An investigative journalist chronicles of the rise of a dangerous marine microorganism in the Mid-Atlantic region of the United States and efforts to contain it.

Ellis, Richard, *The Empty Ocean, Island Press,* **2004.**
The author of more than 10 books on the oceans and a research associate at the American Museum of Natural History in New York uses history, anecdote and stunning facts to chronicle humanity's predation on the oceans.

Fujita, Rodney M., *Heal the Ocean: Solutions for Saving Our Seas, New Society Publishers,* **2003.**
A marine ecologist describes successful efforts to confront the problems in the world's oceans.

Meinesz, Alexandre, *Killer Algae: The True Tale of a Biological Invasion, University of Chicago Press,* **1999.**
The scientist who discovered the problem of *Caulerpa taxifolia,* the "killer seaweed" that is taking over the Mediterranean, gives a first-hand account of how bad an invading species can be.

Molyneaux, Paul, *The Doryman's Reflection: A Fisherman's Life, Avalon,* **2005.**
A former commercial fisherman gives a personal account of the collapse of U.S. fisheries, with critical insights into the mindset and values that destroyed a beloved culture.

Warner, William, *Distant Water: The Fate of the North Atlantic Fishermen, Little, Brown,* **1977.**
The classic account of the rise of factory trawlers and the damage they did prior to the advent of 200-mile limits.

Woodard, Colin, *Ocean's End: Travels through Endangered Seas, Basic Books,* **2000.**
The author, a freelance journalist specializing in ocean issues, describes the degradation of the world's oceans.

Articles

Garrison, Virginia, et al., "African and Asian dust: from desert soils to coral reefs," *Bioscience*, **May 1, 2003.**
Scientists hypothesize that the world's coral reefs may be dying because of dust from African desertification.

Kolbert, Elizabeth, "The Darkening Sea," *The New Yorker*, **Nov. 20, 2006.**
The author provides a detailed and readable account of what carbon emissions are doing to the ocean through acidification.

Kunzig, Robert, "Twilight of the Cod," *Discover*, **April 1995.**
Kunzig chronicles the collapse of the New England and Newfoundland cod fisheries in the late 1980s.

Weiss, Kenneth R., et al., "Altered Oceans," *Los Angeles Times*, **July 30-Aug. 3, 2006.**
In a Pulitzer Prize-winning series, Weiss and others describe the oceans' demise, with emphasis on the "rise of slime."

Reports and Studies

Dorsey, Eleanor, and Judith Pederson (eds.), *Effects of Fishing Gear on the Sea Floor of New England*, **Conservation Law Foundation, 1998.**
This report catalogs the damage caused by bottom trawlers, as viewed by scientists, environmentalists and fishermen.

Harvey, Janice, and David Coon, "Beyond the Crisis in the Fisheries: A proposal for community-based ecological fisheries management," *Conservation Council of New Brunswick*, **1997.**
A groundbreaking report by the Canadian conservation council argues for giving proprietary ownership of fishing resources to the local communities that have relied on them.

***Pew Oceans Commission*, "America's Living Oceans: Charting a Course for Sea Change," May 2003.**
The commission describes the critical state of the world's oceans and recommends an ecosystem-based approach to future ocean management.

***United Nations Food and Agriculture Organization*, "State of the World's Fisheries and Aquaculture 2006," 2007, www.fao.org/docrep/009/A0699e/ A0699e00.htm.**
The FAO's latest official report on the state of world fisheries says a quarter of the commercial fish stocks have been over-exploited or depleted and about half are fully exploited.

***U.S. Commission on Ocean Policy*, "An Ocean Blueprint for the 21st Century," 2004.**
The recommendations of a panel established by Congress echo those of the Pew Oceans Commission, while extending analysis to energy, environmental education and the issues afflicting the Great Lakes.

For More Information

Belize Coastal Zone Management Institute, P.O. Box 1884, Belize City, Belize, Central America; +1-501-223-0719; www.coastalzonebelize.org. Coordinates policies that will affect the health of Belize's barrier reef system.

Black Sea Ecosystem Recovery Project, www.undp-drp .org/drp/project_cooperation_BSERP.html. A network of scientists and policy experts sponsored by the U.N. Development Program.

Canadian Department of Fisheries and Oceans, 200 Kent St., 13th Floor, Station 13228, Ottawa, Ontario, Canada K1A 0E6; 613-993-0999; www.dfo-mpo.gc.ca. Manages Canada's fisheries, oceans and marine research.

International Whaling Commission, The Red House, 135 Station Road, Impington, Cambridge, CB24 9NP, United Kingdom; +44-1223-233-971; www.iwcoffice.org. Regulates whaling and the conservation of whales.

Joint Ocean Commission Initiative, c/o Meridian Institute,1920 L St., N.W., Suite 500, Washington, DC 20036-5037; (202) 354-6444; www.jointoceancommission.org. A vehicle for the chairs of the Pew Oceans Commission and U.S. Commission on Ocean Policy to push implementation of their recommendations.

National Fisheries Institute, 7918 Jones Branch Dr., Suite 700, McLean, VA 22102; (703) 752-8880; www.about seafood.com. The main lobbying and advocacy association for commercial fishing and seafood processing industries in the United States.

National Marine Fisheries Service, 1315 East-West Highway, Silver Spring, MD 20910; (301) 713-2239; www .nmfs.noaa.gov. U.S. federal agency responsible for the management of fisheries and international fishing agreements.

Oceana, 2501 M Street, N.W., Suite 300, Washington, DC 20037-1311; (202) 833-3900; www.oceana.org. The world's largest oceans-based environmental group, with branch offices in Europe, South America and the U.S. West Coast.

Ocean Conservancy, 1300 19th St., N.W., Washington, DC 20036; (202) 429-5609; www.oceanconservancy.org. Nonprofit organization promoting healthy and diverse ocean ecosystems and opposing practices that threaten ocean life.

Pew Institute for Ocean Science, 126 East 56th St., New York, NY 10022; (212) 756-0042; www.pewoceanscience.org. A Pew-funded body that conducts, supports, and disseminates scientific information on protecting the world's oceans.

Seaweb, 8401 Colesville Road, Suite 500, Silver Spring, MD 20910; (301) 495-9570; www.seaweb.org. Environmental advocacy group promoting ocean conservation, with branch offices in London and Paris.

The Shark Alliance, Rue Montoyer 39, 1000 Brussels, Belgium; www.sharkalliance.org. A continent-wide coalition of nongovernment organizations working to save Europe's sharks.

University of British Columbia Fisheries Centre, 2202 Main Mall, University of British Columbia, Vancouver, B.C.; Canada V6T 1Z4; 604-822-2731; www.fisheries.ubc .ca. Leading fisheries research institution and home to the scientists who predict the world is facing "seas of slime" and may end up "fishing down the marine food webs."

11

Avian Flu Threat

Are We Prepared for the Next Pandemic?

Sarah Glazer

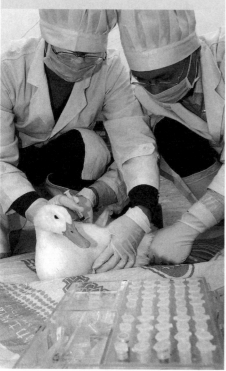

Health workers take blood samples from a duck in Sichuan Province, China, on Nov. 11, 2005, to see if it is infected with bird flu. Since 1997, the disease has infected millions of poultry in Asia and Europe. So far, about 75 of the more than 145 people known to be infected by the disease have died.

From *CQ Researcher*,
January 13, 2006

Chickens started dying mysteriously in Srisomboon, in northern Thailand, in August 2004. Like most children in the sleepy village, 11-year-old Sakuntula had daily contact with the birds. When she developed a stomachache and fever, the nurse at a nearby clinic dismissed her symptoms as a bad cold.

Five days later, Sakuntula began coughing up blood and was rushed to the district hospital. Her mother, Pranee Thongchan, was summoned from her job at a garment factory near Bangkok and found her daughter gasping for breath. The child died that night. Two weeks later, Pranee, 26, died, suffering from muscle aches and exhaustion, which were blamed on grief.* Viral pneumonia was listed as the official cause of death, however.[1]

Then, on Sept. 28, 2004, the World Health Organization (WHO) announced that the mother's death represented the first person-to-person transmission of the avian flu strain known as H5N1.

Researchers received the news with understandable concern. If H5N1 becomes easily transmissible from human to human, a worldwide epidemic — or pandemic — could occur, causing widespread infection and death from a virus to which most humans are believed to have little natural immunity.

The WHO has reassuringly called the Thongchans' daughter-to-mother transmission a "viral dead-end," because the virus does not appear to have mutated into a form that is easily passed from human to human.[2]

---

* Symptoms of avian flu in humans have ranged from no symptoms to typical flu-like symptoms (fever, cough, sore throat and muscle aches) to eye infections, pneumonia, severe respiratory diseases and other life-threatening complications.

Migratory Birds May Spread Virus

Migratory birds may be spreading avian flu as it moves westward from Asia to Europe. Researchers say migratory-bird densities were at their peak when most of the outbreaks in Southeast Asia occurred in 2003-2004. The pattern of H5N1 outbreaks worldwide, however, does not track the migratory flyways of wild birds in all countries.

Flight Patterns of Migratory Birds

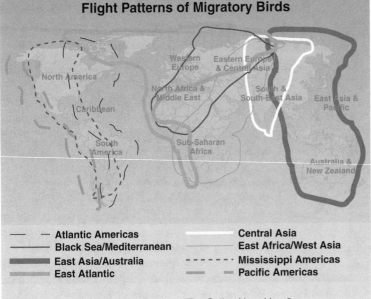

— — Atlantic Americas	Central Asia
——— Black Sea/Mediterranean	East Africa/West Asia
▬▬ East Asia/Australia	- - - - Mississippi Americas
▬▬ East Atlantic	- - Pacific Americas

Source: Public Broadcasting Service, "The Online NewsHour"

Today, the H5N1 virus is "like a key that doesn't quite fit the lock" of human-to-human contagion, explains Michael T. Osterholm, a professor at the University of Minnesota's School of Public Health. "But if you jiggle the key enough times, occasionally it will open the door. The virus is moving closer to the key that would really open the door. That's when you get sustained human-to-human transmission."

And each new human case gives the virus an opportunity to mutate into a fully transmissible strain among people, according to the WHO. International health officials were particularly alarmed by this month's deaths of three children in Turkey, the first victims of the disease reported outside of East Asia. Within a week, more Turks had contracted the disease, apparently after handling infected birds. About 50 others were hospitalized with suspected cases of the bird flu — 20 of them near Ankara, a major metropolitan city that is relatively well off and

where humans and animals do not customarily share the same living quarters. By Jan. 9, at least 10 of 81 Turkish provinces reported having found sick birds, compared to only three provinces a few days earlier.[3]

Currently, there is no government-approved vaccine for human avian flu, although there is one for the version that attacks poultry. If a pandemic flu were to hit the United States tomorrow, it could take up to a year after the virus strain was identified to manufacture a targeted vaccine, but domestic-manufacturing capacity would only be able to produce enough doses to cover barely a tenth of the nation's population.*

Currently, the only treatment for the disease is thought to be Tamiflu and Relenza, antiviral medications known to work against seasonal flu. But no one knows for sure how effective they would be against a new pandemic flu strain.

Since 1997, H5N1 outbreaks have infected millions of poultry and more than 140 humans around the world as it has spread from flocks in Southeast Asia to Central Asia and Europe. ** More than 75 people have died, about half of those said to be infected. The high 50-percent mortality rate worries experts. However, many think it is probably overstated because milder cases probably are not being reported. And some infected people who may have developed antibodies won't show any symptoms. By contrast, a worldwide flu outbreak in 1918 — the most lethal in

---

* To create sufficient capacity to cover the entire population, most experts agree the nation needs to convert to new cell-based technology, which has more flexibility to expand the number of doses than current egg-based technology. It would take 2-5 years to get government approval for the new method and to build plants using the new technology.

** Infected birds shed large quantities of the virus in their feces, creating abundant opportunities for exposure. Exposure is considered most likely during slaughter, defeathering, butchering and preparation of poultry for cooking.

recent history — killed only 2.5 percent of its victims, but that amounted to 40 million to 100 million worldwide — including about 675,000 Americans.[4]

But some experts think the avian flu will never mutate into a humanly transmissible virus. Michael Fumento, a senior fellow at the conservative Hudson Institute, maintains that H5N1 was first discovered in Scottish chickens in 1959. "It's therefore been mutating and making contact with humans for 47 years. If it hasn't become transmissible between humans in all that time, it almost certainly won't," he writes. (*See "At Issue," p. 303.*)

Because no one knows whether or when an avian flu pandemic might occur, the U.S. government is in a quandary over how aggressively to act. Some experts believe a global disaster threatens. "The situation right now in Asia is ripe for a perfect storm," says Osterholm. "You've got the virus circulating, you've got it moving closer to human pathogens and you've got a world ill-prepared."

Modern transportation permits a single person to spread disease to several continents within days, as the rapid spread of SARS demonstrated in 2003, when an infected doctor traveling out of China managed to spread the disease to Vietnam, Singapore and Canada within a month.[5] (Although SARS never became the worldwide epidemic that was predicted, before it was effectively contained it had spread to 30 countries, infected 8,000 people and killed 800.)

If a new avian flu pandemic develops, Osterholm paints a bleak picture of nations closing their borders and disrupting global economic trade in self-protection. And since the United States imports 80 percent of the raw materials used to produce crucial pharmaceuticals, he says, medicine would be scarce.

Efforts to contain the disease in Asia — including China's efforts to vaccinate every one of its 14 billion poultry — won't work, some experts say, because some vaccines are likely to be fake or overly diluted.[6] In a

At Least 78 Deaths Reported

The number of humans infected with avian flu doubled between 2004 and 2005, but the outbreak remained in Asia. On Jan. 10, 2006, Turkish health officials reported 15 patients confirmed with the disease and more hospitalized with symptoms suggesting the avian flu — more cases than the World Health Organization's totals (below). Three children in Turkey had died from the infection as of Jan. 10.

Confirmed Avian Flu Cases and Deaths

	2003 cases/ deaths	2004 cases/ deaths	2005 cases/ deaths	2006 cases/ deaths	Total
Cambodia	0/0	0/0	4/4	0/0	4/4
China	0/0	0/0	7/5	1/0	8/5
Indonesia	0/0	0/0	16/11	0/0	16/11
Thailand	0/0	17/12	5/2	0/0	22/14
Turkey	0/0	0/0	0/0	4/2	4/2
Vietnam	3/3	29/20	61/19	0/0	93/42
Total	**3/3**	**46/32**	**93/41**	**5/2**	**147/78**

Source: World Health Organization

phone interview from Hong Kong, virologist Robert Webster of St. Jude Children's Research Hospital in Memphis, Tenn., and one of the world's leading authorities on bird flu, said "crap vaccines" already are being used in China. There are no international standards for agricultural vaccines, he notes.

Administering a weak vaccine causes a "bloody disaster," he explains, because only the symptoms, not the virus itself, tend to disappear. "The chicken doesn't die; instead, if it's infected it goes on pooping out virus for days and days and spreads the virus and increases the rate of evolution" of the virus, he says.

H5N1 has also been found in migratory birds, which may explain its spread to Europe, and in ducks, which do not show symptoms but may play an increased role in transmitting H5N1 to both poultry and humans.[7]

The situation looks dire to some advocates. The National Institutes of Health (NIH) is testing an experimental vaccine against a Vietnamese strain of H5N1 that infects humans, and the government has ordered more doses of it to be made. But it will be two to five

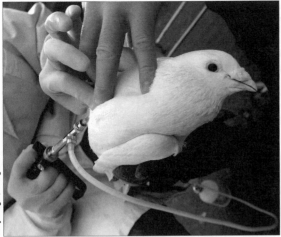

A pigeon is vaccinated in Beijing in an effort to curb the spread of bird flu. China plans to vaccinate every one of its 14 billion birds. There is no approved vaccine yet for the human version of the disease.

years before the United States could build enough capacity to vaccinate everyone in the country.

Meanwhile, the government has begun stockpiling Tamiflu, but has only ordered enough to treat 5 percent of the population. (While Relenza is considered as effective as the Tamiflu capsule, it must be inhaled using a special inhaler, making it a less desirable medicine for mass distribution and stockpiling.)

"You can't prevent it if you don't have the vaccine; you can't treat it if you don't have the medication," says Kim Elliott, deputy director of the Trust for America's Health, a public-health advocacy group.[8]

That leaves isolating infected people as the only strategy for preventing spread of the disease. The Centers for Disease Control and Prevention (CDC) has proposed new regulations giving it authority to stop sick travelers from getting off international flights. But, unlike SARS, people with the flu are contagious for about a day before they have symptoms.

"When people push me, I say if society comes apart you have to be prepared to exist for three months with what you have in your house," says Webster. "It won't work, but what else have we got?"

"To have effective quarantine, you have to tell everyone to stay home [because we won't know] who's sick. That's just not possible," says Elliott.

In November 2005, President Bush proposed $7.1 billion in emergency funding to prepare for a flu pandemic, mainly to produce and stockpile vaccines and antiviral drugs and to improve reporting of bird flu cases at home and abroad. In December, Congress approved half that amount — $3.8 billion for 2006 — enough to "jump start" the plan this year, according to the Trust for America's Health.[9] The legislation also created sweeping protection from lawsuits for pandemic-vaccine manufacturers, which consumer groups blasted as an "unprecedented giveaway" to drug companies.[10]

But some critics say even the president's full request was too little too late. "That's less than the cost of an aircraft carrier," observes Tara O'Toole, director of the Center for Biosecurity at the University of Pittsburgh Medical School. "If we don't deal with this, we are facing a potential destabilizing and existential threat. You have to have countermeasures. That will require spending real money — money that you measure in [national] defense terms."

Other experts agree with Fumento and doubt this strain of flu will jump from birds to humans. Some believe it could evolve into something no more lethal than typical seasonal flu. "I'm just not persuaded this is a clear-cut case of avian virus waiting to cause the next pandemic," says Peter Palese, a leading microbiologist at Mount Sinai School of Medicine in New York. Like most scientists, Palese expects a flu pandemic of some kind eventually to occur as successive generations lose immunity to older viruses, but he says it could be 20 years from now and bear little relation to H5N1.

Of the 20th century's three flu pandemics, only the 1918 outbreak was extremely lethal. The 1957 and 1968 outbreaks caused about 75,000 and 34,000 U.S. deaths, respectively. Today, a mild pandemic on that scale would cause about 100,000 deaths in the United States — about three times the estimated 36,000 deaths that occur annually from seasonal flu, the Congressional Budget Office (CBO) projects.

Based on the historical frequency of pandemics over the past 300 years, in which mild pandemics have predominated, the chances of a severe pandemic occurring in the future are very small — only 0.3 percent, according to the CBO.[11]

A 1918-scale flu, nonetheless, would infect about 90 million people in the United States and cause 2 million U.S. deaths, according to the CBO.

If a pandemic were to hit tomorrow, most agree our medical system would be woefully unprepared. "If this is anything like 1918, hospitals will be overwhelmed; if hospital workers are home sick with the flu, how you increase capacity becomes almost insoluble," says O'Toole, noting that most hospitals already run at close to 100 percent capacity. "If you ask them to double or triple their capacity, they collapse," she says.

Yet if the president were to start an even more ambitious pandemic-preparedness effort today — such as building new hospitals — the effort would be both costly and possibly unnecessary, as President Gerald Ford discovered with "swine flu." In 1976, the new strain of flu was projected to kill 1 million people, and Ford pushed for a mass-vaccination campaign. But only a few deaths occurred from the swine flu, and the government had to spend millions to compensate hundreds hurt or killed by the vaccine.

President Bush seemed to take note of this inevitable uncertainty when he unveiled his pandemic flu plan on Nov. 1. "While avian flu has not yet acquired the ability to spread easily from human to human, there is still cause for vigilance," he said. "Our country has been given fair warning of this danger to our homeland — and time to prepare. It's my responsibility as president to take measures now to protect the American people from the possibility that human-to-human transmission may occur."[12]

So why is Bush so concerned about preparing for a pandemic? "I have one word for you — [Hurricane] Katrina," says Michael Fumento, a senior fellow at the conservative Hudson Institute, who believes the current bird flu strain will never become a human pandemic.

Yet if a pandemic does arrive soon — whether from this bird flu or another virus — many experts say it could be a disaster, given the nation's beleaguered public health system, inadequate vaccine-production capacity and insufficient stores of antiviral medicine.

Here are some of the questions being debated in Congress, the scientific community and international organizations:

Is the United States prepared for a pandemic?

Top federal health officials have candidly admitted that if a pandemic arrived tomorrow the United States would not be prepared.[13] However, they contend that President Bush's proposal to spend billions on preparation, together with the detailed action plan released by the Department of Health and Human Services (HHS) in November, are

steps in the right direction. About 95 percent of the president's proposal would go toward producing and stockpiling vaccines, antiviral drugs and other medical supplies and improving systems for detecting and reporting flu cases here and abroad.[14]

Critics charge that the administration's failure to stockpile antiviral medication earlier or to encourage the development of pre-pandemic vaccines has put the U.S. far behind European countries, which are competing with us for scarce anti-flu medications.

Under the HHS plan, $4.7 billion would be spent to help private companies create production capacity for pandemic influenza vaccine and to build a stockpile. The ultimate goal is to have the capacity to produce enough vaccine for the entire U.S. population — almost 300 million people — within six months of an outbreak.

But current U.S. production capacity falls far short of that goal. The major flu vaccine manufacturer located in the United States is sanofi pasteur, the vaccine-producing arm of the French pharmaceuticals group Sanofi Aventis, which can produce only about 60 million doses each winter. According to most experts, 600 million doses — two shots for every American — would be needed to protect against a pandemic. "You do the math; it's frightening," says Elliott.

Moreover, there is no federally approved vaccine in the United States to protect against the bird flu strains circulating in Asia. The federal government has tested an experimental H5N1 vaccine in healthy people and is stockpiling the active ingredient needed for the vaccine, known as an antigen, in bulk form. The vaccine requires 12 times as much antigen per dose as seasonal flu vaccine and is expected to require two shots. Based on this formula, some experts say the government will only have enough H5N1 antigen to protect 4 million people by February 2006.[15]

The administration is hoping to stretch that supply with two methods shown in ongoing studies to enhance the immune response — diluting the vaccine with additives known as adjuvants and administering it into the skin rather than the muscle. However, it's unclear how far the supply can be stretched using these methods, according to Bruce Gellin, director of the National Vaccine Program Office, which authored the HHS plan.[16]

It is also unclear whether the H5N1 vaccine being tested by NIH will work against whatever virus appears

How Dangerous Is the Virus?

The lethal 1918 "Spanish flu" virus was probably descended from an avian virus and shares some genetic features with today's H5N1 bird flu, but its exact origin remains mysterious, according to molecular pathologist Jeffery K. Taubenberger. He and his research team at the Armed Forces Institute of Pathology recently reconstructed the deadly virus from frozen tissue samples.[1]

Their genetic analysis, published in October 2005, suggested that all eight genes of the 1918 flu came directly from a bird virus and moved into humans after gradually mutating. Federal health officials said at the time that H5N1 flu has already acquired some of the genetic-sequence changes that apparently allowed the 1918 virus to become easily transmissible among humans.[2]

Of the more than 140 people infected with H5N1, most had contact with infected poultry. The potential similarities between the catastrophic 1918 flu and the H5N1 flu — which has caused at least 75 deaths so far — have put the global public health community on edge.[3]

If, as Taubenberger suggests, the 1918 flu was a completely novel virus to which humans had never been exposed — and therefore had developed no immunity — that might help explain why so many people became sick and died. By contrast, the milder pandemics of 1957 and 1968 are believed to have been the combined product of a human flu and an avian virus that exchanged genes after either a human or a pig caught both viruses.

However, this explanation for the greater lethality of the 1918 flu is not universally accepted. It's also possible that the 1918 virus or versions of it had circulated in humans or other animals before it became pandemic, skeptics argue.

Because no genetic information exists about any pre-1918 human viruses, no one can know for sure whether the 1918 virus was unique in makeup or whether it may have infected humans at some earlier point.

One of the skeptics, Mount Sinai School of Medicine microbiologist Peter Palese, says, "I don't think we can say [the 1918 flu] was an avian virus that jumped into humans." It's "equally likely" that the 1918 flu was a product of both human and avian viruses, like the 1957 and 1968 pandemics, he says.

Palese is one of several scientists who are not convinced that H5N1 will become a human virus, citing research dating from 1992 indicating that many Chinese already have antibodies to it. "The H5 virus has had ample opportunity to jump from avian populations into humans," he says.

What about mounting reports of humans contracting bird flu since 2003, half of whom have died? Palese thinks the widespread perception from media reports that there has been a jump in cases and a high fatality rate is erroneous. Many bird flu cases probably are not being reported, he says, because they are either mild or asymptomatic (in the case of people with antibodies). So the fatality rate is probably much lower than the apparent 50 percent rate, he says.

Many other scientists also suspect that cases of bird flu are being underreported, especially in China. For example, by the end of 2005, Vietnam had announced more than 90 cases of bird flu, while China — vastly larger than Vietnam — had reported only seven.[4] Some experts, like Palese, suspect that the numbers infected in China are actually in the hundreds.[5]

on our shores. Virologist Webster doubts that it will prevent people from getting sick, though it may prevent deaths. "The viruses that are circulating out here are no longer closely related to the vaccine strain," he said in December, speaking by phone from Hong Kong.

In any case, it will probably be another two to five years before the United States can develop a vaccine and manufacturers can build enough production capacity to vaccinate everyone for a pandemic. (*See sidebar, p. 300.*)

Antiviral medications — such as Tamiflu, which helps people recover from the flu and acts as a preventive — are the second pillar of the administration's pandemic strategy. Under the plan, $1 billion would go toward purchasing enough antiviral drugs for a quarter of the U.S. population — the proportion recommended by the WHO.

However, as of December 2005, the administration had stockpiled only 4.3 million courses of Tamiflu, according to Gellin, far short of the 75 million needed.

Nevertheless, the U.S. government is planning for a worst-case scenario with a 2.5 percent death rate, as experienced in 1918. Since influenza viruses also tend to lose lethality over time, some scientists argue that any increase in transmissibility will produce a massive drop in virulence, because killing the host (i.e. humans) impedes a virus' evolution into a more lethal strain.[6]

No one can predict whether the virus will become humanly transmissible, or how virulent it will be, including Robert G. Webster, the scientist at St. Jude Children's Research Hospital in Memphis, Tenn., who has been warning of its potential dangers for years. When asked how serious it might be, all he can do is "hand wave" a guess. "My hand-waving would be if it does go human-to-human, the first wave will be a catastrophe for the world — for two, three, four months," he suggests. "The second wave will be less pathogenic and the third wave will go back to being somewhat benign." This is similar to the pattern observed in ducks, Webster says.

This month, however, Taubenberger and epidemiologist David M. Morens of the National Institutes of Health played down the similarities between the 1918 flu and H5N1. They noted that while the 1918 virus is "avianlike," researchers have been unable to trace the 1918 virus to any particular bird and that there is no historical data indicating that a precursor virus attacked domestic poultry in large numbers, as H5N1 has. No highly pathogenic avian virus has ever been known to cause a human pandemic, they noted. And despite Taubenberger's genetic-sequencing work, the biological basis for converting a virus into a humanly transmissible form — the prerequisite for a human pandemic — remains "unknown," they said.[7]

"The 1918 virus acquired this trait, but we do not know how, and we currently have no way of knowing whether H5N1 viruses are now in a parallel process of acquiring human-to-human transmissibility," they wrote. "Despite an explosion of data on the 1918 virus during the past decade, we are not much closer to understanding pandemic emergence in 2006 than we were in understanding the risk of H1N1 'swine flu' emergence in 1976," which turned out to be a false alarm.[8]

On the reassuring side, if H5N1 were to become a pandemic flu, the availability of modern antibiotics, which did not exist in 1918, would combat secondary bacterial infections, which caused many of the deaths in 1918.

But other unprecedented aspects of the virus worry scientists. The infection now has been found in tigers and domestic cats and in migratory birds, previously considered safe from such viruses. "We have to accept the fact that we're watching the evolution of this virus," says Webster. "Will it ever go human-to-human? Let's hope not. But we'd better be prepared for it."

---

[1] J. K. Taubenberger, *et al.*, "Characterization of the 1918 influenza virus polymerase genes," *Nature*, Oct. 6, 2005, pp. 889-893.

[2] "Bird Flu and the 1918 Pandemic," editorial, *The New York Times*, Oct. 8, 2005, p. A14.

[3] Congressional Research Service, "Pandemic Influenza: Domestic Preparedness Efforts," Nov. 10, 2005, p. 6.

[4] WHO, "Confirmed number of human cases," Dec. 19, 2005, www.who.int.

[5] See Elisabeth Rosenthal, "Experts Doubt Bird Flu Tallies from China and Elsewhere," *The New York Times*, Dec. 2, 2005, p. A8.

[6] Dennis Normile, "Pandemic Skeptics Warn Against Crying Wolf," *Science*, Nov. 18, 2005, pp. 1112-1113.

[7] Jeffery K. Taubenberger and David M. Morens, "1918 Influenza," *Emerging Infectious Diseases*, January 2006; www.cdc.gov/ncidod/EID/vol12no01/05-0979.htm.

[8] *Ibid.*

"There's no question more than 4 million Americans would become sick. We're woefully under-stockpiled there," says Elliott.

In response, Gellin cites computer simulations suggesting a pandemic could be stopped in its tracks by using Tamiflu to treat the small number of people initially infected and by giving it as a preventive to those in the surrounding area. "Three million treatment courses in one model has been shown to be the amount that's needed," he says, adding that the government hopes soon to have enough to treat twice that number of people. However, some experts doubt the government would be able to act fast enough to contain a pandemic this way. (Tamiflu must be taken within 48 hours of becoming ill.)

The United States has ordered 12 million treatment courses of Tamiflu from Roche, the Swiss pharmaceutical giant that developed the drug, but critics say the administration was so slow in placing its order that it is far down on the two-year waiting list behind other countries. And its order would only cover 5 percent of the population. Gellin responds that while the order won't be complete until sometime in 2007, the government will continue to get partial shipments in the intervening months.*

However, as governments were racing to buy Tamiflu, doubts suddenly emerged in late December 2005 about its efficacy, at current doses, after the prestigious *New England Journal of Medicine* reported that half of eight bird flu patients in Vietnam who were treated with Tamiflu had died — including two who developed resistance to the drug.[17]

Under the HHS plan, state and local governments would be largely responsible for distributing vaccines, anti-viral drugs and other medical supplies. But critics say state and local health departments, crippled by years of budget cuts and often sorely understaffed, will be hard-pressed to shoulder the burden. Many said the plan provided too little money for planning and none for implementation. Other critics say many states can't afford the 75 percent share the government is expecting them to kick in to buy 31 million courses of Tamiflu.

"I don't know where the states are going to come up with the money," says Elliott, who calculates the states' share of the cost at $510 million. "Look at Louisiana and Mississippi [post-Katrina]," she says. "They don't have it. It should not matter where you live or what your state's fiscal health is as to whether you get treated during a pandemic."

The administration argues that some $15 billion appropriated since 2001 to counter bioterrorism have helped states build up the same kind of public health capacities that would be needed in a flu pandemic. "Since 9/11 there's been a substantial investment to enhance that infrastructure," says Gellin. "A lot of those investments are helping precisely for the kind of threats we're facing now." Moreover, he says, pandemic planning should be a "shared responsibility" with the states.

But state officials say bioterrorism funds don't make up for cuts in their most crucial resource — people. "The tragedy is the hole was so big that the billions for public health preparedness are not enough when you cut school health programs. When something bad happens, that's where you

get your nurses from," says Georges C. Benjamin, executive director of the American Public Health Association. "If the resources aren't there, you end up with a big bottle of Tamiflu and no one to manage it."

In a pandemic, up to 5-10 million Americans would need hospitalization — far exceeding the nation's 900,000 staffed hospitals beds. And the flood of patients would overwhelm the need for crucial equipment, such as the nation's 100,000 ventilators, according to the CBO.[18]

The administration's plan contains a long list of recommendations for how hospitals should handle the overflow patients during a pandemic. But "there's no way hospitals could implement even a fraction of what's recommended without federal funds," which are absent from the administration's plan, says the Center for Biosecurity's O'Toole.

Some experts say the administration should put more emphasis on quarantine. "If our states and federal government are only focused on vaccines, and there's no plan for the interim to slow the spread of disease, then it will spread like wildfire," says David Heyman, director of the homeland security program at the Center for Strategic and International Studies and author of a study proposing quarantine guidelines. State officials have been calling him for advice, he said, because they've received so little guidance from the federal government.[19]

But many experts say a quarantine to control pandemic flu won't work. Unlike SARS, people infected with flu can be contagious before they show any symptoms, and some carriers may never show symptoms at all.

However, skeptics like Fumento, at the Hudson Institute, say H5N1 is unlikely to mutate into a human form. And if the next pandemic is not an avian flu, then all the government vaccine efforts aimed at producing an H5N1 vaccine "will be completely useless."

As for the administration's plan in general, "A lot of this is going to be wasted," Fumento says. "It's true of any government crash program. That's how you get $500 toilet seats."

Will liability protection encourage more companies to manufacture vaccines?

"In the past three decades, the number of vaccine manufacturers in America has plummeted, as the industry has been flooded with lawsuits," President Bush declared in his Nov. 1 pandemic speech. The fact that only one

---

* Under pressure from the global community, Roche agreed last fall that it would license partner companies to produce Tamiflu.

major company now manufactures flu vaccine on U.S. soil, Bush said, leaves "our nation vulnerable in the event of a pandemic."[20]

He urged Congress to shield drug makers from lawsuits in order to encourage more of them to manufacture vaccine. A provision providing sweeping protection from liability was approved by Congress in December (see p. 304).

The number of manufacturers producing vaccine for the U.S. market has declined precipitously — from 26 companies in 1967 to five today — for all types of vaccines. Only three companies produce flu vaccine for the U.S. market — sanofi pasteur, in Swiftwater, Pa., Chiron, which manufactures its vaccines in England, and MedImmune, based in Gaithersburg, Md.

While thousands of lawsuits claiming vaccine-related injuries to children have flooded the courts in recent years, there have been very few lawsuits — only 10 in the last 20 years — over flu vaccines, according to a recent study in the *Journal of the American Medical Association* (*JAMA*). While two resulted in awards — of $1.9 million and $13.5 million — the rest were settled for much smaller amounts or were dismissed on summary judgment.[21]

Some experts argue that market factors have been more important in discouraging drug makers than liability fears, including the uncertain seasonal demand and the low profitability. Profit margins are much lower for vaccines, which patients receive only once a year, than for drugs for chronic conditions like high blood pressure, which are often taken daily. Indeed, when Wyeth Pharmaceuticals stopped making flu vaccine in 2002, its reasons were "not specifically related to liability," says Wyeth Vice President Peter Paradiso. "We were unable to sell 8-10 million doses out of 20 million in 2002," he says. "It became clear there wasn't a demand for our product."

Nevertheless, insurers' perception of litigation threats has made it difficult for manufacturers to obtain insurance, and a similar perception among manufacturers may have been as important as the reality, the *JAMA* study's authors suggest.

"The economics have not always been favorable, and liability has been a factor in determining the profitability of participating in vaccine manufacturing," says sanofi pasteur spokesman Len Lavenda. "For example, today there are thousands of lawsuits pending against manufacturers of thimerosol" — a mercury additive in childhood vaccines.

But Howard Shlevin, president and CEO of Solvay Pharmaceuticals, in Marietta, Ga., said his company decided in 1998 to build a U.S. flu vaccine plant utilizing the newest cell-based technology, before there was any talk of liability protection. "From Solvay's perspective, if someone wants to give me a free ride, that's nice, but that's not what I'm looking for," he said. The company has, however, applied for a federal grant to help build the new plant, he said.

In any case, most agree that drug companies will need some protection from litigation when it comes to producing a vaccine specifically for a flu pandemic. In a pandemic, there probably won't be enough time to test it extensively for side effects. In addition, notes Lavenda, "When we're talking about a new vaccine combined with a particularly virulent disease and immunizing perhaps 300 million individuals, we have the ingredients for liability exposure far in excess of that normally associated with immunization programs. That's why congressional liability protection is essential for companies supplying pandemic vaccines."

But consumer groups and public health workers' unions maintain that the threat of lawsuits prevents shoddy practices and that the government should not abolish citizens' ability to sue in court unless it also compensates those hurt by the vaccines.

Members of an expert panel convened by the Institute of Medicine (IOM) in 2003 say there are better ways than liability protection to encourage drug companies to produce vaccines. To provide greater supply and price certainty, they recommended the government guarantee an advance purchase of vaccines at a negotiated price. To encourage universal vaccination, they proposed the government require health insurers to cover vaccination and provide government vouchers to people without health insurance.[22]

"Make it worth the manufacturer's while to produce the vaccine. The way other nations do it is by guaranteeing the supply and purchase," says panel member Sara Rosenbaum, chairwoman of the Department of Health Policy at George Washington University. "Until we're ready to do this, I really don't think that an incentive that's speculative at best and meaningless at worst will contribute much to the problem," she said of a sweeping liability approach. The U.S. government already contracts with manufacturers to purchase certain childhood vaccines, which it provides free to children without health insurance under the Vaccines for Children program launched in 1994.[23] Since then, the market for those vaccines has been "robust," according to Rosenbaum.*

Duke University Professor of economics Frank Sloan, who chaired the IOM committee, attributes drug-makers' antipathy to vaccines to low profits, uncertainty about sales and high regulatory costs. "Just taking tort rights away is unjust," he says. "The government regulation of drug companies should be the first guard against contamination" of vaccines like that discovered at Chiron's British plant in 2004. "But suppose it failed? Then you should have tort as a backup."[24]

Should the U.S. government do more to combat avian flu overseas?

Like other wealthy governments, the Bush administration has made its first priority stockpiling enough vaccine to inoculate everyone in the country and enough antiviral medication for those who get the flu. But that approach concentrates most of the world's medical supplies in rich countries. The poorer countries of Asia, like steerage passengers on the doomed *Titanic*, will be left without any lifeboats.

Fewer than 10 countries have domestic vaccine companies working on a pandemic vaccine. Based on present trends, the majority of developing countries would have no access to a vaccine during the first wave of a pandemic and possibly its entire duration, according to the World Health Organization (WHO). Some 23 countries have ordered antiviral drugs for national stockpiles, but the principal manufacturer, Swiss drugmaker Roche, will not be able to fill all orders for at least another year, according to the WHO.[25]

One solution to this bottleneck would be for the government to suspend Roche's Tamiflu patent so other companies could produce it. In October, Sen. Charles E. Schumer, D-N.Y., threatened legislation to this effect unless Roche issued licenses to other companies.[26]

---

* The government also limited the liability of childhood vaccine manufacturers in 1986, when it required families of children injured by routine childhood vaccines to first seek relief through the federal Vaccine Injury Compensation Program before seeking redress in the courts. Seasonal flu vaccines were added to the program in 2004, but vaccines for use in pandemics were not covered.

Bowing to international criticism, Roche agreed to license its product to 12 new partners out of 200 interested companies globally to help a number of countries meet their stockpile needs.

For its part, the WHO has recommended that wealthy countries contribute to an international stockpile of antiviral medications and cooperatively develop a "world vaccine." But so far, there's been more talk of coordination than action, according to David Nabarro, the new United Nations official in charge of avian flu.[27]

One computer model suggests that a big flu outbreak in rural Thailand could be contained within a month by giving antiviral medications to the first group of people infected and to uninfected people in the surrounding area. "Several million courses sent to Thailand would be more effective than hoarding [doses] for 300 million people" in the United States, said the model's creator, Emory University Professor of biostatistics Ira Longini.[28]

However, most Asian countries where avian flu has become endemic don't have big stockpiles of the drugs. Cambodia has only 150 doses of Tamiflu, enough for one dose per province, according to CBS' "60 Minutes."[29]

The limited supplies raise a major ethical as well as practical dilemma: Should the United States be prepared to hand over its stockpile of a few million antivirals to a country like Cambodia if the disease emerges there first — if only to protect itself?

A blunt "no," answers Osterholm, because he considers Longini's predictions of stopping the disease "a fairy tale."

For the strategy to work, the first human clusters of virus would have to be rapidly detected, reported and diagnosed. But in far-flung rural villages, local clinic staff usually do not recognize an unusual virus, and lengthy waits are common to get diagnoses from far-off laboratories. "I see no reasonable way to stop the virus in Asia," the University of Minnesota's Osterholm says.

He also doubts it will be possible to keep people from leaving a cordoned-off area. "People are going to flee," he says. Moreover, he asks, what government would be willing to announce that it's the first site of a deadly contagious virus when that news will instantly ostracize them economically?

Conventional wisdom dictates that Tamiflu must be taken within 48 hours of getting sick to be effective, but some recent research suggests that it must be taken within hours of infection, Osterholm says, a near-impossibility in a backward, rural area. And handing out Tamiflu

CHRONOLOGY

1900s-1970s *"Spanish flu" pandemic kills millions; vaccines and antibiotics become available later.*

1918 "Spanish flu" kills up to 100 million, including 675,000 in U.S.

1957 Asian flu kills 75,000 in U.S.

1968 Hong Kong flu kills 700,000 worldwide, 34,000 in U.S.

1976 President Gerald R. Ford orders mass vaccination for "swine flu." Pandemic fizzles, but vaccinations kill 32 and make hundreds sick.

1977 Russian flu, another pandemic that never materializes, infects children and young adults in U.S.

1990s *H5N1 bird flu is isolated in humans; new antiviral medications enter market.*

1997 H5N1 is first isolated in humans; infects 18 in Hong Kong; six die. Hong Kong slaughters all chickens.

1999 New antiviral drugs, Relenza and Tamiflu, licensed in U.S., Europe.

Early 2000s *Terrorist attacks in U.S. raise concern about possible bioterrorism; bird flu reappears in Asia.*

December 2002 President Bush orders smallpox vaccinations for health workers and military; few sign up.

February 2003 Two people contract H5N1 virus in Hong Kong; one dies.

Mid-2003 First wave of H5N1 infection begins with outbreaks in animals in Asia.

December 2003 Bush administration compensates those injured by smallpox vaccine. South Korea reports first avian flu outbreak in chickens.

2004 *Avian flu spreads through Southeast Asia, killing 32 people in Thailand, Vietnam.*

January 2004 Bird flu appears in poultry in Vietnam, Japan, Thailand; fatalities reported in Vietnam.

Summer 2004 Second wave of H5N1 infection strikes poultry in China, Indonesia, Thailand, Vietnam. Eight more fatalities occur in Thailand, Vietnam.

November 2004 World Health Organization (WHO) warns of possible pandemic.

December 2004 Third wave of infection occurs among poultry in Indonesia, Thailand and Vietnam; new human case reported in Vietnam.

2005 *Congress approves crash plan to develop and manufacture vaccine and handle a pandemic, as bird flu spreads to more than 20 countries. . . . Cumulative worldwide totals reach more than 140 cases and 75 deaths.*

January 2005 First account of human-to-human transmission of avian flu published by *New England Journal of Medicine.*

March 2005 Bird flu has spread to 20 countries and killed 50 million chickens.

July 2005 Research on dead migratory birds suggests virus is carried along winter migration routes of geese. . . . Russia becomes first European country with virus outbreak in poultry.

October 2005 Virus confirmed in poultry in Turkey, Romania, Croatia.

November 2005 President Bush requests $7.1 billion to boost vaccine capacity, buy drugs.

December 2005 Congress approves $3.8 billion for flu plan, enacts liability protection for vaccine manufacturers. . . . Two cases of resistance to Tamiflu reported in Vietnam.

2006 *First human victims of H5N1 infection reported outside Asia.*

Jan. 5, 2006 Three children die from H5N1 in Turkey. . . . U.S farmers begin testing chickens for flu. . . . WHO reports 144 infected to date, including 76 fatalities.

willy-nilly raises the threat that resistance will develop. "Trying to use Tamiflu wisely now is like trying to land a 747 on an aircraft carrier," he maintains.

The WHO acknowledges many of these difficulties in its report recommending shipping Tamiflu from an international stockpile to the first region where the virus takes hold. "While pursuit of this option . . . has no guarantee of success, it nonetheless needs to be undertaken, as it represents one of the few preventive options," the WHO report says. Even if this doesn't stop the virus dead in its tracks, a delay would at least give other countries time to get prepared, it argues.[30]

Once a pandemic hits, nations with vaccine manufacturers are sure to nationalize those industries, preventing any domestically produced vaccine from leaving their borders, warns the Center for Biosecurity's O'Toole, unless some international cooperation forestalls them.

"There's nothing in the president's speech or the [HHS] plan that indicates the United States is going to try to lead a coalition of the world's vaccine manufacturers to maximize the global vaccine supply or has any intention of giving our vaccine away to countries that might be at the center of the storm," she notes. "The blowback from the United States acting as fortress America and having made no attempt to help less developed countries will harm America's standing in the world for a generation."

O'Toole knows it will be hard to persuade government leaders to share scarce vaccine. Her organization recently held a role-playing exercise to find out what would happen if bioterrorists attacked nations with smallpox. Former Secretary of State Madeleine K. Albright played the role of a U.S. president, and former prime ministers played other countries' leaders.

"We saw that national leaders become very ungenerous when their own stocks of vaccine are limited," O'Toole reports. In one scenario, Albright was prepared to share vaccine with Turkey. But when an American city was also attacked, Albright refused to send vaccine, saying, "'We paid for this,'" says O'Toole. "All the other countries did the same thing."

BACKGROUND

'Spanish Flu'

Worldwide influenza epidemics — called pandemics — were first documented about 300 years ago, and since

then an estimated 10-13 pandemics have occurred. The 20th century saw three flu pandemics: Two were mild, but the 1918-1919 "Spanish flu" epidemic infected an estimated 25-30 percent of the world's population. About 675,000 Americans died from the flu in 1918 — nearly half of all U.S. deaths that year. Worldwide, from 40 million up to 100 million people died.[31]

The 1918 flu was unusual in its high rate of mortality and the large percentage of deaths among young adults between ages 15 and 35, often within hours after the first symptoms appeared. Young people have the strongest immune systems of any age group, and, paradoxically, their immune system response to the foreign virus was so powerful that it killed them, explains author and chronicler of the 1918 epidemic John M. Barry. Many young adults suffered from acute respiratory distress syndrome, in which disease-fighting cells overreact, filling the lungs with fluid and debris, and ultimately suffocating the victim.

In 1997, pathologists noticed something similar in the first six people who died from H5N1 in Hong Kong. Many of the victims' organs were under attack from a "renegade" immune system, Barry writes. Indeed, the deaths reported so far from H5N1 have largely occurred in children and young, healthy adults — a similarity that worries some scientists.[32]

The two milder 20th-century pandemics — in 1957 and 1968 — probably were caused by the exchange of genes between human and avian flu viruses, known as reassortment, which occurred after either a human or a pig caught both viruses.

The second principal mechanism by which flu becomes easily contagious among humans is called adaptive mutation, a more gradual process in which the virus' ability to bind to human cells increases during subsequent infections of humans. Some scientists have suggested that the 1918 flu falls into the latter category.

The 1957 Asian flu outbreak, so-called because it was first identified in Asia, spread to the United States during the summer, killing about 70,000 people. Health officials responded quickly, and limited vaccine supplies were available by August. The 1968 Hong Kong flu killed 33,800 people in the United States, making it the mildest pandemic of the 20th century. A normal seasonal flu outbreak kills about 36,000 Americans each year.

The '57 and '68 pandemics were mild partly because the viruses were less virulent and partly because of advances in medicine. Global detection had improved, allowing public health officials to quickly isolate the viruses, and manufacturers were able to provide vaccines for the two strains. Antibiotics were also widely available to treat secondary bacterial infections, in contrast to 1918, and there were fewer cases of viral pneumonia.

Recent Flu Scares

Several 20th-century flu scares failed to live up to their billing. The 1976 "swine flu" scare began when an 18-year-old soldier at Fort Dix in New Jersey succumbed to a novel virus thought to be related to the Spanish flu virus. After health officials predicted a 1918-scale epidemic, President Ford initiated a program to inoculate every American.

But the pandemic never arrived. Moreover, the vaccination program was stopped after hundreds of people suffered from a rare neurological disorder — Guillain-Barre syndrome — later linked to the vaccine, which killed 32. Congress provided liability protection for the manufacturers and $90 million in compensation for those claiming injuries.[33]

Ever since, the swine flu incident has stood as a cautionary tale to public officials fearful of crying wolf. "In this case, the consequences of being wrong about an epidemic were so devastating in people's minds that it wasn't possible to focus properly on the issue of likelihood," Harvey V. Fineberg, now president of the Institute of Medicine, concluded later. "Nobody could really estimate the likelihood then or now. . . . And at a higher level [The White House] the two — likelihood and consequence — got meshed."[34] In 1977, the so-called Russian flu involved a virus strain that had been in circulation before 1957. The virus primarily sickened children and young adults, who lacked prior immunity to it.

H5N1 Emerges

The current concern about the H5N1 virus dates from 1997, when outbreaks of the highly pathogenic virus occurred in chickens and humans in Hong Kong. Six people died — out of 18 who became sick after handling infected poultry. To prevent further outbreak, Hong Kong's chicken population was slaughtered in three days. Researchers later found that the virus had originated among Chinese geese and found its way into Hong Kong's poultry markets before infecting the first humans.[35]

After several quiet years, the virus reappeared in 2003 — among birds in several Chinese mainland provinces.

Alarm bells again sounded that February, when H5N1 infected two people in Hong Kong, killing one. In December, the virus killed two tigers and two leopards in a Thai zoo that had been fed fresh chicken carcasses; it was the first report of influenza causing disease and death in big cats. In January 2004, Vietnam and Thailand reported their first cases of human infection with H5N1.[36]

A second wave of infections began in summer 2004, with reports of infected poultry in China, Indonesia, Thailand and Vietnam. Research showed that H5N1 had become progressively more lethal for mammals and could kill wild waterfowl, long considered a disease-free natural reservoir. More human cases — eight fatal — were reported in Thailand and Vietnam.

In September 2004, researchers found that domestic cats experimentally infected with H5N1 could spread infection to other cats, previously considered resistant to all influenza A viruses — the broad category that includes H5N1. The following month, H5N1 was confirmed in two eagles illegally imported to Brussels, Belgium, from Thailand, and research confirmed that ducks were excreting large quantities of the virus without showing any signs of illness.[37]

The WHO warned in November 2004 that the H5N1 bird flu virus might spark a deadly pandemic.[38] And in 2005 the Institute of Medicine reported H5N1 apparently had accumulated mutations making it both increasingly infectious and deadly in mammals.[39]

Poultry outbreaks in Indonesia, Thailand and Vietnam in December 2004 marked the beginning of a third wave of worldwide infection, according to the WHO. The first — and so far only — human-to-human transmission of avian flu occurred in Thailand in September 2004, according to an early 2005 report in *The New England Journal of Medicine*.[40] Cambodia then reported its first human cases, all fatal, as did Indonesia.

Last April, wild birds began dying at Quinghai Lake in Central China, where hundreds of thousands of migratory birds congregate. More than 6,000 birds died in the ensuing weeks. In July, researchers found transmission of the virus among migratory geese and suggested it may be carried along winter migratory routes.[41] (*See map, p. 288.*)

On July 23, 2005, Russia became the first European country to report an outbreak of the virus — in poultry in Western Siberia — followed by Kazahkstan the next month. By October, the virus was confirmed among poultry in Turkey, Romania and Croatia.

New Technique Could Speed Up Vaccine Production

If a flu pandemic were to break out tomorrow, it would take up to a year to develop a vaccine against the virus, by which time it could have circled the globe, creating death and economic havoc worldwide.

Why does it take so long to develop a vaccine? For every dose of flu vaccine, a manufacturer must infect a chicken egg with the particular influenza virus that is causing the new flu epidemic. Using a laborious process that hasn't been updated since the 1950s, a manufacturer aiming to make 20 million doses of a new vaccine must first order 20 million chicken eggs many months before the flu even hits.

"You have to plan in advance for egg deliveries, but there's no assurance you will get them," says Harold Shlevin, CEO of Solvay Pharmaceuticals in Marietta, Ga. "Just the logistics of getting 20 million eggs that you hope will grow properly, isolating and processing them [takes] closer to 9-12 months." Further complicating matters, for a virus that attacks birds as well as humans — such as the H5N1 avian flu now circulating in Asia — the virus could kill the eggs. So manufacturers today face the prospect of "no chickens, no eggs, no vaccine," says Shlevin.

His company has developed a new way to produce flu vaccine that relies on a line of cells harvested from a cocker spaniel's kidney in 1958 and kept alive ever since. President Bush has proposed a $2.8 billion crash program to accelerate development of vaccines using this approach — called cell-based technology — in order to produce enough flu vaccine for every American within six months after a pandemic hits. But it could be another two-to-five years before the United States has such a capacity — the estimated time manufacturers need to obtain government approval and build plants using the new technology.

Under Shlevin's process, rather than ordering millions of eggs, a manufacturer would only need to go to the freezer, pull out a vial of cells, inoculate them with the virus and place them in a large tank, called a bioreactor, to grow.

"If you want to make more simultaneously, you just need another bioreactor," says Shlevin, who likens it to a tank in which beer is brewed. Once the flu strain is isolated, the process could take as little as 90 days, Shlevin estimates.

Solvay is building a plant in Holland to produce a cell-based flu vaccine and has approval to sell it there. Close behind is Chiron, which is conducting clinical trials with cell-based flu vaccine in Europe and expects to apply for approval to sell the vaccine there in 2007.

Normally, it would take another three-to-four years to get the vaccine approved in the U.S. and possibly longer before new plants could be built here, according to Shlevin. However, representatives from both companies say the Food and Drug Administration (FDA) has been discussing expediting their procedure.

The FDA's vaccine advisory committee was asked if it could speed up some of its approval procedures without endangering safety. Panel member David Markovitz, a professor of infectious diseases at the University of Michigan, said he was favorably disposed after Nov. 16 presentations by Chiron and Solvay. Although the meeting was non-binding, Markovitz said, "The fact that the committee was very much in favor would suggest that it's likely to be licensed soon as technology for making flu vaccines."

Markovitz explains that while the vaccine would probably be safe, the residual dog cells could produce cancer in a vaccine recipient, because the cells are "immortalized"

Then in August the British medical journal *Lancet* reported Relenza was at least as effective as Tamiflu, but with fewer side effects and no evidence of resistance. By contrast, it reported resistance levels in up to 18 percent of those taking Tamiflu. The researchers recommended stockpiling both drugs.[42]

Fear of Vaccine

After the attacks on the World Trade Center and the Pentagon on Sept. 11, 2001, U.S. officials increasingly worried that terrorists might attack with a biological weapon, such as anthrax or smallpox.[43] In December 2002, President

— managed so that they "just keep growing," and often some cells are abnormal. But, he adds, "The odds of that in most of these lines seem quite low."

Meanwhile, other vaccine technologies are being tested. The National Institutes of Health (NIH), for instance, is testing a vaccine against one strain of H5N1 in healthy people and next will test it in the elderly. Like seasonal flu vaccines, it uses a killed, or inactivated, virus. However, during a pandemic an individual influenza strain can undergo changes, a process known as "drift," so a virus stockpiled now might not be effective against a future pandemic strain. For example, the H5N1 strains now circulating in Asia are different from strains that caused the flu in Hong Kong in 1997.

A newer-generation vaccine can be made from a live flu virus that has been weakened, or attenuated, so it cannot cause disease. The NIH is developing a live attenuated vaccine for H5N1 with MedImmune Vaccines Inc., which produces FluMist, a nasal spray made from a live attenuated vaccine currently available in the United States.

Live attenuated vaccines appear to create broader protective immunity against strains that have changed over time than vaccines made from killed viruses, according to Ruth Karron, an influenza vaccine expert at the Johns Hopkins Bloomberg School of Public Health. The school will begin testing MedImmune's new, live attenuated vaccine this spring. "We have evidence that this is true for some of the human influenza viruses that circulate each year," she said. For instance, for unknown reasons, FluMist

Purdue University researcher Suresh Metal examines a cell infected with a bird flu gene. U.S. researchers are trying to develop a vaccine in tissue cultures rather than chicken eggs, thus allowing faster production.

AFP Photo/Jeff Haynes

"seems to work better against drifted strains than inactivated influenza vaccine."[1]

Live attenuated vaccine is currently made using egg-based technology but could be made with cell-based techniques once they are available.

Meanwhile, the idea of a single vaccine to protect against all types of flu has always been the "holy grail" for flu vaccine researchers, but no one knows whether it can be achieved. In the event of a pandemic, a universal vaccine would dramatically reduce the turn-around time needed now to develop a vaccine tailored to a specific strain, according to NIH researcher Gary Nabel, who is exploring this possibility.[2]

Finally, researchers are also in the early stages of investigating a DNA-based vaccine, which would inject the DNA from a flu virus into people instead of the killed virus itself, causing a person's cells to make the virus proteins. Theoretically this could speed up production of a vaccine, because the DNA vaccine could be grown in fast-growing bacteria in a matter of weeks. DNA vaccines work well in mice, but "there's no good evidence they induce enough protective immunity in humans," according to Mount Sinai School of Medicine microbiologist Peter Palese. Given the data available now on DNA vaccines, he says, "I would seriously question whether it's really protective against a pandemic strain."

---

[1] John Hopkins Bloomberg School of Public Health, "Preparing for a Pandemic — Bloomberg School Tests Potential Avian Flu Vaccine," Oct. 19, 2005.

[2] Richard Harris, "Pandemic Flu Spurs Race for New Vaccine Methods," National Public Radio, Dec. 6, 2005, at www.npr.org.

Bush announced that all frontline health-care workers and military personnel should be vaccinated against smallpox, saying countries like Iraq were harboring secret reserves of smallpox and could use it as a biological weapon. However, many health workers and some hospitals refused to go along with the program, saying the vaccine was not safe.[44]

In response, Congress passed legislation in early 2003 to compensate people injured as a result of receiving the smallpox vaccine. But the compensation program was not launched until the end of that year, which critics said came too late to convince most health-care personnel, and the program fell far short of its goal.[45] Only about

How to Avoid Risk

- Poultry and eggs should be fully cooked — no "pink" parts and no runny yolks. Normal temperatures used for cooking poultry (158 degrees F. in all parts of the food) will kill the virus.

- If handling raw poultry in the kitchen, wash hands and disinfect cooking surfaces with hot water and soap. Raw poultry juices should never mix with food eaten raw.

- If you have no contact with birds, the risk is "almost non-existent," according to the World Health Organization.

Source: World Health Organization

40,000 individuals out of the 500,000 to several million health workers targeted have been vaccinated to date.[46] Labor unions and consumers have cited this failure in arguing that any successful mass-vaccination program for flu must include compensation for injuries.

CURRENT SITUATION

Global Efforts

The most dramatic effort to stem the H5N1 virus is taking place in China, where the government is trying to vaccinate an estimated 14 billion domestic chickens and ducks against the virus. In theory, the virus could be stopped this way.

In 2004, when H5N1 was rampant in Asia, Hong Kong did not have a single case in poultry or humans because it "used good vaccines and monitored to see that every chicken imported into Hong Kong was vaccinated with H5N1 vaccine," according to Memphis virologist Webster. But Hong Kong is a small, wealthy city surrounded by water, making it relatively easy to stop every poultry delivery.

By contrast, China is an enormous country, where people — especially in far-flung rural areas — live in close proximity to their poultry and where the prevalence

of fake vaccines worries scientists. Government vaccinators have also been seen inoculating birds without wearing gloves and discarding used needles on the ground — raising the potential of further spreading the disease.[47]

When it comes to detecting the virus, the world's early warning system is "weak," the WHO reported last year. Since the countries most affected by avian flu cannot afford to compensate farmers adequately for killing their infected poultry, farmers have little incentive to report outbreaks in the rural areas where most human cases have occurred, WHO concluded. Farmers have suffered more than $10 billion in economic losses already, the organization estimates.[48]

The deadly consequences of failing to report bird flu outbreaks were illustrated in early January 2006, when human cases of bird flu began to multiply in rural eastern Turkey. International health officials said they believed the disease had existed among poultry for months, but because there were no earlier reports of bird flu in the area, humans had no way of knowing they were at risk in handling poultry.[49]

The United States is helping to prevent the spread of H5N1 by funding detection, reporting and education programs.[50] The U.S. Agency for International Development is spending $13.7 million to control and prevent avian flu in Asia, and the Centers for Disease Control and Prevention is spending $6 million on international detection and reporting. But a November 2005 report prepared by the U.N. Food and Agriculture Organization suggested that the amounts committed by member nations so far have been insufficient to control avian flu in animals.[51]

Moreover, the WHO's efforts to get developed countries to cooperate in providing vaccines to developing countries and building an international stockpile of antiviral medications, have had only limited success.[52]

Worldwide, current manufacturers could only produce enough H5N1 bird flu vaccine to inoculate about 1.5 percent of the world's population, which the University of Minnesota's Osterholm says would be "like trying to fill Lake Superior with a garden hose."[53] The scientific journal *Nature* says WHO's fledgling international effort to establish a coalition to fight the spread of the disease is "shaky and far from united or sure in its purpose" and "grossly underfunded."[54]

Is there a serious risk of a human pandemic of avian flu?

YES
Michael T. Osterholm
Director, Center for Infectious Disease Research and Policy, University of Minnesota

From testimony before House Committee on International Relations, Dec. 7, 2005

We must never forget that influenza pandemics are like earthquakes, hurricanes and tsunamis; they occur. The most recent came in 1957-58 and 1968-69, and although tens of thousands of Americans died in each one, these were considered mild compared to others. According to a recent analysis, [the 1918-19 pandemic] killed 50-100 million people globally. Today, with a population of 6.5 billion — more than three times that of 1918 — even a mild pandemic could kill many millions.

A number of recent events and factors have heightened our concern that a specific near-term pandemic may be imminent. Some important preparatory efforts are under way, but much more needs to be done throughout the world.

Based on our past experiences with outbreaks such as SARS, if an influenza pandemic began today, borders will close, the global economy will shut down, pharmaceutical supplies — including important childhood vaccines — will be in extreme short supply, health-care systems will be overwhelmed and panic will reign. Access to pandemic influenza vaccines and effective antiviral drug treatments will be limited for the entire world for years to come because of our lack of modern vaccines and a grossly inadequate worldwide production capability.

An influenza pandemic will be like a 12-to-18-month global blizzard that will ultimately change the world as we know it today. Foreign trade and travel will be reduced or even ended in an attempt to stop the virus from entering new countries — even though such efforts will probably fail, given the infectiousness of influenza and the volume of illegal crossings that occur at most borders.

One part of pandemic preparedness planning that must receive immediate attention is the implementation of a concept that I have called "critical product continuity" (CPC) — the determination of those products and services that must be available during a pandemic in order to minimize potentially catastrophic collateral health and security consequences — and the subsequent comprehensive actions that must be taken by both governments and the private sector to ensure their availability.

While I have chosen to highlight the issue of critical product continuity and the pharmaceutical industry, there are many other product areas that must be considered as we plan for getting through the next 12-to-18-month pandemic.

NO
Michael Fumento
Senior Fellow, Hudson Institute

Written for the *CQ Researcher*, Jan. 4, 2006

It is only a matter of time before an avian flu virus — most likely H5N1 — acquires the ability to be transmitted from human to human, sparking the outbreak of human pandemic influenza." So declared Dr. Lee Jong-wook, director-general of the World Health Organization.

Terrifying statement. False statement.

It is the best-kept secret of the pandemic panic purveyors that H5N1 hasn't just been around since its Hong Kong appearance in 1997 but actually was discovered in Scottish chickens in 1959. It's therefore been mutating and making contact with humans for 47 years. If it hasn't become transmissible between humans in all that time, it almost certainly won't.

Despite what you've been told, H5N1 isn't even slowly mutating in the direction of becoming pandemic. There are no evolutionary pressures upon it to either become more efficiently transmitted from bird to man or man to man. Rather, as one mutation draws the virus closer to human transmissibility, another is as likely to draw it farther away.

Certainly an avian flu pandemic won't let media hysteria dictate its appearance and therefore be upon us before effective vaccines become widely available in a couple of years. If "a matter of time" means several years from now, we'll be quite prepared, thank you.

But aren't we "overdue" for a pandemic, with H5N1 the likeliest cause? Google "avian flu," "pandemic," and "overdue," and you'll get more than 35,000 hits. Anthony Fauci, director of the National Institute of Allergies and Infectious Diseases, insists we're "overdue," explaining that there were three pandemics in the 20th century, the last one 38 years ago.

Yet the time between the second and third pandemics was only 11 years. There's no cycle. As risk-communication expert Peter Sandman of Rutgers University says, the "overdue pandemic" is mere superstition.

None of which should discourage such sensible measures as mass poultry vaccinations, killing infected flocks and teaching Asian farmers to have as little contact with their birds and bird droppings as possible. These steps can reduce or even eliminate the few human cases now occurring and cut the chance of pandemic from nearly zero to zero.

But there is no gain in spreading an epidemic of hysteria. The false fears we sow today we shall reap in the future as public complacency when a monster is truly at the door.

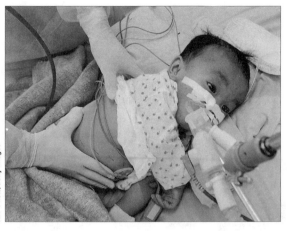

A Vietnamese infant receives avian flu treatment in Hanoi. Health experts say antiviral medications like Tamiflu could lessen the severity of the disease. However, some bird flu patients in Vietnam who took Tamiflu died.

The discovery in 2004 of the two infected eagles smuggled into Belgium from Thailand in airline carry-on baggage highlighted the severely under-policed illegal trade in exotic animals — second in size only to the drug trade — as another possible vector for spread of the disease. Robert A. Cook, vice president and chief veterinarian at the Wildlife Conservation Society, calls U.S. laws governing the import of illegal animals "dangerously lax."[55]

Increasingly, new human diseases — such as AIDS and SARS — have originated in wild animals, according to Cook. "You take these animals out of the wild, and they [bring] with them a whole new range of diseases we haven't seen before," he says.

Washington imposed some new import restrictions after monkey pox, which causes fevers and ulcers, infected 71 Midwesterners in 2003. The outbreak was triggered when imported African rodents infected prairie dogs at a pet shop. But it is still legal in the United States to import most exotic species.

Domestic Efforts

On Nov. 1, recalling that the 1918 flu infected one-third of Americans, President Bush unveiled his pandemic plan to the nation. "If history is our guide, there is reason to be concerned," he said.[56]

But in December, when Congress approved only $3.8 billion for pandemic spending — about half the president's $7.1 billion request — lawmakers said the money was enough to get the program started in 2006.[57] Public health advocates hope Congress will appropriate the rest of Bush's request next year.

Of the total, $3 billion is earmarked to prepare for a pandemic, including the purchase of vaccines and antiviral drugs, $350 million for state and local preparedness — more than Bush had requested — and $267 million for overseas detection and reporting of flu cases. The legislation also allows HHS to negotiate contracts with vendors through which states could order antiviral drugs and be reimbursed by the federal government. The legislation would permit the use of federal funds to construct or renovate private facilities for the production of vaccines.

Critics immediately complained that the plan did not specify what localities should do once their hospitals are filled to capacity. European nations are far ahead of the United States in planning so-called surge capacity, according to Elliott, of the Trust for America's Health. "Every single hotel in Great Britain knows whether or not they're going to be a surge hospital," she says.

The plan says health workers should get top priority for vaccinations and allows states to decide who should be in subsequent priority groups. George E. Hardy, Jr., executive director of the Association of State and Territorial Health Officials, says states would like more consistency on who is at the top of the list.

"Whether you live in Alabama or Montana, the priority groups should be the same," he says.

Liability

In December, Congress approved sweeping provisions shielding manufacturers of pandemic vaccines from liability lawsuits.[58] President Bush and GOP lawmakers had argued that the liability protection was necessary to encourage drug makers to get into the vaccine business.

Tacked onto the Defense appropriations bill in the middle of the night, the liability language was immediately attacked as a "backroom deal" by consumer groups complaining that the provision was never subjected to a separate floor vote or discussion.

Senate Majority Leader Bill Frist, R-Tenn., described the measure as "targeted liability protection." Lawsuits could only be brought if the federal government sues on behalf of a patient's wrongful death or serious injury. But the suits can only be brought for "willful misconduct," and negligence or recklessness are not defined as willful misconduct.

"There's no reason to immunize a company against recklessness," says Amy Widman, a lawyer for the Center for Justice and Democracy, arguing that a threat of lawsuits checks corporate irresponsibility.

The center was part of a coalition of five consumer groups that complained to senators that under this narrow definition drug companies would only be held responsible if "the company had actual knowledge the product would kill someone."

The legislation would exempt companies from liability for "countermeasures" — drugs, vaccines or medical devices — designed to protect Americans in public "emergencies," to be defined by the HHS secretary. Consumer advocates said the legislation could cover everything from cholesterol drugs to Tylenol. Widman calls it "a giveaway to drug companies" seeking to incorporate "a lot of things they've been trying to get for many, many years."

"The Republican leadership in Congress cut a backroom deal to give a massive Christmas bonus to the drug companies," Sen. Edward M. Kennedy, D-Mass., said in a statement after the House vote.[59]

But Frist said he was "proud" of the provisions that had been incorporated into the defense appropriations bill. "The bill strikes a reasonable balance where those who are harmed will be fairly compensated and life-saving products will be available in ample supply to protect and treat as many Americans as possible," he said.[60]

The new law directs HHS to sets up a compensation fund to reimburse anyone injured by a vaccine or other medication covered by the legislation. Consumer and labor groups, however, pointed out that no money was appropriated for the fund, which would be inoperable until funded.

Without funding for compensation, said Barbara Coufal, legislative affairs specialist for the American Federation of State, County and Municipal Employees (AFSCME), "We're worried [that] it may never be realized."

Quarantines

In the event of a pandemic, say many public health experts, it may be nearly impossible to isolate the infected from the well, since people infected with the flu are contagious for at least a day before they show symptoms. The more likely scenario would be a wholesale shutdown of public places like schools, workplaces, shopping malls and theatres.

In November, the CDC proposed new quarantine rules that include influenza as one of the illnesses subject to a quarantine ordered by the president. The new rules would also require airlines to keep copies of passenger manifests for 60 days, which could be made available to the CDC within 12 hours if ill passengers arrive on international or domestic flights.[61] But experts say preventing sick or exposed persons from getting off airplanes is unlikely to prevent avian flu from entering the country.

"What if I fly from Thailand to Europe to Canada and drive to Seattle? Are they going to flag me and stop me?" asks the University of Minnesota's Osterholm. "I don't think we're going to stop it."

On Nov. 1, New York City's health department offered free flu vaccines to anyone who showed up at a downtown clinic in an experiment aimed at simulating what might happen during a major outbreak. Many people waited more than three hours, prompting some to wonder whether the city could handle a real emergency.[62]

"Most state and local public health agencies lack the people, money and political clout to manage an epidemic," according to the Center for Biosecurity at the University of Pittsburgh.[63]

Governors have put most of their health dollars into mandatory programs like Medicaid, according to Elliott rather than public health departments where spending is discretionary. "We have an aging work force and not a lot of new blood coming in because it's not a lucrative profession," she says. There are not enough workers now to handle regular vaccinations and health needs, she points out.

On the other hand, since 9/11, every state has developed a federally funded plan for responding to a bioterrorist attack. "We're much better prepared than we were a year ago," says Hardy of the Association of State and Territorial Health Officials. However, federal funds for state and local bioterrorism preparedness programs were cut 14 percent in the fiscal 2006 appropriations bill, which the Trust for America called "ill-advised" in view of their pandemic responsibilities.

"The first thing we learned in Hurricane Katrina is you put public health leaders in charge of a health crisis, not first responders" like police, says Elliott, of the Trust for America's Health. "Otherwise we have situations like triaging folks in an airport and putting masses of people in a convention center with no water or sanitary facilities. Public health officials would never have done that."

Late-Breaking News

Multiplying human cases of bird flu appeared in early January 2006 in Turkey, putting health officials in Europe on "high alert." An unusual cluster of human cases (15 confirmed as of Jan. 10), including some 50 other people hospitalized for possible H5N1, raised the possibility that the virus might have mutated to become more contagious to humans. But as of Jan. 11, WHO scientists had detected no changes in the H5N1 virus samples from Turkey that might make it more transmissible to humans.[64]

American chicken farmers apparently are taking the disease more seriously, given the announcement that nearly all flocks would be tested for avian flu starting Jan. 16.[65] With the fall bird migration ended, some experts declared that North America had dodged the bird flu — at least for the 2005-2006 winter flu season. But international health officials warned that Europe might still be vulnerable from the spring 2006 migration.[66]

OUTLOOK

Economic Disaster?

Many experts hope a pandemic doesn't arrive for another five years or so, which would give the United States time to increase manufacturing capacity for vaccines. The administration is pinning its hopes on the new cell-based vaccines that would take less lead time than today's old-fashioned technology.

Meanwhile, NIH researchers are working on developing a universal vaccine that would prevent all flu strains — considered the holy grail of vaccine researchers.

Many agree that new, more effective antiviral medications need to be developed, especially if resistance develops in whatever flu strain hits our shores. But others say it's most important to rebuild the U.S. public health system, so there will be enough workers to vaccinate and treat the sick.

The gloomiest forecast is painted by the University of Minnesota's Osterholm, who foresees a collapse in our increasingly global economy if a pandemic forces nations to shut down their borders. For instance, most masks, gloves and syringes are manufactured offshore, as are the raw materials for antibiotics. As a result, modern medicine's advantages won't really be available, he predicts.

"When a pandemic flu hits, we'll go back to 1918 medicine; we're going to care for people in large gyms and stadiums; we will have a major shortage of intravenous equipment; we'll have a shortage of antibiotics and health-care workers, and no masks are being stockpiled. So you tell me how that's different from 1918. If you don't call that a perfect storm, I don't know what is."

But some economists say the U.S. economy is so resilient that even a severe pandemic — like that in 1918 — would not produce an economic disaster. A mild pandemic like that in 1968 would "probably not cause a recession and might not be distinguishable from the normal variation in economic activity," according to a recent CBO report.[67]

There are so many gaps in the scientific knowledge about viruses that "there is no scientific basis to predict anything," according to Masato Tashiro, director of the WHO's Collaborative Center for Influenza Surveillance and Research at Japan's National Institute of Infectious Diseases in Tokyo.[68]

Although some scientists are skeptical that H5N1 bird flu will cause the next pandemic, and others believe it will be mild, virtually everyone agrees there will be another flu pandemic eventually, and that the country should start preparing now.

NOTES

1. This description is from Mike Davis, *The Monster at Our Door* (2005), pp. 4-8.

2. *Ibid.*, p. 7.

3. Elisabeth Rosenthal, "Bird Flu Reports Multiply in Turkey, Faster Than Expected," *The New York Times*, Jan. 9, 2006, p. A4.

4. Institute of Medicine, *The Threat of Pandemic Influenza: Are We Ready? A Workshop Summary* (2005), p. 8.

5. For background, see Mary H. Cooper, "Fighting SARS," *CQ Researcher*, June 20, 2003, pp. 569-592.

6. That is the number needed in order to kill all poultry in China over a year's time.

7. Institute of Medicine, *op. cit.*, p. 19.

8. http://healthyamericans.org.

9. Trust for America's Health, press release, "TFAH commends U.S. House of Representatives for Passing Down Payment," Dec. 19, 2005.

10. "Don't Support a Defense Spending Bill that Has Backroom Special Interest Protections," Dec. 20, 2005, letter to senators from U.S. PIRG and other interest groups at www.uspirg.org.

11. Congressional Budget Office (CBO), "A Potential Influenza Pandemic: Possible Macroeconomic Effects and Policy Issues," Dec. 8, 2005, p. 6.

12. White House, "President Outlines Pandemic Influenza Preparations and Response," Nov. 1, 2005, at www.whitehouse.gov/news/releases/2005/11/20051101-1.html.

13. See for example, comments by Anthony Fauci on CBS' "60 Minutes:" "Right now . . . if we had an explosion of H5N1 we would not be prepared for that;" "Chasing the Flu," Dec.4, 2005, at www.cbsnews.com/stories/2005/12/02/60minutes/main1094515.shtml.

14. The president's proposal and HHS plan can be found at www.pandemicflu.gov.

15. Congressional Budget Office, *op. cit.*, p. 22.

16. Sanofi pasteur announced Dec. 15 study results showing it could produce an H5N1 vaccine requiring only four times as much antigen using adjuvants. See "Sanofi says H5N1 vaccine with adjuvant may go further," Dec. 15, 2005, at www.cidrap.umn.edu.

17. Andrew Jack, "Deaths cast doubt over use of Tamiflu," *Financial Times*, Dec. 22, 2005, p. 6.

18. CBO, *op. cit.*, p. 29.

19. David Heyman, "Model Operational Guidelines for Disease Exposure Control," Nov. 2, 2005, at www.csis.org/index.php?option=com_csis_pubs&task=view&id=2504.

20. White House press release, "President Outlines Pandemic Influenza Preparations and Response," Nov. 1, 2005.

21. Michelle M. Mello and Troyen A. Brennan, "Legal Concerns and the Influenza Vaccine Shortage," *JAMA*, Oct. 12, 2005, pp. 1817-1820.

22. Institute of Medicine, *Financing Vaccines in the 21st Century: Assuring Access and Availability* (2003), at www.nap.edu.

23. www.cdc.gov/nip/vfc/Parent/parent_home.htm#1.

24. In October 2004, British government regulators withdrew the license from Liverpool, England, flu vaccine manufacturer Chiron after 4 million doses were found to be contaminated. On Oct. 5, 2004, Chiron announced that it could not provide its expected production of 46-48 million doses of flu vaccine — about half the expected U.S. influenza vaccine supply — setting off a major shortage of flu vaccine in the winter flu season of 2004.

25. World Health Organization (WHO), *Responding to the Avian Influenza Pandemic Threat: Recommended Strategic Actions* (2005), p. 2. Also see Ira M. Longini, Jr., *et al.*, "Containing Pandemic Influenza at the Source," *Science*, Aug. 12, 2005, pp. 1083-1087.

26. See press releases from Sen. Schumer "As Avian Flu Closes in on U.S. Schumer Calls for Immediate Action: Demands Suspension of Tamiflu Patent So Vaccine Can be Mass-Produced," Oct. 16, 2005, and "Schumer Praises Roche Agreements with 2 Major U.S. Generic Drug Companies," Dec. 8, 2005.

27. See Council on Foreign Relations, Conference on the Global Threat of Pandemic Influenza, Session 2: Containment and Control, Nov. 16, 2005 at www.cfr.org/publication/9244/council_on_foreign_relations_conference_on_the_global_threat_of_pandemic_influenza_session_2.html. David Nabarro is U.N. System Coordinator for Avian and Human Influenza.

28. Quoted in Michael Fumento, "Fuss and Feathers: Pandemic Panic Over the Avian Flu," *The Weekly Standard*, Nov. 21, 2005.

29. "60 Minutes," *op. cit.*

30. WHO, *op. cit.*, p. 12.

31. CBO, *op. cit.*, p. 6. It is unclear why the outbreak was called the "Spanish flu," since it did not originate in Spain or hit that country particularly hard. Some theorize that the term arose because of heavy coverage by Spanish newspapers.

32. John M. Barry, *The Great Influenza* (2004), p. 250.

33. Laurie Garrett, "The Next Pandemic?" *Foreign Affairs*, July/August 2005, pp. 3-23.

34. Quoted in *ibid.*, p. 10.

35. *Ibid.*; also see Institute of Medicine (2005), p. 13.

36. WHO, "H5N1 Avian Influenza: Timeline," Oct. 28, 2005.

37. *Ibid.*

38. "Avian Flu Timeline," *Nature* Web site at www.nature.com/nature/focus/avianflu/timeline.html.

39. Institute of Medicine (2005), p. 12.

40. K. Ungchusak, *et al.*, "Probable Person-to-person Transmission of Avian Influenza A (H5N1)," *The New England Journal of Medicine*, Jan. 27, 2005, pp. 333-40.

41. WHO, *ibid.*

42. *Nature* Web site, *op. cit.*

43. For background, see David Masci, "Smallpox Threat," *CQ Researcher*, Feb. 7, 2003, pp. 105-128.

44. Jeffrey Gettleman, "Threats and Responses: Biological Defenses," *The New York Times*, Dec. 19, 2002, p. A19.

45. The program hoped to vaccinate 500,000 people, but by October 2003 only 37,901 had been vaccinated. A hundred people suffered injuries. See *CIDRAP News*, "Study shows few serious problems among smallpox vaccinees," Dec. 14, 2005, at www.cidrap.umn.edu.

46. CBO, *op. cit.*, p. 27.

47. Howard W. French, "Bird by Bird China Tackles Vast Flu Task," *The New York Times*, Dec. 2, 2005, p. A1.

48. WHO, "Responding to the Avian Influenza Pandemic Threat," *op. cit.*

49. Elisabeth Rosenthal, "Bird Flu Reports Multiply in Turkey, Faster Than Expected," *New York Times*, Jan. 9, 2006, p. A4.

50. In September, Bush announced an International Partnership on Avian and Pandemic Influenza, a global network that requires participating countries that face an outbreak to provide samples to the WHO. As of Nov. 1, 88 countries had joined the effort.

51. *Ibid.*

52. Congressional Research Service, *Pandemic Influenza: Domestic Preparedness Efforts*, Nov. 10, 2005, p. 17.

53. Based on current doses of H5N1 vaccine, Osterholm calculates that capacity exists for about 100 million of the world's population of about 6.5 billion.

54. "On a Wing and a Prayer," *Nature*, May 26, 2005, pp. 385-386, www.nature.com/nature.

55. William B. Karesh and Robert Cook, "The Human-Animal Link," *Foreign Affairs*, July/August 2005, pp. 38-50.

56. White House, "President Outlines Pandemic Influenza Preparations and Response," Nov. 1, 2005.

57. "House Approves Pandemic Funding Far Below Bush Request," *CIDRAP News* at www.cidrap.umn.edu/cidrap/content/influenza/panflu/news/dec1905funding.html.

58. Sheryl Gay Stolberg, "Legal Shield for Vaccine Makers is Inserted into Military Bill," *The New York Times*, Dec. 20, 2005, p. A26.

59. *Ibid.*

60. Sen. Bill Frist press release, "Frist Hails Passage of FY06 Defense Appropriations Conference Report," Dec. 21, 2005.

61. Lawrence K. Altman, "C.D.C. Proposes New Rules in Effort to Prevent Disease Outbreak," *The New York Times*, Nov. 23, 2005, p. A22.

62. Shadi Rahimi, "Just a Drill, But Flu Shots were Real, And Popular," *The New York Times*, Nov. 2, 2005, p. A1.

63. Center for Biosecurity, "National Strategy for Pandemic Influenza," Nov. 7, 2005.

64. See Rosenthal, *op. cit.*, Jan. 9, 2006; Reuters, "Turkey Struggles with Bird Flu as Children Fall Ill," *The New York Times*, Jan. 7, 2006, and Elisabeth Rosenthal, "New Bird Flu Cases in Turkey Put Europe on 'High Alert,'" *The New York Times*, Jan. 7, 2006, p. A3.

65. Donald G. McNeil Jr., "U.S. Farmers to Begin Testing Chickens for Flu," *The New York Times*, Jan. 6, 2006, p. A19.

66. See "If the Avian Flu Hasn't Hit, Here's Why. Maybe," *The New York Times*, Jan. 1, 2006, "News of the Week in Review," p. 10, and U.N. Food and Agriculture Organization, "Wild Birds and Avian Influenza," at www.fao.org/ag/againfo/subjects/en/health/diseases-cards/avian_HPAIrisk.html.

67. CBO, *op. cit.*, pp. 1-2.

68. Dennis Normile, "Pandemic Skeptics Warn Against Crying Wolf," *Science*, Nov. 18, 2005, p. 1113.

BIBLIOGRAPHY

Books

Barry, John M., *The Great Influenza: The Epic Story of the Deadliest Plague in History*, Penguin Books, 2004.
This history of the deadly 1918 influenza pandemic cites similarities with the H5N1 bird flu now in Asia. Barry is a distinguished visiting scholar at the Center for Bioenvironmental Research of Tulane and Xavier universities.

Davis, Mike, *The Monster at Our Door: The Global Threat of Avian Flu*, The New Press, 2005.
Science writer Davis expresses outrage at poor countries' lack of access to vaccines and antiviral medicines and recommends governments take over their manufacture if the free market can't distribute them cheaply.

Garrett, Laurie, *The Coming Plague: Newly Emerging Diseases in a World Out of Balance*, Penguin Books, 1994.
In a wide-ranging look at modern diseases that some have compared to Rachel Carson's celebrated *Silent Spring*, a Pulitzer Prize-winning journalist warns that infectious microbes pose increasing danger as humans disrupt the Earth's ecology.

Articles

Fumento, Michael, "Fuss and Feathers: Pandemic Panic over the Avian Flu," *The Weekly Standard*, Nov. 21, 2005; www.weeklystandard.com.
A senior fellow at the conservative Hudson Institute downplays the risk of bird flu and charges that politicians, public health officials and the press are crossing the line between informing the public and starting a panic.

Garrett, Laurie, "The Next Pandemic?" *Foreign Affairs*, July/August 2005, pp. 3-23.
Journalist Garrett, now a senior fellow at the Council on Foreign Relations, describes the recent history of H5N1 and why it might create the next pandemic.

Karesh, William B., and Robert A. Cook, "The Human-Animal Link," *Foreign Affairs*, July/August 2005, pp. 38-50.
Two veterinarians explain why diseases like bird flu that originate in animals are a growing threat to humans.

Normile, Dennis, "Pandemic Skeptics Warn Against Crying Wolf," *Science*, Nov. 18, 2005, pp. 1112-1113.
Some scientists doubt that H5N1 bird flu will become the next human pandemic and worry the "current hype" could undermine efforts to prepare for the next genuine pandemic.

Orent, Wendy, "Chicken Little," *The New Republic*, Sept. 12, 2005; www.tnr.com.
Those warning of a new H5N1 epidemic are being alarmists, the author says.

Osterholm, Michael T., "Preparing for the Next Pandemic," *Foreign Affairs*, July/August 2004, pp. 24-37.
A professor of public health at the University of Minnesota discusses why the world is unprepared for a pandemic and what steps should be taken.

Taubenberger, Jeffery K., and David M. Morens, "1918 Influenza: The Mother of All Pandemics," *Emerging Infectious Diseases*, January 2006; www.cdc.gov/ncidod/EID/vol12no01/05-0979.htm.
Taubenberger, the scientist who sequenced the genes of the 1918 flu, and epidemiologist Morens downplay earlier reported similarities between the 1918 virus and H5N1 virus.

Reports and Studies

***Congressional Budget Office, A Potential Influenza Pandemic: Possible Macroeconomic Effects and Policy Issues*, Dec. 8, 2005; www.cbo.gov.**
A severe flu pandemic would cause a recession, the CBO concludes in this up-to-date summary of policy debates over avian flu.

***Congressional Research Service, Pandemic Influenza: Domestic Preparedness Effort*, Nov. 10, 2005; www.fas.org/sgp/crs/homesec/RL33145.pdf.**
The CRS provides a good overview of efforts by domestic and international agencies to prepare for a pandemic as well as proposed legislative approaches.

***Institute of Medicine, Financing Vaccines in the 21st Century: Assuring Access and Availability*, 2003; www.nap.edu.**
A panel of experts recommended that the government mandate health-insurance coverage of vaccination in order to encourage drug companies to get into the vaccine market.

Institute of Medicine, The Threat of Pandemic Influenza: Are We Ready?, 2005; www.nap.edu.
This report, which grew out of a 2004 workshop at the Institute of Medicine, contains papers by contributors as well as recommendations on how to prepare for a pandemic.

World Health Organization, Responding to the Avian Influenza Pandemic Threat: Recommended Strategic Actions, 2005; www.who.int/csr/resources/publications/influenza/WHO_CDS_CSR_GIP_05_8-EN.pdf.
After assessing the global threat of H5N1 flu virus, this report recommends that nations contribute to a worldwide stockpile of antiviral medications, among other steps.

For More Information

American Public Health Association, 800 I St., N.W., Washington, DC 20001-3710; (202) 777-APHA; www.apha.org. Represents public health professionals worldwide.

Association of State and Territorial Health Officials, 1275 K St., N.W., Suite 800, Washington, DC 20005-4006; (202) 371-9090; www.astho.org. Represents chief health officials.

Center for Biosecurity, University of Pittsburgh Medical Center, The Pier IV Building, 621 E. Pratt St., Suite 210, Baltimore, MD 21202; (443) 573-3304; www.upmc-biosecurity.org. An independent organization concerned with epidemics caused by natural and terrorist agents.

Center for Infectious Disease Research & Policy, University of Minnesota, Academic Health Center, 420 Delaware St., S.E., MMC 263, Minneapolis, MN 55455; (612) 626-6770; www.cidrap.umn.edu. Carries daily breaking news on avian flu on its Web site.

Center for Justice and Democracy, 80 Broad St., Suite 1600, New York, NY 10004; (212) 267-2801; http://centerjd.org. A consumer group active on liability issues involving vaccine manufacturers.

pandemicflu.gov. The official U.S. government Web site on pandemic flu and avian flu is managed by the Department of Health and Human Services, with links to the White House and other federal agencies.

Pharmaceutical Research and Manufacturers Association of America, 1100 15th St., N.W., Washington, DC 20005; (202) 835-3400. www.phrma.org. Represents the country's leading pharmaceutical research and biotechnology companies.

Trust for America's Health, 1707 H St., N.W., 7th Floor, Washington, DC 20006; (202) 223-9870; http://healthyamericans.org. A nonprofit public health advocacy group.

U.S. Centers for Disease Control and Prevention, 1600 Clifton Rd., Atlanta, GA 30333; (404) 639-3534; www.cdc.gov. The chief federal health agency dealing with avian flu.

12

Anti-Americanism

Is Anger at the U.S. Growing?

Samuel Loewenberg

President George W. Bush lands on the aircraft carrier *USS Abraham Lincoln* in May 2003 and declares the formal end to combat in Iraq. Many critics abroad blame Bush and the Iraq War — now entering its fifth year — for the decline in U.S. prestige.

From *CQ Researcher*, March 2007.

oon after the Sept. 11, 2001, terrorist attacks, the cover of *Newsweek* pictured a turbaned child holding a toy machine gun. The headline read: "The Politics of Rage: Why Do They Hate Us?"[1]

Since then, versions of that question — simultaneously plaintive and rhetorical — have been repeated throughout the U.S. media. The most common answer often reflected the views of Harvard scholar Samuel P. Huntington, who described an inevitable schism between Christianity and Islam in his seminal 1993 essay, "Clash of Civilizations."[2]

But America's critics are far more diverse, and their criticisms more differentiated, than can be explained away by a simple East vs. West conflict. Today not only radical Eastern Islamists but also more and more Latin Americans and former close allies in Europe are finding America and its policies reprehensible.

Some of the most outspoken voices come from Europe, where dismissive attitudes about the mixing bowl of people in the New World have long been a staple of intellectual preening. Since the 17th century, America has been depicted as a haven for uncouth debauchers, religious zealots and puffed-up nationalists. Only after World War II, when America emerged into a position of military and economic might, did it became an object of both desire and envy.

As the United States flexed its muscles over the subsequent decades, others began to perceive it as a threat to their own national sovereignty and identity. America was too big, too influential, too sure of its virtues. Protesters around the world began to attack all three facets of American influence — economic, political and cultural. By the end of the Cold War, the United States was the only remaining superpower, and even more vulnerable to accusations of arrogance and bullying.

In 1999 this sole superpower was symbolically attacked on a much smaller — and non-lethal — scale than it was on Sept. 11, 2001, when French protesters dismantled a McDonald's restaurant in the town of Millau, turning farmer and union leader José Bové into an international hero.[3]

"Look," Bové said later, "cooking is culture. All over the world. Every nation, every region, has its own food cultures. Food and farming define people. We cannot let it all go, to be replaced with hamburgers. People will not let it happen."[4]

That act of cultural theater preceded many others, and by 2003, as the United States led the invasion into Iraq, America was regularly being pilloried as an international villain, damned for its military excursions and held up as a convenient target for all sorts of global discontent.[5]

The indictment against America, writes Andrei S. Markovits, a Romania-born professor of comparative European politics at the University of Michigan, "accuses America of being retrograde on three levels":

- Moral: America is viewed as the purveyor of the death penalty and of religious fundamentalism, while Europe abolished the death penalty in favor of rehabilitation and adheres to an enlightened secularism;
- Social: America is viewed as the bastion of unbridled "predatory capitalism," as former German Chancellor Helmut Schmidt put it, while Europe is the home of the considerate welfare state; and
- Cultural: America is viewed as common, prudish and prurient, Europe as refined, savvy and wise.[6]

Those bleak assessments of the United States have played out in innumerable protests in recent years. When tens of thousands of leftist protesters from around the world gathered in Porto Alegre, Brazil, during the World Economic Forum in February 2002, they waved signs declaring "No blood for oil," and "Bush is #1 Terrorist." Raucous anti-globalization protests have followed the meetings of the World Trade Organization and the G8 from Doha to Davos to Seattle.

When 70,000 protesters gathered in Berlin's Alexanderplatz in March 2003, a banner proclaimed: "We Aren't Allowed to Compare Bush to Hitler. Too Bad!"[7]

When 2,000 Pakistanis in Islamabad rallied against Danish cartoons that had caricatured the Prophet Muhammad in 2006, they also shouted "Death to America!" and torched an effigy of President George W. Bush, as if Bush himself had commissioned the works.[8]

This was a long way from the moment after the 9/11 attacks, when the globe was in brief solidarity with the United States, as epitomized by the famous banner headline in the French newspaper *Le Monde*, "We are all Americans."[9]

Something had changed.

In just a few years, what once seemed to be a clash of two halves of the globe had metastasized into a clash between America and the rest of the world. These sentiments were not coming from isolated pockets of religious fundamentalists but from America's longstanding allies throughout the world. In Europe, anti-U.S. sentiment had reached record levels.

The Iraq invasion "did not create anti-Americanism but it increased it and gave it form," according to Professor Gérard Grunberg, deputy director of Sciences Po, a political institute in Paris.[10]

Many clearly think that negative attitudes toward the United States are now at an all-time high. "Anti-Americanism is deeper and broader now than at any time in modern history. It is most acute in the Muslim world, but it spans the globe," according to a recent survey by the Pew Research Center for People & the Press.[11] In another Pew poll, Europeans gave higher approval ratings to China than to the United States.[12]

Yet much of the anti-American hostility disguises the fact that many of the most vociferous European critics really don't know much about the USA. As British scholar Tony Judt, director of the Remarque Institute at New York University, points out, Europeans complain about their own governments' policies by saying they have been influenced by America.[13]

But on both sides of the Atlantic, says Judt, even in the supposed age of "globalization," there is a massive ignorance about the reality of politics, and of everyday life. "We don't actually understand each other any better than we did in the 1930s."

How did America go, in the eyes of many, from being the symbol of democracy, freedom and opportunity — an ideal to strive for — to an example to be avoided? Judt calls anti-Americanism the "master narrative" of the current age, in which declared opposition to the United States became a uniting factor for disparate critics of economic, cultural and foreign policies around the globe. In America they had found "a common target."

But these days, the overwhelming source of anti-American sentiment, not only in Europe but also throughout the world, is U.S. foreign policy, especially the Bush administration's pursuit of the war in Iraq.

Resentment of the policies and personalities in the Bush administration cannot be overstated. Even President Richard M. Nixon's transgressions were mostly identified as domestic problems (the Watergate scandal), while the Vietnam War was seen as part of larger Cold War politics and did not evoke the same strong anti-American sentiment as Iraq does today.

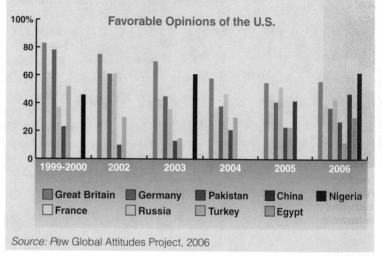

America's Global Image Slips

Since the beginning of the Bush administration in 2001, favorable opinions of the United States have declined in many countries. In Great Britain — an ally in the war in Iraq — approval levels fell from 83 percent in 1999-2000 to 56 percent in 2006.

Favorable Opinions of the U.S.

Legend: Great Britain, Germany, Pakistan, China, Nigeria, France, Russia, Turkey, Egypt

Source: Pew Global Attitudes Project, 2006

Although there certainly was European criticism about the American war in Vietnam, Americans did not hear about it on a daily basis, as they do with criticisms of the war in Iraq. Instant television reporting and the Internet bring the war as well as its critics into homes every hour. Now, says Judt, "Whatever catastrophes the Americans are involved in overseas are immediately visible, with no time lag."

Another foreign conflict strongly identified with the United States and a recurrent theme at anti-war protests around the globe is the Israeli-Palestinian stalemate. European and Middle Eastern criticism of U.S. support of Israel ranges from humanitarian concerns about Palestinian rights to demagoguery invoking a Jewish-American-capitalist conspiracy.

"This didn't come from nothing," says Markovits. In his new book, *Uncouth Nation: Why Europe Dislikes America*, he traces the origins of anti-American sentiment to the 19th century, when European elites feared the pugnacious, young country.

For Americans, it is easy to dismiss criticism of U.S. policies as simply an irrational ideology, Markovits writes. But the term "anti-Americanism" is misleading,

he says, because it lumps together rational criticisms, whether one agrees with them or not, with a disembodied, ideological opposition to an idea of America, in which the country stands as a symbol for a variety of foreign, cultural and political discontents.

As Markovits notes, "Anti-Americanism is a particularly murky concept because it invariably merges antipathy toward what America does with what America is — or rather is projected to be in the eyes of its beholders." In contrast to classical stereotypes, which usually depict powerless minorities, the United States does, in fact, have great political, economic and cultural power. This makes it especially difficult to disentangle the perception from the reality. Critics of America assume that the expansion of this power, rather than a more benign exercise of it, is always the top priority of the American government. This is particularly true when it comes to the view, shared by much of the globe, that the United States is too tightly connected to Israel.

As Beirut's *Daily Star* said after the United States deposed Saddam Hussein: "Having waged an 'illegitimate' war on Iraq that has stoked anti-American feelings around the world, challenged and ignored international

French activist and farmer José Bové has a following in Solomiac, France, after attempting to rip up a crop of genetically modified maize. Bové gained fame for destroying a French McDonald's restaurant in 1999.

AFP/Getty Images/Eric Cabanis

law and the United Nations . . . the Bush administration is not about to 'offer Iraq on a golden platter to an opposition group or to the U.N. Security Council.'

"It will deny others a say in shaping post-war Iraq, and it won't withdraw its forces on request . . . . Israel, of course, will be an exception, and is the only U.S. partner whose participation in shaping post-war Iraq is 'guaranteed.' That is because Israel was the main reason for which the war was waged."[14]

Trying to sort out real criticisms of the United States from the political symbolism that makes up much anti-Americanism is a daunting task. But for America's many critics around the globe, the daily carnage in Iraq has confirmed that America, having found no weapons of mass destruction in Iraq, is now on a reckless crusade.

In the week after the Sept. 11, attacks, Bush declared, "this crusade, this war on terrorism, is going to take a while."[15] While the term "crusade" went largely unnoticed in the United States, it alarmed many around the world with its evocation of the ancient wars between Christianity and Islam.

As Americans seek to understand global criticism of the United States, here are some of the key issues being debated:

Is the United States the primary force behind globalization policies that harm other countries?

Before there was anti-Americanism there was anti-globalization. For many critics, they are mostly the same.[16]

Globalization is the umbrella term for the rapidly increasing social, technological, cultural and political integration of nation-states, corporations and organizations around the world.

Its supporters believe that globalization is a positive engine of commerce that brings increased standards of living, universal values, multiculturalism and technology to developing countries. Globalization's critics claim it is a slave to corporate interests, harms the environment and tramples human rights and the economic and ethical claims of the poor and working classes.

It's no surprise, then, that America has become the country most vilified by the anti-globalization movement. After all, U.S. brands like McDonald's, Marlboro and Nike are among the most recognized in the world.

Globalization does have its defenders, and at least one links the movement to an old socialist tradition in Europe. "Globalization simply means freedom of movement for goods and people," wrote the late French journalist and philosopher Jean-Francois Revel, "and it is hard to be violently hostile to that.

"But behind the opposition to globalization lies an older and more fundamental struggle against economic liberalization and its chief representative, the United States. Anti-globalism protests often feature an Uncle Sam in a stars-and-stripes costume as their supreme scapegoat."

Lashing out at America through targeting its products had roots in the Cold War. For example, some Eastern Bloc countries prohibited Coca-Cola but not Pepsi, because Coke was so strongly identified with the United States. But the movement reached its peak at the turn of the 21st century with global protests against the World Trade Organization, against the incursion of McDonald's and Starbucks and against acceptance of genetically modified foods from the United States.[17]

Championing the pure-food cause was Great Britain's Prince Charles. In 1999, after representatives of 20 African countries had published a statement denying that gene technologies would help farmers to produce the food they needed, Charles came to their defense: "Are we going to allow the industrialization of life itself, redesigning the natural world for the sake of convenience? Or should we be adopting a gentler, more considered approach, seeking always to work with the grain of nature?"[18]

Reluctance to accept American products and economic power has brought together critics from the left and the right. For both, "America represents the ideal of unfettered capitalism itself," says Fernando Vallespin, director of the Sociological Research Centre of Spain, a nonpartisan think tank in Madrid. "For those on the left, the concern is for labor exploitation. For those on the right, it is the loss of national sovereignty."

Resentment of the American economic model is particularly strong in Europe, which is currently confronting painful and unpopular adjustments to its own long-held social-welfare state model. Politicians, unions and disenfranchised workers in France, Italy and Spain say they do not want to adopt the "Anglo-Saxon" model, a reference not to Germany or England but to the United States. Spaniards are vociferous critics of the American way of life, says Vallespin, "but on the other hand we are probably one of the most American in terms of our patterns of consumption."

Cost-cutting proposals that seem to erode Europe's time-honored cradle-to-grave welfare privileges — such as fees for seeing a doctor or reducing the meal allowances of factory workers — have been denounced as "American." But in truth, most policies are still far from American-style capitalism.

In Germany, American business interests are seen as a double threat. After a recent buying spree of distressed companies by hedge funds, most of them American, German Vice Chancellor Franz Muentefering said the funds "fall like a plague of locusts over our companies, devour everything, then fly on to the next one."

Muentefering's statement was widely scrutinized, with some critics suggesting that the image of locusts preying on German companies evoked sentiments that were not only anti-American but also anti-Semitic.

There is no doubt the United States has been leading the current charge to deregulate markets, but it is still wrong to blame it for the world's economic inequalities, says Charles Kupchan, a professor of international affairs at Georgetown University and the former director for European affairs at the National Security Council during the Clinton administration.

He points out that large corporations in nearly every European country have been globalizing. In fact, the precursor

Yankee mice Mickey and Minnie reign at Disneyland Paris during Disney's 100th anniversary. Despite protests against American cultural imports by French intellectuals, more people visit the Paris theme park than any other Disney attraction in the world.

to modern globalization was not the commercial efforts of the United States but European imperialism of the past 500 years. A large part of that was the economic domination and exploitation of Latin America and Africa.

The remnants of Europe's imperialist past continue to earn big profits for European countries, with Spain holding powerful telecom and banking concessions in Latin America, and the French profiting off mining and agricultural interests in their former colonies in Africa. Yet, curiously, the focus of the anti-globalization debate continues to revolve around the United States.

"There is an unjustifiable equation between globalization and Americanization," says Kupchan.

Spanish Blame Bombing on War in Iraq

Spain's support of U.S. seen as critical factor

On the morning of March 11, 2004, a coordinated bomb attack on four rush-hour trains in Madrid killed 191 people and injured more than 1,700.

Spain had lived through decades of terrorism from the Basque separatist group ETA, but these bombers were not seeking independence; they were attempting to intimidate the Spanish government. In February 2007, Spanish authorities put 29 men on trial for the bombings, claiming they belonged to a local cell of Islamic militants aligned with al Qaeda.

In sharp contrast to the American reaction after the Sept. 11, 2001, terrorist attacks, Spanish citizens did not view the assault as part of a war between Islam and the West. Instead, many turned their anger toward the United States and their own government, which had supported the U.S.-led invasion of Iraq.

"We didn't want to go to war, but we did because of [former Prime Minister José Maria] Aznar," said Miguel Barrios, a 45-year-old maintenance worker who was in one of the bombed trains. "They didn't pay attention to the anti-war movement."[1]

It became clear that in an effort to stay aligned with the interests of the United States, the world's sole superpower, the Spanish government had run against the will of its own people. In the wake of the railroad attacks that Spanish government was voted out. The new prime minister, José Luis Rodriguez Zapatero, withdrew Spain's 1,300 troops from Iraq within weeks, risking a rupture of the close alliance Spain had enjoyed with the U.S.

"Mr. Bush and Mr. Blair will reflect on our decision," said Zapatero. "You cannot justify a war with lies. It cannot be."

People felt the war in Iraq had never been Spain's business, said Miguel Bastenier, a columnist for *El Pais*, Spain's largest newspaper. "Aznar was doing what Bush wanted without any particular reason for Spain to be there.

"There was undoubtedly the feeling that Spain was being punished for its association with the aggressive policies of the United States," and that "their country had been targeted by Muslim terrorists because it was now seen as being allied with the Jewish state."

In 2002, when war in Iraq was still only imminent, millions of Spaniards had taken to the streets to protest the coming invasion; polls showed more than 80 percent opposed to supporting the United States.

"Bush wants to go into Iraq to get the oil," said Virgilio Salcedo, a 29-year-old computer programmer who came to the rally in Madrid with his parents. "Everybody knows

At the same time, the U.S. government, under both the current Bush administration and the Clinton presidency, pushed often and hard on behalf of U.S. business interests.

The most famous attempt, which failed spectacularly, was the U.S. attempt to open Britain to bioengineered foods. The lobbying attempt, led by former Clinton U.S. Trade Representative Mickey Kantor, ran up against deeply held British attitudes of reverence for pristine nature.

"These senior executives thought they could just walk in and buy [British officials] a glass of champagne and charm them," said Evie Soames, a British lobbyist who represented the U.S. company Monsanto, which was attempting to sell its genetically modified seeds in England for several years.[19]

More recent American lobbying efforts have borne fruit. In 2001 the European Union tried to impose a strict safety-testing regime on chemical manufacturers; the Bush administration mounted a massive lobbying campaign that mobilized American embassies across Europe and Asia. The final, much scaled-back, version of the testing regime will save U.S. chemical companies billions of dollars.

Perhaps the biggest global concern about U.S. economic interests has been the perception that the U.S.-led invasion of Iraq was driven by America's thirst for petroleum. Notably, the most ubiquitous slogan, "No blood for oil," popped up at protests in the United States and abroad during the first Persian Gulf War in 1991 as well as the current war.

In a scathing commentary about President Bush's belief that he is on a direct mission from God, Henry

that he doesn't want to help the people there."

"We think our president has sold out the country to the Americans," said Susanna Polo, a 30-year-old economist.

"Aznar is Bush's dog," added Raquel Hurtado, a 19-year-old economics student.[2]

Even for those most deeply affected by 9/11, like 53-year-old Rosalinda Arias, whose sister died in the World Trade Center attacks, U.S. motives were suspect. "It is all business. They want petroleum; they want to bring U.S. imperialism," said Arias, owner of a restaurant in Madrid.

For the many older people attending the rally, memories of the Franco dictatorship were still fresh, including America's support of the fascist regime in the 1930s. Now they had little faith in Bush administration claims that America was going to liberate Iraq.

"There are lots of dictatorships that have been backed by the USA," said Carlos Martin, a 67-year-old

A tear rolls down a girl's cheek during a rally in Madrid following terrorist bombings in March 2004 that killed nearly 200 people. Her message: "Peace, not terrorism."

Getty Images/Ian Waldie

translator of Italian literature. "I can't imagine how the Iraqi people are feeling now. They were bombed in 1991, then they had 12 years of horrible sanctions, and now they are being bombed again. I can't imagine they will look at the Americans as liberators."

Some of the protesters' worst fears were realized as the U.S. Coalition Forces invaded and subdued Baghdad in 2003, then settled into the current quagmire.

But Spain did not seek revenge against the killing of 191 of its citizens. A 40-year-old teacher named Valeria Suarez Marsa gave a softer voice to the public mood. "It is more important then ever to call for peace," she said. "The bombs reminded us of that urgency."

---

[1] The author covered the Madrid protests in 2002.

[2] Quoted in Samuel Loewenberg, "A Vote for Honesty," *The Nation*, March 18, 2004.

A. Giroux, a professor of communications at Canada's McMaster University, wrote: "Surrounded by born-again missionaries . . . Bush has relentlessly developed policies based less on social needs than on a highly personal and narrowly moral sense of divine purpose."[20]

In the months before the invasion of Iraq in March 2003, *The Economist* summed up the anti-Bush sentiment: "Only one thing unsettles George Bush's critics more than the possibility that his foreign policy is secretly driven by greed. That is the possibility that it is secretly driven by God . . . . War for oil would merely be bad. War for God would be catastrophic."[21]

Is the United States threatening other cultures?

Any American who has traveled abroad for any length of time will be familiar with the following exchange: "Oh,

you're American. I hate Americans." Or, the rhetorical litmus-test question: "What do you think of your president?" This, however, is soon followed by "I love New York" or "Have you ever been to Disneyland?"

For decades, America's most influential export has not been cars or televisions, but culture. This can be mass media like Hollywood movies and hip-hop music, fast-food restaurants that are often seen as crass and objectionable, or soft drinks such as Coca-Cola.

While these cultural products have long been embraced on a worldwide scale, they have also raised concerns that their appeal would diminish traditions and habits that other cultures hold dear. This love-hate relationship with American popular culture and consumerism was reflected in a 2005 Pew study that found "72 percent of French, 70 percent of Germans and 56

U.S. Lags in Foreign Aid

When foreign aid donations are measured as a percentage of gross national income, the U.S. ranks behind 20 other major donors.

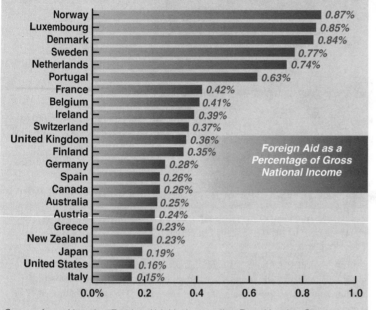

Foreign Aid as a Percentage of Gross National Income

Country	Percentage
Norway	0.87%
Luxembourg	0.85%
Denmark	0.84%
Sweden	0.77%
Netherlands	0.74%
Portugal	0.63%
France	0.42%
Belgium	0.41%
Ireland	0.39%
Switzerland	0.37%
United Kingdom	0.36%
Finland	0.35%
Germany	0.28%
Spain	0.26%
Canada	0.26%
Australia	0.25%
Austria	0.24%
Greece	0.23%
New Zealand	0.23%
Japan	0.19%
United States	0.16%
Italy	0.15%

Source: Larry Nowels, "Foreign Aid: Understanding Data Used to Compare Donors," Congressional Research Service, May 23, 2005

percent of Britons regard the spread of American culture negatively. In all of these countries, paradoxically, large majorities of respondents — especially young people — say they like American movies and other cultural exports."[22]

The University of Michigan's Markovits says resentment of U.S. culture has deep roots among European elites. "Many of the components of European anti-Americanism have been alive and well in Europe's intellectual discourse since the late 18th century," he writes. "The tropes about Americans' alleged venality, mediocrity, uncouthness, lack of culture and above all inauthenticity have been integral and ubiquitous to European elite opinion for well over 200 years. All of these 'Americanizations' bemoan an alleged loss of purity and authenticity for Europeans at the hands of a threatening and unwelcome intruder who — to make matters worse — exhibits a flaring cultural inferiority."[23]

"The fear is that what's happening in America will happen in Europe, and that left to their own devices

people will go to vulgar theme parks and shop at Wal-Mart," says Nick Cohen, a liberal British columnist. At its roots, this strain of anti-Americanism is a conservative ideology, he says. European elites were concerned that Americans had forsaken the church and the social hierarchy, according to Cohen, the author of a book reassessing European social liberals, *What's Left? How Liberals Lost Their Way.*

Nowhere is the ambivalence toward American culture more apparent than in France. When a Walt Disney theme park opened near Paris in 1994, French critics called it "a cultural Chernobyl." Yet today it rivals the Eiffel Tower as the country's most popular tourist destination. Without doubt, the biggest symbol of American cultural effrontery for the French is McDonald's. Yet the French are the biggest consumers of Big Macs in Europe.[24]

When France was making a national celebrity of farmer-activist Bové in 1999, the quality of McDonald's cheeseburgers was not the big issue; the enemy was the corporation. But food in France has deep and sentimental roots.

At a protest gathering on Bové's behalf, *The New York Times* interviewed a 16-year-old French lad who had come mostly for the carnival atmosphere. "But my father was a farmer," he said, "and I am here representing my family, too. We believe in what Mr. Bové believes in. We don't want the multinationals to tell us what to eat."[25]

In the 19th and early 20th centuries, when millions of Europeans sought their fortunes in the United States, American culture promised relief from the restrictions of European social hierarchies. "America was a hope, especially for the lower classes, in those times," says Detlev Claussen, a professor of social theory, cultural studies and sociology at Germany's Leibniz Hannover University. In the wake of World War I, Germans embraced American jazz, literature and art.

Nazi propaganda enthusiastically portrayed Americans as evil capitalists during World War II, but attitudes mellowed after the war when, despite the continued presence of the American military, the U.S. Marshall Plan helped rebuild Europe. Even in the 1960s and '70s, Germans were enthralled by American history and pop culture and established hundreds of re-enactment clubs that staged "Wild-West" shootouts and sympathetic portrayals of Indians.

The positive view of America began to change only in the Vietnam War era of the late 1960s, says Claussen. Even then, Germans made a distinction between disdain for American policies and adoration of cultural icons like Bob Dylan and the Rev. Martin Luther King Jr.

Now even those distinctions are eroding. The new anti-Americanism, Claussen says, stems from a sense of disappointment in the American utopia, tinged with envy of its political and economic power. Many Germans, he says, have simply given up on the idea of a virtuous America as a land of promise.

"When you can make no distinction between politics and culture, when you say, 'I don't like America, full stop,' that's real anti-Americanism," he says.

Is the "American Century" over?

On Feb. 7, 1941, in an editorial in *Life* magazine entitled "The American Century," media magnate Henry Luce advocated that the United States enter World War II and begin a global crusade on behalf of the values of freedom, opportunity, self-reliance and democracy.[26]

The concept of the "American Century," a potent ideal even before Luce's epochal essay, encompasses the modern history of American dominance, from the Spanish-American War to World War II, the Cold War and America's emergence as the world's only superpower in the 1990s.

These days, many are questioning whether the United States has squandered its position atop the global hierarchy. Rivals have emerged, even as the Soviet Union, once a contender, has dissolved. The European Union has been revitalized by the membership of new former Soviet-bloc countries. China and India, with their massive populations, are rapidly becoming developed countries. Perhaps the American "empire," like the Roman Empire and others before it, is already locked into inevitable decline.

Time recently devoted a cover story to China which concluded that, "in this century the relative power of the U.S. is going to decline, and that of China is going to rise. That cake was baked long ago."[27]

For the time being, however, the United States is the world's richest country and leading economy, with a gross domestic product (GDP) of $13 trillion. Its armed forces are stationed in 40 countries, its corporations and its charities operate throughout the globe and its technology arguably remains the most innovative. America is still a magnet for millions around the world, but its image has been badly tarnished by the Iraq War.

"There is a perception in the rest of the world that the U.S. is no longer capable of being the global leader that it once was," says Julia E. Sweig, director of Latin America studies at the Council on Foreign Relations and author of the 2006 book *Friendly Fire: Losing Friends and Making Enemies in the Anti-American Century.*

For many, that would be no great loss. No one likes the king of the hill for long. America (at least as a concept) is genuinely unpopular. A Pew survey found that "favorability ratings for the United States continue to trail those of other major countries. In Europe, as well as in predominantly Muslim countries, the U.S. is generally less popular than Germany, France, Japan and even China. In Western Europe, attitudes toward America remain considerably more negative than they were in 2002, prior to the Iraq War."[28]

"The tendency now is to view the U.S. as a threat to international stability," says Georgetown University's Kupchan.

Muslims in Southeast Asia, for example, no longer look up to the United States, says Farish A. Noor, a history professor at the Centre for Modern Oriental Studies in Berlin. "That's gone. It's completely erased now. An entirely new image of America has been constructed by the Islamists."

Of course, the damage to America's status did not begin with the invasion of Iraq. Still alive is the memory of the war in Vietnam, as well as America's Cold War support of totalitarian regimes, such as Augusto Pinochet's in Chile and Saddam Hussein's in Iraq (when Iraq was fighting Iran). In Latin America, many blamed the United States for encouraging the "dirty war" of the 1970s and '80s in Argentina and for supporting right-wing paramilitary squads in Nicaragua against the Marxist Sandinista junta.

At the same time, the United States cut back many "soft power" programs in cultural, economic and humanitarian

CHRONOLOGY

1700s-1800s *Europeans express disdain over U.S. independence.*

1768 Dutch philosopher Cornelius de Pauw describes America as "a Moronic Spirit" and the people "either degenerate or monstrous."

1776 English radical Thomas Day decries American hypocrisy: "If there be an object truly ridiculous in nature, it is an American patriot, signing resolutions of independency with the one hand, and with the other brandishing a whip over his affrighted slaves."

1842 British writer Charles Dickens lambastes oppressive Northern cities, Southern ignorance and Mississippi River pollution in *American Notes.*

1901-1980 *U.S. industrial power helps win world wars; Cold War begins.*

1919 Allies defeat Germany in World War I after U.S. enters war in 1917.

June 6, 1944 American forces lead invasion of Europe on D-Day; millions extend thanks to GIs.

August 1945 U.S. drops atomic bombs on Hiroshima and Nagasaki, forcing Japan to surrender. . . . Post-war U.S.-funded Marshall Plan provides development assistance to war-ravaged Europe.

1961 U.S. involvement in Vietnam begins, sparking anti-U.S. sentiment.

1967 Israel wins Six-Day War against Egypt, Jordan and Syria, begins occupation of West Bank and Gaza Strip. U.S. support for Israel feeds anti-Americanism.

1979 Shah overthrown in Iran. U.S. declared "The Great Satan."

1980s-1990s *Soviet Union collapses. U.S. involvement in Central America misfires. Resentment of world's sole superpower grows.*

1981 U.S.-trained Salvadoran soldiers massacre 800 women and children and elderly people in the country's bloody civil war; U.S. blamed.

Nov. 9, 1989 Berlin Wall falls. Citizens of newly reunited German capital dance to American TV star David Hasselhoff's "Looking for Freedom."

1989 U.S. arrests former American ally Gen. Manuel Noriega of Panama for drug trafficking.

1999 Negotiations conclude for Kyoto global warming pact; U.S. signs but Congress refuses to ratify.

1999 Farmer José Bové destroys a McDonald's in southern France as a consumer protest. Protests are held against globalization, multinational corporations and U.S. products.

2000s *President George W. Bush begins a unilateralist foreign policy, alienating allies.*

Sept. 11, 2001 Terrorists hijack four airplanes and crash three into the World Trade Center and the Pentagon. . . . In October a worldwide, U.S.-led coalition invades Afghanistan.

2002 In France, Thierry Meyssan's bestseller *L'Effroyable Imposture* (*The Terrible Fraud*) alleges the U.S. was behind the Sept. 11 attacks. . . . Venezuelan strongman Hugo Chavez, temporarily toppled in an aborted coup, accuses Bush administration of backing the revolt. . . . American companies abroad are vandalized.

2003 Millions march in Europe to protest U.S-led invasion of Iraq. . . .

2004 U.N. Secretary-General Kofi Annan calls Iraq invasion "illegal." . . . Abu Ghraib prison abuses shock the world. . . . Terrorists bomb Madrid trains.

2005 U.S. sends disaster aid to Indonesia and Pakistan, gaining goodwill. . . . Terrorists bomb London buses.

2006 British television airs a mock documentary about the imagined assassination of President Bush.

Feb. 10, 2007 Russian President Vladimir Putin denounces U.S. expansionism and military spending.

March 8, 2007 President Bush begins five-nation Latin American tour, sparking protests across the region.

aid in Latin America. Many of these were replaced with aggressive law-and-order programs that were part of the American government's war on drugs, and, after Sept. 11, the "war on terror."

And even before al Qaeda's 9/11 attacks, foreigners were critical of the U.S. rejection of global treaties, including the Kyoto Protocol for climate change, the creation of the International Criminal Court and rules for curbing biological weapons. Some of these treaties were actually rejected during the Clinton administration. The impression was strong that the United States would go it alone, because it thought it could.

It was at that point that many nations began to view the United States as "a delinquent international citizen."[29]

Some analysts wonder if the end of the American Century will begin in the Americas. Stepping into the hemispheric leadership vacuum, leftist President Hugo Chavez of Venezuela mocks President Bush as "the little gentleman" from the North and works at consolidating the region under his own oil-rich leadership.

American involvement in Latin America, long treated as a vast raw-material commodities mart by U.S. businesses, had already alienated many South and Central American countries, and, more recently, many Latin Americans have blamed U.S.-backed free-market economic policies for destabilizing their economies.

In 2005 Chavez even attempted to turn old-style American "soft power" on its head, offering and delivering 17 million gallons of heating oil to low-income families in New York and New England.

President Bush's March 2007 diplomatic swing through Latin American was intended to soothe feelings, but his administration's neglect, says Sweig, "has ripped off the Band-Aid that had covered up latent wounds for a long time."

As Bush was addressing an audience in Uruguay on March 10, Chavez led a counter rally in Argentina in which he called Bush a "political corpse." Alluding to the fact that he had previously called Bush "the devil" at the United Nations, Chavez bragged that, "He does not even smell of sulfur anymore; what [smells] is the scent of political death, and within a very short time it will become cosmic dust and disappear."[30]

In Muslim nations, the fiery rhetoric of the Bush administration's war on terror sparked a new depth of hostility. Among predominantly Islamic countries in Southeast Asia, which had previously looked on the U.S. as liberators, the Bush administration "squandered five decades of goodwill," says Noor. "So much of this has been personalized in Bush. He is like an icon of everything that is bad about the U.S."

Because of the war in Iraq and the festering Palestinian question, hatred for America on the Arab "street," as well as among Islamists, is raw and without nuance. But it is instructive to hear voices from a recent *New York Times* report about a new al Qaeda training camp for jihadists at a Palestinian refugee camp north of Beirut.

" 'The United States is oppressing a lot of people,' the group's deputy commander, Abu Sharif, said in a room strewn with Kalashnikovs. 'They are killing a lot of innocents, but one day they are getting paid back.'

" 'I was happy,' Hamad Mustaf Ayasin, 70, recalled in hearing last fall that his 35-year-old son, Ahmed, had died in Iraq fighting American troops near the Syrian border. 'The U.S. is against Muslims all over the world.'

"On the streets of the camp, one young man after another said dying in Iraq was no longer their only dream."

It was suicide.

" 'If I had the chance to do any kind of operation against anyone who is against Islam, inside or outside of the U.S., I would do the operation,' " said 18-year-old Mohamed.[31]

In England, *The Guardian* noted the continuing concern about the United States' use of its power during the months leading up to the invasion of Iraq. "Of course, enemies of the U.S. have shaken their fist at its 'imperialism' for decades," the paper editorialized. "They are doing it again now, as Washington wages a global 'war against terror' and braces itself for a campaign aimed at 'regime change' in a foreign, sovereign state.

"What is more surprising, and much newer, is that the notion of an American empire has suddenly become a live debate inside the U.S. And not just among Europhile liberals either, but across the range — from left to right."[32]

BACKGROUND

The Ungrateful Son

The story begins in Europe. The roots of antagonism toward the New World grew among the nations that first

At a Berlin Café, Musing About America

"We were hoping America would not elect Bush"

Prenzlauer Berg was once on the gritty side of town, in East Berlin, when Berlin was a divided city. The Berlin Wall was torn down nearly 20 years ago, and few signs of it remain.

Prenzlauer Berg is now fashionable, but there's still a certain working-class feel to it. On a rainy afternoon last February three friends met for coffee at the Wasser und Brot (Water and Bread), a barely decorated neighborhood café frequented mostly by local workmen, artists, students and retirees.

Baerbel Boesking *is a 45-year-old actress, originally from Lower Saxony;* Robert Lingnau, *33, is a composer and writer.* Petra Lanthaler, *30, is a psychologist. She came to Berlin four years ago from northern Italy.*

They sipped tea and coffee and smoked, musing about the United States, George Bush and the future of relations with those increasingly alienating Americans:

Is America different from other countries?

ROBERT: America is very powerful so it has more impact on us than any other country. All of the oil stuff, all of the pollution, the politics.

BAERBEL: Since the student protests here in the 60s, many people still think of the United States as an imperialist, capitalist power. People think Americans are just superficial, and Bush has only made that worse. But I know that not all Americans are superficial, like [filmmaker] Michael Moore, for instance.

PETRA: I don't think the American people are superficial. As far as I know, there are also many people in the United States who are rebelling against Bush.

Did your impression of America change after Sept. 11?

ROBERT: I think that the American government in some way participated or co-arranged for 9/11, or at least they knew certain things in advance and didn't act to prevent it. They wanted to install the Patriot Act, so that the government could take more control over people's lives. With the terrorist threat, people let the Patriot Act go through. Meanwhile, Bush is cutting billions from Medicare but putting more and more money into the war in Iraq.

BAERBEL: I often hear things like this from my friends. Many of them have the opinion that this whole thing, 9/11, was self-done by the U.S. itself. These are really educated people, it's horrible. This is an unbelievable point of view, like people who believe that the landing on the moon was just a Hollywood production.

ROBERT: I have two degrees actually. I think the Americans landed on the moon, but I don't think the

colonized it. America was the repository of the old world's disenfranchised and discontented, after all.

It was 18th-century British author Samuel Johnson who famously declared, "I am willing to love all mankind except an American." And another Briton, the 19th-century playwright George Bernard Shaw, quipped that "an asylum for the sane would be empty in America." Austria's Sigmund Freud, the father of psychoanalysis, was not enamored of the United States either. "A mistake," he called it, "a gigantic mistake."[33]

While some Americans might take pride in being loathed by European intellectuals, most have been mystified by, if not indifferent to the barbs. European anti-American feeling, argues the University of Michigan's Markovits, stems from the Europeans' sense that they have lost their own power and influence, and the subsequent search for a contemporary identity in a differently aligned global pecking order.

"Unlike elsewhere in the world," he said, "at least until very recently, America represented a particularly loaded concept and complex entity to Europeans precisely because it was, of course, a European creation."

The son, in other words, had rejected the father; America had "consciously defected from its European origins," Markovits says.

European conservatives and elites were miffed at America's rejection of the strictures of European class and religious hierarchies, the very things that people rebelled against when they emigrated to America.

One of the first Anti-American sentiments was the "degeneracy hypothesis," the belief that humidity and other atmospheric conditions in America created weak and

government did their best to prevent what happened. I don't think they wrote the script for what happened, but in a way they participated in order to get the Patriot Act through and for what came after.

PETRA: I don't want to believe that a government would do that. It's true that after 9/11 the U.S. took advantage of these fears of terrorism.

Anti-war demonstrators sometimes have signs comparing Bush to Hitler.

BAERBEL: Bush is not equal to Hitler. You can't compare somebody to Hitler.

ROBERT: You can compare Stalin to Hitler, but not Bush.

BAERBEL: You can compare Mao, this new guy in Korea and Saddam Hussein, but it is crazy to say that Bush is like Hitler.

BAERBEL: I was watching a television debate between Bush and [Sen. John] Kerry [D-Mass.], and Bush said that his role model was Jesus. He's got a long way to go. I don't think Jesus would have started a war with Iraq. I'm a Christian, too.

What do you think about American culture?

PETRA: The first words that come into my mind are big size. The shops are much bigger, the portions are much bigger, everything is bigger. People are bigger. But I know that's a really superficial answer because I've never actually been to America. I am impressed by their

scientific research. They think much more globally than Europeans do.

ROBERT: They don't seem to think globally about pollution and global warming. For me, there are two things that constitute my everyday life: that's jazz music and Apple Macintosh. That's what I think of when I think about U.S. culture. Both native American art forms.

BAERBEL: I had an American boyfriend once. From Kansas.

Do you think relations between America and Europe will improve with a new president in 2008?

BAERBEL: Yes, if it's a Democrat. It's really good you have term limits in the United States. We had Helmut Kohl for 16 years.

ROBERT: But if Jeb Bush gets elected, this is like 16 years of Kohl.

PETRA: All of my friends, most everybody I knew, we were really hoping that America would not elect Bush for the second term. It was really disappointing.

ROBERT: My hope for the next president is that he didn't study at Yale and that he hasn't been a member of Skull and Bones [the exclusive secret society].

It was still raining and cold when the friends left the smoky warmth of the Wasser und Brot. It wasn't their anti-Americanism that stood out but how much they knew about America and American life. And it begged the question: Would Americans know half as much about Germany, even the name of the chancellor?

---

morally inferior animals and human beings. The court philosopher to Frederick II of Prussia, Cornelius de Pauw, argued in 1768 about Americans that, "the weakest European could crush them with ease."[34]

As American industry rose in the late 19th century, the speed of American life became a major threat to European traditions of craftsmanship. "The breathless haste with which they work — the distinctive vice of the new world — is already beginning ferociously to infect old Europe and is spreading a spiritual emptiness over the continent," observed the German philosopher Friedrich Nietzsche.[35]

The notion that the mixing of races was bringing down the level of capability in Americans was another major thrust of anti-Americanism. Blacks and "low quality" immigrants, it was said in European salons, would lead to ultimate dissolution.

Arthur de Gobineau, a French social thinker, declared that America was creating the "greatest mediocrity in all fields: mediocrity of physical strength, mediocrity of beauty, mediocrity of intellectual capacities — we could almost say nothingness."[36]

After World War I, allies of the United States, France and Great Britain, found themselves massively in debt to the brash and newly powerful Americans, which generated resentment. These sentiments spread during the Great Depression. Sometimes the bias took on anti-Semitic overtones, including the widely held theory that the American government was ruled by a Jewish conspiracy.[37]

After World War II, the U.S. Marshall Plan helped rebuild Europe. Yet as American power grew while Europe licked its wounds, the United States became a scapegoat for an increasing sense of weakness among those nostalgic

Pakistani protesters burn the American flag and a mock Israeli flag to protest the Israeli attack on southern Lebanon in August 2006. Anti-American sentiment often ties the U.S. and Israel together as partners in the exploitation and humiliation of other countries.

for their former empires. It was then that the global spread of American cultural, economic, and political power — rock 'n' roll, McDonald's and U.S. military bases — established the United States as a symbol of global authority, and one to be resisted.

Religious Differences

The staying power of American religiosity created another divide between Europe and the United States. Historian Huntington's "clash of civilizations" theory postulated that the big divide was between Christianity and Islam. But one of the deepest rifts between Europe and the United States centered on the relationship between religion and government.

Europeans had begun abandoning churchgoing in the 1950s and no longer felt that religion should play a role in political affairs.[38] But a large majority of Americans not only continued to go to church but also maintained the belief that religious tenets should provide moral direction to their elected leaders.

Many Europeans have been aghast at what they viewed as American religious fervor, particularly when it has seemed to influence government policy. "An American president who conducts Bible study at the White House and begins Cabinet sessions with a prayer may seem a curious anachronism to his European allies, but he is in tune with his constituents," write Judt and French scholar Denis Lacorne.[39]

Even in Spain, which has one of the most conservative religious establishments in Europe, American evangelicals'

penchant for focusing on sexual issues does not resonate. In 2005, for example, a large majority of the Spanish population voted to legalize gay marriage, a key moral issue to some conservative American Christians.

Policies and traditions that regularly mix church and state in the United States — prayer in schools, God in the Pledge of Allegiance and the open displays of faith by President Bush — "were really shocking to the average Spaniard," says Charles Powell Solares, a deputy director at the Elcano Royal Institute, a think tank in Madrid. He says that 90 percent of Spaniards are in favor of a radical separation between church and state.

On the other hand, polls in Indonesia, Pakistan, Lebanon and Turkey reveal that the majority of people in Muslim countries believe the United States is secular and ungodly.[40]

Foreign Affairs Bully?

Muslims and Americans have not always been adversaries. The United States, after all, supported Islamists in Afghanistan in their fight against the Soviet Union in the 1980s, as well as Bosnian Muslims against Christian Orthodox Serbia in the 1990s.

Moreover, the United States maintains strong relationships with Saudi Arabia, Jordan and Egypt, and Muslim immigrants continue to flow into America — from Pakistan, Bangladesh, Afghanistan, India and even Iraq.

In Indonesia and Malaysia, home to some of the world's largest Muslim populations, anti-Americanism is a recent phenomenon. For most of the postwar 20th century, the United States was seen as an anti-colonial power because of its role in liberating those countries from Japan.

"It's not a coincidence that the Malaysian flag looks like the American flag," says Noor of Berlin's Centre for Modern Oriental Studies.

The advance of high-speed communications has been a key factor in the attitude shift in Southeast Asia. "New media, especially satellite television and the Internet, reinforce negative images of the U.S. through a flood of compelling, highly graphic images," said Steven Simon, a Middle East scholar at the Council on Foreign Relations. "Some of these images present the Muslims as victims; others as victors. All tend to frame events as segments of an ongoing drama between good and evil."[41]

This "us vs. them" dynamic had its genesis in Europe. "Many of these originated outside the Muslim world entirely," Simon told the House International Relations Committee. They were "introduced to the region by Nazi and Soviet propaganda in mid-20th century."

Most notoriously, the British-appointed mufti of Jerusalem, Haj Amin al-Husayni, made a pact with the German government in the 1930s and spread ill will throughout the region against the Western allies, including the United States. Great Britain, of course, was already an object of scorn and resentment for its heavy-handed colonial administration of Muslim territory.

Simon also noted that after Britain pulled out of the Middle East in the 1940s and America began to vie for influence during the Cold War, the United States inherited the animosity that Muslim countries had against Britain, their former conquerors. "The substitution of American power in the region for British authority was bound to tar the U.S. with the imperialist brush," Simon said.

American Exceptionalism

Americans' self-image has been rooted in the certitude that their country is different — a beacon of personal, political and economic freedom in the world. This idea really came of age during World War II, when American industrial power, along with Soviet manpower, liberated Europe. Then the Yanks were cheered and admired, but some scholars believe that the roots of anti-American feelings by many Europeans stem from this U.S. "salvation."

A residue of that feeling remains in France, which truly had been liberated. Germany, however, had been the enemy, and even during the height of the Cold War in the 1960s and '70s, many West Germans deeply resented the presence of American military bases.

Even though the American army's airlift of supplies had saved West Berlin, few thought of the United States as having saved them from the Nazis or the Soviets, says Claussen, at Leibniz Hannover University, and West German politicians were loath to suggest that "America has liberated us."

Spain until recently was America's closest ally in continental Europe, but enmity toward the United States has existed since the 1950s, says Powell Solares, at Madrid's Elcano Royal Institute. Spain never viewed America as a liberator because the country was largely uninvolved with World War II. Instead, they tend to condemn the U.S. for supporting fascist Gen. Francisco Franco as part of its Cold War policy.

A female U.S. Army soldiers frisks a Kurdish woman at a checkpoint in Ramadi, Iraq, in October 2004. Several people had been killed in clashes between rebels and U.S. troops. The War in Iraq underlies much of the spiraling anti-American sentiment around the world today.

AFP/Getty Images/Patrick Baz

"And that means that Spaniards have never associated the U.S. with freedom and democracy," says Powell Solares, citing polls from the 1960s and '70s in which Spaniards viewed the United States as a bigger threat to world peace than the Soviet Union.

After the collapse of the Soviet Union in 1991 the former republics of the Soviet Union and its satellite nations emerged with more solidarity with the United States than most of the countries of Western Europe. Except for Great Britain, Eastern European nations have contributed more troops per capita to the Coalition Forces in the invasions of Afghanistan and Iraq. Several have allegedly allowed controversial secret CIA prisons on their soil.

When U.S. Secretary of Defense Donald Rumsfeld distinguished between the "Old Europe" and "New Europe" in 2003, he was paying homage to the willingness of the newly liberated nations to aid the United States, in contrast to the recalcitrance of Germany and France — Old Europe.[42] French officials labeled the secretary's bluntness as "arrogance."

Anti-Americanism got only a short reprieve in the aftermath of the 9/11 attacks.

"Initially, there was a spontaneous outpouring of sympathy and support for the United States," Pew researchers found. "Even in some parts of the Middle East, hostility toward the U.S. appeared to soften a bit. But this reaction proved short-lived. Just a few months after the attacks, a Global Attitudes Project survey of opinion leaders around

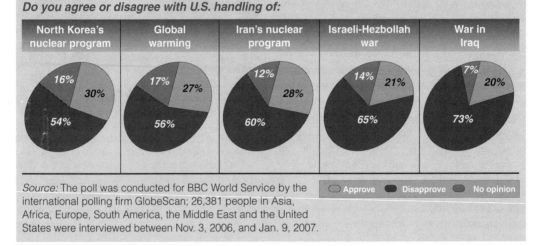

Disapproval of American Policies Is Widespread

More than half of the 26,000 people surveyed in 25 countries disapprove of the United States' role in several foreign-policy areas. Fifty-six percent disagree with the U.S. approach toward global warming, while nearly three-quarters are critical of the war in Iraq.

Do you agree or disagree with U.S. handling of:

North Korea's nuclear program	Global warming	Iran's nuclear program	Israeli-Hezbollah war	War in Iraq
16% / 30% / 54%	17% / 27% / 56%	12% / 28% / 60%	14% / 21% / 65%	7% / 20% / 73%

○ Approve   ● Disapprove   ◐ No opinion

Source: The poll was conducted for BBC World Service by the international polling firm GlobeScan; 26,381 people in Asia, Africa, Europe, South America, the Middle East and the United States were interviewed between Nov. 3, 2006, and Jan. 9, 2007.

the world found that, outside Western Europe, there was a widespread sense that U.S. policies were a major cause of the attacks."

In Venezuela, President Chavez cynically suggested, "The hypothesis that is gaining strength . . . is that it was the same U.S. imperial power that planned and carried out this terrible terrorist attack or act against its own people and against citizens of all over the world. Why? To justify the aggressions that immediately were unleashed on Afghanistan, on Iraq."[43]

CURRENT SITUATION

Missteps and Failures

Because of their self-proclaimed virtues and their emphasis on human rights, Americans are often held to higher expectations on the world stage than are other nations. When they fail to perform to those standards, they are doubly condemned. Many who see U.S. foreign policy floundering are as disappointed as they are angry.

Some of the criticisms of the United States — such as the allegations that the government was behind the 9/11 attacks — are so irrational that there is no way to answer them. But there are inescapable realities that will not go away.

America's credibility on human rights has been severely damaged by prisoner abuse at Abu Ghraib, the U.S.-run Baghdad prison for terrorism suspects, and alleged mistreatment at the Guantanamo Bay detention camp in Cuba, as well as by CIA renditions and secret detention camps in Eastern Europe.[44] Its reputation for competence has been trampled by revelations that Iraq's alleged weapons of mass destruction had been trumped up by an overeager White House yearning for battle. Most jarring of all is the bloodshed in Iraq that has claimed at least 34,000 Iraqis and more than 3,000 American troops.[45]

After the revelations at Abu Ghraib, Patrick Sabatier of the French newspaper *Liberation* wrote, "One can lose a war in places other than battlegrounds. The torture that took place in the Abu Ghraib prison is a major defeat for the U.S. The photographs fan the fires of anti-American hate in the Arab world. Elsewhere they trigger reactions of disgust, and take away from the coalition's small dose of moral legitimacy, gained by toppling Saddam's regime."[46]

Even Americans themselves no longer defend the U.S position in Iraq, Pew researchers found. "As to whether the removal of Saddam Hussein from power made the world a safer place," the survey said, "views are also lopsidedly negative. In no country surveyed, including the

Will anti-Americanism wane after President Bush leaves office?

YES
Dr. Farish A. Noor
Professor of history, Centre for Modern Oriental Studies, Berlin

Written for *CQ Global Researcher*, March 2007

It is undeniable that the image of the United States of America has declined significantly in Southeast Asia during President George Bush's term. Over the past two years I have witnessed more than two-dozen anti-American demonstrations in Malaysia and Indonesia, where the issues ranged from Malaysia's protracted negotiations with the USA on the Free Trade Agreement to America's actions in Afghanistan and Iraq. At almost all of these demonstrations effigies of George Bush and Condoleeza Rice were paraded and sometimes set alight.

Historically America was seen as a liberator and savior in the Southeast Asian region, especially in its role against the Japanese imperial army during the Second World War and its efforts to prevent the Western European colonial powers (Britain, France and the Netherlands) from recolonizing their former colonies Malaya, Indonesia, Vietnam, Burma and the Philippines.

Admiration for America, the American way of life and American values was at its peak during the postcolonial developmental era of the 1960s to 1980s, when Southeast Asian countries sent tens of thousands of students to the U.S. for further education. The American economic model became the framework for the postcolonial economies of the region; and America was doubly thanked for helping to keep the region safe from communism.

Yet, America today is seen as the enemy of Islam, and for Muslim-majority countries like Malaysia, Indonesia and Brunei this poses new problems for bilateral relations. One major factor that has worsened the situation was the use of bellicose rhetoric by the Bush administration in its unilateral "war on terror," which was couched in terms of a "crusade." Subsequent actions and misjudgments (such as the invasion of Iraq without sufficient consultation with Muslim countries) and the deteriorating security condition in Iraq and Afghanistan have merely compounded the problem even more.

Much of the damage, however, is due to the unilateralist character of a Bush administration that was seen as cavalier, gung-ho and insensitive to Muslim concerns. Thanks in part to the overreach and over-projection of the image of Bush in this campaign, however, much of the controversy surrounding the war on terror, the invasion of Afghanistan and Iraq, etc. has been associated with President Bush himself on a personal level.

There is every reason to believe that some of the anti-Americanism we see in Southeast Asia today will wane with a change of administration. But this also depends on whether the next U.S. government can bring the campaigns in Afghanistan and Iraq to a close with minimum loss of life.

NO
Manjeet Kripalani
Edward R. Murrow Press Fellow, Council on Foreign Relations; India Bureau Chief, Business Week

Written for *CQ Global Researcher*, March 2007

The favorability rating of the U.S. in the eyes of the world has fallen precipitously since the Iraq invasion, and continues to decline as the war wears on.

Will America ever recover its lost reputation? Perhaps, but it will take years. The perception of the U.S. is that of a power in descent, a nation spent in the ignominious and outmoded task of building Empire. The ideals and positive force that the U.S. represented have been discredited since 2003, given the fundamentalist fervor with which they have been pursued.

That's not the best option in an increasingly complex world. Getting a global consensus on crises like Darfur, trade imbalances, terrorism and Middle East peace in a world without the powerful moral authority of the U.S. will be more difficult. But it has created space for other leadership to step up to the task.

This ascendant world comprises powers like Russia, but more widely the countries of Asia — notably China, India and even Japan. As the beneficiary of past American ideals, Japan has developed goodwill over decades through aid, anti-war sensitivities and the potential to be the stable "America" in Asia.

China and India are both poor, developing countries — but much of today's world looks more like them than it does the U.S.-dominated developed world. Their experiences are being closely watched by their peers, with whom there are centuries-old cultural and historic ties.

In this new world order, the U.S.' tarnished image really doesn't matter. America is still a powerful country, and these same ascendant nations are meshed with it economically and politically. China is in a tight economic embrace with America. Japan is still militarily protected by the U.S. and is its strongest, staunchest ally in Asia.

India, after years of hostile relations with the U.S., has turned pragmatic. Since 2001, America's popularity in India has been on the rise. That's because Indians, affected by terrorism for decades, view Washington as fighting their war for them. And despite domestic pressure, President Bush has continued to support the outsourcing of back-office jobs to India. The signing of the nuclear deal last December is surely good for U.S. business and Indian consumers. But its symbolism is far greater: Its confidence in India's non-proliferation record has ensured that democratic India will wholeheartedly embrace the U.S. economically, technologically and politically.

This ensures that in the future, no matter how much moral authority the U.S. loses, its wagon is hitched firmly to the stars of these ascendant nations — and vice versa.

Political theater plays out in Paris as orange-jump-suited Amnesty International protesters call on the United States to close the Guantanamo Bay, Cuba, prison camp.

United States, does a majority think the Iraq leader's overthrow has increased global security."[47]

Another strike against the American war in Iraq is its duration — longer now than World War II. And the carnage can be seen daily on television. "If the war had had a quick or favorable ending, people would have forgotten about it. But it is in the news every day," says Vallespin, at the Sociological Research Centre of Spain.

Support for Israel

For many Americans and Europeans, Israel cannot be forsaken. It is a place of immense historical and spiritual importance, and was established to right grievous historic wrongs. This is felt not only by America's 3 million Jews but also by an overwhelming number of the country's Christians.

Muslim nations, however, and many other non-Muslim countries, see Israel as a regional bully propped up by the United States. Pew surveys found that many people "suspect the United States of deliberately targeting Muslim nations and using the war on terror to protect Israel," as well as to gain control of Middle East oil.[48]

Clear evidence of a biased relationship was seen in the fact that the United States announced a $10 billion military-aid package to Israel on the same day that the U.S. military began its assault on Iraq in 2003.

"To announce this package on the same day that Iraq is bombed is as stupid as it is arrogant," said Nabeel Ghanyoum, a military analyst in Syria. "This is effectively telling the Arab world, 'Look we are bombing Iraq as we please, and we are giving Israel as much financial aid [as] it wants.'"[49]

In his study of the links between anti-Israeli sentiment and anti-Americanism, the University of Michigan's Markovits found that the crucial link was made after the Israeli victory in the 1967 war, while America was embroiled in Vietnam.

"Israel became little more than an extension of American power to many, especially on Europe's political left," he wrote. "Israel was disliked, especially by the left, not so much because it was Jewish but because it was American. And as such it was powerful."[50]

A Good Neighbor?

There have been positive moments in the past few years. The Council on Foreign Relations' Simon says that there was an upsurge in America's standing in 2004, when it provided substantial aid in the wake of the devastating Southeast Asian tsunami. The perception that this aid was "unconditional," he said, had a "sharply positive effect" on perceptions of the United States.

Noor at the Centre for Modern Oriental Studies in Berlin disagrees. He says he visited storm-damaged areas of Indonesia and Pakistan after the disaster and perceived even this seemingly altruistic venture was a public-relations disaster for the United States.

"They showed up on aircraft carriers and other warships," he says, "and the soldiers sent to help the victims were still wearing their combat fatigues from the Iraq War." It would have been far wiser to send civilian aid workers rather than the military, he says, who were regarded by many storm victims as emissaries of the imperial United States. "America is now seen [there] as something alien."

The Remarque Institute's Judt says that the U.S. government's disdain for international institutions has had a lasting negative effect, particularly among America's longtime allies. The Bush administration created an "in-your-face America," he says, that conveyed the message: "Not only do the things we do annoy you, but we don't care. We are going to do what we do, and you can take it or leave it."

For example, during his short stint as U.S. envoy to the United Nations, Ambassador John Bolton was criticized — and also praised — for his straight-from-the-shoulder diplomacy, including his disparagement of the United Nations itself. "The Secretariat building in New York has 38 stories," he famously once said. "If it lost 10 stories, it wouldn't make a bit of difference."[51] Bolton was blamed by some U.N. officials for quietly sabotaging the organization's reform initiative by stirring differences between poor and rich countries.

"He sometimes makes it very difficult to build bridges because he is a very honest and blunt person," said South Africa's ambassador, Dumisani Shadrack Kumalo, chairman of a coalition of developing nations. He said it sometimes appeared that "Ambassador Bolton wants to prove nothing works at the United Nations."[52] Bolton resigned in December 2006.

In addition, both Noor and Latin America expert Sweig at the Council on Foreign Relations say the U.S. reputation for generosity has been hurt by drastic cuts in foreign-assistance programs under the U.S. Agency for International Development (AID), as well as cuts in funds for libraries, scholarships and other cultural activities. Private giving by Americans remains the highest per capita in the world, and American foreign-development aid is the highest in the developed world in pure dollar terms, but the level of aid sinks very low when measured as a percentage of GDP.[53]

Such aid programs in many cases were replaced by "War on Terrorism" initiatives, including a $300 million propaganda campaign from the Pentagon. The psychological-warfare operation included plans for placing pro-American messages in foreign media outlets without disclosing the U.S. government as the source.[54]

Alarmist rhetoric is a poor substitute for help, says Noor, because the United States no longer has people on the ground in Muslim countries who know the cultures and the languages. When they were in effect and fully funded, he says, U.S. aid programs were so successful that Islamist movements in those countries have mimicked them. "They borrowed the tactics of the Peace Corps."

Missed Opportunities

By linking Israel and the United States into a single, fearsome conspiracy, anti-American activists have created strange bedfellows: fundamentalist Muslims, socialists and Western pacifists. Left-leaning groups used to find common cause in socialist ideals. Now, "anti-Americanism is the glue that holds them together, and hatred of Israel is one aspect," said Emmanuele Ottolenghi, a research fellow at the Centre for Hebrew and Jewish studies at Oxford University in England.[55]

While America's close relationship with Israel was often questioned outside the United States, the U.S. role in opposing the Soviet Union during the Cold War more

Venezuelan President Hugo Chavez fulminates about the United States at Miraflores Palace, Caracas, in 2006. Chavez, who is attempting to form an alternative coalition of South American countries opposed to the United States, insults and belittles the American president at every opportunity.

than outweighed it, says Georgetown University's Kupchan. Now, he says, the old bonds don't count for so much.

"The World War II generation is dying off; the reflexive support of the transatlantic partnership of that generation is disappearing. You have a new generation of Europeans for whom the United States is not the savior from the Nazis and the Soviets that it was for their parents," says Kupchan.

Meanwhile, even with a new U.S. presidential election nearing, fears remain strong in Europe about the actions of the Bush administration in its remaining months. Of particular concern is the possibility of a dangerous new U.S. offensive against Iran, which says it will continue developing nuclear energy.

"We think that the growing tensions between the two countries are made more dangerous by George Bush's detachment from the electorate: There's a real risk that he may strike at Iran before he leaves power," John Micklethwait, editor of *The Economist*, recently wrote.[56]

OUTLOOK

Lasting Damage?

When prosecutors in Munich decided in January to charge CIA counterterrorism operatives with kidnapping a German citizen, Khalid el-Masri, the newspaper *Sueddeutsche Zeitung* declared: "The great ally is not allowed to simply send its thugs out into Europe's streets." Indeed,

Craig Whitlock reported, the decision "won widespread applause from German politicians and the public."[57]

In the wake of such incidents, many at home and abroad are asking how — and even if — the United States can repair its image and its relations with its allies. Some analysts believe that the coming new presidential administration, whether Republican or Democratic, can do it through diligent cooperation and outreach. Others say the damage is so severe that it would take decades.

"When Bush goes, assuming that there isn't a war with Iran, it will be possible for the next president to exercise damage control," says Remarque Institute Director Judt.

Sweig of the Council on Foreign Relations sees a longer road ahead. "It will be the work of a generation to turn this around," she says.

Gerard Baker, U.S. editor for the *Times of London*, posits a more complex future. "Somewhere, deep down," he writes, "tucked away underneath their loathing for George Bush, in a secret place where the lights of smart dinner-party conversation and clever debating-society repartee never shine, the growing hordes of America-bashers must dread the moment he leaves office.

"When President Bush goes into the Texas sunset, and especially if he is replaced by an enlightened, world-embracing Democrat, their one excuse, their sole explanation for all human suffering in the world will disappear too. And they may just find that the world is not as simple as they thought it was."[58]

Critics agree that as long as the United States remains the world's greatest economic and military force, it will often be blamed for its negative impact on other countries, and seldom thanked for positive contributions. The inferiority complex that the University of Michigan's Markovits says drives Europe's brand of anti-Americanism will probably continue to fester until the EU can learn to assert itself in global affairs when humanitarian as well as military demands are compelling.

The Israeli-Palestinian conflict also will remain a problem and a source of agitation against U.S. policy, as long as Israel insists on occupying Palestinian land, America supports its right to do so and Palestinian politicians are unable to bring their angry streets to a compromise solution for statehood. The problem is multi-faceted.

But, as Powell Solares at Madrid's Elcano Royal Institute points out, much of the global public sees only one thing: "The perception that the main problem with the Arab-Israeli conflict is that the U.S. will always back Israel."

Iraq looms over all questions about the future. "The U.S. presence in Iraq will seriously impede American efforts to influence hearts and minds," Simon, the Middle East expert at the Council on Foreign Relations, told a House subcommittee last September. "Our occupation will reinforce regional images of the United States as both excessively violent and ineffectual."[59]

But what will follow the "American Century" in the near future if the United States has lost the trust of the world?

"It may be that the United States has not shown itself worthy or capable of ensuring the unity of a civilization whose laws have governed the world, at least for the last few centuries," writes Jean Daniel in *Le Nouvel Observateur* in Paris.

"But since a united Europe capable of taking over this mission hasn't yet emerged," Daniel continues, "all we can do is hope that the American people will wake up and rapidly call a halt to these crude interventionist utopias carelessly dredged out of the Theodore Roosevelt tradition. Utopias that, in the words of an American diplomat, have made George W. Bush and his brain trust 'lose their intelligence as they turned into ideologues.' "[60]

NOTES

1. See Fareed Zakaria, "The Politics of Rage: Why Do They Hate Us?" *Newsweek*, Sept. 24, 2001.

2. Samuel P. Huntington, "The Clash of Civilizations?" *Foreign Affairs*, summer 1993; www.foreignaffairs.org/19930601faessay5188/samuel-p-huntington/the-clash-of-civilizations.html.

3. James Keaten, "French Farmer José Bové Leads New McDonald's Protest," The Associated Press, Aug. 13, 2001; www.mcspotlight.org/media/press/mcds/theassociatedpr130801.html.

4. Quoted in David Morse, "Striking the Golden Arches: French Farmers Protest McDonald's Globalization," *The Ecologist*, Dec. 31, 2002, p. 2; www.socsci.uci.edu/~cohenp/food/frenchfarmers.pdf.

5. For background, see Mary H. Cooper, "Hating America," *CQ Researcher*, Nov. 23, 2001, pp. 969-992.

6. Andrei S. Markovits, "European Anti-Americanism (and Anti-Semitism): Ever Present Though Always Denied," Working Paper Series #108. Markovits is Karl W. Deutsch Collegiate Professor of Comparative Politics and German Studies at the University of Michigan.

7. Paul Hockenos, "Dispatch From Germany," *The Nation*, April 14, 2003; www.thenation.com/doc/20030414/hockenos.

8. "Pakistani Cartoon Protesters Chant Anti-American Slogans," FoxNews.com, Feb. 21, 2006; www.foxnews.com/story/0,2933,185503,00.html.

9. Jean-Marie Colombani, "We Are All Americans," *Le Monde*, Sept. 12, 2001.

10. Quoted in Denis Lacorne and Tony Judt, *eds., With Us or Against Us: Studies in Global Anti-Americanism* (2005).

11. "Global Opinion: The Spread of Anti-Americanism," *Trends 2005*, p. 106; Pew Research Center for People and the Press, Jan. 24, 2005; http://people-press.org/commentary/display.php3?Analysis ID=104.

12. "U.S. Image Up Slightly, But Still Negative American Character Gets Mixed Reviews," Pew Research Center for People and the Press, June 23, 2005; http://pewglobal.org/reports/display.php?Report ID=247.

13. Lacorne and Judt, *op. cit.*

14. "War in Iraq: Winning the Peace," *The* [Beirut] *Daily Star*, April 6, 2006, from Worldpress.com; www.worldpress.org/Mideast/1041.cfm.

15. Peter Ford, "Europe Cringes at Bush 'Crusade' Against Terrorists," *The Christian Science Monitor*, Sept. 19, 2001.

16. For background, see "Brian Hansen, "Globalization Backlash," *CQ Researcher*, Sept. 28, 2001, pp. 961-784.

17. For background, see Sarah Glazer, "Slow Food Movement," *CQ Researcher*, Jan. 26, 2007, pp. 73-96, and David Hosansky, "Food Safety," *CQ Researcher*, Nov. 1, 2002, pp. 897-920.

18. Quoted in *The Daily Mail*, June 1, 1999, BBC Online Network; http://news.bbc.co.uk/2/hi/uk_news/358291.stm.

19. Quoted in Sam Loewenberg, "Lobbying Euro-Style," *The National Journal*, Sept. 8, 2001.

20. Henry A. Giroux, "George Bush's Religious Crusade Against Democracy: Fundamentalism as Cultural Politics," *Dissident Voice*, Aug. 4, 2004; www.dissidentvoice.org/Aug04/Giroux0804.htm.

21. "God and American diplomacy," *The Economist*, Feb. 8, 2003.

22. Pew Research Center, *op. cit.*, Jan. 24, 2005.

23. Markovits, *op. cit.*

24. "Burger and fries à la française," *The Economist*, April 15, 2004.

25. Suzanne Daley, "French Turn Vandal Into Hero Against US." *The New York Times*, July 1, 2000.

26. Henry Luce, "The American Century," *Life*, Feb. 7, 1941.

27. Michael Elliott, "China Takes on the World," *Time*, Jan. 11, 2007.

28. "America's Image Slips, But Allies Share U.S. Concerns Over Iran, Hamas; No Global Warming Alarm in the U.S., China," Pew Research Center for People and the Press, June 13, 2006; http://pewglobal.org.

29. Lacorne and Judt, *op. cit.*

30. "Hugo Chavez: Latin America Rises Against the Empire," March 10, 2007, from audio transcript on TeleSUR; http://latinhacker.gnn.tv/blogs/22178/Hugo_Chavez_Latin_America_Rises_Against_the_Empire.

31. Souad Mekhennet and Michael Moss, "New Face of Jihad Vows Attacks," *The New York Times*, March 16, 2007.

32. "Rome AD . . . Rome DC?" *The Guardian*, Sept. 18, 2002; www.guardian.co.uk/usa/story/0,12271,794163,00.html.

33. Quoted in Judy Colp Rubin, "Is Bush Really Responsible for Anti-Americanism Around the World," Sept. 27, 2004, George Mason University's History Network; http://hnn.us/articles/7288.html.

34. Cornelius de Pauw, "Recherches philosophiques sur les Américains ou Mémoires interessants pour servir à l'histoire de l'espèce humaine," London, 1768.

35. Friedrich Nietzsche, *The Gay Science*, sec. 329 (1882).

36. Arthur Gobineau, (Count Joseph Arthur de Gobineau) and Adrian Collins [1853-55] 1983. *The Inequality of Human Races*, Second edition, reprint.

37. Barry Rubin and Judith Colp Rubin, *Hating America: A History* (2004).

38. Lacorne and Judt, *op. cit.*, p. 26.

39. *Ibid.*

40. Pew Research Center, *op. cit.*, June 23, 2005.

41. Testimony before House International Relations Committee, Sept. 14, 2006.

42. Quoted in "Outrage at 'Old Europe' Remarks," BBC Online, Jan. 23, 2003.

43. "Theory That U.S. Orchestrated Sept. 11 Attacks 'Not Absurd,' " The Associated Press, Sept. 12, 2001, www.breitbart.com/.

44. For background, see Peter Katel and Kenneth Jost, "Treatment of Detainees," *CQ Researcher*, Aug. 25, 2006, pp. 673-696.

45. For background, see Peter Katel, "New Strategy in Iraq," *CQ Researcher*, Feb. 23, 2007, pp. 169-192.

46. Patrick Sabatier, Liberation, Paris, Quoted in WorldPress.com, "Iraq Prisoner Abuse Draws International Media Outrage," May 12, 2004; www.worldpress.org/Mideast/1861.cfm.

47. Pew Research Center, *op. cit.*, June 23, 2005.

48. Pew Research Center, *op. cit.*, Jan. 24, 2005.

49. Firas Al-Atraqchi, "Disillusion, Anger on the Arab Street," *Dissident Voice Online*, March 21, 2007; www.dissidentvoice.org/Articles3/Atraqchi_Arab Street.htm.

50. Markovits, *op. cit.*

51. Quoted in Anne Applebaum, "Defending Bolton," *The Washington Post*, March 9, 2005, p. A21.

52. Quoted in Peter Baker and Glenn Kessler, "U.N. Ambassador Bolton Won't Stay," *The Washington Post*, Dec. 6, 2006, p. A1.

53. "Review of the Development Cooperation Policies and Programmes of United States," Organization for Economic Cooperation and Development, 2006.

54. Matt Kelley, "Pentagon Rolls Out Stealth PR," *USA Today*, Dec. 14, 2005.

55. Glenn Frankel, "In Britain, War Concern Grows Into Resentment of U.S. Power; Anxiety Over Attack on Iraq Moves to Political Mainstream," *The Washington Post*, Jan. 26, 2003, p. A14.

56. John Micklethwait, "Letter to Readers," *The Economist*, Feb. 8, 2007.

57. Craig Whitlock, "In Another CIA Abduction, Germany Has an Uneasy Role," *The Washington Post*, Feb. 5, 2007, p. A11.

58. Gerard Baker, "When Bush Leaves Office," *Times of London*, TimesOnline, March 2, 2007.

59. Testimony before International Relations Subcommittee on the Middle East, Sept. 14, 2006.

60. Jean Daniel, "Our American 'Enemies,' " *La Nouvel Observateur*, Sept. 23, 2003, quoted on WorldPress.org.

BIBLIOGRAPHY

Books

Cohen, Nick, *What's Left? How Liberals Lost Their Way,* **Fourth Estate, 2007.**
A well-known liberal British columnist for *The Observer* and *The New Statesman* gives a scathing critique of anti-Americanism among the British Left, the anti-globalization movement and intellectuals who have become apologists for militant Islam.

Garton Ash, Timothy, *Free World: America, Europe and the Surprising Future of the West,* **Random House, 2004.**
In an engaging critique of anti-American sentiment, a former journalist who runs the European Studies Centre at Oxford University argues that in the post-Cold War world, America is the "other" against which Europeans try to define their own identity.

Joffe, Josef, *Uberpower: The Imperial Temptation of America,* **W. W. Norton, 2006.**
The editor and publisher of *Die Zeit,* a German weekly, and a fellow in international relations at the Hoover Institution, provides a European intellectual's insight into the envy at the heart of anti-Americanism and its parallels with classical anti-Semitism.

Katzenstein, Peter, and Robert Keohane, eds., *Anti-Americanisms in World Politics,* **Cornell University Press, 2006.**

Two international-relations scholars bring together the insights of historians, social scientists and political scientists.

Kohut, Andrew, and Bruce Stokes, *America Against the World: How We Are Different and Why We Are Disliked,* **Times Books, 2006.**

Kohut, director of the Pew Research Center for the People and the Press, and Stokes, international economics columnist for *National Journal,* provide a comprehensive survey of public opinions about America from around the world.

Kupchan, Charles, *The End of the American Era: U.S. Foreign Policy and the Geopolitics of the Twenty-first Century,* **Vintage, 2003.**

A former National Security Council staffer and a senior fellow at the Council on Relations argues that with the rise of China and the European Union America can no longer afford to have a unilateralist foreign policy.

Lacorne, Denis, and Tony Judt, eds., *With Us or Against Us: Studies in Global Anti-Americanism,* **Palgrave Macmillan, 2005.**

Essays by 11 scholars analyze anti-American sentiment in Western and Eastern Europe, the Middle East and Asia.

Markovits, Andrei S., *Uncouth Nation: Why Europe Dislikes America,* **Princeton University Press, 2007.**

A professor of comparative politics and German studies at the University of Michigan, Ann Arbor, writes provocatively about the anti-Americanism in everyday European life.

Revel, Jean-Francois, *Anti-Americanism,* **Encounter Books, 2003.**

Revel, a leading French intellectual, castigates his countrymen for pointing their fingers at America when they should be dealing with their own current and historical problems.

Sweig, Julia, *Friendly Fire: Losing Friends and Making Enemies in the Anti-American Century,* **Public Affairs, 2006.**

The director of Latin American studies at the Council on Foreign Relations argues that American policies in Latin America, including sponsoring dictators and condoning human-rights violations, set the stage for the current animosity toward the U.S.

Articles

Judt, Tony, "Anti-Americans Abroad," *The New York Review of Books,* **May 2003.**

The director of the Remarque Institute at New York University examines the rage for new books in France attacking America.

Reports and Studies

"America's Image Slips, But Allies Share U.S. Concerns Over Iran, Hamas," *Pew Research Center,* **2006; http://pewglobal.org/reports/display.php?ReportID=252.**

The latest poll by the Pew Global Attitudes Project finds that while anti-Americanism had dipped in 2005, it began rising again.

"Foreign Aid: An Introductory Overview of U.S. Programs and Policy," *Congressional Research Service, Library of Congress,* **2004; http://fpc.state.gov/documents/organization/31987.pdf.**

This study of American foreign aid includes data on humanitarian, military and bilateral-development aid.

"Worldviews 2002," *German Marshall Fund of the United States and The Chicago Council on Foreign Relations,* **2002; www.worldviews.org.**

A comprehensive survey of contrasting European and American public opinion following the Sept. 11 terrorist attacks finds that Europeans believed U.S. foreign policy contributed to the attacks.

For More Information

Centre for Modern Oriental Studies, Kirchweg 33, 14129 Berlin, Germany; +49-(0)-30-80307-0; www.zmo.de. German think tank conducting comparative and interdisciplinary studies of the Middle East, Africa, South and Southeast Asia.

Council on Foreign Relations, 58 E. 68th St., New York, NY 10065; (212) 434-9400; www.cfr.org. Promotes a better understanding of the foreign-policy choices facing the United States and other governments.

Elcano Royal Institute, Príncipe de Vergara, 51, 28006 Madrid, Spain; +34-91-781-6770; www.realinstitutoelcano .org. Non-partisan Spanish institution generating policy ideas in the interest of international peace.

Pew Global Attitudes Project, 1615 L St., N.W., Suite 700, Washington, DC 20036; (202) 419-4400; www .pewglobal.org. Assesses worldwide opinions on the current state of foreign affairs and other important issues.

USC Center on Public Diplomacy, USC Annenberg School, University of Southern California, 3502 Watt Way, Suite 103, Los Angeles, CA 90089-0281; (213) 821-2078; http://uscpublicdiplomacy.com. Studies the impact of government-sponsored programs as well as private activities on foreign policy and national security.

Supporting researchers for more than 40 years

Research methods have always been at the core of SAGE's publishing program. Founder Sara Miller McCune published SAGE's first methods book, *Public Policy Evaluation*, in 1970. Soon after, she launched the *Quantitative Applications in the Social Sciences* series—affectionately known as the "little green books."

Always at the forefront of developing and supporting new approaches in methods, SAGE published early groundbreaking texts and journals in the fields of qualitative methods and evaluation.

Today, more than 40 years and two million little green books later, SAGE continues to push the boundaries with a growing list of more than 1,200 research methods books, journals, and reference works across the social, behavioral, and health sciences. Its imprints—Pine Forge Press, home of innovative textbooks in sociology, and Corwin, publisher of PreK–12 resources for teachers and administrators—broaden SAGE's range of offerings in methods. SAGE further extended its impact in 2008 when it acquired CQ Press and its best-selling and highly respected political science research methods list.

From qualitative, quantitative, and mixed methods to evaluation, SAGE is the essential resource for academics and practitioners looking for the latest methods by leading scholars.

For more information, visit **www.sagepub.com**.